C000183229

STREET ATLAS
East Kent

First published in 1989 by

Philip's, a division of
Octopus Publishing Group Ltd
2–4 Heron Quays, London E14 4JP

Second colour edition 2001
Second impression with revisions 2002

ISBN 0-540-07977-4 (hardback)
ISBN 0-540-07978-2 (spiral)

© Philip's 2002

Ordnance Survey®

This product includes mapping data licensed from Ordnance Survey® with the permission of the Controller of Her Majesty's Stationery Office. © Crown copyright 2002. All rights reserved. Licence number 100011710

Printed and bound in Spain
by Cayfosa-Quebecor

Contents

Digital Data

The exceptionally high-quality mapping found in this atlas is available as digital data in TIFF format, which is easily convertible to other bitmapped (raster) image formats.

The index is also available in digital form as a standard database table. It contains all the details found in the printed index together with the National Grid reference for the map square in which each entry is named.

For further information and to discuss your requirements, please contact Philip's on 020 7531 8439 or ruth.king@philips-maps.co.uk

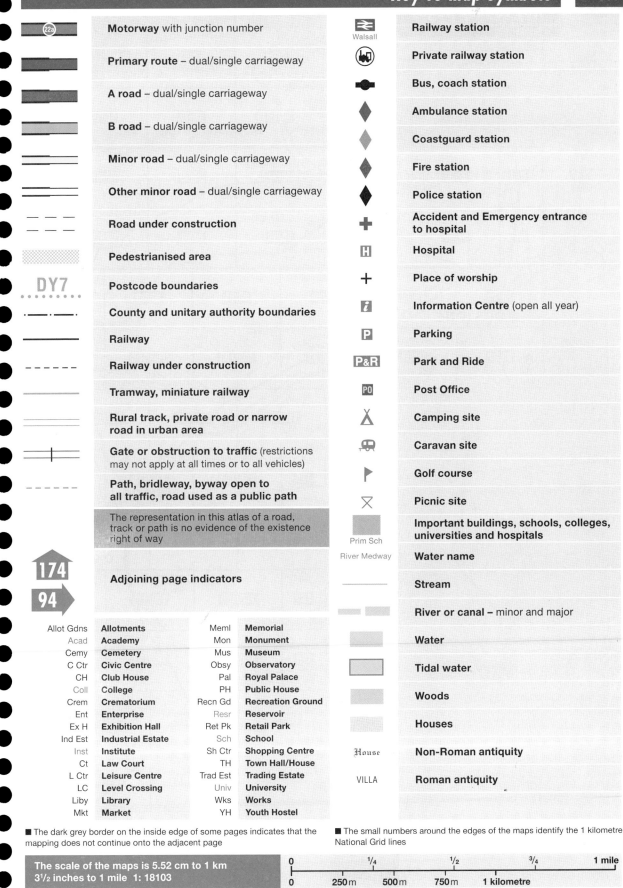

Motorway with junction number

Primary route – dual/single carriageway

A road – dual/single carriageway

B road – dual/single carriageway

Minor road – dual/single carriageway

Other minor road – dual/single carriageway

Road under construction

Pedestrianised area

DY7   Postcode boundaries

County and unitary authority boundaries

Railway

Railway under construction

Tramway, miniature railway

Rural track, private road or narrow road in urban area

Gate or obstruction to traffic (restrictions may not apply at all times or to all vehicles)

Path, bridleway, byway open to all traffic, road used as a public path

The representation in this atlas of a road, track or path is no evidence of the existence right of way

174
94   Adjoining page indicators

Allot Gdns	**Allotments**	Meml	**Memorial**
Acad	**Academy**	Mon	**Monument**
Cemy	**Cemetery**	Mus	**Museum**
C Ctr	**Civic Centre**	Obsy	**Observatory**
CH	**Club House**	Pal	**Royal Palace**
Coll	**College**	PH	**Public House**
Crem	**Crematorium**	Recn Gd	**Recreation Ground**
Ent	**Enterprise**	Resr	**Reservoir**
Ex H	**Exhibition Hall**	Ret Pk	**Retail Park**
Ind Est	**Industrial Estate**	Sch	**School**
Inst	**Institute**	Sh Ctr	**Shopping Centre**
Ct	**Law Court**	TH	**Town Hall/House**
L Ctr	**Leisure Centre**	Trad Est	**Trading Estate**
LC	**Level Crossing**	Univ	**University**
Liby	**Library**	Wks	**Works**
Mkt	**Market**	YH	**Youth Hostel**

Walsall   Railway station

Private railway station

Bus, coach station

Ambulance station

Coastguard station

Fire station

Police station

Accident and Emergency entrance to hospital

Hospital

Place of worship

Information Centre (open all year)

Parking

P&R   Park and Ride

PO   Post Office

Camping site

Caravan site

Golf course

Picnic site

Important buildings, schools, colleges, universities and hospitals

Prim Sch

River Medway   Water name

Stream

River or canal – minor and major

Water

Tidal water

Woods

Houses

House   Non-Roman antiquity

VILLA   Roman antiquity

■ The dark grey border on the inside edge of some pages indicates that the mapping does not continue onto the adjacent page

■ The small numbers around the edges of the maps identify the 1 kilometre National Grid lines

The scale of the maps is 5.52 cm to 1 km
3¹/₂ inches to 1 mile 1: 18103

0	¼	½	¾	1 mile
0	250 m	500 m	750 m	1 kilometre

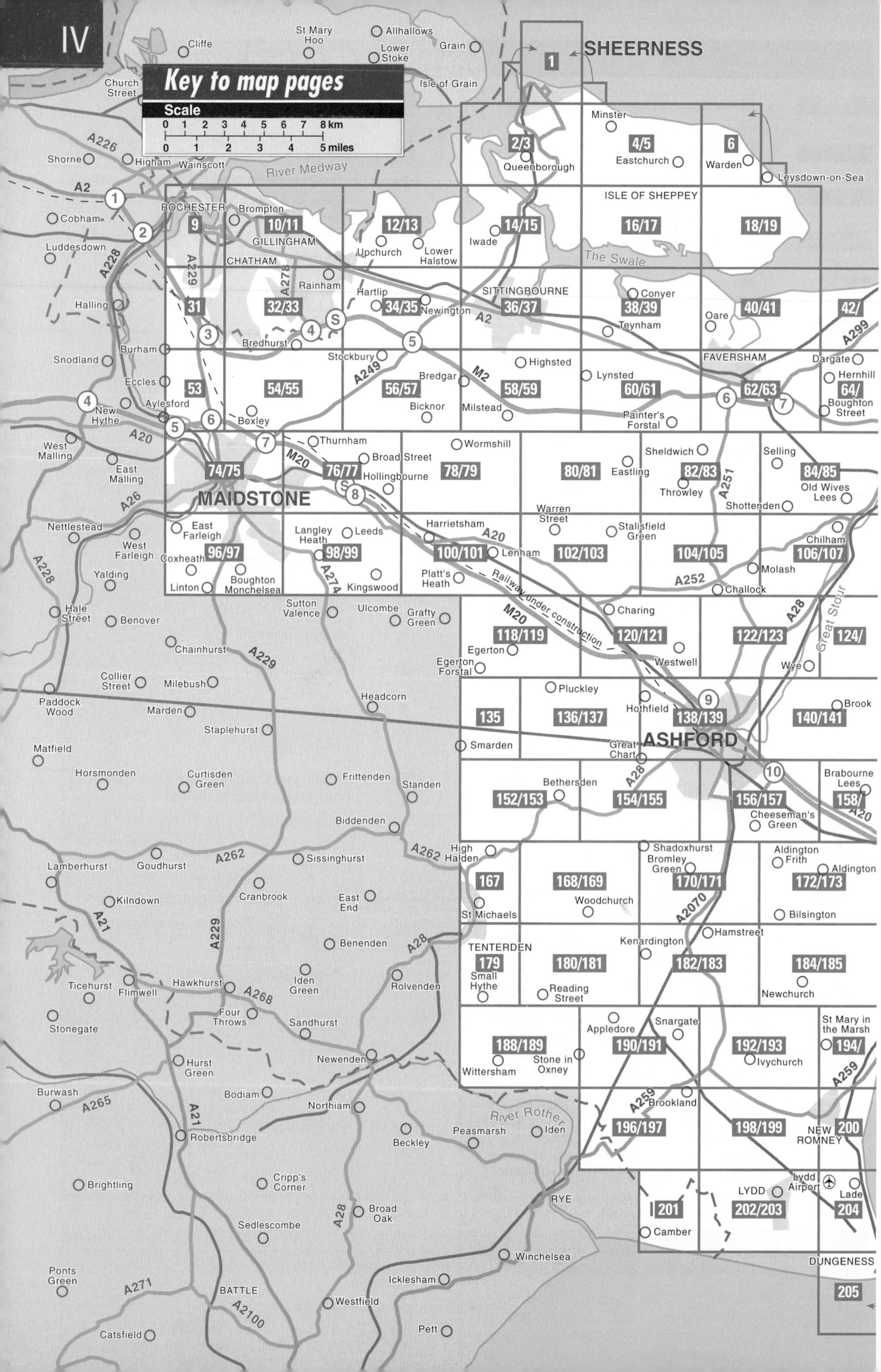
Key to map pages
Scale
0 1 2 3 4 5 6 7 8 km
0 1 2 3 4 5 miles
SHEERNESS
1
Minster
2/3
Queenborough
4/5
Eastchurch
6
Warden
Leysdown-on-Sea
ISLE OF SHEPPEY
St Mary Hoo
Allhallows
Lower Stoke
Grain
Isle of Grain
Cliffe
Church Street
Shorne
Higham
Wainscott
River Medway
A226
A2
Cobham
Luddesdown
A228
A229
A278
ROCHESTER
Brompton
9
10/11
GILLINGHAM
CHATHAM
12/13
Upchurch
Lower Halstow
Iwade
14/15
16/17
18/19
The Swale
Rainham
Hartlip
31
32/33
34/35
Newington
A2
SITTINGBOURNE
36/37
Conyer
38/39
Teynham
Oare
40/41
42/
A299
Halling
Burham
Snodland
Bredhurst
Stockbury
A249
M2
Bredgar
Highsted
Lynsted
FAVERSHAM
Dargate
Hernhill
53
54/55
56/57
58/59
60/61
62/63
64/
Boughton Street
Eccles
Aylesford
New Hythe
Boxley
Bicknor
Milstead
Painter's Forstal
West Malling
A20
East Malling
Thurnham
Broad Street
Wormshill
Sheldwich
Selling
M20
74/75
76/77
Hollingbourne
78/79
80/81
Eastling
82/83
Throwley
A251
84/85
Old Wives Lees
Shottenden
MAIDSTONE
A26
Nettlestead
East Farleigh
West Farleigh
Warren Street
Stalisfield Green
Harrietsham
Langley Heath
Leeds
Chilham
96/97
98/99
100/101
Lenham
102/103
104/105
106/107
Coxheath
Linton
Boughton Monchelsea
A274
Kingswood
Platt's Heath
Railway under construction
A252
Molash
Challock
Yalding
Hale Street
Benover
Sutton Valence
Ulcombe
Grafty Green
Charing
118/119
120/121
122/123
124/
A28
Great Stour
Egerton
Egerton Forstal
Westwell
Wye
Chainhurst
A229
Collier Street
Milebush
Paddock Wood
Marden
Headcorn
Pluckley
Hothfield
Brook
135
136/137
138/139
140/141
Staplehurst
Smarden
Great Chart
ASHFORD
Matfield
Horsmonden
Curtisden Green
Frittenden
Standen
Bethersden
Brabourne Lees
152/153
154/155
156/157
158/
Cheeseman's Green
Biddenden
High Halden
Shadoxhurst
Bromley Green
Aldington Frith
Aldington
Lamberhurst
Goudhurst
A262
Sissinghurst
167
168/169
170/171
172/173
Kilndown
Cranbrook
East End
Woodchurch
A2070
Bilsington
St Michaels
Hamstreet
A21
Benenden
TENTERDEN
Kenardington
179
180/181
182/183
184/185
Small Hythe
Reading Street
Newchurch
Ticehurst
Flimwell
Hawkhurst
A268
Iden Green
Rolvenden
Stonegate
Four Throws
Sandhurst
Appledore
Snargate
St Mary in the Marsh
188/189
190/191
192/193
194/
Wittersham
Stone in Oxney
Ivychurch
A259
Hurst Green
Newenden
Burwash
A265
Bodiam
Northiam
River Rother
Brookland
196/197
198/199
NEW ROMNEY
200
Robertsbridge
Beckley
Peasmarsh
Iden
Brightling
Cripp's Corner
Broad Oak
RYE
Lydd Airport
LYDD
Lade
201
202/203
204
Sedlescombe
Camber
Winchelsea
DUNGENESS
Ponts Green
A271
Icklesham
205
BATTLE
A2100
Westfield
Catsfield
Pett

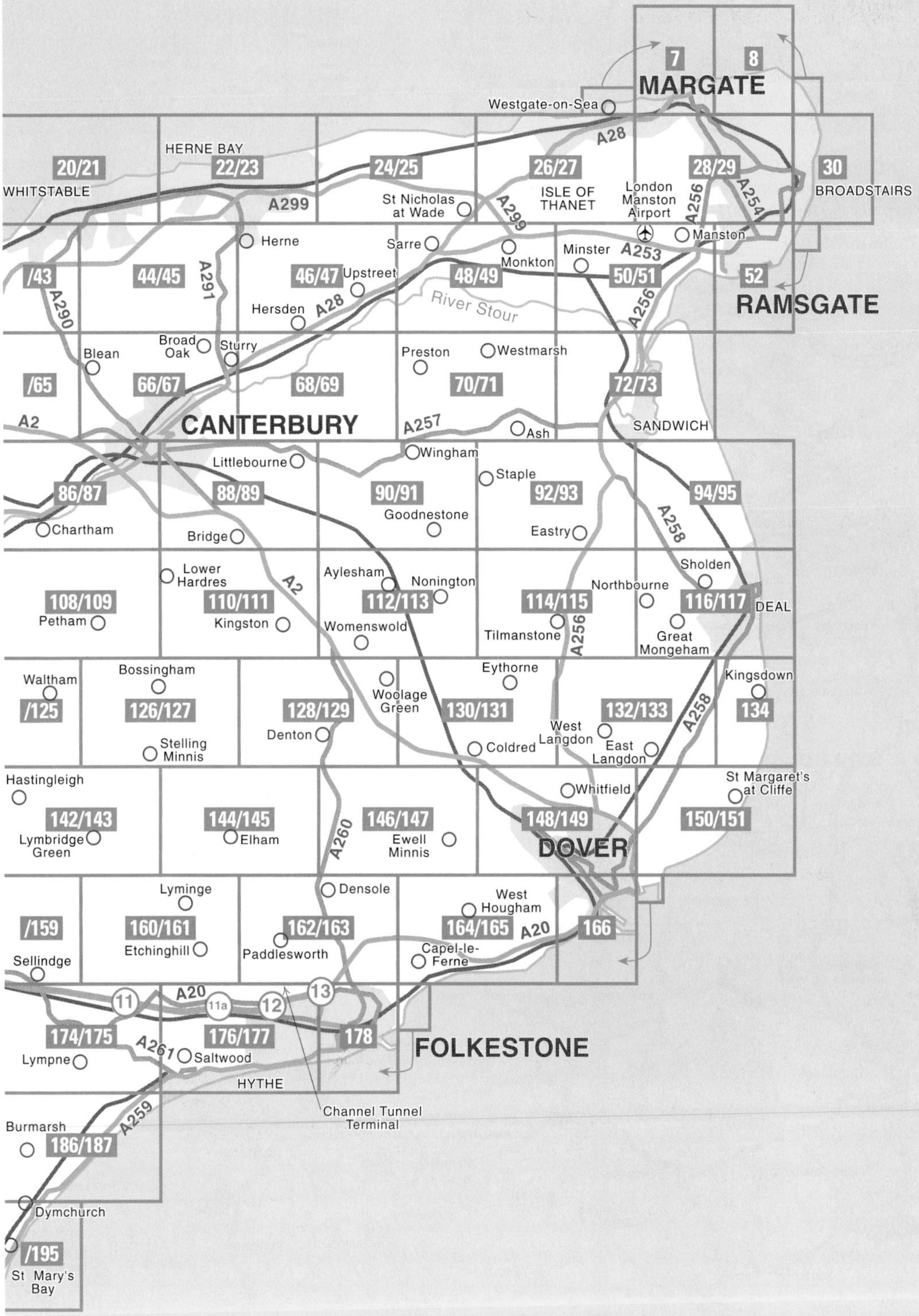
7
8
MARGATE
Westgate-on-Sea
A28
20/21
WHITSTABLE
HERNE BAY
22/23
A299
24/25
St Nicholas at Wade
26/27
ISLE OF THANET
London Manston Airport
28/29
A256
A254
30
BROADSTAIRS
Herne
Sarre
Monkton
Minster
A253
Manston
/43
A290
44/45
A291
46/47
Upstreet
48/49
50/51
A256
52
RAMSGATE
Hersden
A28
River Stour
Blean
Broad Oak
Sturry
Preston
Westmarsh
/65
66/67
68/69
70/71
72/73
A2
CANTERBURY
A257
Ash
SANDWICH
Littlebourne
Wingham
Staple
86/87
88/89
90/91
92/93
94/95
Chartham
Bridge
Goodnestone
Eastry
A258
Sholden
Lower Hardres
A2
Aylesham
Nonington
Northbourne
108/109
110/111
112/113
114/115
116/117
DEAL
Petham
Kingston
Womenswold
Tilmanstone
A256
Great Mongeham
Waltham
Bossingham
Eythorne
Kingsdown
/125
126/127
128/129
Woolage Green
130/131
132/133
A258
134
Denton
West Langdon
East Langdon
Coldred
Stelling Minnis
Hastingleigh
Whitfield
St Margaret's at Cliffe
142/143
144/145
146/147
148/149
150/151
Lymbridge Green
Elham
A260
Ewell Minnis
DOVER
Lyminge
Densole
West Hougham
/159
160/161
162/163
164/165
A20
166
Sellindge
Etchinghill
Paddlesworth
Capel-le-Ferne
11
A20
11a
12
13
174/175
A261
176/177
178
FOLKESTONE
Lympne
Saltwood
HYTHE
Channel Tunnel Terminal
Burmarsh
A259
186/187
Dymchurch
/195
St Mary's Bay

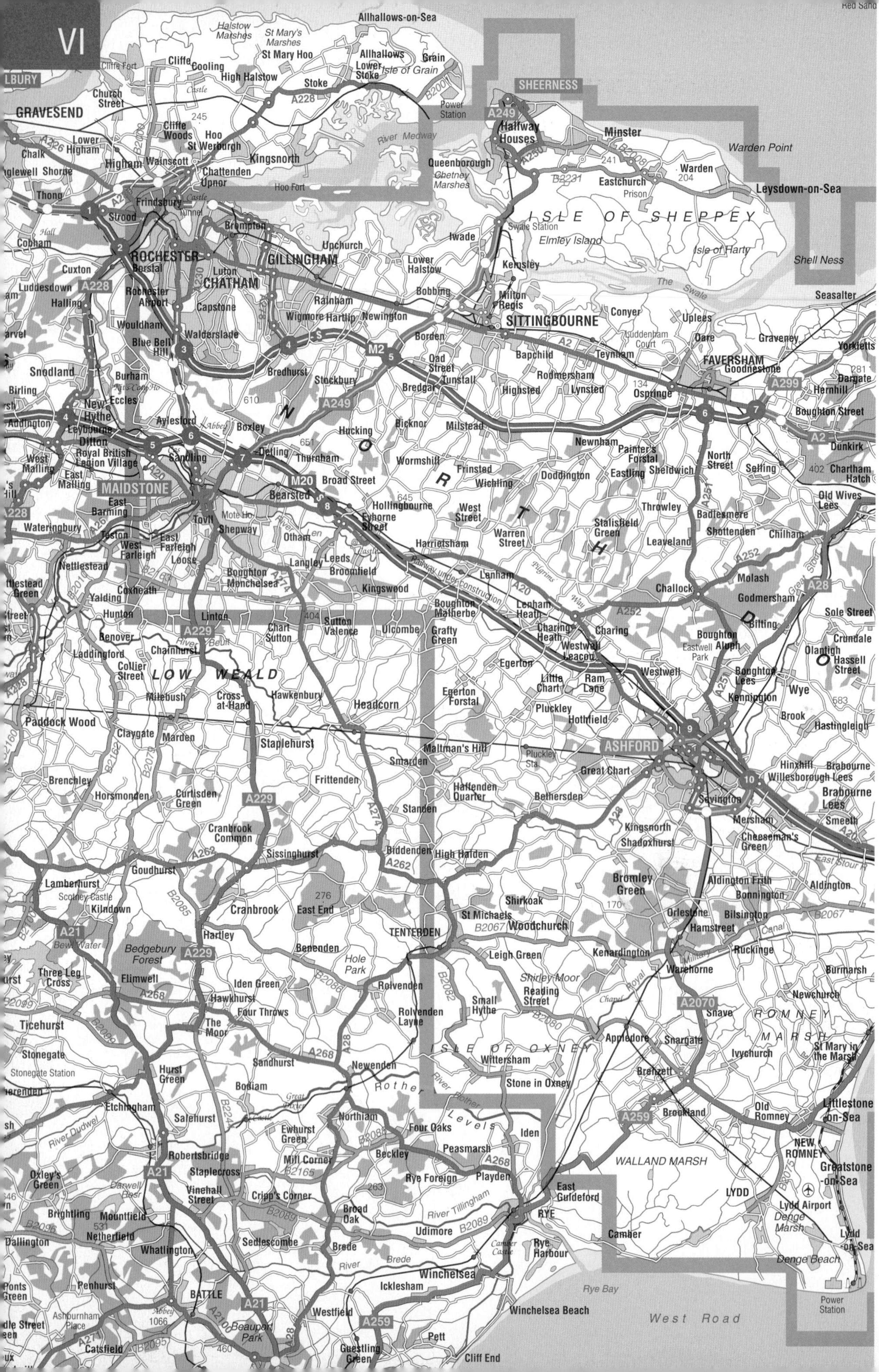

GRAVESEND

Halstow Marshes
St Mary's Marshes
Allhallows-on-Sea
St Mary Hoo
Allhallows
Grain
Lower Stoke
Isle of Grain
Cliffe Fort
Cliffe
Cooling
High Halstow
Stoke
Church Street
LBURY
245
Lower Higham
Chalk
nglewell Shorne
Hall Copham
Cliffe Woods
Hoo St Werburgh
Kingsnorth
Power Station
SHEERNESS
Halfway Houses
Minster
Warden Point
Luddesdown
Cuxton
Borstal
ROCHESTER
Rochester Airport
GILLINGHAM
CHATHAM
Upnor
Frindsbury
Strood
Brompton
Upchurch
Queenborough
Chetney Marshes
Eastchurch
Prison
Warden
Leysdown-on-Sea
ISLE OF SHEPPEY
Elmley Island
Isle of Harty
Shell Ness
Seasalter
Snodland
Burham
Wouldham
Blue Bell Hill
Walderslade
Capstone
Rainham
Wigmore Hartlip
Newington
Borden
Bobbing
Milton Regis
SITTINGBOURNE
Conyer
Oare
Uplees
Graveney
Yorkletts
FAVERSHAM
Goodnestone
Dargate
Hernhill
Boughton Street

New Hythe
Leybourne
Ditton
Royal British Legion Village
East Malling
Aylesford
Boxley
Sandling
Detling
Thurnham
Hucking
Bicknor
Milstead
Bredhurst
Stockbury
Bredgar
Oad Street
Tunstall
Highsted
Rodmersham
Lynsted
Teynham
Ospringe
Newnham
Painter's Forstal
Eastling
Sheldwich
North Street
Selling
Dunkirk
Chartham Hatch
Old Wives Lees
Chilham

MAIDSTONE
East Barming
West Farleigh
East Farleigh
Loose
Tovil
Shepway
Otham
Bearsted
Hollingbourne
Evhorne Street
Broad Street
Wormshill
Frinsted
Wichling
West Street
Doddington
Throwley
Leaveland
Badlesmere
Shottenden
Molash
Godmersham
Bitting
Sole Street
Crundale
Olantigh
Hassell Street
Wye
Brook
Hastingleigh

Wateringbury
Nettlestead
Yalding
Coxheath
Hunton
Benover
Laddingford
Collier Street
Linton
Chart Sutton
Sutton Valence
Ulcombe
Grafty Green
Egerton
Boughton Malherbe
Lenham
Lenham Heath
Charing Heath
Charing
Westwell Leacon
Westwell
Eastwell Park
Boughton Aluph
Boughton Lees
Kennington

LOW WEALD
Chainhurst
Milebush
Cross-at-Hand
Hawkenbury
Headcorn
Little Chart
Ram Lane
Egerton Forstal
Pluckley
Hothfield
ASHFORD
Great Chart
Sevington
Hinxhill
Brabourne
Willesborough Lees
Brabourne Lees
Smeeth
Mersham

Paddock Wood
Claygate
Marden
Staplehurst
Smarden
Maltman's Hill
Pluckley Sta.
Frittenden
Standen
Haffenden Quarter
Bethersden
Kingsnorth
Shadoxhurst
Cheeseman's Green

Brenchley
Horsmonden
Curtisden Green
Cranbrook Common
Sissinghurst
Biddenden
High Halden
Shirkoak
St Michaels
Woodchurch
Bromley Green
Aldington Frith
Bonnington
Aldington
Lamberhurst
Scotney Castle
Kilndown
Goudhurst
Cranbrook
East End
TENTERDEN
Leigh Green
Kenardington
Orlestone
Hamstreet
Bilsington
Ruckinge
Burmarsh

A21
Three Leg Cross
Flimwell
Bedgebury Forest
Hartley
Benenden
Hole Park
Rolvenden
Rolvenden Layne
Small Hythe
Reading Street
Shirley Moor
Warehorne
Newchurch

Ticehurst
Stonegate
Stonegate Station
Hawkhurst
Four Throws
The Moor
Iden Green
ISLE OF OXNEY
Wittersham
Appledore
Snargate
Snave
ROMNEY MARSH
Ivychurch
St Mary in the Marsh

Etchingham
Hurst Green
Salehurst
Sandhurst
Bodiam
Newenden
Stone in Oxney
Brenzett
Brookland
Old Romney
Littlestone-on-Sea

Oxley's Green
Brightling
Mountfield
Robertsbridge
Staplecross
Northiam
Four Oaks
Peasmarsh
Iden
WALLAND MARSH
NEW ROMNEY
Greatstone-on-Sea

Dallington
Netherfield
Whatlington
Vinehall Street
Mill Corner
Beckley
Rye Foreign
Playden
East Guldeford
LYDD
Lydd Airport
Denge Marsh
Lydd-on-Sea

Penhurst
Catsfield
BATTLE
Beaupont Park
Sedlescombe
Cripp's Corner
Broad Oak
Brede
Udimore
RYE
Camber
Rye Harbour
Denge Beach

Westfield
Guestling Green
Pett
Icklesham
Winchelsea
Winchelsea Beach
Rye Bay
West Road
Power Station
Cliff End

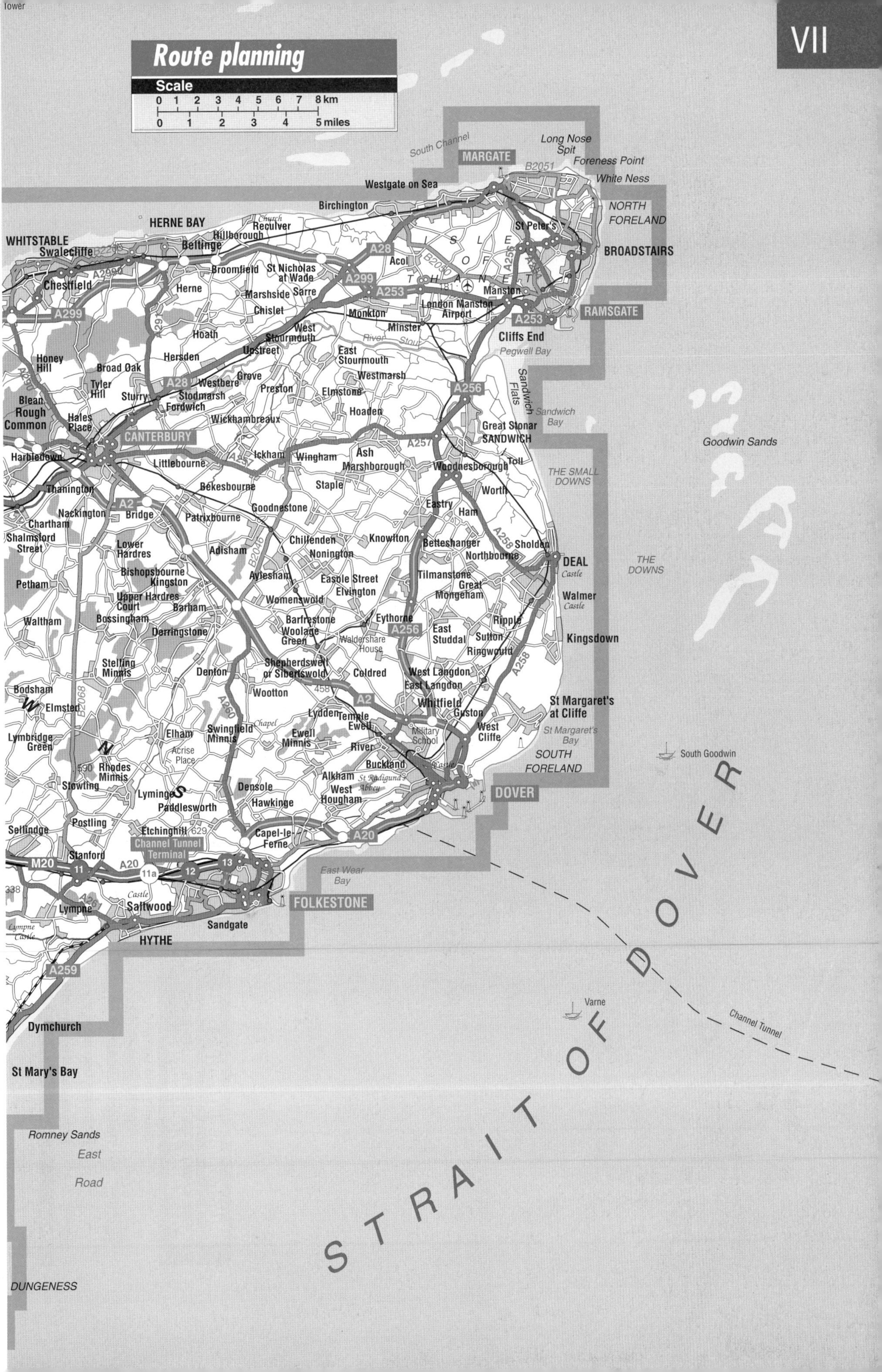

Route planning

Scale

0 1 2 3 4 5 6 7 8 km
0 1 2 3 4 5 miles

South Channel

MARGATE

Long Nose Spit
Foreness Point
White Ness

Westgate on Sea

B2051

Birchington

NORTH FORELAND

HERNE BAY
Church
Reculver
Hillborough

St Peter's

WHITSTABLE
Swalecliffe
Beltinge

BROADSTAIRS

Chestfield

A299

A2990

Broomfield
St Nicholas
at Wade
Marshside Sarre
Herne

Acol

B2050

ISLE

RAMSGATE

A299

Chislet
Monkton

A253

A253

London Manston
Airport
Manston

Honey
Hill

Hoath

A28

West
Stourmouth
Upstreet
Hersden

Minster

River Stour

OF

Cliffs End
Pegwell Bay

Broad Oak

Grove
Westbere

East
Stourmouth

THANET

Tyler
Hill

Preston

Westmarsh

Sandwich
Flats

Blean
Rough
Common
Hales
Place

Sturry
Stodmarsh
Fordwich

Elmstone

A28

Hoaden

Westmarsh

A256

Sandwich
Bay

Harbledown

CANTERBURY

Wickhambreaux

Great Stonar

SANDWICH

Goodwin Sands

Littlebourne
Ickham
Wingham

Ash

Toll

Thanington

A257

Marshborough

A257

Woodnesborough

THE SMALL
DOWNS

Nackington
Bridge
Bekesbourne
Staple

A2

Patrixbourne

Goodnestone

Eastry
Ham

Worth

Chartham
Shalmsford
Street

Lower
Hardres

Adisham

Chillenden
Nonington

Knowlton

A256

Betteshanger
Northbourne

Sholden

A258

Petham

Bishopsbourne
Kingston

Aylesham

Easole Street
Elvington

Tilmanstone
Great
Mongeham

DEAL
Castle

THE
DOWNS

Waltham

Upper Hardres
Court
Bossingham
Barham

Womenswold

Walmer
Castle

B2046

Derringstone

Barfrestone
Woolage
Green

Eythorne

A256

East
Studdal
Sutton

Ripple

Kingsdown

Ringwould

Stelling
Minnis

Denton

Waldershare
House

Coldred

West Langdon
East Langdon

St Margaret's
at Cliffe

Bodsham
Elmsted

Shepherdswell
or Sibertswold

458

A2

Whitfield

St Margaret's
Bay

Lymbridge
Green

Wootton

Guston

West
Cliffe

B2068

Stelling

Lydden
Temple
Ewell

Military
School

SOUTH
FORELAND

South Goodwin

A260

Swingfield
Minnis
Ewell
Minnis

River

Buckland

Elham

Acrise
Place

Densole

Alkham

St Radigund's
Abbey

M20

Rhodes
Minnis

West
Houghan

Castle

DOVER

Stowting

Lyminge
Paddlesworth

Hawkinge

Sellindge

Postling

Etchinghill
629

Capel-le-
Ferne

A260

East Wear
Bay

STRAIT

Stanford

Channel Tunnel
Terminal

A20

M20
11
A20
11a
12
13

FOLKESTONE

OF

Lympne
Castle
Saltwood

Sandgate

Lympne

HYTHE

Varne

DOVER

Channel Tunnel

A259

Dymchurch

St Mary's Bay

Romney Sands
East

STRAIT OF DOVER

Road

DUNGENESS

338

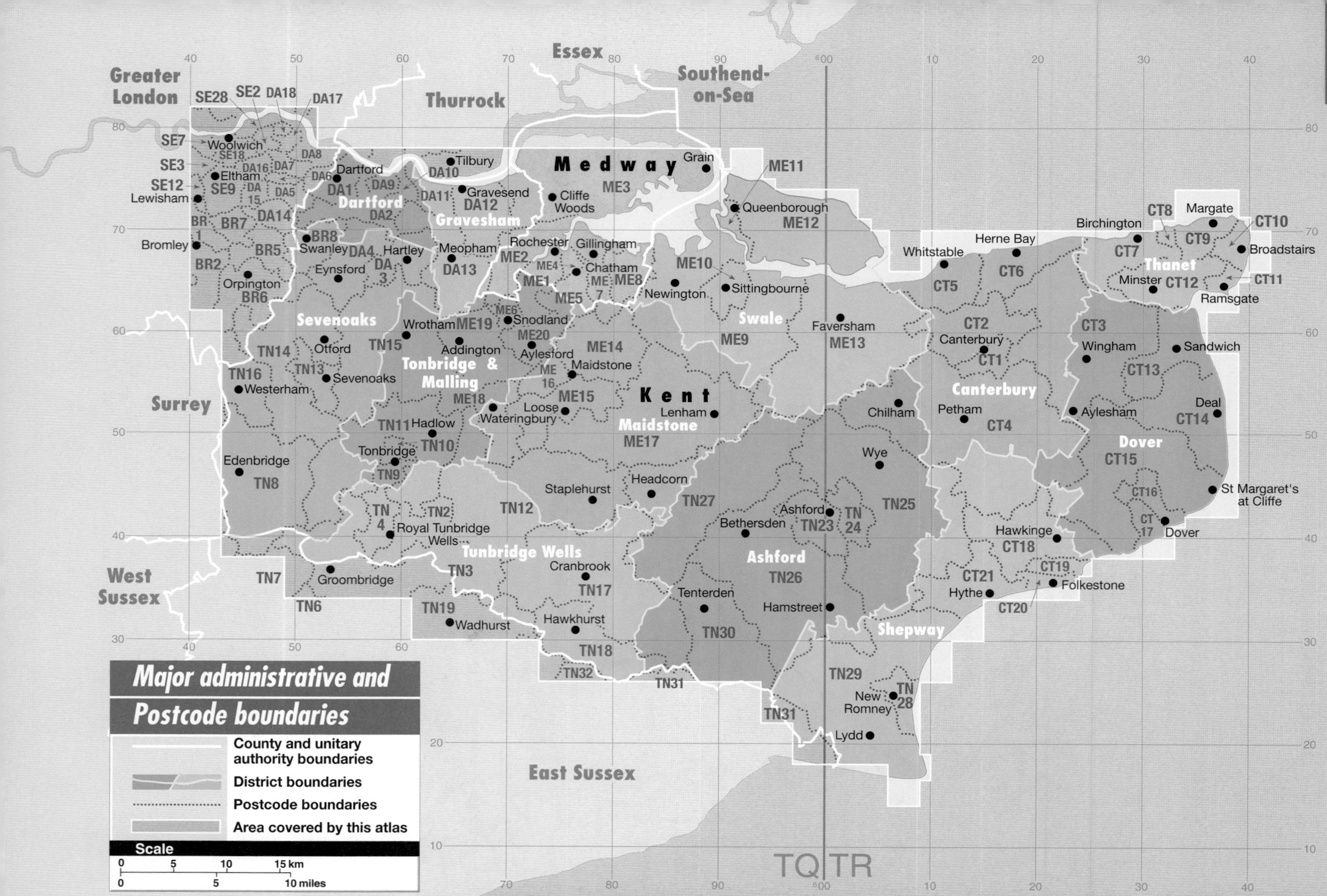

Major administrative and Postcode boundaries

Scale

| County and unitary authority boundaries |
| District boundaries |
| Postcode boundaries |
| Area covered by this atlas |

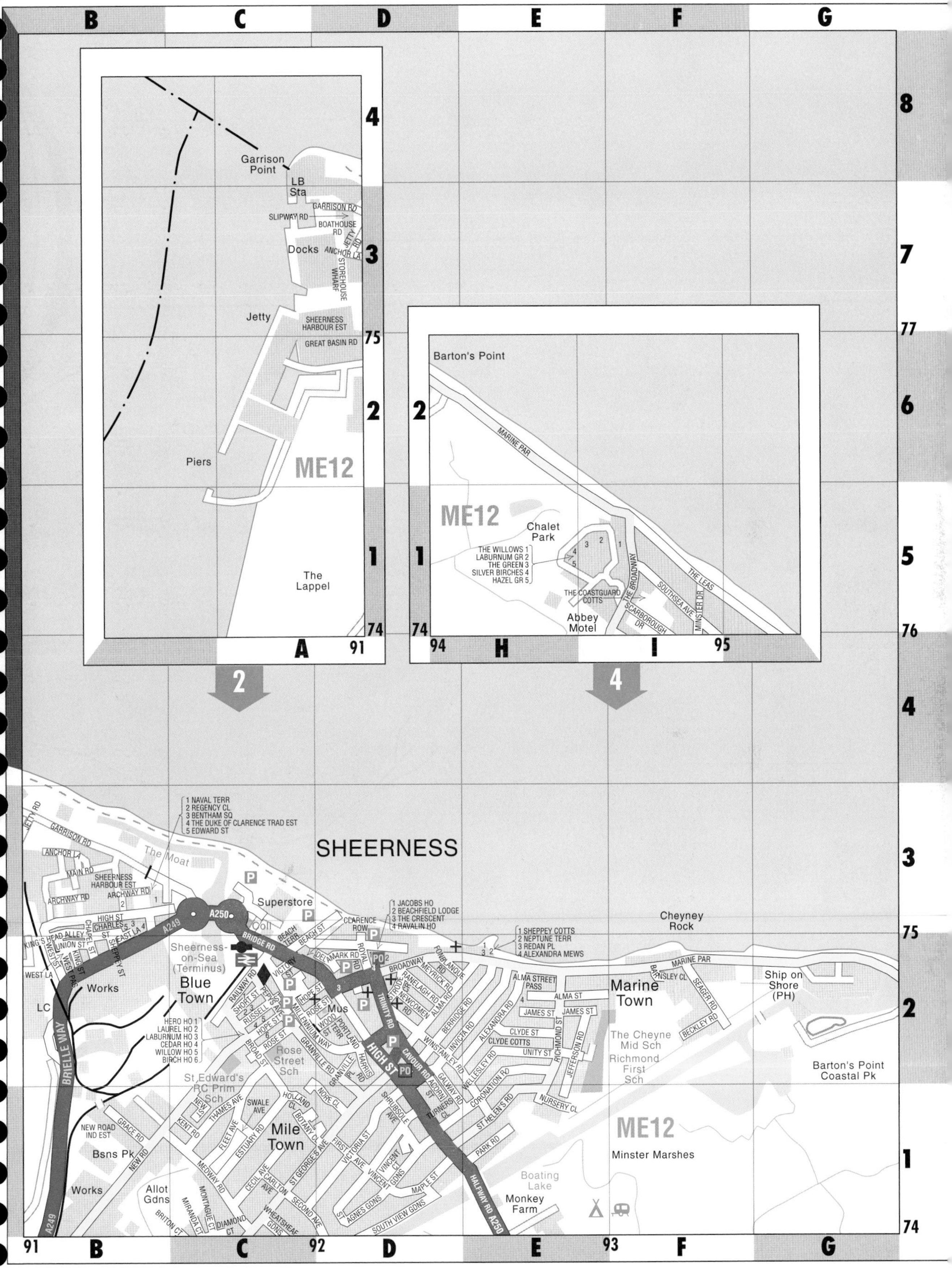

SHEERNESS
Garrison Point
LB Sta
GARRISON RD
SLIPWAY RD
BOATHOUSE RD
JETTY RD
Docks
ANCHOR LA
STOREHOUSE WHARF
Jetty
SHEERNESS HARBOUR EST
GREAT BASIN RD
Piers
ME12
The Lappel
Barton's Point
MARINE PAR
Chalet Park
THE WILLOWS 1
LABURNUM GR 2
THE GREEN 3
SILVER BIRCHES 4
HAZEL GR 5
THE COASTGUARD COTTS
THE BROADWAY
SOUTHSEA AVE
THE LEAS
SCARBOROUGH DR
MINSTER DR
Abbey Motel
1 NAVAL TERR
2 REGENCY CL
3 BENTHAM SQ
4 THE DUKE OF CLARENCE TRAD EST
5 EDWARD ST
The Moat
Superstore
Coll
Sheerness-on-Sea (Terminus)
Blue Town
Works
LC
BRIELLE WAY
A249
A250
BRIDGE RD
1 JACOBS HO
2 BEACHFIELD LODGE
3 THE CRESCENT
4 RAVALIN HO
CLARENCE ROW
1 SHEPPEY COTTS
2 NEPTUNE TERR
3 REDAN PL
4 ALEXANDRA MEWS
Cheyney Rock
Marine Town
ALMA STREET PASS
ALMA ST
JAMES ST
CLYDE ST
CLYDE COTTS
UNITY ST
RICHMOND ST
JEFFERSON RD
The Cheyne Mid Sch
Richmond First Sch
Ship on Shore (PH)
Barton's Point Coastal Pk
BECKLEY RD
SEAGER RD
BARNSLEY CL
HERO HO 1
LAUREL HO 2
LABURNUM HO 3
CEDAR HO 4
WILLOW HO 5
BIRCH HO 6
Mus
Rose Street Sch
St Edward's RC Prim Sch
HIGH ST
TRINITY RD
CAVOUR RD
HALFWAY RD
Mile Town
NEW ROAD IND EST
Bsns Pk
Allot Gdns
Works
Boating Lake
Monkey Farm
Minster Marshes
NURSERY CL
CORONATION RD
ST HELEN'S RD
PARK RD
WELLESLEY RD
ALEXANDRA RD
INVICTA RD
BERRIDGE RD
WINSTANLEY RD
GALWAY RD
TURNERS CL
ACORN ST
SHRUBSOLE AVE
VICTORIA ST
FIRST AVE
VINCENT GDNS
MAPLE ST
SOUTH VIEW GDNS
AGNES GDNS
SECOND AVE
ST GEORGE'S AVE
CARLTON AVE
CECIL AVE
WHEATSHEAF GDNS
DIAMOND CT
MIRANDA CT
MONTAGUE CT
MEDWAY RD
BRITON CT
NEW RD
GRACE RD
ESTUARY RD
FLEET AVE
THAMES AVE
SWALE AVE
KENT RD
HOLLAND CL
BOTANY CL
NORE CL
GRANVILLE RD
HARRIS RD
PORTLAND AVE
WOOD ST
ROSE ST
HOPE ST
MILLENNIUM WAY
RUSSELL ST
SHORT ST
RAILWAY RD
BROAD ST
VICTORY ST
BEACH ST
ROYAL RD
MEYRICK RD
RANELAGH RD
NEWCOMEN RD
ALMA RD
FONBLANQUE RD
BROADWAY
HIGH ST
CHARLES ST
EAST LA
KING'S HEAD ALLEY
UNION ST
WEST ST
WEST LA
KING ST
SHEPPEY ST
ARCHWAY RD
MAIN RD
JETTY RD

2
4
3

1

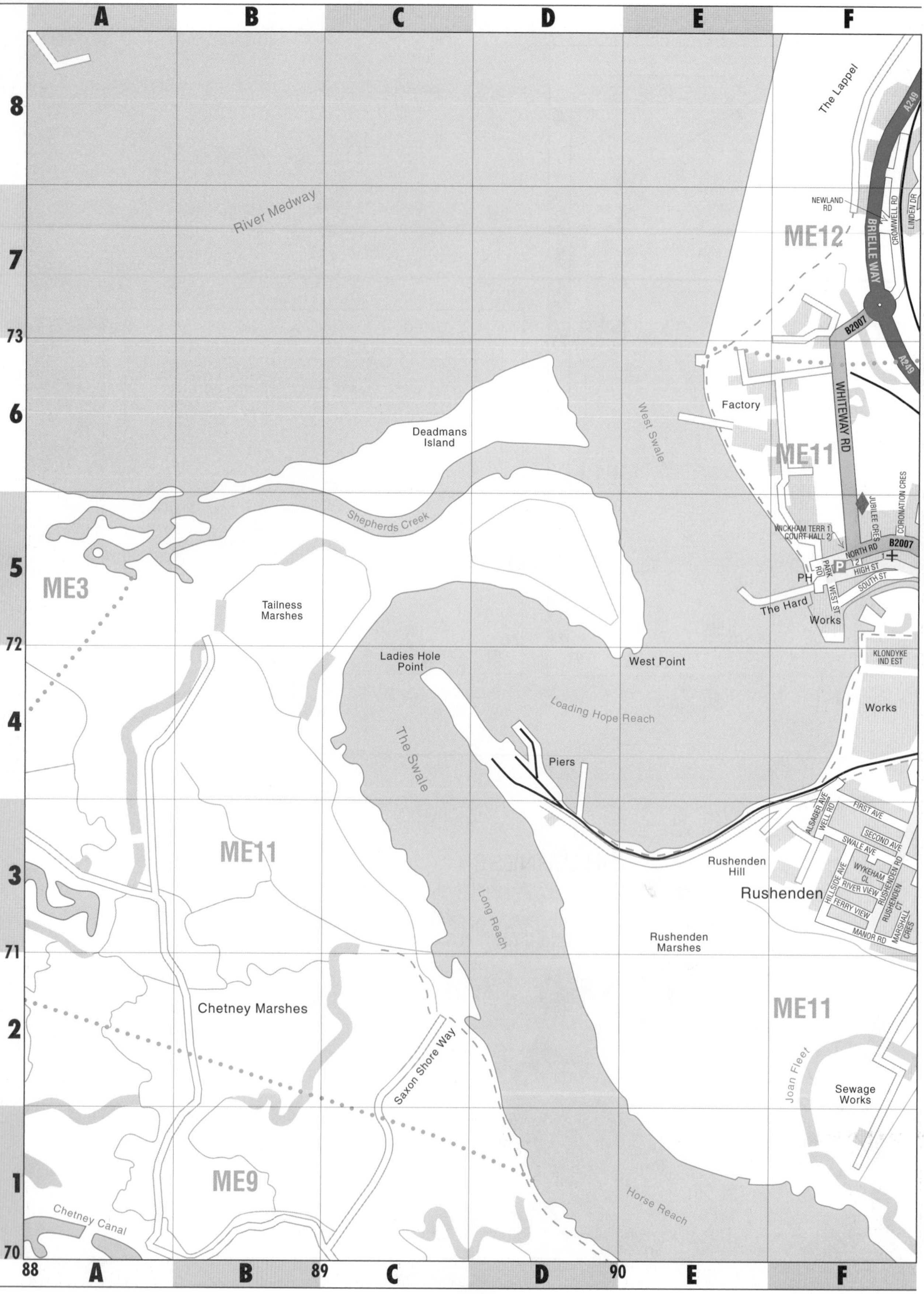
A
B
C
D
E
F
8
7
73
6
5
72
4
3
71
2
1
70
88
89
90
The Lappel
A249
NEWLAND RD
CROMWELL RD
LINDEN DR
BRIELLE WAY
ME12
B2007
A249
River Medway
Factory
WHITEWAY RD
West Swale
Deadmans Island
ME11
JUBILEE CRES
CORONATION CRES
WICKHAM TERR 1
COURT HALL 2
B2007
NORTH RD
Shepherds Creek
HIGH ST
SOUTH ST
PARK RD
WEST ST
PH
ME3
The Hard
Works
Tailness Marshes
KLONDYKE IND EST
Ladies Hole Point
West Point
Works
Loading Hope Reach
The Swale
Piers
ALSAGER AVE
WELL RD
FIRST AVE
SECOND AVE
SWALE AVE
ME11
Rushenden Hill
WYKEHAM CL
HILLSIDE AVE
RIVER VIEW
RUSHENDEN RD
Rushenden
FERRY VIEW
RUSHENDEN CT
MARSHALL CRES
MANOR RD
Long Reach
Rushenden Marshes
Chetney Marshes
ME11
Saxon Shore Way
Joan Fleet
Sewage Works
ME9
Horse Reach
Chetney Canal

14

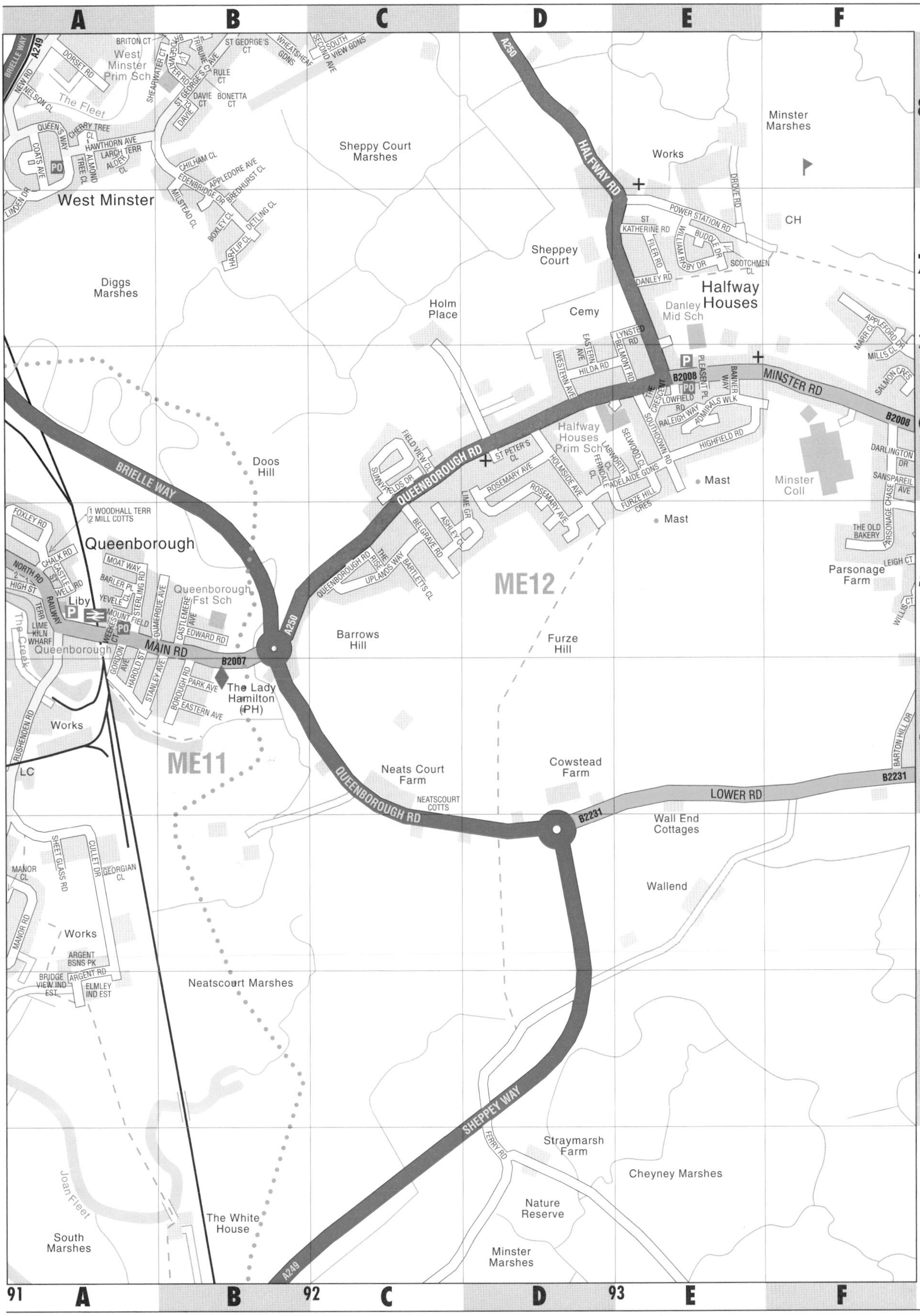

| A | B | C | D | E | F |

8

7

73

6

ME12

5

72

4

3

71

2

1

70

91   92   93

A   B   C   D   E   F

A249 BRIELLE WAY · NEW RD · NELSON CL · DORSET RD · LINDEN DR · COATS AVE · QUEEN'S WAY · HAWTHORN AVE · CHERRY TREE CL · ALMOND AVE · LARCH TERR · ALDER CL · The Fleet

West Minster Prim Sch · BRITON CT · West Minster · SHEARWATER CT · TRIBUNE CT · ST GEORGE'S CT · SECOND AVE · SOUTH VIEW GDNS · WHEATSHEAF GDNS · RULE CT · ST GEORGES CT · DAVIE CT · BONETTA CT · MILLSTEAD CL · EDENBRIDGE DR · BREDHURST CL · APPLEDORE AVE · CHILHAM CL · BOXLEY CL · HARTLIP CL · DETLING CL

Sheppy Court Marshes

A250 HALFWAY RD · Works · Minster Marshes

Diggs Marshes

Sheppey Court · Holm Place · Cemy · Danley Rd · ST KATHERINE RD · FILER RD · POWER STATION RD · WILLIAM RIGBY DR · DROVER RD · CH · BUDDLE DR · SCOTCHMEN CL · Halfway Houses · Danley Mid Sch

Doos Hill

EASTERN AVE · WESTERN AVE · HILDA RD · LYNSTED RD · BELMONT RD · P · PLEASENT PL · B2008 · PO · FLOWFIELD RD · CRESSET RD · RALEIGH WAY · ADMIRALS WLK · BANNER WAY · MINSTER RD · B2008 · APPLEFORD DR · MARII CL · MILLS CL · SALMON CRES

BRIELLE WAY

QUEENBOROUGH RD · SUNNYFIELDS DR · FIELD VIEW CL · St Peter's CL · Halfway Houses Prim Sch · LABURNTH · ADELAIDE GDNS · SOUTHDOWN RD · HIGHFIELD RD · Mast · DARLINGTON DR · SANSPAREIL AVE · PARSONAGE CHASE · LEIGH CT

1 WOODHALL TERR · 2 MILL COTTS · Queenborough · QUEENBOROUGH RD · THE UPLANDS · BARTLETT'S CL · LIME GR · BELGRAVE RD · ASHLEY CL · ROSEMARY AVE · Rosemary Ave · FURZE HILL CRES · Mast · Minster Coll · THE OLD BAKERY · Parsonage Farm · WILLIS CT

FOXLEY RD · NORTH RD · HIGH ST · CHALK RD · CASTLE · Queenborough Fst Sch · BARLER PL · YEVELE · STERLING RD · CASTLEMERE · DUMERGUE AVE · EDWARD RD · Liby · P · RAILWAY · MOAT WAY · MOUNT · FIELD · ME12 · Barrows Hill · Furze Hill · BARTON HILL DR

LIME KILN WHARF · Queenborough · The Creek · MERSEY RD · PO · MAIN RD · GORDON AVE · HAROLD ST · STANLEY AVE · BOROUGH RD · PARK AVE · EASTERN AVE · B2007 · The Lady Hamilton (PH) · A250

Works · RUSHENDEN RD · LC · ME11 · Neats Court Farm · NEATSCOURT COTTS · Cowstead Farm · B2231 · Wall End Cottages · LOWER RD · B2231

MANOR CL · MANOR RD · SHEET GLASS RD · CULLET DR · GEORGIAN CL · Works · ARGENT BSNS PK · ARGENT RD · BRIDGE VIEW IND EST · ELMLEY IND EST · Neatscourt Marshes · QUEENBOROUGH RD · Wallend

Joan Fleet · South Marshes · The White House · A249 · SHEPPEY WAY · FERRY RD · Straymarsh Farm · Nature Reserve · Minster Marshes · Cheyney Marshes

A B C D E F

8

Ripney Hill Farm

Royal Oak Point

Merryman's Hill

7

Elliott Park Sch

Minster

Round Hill

Seacliff

East End Farm

Caravan Pk

Sheppey H

73

The Rowans

Queenborough Dr

Abbeyview Dr

Minster-Sheppey Prim Sch

Minster Abbey

Cliff Gdns

Mill Hill

Chequers Rd

Oak Ave

Pigtail Cnr

Danedale Ave

B2008

Plough Rd

Eastchurch Rd

The Maples

Shurland Ave

Saxon Ave

Trafalgar Par

Liby

Waterloo Hill

HIGH ST BACK LA

Mus

CHAPEL ST

Windmill Rise

6

B2008

MINSTER RD

Worcester

New Rd

Petfield

Prince Charles Ave

Sports Gd

St George's CE Mid Sch

British Queen (PH)

Sheppey Terr

Darlington Dr

Dreadnought Ave

Fleetwood

Blatcher Cl

George Parris Ct

Copland Rd

Bramston Rd

Hofsing Rd

Nelson Ave

Tadwell Farm

Sanspareil Ave

Harps Ave

Summerville Ave

Lapwing Cl

Heron Dr

Scocles Rd

Drake Ave

Elm La

Woottons Farm

The Mount

5

Hilltop Rd

Plover Rd

Barton Hill Dr

1 Murthwaite Ct
2 Menzies Ct
3 Turmine Ct

Thistle Hill Way

Scocles Cotts

Boarers Farm

Rape Hill

Scocles Farm

ME12

Brambledown

Shrubsoles Hill

72

Thistle Hill

Bellflower Ave

Buckthorne

Penny Cress Rd

Orchid Cl

Harebell Cl

Hazel Hill Way

Shardens Farm

4

B2231

LOWER RD

FORTY ACRES HILL

LOWER RD

Brambledown Spring

Marshlands Farm

Piggery

Elm Tree Inn (PH)

Primrose Cottage

B2231

3

Flatcreek Head

South Lees

Elmley Rd

71

2

Poors

Windmill Quay Rd

New Hook Farm

Old Hook Rd

1

Southlees Marshes

Newhook Marshes

Old Hook Farm

70

94 A B 95 C D 96 E F

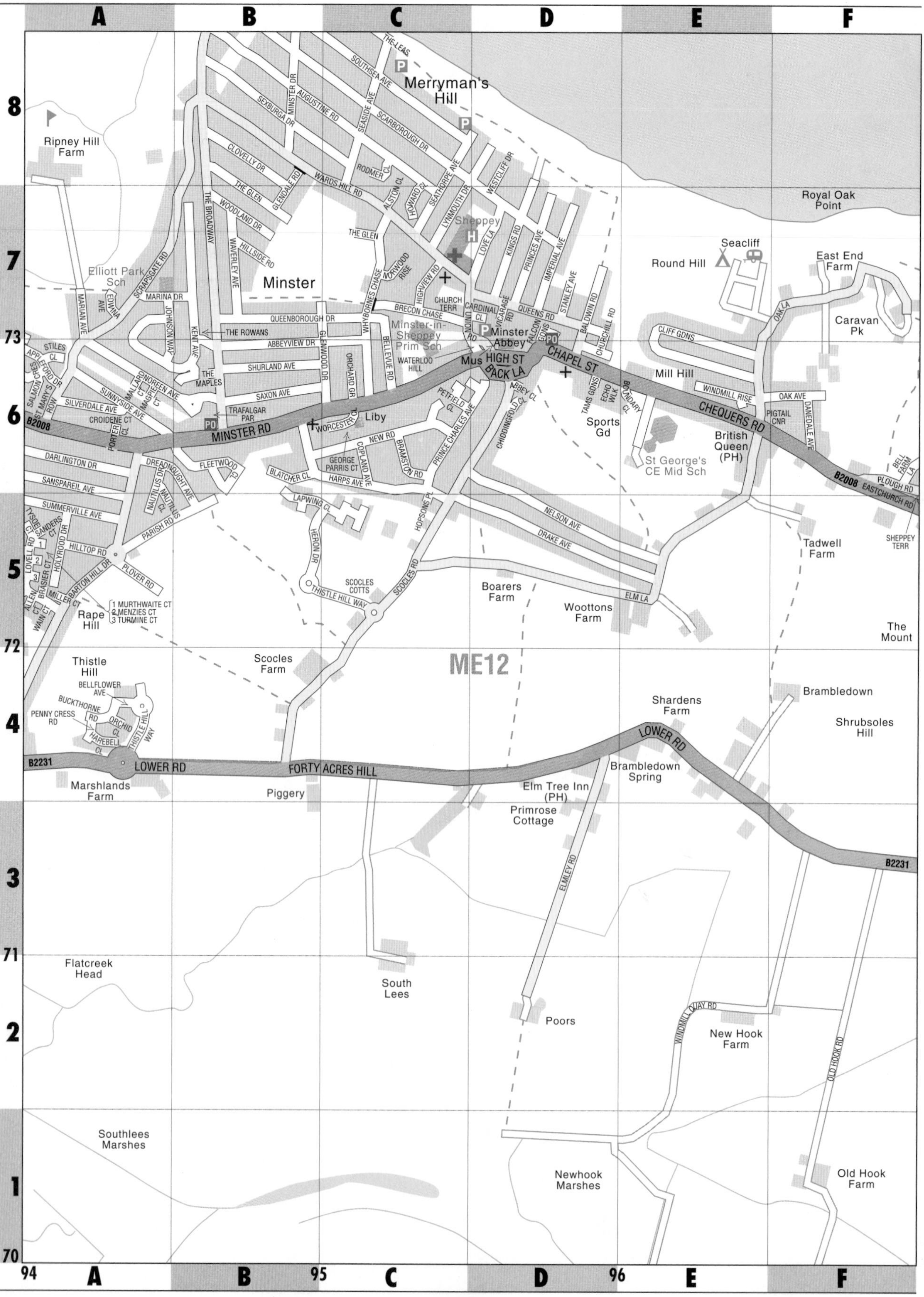

6

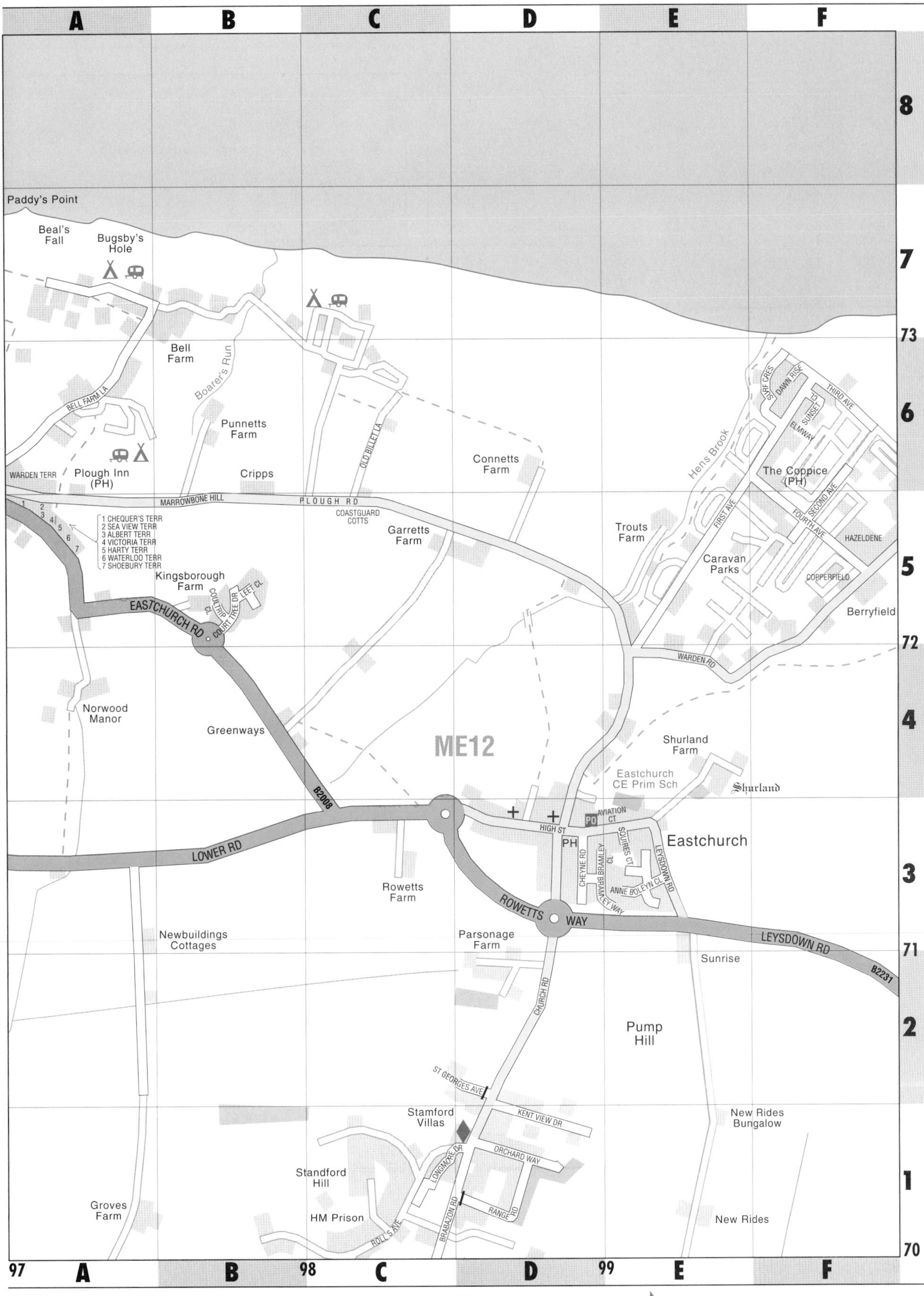
A
B
C
D
E
F
8
7
73
6
5
72
4
3
71
2
1
70
97
98
99
Paddy's Point
Beal's Fall
Bugsby's Hole
Bell Farm
Boarer's Run
BELL FARM LA
Punnetts Farm
OLD BILLET LA
Connetts Farm
WARDEN TERR
Plough Inn (PH)
Cripps
MARROWBONE HILL
PLOUGH RD
COASTGUARD COTTS
Garretts Farm
1 CHEQUER'S TERR
2 SEA VIEW TERR
3 ALBERT TERR
4 VICTORIA TERR
5 HARTY TERR
6 WATERLOO TERR
7 SHOEBURY TERR
Kingsborough Farm
COULTRIP CL
COURT TREE DR
LEET CL
EASTCHURCH RD
Norwood Manor
Greenways
ME12
B2008
LOWER RD
Rowetts Farm
Newbuildings Cottages
Parsonage Farm
ROWETTS WAY
HIGH ST
PH
PO
AVIATION CT
CHEYNE RD
BRAMLEY CL
BRAMLEY WAY
SQUIRES CT
ANNE BOLEYN CL
LEYSDOWN RD
Eastchurch
Eastchurch CE Prim Sch
Shurland Farm
Shurland
Hens Brook
SURF CRES
DAWN RISE
THIRD AVE
SUNSET CL
ELMWAY
FIRST AVE
The Coppice (PH)
SECOND AVE
FOURTH AVE
HAZELDENE
COPPERFIELD
Trouts Farm
Caravan Parks
Berryfield
WARDEN RD
Sunrise
B2231
CHURCH RD
Pump Hill
ST GEORGES AVE
KENT VIEW DR
Stamford Villas
ORCHARD WAY
LONGMORE DR
Standford Hill
RANGE RD
BRABAZON RD
ROLL'S AVE
HM Prison
Groves Farm
New Rides Bungalow
New Rides

17

6

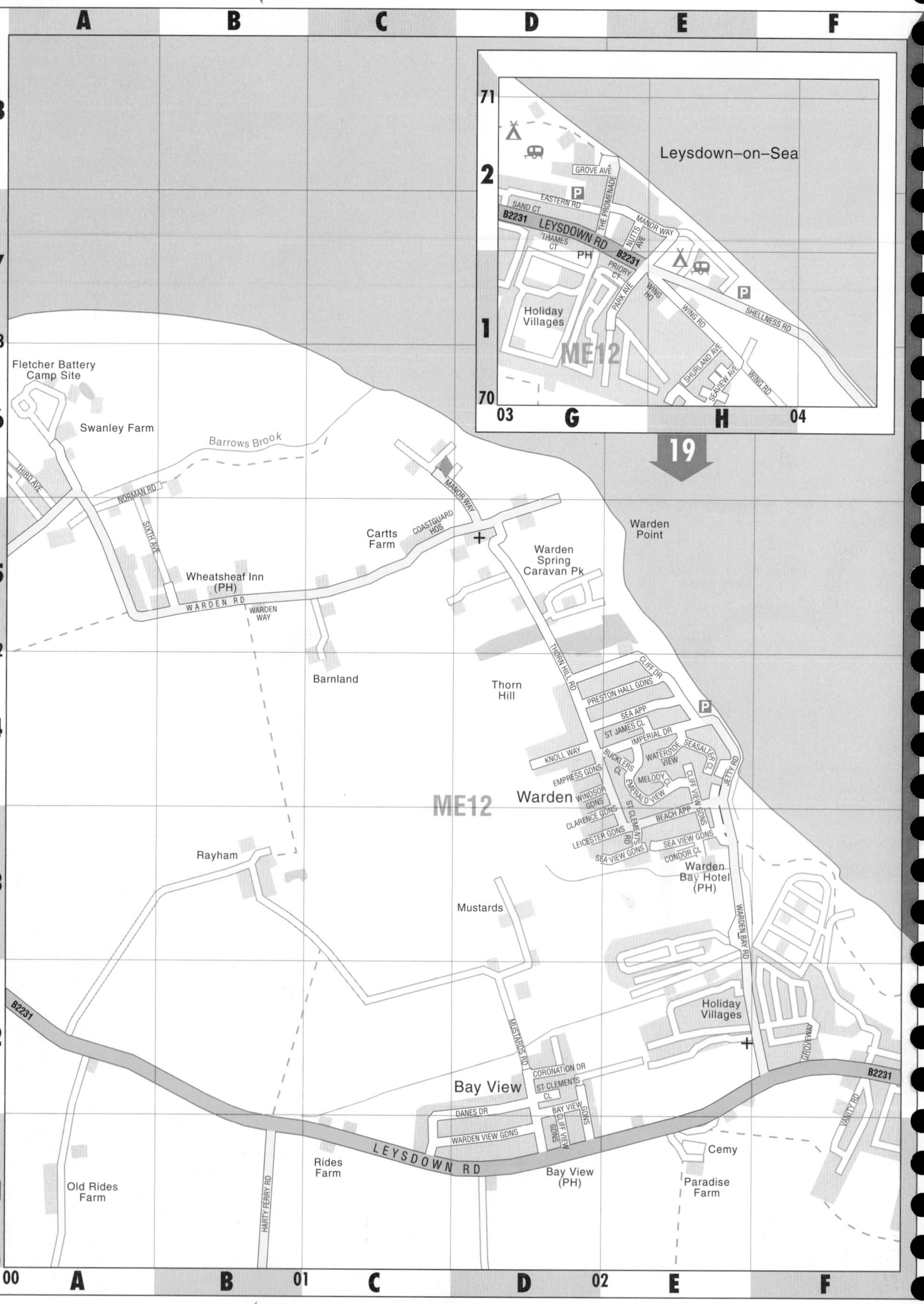

Leysdown–on–Sea

Holiday Villages

ME12

19

Fletcher Battery Camp Site

Swanley Farm

Barrows Brook

Cartts Farm

COASTGUARD HOS

Warden Point

Warden Spring Caravan Pk

Wheatsheaf Inn (PH)

WARDEN RD

WARDEN WAY

Barnland

Thorn Hill

CLIFF DR

PRESTON HALL GDNS

SEA APP

ST JAMES CL

KNOLL WAY

IMPERIAL DR

BUCKLERS CL

WATERSIDE VIEW

SEASALTER

JETTY RD

CLIFF VIEW GDNS

EMPRESS GDNS

WINDSOR GDNS

MELODY

EMERALD VIEW

Warden

CLARENCE GDNS

ST CLEMENTS

BEACH APP

LEICESTER GDNS

SEA VIEW GDNS

SEA VIEW GDNS

CONDOR CL

ME12

Rayham

Mustards

Warden Bay Hotel (PH)

WARDEN BAY RD

B2231

Holiday Villages

MUSTARDS RD

Bay View

CORONATION DR

ST CLEMENTS CL

BAY VIEW GDNS

DANES DR

CLIFF VIEW GDNS

WARDEN VIEW GDNS

GROVE WAY

B2231

TRINITY RD

Cemy

LEYSDOWN RD

Rides Farm

Bay View (PH)

Paradise Farm

HARTY FERRY RD

Old Rides Farm

THIRD AVE

NORMAN RD

SIXTH AVE

MANOR WAY

THORN HILL RD

GROVE AVE

EASTERN RD

SAND CT

B2231

THAMES CT

LEYSDOWN RD

THE PROMENADE

NUTTS AVE

MANOR WAY

B2231

PH

PRIORY CL

PARK AVE

WING RD

WING RD

SKURLAND AVE

SEAVIEW AVE

SHELLNESS RD

03 G 04 H

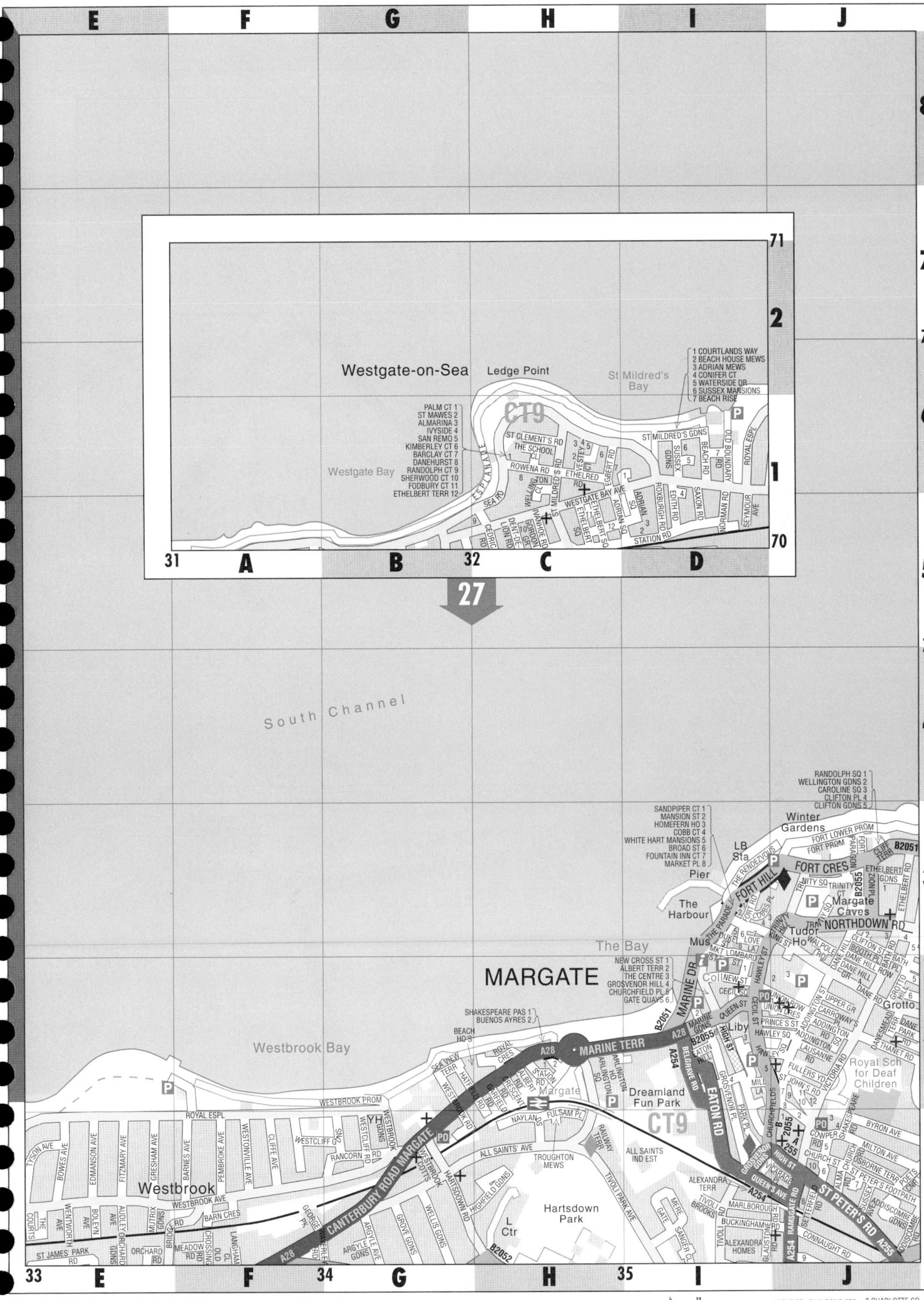

8

Westgate-on-Sea Ledge Point

St Mildred's Bay

CT9

Westgate Bay

1 PALM CT 1
ST MAWES 2
ALMARINA 3
IVYSIDE 4
SAN REMO 5
KIMBERLEY CT 6
BARCLAY CT 7
DANEHURST 8
RANDOLPH CT 9
SHERWOOD CT 10
FODBURY CT 11
ETHELBERT TERR 12

1 COURTLANDS WAY
2 BEACH HOUSE MEWS
3 ADRIAN MEWS
4 CONIFER CT
5 WATERSIDE DR
6 SUSSEX MANSIONS
7 BEACH RISE

27

South Channel

RANDOLPH SQ 1
WELLINGTON GDNS 2
CAROLINE SQ 3
CLIFTON PL 4
CLIFTON GDNS 5

Winter Gardens

SANDPIPER CT 1
MANSION ST 2
HOMEFERN HO 3
COBB CT 4
WHITE HART MANSIONS 5
BROAD ST 6
FOUNTAIN INN CT 7
MARKET PL 8

FORT CRES

Margate Caves

NORTHDOWN RD

Pier

The Harbour

The Bay

MARGATE

NEW CROSS ST 1
ALBERT TERR 2
THE CENTRE 3
GROSVENOR HILL 4
CHURCHFIELD PL 5
GATE QUAYS 6

Grotto

Royal Sch for Deaf Children

SHAKESPEARE PAS 1
BUENOS AYRES 2

Westbrook Bay

Dreamland Fun Park

CT9

Westbrook

Hartsdown Park

28

8

J1
1 GEORGE WARREN CT
2 CHARLOTTE PL
3 SPARROW CASTLE
4 MILTON SQ
5 ARNOLD RD
6 OXFORD ST
7 HOMESTEAD CL
8 VICARAGE CRES
9 CONNAUGHT GDNS
10 THE ST JOHN BSNS CTR
J2
1 PUMP LA
2 COLLEGE SQ
3 COLLEGE WLK
4 ANCHOR HILL
5 GROTTO RD
6 GROTTO GDNS
7 ST JOHN'S ST
8 CHARLOTTE SQ
9 WINDSOR MEWS
10 PRINCES CRES
11 LAUSANNE TERR
12 VENTNOR LA

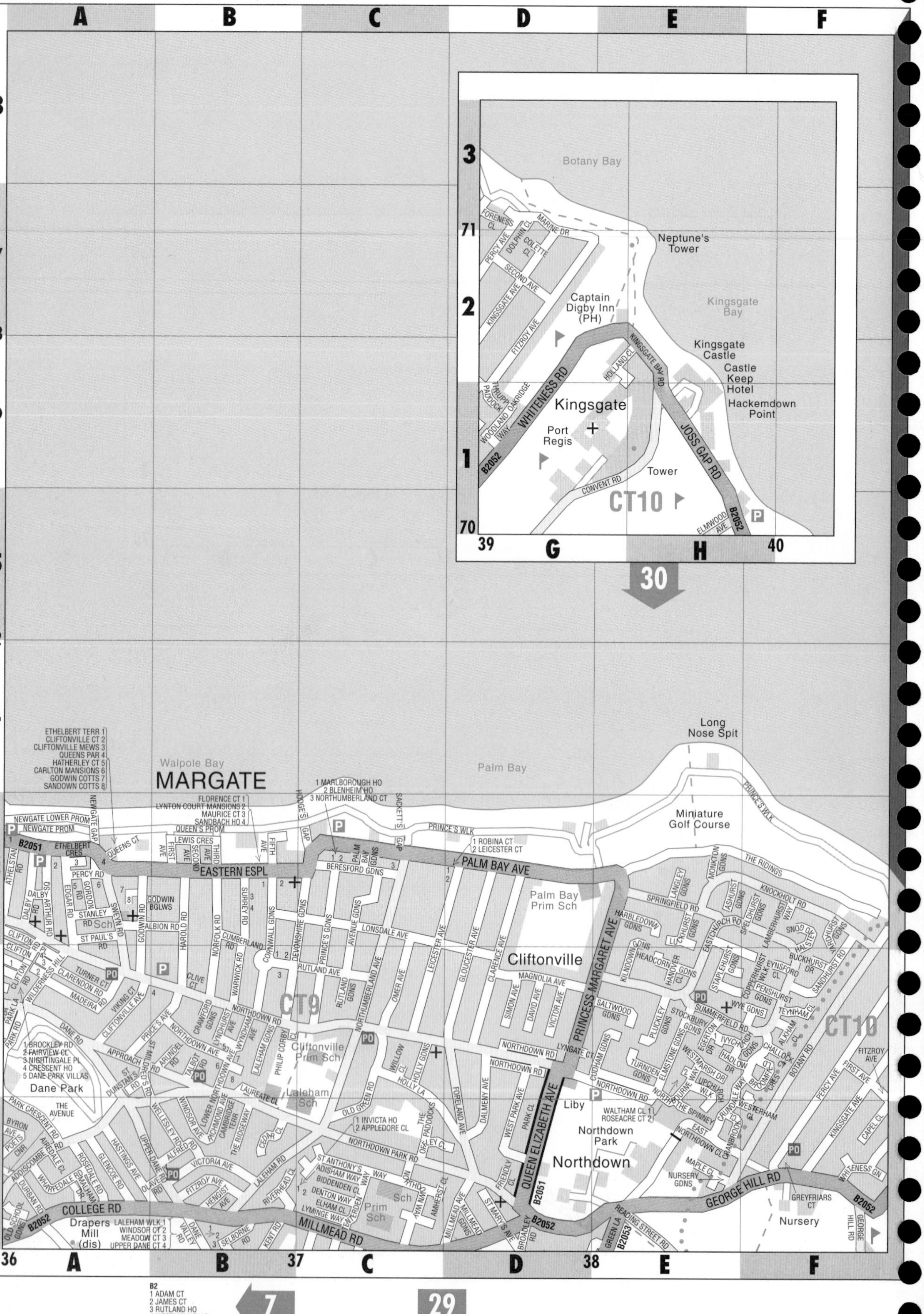

A B C D E F

8

7

73

6

5

72

4

3

71

2

1

70

3

71

2

1

70

39 G H 40

Botany Bay

FORENERS CL

MARINE DR

PERCY AVE

DOG PEN CL

COLETTE

Neptune's Tower

KINGSGATE AVE

SECOND AVE

Kingsgate Bay

Captain Digby Inn (PH)

FITZROY AVE

WHITENESS RD

HOLLAND CL

KINGSGATE BAY RD

Kingsgate Castle

Castle Keep Hotel

Hackemdown Point

THRUMPTON CL

PADDOCKS

WOODLAND WAY

OAKRIDGE

Kingsgate

JOSS GAP RD

Port Regis

B2052

CONVENT RD

Tower

CT10

ELMWOOD AVE

B2052

P

30

Main map (Margate / Cliftonville):

Long Nose Spit

ETHELBERT TERR 1
CLIFTONVILLE CT 2
CLIFTONVILLE MEWS 3
QUEENS PAR 4
HATHERLEY CT 5
CARLTON MANSIONS 6
GODWIN COTTS 7
SANDOWN COTTS 8

Walpole Bay

MARGATE

Palm Bay

1 MARLBOROUGH HO
2 BLENHEIM HO
3 NORTHUMBERLAND CT

Miniature Golf Course

PRINCE'S WLK

FLORENCE CT 1
LYNTON COURT MANSIONS 2
MAURICE CT 3
SANDBACH HO 4

THE RIDINGS

NEWGATE LOWER PROM

NEWGATE PROM

P

QUEEN'S PROM

PRINCE'S WLK

B2051

ETHELBERT CRES

QUEENS CT

LEWIS CRES

PALM BAY AVE

1 ROBINA CT
2 LEICESTER CT

ATHELSTAN RD

DALBY

PERCY RD

FIRST AVE

SECOND AVE

THIRD AVE

FIFTH AVE

BERESFORD GDNS

PALM BAY

GAP

SACKETT'S

EASTERN ESPL

Palm Bay Prim Sch

DALBY RD

ARTHUR RD

EDGAR RD

GORDON RD

STANLEY RD

GODWIN RD

ST PAULS RD

GODWIN BGLWS

ALBION RD

O'DOND RD

NORFOLK RD

SURREY RD

CORNWALL GDNS

DEVONSHIRE GDNS

PRINCE'S GDNS

AVENUE GDNS

LONSDALE AVE

LEICESTER AVE

GLOUCESTER AVE

CLARENCE AVE

Cliftonville

HARBLEDOWN GDNS

SPRINGFIELD RD

LANGLEY GDNS

MONKTON GDNS

KNOCKHOLT RD

CLIFTON

CLIFTON RD

TURNER RD

MADEIRA RD

VIKING AVE

CLIFTONVILLE AVE

WARWICK RD

CLIVE AVE

RUTLAND AVE

OMER AVE

SIMON AVE

IDAVO AVE

VICTOR AVE

Magnolia AVE

SALTWOOD GDNS

KILNDOWN GDNS

HEADCORNER

HANVER GDNS

EASTCHURCH RD

SPELDHURST GDNS

LAMBERHURST GDNS

ASHURST GDNS

SNO DR

BUCKHURST DR

EYNSFORD CL

CT9

PRICE'S AVE

NORTHDOWN AVE

CRAWFORD GDNS

RUTLAND AVE

NORTHUMBERLAND AVE

WYTHAM AVE

HOLLY GDNS

WILLOW

LYNGATE CT

NORTHDOWN RD

PRINCESS MARGARET AVE

PLUCKLEY GDNS

STOCKBURY GDNS

SUMMERFIELD RD

WYE GDNS

COPPERHURST

PENSHURST CL

WESTGATE

TEYNHAM CL

CT10

BROCKLEY RD
FAIRVIEW CL
NIGHTINGALE PL
CRESCENT HO
DANE PARK VILLAS

DANE RD

ARKLEY RD

DUNSTAN'S

THE PADDOCKS

INVICTA HO
APPLEDORE CL

NORTHDOWN RD

MAGNOLIA AVE

SIMON AVE

LYDIA DO AVE

VICTOR AVE

ELMSTONE GDNS

TURNDEN GDNS

WICKHAM CL

IVYCHURCH GDNS

CHALLOCK CL

FITZROY AVE

FIRST AVE

Dane Park

THE AVENUE

LAUREATE AVE

LALEHAM RD

Laleham Sch

OLD GREEN RD

DALMENY AVE

FORELAND AVE

WEST PARK AVE

PARK CL

SALTWOOD GDNS

NORTH DOWN RD

THE SPINNEY

WLK

WESTGATE

HADLOW

VIRGINIA RD

WESTERHAM CL

EAST

NORTHDOWN CL

CRIMBELL MANOR

BOTANY RD

KINGSGATE AVE

PERCY AVE

BYRON AVE

POE'S

ADDISCOMBE RD

WHARFEDALE RD

GLENCOE RD

HASTINGS AVE

UPPER DANE RD

VICTORIA AVE

ALFRED RD

WELLESLEY RD

CAMBRIDGE TERR

THE RIDGEWAY

ST ANTHONY'S WAY

ADISHAM WAY

BIDDENDEN CL

DENTON WAY

LYMINGE WAY

Northdown Park

QUEEN ELIZABETH AVE

Liby

B2051

WALTHAM CL 1
ROSEACRE CT 2

Northdown Park

Northdown

MAPLE CL

NURSERY GDNS

CAPEL CL

WHITENESS GN

P

WEST PARK AVE

PARK CRESCENT RD

AIREDALE RD

PARK RD

DURBAN RD

OLD SCH CL

B2052

Drapers Mill (dis)

COLLEGE RD

LALEHAM WLK 1
WINDSOR CT 2
MEADOW CT 3
UPPER DANE CT 4

SELBORNE RD

KENT RD

HENGIST AVE

FITZROY AVE

RIVERHEAD

RICHMOND AVE

ST MARY'S AVE

FRIEND'S AVE

MILLMEAD RD

Prim Sch

NORTHDOWN PARK RD

HAMMERET CL

MILLMEAD AVE

B2052

BROADLEY RD

GREEN LA

B2053

READING STREET RD

GEORGE HILL RD

GREYFRIARS CT

B2052

Nursery

GEORGE HILL RD

A B 37 C D 38 E F

70

36

B2
1 ADAM CT
2 JAMES CT
3 RUTLAND HO
4 WESTMOUNT HO
5 HIGHFIELD CT
6 REBECCA CT
7 RICHARD CT
8 LEONA CT

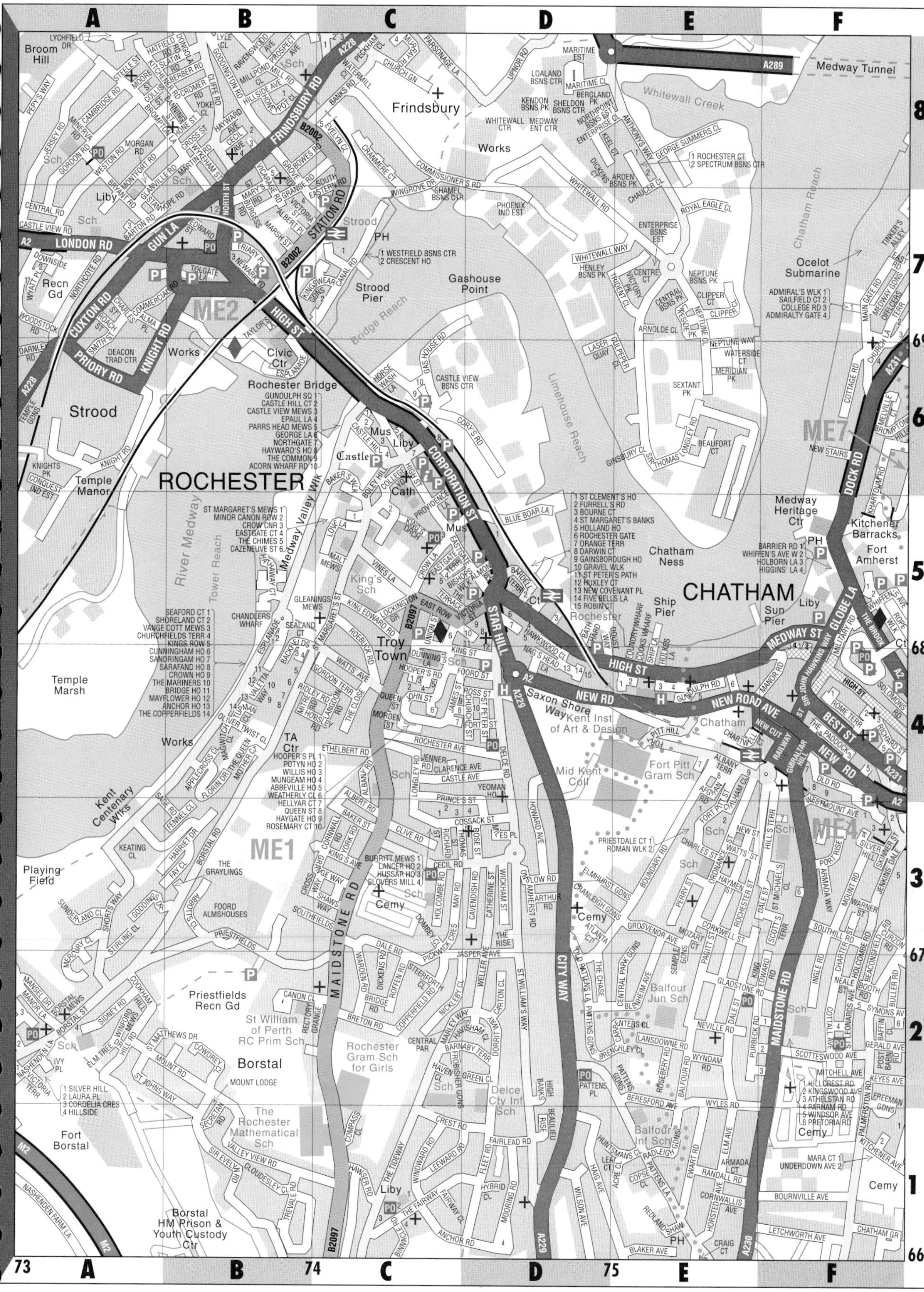

A7
1 WYATT HO
2 HILLSIDE CT
3 WARBLERS CL

B7
1 NEWARK CT
2 AVELING CT
3 FRIARY PREC
4 GROVE CT

B8
1 ALEXANDER CT
2 EPPE CL
3 FLORENCE ST
4 ARCHWAY CT
5 ST MICHAEL'S CT

C8
1 BILL STREET RD
2 MAYFAIR
3 CHRISTIAN CT
4 PEMBERTON SQ
5 EVELYN HO

C1
1 BAKENHAM HO
2 LEEKE HO
3 TRANSOM HO
4 SPINNAKER CT

E4
1 BINGLEY RD
2 ST BARTHOLOMEW'S TERR
3 HOSPITAL LA
4 ST BARTHOLOMEW'S LA
5 MEDWAY HEIGHTS
6 HAMOND HILL
7 CRESSEY CT
8 LUMSDEN TERR
9 ORDNANCE TERR

F3
1 ORCHARD VILLAS
2 CLAREMONT WAY
3 MOUNT VIEW CT
4 SILVER HILL GDNS
5 CORONATION FLATS
6 RIVER VIEW CL
7 SAUNDERS ST

F4
1 CAMBRIDGE TERR
2 MEETING HOUSE LA
3 CLOVER ST
4 MILLWOOD CT
5 JAMES ST
6 COPPERFIELD HO
7 SPRINGFIELD TERR
8 BERKELEY MOUNT
9 LANSDOWNE CT

9

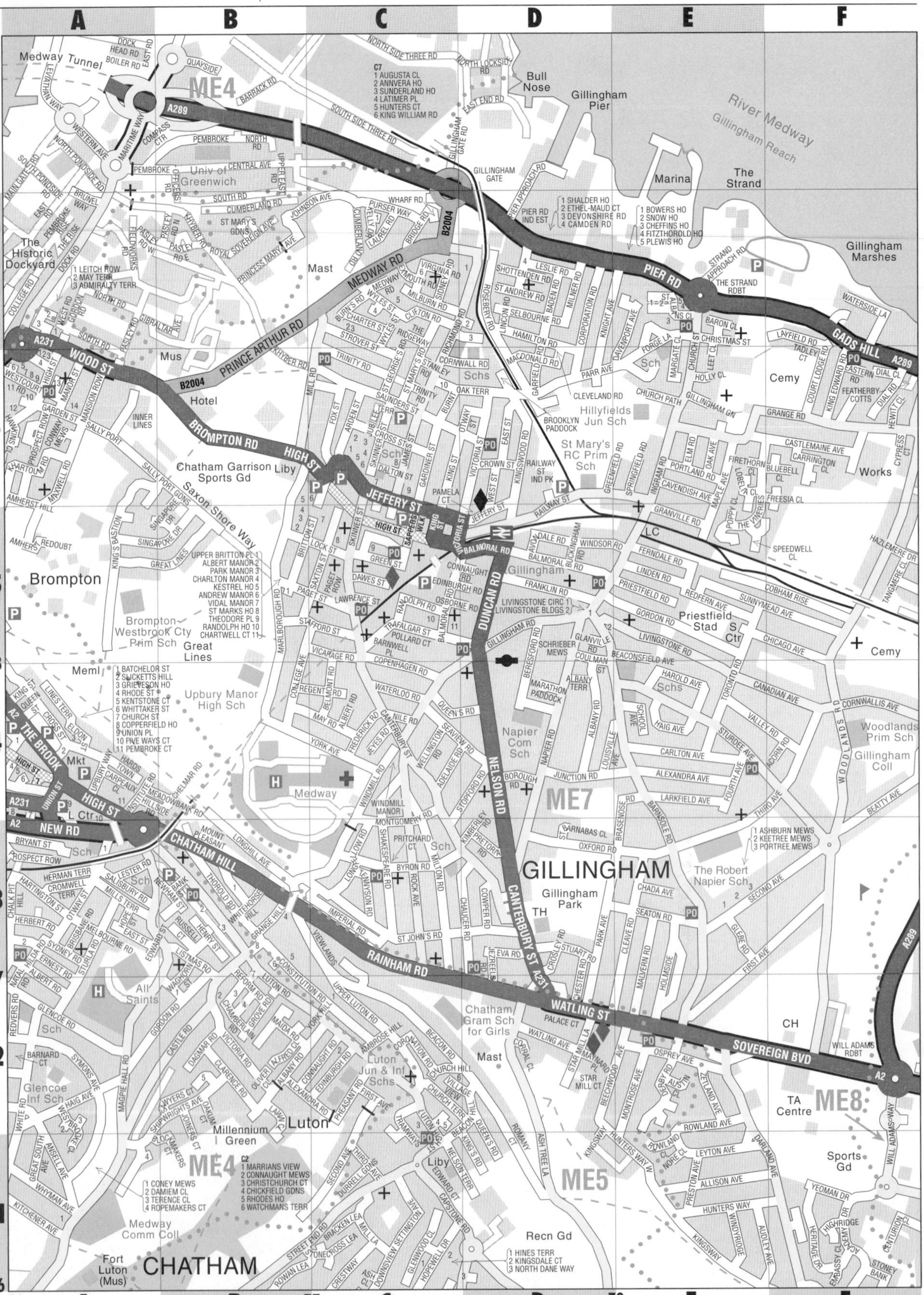

C7
1 AUGUSTA CL
2 ANNVERA HO
3 SUNDERLAND HO
4 LATIMER PL
5 HUNTERS CT
6 KING WILLIAM RD

1 SHALDER HO
2 ETHEL-MAUD CT
3 DEVONSHIRE CT
4 CAMDEN RD

1 BOWERS HO
2 SNOW HO
3 CHEFFINS HO
4 FITZTHOROLD HO
5 PLEWIS HO

1 LEITCH ROW
2 MAY TERR
3 ADMIRALTY TERR

UPPER BRITTON PL 1
ALBERT MANOR 2
PARK MANOR 3
CHARLTON MANOR 4
KESTREL HO 5
ANDREW MANOR 6
VIDAL MANOR 7
ST MARKS HO 8
THEODORE PL 9
RANDOLPH HO 10
CHARTWELL CT 11

1 BATCHELOR ST
2 SUCKETTS HILL
3 GRIEVES HO
4 RHODE ST
5 KENTSTONE CT
6 WHITTAKER ST
7 CHURCH ST
8 COPPERFIELD HO
9 UNION PL
10 FIVE WAYS CT
11 PEMBROKE CT

1 ASHBURN MEWS
2 KEETREE MEWS
3 PORTREE MEWS

C2
1 CONEY MEWS
2 DAMIEM CL
3 TERENCE CL
4 ROPEMAKERS CT

C2
1 MARRIANS VIEW
2 CONNAUGHT MEWS
3 CHRISTCHURCH CT
4 CHICKFIELD GDNS
5 RHODES HO
6 WATCHMANS TERR

1 HINES TERR
2 KINGSDALE CT
3 NORTH DANE WAY

9   32

A3
1 OTWAY TERR
2 LEOPOLD RD
A6
1 VICTORY MANOR
2 TEMERAIRE MANOR
3 BARFLEUR MANOR
4 MIDDLE ST
5 CAMPERDOWN MANOR
6 RIVER ST

7 DAWSON CT
8 MCCUDDEN ROW
9 PERIE ROW
10 PLEASANT ROW
11 LENDRIM CL
12 MELVILLE CT
13 FLAXMANS CT
14 MANOR HO

B2
1 PORTLAND ST
2 LISTMAS RD
3 BRIGHT RD
4 COBDEN RD
5 SAILMAKERS CT

B3
1 SEYMOUR RD
2 HARE ST
3 SHORT ST
4 THE PICCADILLY
5 WEALDEN CT
6 OCELOT CT
7 LEONARD RD
8 CONSTITUTION HILL

C6
1 PADSTOW MANOR
2 CAMBORNE MANOR
3 REDRUTH MANOR
4 PENRYN MANOR
5 AUSTELL MANOR
6 TINTAGEL MANOR
7 GRAND CT
8 DEANE CT
9 WILL ADAMS CT

10 CHATSWORTH RD

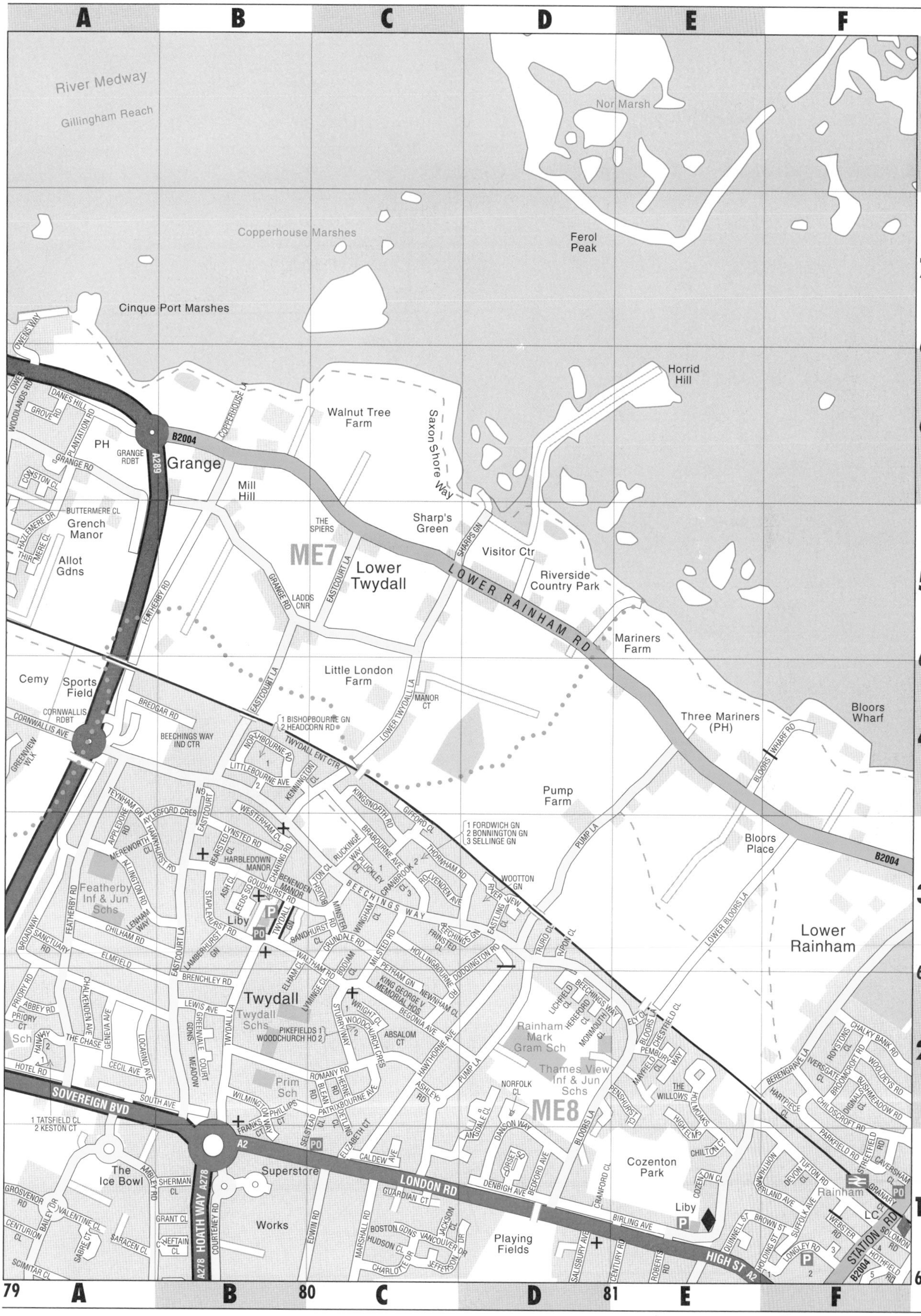

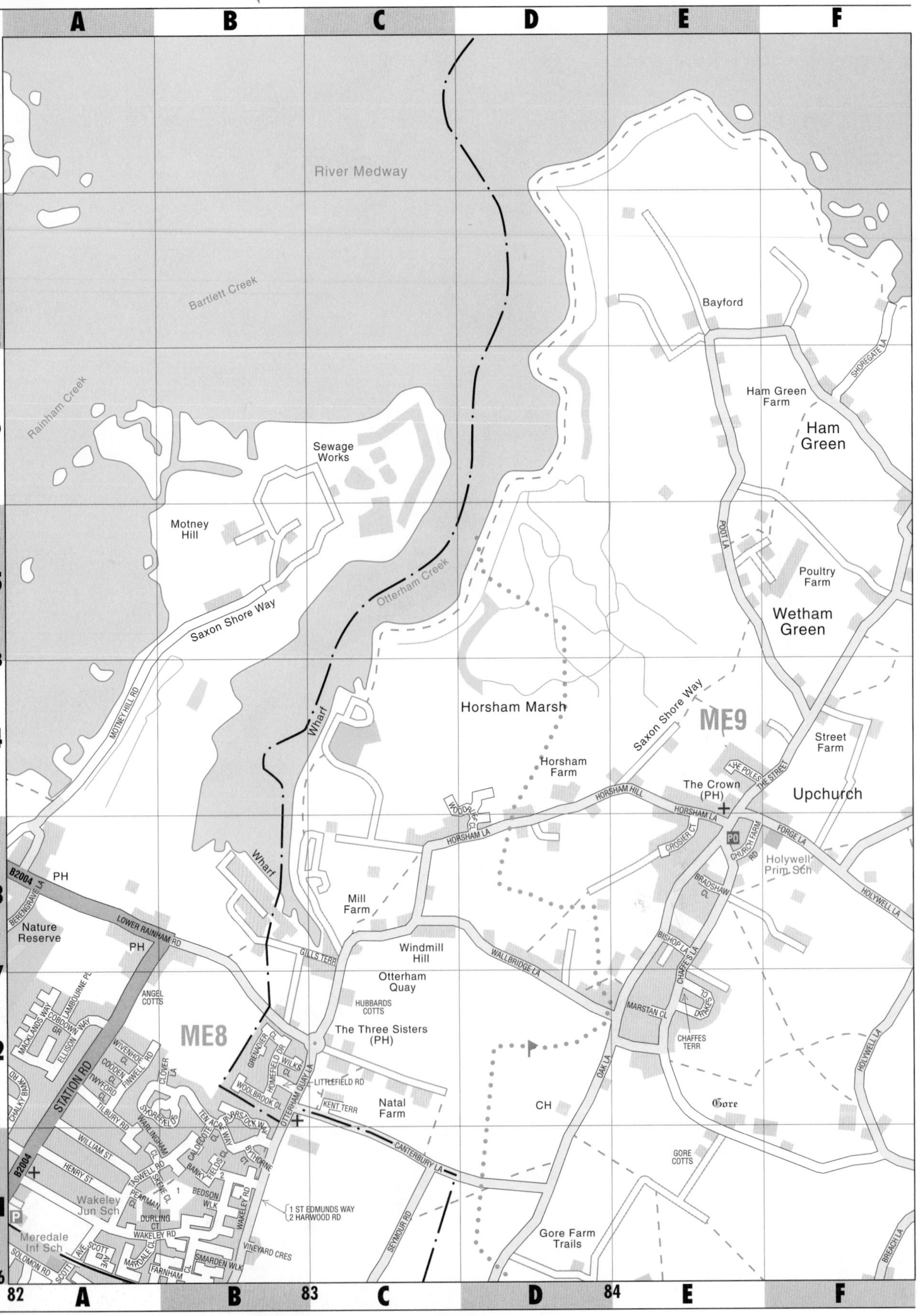

A B C D E F

8

River Medway

7

Bartlett Creek

69

Rainham Creek

6

Sewage Works

Motney Hill

Ham Green Farm

Ham Green

Otterham Creek

5

Saxon Shore Way

POOT LA

Poultry Farm

Wetham Green

SHOREGATE LA

Bayford

68

Wharf

Horsham Marsh

Saxon Shore Way

ME9

Street Farm

4

Horsham Farm

THE POLES

THE STREET

The Crown (PH)

Upchurch

Wharf

HORSHAM HILL

HORSHAM LA

WOODE

HORSHAM LA

CROSIER CT

PO

CHURCH FARM

FORGE LA

HOLYWELL LA

Holywell Prim Sch

B2004

PH

LOWER RAINHAM RD

GILLS TERR

Mill Farm

BRADSHAW CL

BISHOP LA

CHAPEL ST

3

BERENGRAVE LA

MOTNEY HILL RD

Nature Reserve

PH

Windmill Hill

WALLBRIDGE LA

HOLYWELL LA

67

Otterham Quay

HUBBARDS COTTS

Angel Cotts

OTTERHAM QUAY LA

GREENLEES

WIVENHOE

WILKS

Marstan Cl

Chaffes Terr

DRAKES

ME8

The Three Sisters (PH)

CH

Gore

2

MACKLANDS WAY

GR

ELLSON WAY

GIBSON

CLOVER

WIVENHOE

PINFOLD RD

FINWELL RD

GREENFIELD DR

LITTLEFIELD RD

KENT TERR

Natal Farm

OAK LA

Gore Cotts

STATION RD

CHALKY BANK RD

TWYFORD CL

COGDEN CL

TILBURY RD

SHOREFIELDS

TEN ACRE WAY

BURRSTOCK WAY

BLYTHORNE

BANKY FIELDS CT

CANTERBURY LA

WILLIAM ST

CALDECOTE CL

WAN INGHAM

WAKELEY RD

1

B2004

HENRY ST

TASWELL RD

STONE CL

PEARMAN CL

BEDSON WLK

DURLING CT

SEYMOUR RD

1 ST EDMUNDS WAY

2 HARWOOD RD

Gore Farm Trails

P

Meredale Inf Sch

SOLOMON RD

Wakeley Jun Sch

SCOTT AVE

SCOTT CL

PR

WAKELEY RD

MARSHALL CL

FARNHAM CL

SMARDEN WLK

VINEYARD CRES

BREACH LA

66

82 A 83 B C 84 D E F

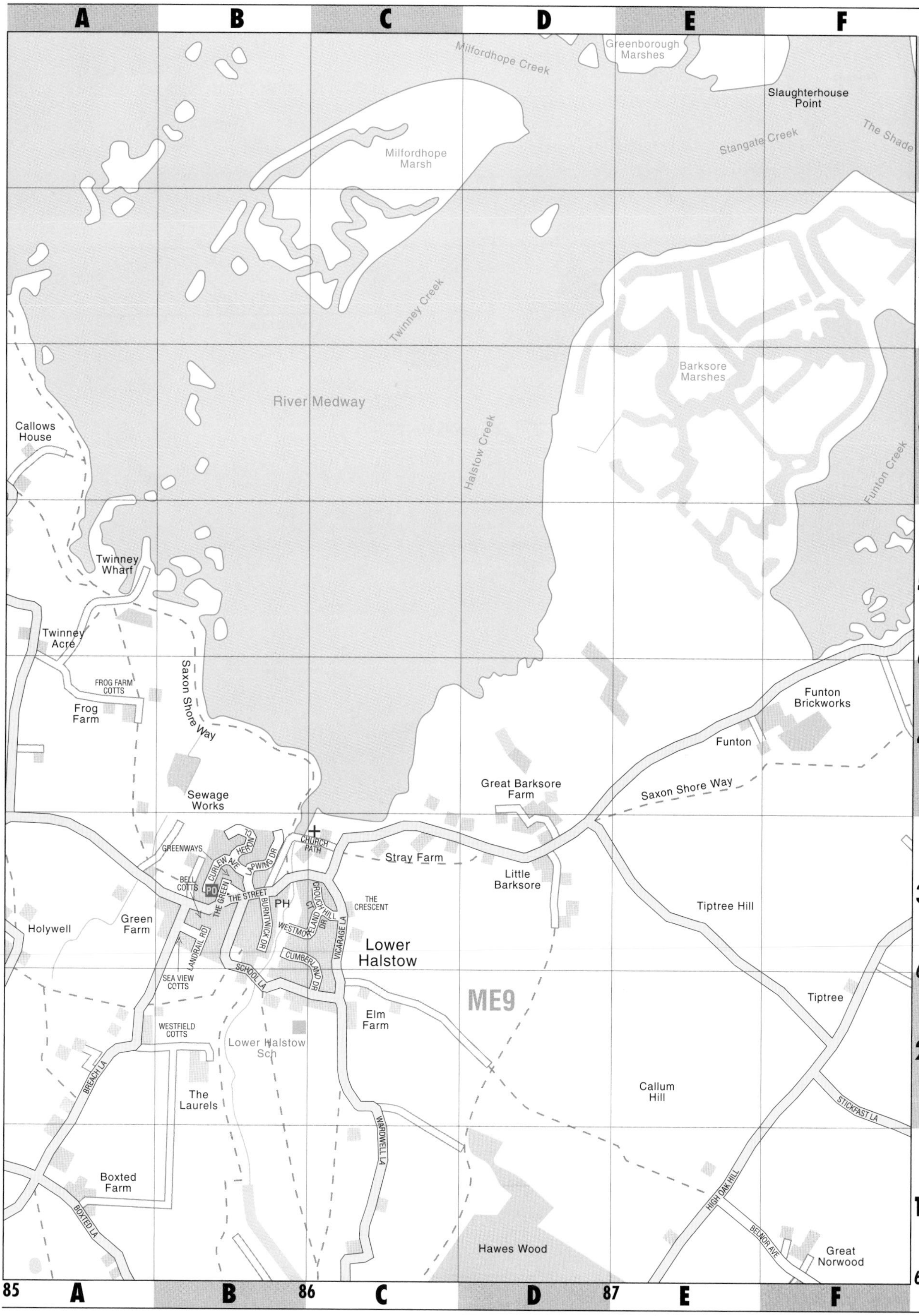

A B C D E F

8
7
69
6
5
68
4
3
67
2
1
66

Milfordhope Creek
Greenborough Marshes
Slaughterhouse Point
The Shade
Stangate Creek
Milfordhope Marsh

Twinney Creek

Barksore Marshes

River Medway

Halstow Creek

Funton Creek

Callows House

Twinney Wharf

Twinney Acre

FROG FARM COTTS

Frog Farm

Saxon Shore Way

Sewage Works

Funton Brickworks

Funton

Saxon Shore Way

Great Barksore Farm

Little Barksore

Tiptree Hill

GREENWAYS
BELL COTTS
PO
CHURCH PATH
Stray Farm
Green Farm
Holywell
PH
THE CRESCENT
Lower Halstow
THE STREET
CURLEN AVE
LAPWING DR
THE GREEN
HERON
WESTMOR
BURNTWICK DR
GROUCH HILL
LANDRAIL RD
CUMBERLAND DR
VICARAGE LA
SCHOOL LA

SEA VIEW COTTS

ME9

Tiptree

WESTFIELD COTTS

Lower Halstow Sch

Elm Farm

BREACH LA

The Laurels

Callum Hill

STICKFAST LA

WARDWELL LA

Boxted Farm

BOXTED LA

HIGH OAK HILL

BELMOR AVE

Hawes Wood

Great Norwood

A   B   C   D   E   F

8

Chetney Hill

The Shade

Horse Reach

Saxon Shore Way

Ferry Marshes

7

Funton Reach

Saxon Shore Way

69

River Medway

Marshbank

OLD FERRY RD

Ridham Fleet

Chetney Cottages

Willow Cottages

6

Raspberry Hill

RASPBERRY HILL LA

SHEPPEY WAY

A249

Raspberry Hill Park

5

Saxon Shore Way

THE STREET

68

Iwade Com Prim Sch

Wool Pack Inn

ME9

EVERGREEN CL
MEADOW CL
FANS LA

4

LINK WAY
SPRINGVALE

PO
WOODPECKER DR

TURNSTONE CL

FERRY RD

HELEN THOMPSON CL

KINGFISHER

SCHOOL LA

MEADOW RISE

ERSTONE

Iwade

COLESHALL COTTS

PINK'S CNR

Moat Farm Cottages

3

Culnell's Cottages

Coleshall Farm

Coleshall

Orchard Farm

67

FEATHERBED LA

B2005

LC

Culnells

2

Great Grovehurst Farm

GROVEHURST RD

ME10

1 OSTEND CT
2 BRUGES CT
3 MELLOR ROW

SHEPPEY WAY

Corbiere

DANES MEAD
GODWIN CL

The Kemsley Arms (PH)

MONS CT

RIDHAM AVE

Pheasants

Kemsley

PO

HURS

FLANDERS
1 CL

COLDHARBOUR LA

Cambray Farm

1

STICKFAST LA

WOODSDALE COTTS

LIEGE CL

CASTLE ROUGH

GLOVER CL

CREATION WAY

Cambray Cottages

PARSONAGE LA

A249

BRAMBLEFIELD LA

Kemsley

COLEMAN DR

B2005

66

LAYFIELD COTTS

SANDSTONE DR

88   **A**   89   **B**   **C**   **D**   90   **E**   **F**

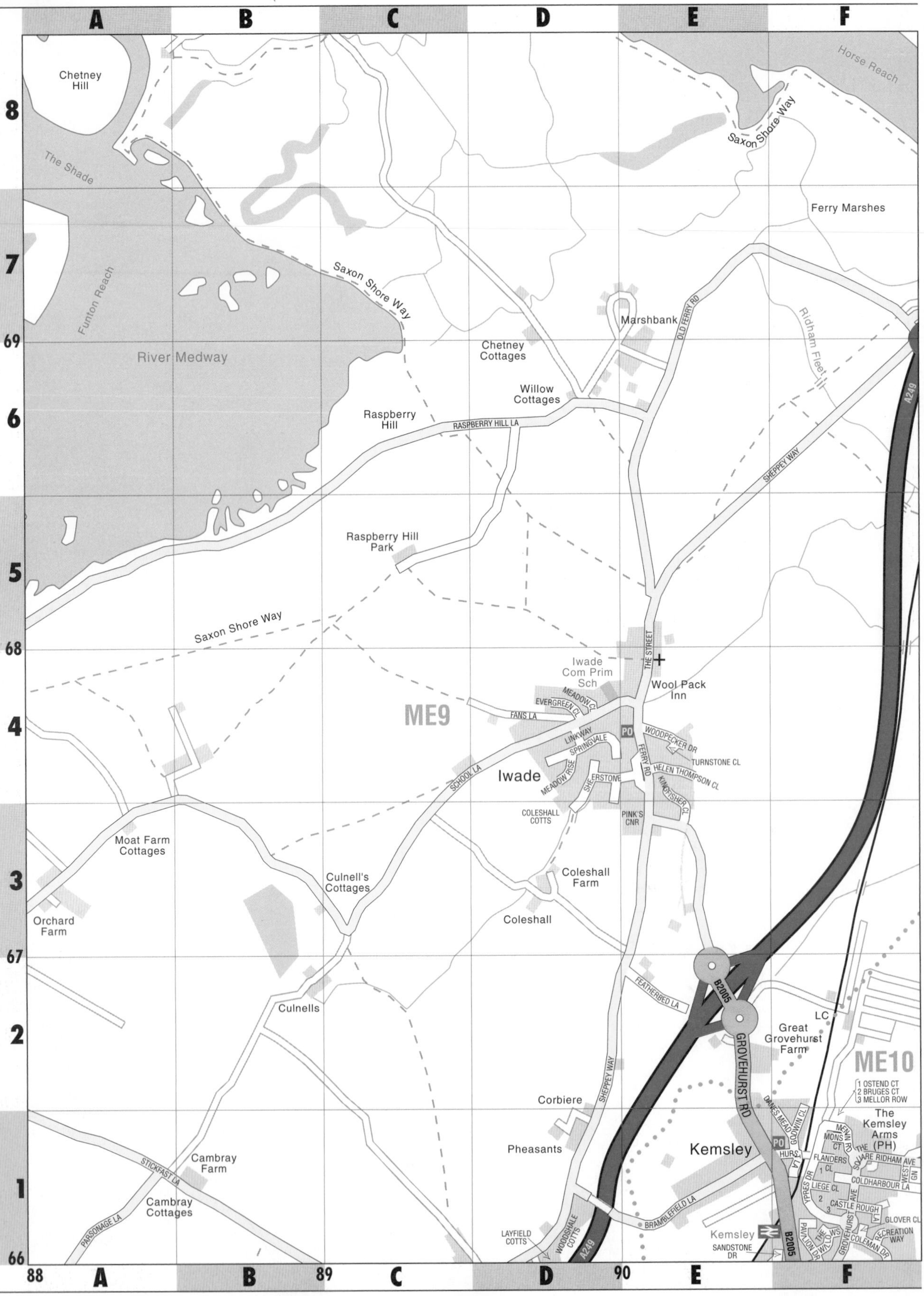

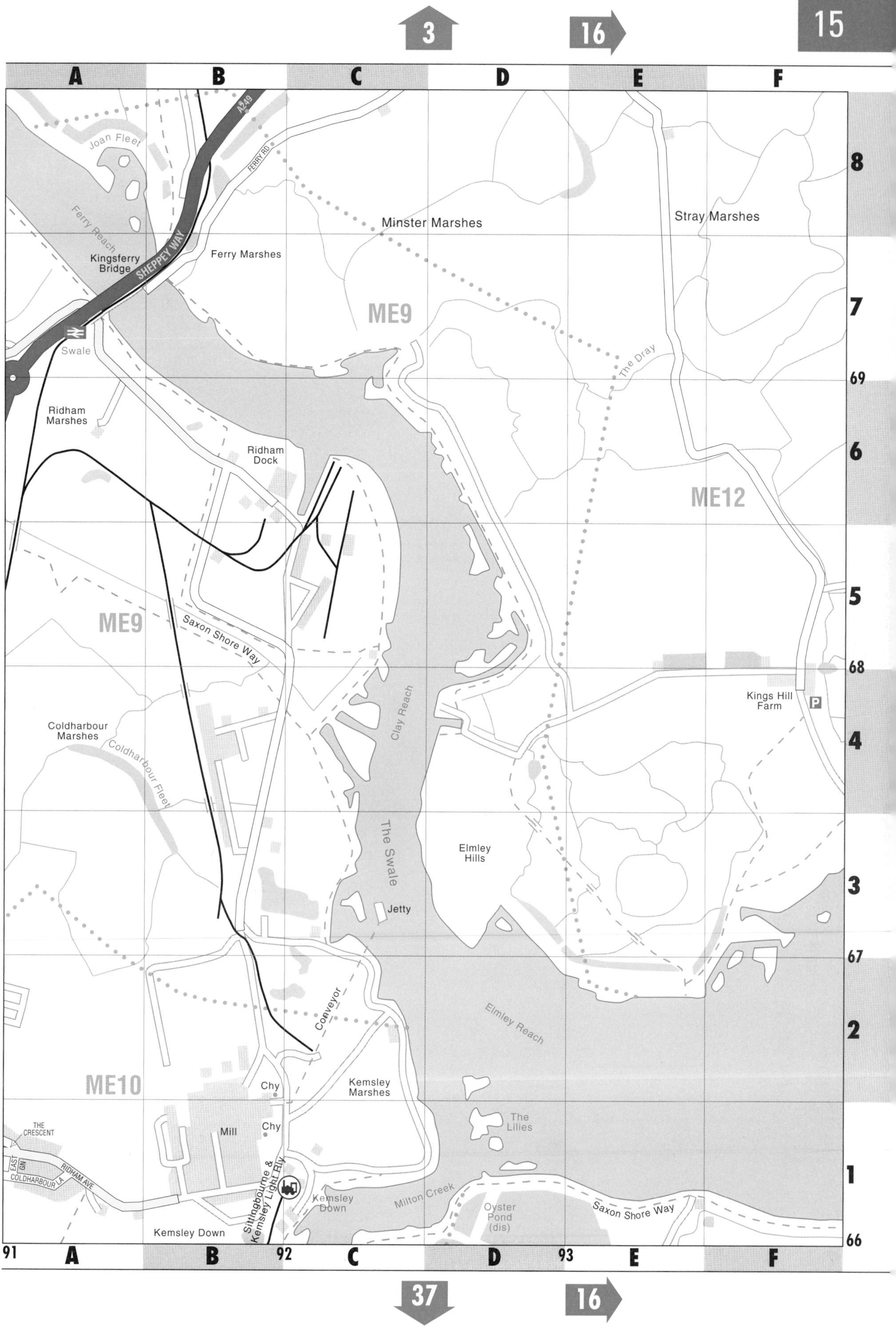

A   B   C   D   E   F

8

Joan Fleet

Minster Marshes

Stray Marshes

Ferry Reach

Ferry Marshes

Kingsferry
Bridge   SHEPPEY WAY

ME9   7

Swale   69

The Dray

Ridham
Marshes   6

Ridham
Dock   ME12

Saxon Shore Way   5

ME9   68

Coldharbour
Marshes   Kings Hill
Farm   P

Coldharbour Fleet   4

Clay Reach

The Swale   Elmley
Hills   3

Jetty   67

Conveyor   Elmley Reach   2

ME10   Kemsley
Marshes

THE
CRESCENT   Chy   The
Lilies

EAST
GN   Mill   Chy   1

RIDHAM AVE   Kemsley
Down   Milton Creek   Oyster
Pond
(dis)   Saxon Shore Way

COLDHARBOUR LA   Sittingbourne & Kemsley Light Rly   66

Kemsley Down

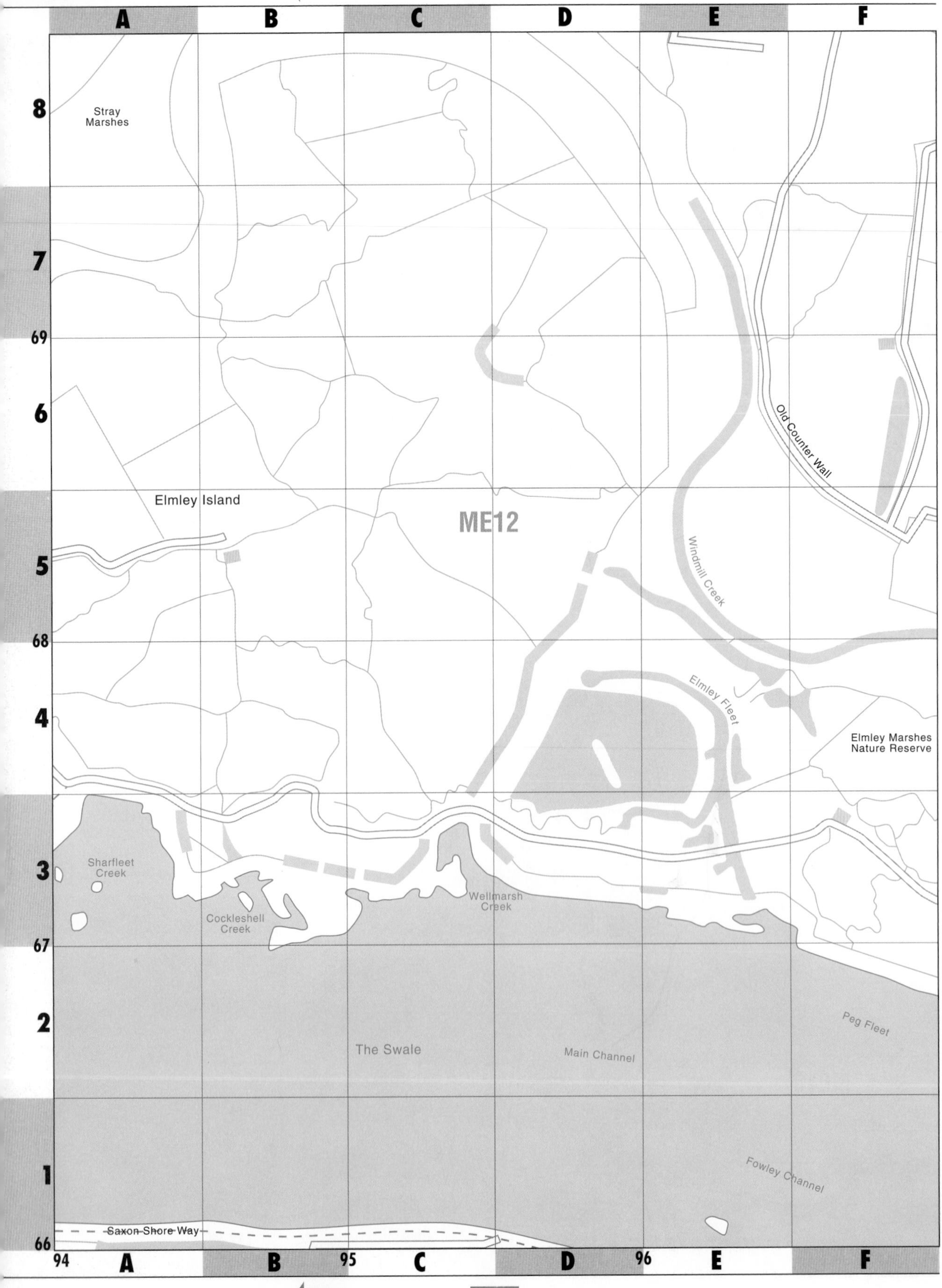

15
4

A   B   C   D   E   F

8

Stray
Marshes

7

69

6

Elmley Island

ME12

Old Counter Wall

5

Windmill Creek

68

4

Elmley Fleet

Elmley Marshes
Nature Reserve

Sharfleet
Creek

3

Cockleshell
Creek

Wellmarsh
Creek

67

2

Peg Fleet

The Swale

Main Channel

1

Fowley Channel

66

Saxon Shore Way

94   A   B   95   C   D   96   E   F

15
38

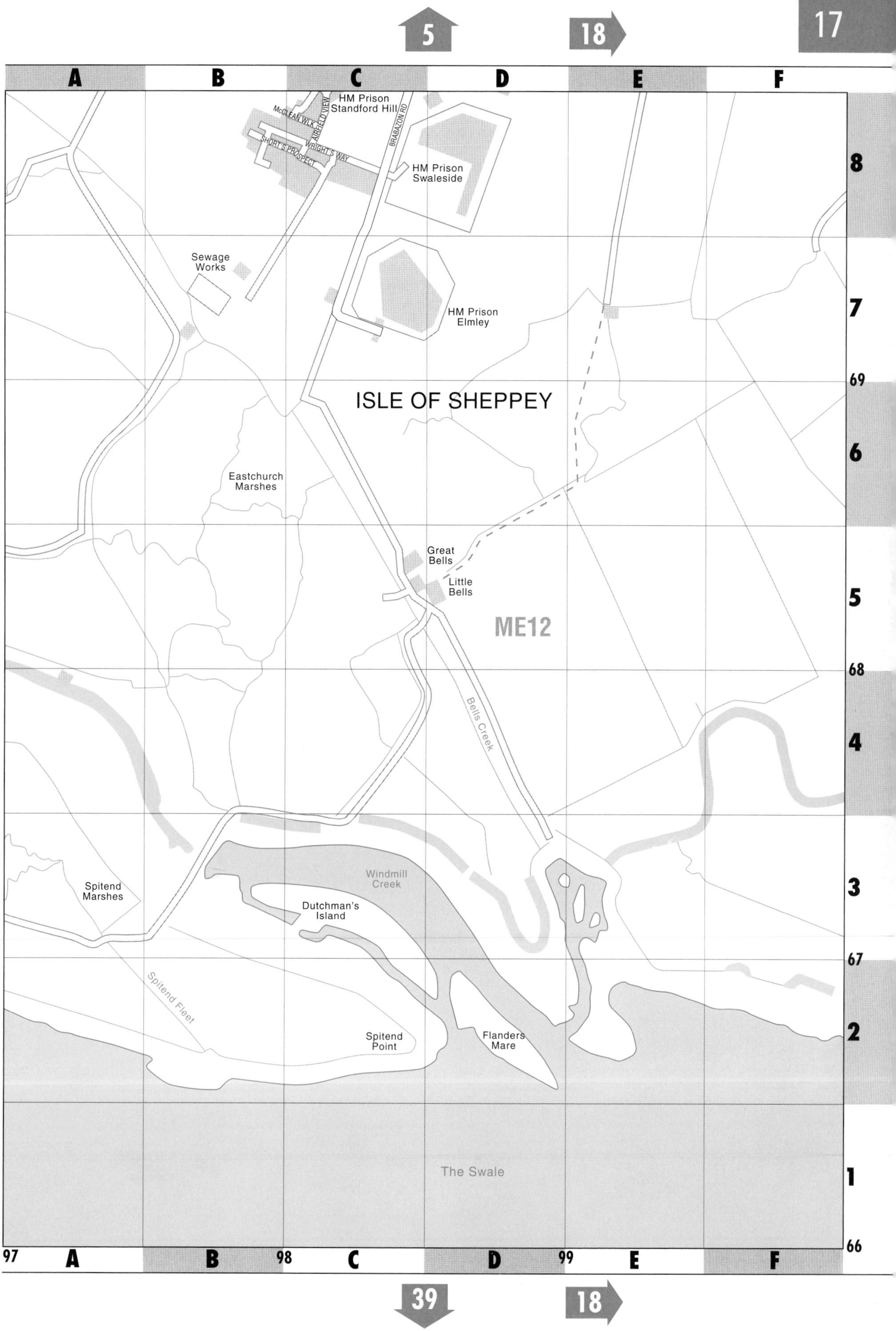

A B C D E F

8
7
69
6
5
68
4
3
67
2
1
66

McCLEAN WLK
WRIGHT'S WAY
AIRFIELD VIEW
SHORT'S PROSPECT
BRABAZON RD

HM Prison
Standford Hill

HM Prison
Swaleside

Sewage
Works

HM Prison
Elmley

ISLE OF SHEPPEY

Eastchurch
Marshes

Great
Bells

Little
Bells

ME12

Bells Creek

Spitend
Marshes

Windmill
Creek

Dutchman's
Island

Spitend Fleet

Spitend
Point

Flanders
Mare

The Swale

97 A B 98 C D 99 E F

17
6

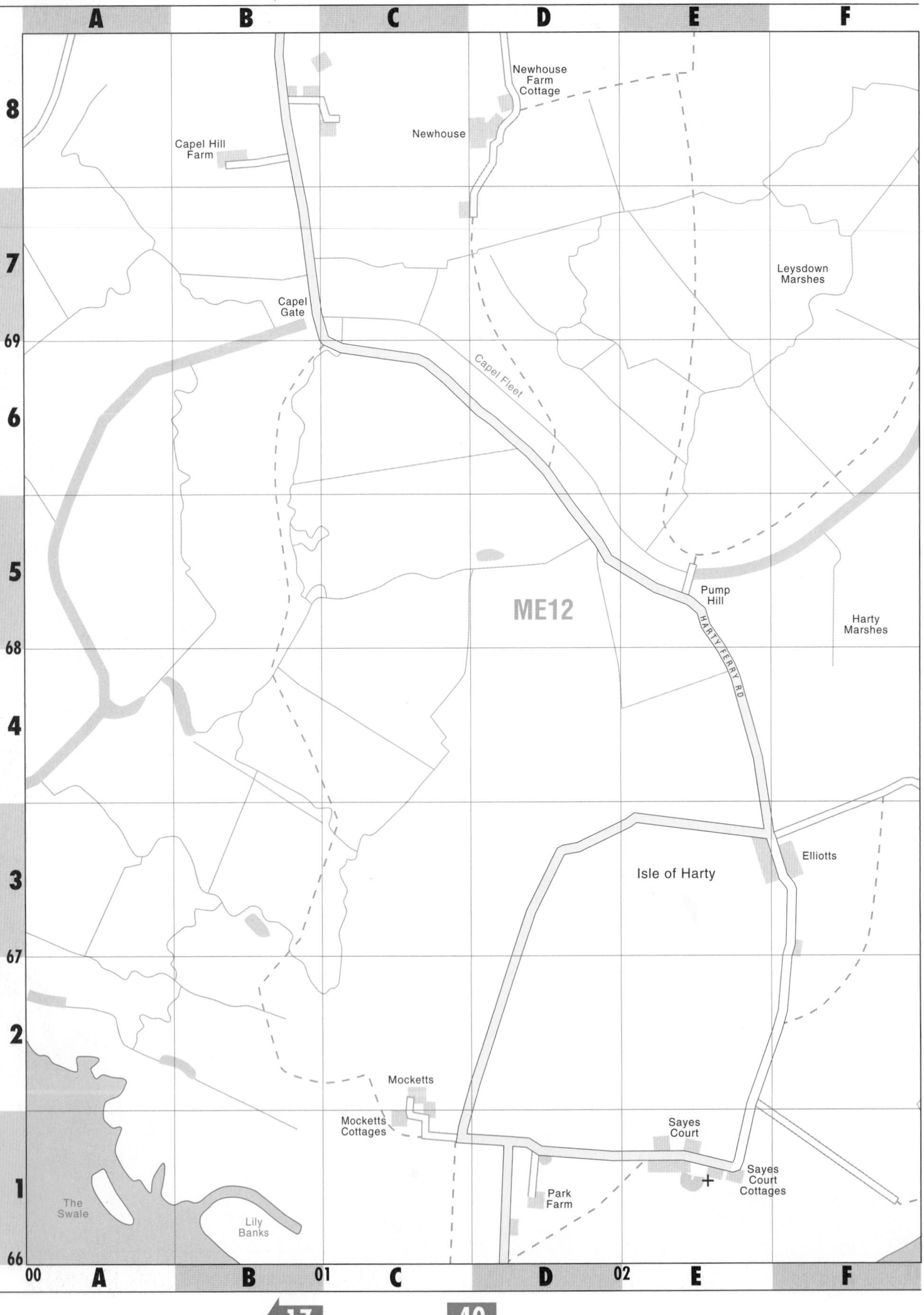

A   B   C   D   E   F

8

Newhouse
Farm
Cottage

Newhouse

Capel Hill
Farm

7

Leysdown
Marshes

Capel
Gate

69

Capel Fleet

6

ME12

5

Pump
Hill

Harty
Marshes

HARTY FERRY RD

68

4

3

Isle of Harty

Elliotts

67

2

Mocketts

Sayes
Court

Mocketts
Cottages

Sayes
Court
Cottages

1

The
Swale

Lily
Banks

Park
Farm

66

00   A   B   01   C   D   02   E   F

17
40

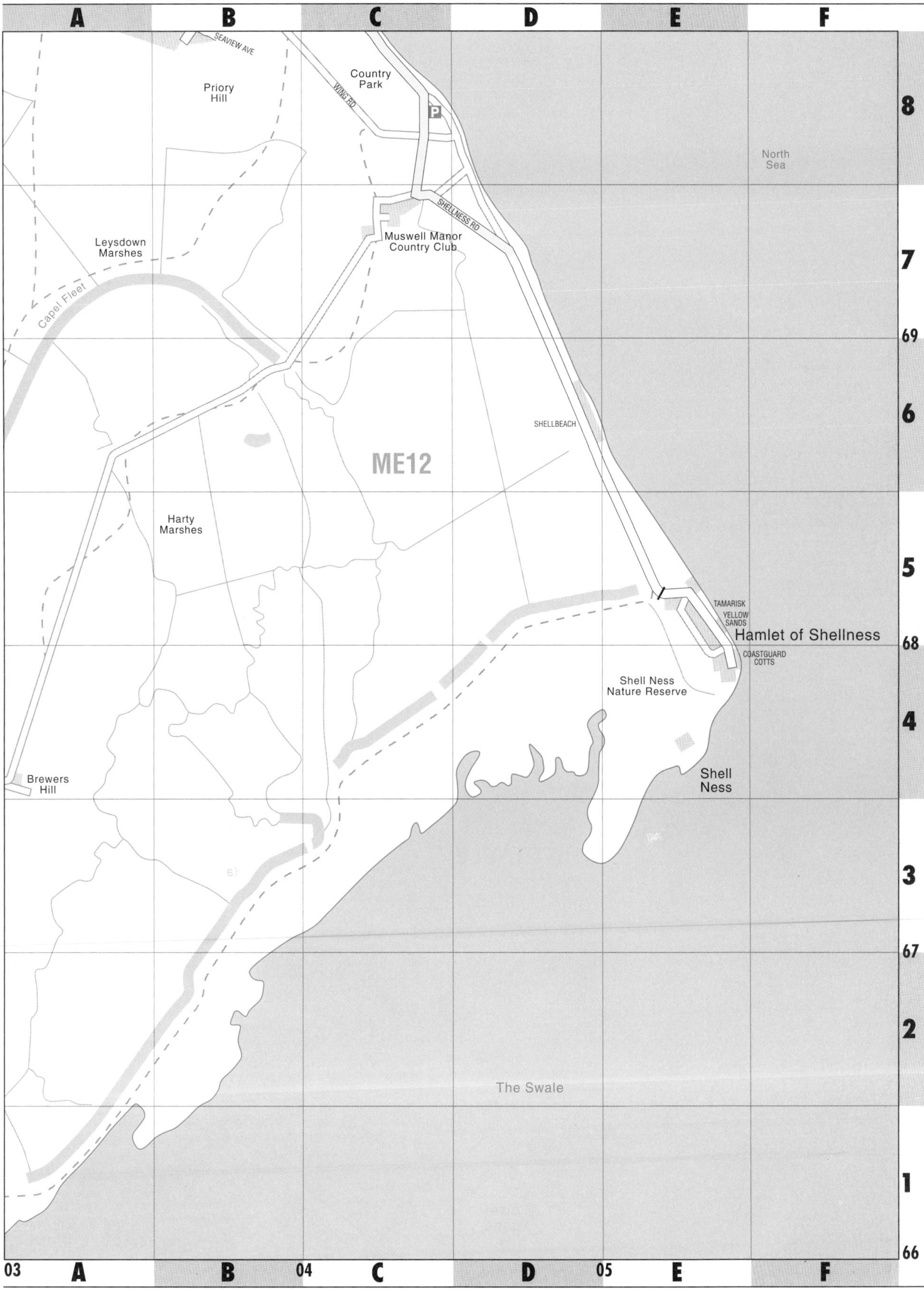

A B C D E F

8

North
Sea

SEAVIEW AVE

Country
Park

WING RD

Priory
Hill

P

SHELLNESS RD

Muswell Manor
Country Club

Leysdown
Marshes

7

Capel Fleet

69

6

SHELLBEACH

ME12

Harty
Marshes

5

TAMARISK
YELLOW
SANDS

Hamlet of Shellness

68

COASTGUARD
COTTS

Shell Ness
Nature Reserve

4

Brewers
Hill

Shell
Ness

3

67

2

The Swale

1

66

03 A B 04 C D 05 E F

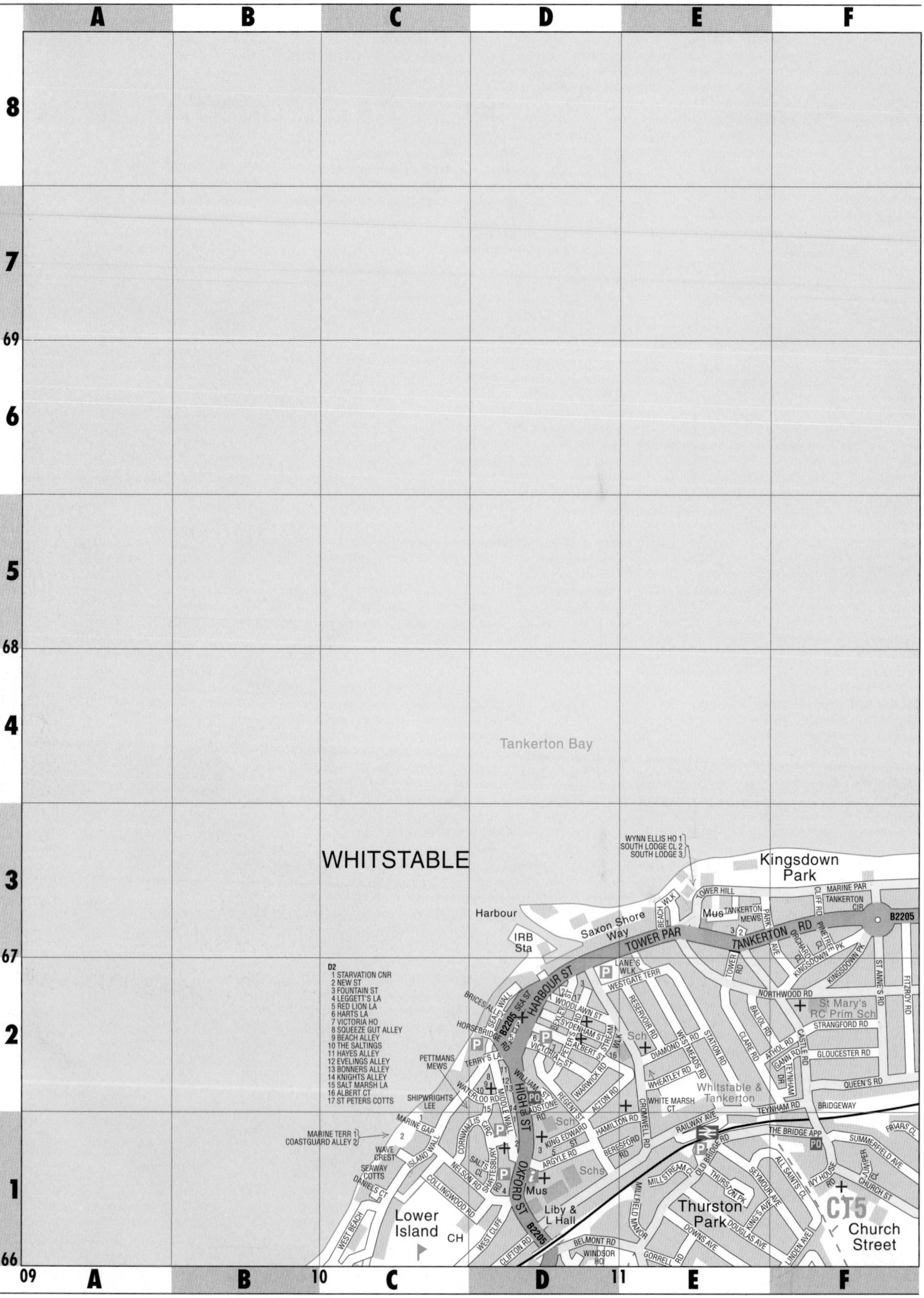

WHITSTABLE

Tankerton Bay

Kingsdown
Park

WYNN ELLIS HO 1
SOUTH LODGE CL 2
SOUTH LODGE 3

Harbour

Saxon Shore
Way

MARINE PAR
TANKERTON
CIR

B2205

TOWER PAR

TANKERTON RD

Mus

IRB
Sta

TOWER HILL

BEACH WLK

TANKERTON
MEWS

D2
1 STARVATION CNR
2 NEW ST
3 FOUNTAIN ST
4 LEGGETT'S LA
5 RED LION LA
6 HARTS LA
7 VICTORIA HO
8 SQUEEZE GUT ALLEY
9 BEACH ALLEY
10 THE SALTINGS
11 HAYES ALLEY
12 EVELINGS ALLEY
13 BONNERS ALLEY
14 KNIGHTS ALLEY
15 SALT MARSH LA
16 ALBERT CT
17 ST PETERS COTTS

LANE'S
WLK

WESTGATE TERR

NORTHWOOD RD

St Mary's
RC Prim Sch

HARBOUR ST

WOODLAWN RD

STRANGFORD RD

RESERVOIR RD

HORSEBRIDGE

B2205

SYDENHAM ST

Sch

DIAMOND RD

GLOUCESTER RD

PETTMANS
MEWS

VICTORIA ST

ALBERT ST

WHEATLEY RD

Whitstable &
Tankerton

QUEEN'S RD

TERRY'S LA

WARWICK ST

WHITE MARSH
CT

BRIDGEWAY

SHIPWRIGHTS
LEE

WATERLOO RD

HIGH ST

REGENT ST

ACTON RD

Railway AVE

TEYNHAM RD

GLADSTONE

Sch

HAMILTON RD

CROWELL RD

THE BRIDGE APP

FRIARS CL

MARINE TERR 1
COASTGUARD ALLEY 2

CORNWALLIS

KING EDWARD

BERESFORD
RD

SUMMERFIELD AVE

MARINE GAP

WAVE
CREST

ISLAND WALL

SALT'S AV

ARGYLE RD

Sch

ALL SAINTS' CL

SEAWAY
COTTS

NELSON RD

OXFORD ST

Mus

CT5

Church
Street

DANIELS CT

COLLINGWOOD RD

B2205

Liby &
L Hall

Thurston
Park

WEST BEACH

Lower
Island

CH

WEST CLIFF

CLIFTON RD

BELMONT RD

WINDSOR
RD

GORRELL RD

DOWNS AVE

D1
1 REEVES ALLEY
2 KEMP ALLEY
3 SKINNER'S ALLEY
4 OXFORD MANS
5 OXFORD CL

22

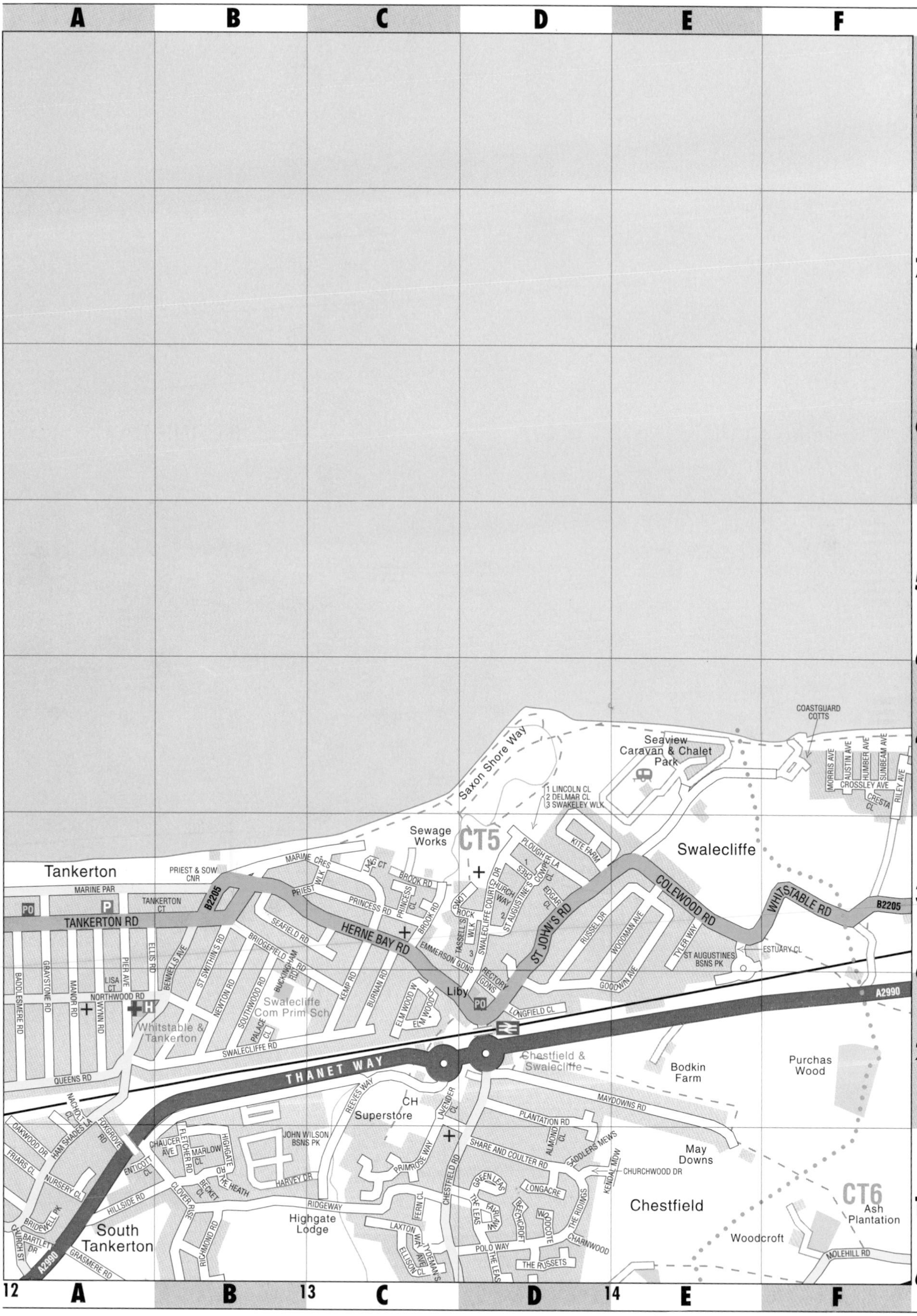
A
B
C
D
E
F
8
7
69
6
5
68
4
3
67
2
1
66
12
13
14
COASTGUARD COTTS
Seaview Caravan & Chalet Park
Saxon Shore Way
1 LINCOLN CL
2 DELMAR CL
3 SWAKELEY WLK
MORRIS AVE
AUSTIN AVE
HUMBER AVE
SUNBEAM AVE
RILEY AVE
CROSSLEY AVE
CRESTA CL
Sewage Works
CT5
KITE FARM
PLOUGH LA
Swalecliffe
Tankerton
PRIEST & SOW CNR
MARINE CRES
LANG CT
BROOK RD
MARINE PAR
TANKERTON CT
B2205
PRIEST WLK
PRINCESS RD
PRINCESS CL
ST AUGUSTINE'S CRES
COWPER CL
EDGAR CL
CHURCH WAY
SWALECLIFFE COURT DR
ST JOHN'S RD
COLEWOOD RD
WHITSTABLE RD
TANKERTON RD
SEAFIELD RD
HERNE BAY RD
EMMERSON GDNS
RECTORY GDNS
RUSSEL DR
WOODMAN AVE
TYLER WAY
ST AUGUSTINES BSNS PK
ESTUARY CL
GOODWIN AVE
BADDLESMERE RD
GRAYSTONE RD
MANOR RD
LISA CT
PIER AVE
ELLIS RD
BENNELLS AVE
ST SWITHIN'S RD
NEWTON RD
BRIDGEFIELD RD
BUCKINGHAM RD
KEMP RD
BURMAN RD
ELM WOOD W
ELM WOOD CL
NORTHWOOD RD
WYNN RD
Whitstable & Tankerton
SOUTHWOOD RD
PALACE CL
Swalecliffe Com Prim Sch
Liby
PO
LONGFIELD CL
A2990
SWALECLIFFE RD
QUEENS RD
THANET WAY
Chestfield & Swalecliffe
Bodkin Farm
Purchas Wood
REEVES WAY
CH
Superstore
LAVENDER CL
MAYDOWNS RD
PLANTATION RD
NACHOLT CL
HAM SHADES LA
FOXGROVE RD
OAKWOOD DR
FRIARS CL
NURSERY CL
CHAUCER AVE
FLETCHER RD
MARLOW CL
HIGHGATE RD
JOHN WILSON BSNS PK
PRIMROSE WAY
SHARE AND COULTER RD
ALMOND CL
SADDLERS MEWS
May Downs
KENDAL MDW
CHURCHWOOD DR
ENTICOTT CL
THE HEATH
HARVEY DR
HILLSIDE RD
CLOVER RISE
BECKET CL
RIDGEWAY
CHESTFIELD RD
GREEN LEAS
LONGACRE
THE RIDINGS
Chestfield
CT6
Ash Plantation
BRIDEWELL PK
BARTLETT DR
CHURCH ST
South Tankerton
RICHMOND RD
Highgate Lodge
LAXTON WAY
FERN CL
THE LEAS
FAIRWAY
BEECHCROFT
WOODCOTE
CHARNWOOD
Woodcroft
MOLEHILL RD
ELLISON CL
TYDEMAN'S AVE
POLO WAY
THE RUSSETS
GRASMERE RD

44

22

21

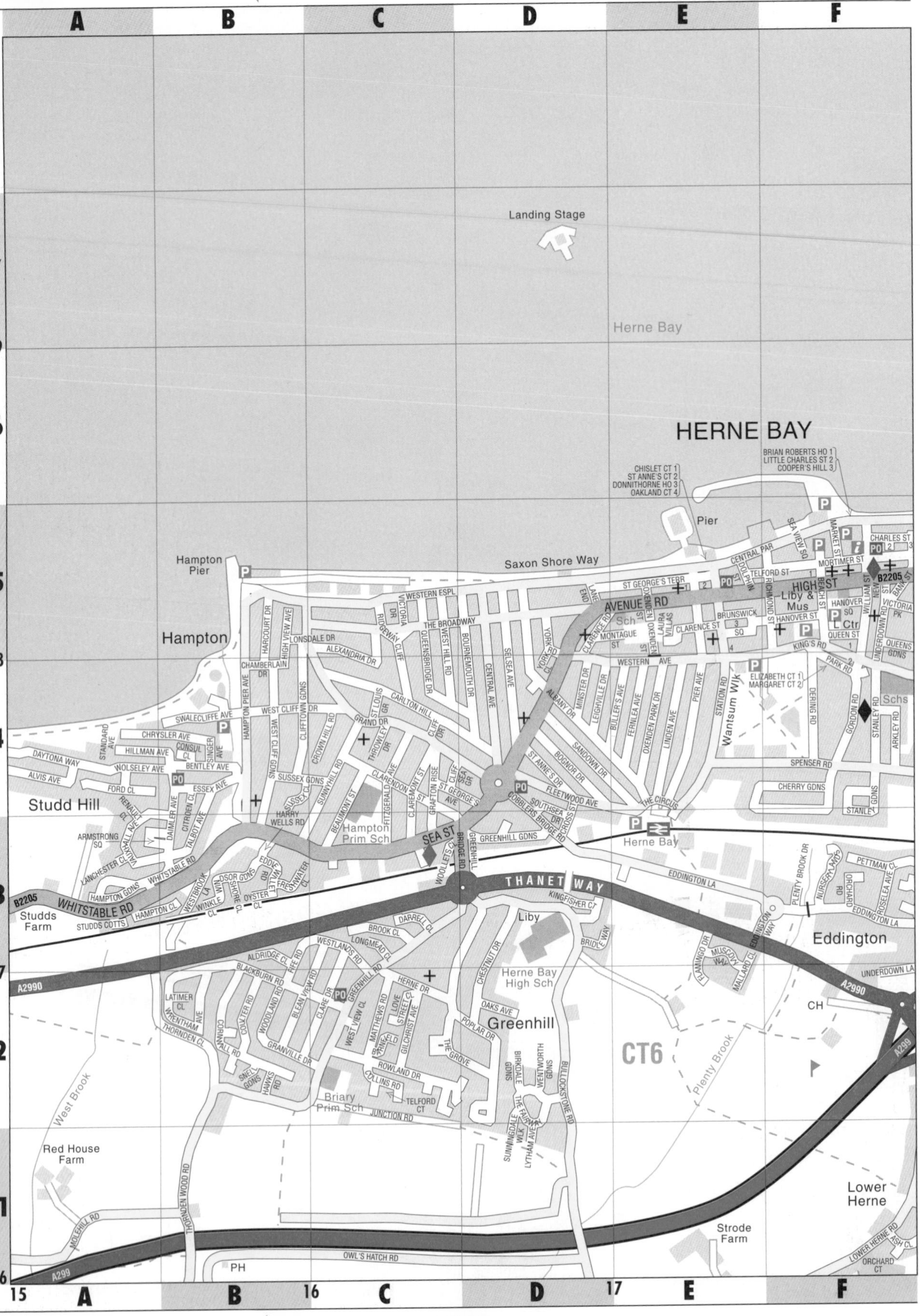

Landing Stage

Herne Bay

HERNE BAY

BRIAN ROBERTS HO 1
LITTLE CHARLES ST 2
COOPER'S HILL 3

CHISLET CT 1
ST ANNE'S CT 2
DONNITHORNE HO 3
OAKLAND CT 4

Pier

CHARLES ST
1
2

Hampton Pier

Hampton

Saxon Shore Way

WESTERN ESPL

THE BROADWAY

AVENUE RD

Sch

HIGH ST

Liby & Mus

Studd Hill

SEA ST

THANET WAY

Herne Bay

Hampton
Prim Sch

Greenhill Gdns

Eddington

Studds
Farm

WHITSTABLE RD

STUDDS COTTS

Liby

Kingfisher Ct

A2990

Herne Bay
High Sch

Oaks Ave

Greenhill

CT6

Eddington

Underdown La

A2990

Briary
Prim Sch

Red House
Farm

West Brook

Plenty Brook

Lower
Herne

Strode
Farm

PH

OWL'S HATCH RD

A299

24

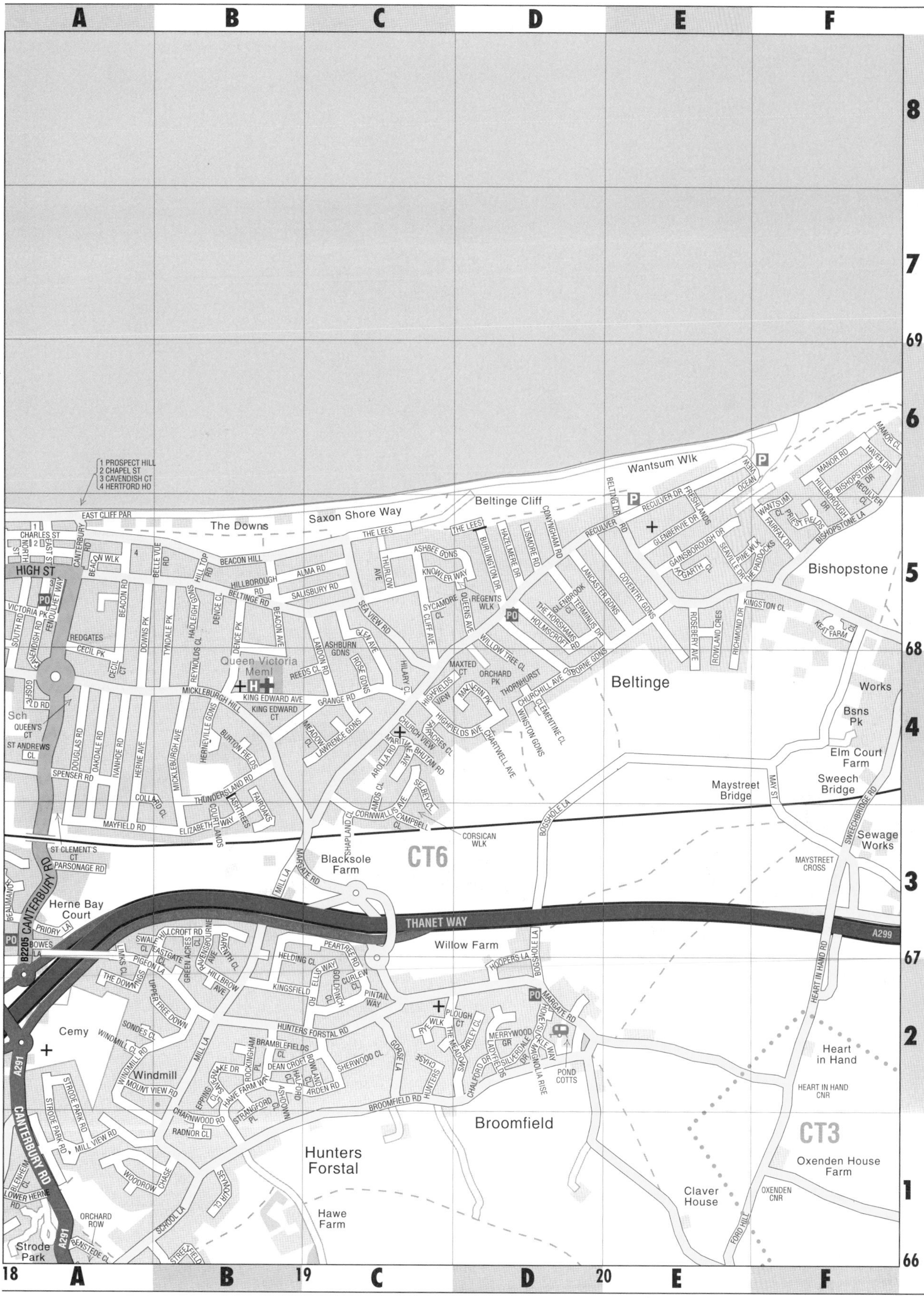

A
B
C
D
E
F
8
7
69
6
5
68
4
3
67
2
1
66
18
19
20
1 PROSPECT HILL
2 CHAPEL ST
3 CAVENDISH CT
4 HERTFORD HO
EAST CLIFF PAR
The Downs
Saxon Shore Way
Beltinge Cliff
Wantsum Wlk
CHARLES ST
NORTH ST
EAST ST
CANTERBURY RD
HIGH ST
BEACON WLK
BELLE VUE RD
HILL TOP RD
BEACON HILL
ALMA RD
HILLBOROUGH RD
BELTINGE RD
SALISBURY RD
THE LEES
THURLOW AVE
ASHBEE GDNS
KNOWLER WAY
BURLINGTON DR
HAZELMERE DR
LISMORE RD
CONYNGHAM RD
BELTING DR
RECULVER RD
RECULVER DR
FRESHLANDS
OCEAN VIEW
GLENBERVIE DR
GAINSBOROUGH DR
HOGARTH CL
SEAVILLE DR
PINE WLK
THE PADDOCKS
WANTSUM CL
PRIEST FIELDS
FAIRFAX DR
MANOR RD
HAVEN DR
MANOR CL
HILLBOROUGH DR
BISHOPSTONE DR
RECULVER CL
BISHOPSTONE LA
Bishopstone
VICTORIA PK
SOUTH RD
CAVENDISH RD
FENOULHET WAY
REDGATES
CECIL PK
CECIL CT
BEACON RD
DOWNS PK
TYNDALE PK
HADLEIGH GDNS
REYNOLDS CL
DENCE CL
DENCE PK
BEACON AVE
LANDON RD
ASHBURN GDNS
GLEN AVE
SEA VIEW RD
ROSE GDNS
HILARY CL
SYCAMORE CL
CLIFF AVE
QUEENS AVE
REGENTS WLK
WILLOW TREE CL
THE HORSHAMS
HOLMSCROFT RD
GLENBROOK CL
TERMINUS DR
LANCASTER GDNS
COVENTRY GDNS
ROSEBERY AVE
ROWLAND CRES
RICHMOND DR
KINGSTON CL
KEAT FARM CL
Queen Victoria Meml
REEDS CL
KING EDWARD AVE
KING EDWARD CT
MICKLEBURGH HILL
GRANGE RD
MAXTED CT
ORCHARD PK
THORNHURST
CHURCHILL AVE
OSBORNE GDNS
Beltinge
Works
Bsns Pk
Elm Court Farm
Sweech Bridge
Maystreet Bridge
MAY ST
GOSFIELD RD
Sch
QUEEN'S CT
ST ANDREWS CL
DOUGLAS RD
OAKDALE RD
IVANHOE RD
HERNE AVE
MICKLEBURGH AVE
HERNEVILLE GDNS
BURTON FIELDS
MEADOW CL
LAWRENCE GDNS
HIGHFIELDS VIEW
MALVERN PK
HIGHFIELDS AVE
CHURCH VIEW
MARTINE AVE
ARCHES CL
BHUTAN RD
AROLLA RD
CLEMENTINE CL
WINSTON GDNS
CHARTWELL AVE
SPENSER RD
COLLARD CL
THUNDERSLAND RD
COURTLANDS
ASHTREES
FAIROAKS
MAYFIELD RD
ELIZABETH WAY
AMOS CL
SELBEY CL
CORNWALLIS AVE
CAMPBELL CL
CORSICAN WLK
SHAPLAND CL
BOGSHOLE LA
SWEECHBRIDGE RD
Sewage Works
MAYSTREET CROSS
ST CLEMENT'S CT
PARSONAGE RD
Blacksole Farm
CT6
MARGATE RD
MILL LA
BEAUMANOR
Herne Bay Court
PRIORY LA
CANTERBURY RD
B2205
BOWES LA
PO
THANET WAY
A299
Willow Farm
HOOPERS LA
BOGSHOLE LA
HEART IN HAND RD
SWALE CL
HILLCROFT RD
EASTGATE CL
GREEN ACRES
RAVENSBOURNE AVE
DARENTH CL
PIGEON LA
LINKS CL
THE DOWNINGS
UPPER FREE DOWN
HILLBROW AVE
HELDING CL
ELLIS WAY
GOLDFINCH CL
CURLEW CL
PEARTREE RD
KINGSFIELD RD
PINTAIL WAY
PLOUGH CT
RYE WLK
THE MEADOWS
BARLEY CL
MERRYWOOD GR
LADYFIELDS
SILKDALE
MAGNOLIA RISE
HONEYSUCKLE WAY
MARGATE RD
POND COTTS
Cemy
SONDES CL
WINDMILL CL
WINDMILL RD
Windmill
MOUNT VIEW RD
HUNTERS FORSTAL RD
BRAMBLEFIELDS CL
ROCKINGHAM PL
DEAN CROFT
HALFORD CL
BOWLAND CL
ARDEN RD
SHERWOOD CL
GORSE LA
HUNTERS CHASE
CHALFORD DR
BROOMFIELD RD
HAWE FARM WAY
EPPING CL
STRANGFORD PL
ASHDOWN CL
CHARNWOOD RD
RADNOR CL
Heart in Hand
HEART IN HAND CNR
CT3
Broomfield
Hunters Forstal
STRODE PARK RD
MILL VIEW RD
WOODROW CHASE
SEYMOUR CL
Oxenden House Farm
OXENDEN CNR
Claver House
A291
CANTERBURY RD
BLENHEIM CL
LOWER HERNE RD
ORCHARD ROW
SCHOOL LA
Hawe Farm
Strode Park
BENSTEDE CL
STREETFIELD
FORD HILL

46

24

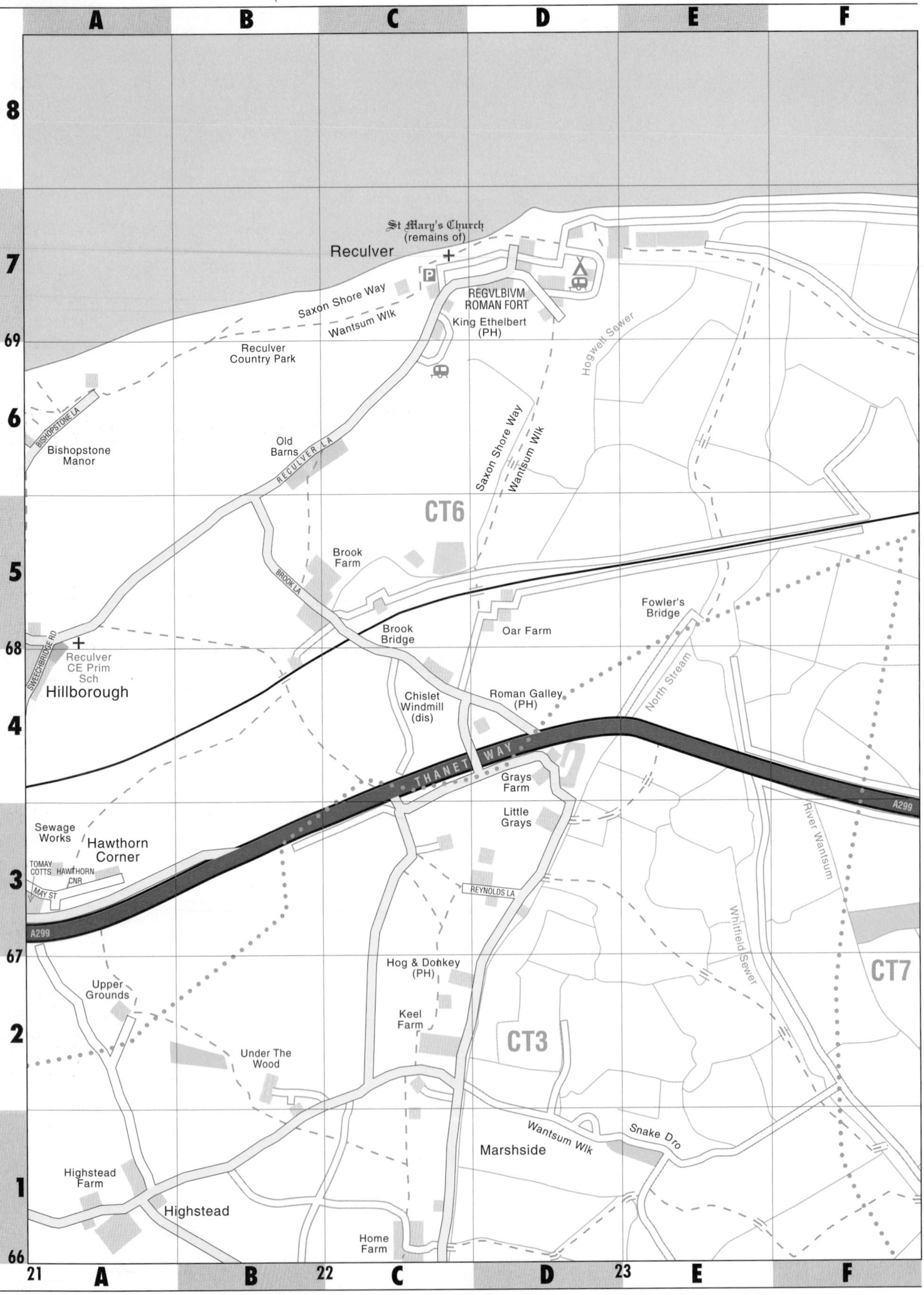

23

A   B   C   D   E   F

8

7

69

6

5

68

4

67

2

1

66

St Mary's Church
(remains of)
Reculver
REGVLBIVM
ROMAN FORT
King Ethelbert
(PH)
Saxon Shore Way
Wantsum Wlk
Hogwell Sewer

Reculver
Country Park
Saxon Shore Way
Wantsum Wlk

BISHOPSTONE LA
Bishopstone
Manor
Old
Barns
RECULVER LA
CT6

BROOK LA
Brook
Farm
Fowler's
Bridge
North Stream

SNEECCHBRIDGE RD
Reculver
CE Prim
Sch
Hillborough
Brook
Bridge
Oar Farm
Roman Galley
(PH)
Chislet
Windmill
(dis)
THANET WAY
A299
River Wantsum

Sewage
Works
Hawthorn
Corner
Grays
Farm
Little
Grays
Whitfield Sewer
CT7
TOMAY
COTTS HAWTHORN
CNR
MAY ST
A299
REYNOLDS LA

Upper
Grounds
Hog & Donkey
(PH)
Keel
Farm
CT3

Under The
Wood
Marshside
Wantsum Wlk
Snake Dro

Highstead
Farm
Highstead
Home
Farm

26

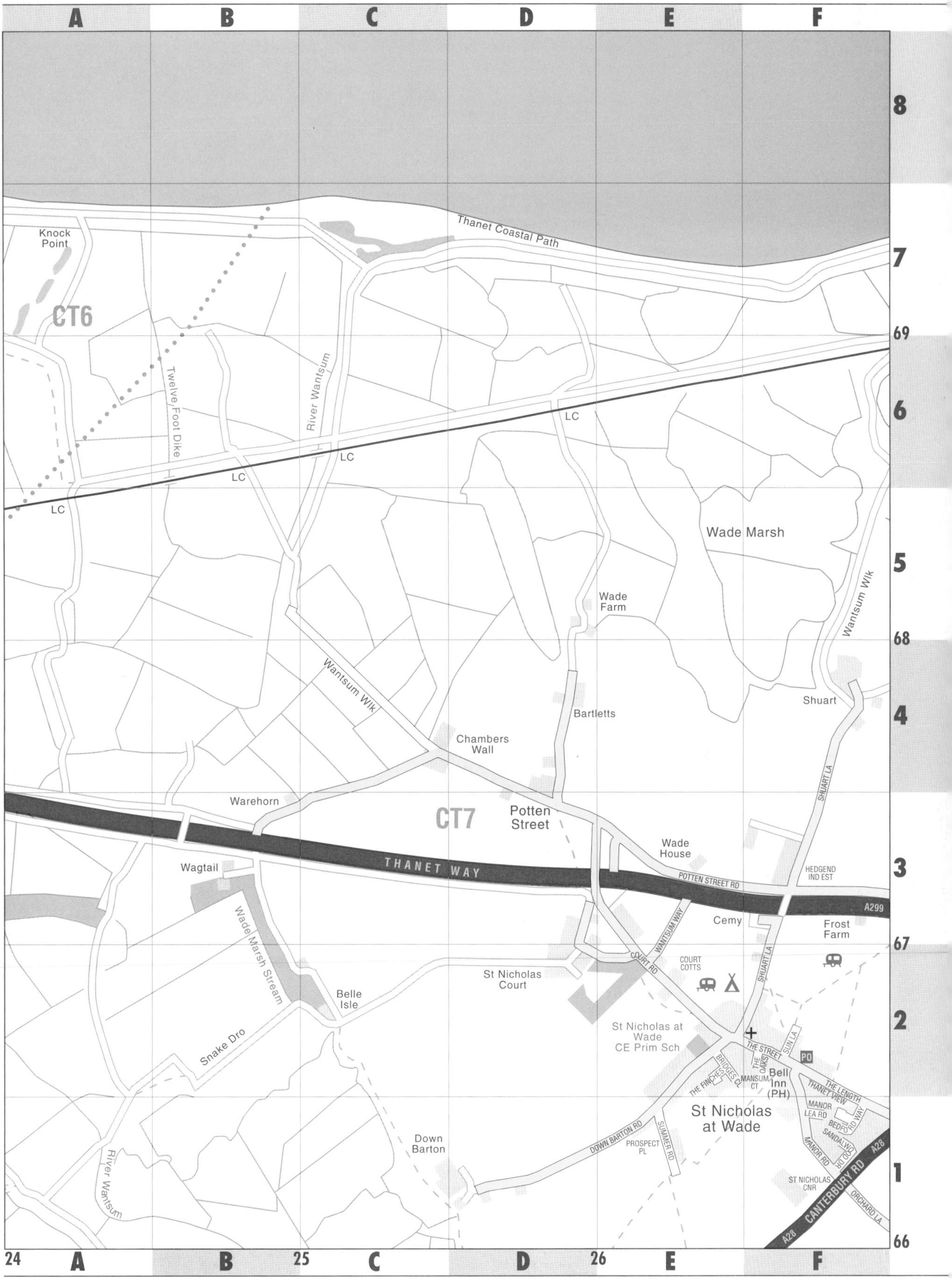

A
B
C
D
E
F
8
7
69
6
5
68
4
3
67
2
1
66
24
25
26
Knock Point
CT6
Thanet Coastal Path
Twelve Foot Dike
River Wantsum
LC
LC
LC
LC
Wade Marsh
Wade Farm
Wantsum Wlk
Wantsum Wlk
Shuart
Bartletts
Chambers Wall
Warehorn
CT7
Potten Street
Wade House
SHUART LA
HEDGEND IND EST
THANET WAY
POTTEN STREET RD
A299
Wagtail
Wade Marsh Stream
WANTSUM WAY
Cemy
Frost Farm
COURT RD
COURT COTTS
St Nicholas Court
SHUART LA
Belle Isle
Snake Dro
St Nicholas at Wade CE Prim Sch
THE STREET
SUN LA
PO
THE OAKS
BRIDGES CL
THE FINCHES
MANSUM CT
Bell Inn (PH)
THE LENGTH
THANET VIEW
MANOR LEA RD
BEDFORD WAY
SANDALWOOD
MANOR RD
St Nicholas at Wade
Down Barton
DOWN BARTON RD
SUMMER RD
PROSPECT PL
River Wantsum
ST NICHOLAS CNR
CANTERBURY RD
A28
A28
ORCHARD LA

48

26

25

A B C D E F

F8
1 DALLINGER RD
2 CARMEL CT
3 SANDPIPER CT
4 GAINSBORO RD
5 LYELL CT
6 HOMEBIRCH HO
7 BERESFORD CT

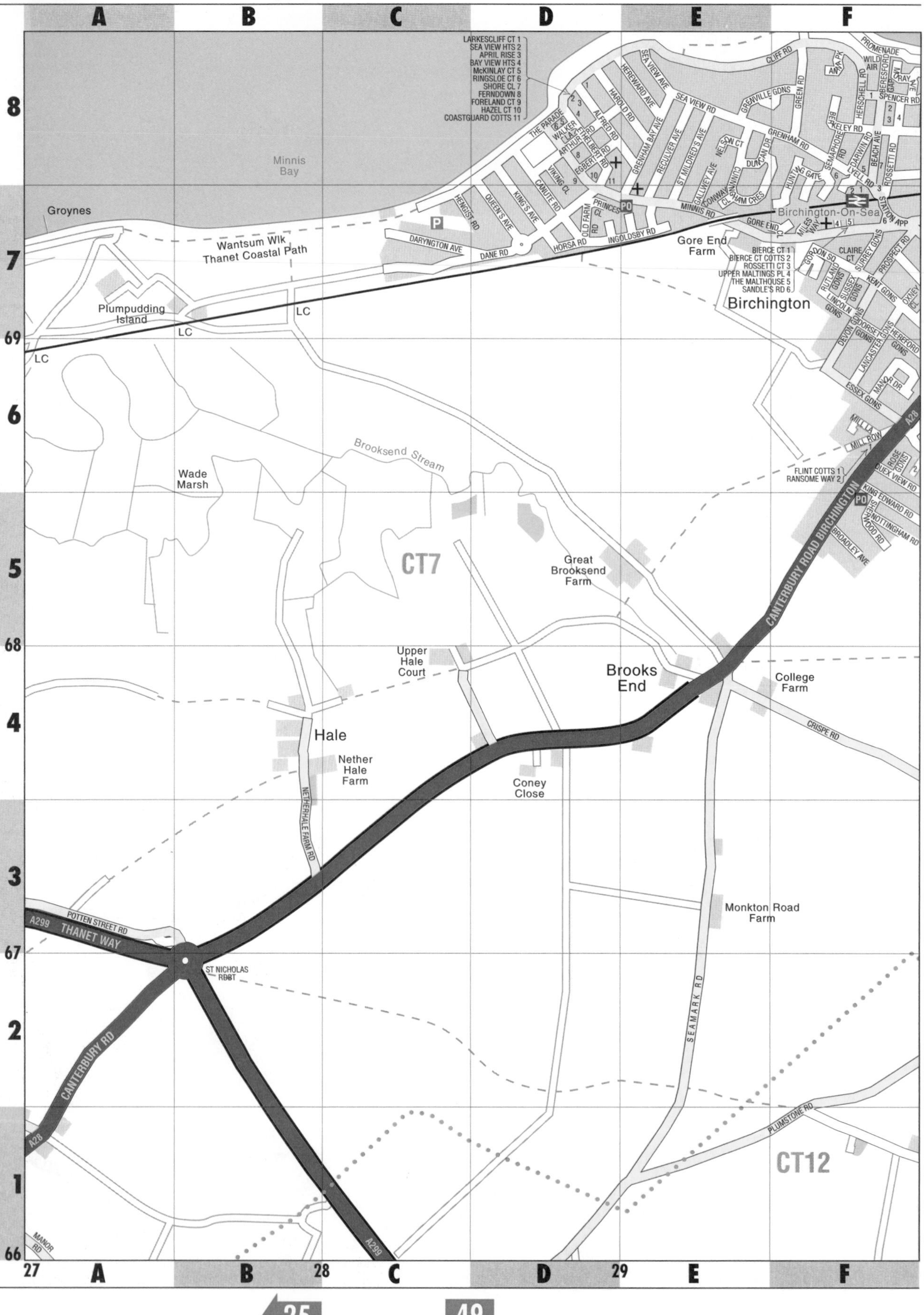

8

LARKESCLIFF CT 1
SEA VIEW HTS 2
APRIL RISE 3
BAY VIEW HTS 4
McKINLAY CT 5
RINGSLOE CT 6
SHORE CL 7
FERNDOWN 8
FORELAND CT 9
HAZEL CT 10
COASTGUARD COTTS 11

Minnis Bay

PROMENADE

Birchington-On-Sea

Groynes

Wantsum Wlk
Thanet Coastal Path

7

Darington Ave

Dane Rd

Horsa Rd

Ingoldsby Rd

Gore End Farm

Birchington

BIERCE CT 1
BIERCE CT COTTS 2
ROSSETTI CT 3
UPPER MALTINGS PL 4
THE MALTHOUSE 5
SANDLE'S RD 6

69

LC

LC

LC

Plumpudding Island

6

Brooksend Stream

Wade Marsh

FLINT COTTS 1
RANSOME WAY 2

MILL ROW

5

CT7

Great Brooksend Farm

CANTERBURY ROAD BIRCHINGTON

A23

68

Upper Hale Court

Brooks End

College Farm

4

Hale

Nether Hale Farm

Coney Close

Crispe Rd

NETHERHALE FARM RD

3

POTTEN STREET RD

THANET WAY

A299

Monkton Road Farm

67

ST NICHOLAS RBBT

SEAMARK RD

2

CANTERBURY RD

PLUMSTONE RD

CT12

A28

1

A299

66

MANOR RD

27 A 28 B C 28 D 29 E F

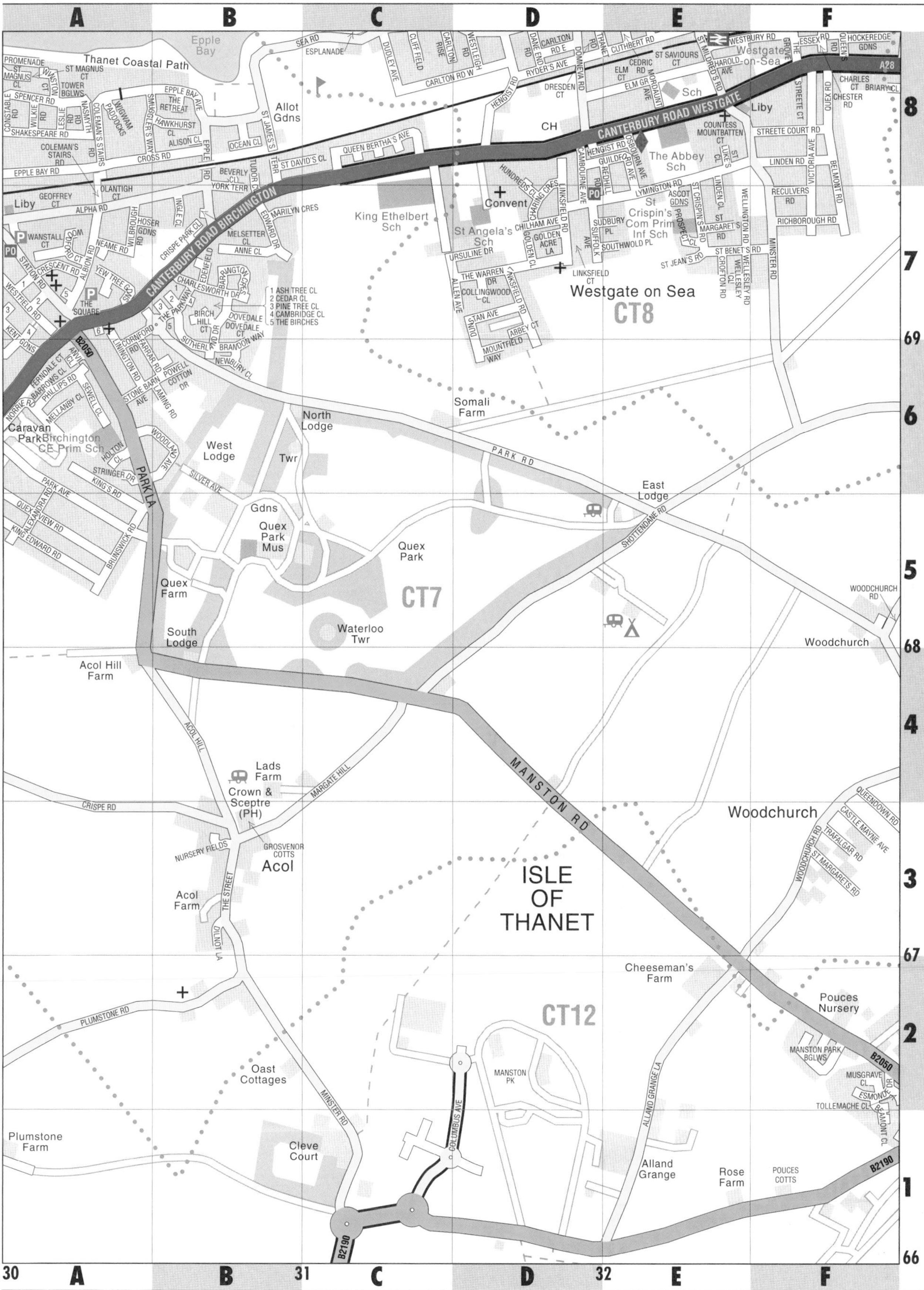

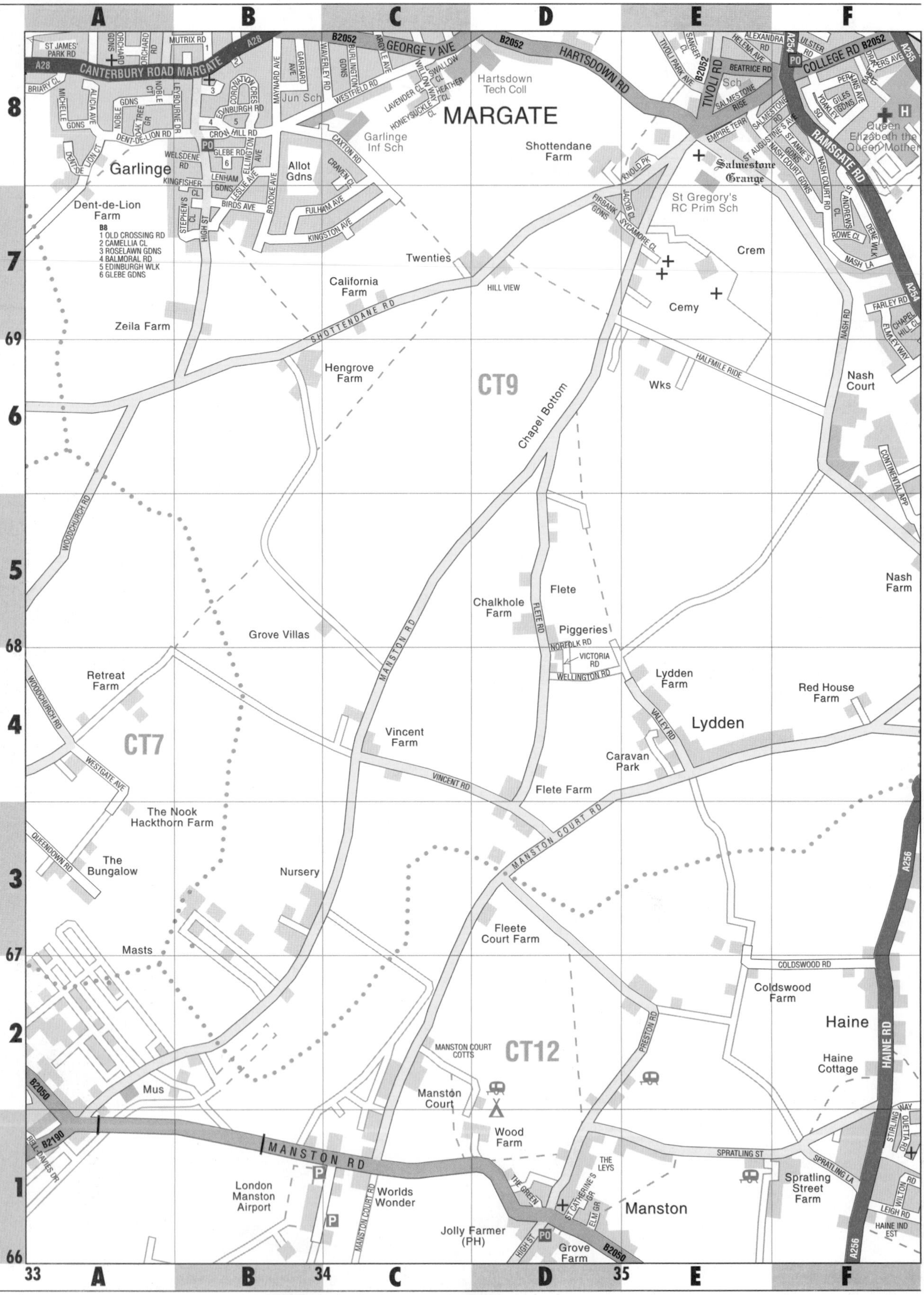

27
7

MARGATE

Garlinge

Dent-de-Lion
Farm

B8
1 OLD CROSSING RD
2 CAMELLIA CL
3 ROSELAWN GDNS
4 BALMORAL RD
5 EDINBURGH WLK
6 GLEBE GDNS

Zeila Farm

California
Farm

Twenties

HILL VIEW

Hengrove
Farm

CT9

Chapel Bottom

Retreat
Farm

Grove Villas

CT7

Vincent
Farm

The Nook
Hackthorn Farm

The
Bungalow

Nursery

Masts

Mus

London
Manston
Airport

Worlds
Wonder

Jolly Farmer
(PH)

MANSTON RD

CT12

Manston Court
Cotts

Manston
Court

Wood
Farm

THE GREEN

Grove
Farm

Manston

THE
LEYS

Fleete
Court Farm

Fleet Farm

Flete

Chalkhole
Farm

Piggeries

NORFOLK RD
VICTORIA
RD
WELLINGTON RD

Lydden
Farm

Caravan
Park

Lydden

Red House
Farm

Coldswood
Farm

Haine

Haine
Cottage

Spratling
Street
Farm

HAINE IND
EST

Shottendane
Farm

St Gregory's
RC Prim Sch

Salmestone
Grange

Crem

Cemy

Wks

Nash
Court

Nash
Farm

Queen
Elizabeth the
Queen Mother

COLLEGE RD

RAMSGATE RD

Hartsdown
Tech Coll

HARTSDOWN RD

Garlinge
Inf Sch

Jun Sch

CANTERBURY ROAD MARGATE

GEORGE V AVE

27   51

8
30

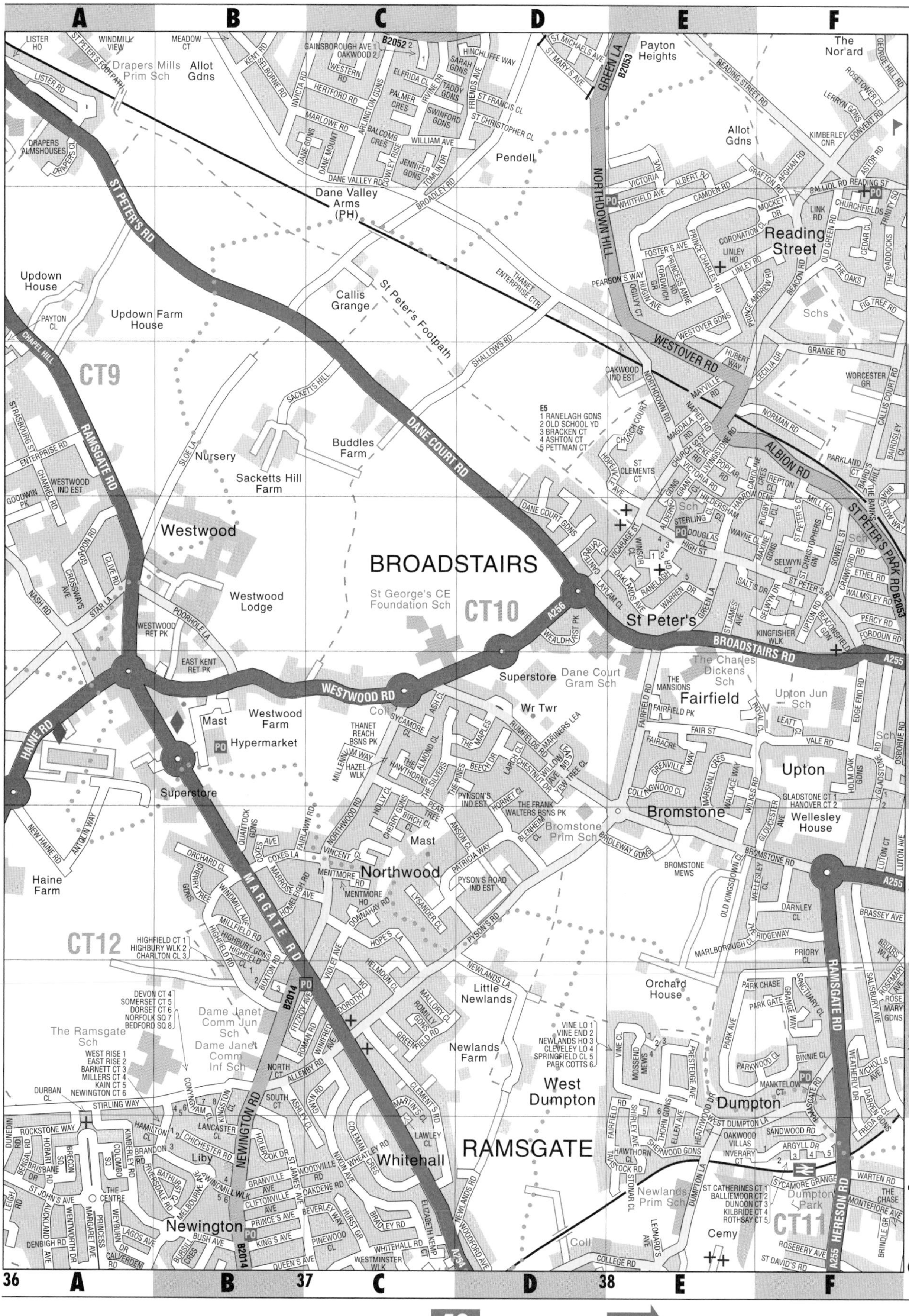
BROADSTAIRS
RAMSGATE
CT9
CT10
CT11
CT12
Westwood
St Peter's
Reading Street
Northwood
Newington
Whitehall
Fairfield
Upton
Bromstone
Dumpton
West Dumpton
Pendell
Payton Heights
The Nor'ard
Updown House
Updown Farm House
Callis Grange
Dane Valley Arms (PH)
Buddles Farm
Sacketts Hill Farm
Westwood Lodge
Westwood Farm
Haine Farm
Little Newlands
Newlands Farm
Orchard House
Wellesley House
Drapers Mills Prim Sch
St George's CE Foundation Sch
Dane Court Gram Sch
The Charles Dickens Sch
Upton Jun Sch
Bromstone Prim Sch
Dame Janet Comm Jun Sch
Dame Janet Comm Inf Sch
The Ramsgate Sch
Newlands Prim Sch
Dumpton Park
Hypermarket
Superstore
St Peter's Footpath
ST PETER'S RD
DANE COURT RD
RAMSGATE RD
MARGATE RD
WESTWOOD RD
BROADSTAIRS RD
NORTHDOWN HILL
WESTOVER RD
ALBION RD
ST PETER'S PARK RD
HAINE RD
NEWINGTON RD
HERESON RD
BROMSTONE RD
PYSON'S RD
A255
A256
A254
B2014
B2052
B2053
36
37
38
66
67
68
69
A
B
C
D
E
F
1
2
3
4
5
6
7
8

52
30

A B C D E F

North
Foreland

CONVENT RD

CH

8 Kingsate
Coll

ELMWOOD AVE

B2052
NORTH FORELAND HILL

Hunton
House

CRESCENT RD

READING ST

Elmwood
Farm

Stella Maris
Convent

ST STEPHEN'S
MANOR

NORTHCLIFFE GDNS

CALLIS COURT RD

7 Mast

VILLIERS HO 1
YARDLEY HO 2
GLENAVON HO 3
FORELAND PARK HO 4
STONE HO 5
STONE HOUSE MEWS 6
MARCROFT 7

FORELAND HEIGHTS

NORTH FORELAND RD

NORTH FORELAND AVE

ST ANNE'S RD

CLIFF PROM

FRANCIS RD

CLIFF RD

69

JULIE CL

DORCAS GDNS

NEWMANS

The
Foreland
Sch

BISHOP'S AVE

ELIZABETH PLACE
PARK CT

THANET

WAINWRIGHT
CT

RHODES GDNS

RAY

TINA GDNS

CORNWALLIS
GDNS

CASTLE AVE

Stone Bay
Sch

CATHERINE WAY

HILLIER CL

SEA VIEW RD

KING'S AVE

QUEEN'S AVE

6

LINDENTHORPE RD

LYNHURST RD

MAGDALEN CT

KNIGHT'S AVE

STONE RD

BEDFORD CT

Thanet Coastal Path

KENDAL RISE

LAURISTON MOUNT

HAMSTMONTH GDNS

CUMBERLAND AVE

DALMAINEY GDNS

CROWTHILL

EAST FINS EST

WING'S CT EST

CHEVIOT CT

East Cliff

5 MASON'S RISE

BRADSTOW WAY

CARLTON AVE

Mus

1 THANET CL
2 STAINES PL
3 FERN CT

WILLOW CT
ROWAN CT

CT10

DICKENS RD

BROADSTAIRS

LLOYD RD

Broadstairs

P

CAERNARVON
GDNS

RECTORY RD

SHUTTLE RD

COPPERFIELD CT

68 Liby
PO
YH

THE BROADWAY A255

HIGH ST

STANLEY RD

PIERREMONT

BELVEDERE RD

DEVONSHIRE

MASH GDNS

ALBION ST

FORT COTTS

HARBOUR ST

Bleak
House

Slipway

B4
1 CHURCH RD
2 CHURCH SQ
3 UNION SQ
4 ELDON PL
5 ST MARY'S RD
6 SEAVIEW COTTS
7 PROSPECT PL
8 CROFT'S PL
9 SERENE PL
10 RAGLAN PL
11 DUNDONALD RD
12 SERENE CT
13 CHARLOTTE ST
14 BUCKINGHAM RD
15 CHANDOS SQ
16 CHANDOS RD
17 YORK AVE
18 JUBILEE CT
19 WROTHAM AVE
20 ASHTON MEWS

4 Sch

MILD CL

PIERREMONT AVE

STEPHEN RD

QUEEN'S RD

THANET RD

VERE RD

DICKENS WLK

JOHN ST

P Pier

Mus

Viking
Bay

A4
1 CLARENDON MEWS
2 SOMERSET CT
3 MANOR RD
4 KENT HO
5 JO-ANN'S CT

CINDER PATH

CLARENDON RD

KING EDWARD AVE

YORK ST

B2052

OSCAR RD

VICTORIA RD

THE VALE

RAMSGATE RD

WROTHAM RD

GRANVILLE RD

Louisa Bay

1 GRANVILLE AVE
2 WEST CLIFF CT
3 WEST CLIFF AVE
4 QUEENS GDNS
5 GRAND MANS
6 CHARLESTON CT
7 SEAVIEW CT

SWINBURNE AVE

HOWARD RD

CHAUCER RD

WEST CLIFF RD

3 A255

Thanet
Coll

1 UPPER APPROACH RD
2 APPROACH RD
3 WOODBERRY FLATS

DAVIDS CL

SEAPOINT RD

PALMERSTON
AVE

South Cliff

NARROW CT

Hereson
Sec
Boys Sch

Bradstow
Sch

67

LEYBOURN
RD

WESTERN ESPL

8 VIKING CT
9 BRAESIDE

Dumpton
Point

2

DUMPTON GAP RD

MINSTER CL

ELHAM WAY

WALDRON RD

CLIFFS

Gap House
Sch

Dumpton
Bay

BAY VW

HURST WAY

COLBURN RD

STAPLEHURST AVE

SEACROFT RD

SOUTH CLIFF PAR

DETLING AVE

1

CLIFFS SIDE DR

Holy Trinity
CE Prim
Sch

OCEAN
VIEW

CT11

MONTEFIORE AVE

66

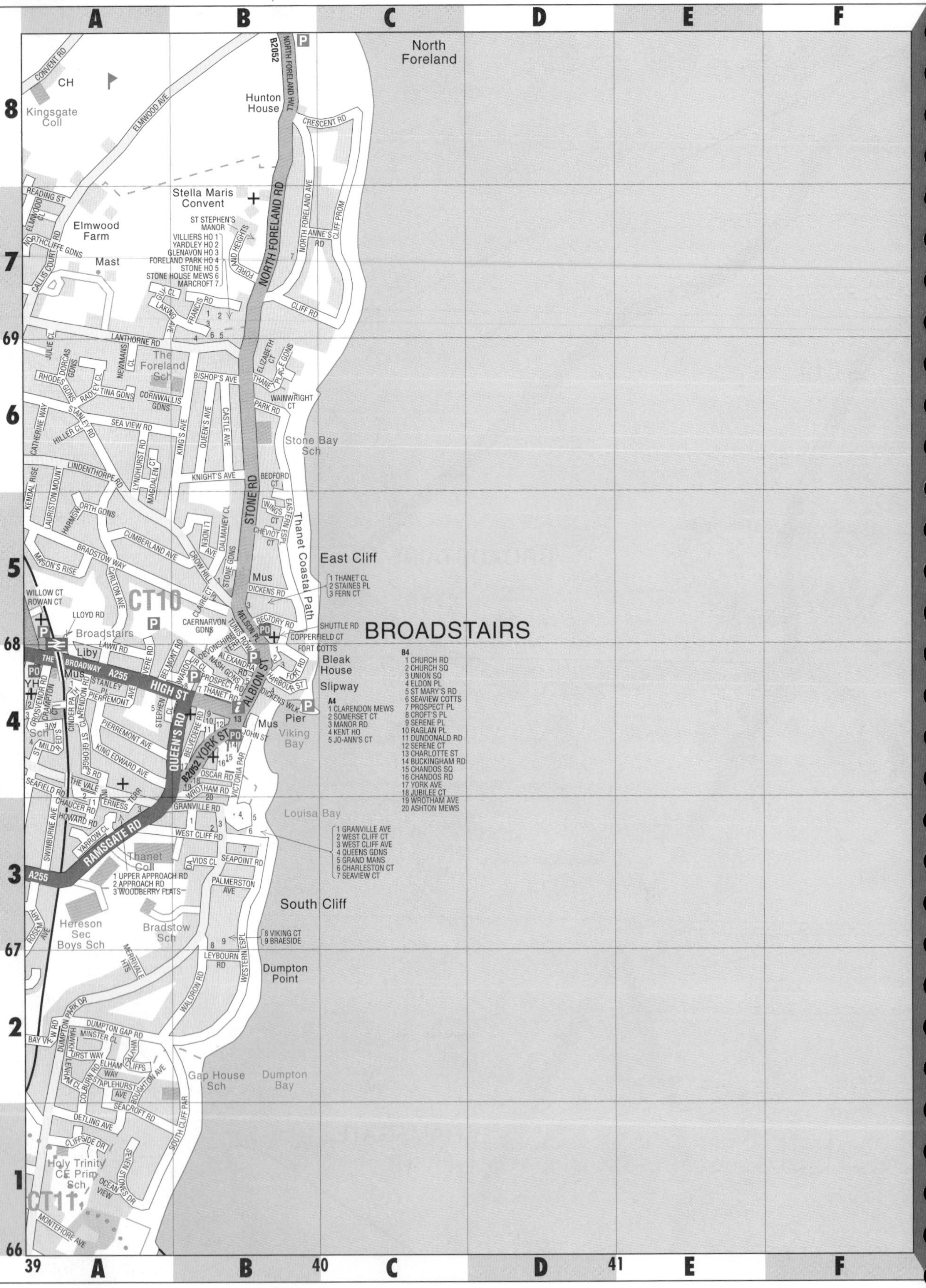

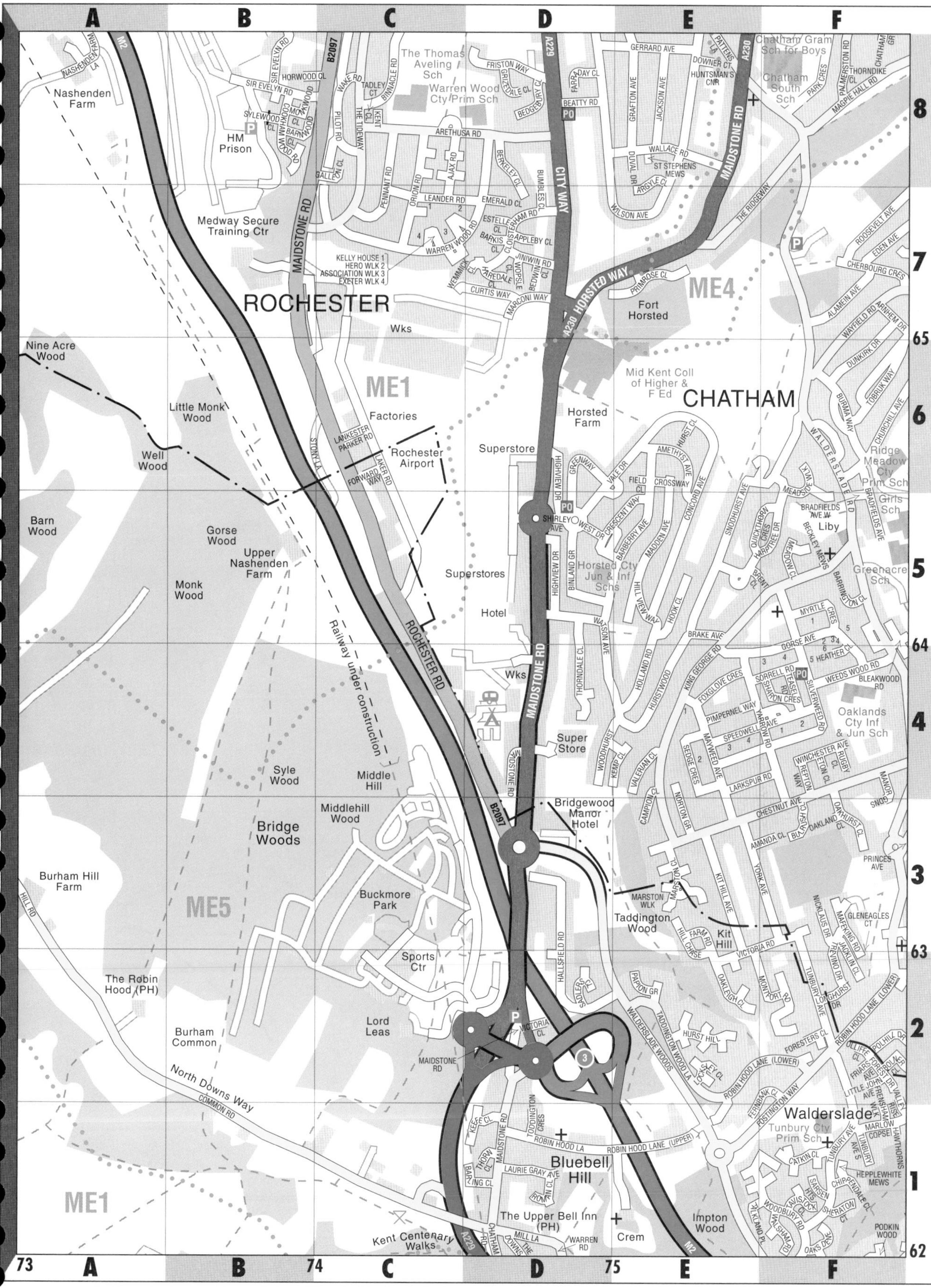

E4	F4	F5
1 LAVENDER CL	1 MALLOW WAY	1 SAFFRON WAY
2 ASPEN WAY	2 JASMINE CL	2 WILLOW HO
3 HONEYSUCKLE CL	3 HAREBELL CL	3 PINE HO
4 GENTIAN CL	4 ROSEMARY CL	4 ROWAN HO
	5 LINDEN HOUSE	5 HAWTHORN HO
	6 OAK HOUSE	

31
10

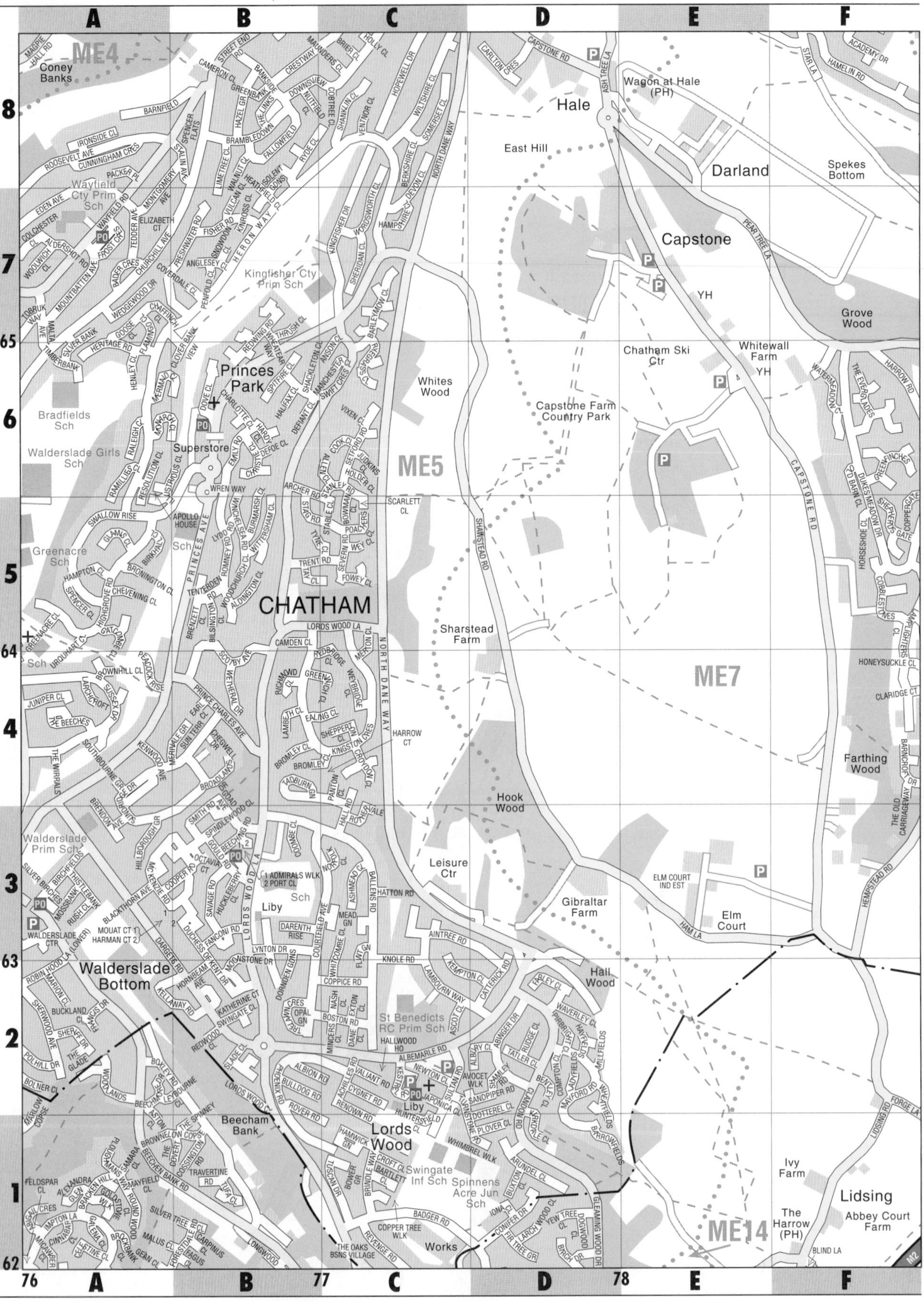
A
B
C
D
E
F
8
7
65
6
5
64
4
3
63
2
1
62
76
77
78
ME4
Coney Banks
Hale
Wagon at Hale (PH)
East Hill
Darland
Spekes Bottom
Capstone
Wayfield Cty Prim Sch
Kingfisher Cty Prim Sch
YH
Grove Wood
Chatham Ski Ctr
Whitewall Farm
Princes Park
Whites Wood
Capstone Farm Country Park
Bradfields Sch
Walderslade Girls Sch
Superstore
ME5
Apollo House
Greenacre Sch
CHATHAM
Sharstead Farm
ME7
Farthing Wood
Hook Wood
Walderslade Prim Sch
Leisure Ctr
Liby
Sch
Gibraltar Farm
Elm Court Ind Est
Elm Court
Walderslade Bottom
Hall Wood
St Benedicts RC Prim Sch
Hallwood Ho
Beecham Bank
Lords Wood
Swingate Inf Sch
Spinnens Acre Jun Sch
Works
Ivy Farm
Lidsing
The Harrow (PH)
Abbey Court Farm
ME14
The Oaks Bsns Village
Capstone Rd
North Dane Way
Princes Ave
Lords Wood La
Sharstead Rd
Ham La
Pear Tree La
Hempstead Rd
Heron Way
Walderslade Ctr
Mouat Ct 1
Harman Ct 2
1 Admirals Wlk
2 Port Cl
Scarlett Cl
Harrow Ct

31
54

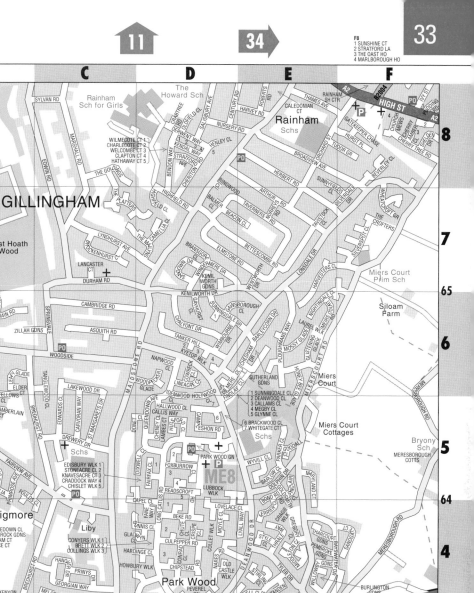

33
12

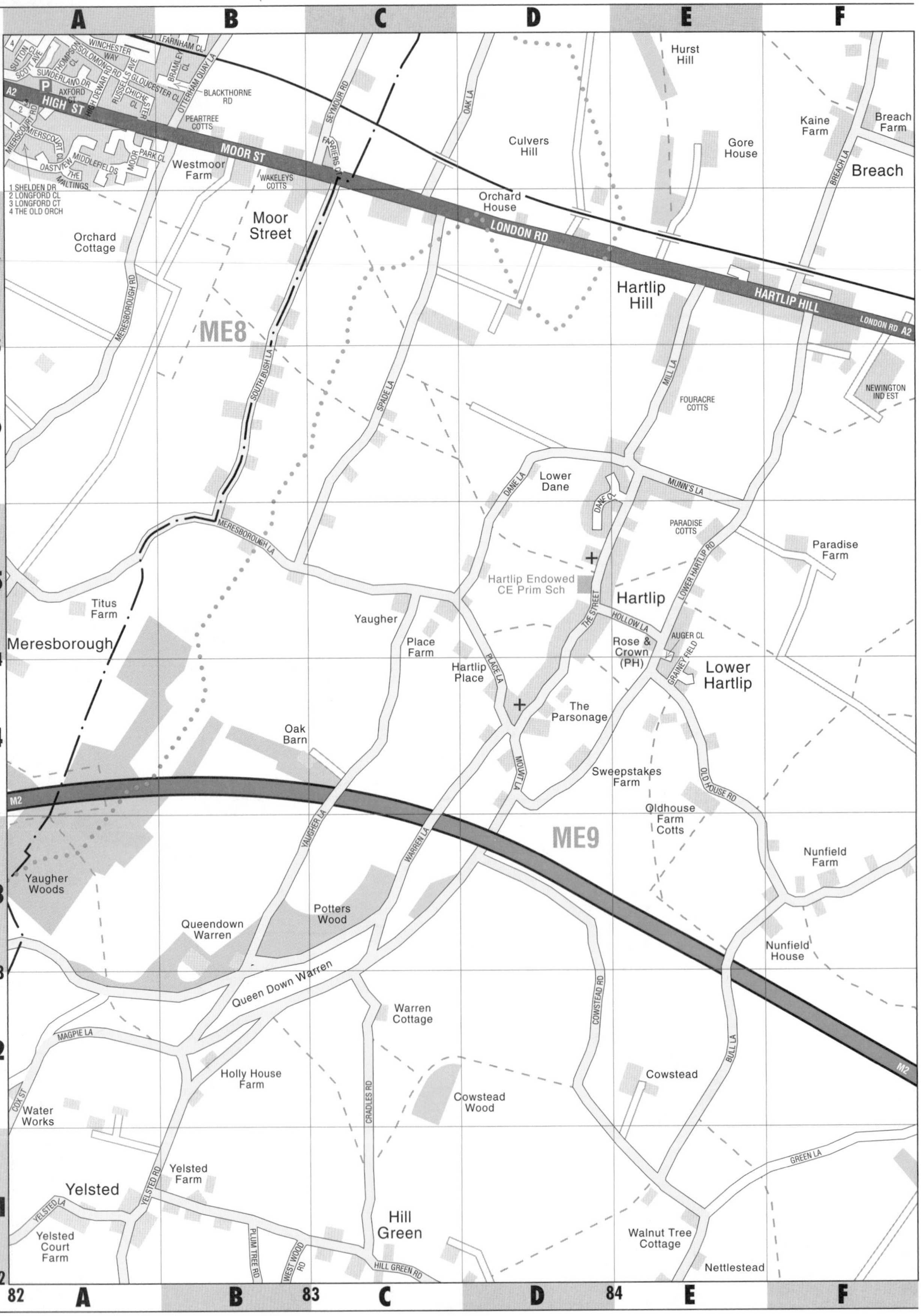
A
B
C
D
E
F
8
7
65
6
5
64
4
3
63
2
1
62
82
83
84
WINCHESTER WAY
SOLOMON RD
THOMPSON CL
SUTTON
SCOTT AVE
SUNDERLAND DR
AXFORD CT
DEWAR RD
RUSSELLS AVE
GLOUCESTER CL
CHICHESTER CL
BRAMLEY CL
FARNHAM CL
OTTERHAM QUAY LA
BLACKTHORNE RD
PEARTREE COTTS
A2
HIGH ST
MIERSCOURT RD
MIERSCOURT CL
OASTVIEW
MIDDLEFIELDS
MOOR PARK CL
THE MALTINGS
1 SHELDEN DR
2 LONGFORD CL
3 LONGFORD CT
4 THE OLD ORCH
Westmoor Farm
MOOR ST
WAKELEYS COTTS
SEYMOUR RD
FARRIERS CL
OAK LA
Culvers Hill
Hurst Hill
Gore House
Kaine Farm
Breach Farm
Breach
BREACH LA
Orchard House
LONDON RD
Orchard Cottage
Moor Street
Hartlip Hill
HARTLIP HILL
LONDON RD A2
ME8
MERESBOROUGH RD
SOUTH BUSH LA
SPADE LA
MILL LA
FOURACRE COTTS
NEWINGTON IND EST
Lower Dane
DANE LA
DANE CL
MUNN'S LA
PARADISE COTTS
Paradise Farm
MERESBOROUGH LA
LOWER HARTLIP RD
Hartlip Endowed CE Prim Sch
Hartlip
Titus Farm
Meresborough
Yaugher
Place Farm
THE STREET
HOLLOW LA
Rose & Crown (PH)
AUGER CL
GRAINEY FIELD
Lower Hartlip
Hartlip Place
PLACE LA
The Parsonage
Oak Barn
Sweepstakes Farm
MOUNT LA
OLD HOUSE RD
M2
Oldhouse Farm Cotts
ME9
YAUGHER LA
WARREN LA
Nunfield Farm
Yaugher Woods
Potters Wood
Queendown Warren
Nunfield House
Queen Down Warren
Warren Cottage
MAGPIE LA
COWSTEAD RD
BULL LA
Holly House Farm
Cowstead
Cowstead Wood
COX ST
Water Works
CRADLES RD
GREEN LA
Yelsted Farm
YELSTED RD
Yelsted
YELSTED LA
Hill Green
Walnut Tree Cottage
Yelsted Court Farm
PLUM TREE RD
WEST WOOD RD
HILL GREEN RD
Nettlestead

33
56

13
36

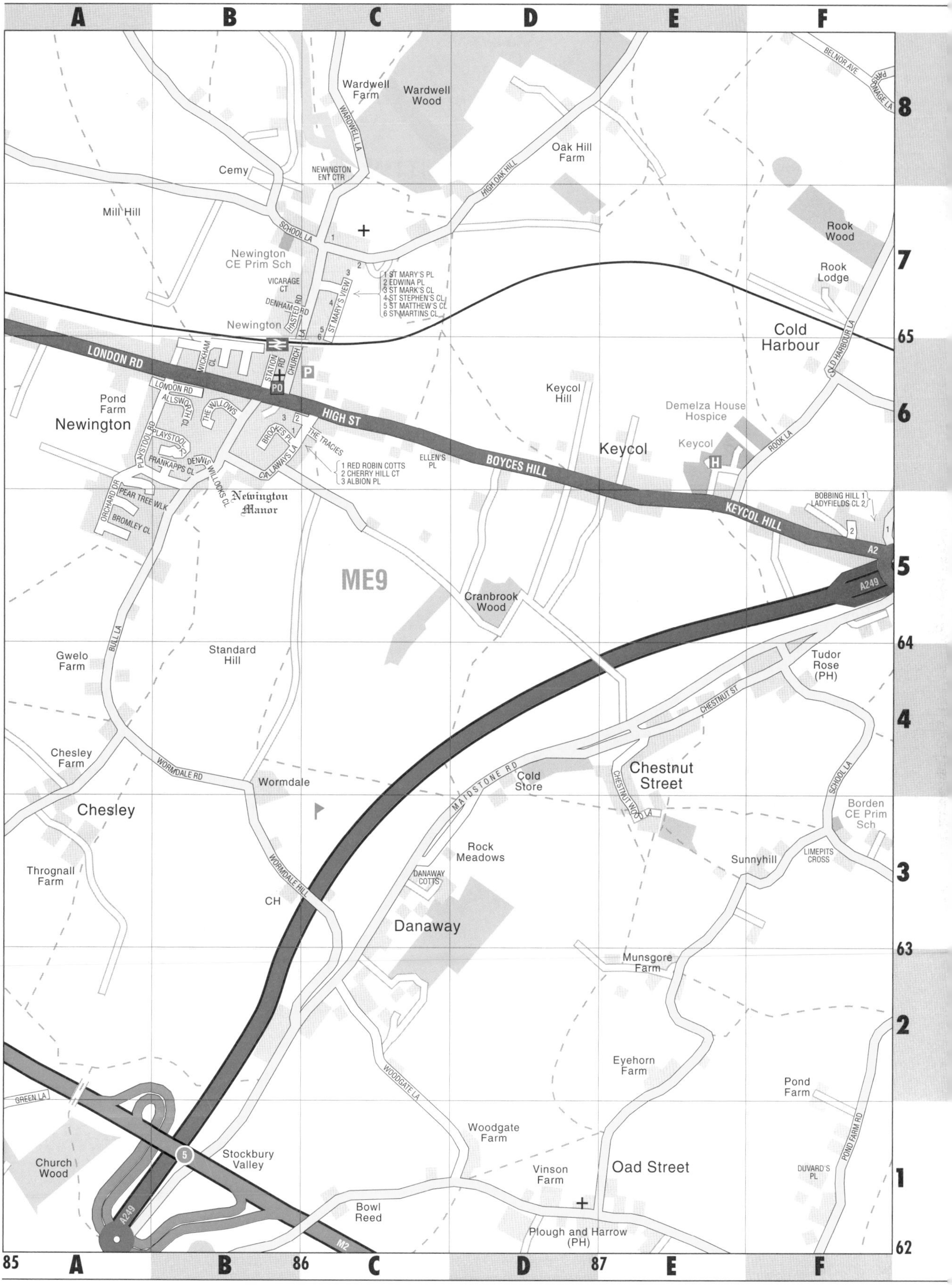
Wardwell Farm
Wardwell Wood
WARDWELL LA
NEWINGTON ENT CTR
Cemy
Mill Hill
Oak Hill Farm
HIGH OAK HILL
SCHOOL LA
Newington CE Prim Sch
VICARAGE CT
DENHAM RD
HASTED RD
ST MARY'S VIEW
1 ST MARY'S PL
2 EDWINA PL
3 ST MARK'S CL
4 ST STEPHEN'S CL
5 ST MATTHEW'S CL
6 ST MARTINS CL
Newington
Rook Wood
Rook Lodge
Cold Harbour
COLD HARBOUR LA
LONDON RD
WICKHAM CL
STATION RD
CHURCH LA
PO
HIGH ST
Pond Farm
Newington
LONDON RD
ALLSWORTH CL
THE WILLOWS
PLAYSTOOL RD
PLAYSTOOL CL
FRANKAPPS CL
DENVIS
WILLOCKS CL
BROOKES PL
THE TRACIES
CALLAWAYS LA
1 RED ROBIN COTTS
2 CHERRY HILL CT
3 ALBION PL
ELLEN'S PL
BOYCES HILL
Keycol Hill
Demelza House Hospice
Keycol
Keycol
ROOK LA
KEYCOL HILL
BOBBING HILL 1
LADYFIELDS CL 2
A2
A249
Newington Manor
ORCHARD DR
PEAR TREE WLK
BROMLEY CL
ME9
Cranbrook Wood
Gwelo Farm
BULL LA
Standard Hill
Tudor Rose (PH)
CHESTNUT ST
Chesley Farm
WORMDALE RD
Wormdale
MAIDSTONE RD
Cold Store
Chestnut Street
CHESTNUT WOOD LA
SCHOOL LA
Borden CE Prim Sch
Chesley
Rock Meadows
Sunnyhill
LIMEPITS CROSS
Thrognall Farm
WORMDALE HILL
CH
DANAWAY COTTS
Danaway
Munsgore Farm
Eyehorn Farm
WOODGATE LA
Pond Farm
GREEN LA
Woodgate Farm
POND FARM RD
Church Wood
Stockbury Valley
5
Vinson Farm
Oad Street
DUVARD'S PL
A249
Bowl Reed
Plough and Harrow (PH)
M2
BELNOR AVE
PARSONAGE LA
A B C D E F
8 7 65 6 5 64 4 3 63 2 1 62
85 86 87

57
36

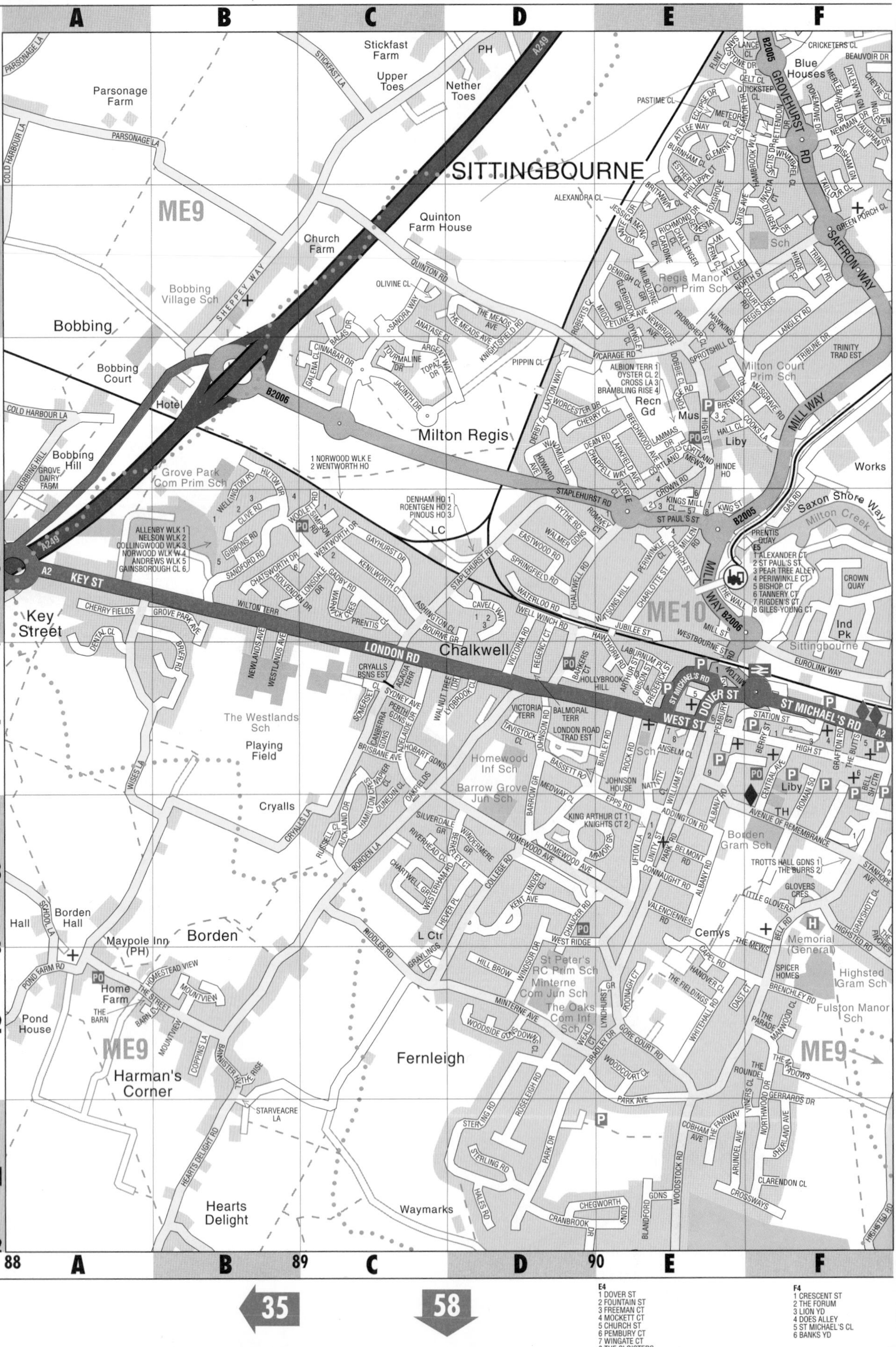

ME9

Parsonage La

Parsonage Farm

PARSONAGE LA

Cold Harbour La

Stickfast Farm

Upper Toes

Nether Toes

PH

SITTINGBOURNE

A249

Quinton Farm House

Church Farm

Bobbing Village Sch

SHEPPEY WAY

Bobbing

QUINTON RD

OLIVINE CL

Bobbing Court

Bobbing Hill

Cold Harbour La

GROVE DAIRY FARM

B2006

Hotel

Grove Park Com Prim Sch

Milton Regis

1 NORWOOD WLK E
2 WENTWORTH HO

DENHAM HO 1
ROENTGEN HO 2
PINOUS HO 3

LC

1 ALLENBY WLK 1
2 NELSON WLK 2
3 COLLINGWOOD WLK 3
4 NORWOOD WLK W 4
5 ANDREWS WLK 5
6 GAINSBOROUGH CL 6

A249

KEY ST

Key Street

CHERRY FIELDS

GROVE PARK AVE

WILTON TERR

LONDON RD

Chalkwell

ME10

Staplehurst Rd

Saxon Shore Way

Milton Creek

St Paul's St

B2005

Prentis Quay
1 ALEXANDER CT
2 ST PAUL'S LA
3 PEAR TREE ALLEY
4 PERIWINKLE CT
5 BISHOP CT
6 TANNERY CT
7 RIGDEN'S CT
8 GILES-YOUNG CT

CROWN QUAY

Ind Pk

Sittingbourne

EUROLINK WAY

MILL WAY

The Westlands Sch

Playing Field

Cryalls

CRYALLS BSNS EST

St Michael's Rd

DOVER ST

WEST ST

St Michael's Rd

Homewood Inf Sch

Barrow Grove Jun Sch

KING ARTHUR CT 1
KNIGHTS CT 2

Borden Gram Sch

AVENUE OF REMEMBRANCE

TH

Liby

TROTTS HALL GDNS 1
THE BURRS 2

GLOVERS CRES

Borden Hall

Hall

Maypole Inn (PH)

Borden

L Ctr

West Ridge

St Peter's RC Prim Sch

Minterne Com Jun Sch

The Oaks Com Inf Sch

Cemys

Memorial (General)

Spicer Homes

Highsted Gram Sch

Home Farm

Pond House

ME9

Harman's Corner

Fernleigh

Fulston Manor Sch

ME9

STARVEACRE LA

Hearts Delight

Waymarks

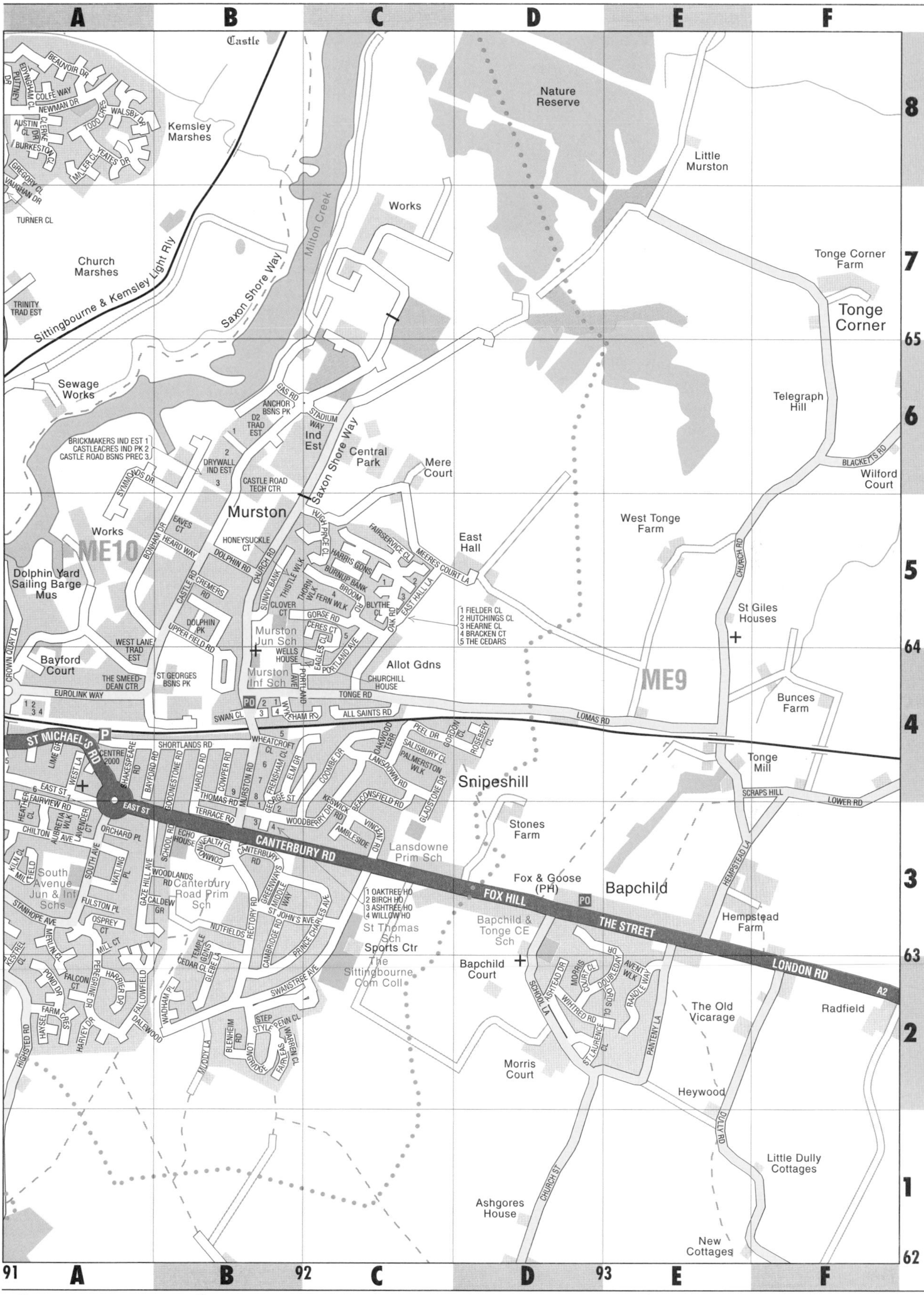

A B C D E F

8 7 65 6 5 64 4 3 63 2 1 62

Castle

Nature Reserve

Kemsley Marshes

Little Murston

Tonge Corner Farm

Church Marshes

Tonge Corner

Milton Creek

Works

Sittingbourne & Kemsley Light Rly

Saxon Shore Way

Telegraph Hill

Sewage Works

TRINITY TRAD EST

GAS RD

ANCHOR BSNS PK

D2 TRAD EST

STADIUM WAY IND EST

Central Park

Mere Court

Blackett's Rd

Wilford Court

BRICKMAKERS IND EST 1
CASTLEACRES IND PK 2
CASTLE ROAD BSNS PREC 3

DRYWALL IND EST

CASTLE ROAD TECH CTR

Saxon Shore Way

West Tonge Farm

Works

ME10

Murston

East Hall

St Giles Houses

Dolphin Yard Sailing Barge Mus

HONEYSUCKLE CT

FAIRSERVICE CL

MEERES COURT LA

1 FIELDER CL
2 HUTCHINGS CL
3 HEARNE CL
4 BRACKEN CT
5 THE CEDARS

ME9

Bayford Court

WEST LANE TRAD EST

Murston Jun Sch

WELLS HOUSE

Allot Gdns

Bunces Farm

THE SMEED-DEAN CTR

ST GEORGES BSNS PK

Murston Inf Sch

CHURCHILL HOUSE

EUROLINK WAY

TONGE RD

SWAN CL

ALL SAINTS RD

LOMAS RD

ST MICHAEL'S RD

SHORTLANDS RD

WHEATCROFT

PEEL DR

Tonge Mill

CANTERBURY RD

Snipeshill

SCRAPS HILL

LOWER RD

EAST ST

Stones Farm

Fox & Goose (PH)

Bapchild

Hempstead Farm

South Avenue Jun & Inf Schs

Canterbury Road Prim Sch

1 OAKTREE HO
2 BIRCH HO
3 ASHTREE HO
4 WILLOW HO

FOX HILL

THE STREET

LONDON RD A2

St Thomas Sch Sports Ctr

Bapchild & Tonge CE Sch

The Sittingbourne Com Coll

Lansdowne Prim Sch

Bapchild Court

The Old Vicarage

Radfield

Morris Court

Heywood

Ashgores House

Little Dully Cottages

New Cottages

37
16

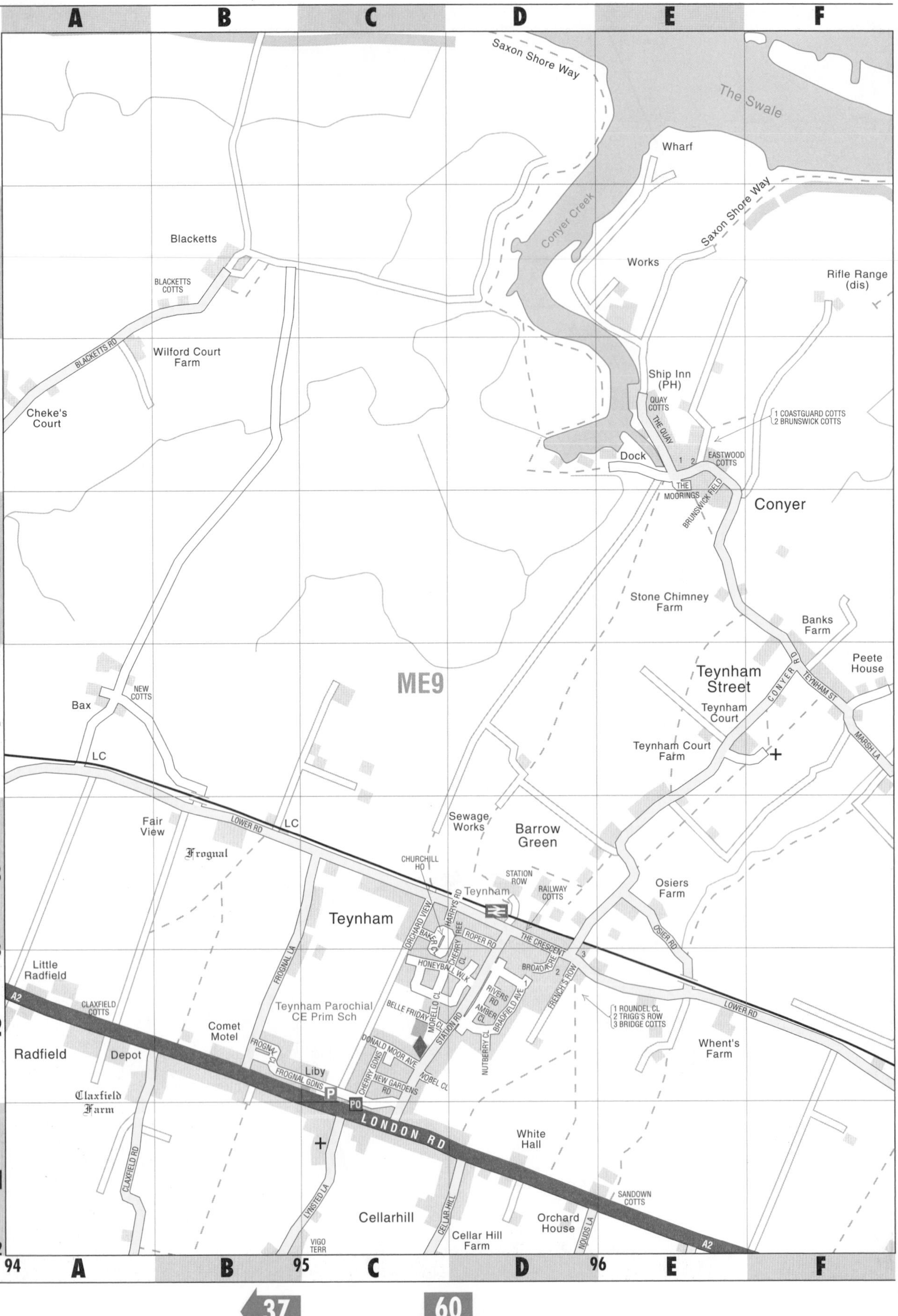

A | B | C | D | E | F

8

Saxon Shore Way

The Swale

Wharf

Conyer Creek

7

Blacketts

BLACKETTS COTTS

Works

Saxon Shore Way

Rifle Range (dis)

65

BLACKETTS RD

Wilford Court Farm

Ship Inn (PH)

QUAY COTTS

1 COASTGUARD COTTS
2 BRUNSWICK COTTS

6

Cheke's Court

THE QUAY

Dock

1   2

EASTWOOD COTTS

THE MOORINGS

BRUNSWICK FIELD

Conyer

5

Stone Chimney Farm

Banks Farm

64

Bax

NEW COTTS

ME9

Teynham Street

Peete House

4

LC

Teynham Court

TEYNHAM ST

CONYER RD

MARSH LA

Teynham Court Farm

Fair View

LOWER RD

LC

Sewage Works

Barrow Green

Osiers Farm

3

Frognal

CHURCHILL HO

STATION ROW

Teynham

Railway Cotts

63

Little Radfield

FROGNAL LA

Teynham

ORCHARD VIEW

BANK

HARRIS'S RD

CHERRY TREE

Roper RD

THE CRESCENT

OSIER RD

LOWER RD

2

A2

CLAXFIELD COTTS

Comet Motel

FROGNAL

Teynham Parochial CE Prim Sch

BELLE FRIDAY

HONEYBALL WLK

MORELLO CL

STATION RD

RIVERS RD

AMBER

BROAD

BEDGELD AVE

FRENCH'S ROW

1 ROUNDEL CL
2 TRIGG'S ROW
3 BRIDGE COTTS

Whent's Farm

Radfield

Depot

Liby

FROGNAL GDNS

DONALD MOOR AVE

CHERRY GDNS

NEW GARDENS RD

NUTBERRY CL

NOBEL CL

Claxfield Farm

CLAXFIELD RD

P

PO

LONDON RD

White Hall

1

LYNSTED LA

CELLAR HILL

Cellarhill

Cellar Hill Farm

Orchard House

NOURIS LA

Sandown Cotts

A2

62

VIGO TERR

94   A   B   95   C   D   96   E   F

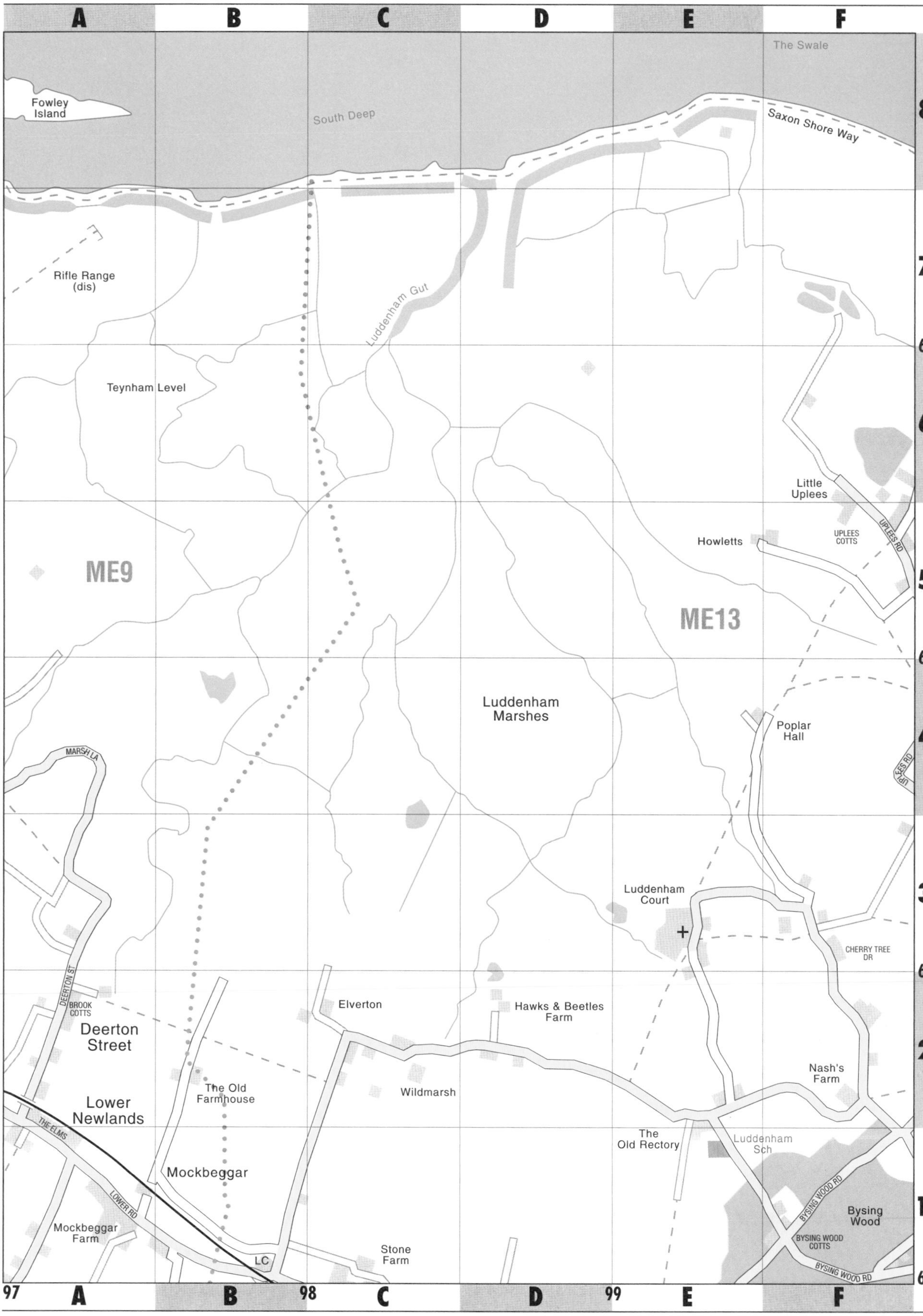

A B C D E F

The Swale

8

Fowley
Island

South Deep

Saxon Shore Way

7

Rifle Range
(dis)

Luddenham Gut

65

Teynham Level

6

Little
Uplees

Howletts

UPLEES
COTTS

UPLEES RD

ME9

5

ME13

64

Luddenham
Marshes

Poplar
Hall

UP LEES RD

4

MARSH LA

Luddenham
Court

+

3

CHERRY TREE
DR

DEERTON ST

BROOK
COTTS

63

Deerton
Street

Elverton

Hawks & Beetles
Farm

Nash's
Farm

2

Lower
Newlands

The Old
Farmhouse

Wildmarsh

The
Old Rectory

Luddenham
Sch

THE ELMS

Mockbeggar

BYSING WOOD RD

Bysing
Wood

1

LOWER RD

Mockbeggar
Farm

Stone
Farm

LC

BYSING WOOD
COTTS

BYSING WOOD RD

62

97 A B 98 C D 99 E F

39
18

A B C D E F

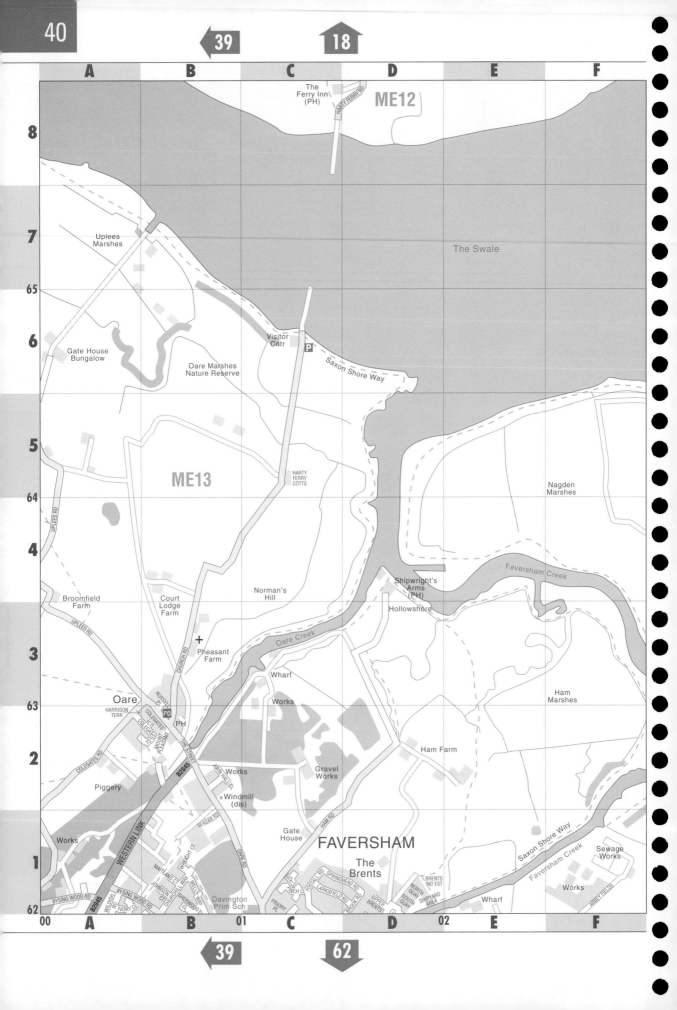
The Ferry Inn (PH)
HARTY FERRY RD
ME12
8
7
Uplees Marshes
The Swale
65
Visitor Cntr
P
6
Gate House Bungalow
Oare Marshes Nature Reserve
Saxon Shore Way
5
ME13
HARTY FERRY COTTS
Nagden Marshes
64
UPLEES RD
4
Faversham Creek
Shipwright's Arms (PH)
Norman's Hill
Broomfield Farm
Court Lodge Farm
Hollowshore
UPLEES RD
Oare Creek
3
Pheasant Farm
CHURCH RD
Wharf
Oare
RUSSELL PL
PO
Works
Ham Marshes
63
HARRISON TERR
COLEGATES CT
COLEGATES CL
MOUNT PLEASANT
PH
THE STREET
Ham Farm
2
COLEGATES RD
B2045
Works
JOHN HALL CL
Gravel Works
Piggery
Windmill (dis)
SEAGAR RD
HAM RD
WESTERN LINK
Works
Gate House
FAVERSHAM
WRIGHT CT
OARE RD
Saxon Shore Way
Sewage Works
1
The Brents
Faversham Creek
MAITLAND CT
JOHNSON CT
CHURCHILL WAY
WELLS WAY
FOSTALL RD
SPRINGHEAD RD
LARKSFIELD RD
BRENTS IND EST
NORTH QUAY
SOUTH QUAY
SHIPYARD AREA
Works
BYSING WOOD RD
WILDISH RD
BYSING WOOD RD
IVORY CL
SHERWOOD CL
Davington Prim Sch
FINCH CL
PRIORY PL
BROOK RD
UPPER BRENTS
Wharf
ABBEY FIELDS
62

00 A B 01 C D 02 E F

39
62

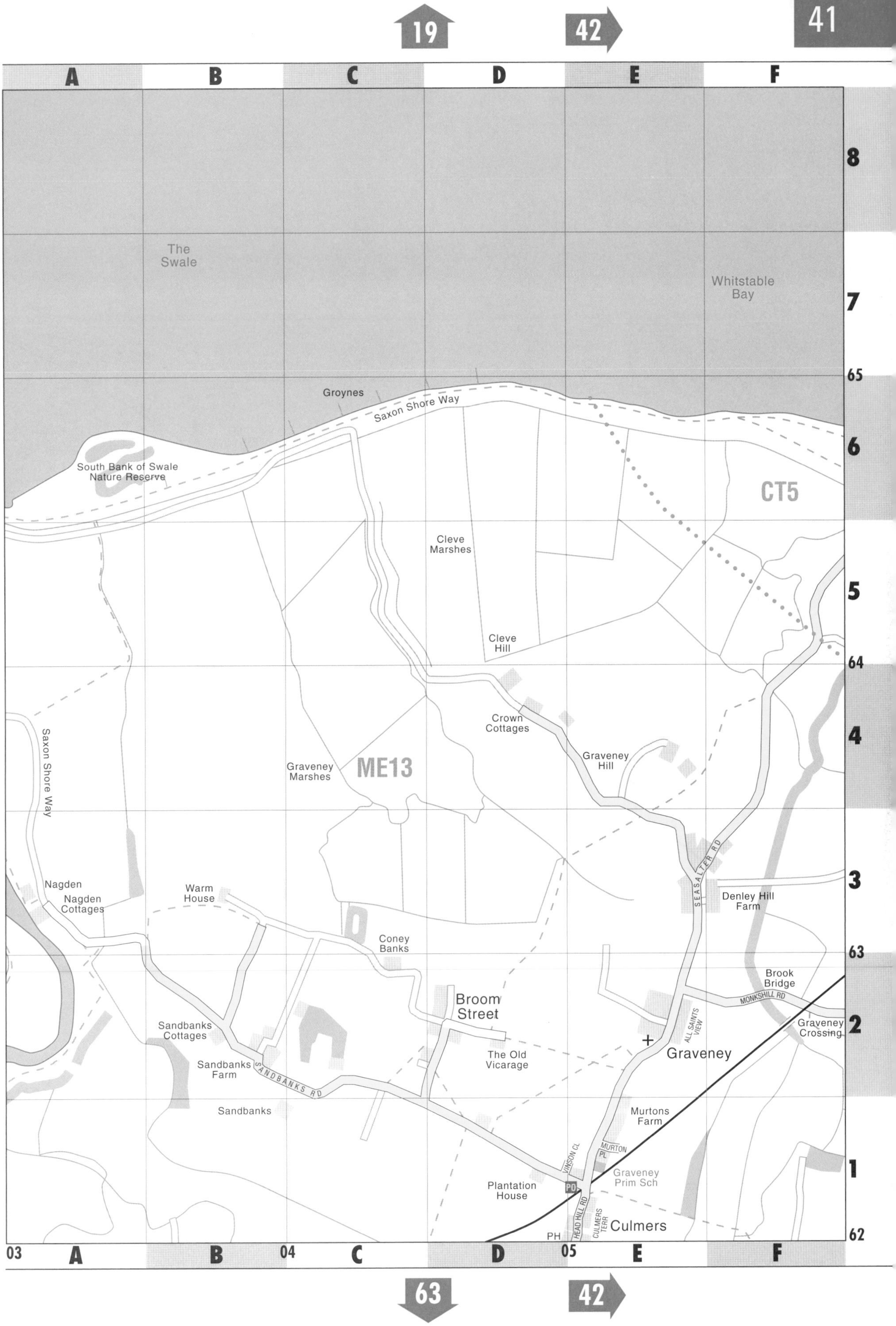
19
42
A
B
C
D
E
F
8
7
6
5
4
3
2
1
65
64
63
62
The Swale
Whitstable Bay
Groynes
Saxon Shore Way
South Bank of Swale Nature Reserve
CT5
Cleve Marshes
Cleve Hill
Crown Cottages
Graveney Hill
Graveney Marshes
ME13
Saxon Shore Way
SEASALTER RD
Denley Hill Farm
Nagden
Nagden Cottages
Warm House
Coney Banks
Brook Bridge
MONKSHILL RD
Broom Street
Sandbanks Cottages
ALL SAINTS VIEW
Graveney Crossing
Graveney
The Old Vicarage
Sandbanks Farm
SANDBANKS RD
Sandbanks
Murtons Farm
VINSON CL
MURTON PL
Graveney Prim Sch
Plantation House
PO
HEAD HILL RD
CULMERS TERR
Culmers
PH
03
04
05
63
42

41

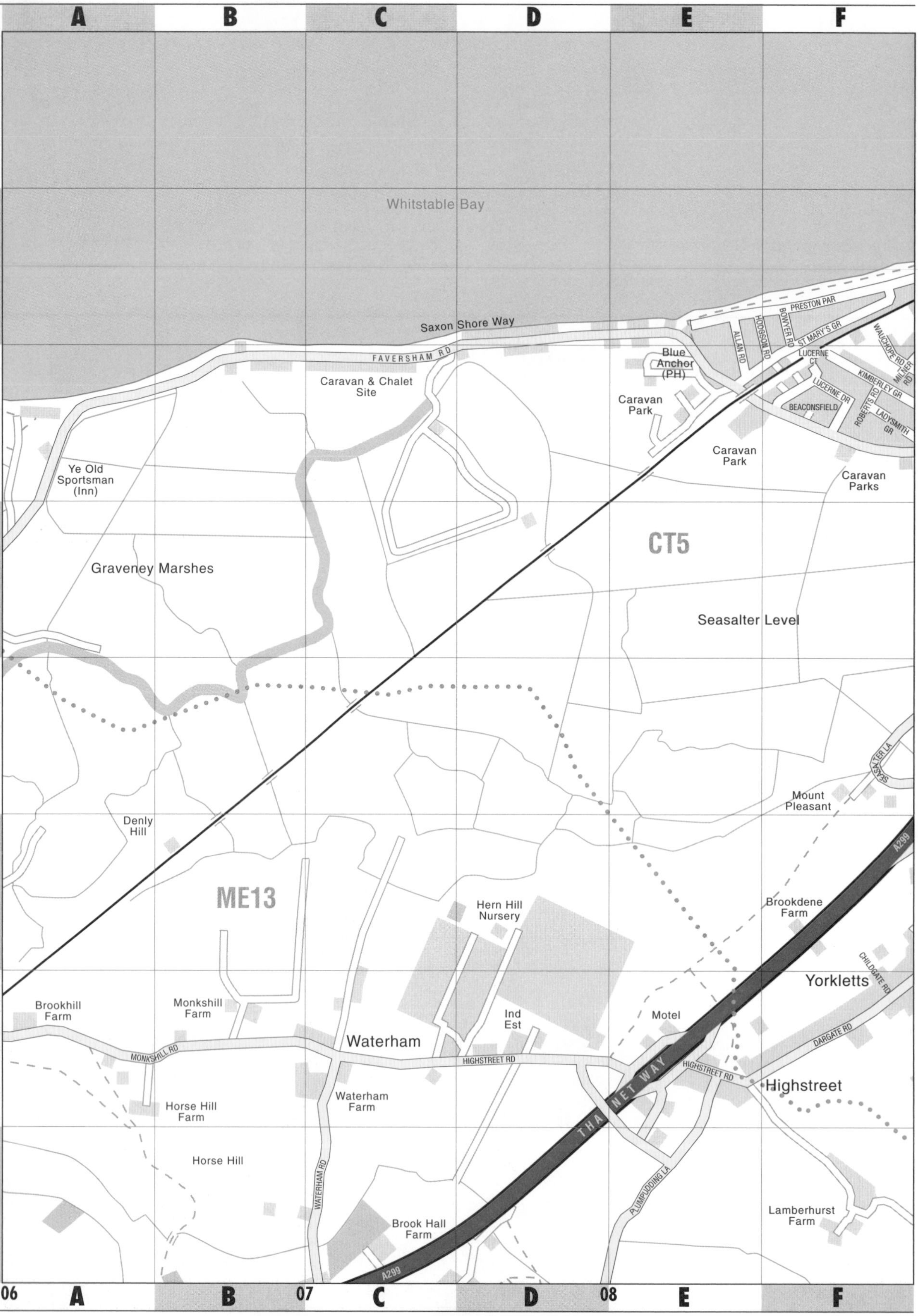

Whitstable Bay

Saxon Shore Way

FAVERSHAM RD

PRESTON PAR

Caravan & Chalet Site

Blue Anchor (PH)

Caravan Park

BOWER RD
HODGSON RD
ST MARY'S GR
ALLAN RD
WALCROFT RD
JUBILEE RD
LUCERNE CT
LUCERNE DR
KIMBERLEY GR
BEACONSFIELD
ROBERTS RD
LADYSMITH GR

CT5

Ye Old Sportsman (Inn)

Caravan Park

Caravan Parks

Graveney Marshes

Seasalter Level

Mount Pleasant

SEASALTER LA

A299

ME13

Denly Hill

Hern Hill Nursery

Brookdene Farm

CHILDGATE RD

Yorkletts

Brookhill Farm

Monkshill Farm

Ind Est

Motel

Waterham

MONKSHILL RD

HIGHSTREET RD

THANET WAY

HIGHSTREET RD

DARGATE RD

Highstreet

Horse Hill Farm

Waterham Farm

WATERHAM RD

Horse Hill

Brook Hall Farm

PLUMPUDDING LA

A299

Lamberhurst Farm

06   A   B   07   C   D   08   E   F

20 44

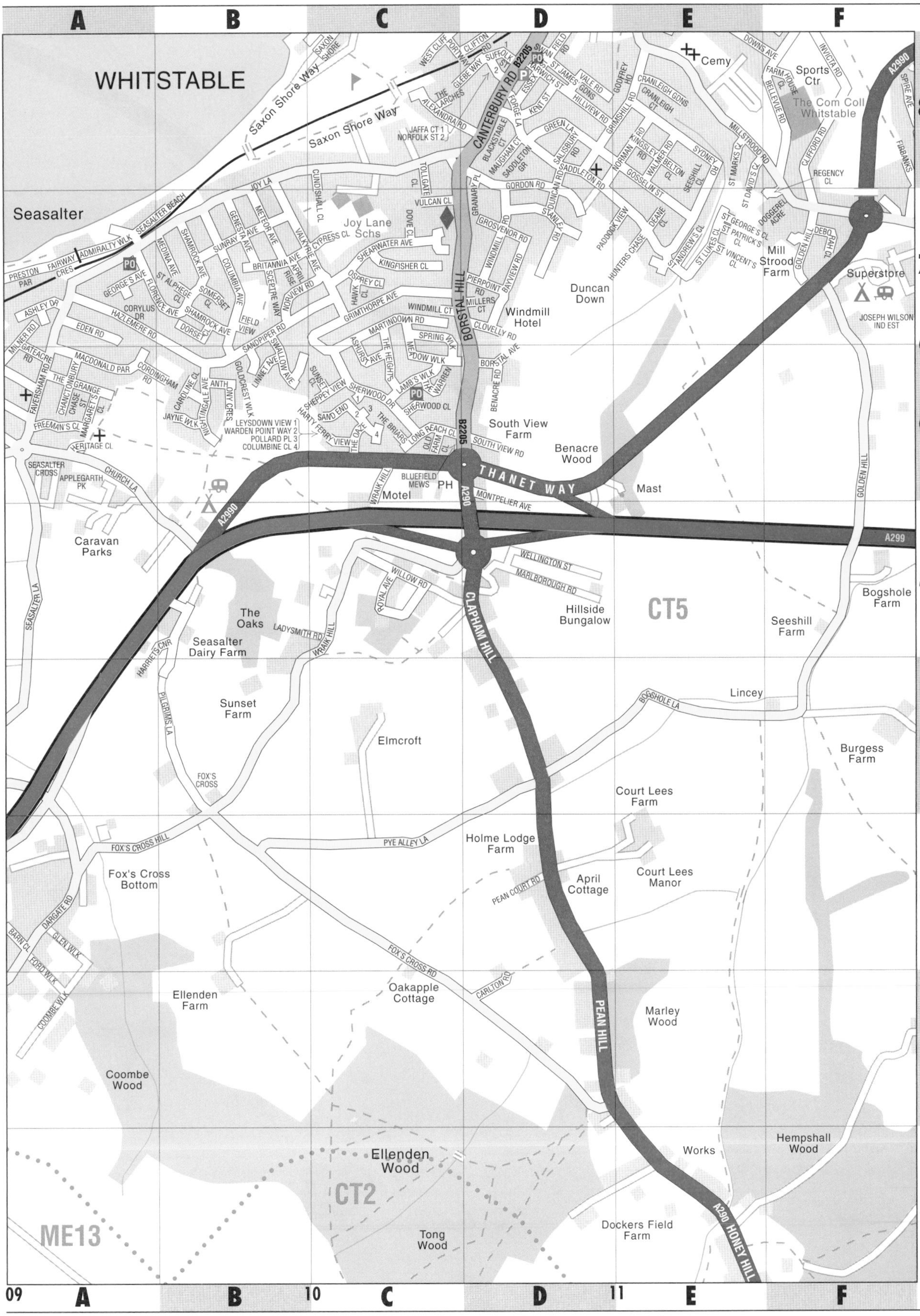
A
B
C
D
E
F
WHITSTABLE
Seasalter
Saxon Shore Way
Saxon Shore Way
Cemy
Sports Ctr
The Com Coll Whitstable
Joy Lane Schs
Duncan Down
Mill Strood Farm
Superstore
JOSEPH WILSON IND EST
Windmill Hotel
South View Farm
Benacre Wood
Mast
Motel
PH
THANET WAY
A2990
A299
A290
B2205
CANTERBURY RD
BORSTAL HILL
CLAPHAM HILL
PEAN HILL
HONEY HILL
Caravan Parks
The Oaks
Seasalter Dairy Farm
Hillside Bungalow
CT5
Seeshill Farm
Bogshole Farm
Lincey
Sunset Farm
Elmcroft
Burgess Farm
Court Lees Farm
Holme Lodge Farm
April Cottage
Court Lees Manor
Fox's Cross Bottom
FOX'S CROSS
FOX'S CROSS HILL
FOX'S CROSS RD
PYE ALLEY LA
BOGSHOLE LA
PEAN COURT RD
CARLTON RD
Ellenden Farm
Oakapple Cottage
Marley Wood
Coombe Wood
Ellenden Wood
CT2
Works
Hempshall Wood
ME13
Tong Wood
Dockers Field Farm
SEASALTER LA
HARRIETS CNR
PILGRIMS LA
LADYSMITH RD
WRAIK HILL
WILLOW RD
ROYAL AVE
WELLINGTON ST
MARLBOROUGH RD
MONTPELIER AVE
GOLDEN HILL
DARGATE RD
BARN CL
GLEN WLK
FORD WLK
COOMBE WLK
SEASALTER CROSS
APPLEGARTH PK
CHURCH LA
HERITAGE CL
FREEMAN'S CL
FAVERSHAM RD
LEYSDOWN VIEW 1
WARDEN POINT WAY 2
POLLARD PL 3
COLUMBINE CL 4
JAFFA CT 1
NORFOLK ST 2
BLUEFIELD MEWS
SOUTH VIEW RD
BORSTAL AVE
BENACRE RD
CLOVELLY RD
MILLERS CT
PIERPOINT RD
WINDMILL RD
BAYVIEW RD
GROSVENOR RD
GRANARY PL
GORDON RD
DUNCAN RD
STANLEY RD
SADDLETON RD
SALISBURY RD
GREEN LA
PADDOCK VIEW
HUNTERS CHASE
DEANE CL
GOSSELIN ST
SEESHILL CL
BELTON CL
WALMER RD
KINGSLEY RD
NORMAN RD
GRIMSHILL RD
GODFREY RD
CRANLEIGH GDNS
CRANLEIGH CT
SYDNEY RD
MILLSTROOD RD
ST MARKS CL
ST DAVID'S CL
DOGGEREL ACRE
ST GEORGE'S CL
ST PATRICK'S CL
ST VINCENT'S CL
ST LUKES CL
ST ANDREW'S CL
REGENCY CL
DEBORAH CL
CLIFFORD RD
BELLEVUE RD
FARM HOUSE CL
DOWNS AVE
INVICTA RD
SPIRE AVE
FIRBANKS
HILLVIEW RD
VALE RD
ST JAMES' GDNS
HARWICH ST
KENT ST
ESSEX ST
FORGE LA
SWAN ST
FIELD RD
SUFFOLK RD
CLIFTON RD
PORTWAY
WEST CLIFF
GLEBE WAY
THE LARCHES
ALEXANDRA RD
BLACKSTABLE CT
MAUGHAM CT
SADDLETON GR
TOLLGATE CL
VULCAN CL
DOVE CL
CUNDISHALL CL
JOY LA
CYPRESS CL
SHEARWATER AVE
KINGFISHER CL
OSPREY CL
HAWK CL
GRIMTHORPE AVE
WINDMILL CT
MARTINDOWN RD
SPRING WLK
MEADOW WLK
THE WARREN
LAMB'S WLK
THE HEIGHTS
ASHURST AVE
SUNSET CL
SHEPPEY VIEW
SHERWOOD DR
SHERWOOD CL
SAND END
HARTY FERRY VIEW
THE OAZE
THE BRIARS
LONG BEACH CL
OLD FARM CL
VALKYRIE AVE
APRIL RISE
NORVIEW RD
SCEPTRE WAY
BRITANNIA AVE
METEOR AVE
SUNRAY AVE
GENESTA AVE
COLUMBIA AVE
SHAMROCK AVE
SOMERSET CL
MEDINA AVE
ST ALPHEGE CL
FLORENCE AVE
SHAMROCK AVE
DORSET CL
FIELD VIEW
SANDPIPER RD
SWALLOW AVE
LINNET AVE
GOLDCREST WLK
ANTHONY CRES
NIGHTINGALE AVE
CAROLINE CL
JAYNE WLK
CORDINGHAM RD
MACDONALD PAR
EDEN RD
HAZLEMERE RD
CORYLUS DR
GEORGE'S AVE
ASHLEY DR
MILNER RD
GATEACRE RD
THE GRANGE
CHANCTONBURY CHASE
ST MARGARET'S CL
PRESTON PAR
FAIRWAY CRES
ADMIRALTY WLK
SEASALTER BEACH
SAXON SHORE
62
63
64
65
1
2
3
4
5
6
7
8
09
10
11

65 44

43
21

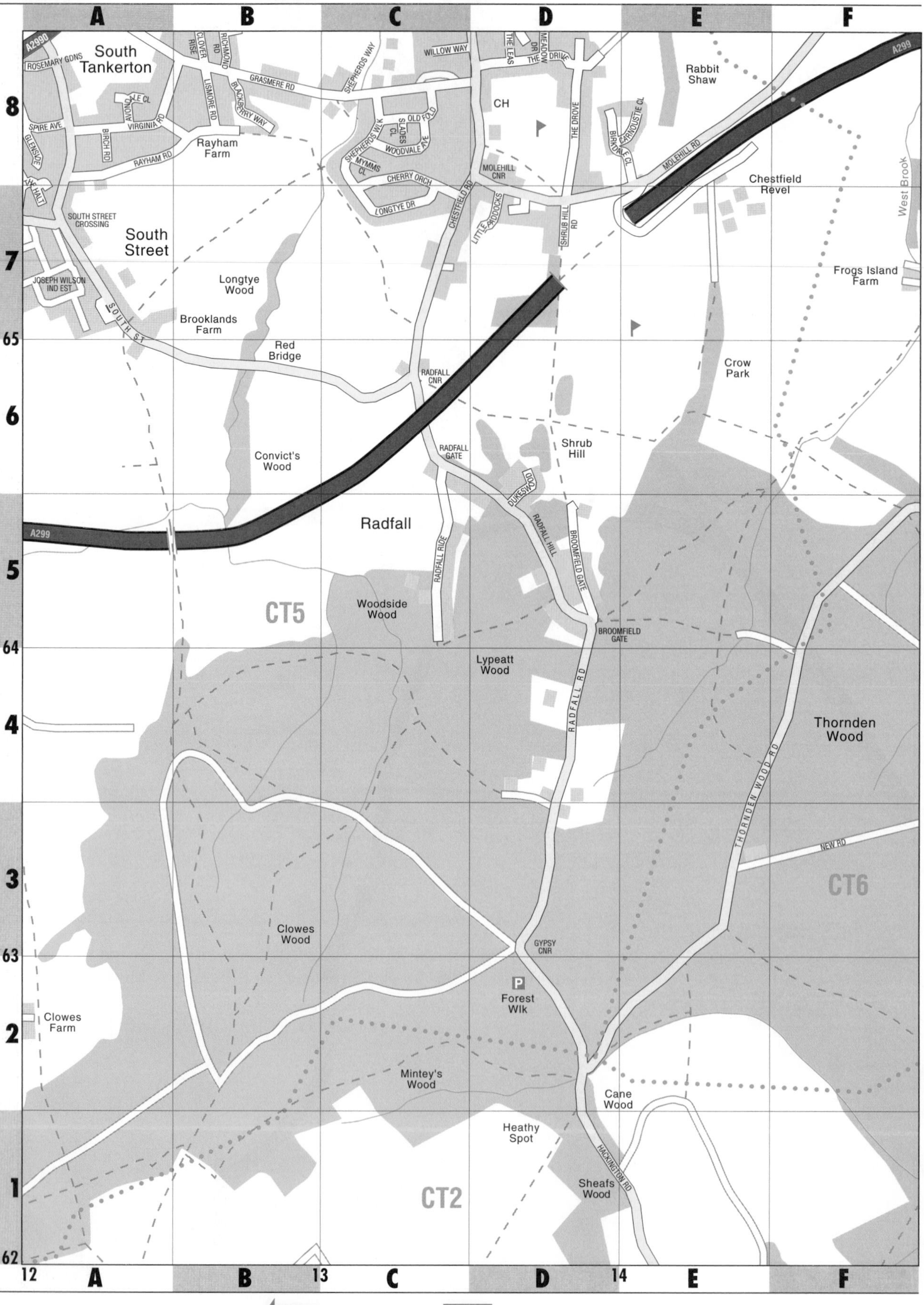
South Tankerton
South Street
Rayham Farm
Longtye Wood
Brooklands Farm
Red Bridge
Convict's Wood
Radfall
Rabbit Shaw
Chestfield Revel
Frogs Island Farm
Crow Park
Shrub Hill
West Brook
CH
CT5
Woodside Wood
Lypeatt Wood
Thornden Wood
CT6
Clowes Wood
Clowes Farm
Forest Wlk
Mintey's Wood
Cane Wood
Heathy Spot
Sheafs Wood
CT2
A2990
A299
ROSEMARY GDNS
SPIRE AVE
GLENSIDE
BIRCH RD
AVONDALE CL
VIRGINIA RD
RAYHAM RD
CLOVER RISE
RICHMOND RD
LISMORE RD
BLACKBERRY WAY
GRASMERE RD
SHEPHERDS WAY
WILLOW WAY
THE LEAS
MEADOW DR
THE DRIVE
THE DROVE
OLD FOLD
SLADES CL
SHEPHERDS WLK
WOODVALE AVE
MYMMS CL
CHERRY ORCH
LONGTYE DR
CHESTFIELD RD
MOLEHILL CNR
LITTLE PADDOCKS
SHRUB HILL RD
BIRKDALE CL
CARNOUSTIE CL
MOLEHILL RD
SOUTH STREET CROSSING
JOSEPH WILSON IND EST
SOUTH ST
RADFALL CNR
RADFALL GATE
DUKESWOOD
RADFALL HILL
BROOMFIELD GATE
RADFALL RIDE
RADFALL RD
THORNDEN WOOD RD
NEW RD
GYPSY CNR
HACKINGTON RD
A
B
C
D
E
F
8
7
65
6
5
64
4
3
63
2
1
62
12
13
14

43
66

22
46

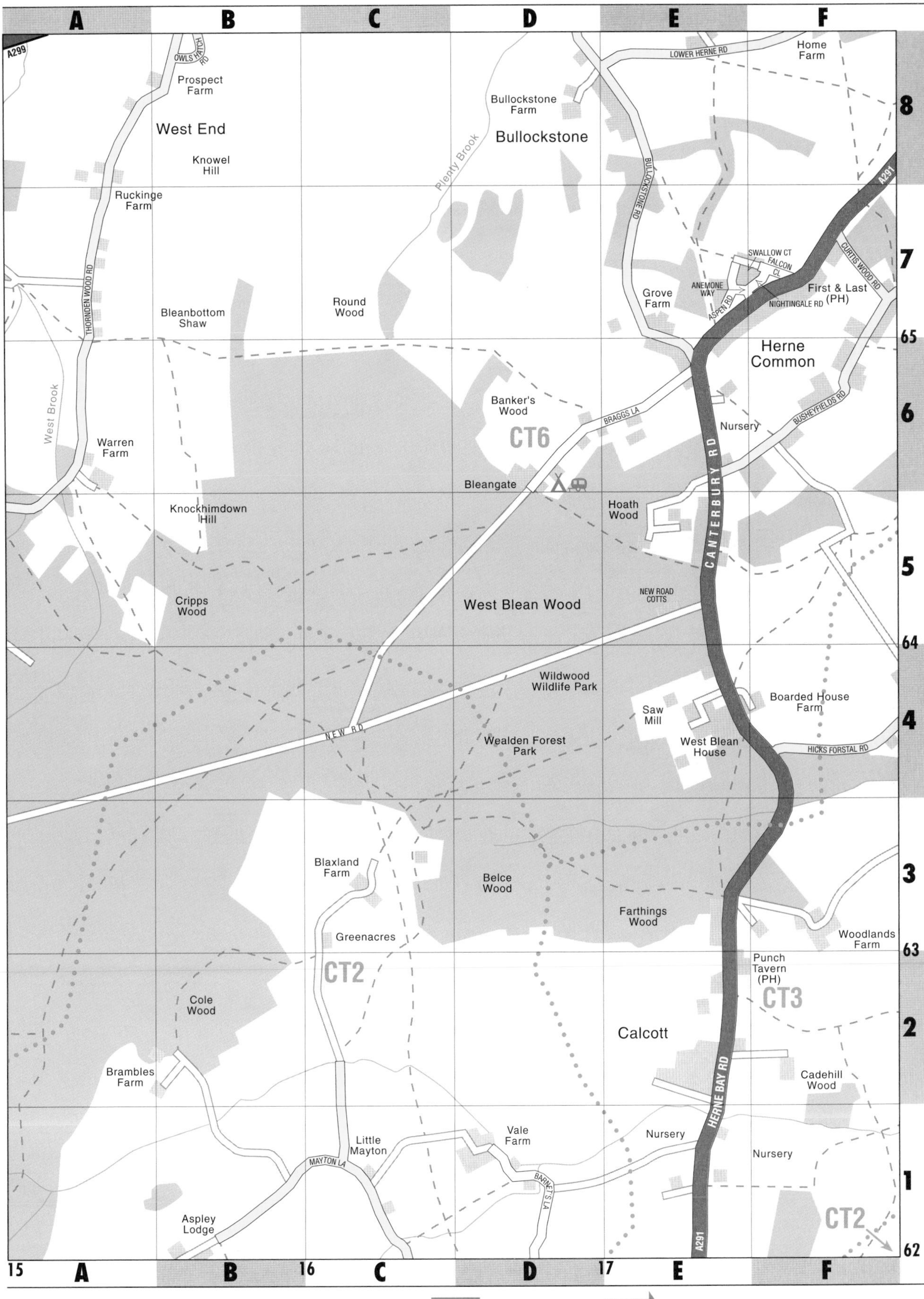
A
B
C
D
E
F
A299
OWLS HATCH RD
Prospect Farm
West End
Knowel Hill
Ruckinge Farm
THORNDEN WOOD RD
Bleanbottom Shaw
Round Wood
Bullockstone Farm
Bullockstone
Plenty Brook
LOWER HERNE RD
Home Farm
BULLOCKSTONE RD
A291
SWALLOW CT
FALCON CL
CURTIS WOOD RD
ANEMONE WAY
ASPEN RD
NIGHTINGALE RD
First & Last (PH)
Grove Farm
Herne Common
West Brook
Warren Farm
Banker's Wood
CT6
BRAGGS LA
Nursery
BUSHEYFIELDS RD
CANTERBURY RD
Bleangate
Hoath Wood
Knockhimdown Hill
Cripps Wood
West Blean Wood
NEW ROAD COTTS
Wildwood Wildlife Park
Saw Mill
Boarded House Farm
NEW RD
Wealden Forest Park
West Blean House
HICKS FORSTAL RD
Blaxland Farm
Belce Wood
Farthings Wood
Woodlands Farm
Greenacres
CT2
Punch Tavern (PH)
CT3
Cole Wood
Calcott
Brambles Farm
HERNE BAY RD
Cadehill Wood
Little Mayton
MAYTON LA
Vale Farm
BARNET'S LA
Nursery
Nursery
Aspley Lodge
A291
CT2
8
7
65
6
5
64
4
3
63
2
1
62
15
16
17

67
46

45 23

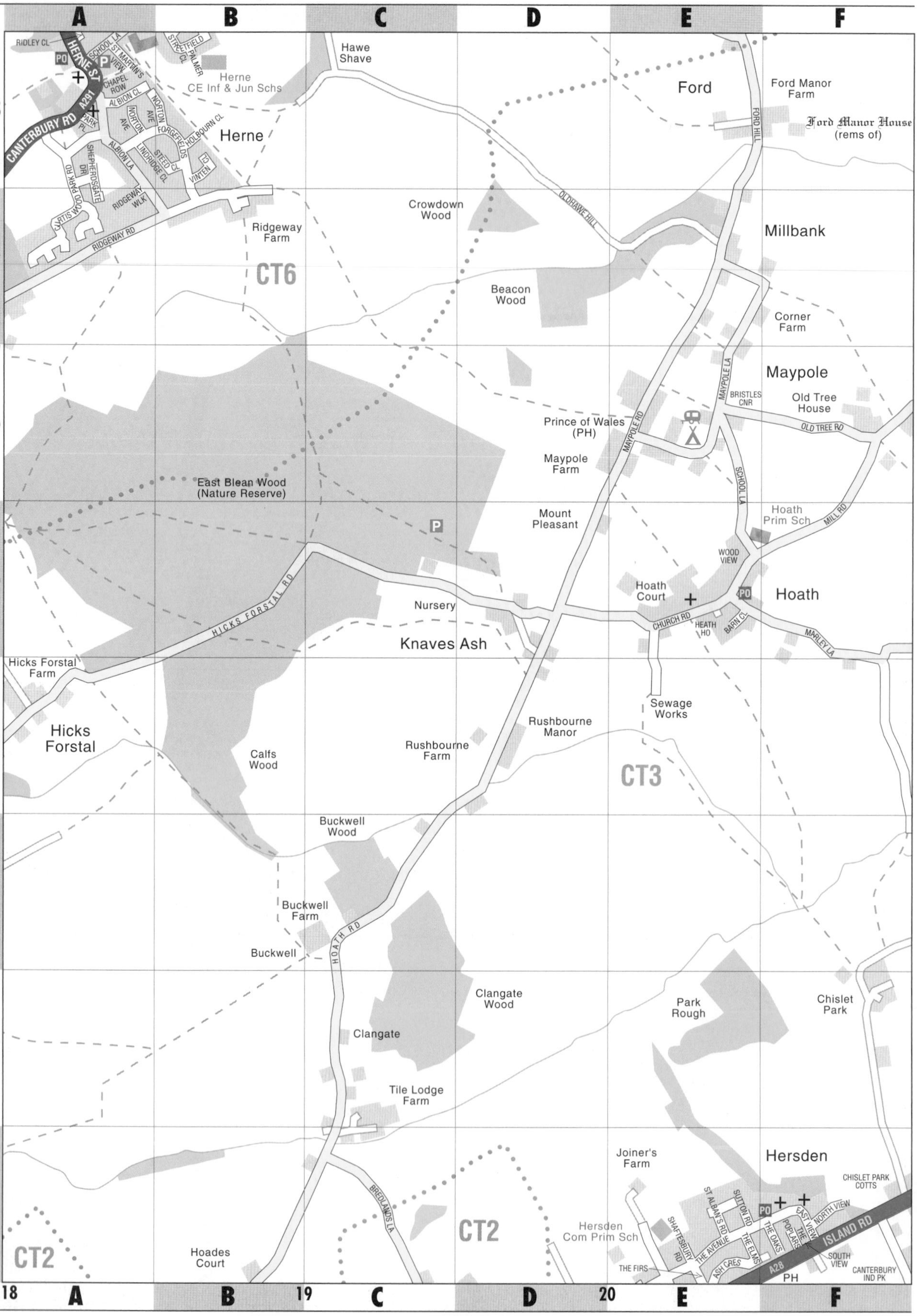

A B C D E F

8

RIDLEY CL
PO
CANTERBURY RD A291
HERNE ST
SCHOOL LA
ST MARTIN'S
STREETFIELD
CHAPEL ROW
Hawe Shave
Herne CE Inf & Jun Schs

Herne

Ford
Ford Manor Farm
Ford Manor House (rems of)
FORD HILL

Millbank

SHEPHERDSGATE DR
CURTIS RD
RIDGEWAY WLK
RIDGEWAY RD
ALBION RD
NORTON CL
AXE
LINDENORE CL
STEED CL
VINTEN
FORGEFIELDS
HOLBOURN CL

Ridgeway Farm

7

CT6

Crowdown Wood

OLD HAWE HILL

Corner Farm

Maypole

MAYPOLE LA
BRISTLES CNR
Old Tree House

65

Beacon Wood

OLD TREE RD

6

East Blean Wood (Nature Reserve)

Prince of Wales (PH)
Maypole Farm

MAYPOLE RD
SCHOOL LA

Hoath Prim Sch
MILL RD

P

Mount Pleasant

WOOD VIEW
Hoath
PO

5

Nursery

Knaves Ash

Hoath Court
CHURCH RD
HEATH HO
BARN CL
MARLEY LA

64

Hicks Forstal Farm

HICKS FORSTAL RD

Rushbourne Manor

Sewage Works

4

Hicks Forstal

Calfs Wood

Rushbourne Farm

CT3

Buckwell Wood

3

Buckwell Farm

HOATH RD

Buckwell

63

Clangate Wood

Park Rough

Chislet Park

2

Clangate

Tile Lodge Farm

1

Joiner's Farm

Hersden

CHISLET PARK COTTS

BREDLANDS LA

CT2

Hersden Com Prim Sch

SHAFTESBURY RD
ST ALBAN'S RD
THE AVENUE
SUTTON RD
THE ELMS
THE OAKS
THE POPLARS
EAST VIEW
NORTH VIEW
PO
ISLAND RD
SOUTH VIEW
CANTERBURY IND PK

62

CT2

Hoades Court

THE FIRS
ASH CRES
A28
PH

18 A B 19 C D 20 E F

45 68

24
48

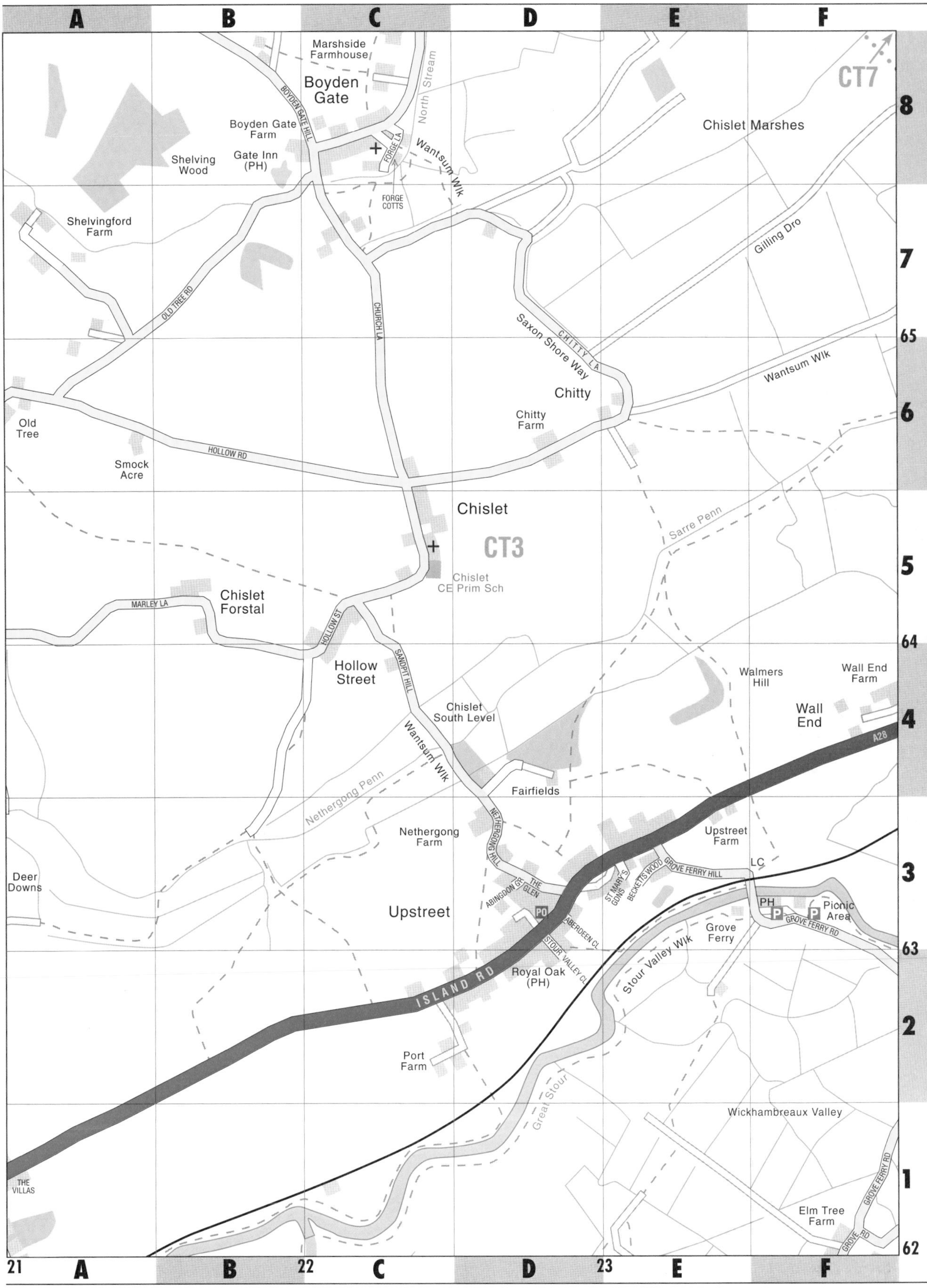
A
B
C
D
E
F
8
7
65
6
5
64
4
3
63
2
1
62
21
22
23
Marshside Farmhouse
Boyden Gate
Boyden Gate Farm
BOYDEN GATE HILL
Gate Inn (PH)
Shelving Wood
North Stream
FORGE LA
Wantsum Wlk
FORGE COTTS
CT7
Chislet Marshes
Shelvingford Farm
Gilling Dro
OLD TREE RD
CHURCH LA
Saxon Shore Way
CHITTY LA
Chitty
Chitty Farm
Wantsum Wlk
Old Tree
Smock Acre
HOLLOW RD
Chislet
CT3
Chislet CE Prim Sch
Sarre Penn
MARLEY LA
Chislet Forstal
HOLLOW ST
Hollow Street
SANDPIT HILL
Chislet South Level
Walmers Hill
Wall End Farm
Wall End
A28
Wantsum Wlk
Nethergong Penn
Fairfields
Nethergong Farm
NETHERGONG HILL
Upstreet Farm
LC
Deer Downs
ABINGDON GR
THE GLEN
PO
ST MARY'S GDNS
BECKETTS WOOD
GROVE FERRY HILL
PH
P
Picnic Area
GROVE FERRY RD
Upstreet
ABERDEEN CL
STOUR VALLEY CL
Stour Valley Wlk
Grove Ferry
Royal Oak (PH)
ISLAND RD
Port Farm
Great Stour
Wickhambreaux Valley
THE VILLAS
Elm Tree Farm
GROVE FERRY RD
GROVE RD

69
48

A | B | C | D | E | F

8

Gilling Dro
Whitfield Sewer
Chislet Marshes
Wantsum Wlk

7

Sarre
Bolingbroke Farm
CHANTRY LA
Crown Inn (PH)
Sarre Mill
CT12

65

Sarre Penn
A253
SARRE CT
OSTLERS LA
A253
MILE RD

6

OLD RD
Sarre Bridge
CLEVEN LO
River Wantsum
CT7
Sevenscore Dike
LC
LC

LC

5

CT3
Sarre Wall
ISLAND RD
Cut End
Great Stour
Sarre Marshes

64

A28

4

A28

Stourmouth Valley
Stour Bridge

Blood Point
Dog & Duck (PH)
Caravan Parks

3

Little Stour
Saxon Shore Way
CT3
Plucks Gutter

63

North Court Farm
Stour Valley Wlk

2

Grove Ferry Rd
Red Bridge
Russell Farm
BREWERY SQ
Stourmouth Stream
Elmstone Valley

West Stourmouth
Dean Farm
Stonehall Farm
SCHOOL LA
Rising Sun (PH)
THE STREET

1

NEWHOUSE CNR
Newhouse Farm
BEGGARS CNR
Poulders Farm
East Stourmouth
SAXON LA

Blue Bridge
Preston Valley
Oast House Farm
PRESTON RD
ROOKSTON CNR

62

Grove Rd

24 | A | B | 25 | C | D | 26 | E | F

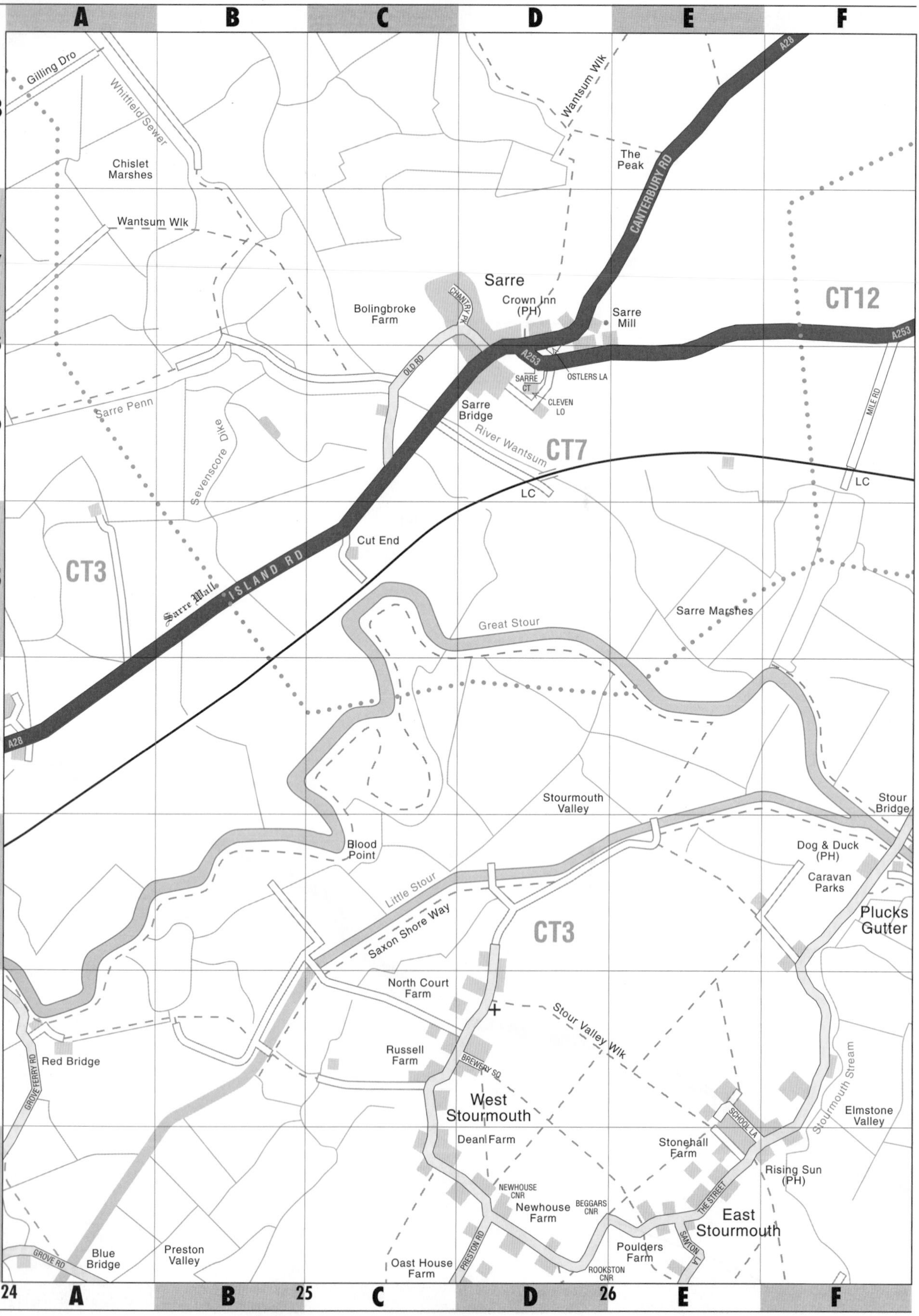

26
50

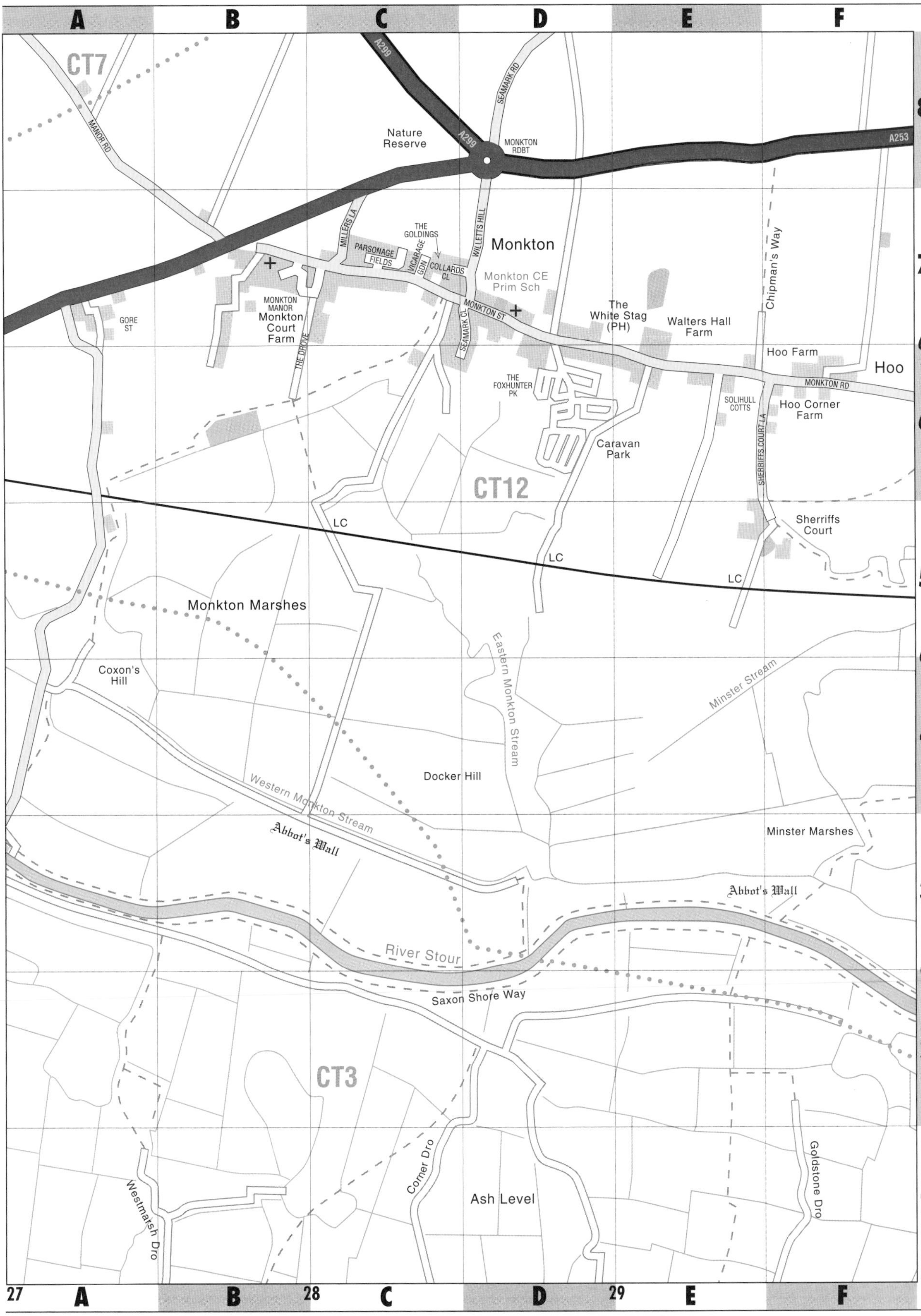
A
B
C
D
E
F
CT7
MANOR RD
A299
SEAMARK RD
Nature Reserve
MONKTON RDBT
A253
8
MILLERS LA
THE GOLDINGS
PARSONAGE FIELDS
VICARAGE GDN
COLLARDS CL
WILLETTS HILL
Monkton
Monkton CE Prim Sch
7
GORE ST
MONKTON MANOR
Monkton Court Farm
THE DROVE
SEAMARK CL
MONKTON ST
The White Stag (PH)
Walters Hall Farm
Chipman's Way
Hoo Farm
Hoo
65
MONKTON RD
THE FOXHUNTER PK
SOLIHULL COTTS
SHERRIFFS COURT LA
Hoo Corner Farm
6
Caravan Park
CT12
LC
LC
LC
Sherriffs Court
5
Monkton Marshes
Coxon's Hill
64
Eastern Monkton Stream
Minster Stream
4
Docker Hill
Western Monkton Stream
Abbot's Wall
Minster Marshes
3
Abbot's Wall
River Stour
63
Saxon Shore Way
2
CT3
Corner Dro
Westmarsh Dro
Ash Level
Goldstone Dro
1
62
27
28
29

71
50

49
27

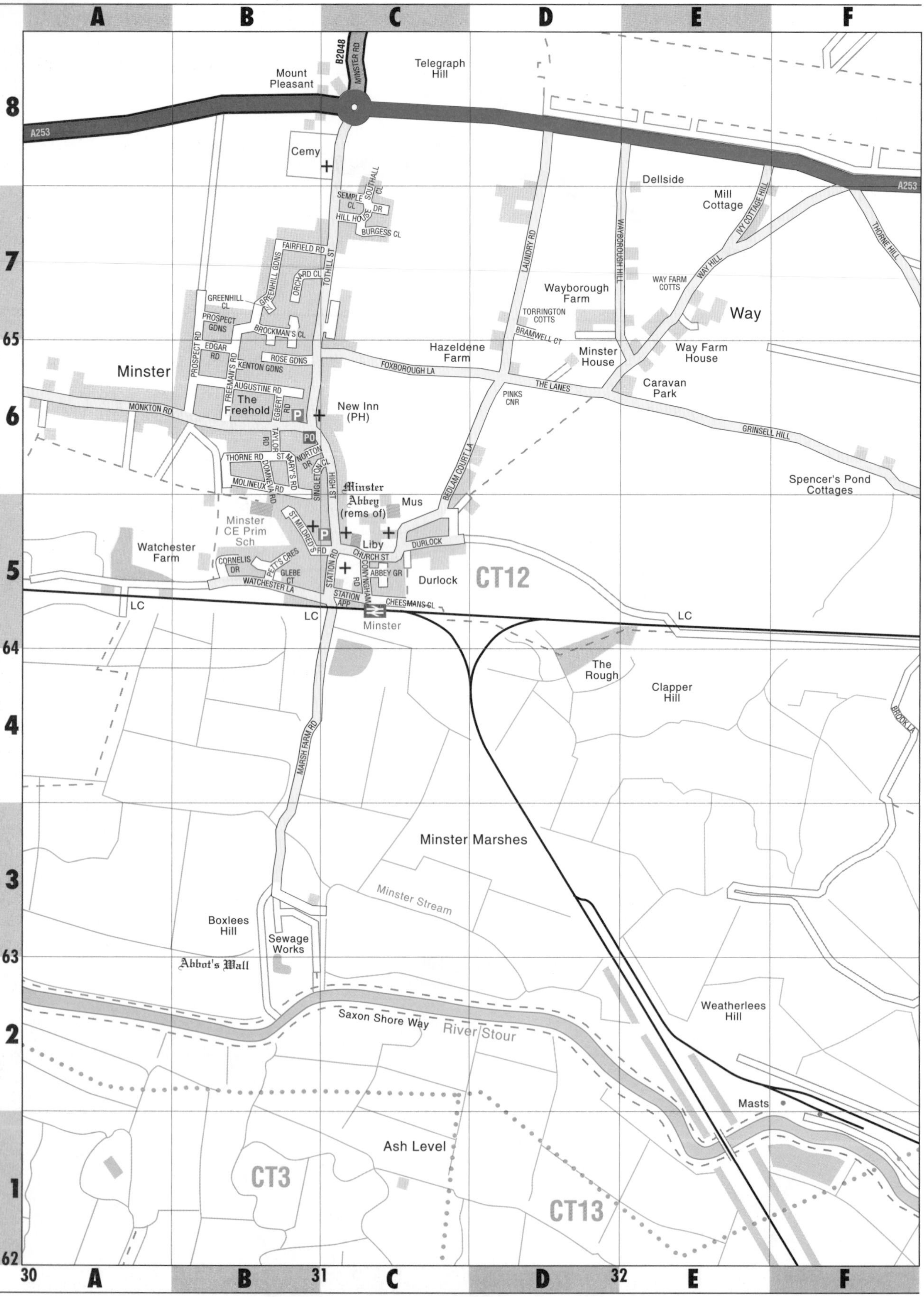
A
B
C
D
E
F
8
7
65
6
5
64
4
3
63
2
1
62
30
31
32
Mount Pleasant
B2048
MINSTER RD
Telegraph Hill
A253
Cemy
Dellside
Mill Cottage
SEMPLE CL
SOUTHALL CL
HILL HOUSE DR
BURGESS CL
FAIRFIELD RD
GREENHILL GDNS
ORCHARD CL
TOTHILL ST
LAUNDRY RD
WAYBOROUGH HILL
IVY COTTAGE HILL
THORNE HILL
WAY HILL
WAY FARM COTTS
Wayborough Farm
Way
GREENHILL CL
PROSPECT GDNS
TORRINGTON COTTS
BRAMWELL CT
BROCKMAN'S CL
PROSPECT RD
EDGAR RD
ROSE GDNS
Hazeldene Farm
Minster House
Way Farm House
Minster
KENTON GDNS
FREEMAN'S RD
FOXBOROUGH LA
AUGUSTINE RD
THE LANES
Caravan Park
MONKTON RD
The Freehold
EGBERT RD
New Inn (PH)
PINKS CNR
GRINSELL HILL
PO
TAYLOR RD
THORNE RD
ST MARY'S RD
NORTON DR
BEDLAM COURT LA
HIGH ST
MOLINEUX RD
DOMNEVA RD
SINGLETON CL
Spencer's Pond Cottages
Minster Abbey (rems of)
Mus
Minster CE Prim Sch
ST MILDRED'S RD
Watchester Farm
Liby
DURLOCK
CHURCH ST
CORNELIS DR
PETT'S CRES
GLEBE CT
STATION RD
ABBEY GR
CONYNGHAM RD
Durlock
CT12
WATCHESTER LA
STATION APP
CHEESMANS CL
LC
Minster
The Rough
Clapper Hill
BROOK LA
MARSH FARM RD
Minster Marshes
Minster Stream
Boxlees Hill
Sewage Works
Abbot's Wall
Weatherlees Hill
Saxon Shore Way
River Stour
Masts
Ash Level
CT3
CT13

49
72

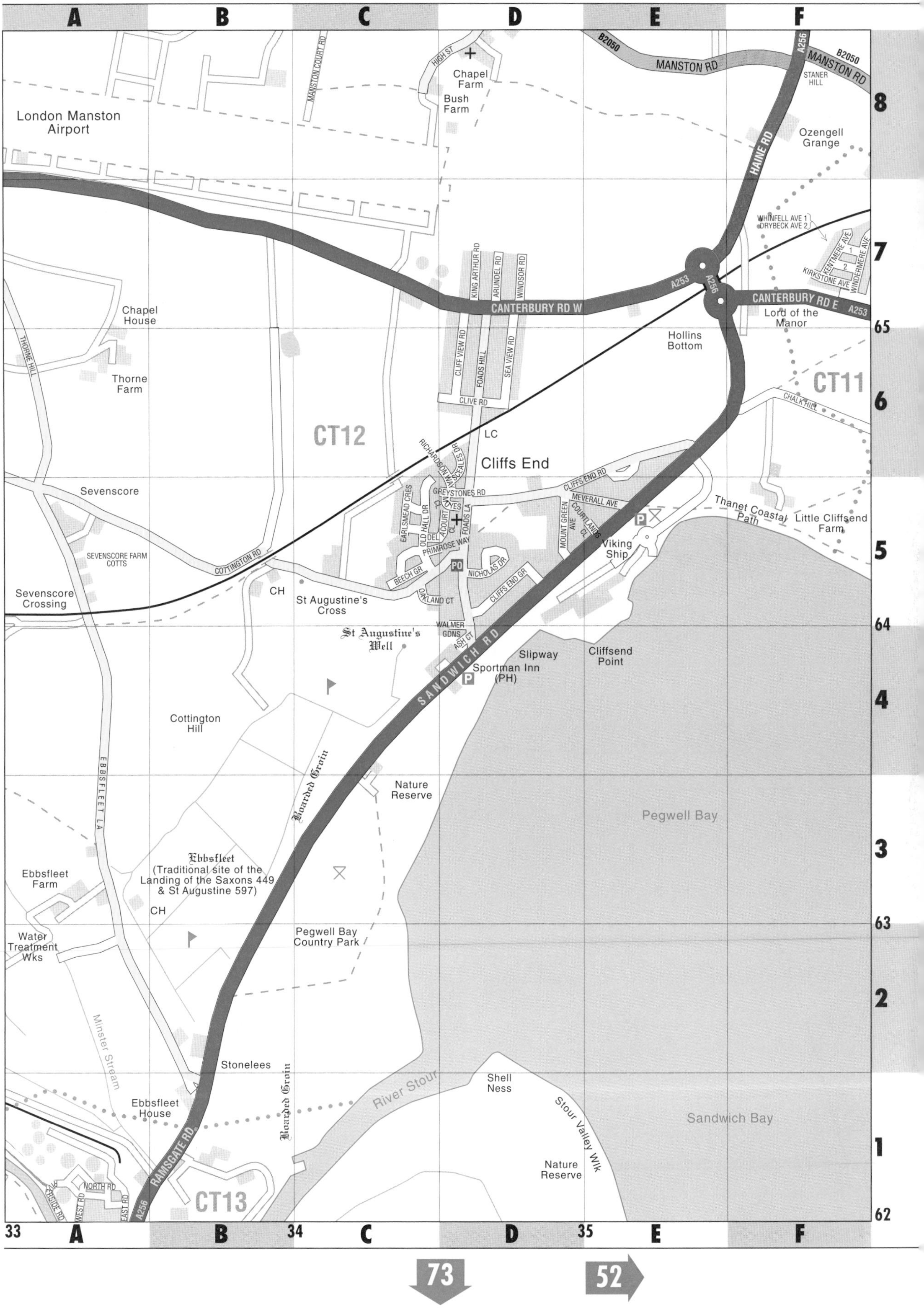
28
52
A
B
C
D
E
F
B2050
MANSTON RD
A256
STANER HILL
HIGH ST
Chapel Farm
Bush Farm
MANSTON COURT RD
London Manston Airport
HAINE RD
Ozengell Grange
WHINFELL AVE 1
DRYBECK AVE 2
KENTMERE AVE
WINDERMERE AVE
KIRKSTONE AVE
KING ARTHUR RD
ARUNDEL RD
WINDSOR RD
A253
CANTERBURY RD W
CANTERBURY RD E
Chapel House
Lord of the Manor
THORNE HILL
Hollins Bottom
Thorne Farm
CLIFF VIEW RD
FOADS HILL
SEA VIEW RD
CT11
CLIVE RD
CHALK HILL
CT12
LC
RICHARDSON WAY
SEALES DR
Cliffs End
CLIFFS END RD
Sevenscore
GREYSTONES RD
MEVERALL AVE
EARLSMEAD CRES
OLD HALL DR
ACOURT CL
FOADS LA
MOYES CL
MOUNT GREEN AVE
COURTLANDS CL
Thanet Coastal Path
Little Cliffsend Farm
SEVENSCORE FARM COTTS
PRIMROSE WAY
Viking Ship
COTTINGTON RD
BEECH GR
PO
NICHOLAS DR
Sevenscore Crossing
CH
St Augustine's Cross
OAKLAND CT
CLIFFS END GR
WALMER GDNS
ASH CT
St Augustine's Well
SANDWICH RD
Slipway
Cliffsend Point
Sportman Inn (PH)
Cottington Hill
EBBSFLEET LA
Boarded Groin
Nature Reserve
Pegwell Bay
Ebbsfleet (Traditional site of the Landing of the Saxons 449 & St Augustine 597)
Ebbsfleet Farm
CH
Water Treatment Wks
Pegwell Bay Country Park
Minster Stream
Stonelees
River Stour
Shell Ness
Ebbsfleet House
Stour Valley Wlk
Sandwich Bay
RAMSGATE RD
Nature Reserve
NORTH RD
WEST RD
EAST RD
CT13
8
7
65
6
5
64
4
3
63
2
1
62
33
34
35
73
52

51

29

E6
1 GUILDFORD LAWN
2 CAVENDISH PL
3 COLEMAN'S YD
4 KING'S PL
5 HIBERNIA ST
6 ALBION HILL
7 PRINCE'S ST
8 WEST CLIFF ARC
9 ROSE HILL
10 GRUNDY'S HILL
11 ST MICHAEL'S ALLEY
12 CORNHILL
13 HARBOUR TWRS
14 HERTFORD HO
15 LIVERPOOL LAWN
16 ADELAIDE GDNS
17 PROSPECT CT
18 PROSPECT TERR

E7
1 PEMBROKE CT
2 LOUGHBOROUGH CT
3 BRUNSWICK CT
4 DALTON CT
5 NEWCASTLE HILL
6 LA BELLE ALLIANCE SQ
7 CAMDEN SQ
8 STAFFORDSHIRE ST
9 UNION ST

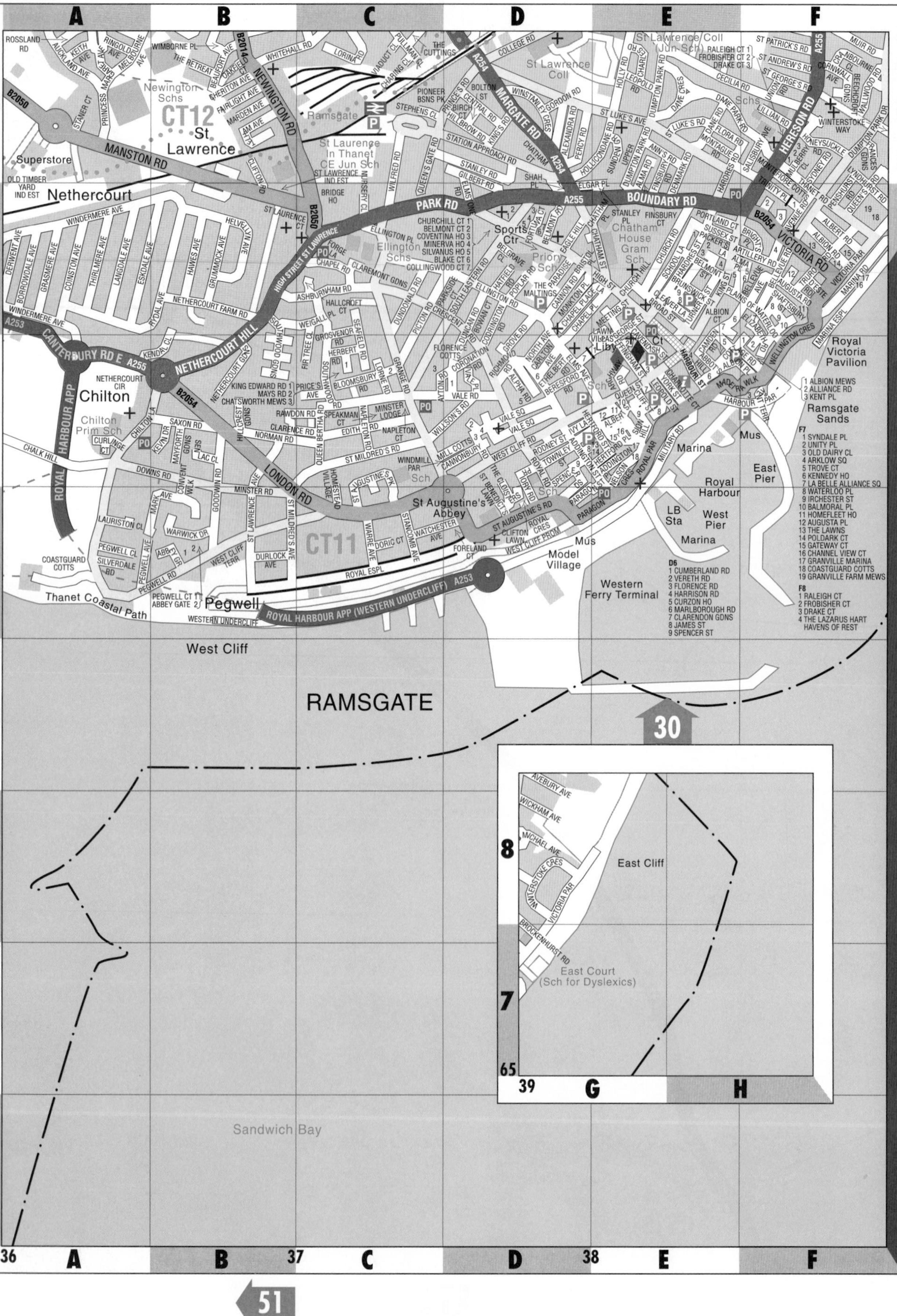

51

31
54

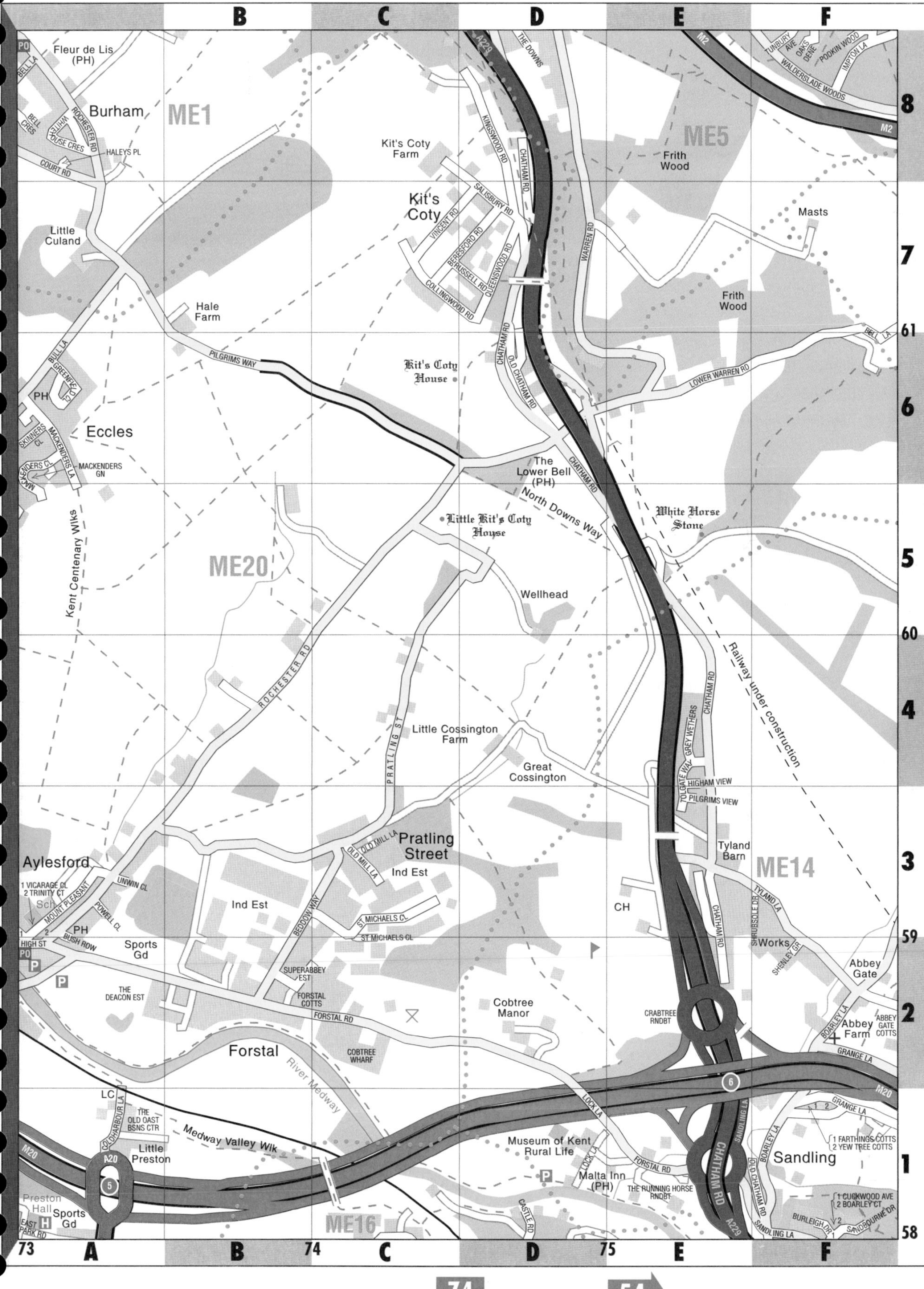
B
C
D
E
F
A
73
74
75
8
7
61
6
5
60
4
3
59
2
1
58
Fleur de Lis
(PH)
PO
BELL LA
Burham
ROCHESTER RD
WHITE HOUSE CRES
BELL CRES
HALEYS PL
COURT RD
ME1
Little
Culand
Hale
Farm
PILGRIMS WAY
BULL LA
GREENFIELD CL
PH
Eccles
SKINNERS CL
MACKENDERS LA
MACKENDERS CL
MACKENDERS GN
Kent Centenary Wlks
ME20
Kit's Coty
Farm
Kit's
Coty
VINCENT RD
BERESFORD RD
RUSSELL RD
COLLINGWOOD RD
QUEENSWOOD RD
SALISBURY RD
KINGSWOOD RD
CHATHAM RD
THE DOWNS
A229
Kit's Coty
House
OLD CHATHAM RD
The
Lower Bell
(PH)
North Downs Way
Little Kit's Coty
House
Wellhead
ROCHESTER RD
PRATLING ST
Little Cossington
Farm
Great
Cossington
WARREN RD
ME5
Frith
Wood
Frith
Wood
Masts
M2
TUNBURY AVE
OAKS DENE
PODKIN WOOD
IMPTON LA
WALDERSLADE WOODS
BELL LA
LOWER WARREN RD
White Horse
Stone
Railway under construction
CHATHAM RD
GREY WETHERS
TOLGATE WAY
HIGHAM VIEW
PILGRIMS VIEW
Tyland
Barn
ME14
TYLAND LA
SHRUBSOLE DR
Works
SHENLEY GR
Abbey
Gate
Aylesford
1 VICARAGE CL
2 TRINITY CT
Sch
MOUNT PLEASANT
UNWIN CL
POWELL CL
PH
HIGH ST
BUSH ROW
Sports
Gd
PO
P
P
THE
DEACON EST
Ind Est
BEDDOW WAY
OLD MILL LA
Pratling
Street
Ind Est
ST MICHAELS CL
ST MICHAELS CL
SUPERABBEY
EST
FORSTAL
COTTS
FORSTAL RD
Forstal
COBTREE
WHARF
River Medway
Cobtree
Manor
CH
CRABTREE
RNDBT
ABBEY
GATE
COTTS
Abbey
Farm
BOARLEY LA
GRANGE LA
M20
6
LC
OLDHARBOUR LA
THE
OLD OAST
BSNS CTR
Little
Preston
Medway Valley Wlk
A20
5
M20
Preston
Hall
H
Sports
Gd
EAST
PARK RD
ME16
Museum of Kent
Rural Life
LOCK LA
P
Malta Inn
(PH)
FORSTAL RD
THE RUNNING HORSE
RNDBT
CASTLE RD
CHATHAM RD
A229
SANDLING LA
OLD CHATHAM RD
BOARLEY LA
GRANGE LA
1 FARTHINGS COTTS
2 YEW TREE COTTS
Sandling
1 CUCKWOOD AVE
2 BOARLEY CT
BURLEIGH DR
SANDBOURNE DR
SANDLING LA

74
54

53
32

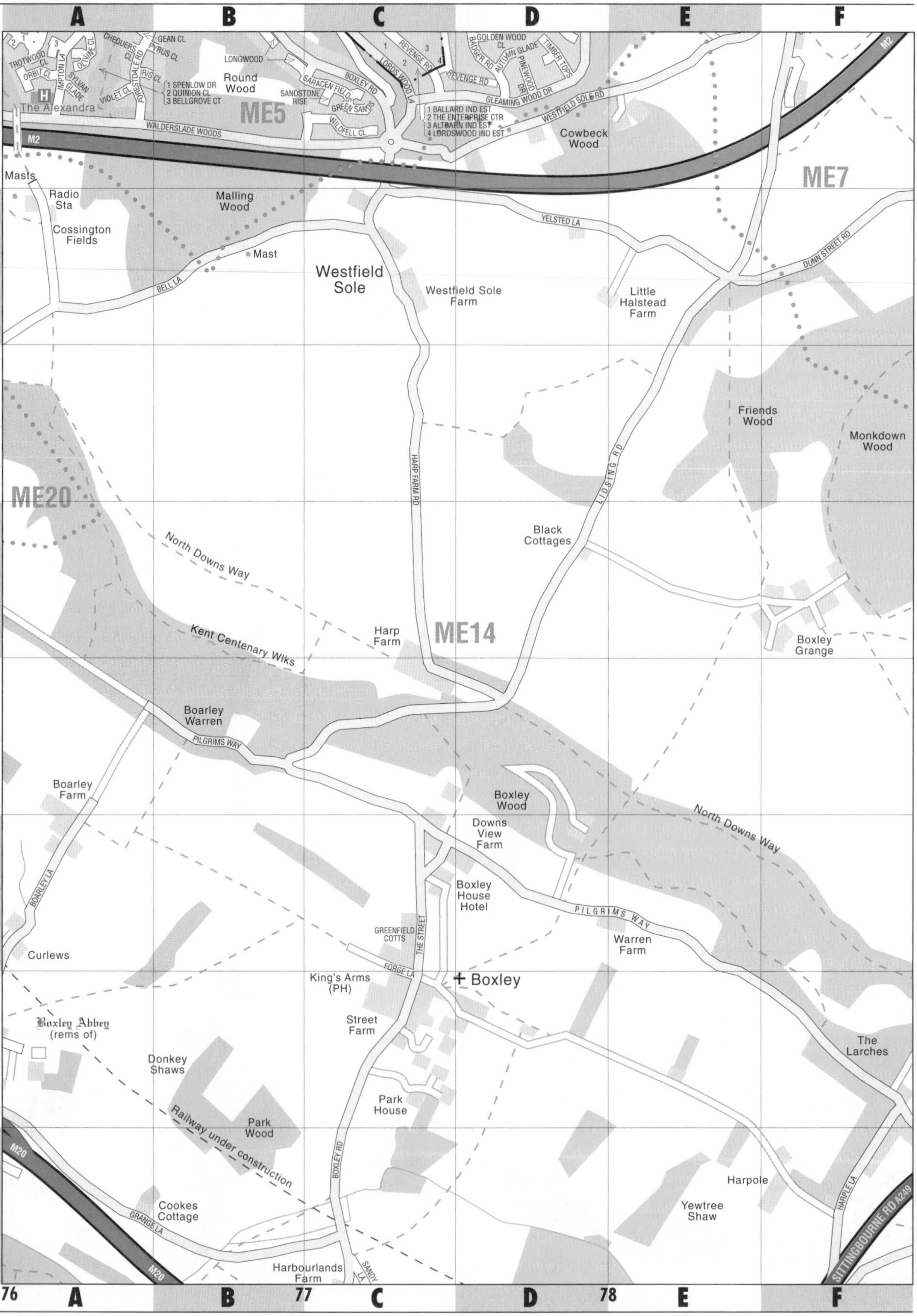

A B C D E F

8

Round Wood

1 SPENLOW DR
2 QUINION CL
3 BELLGROVE CT

TROTWOOD
ORBIT CL
LUPTON LA
CLOVING CL
SYLVAN GLADE
CHEQUERS CL
PYRUS CL
VIOLET CL
IRIS CL
ROSEDALE RD
GEAN CL
LONGWOOD
SARACEN FIELD
SANDSTONE RISE
GREEN SAND
WILDFELL CL
BOXLEY RD
LORDS WOOD LA
REVENGE RD
REVENGE RD
GOLDEN WOOD CL
BADGER RD
AUTUMN GLADE
PINEWOOD
TIMBER TOPS
GLEAMING WOOD DR
WESTFIELD SOLE RD

H
The Alexandra

ME5

1 BALLARD IND EST
2 THE ENTERPRISE CTR
3 ALTBARN IND EST
4 LORDSWOOD IND EST

Cowbeck Wood

M2

WALDERSLADE WOODS

Masts

Radio Sta

Cossington Fields

Malling Wood

ME7

YELSTED LA

DUNN STREET RD

7

Mast

Westfield Sole

Westfield Sole Farm

Little Halstead Farm

BELL LA

61

HARP FARM RD

LLOSING RD

Friends Wood

Monkdown Wood

6

ME20

North Downs Way

Black Cottages

5

Boxley Grange

Kent Centenary Wks

Harp Farm

ME14

60

Boarley Warren

PILGRIMS WAY

4

Boarley Farm

Boxley Wood

Downs View Farm

North Downs Way

3

BOARLE LA

Curlews

Boxley House Hotel

PILGRIMS WAY

Warren Farm

GREENFIELD COTTS

THE STREET

FORGE LA

59

King's Arms (PH)

+ Boxley

Boxley Abbey (rems of)

Street Farm

2

Donkey Shaws

The Larches

Park House

Park Wood

BOXLEY RD

Railway under construction

M20

Harpole

HARPLE LA

1

Cookes Cottage

GRANGE LA

Yewtree Shaw

SITTINGBOURNE RD A249

58

Harbourlands Farm

SANDY LA

76 A B 77 C D 78 E F

53
75

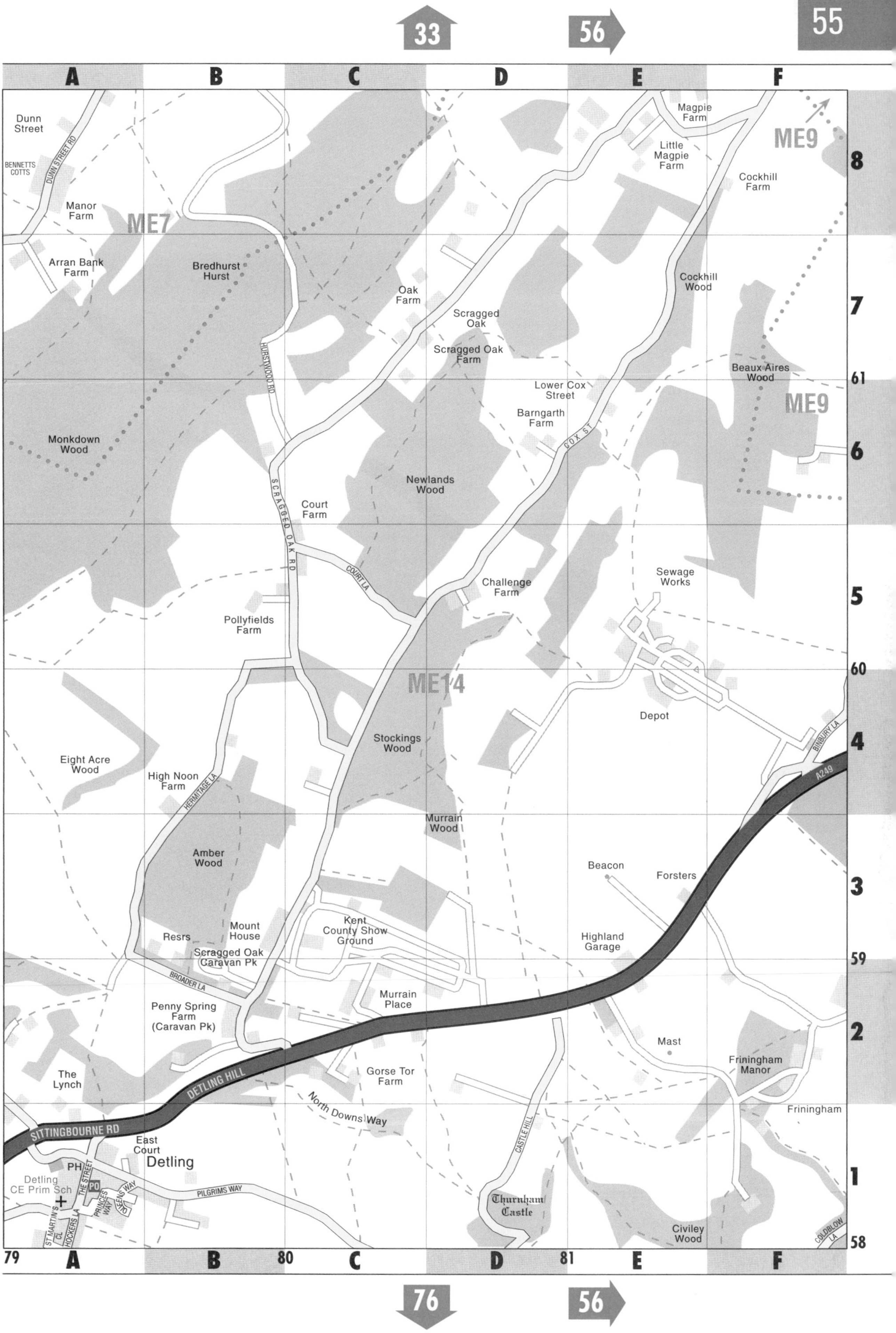
33
56
A
B
C
D
E
F
8
7
61
6
5
60
4
3
59
2
1
58
79
80
81
76
Dunn Street
DUNN STREET RD
BENNETTS COTTS
Manor Farm
ME7
Arran Bank Farm
Bredhurst Hurst
HURSTWOOD RD
Magpie Farm
Little Magpie Farm
ME9
Cockhill Farm
Cockhill Wood
Oak Farm
Scragged Oak
Scragged Oak Farm
Lower Cox Street
Barngarth Farm
COX ST
Beaux Aires Wood
Monkdown Wood
Newlands Wood
Court Farm
SCRAGGED OAK RD
COURT LA
Challenge Farm
Sewage Works
Pollyfields Farm
ME14
Depot
Stockings Wood
BINBURY LA
A249
Eight Acre Wood
High Noon Farm
HERMITAGE LA
Murrain Wood
Amber Wood
Beacon
Forsters
Resrs
Mount House
Kent County Show Ground
Scragged Oak Caravan Pk
Highland Garage
BROADER LA
Murrain Place
Penny Spring Farm (Caravan Pk)
Mast
Fríningham Manor
The Lynch
DETLING HILL
Gorse Tor Farm
North Downs Way
Friningham
SITTINGBOURNE RD
East Court
Detling
PH
THE STREET
PO
Detling CE Prim Sch
PRINCES WAY
QUEENS WAY
PILGRIMS WAY
ST MARTIN'S CL
HOCKERS LA
CASTLE HILL
Thurnham Castle
Civiley Wood
COLDBLOW LA

55 34

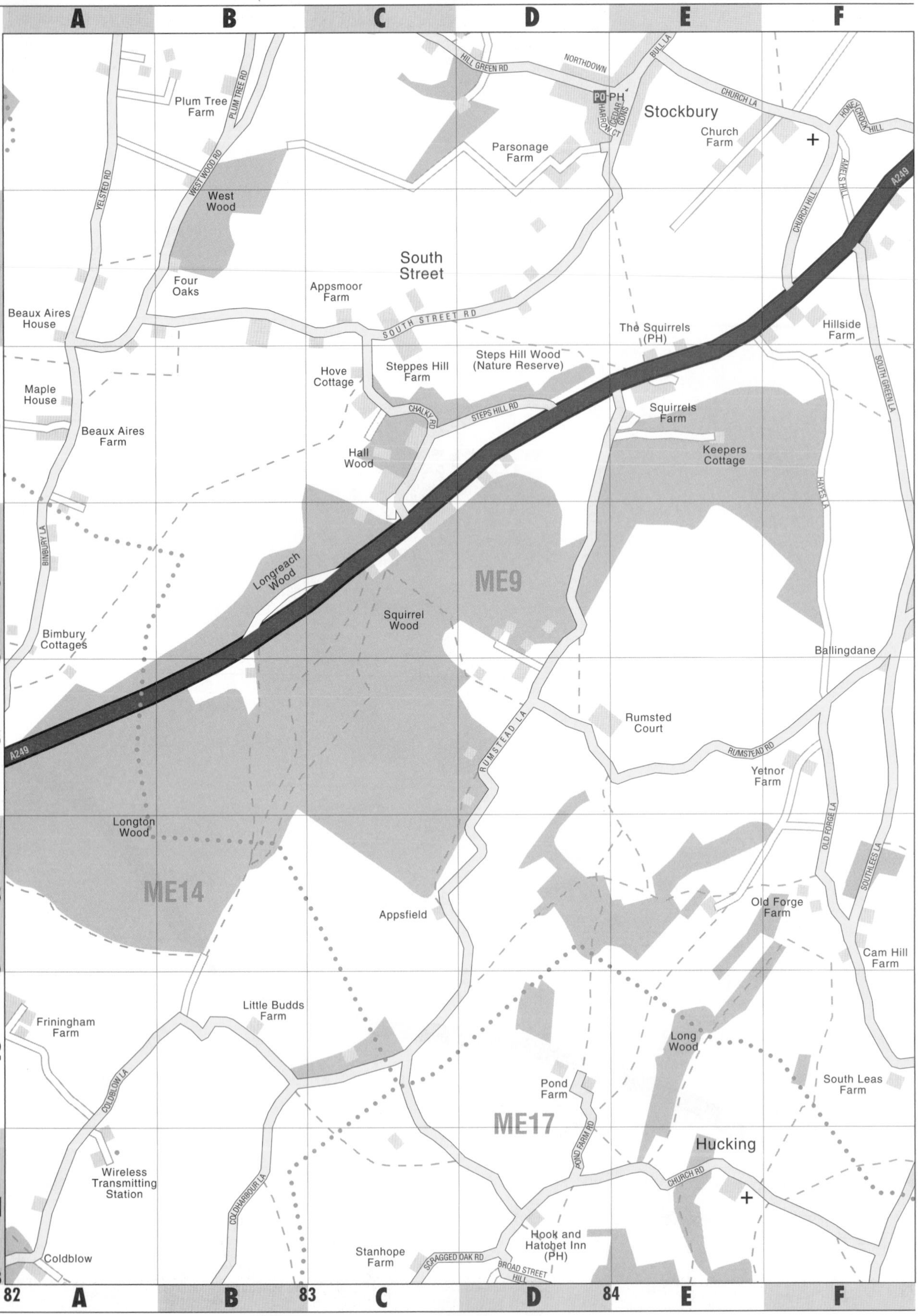

A B C D E F

8

Plum Tree Farm

West Wood

HILL GREEN RD
NORTHDOWN
BULL LA
CHURCH LA
PO PH
SNIP HILL
HARROW CT
Stockbury
Church Farm
HONEYCROCK HILL
JAMES HILL
A249

7

South Street

Four Oaks

Appsmoor Farm

Beaux Aires House

SOUTH STREET RD

The Squirrels (PH)

Hillside Farm

61

Maple House

Hove Cottage

Steppes Hill Farm

Steps Hill Wood (Nature Reserve)

Squirrels Farm

SOUTH GREEN LA

6

Beaux Aires Farm

CHALKY RD

STEPS HILL RD

Keepers Cottage

Hall Wood

HAYES LA

BINBURY LA

Longreach Wood

ME9

5

Squirrel Wood

Bimbury Cottages

Ballingdane

60

A249

Rumsted Court

RUMSTEAD RD

Yetnor Farm

4

RUMSTEAD LA

OLD FORGE LA

Longton Wood

ME14

Old Forge Farm

SOUTH LEES LA

3

Appsfield

Cam Hill Farm

59

Little Budds Farm

Frininghm Farm

Long Wood

2

COLDBLOW LA

Pond Farm

South Leas Farm

ME17

Hucking

Wireless Transmitting Station

COLDHARBOUR LA

POND FARM RD

CHURCH RD

1

Coldblow

Stanhope Farm

SCRAGGED OAK RD

Hook and Hatchet Inn (PH)

BROAD STREET HILL

58

82 A B 83 C D 84 E F

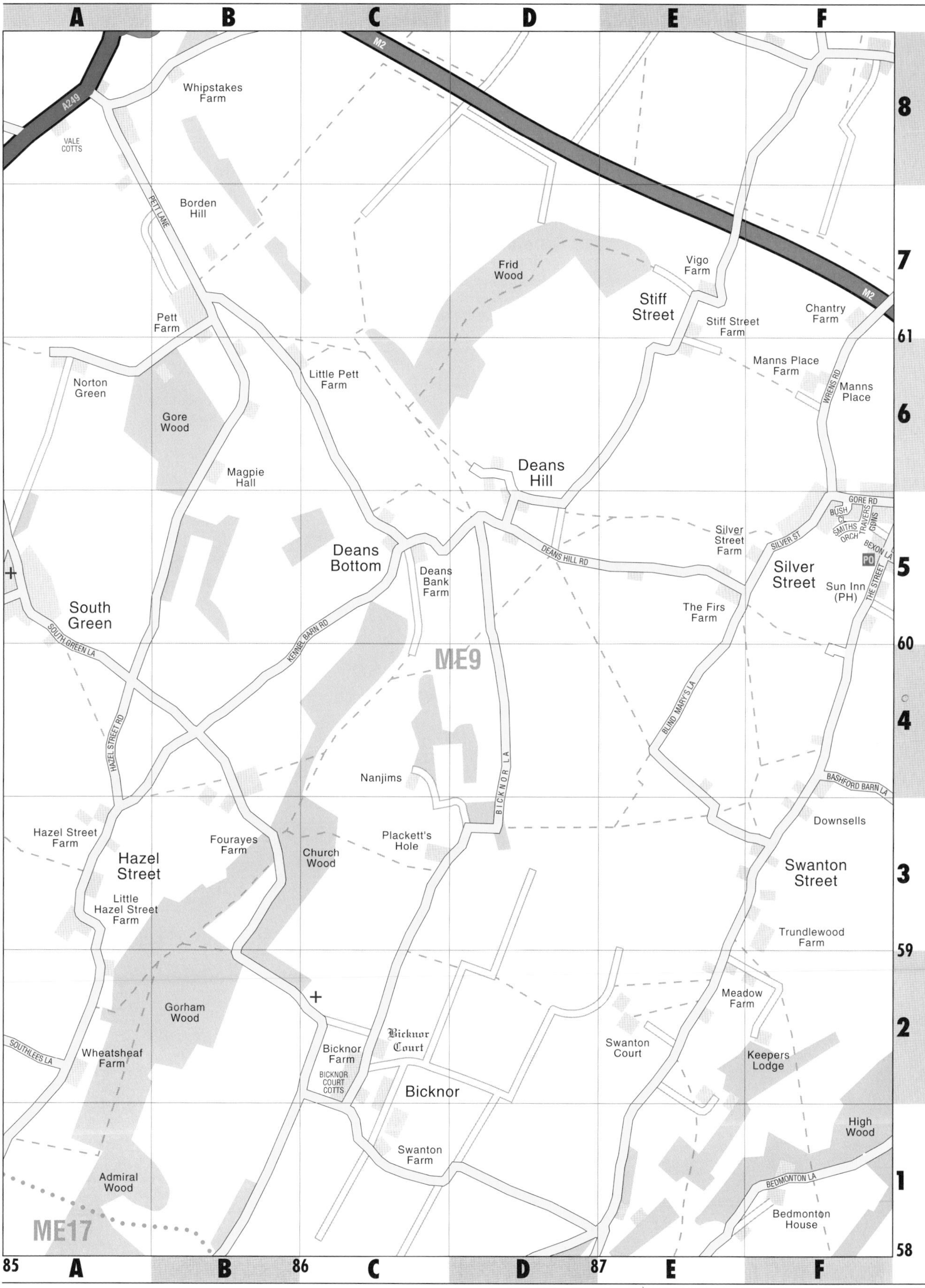

A B C D E F

8
7
61
6
5
60
4
3
59
2
1
58

M2

A249

VALE COTTS

Whipstakes Farm

PETT LANE

Borden Hill

Pett Farm

Norton Green

Gore Wood

Little Pett Farm

Magpie Hall

Frid Wood

Stiff Street

Vigo Farm

Stiff Street Farm

Chantry Farm

Manns Place Farm

WREN'S RD

Manns Place

GORE RD

BUSH CT

SMITHS ORCH

TRAVERS GDNS

BEXON LA

THE STREET

Silver Street Farm

SILVER ST

Silver Street

PO

Sun Inn (PH)

Deans Hill

DEANS HILL RD

Deans Bottom

KENNEL BARN RD

Deans Bank Farm

The Firs Farm

ME9

South Green

SOUTH GREEN LA

HAZEL STREET RD

BLIND MARY'S LA

60

BASHFORD BARN LA

Downsells

Swanton Street

Nanjims

BICKNOR LA

Plackett's Hole

Hazel Street Farm

Fourayes Farm

Church Wood

Hazel Street

Little Hazel Street Farm

Trundlewood Farm

Meadow Farm

Keepers Lodge

Gorham Wood

SOUTHLEES LA

Wheatsheaf Farm

Bicknor Farm

BICKNOR COURT COTTS

Bicknor Court

Bicknor

Swanton Court

High Wood

Swanton Farm

Admiral Wood

ME17

BEDMONTON LA

Bedmonton House

85 A B 86 C D 87 E F

57
36

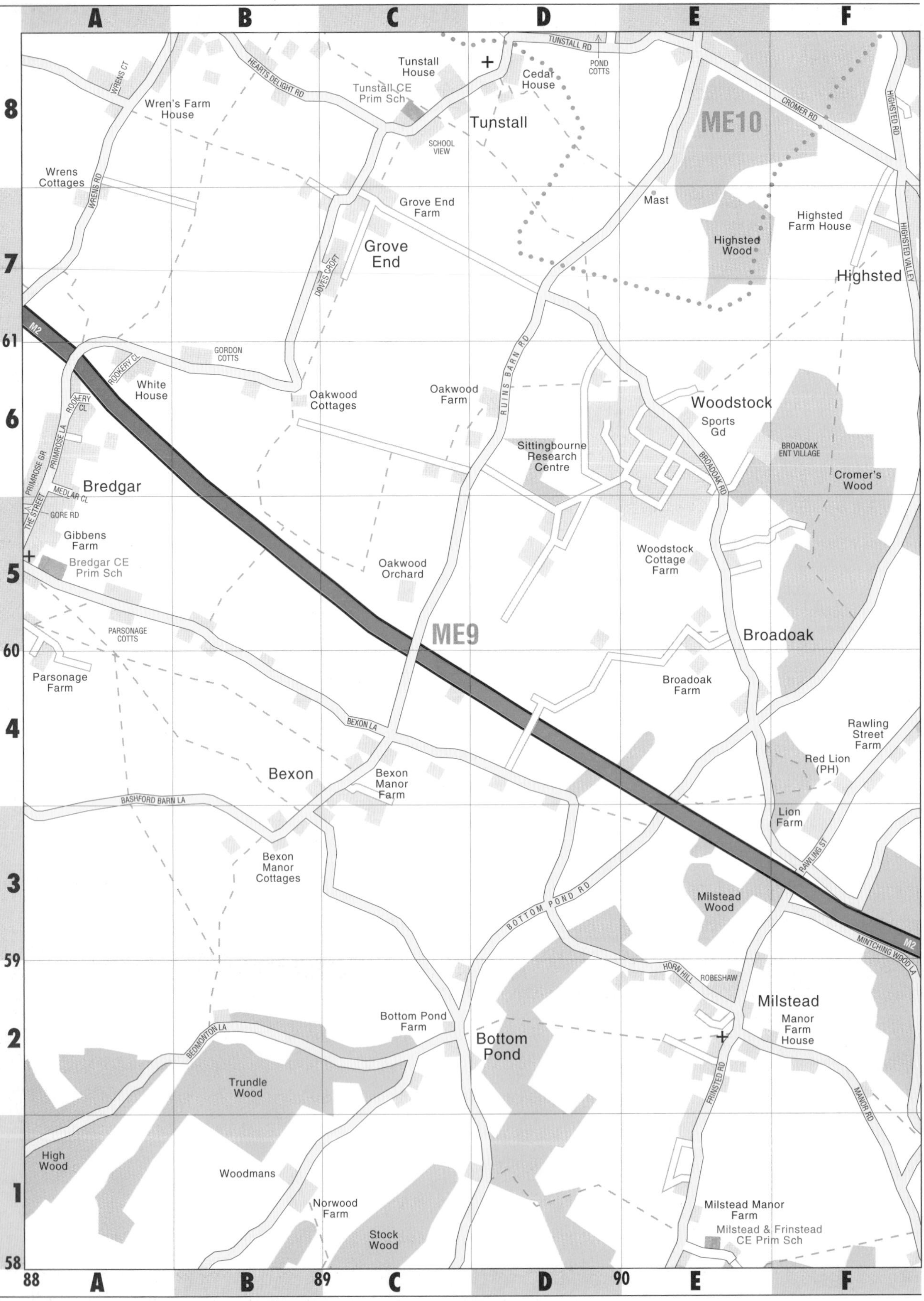

A **B** **C** **D** **E** **F**

8

Wren's Farm House

Wrens Cottages

WRENS CT

HEART'S DELIGHT RD

Tunstall House

Tunstall CE Prim Sch

SCHOOL VIEW

Tunstall

Cedar House

TUNSTALL RD

POND COTTS

CROMER RD

ME10

Mast

Highsted Farm House

Highsted Wood

Highsted

HIGHSTED RD

HIGHSTED VALLEY

7

Grove End Farm

Grove End

DRIVES CROFT

61

M2

GORDON COTTS

White House

ROOKERY CL

Oakwood Cottages

Oakwood Farm

RUINS BARN RD

Woodstock

Sports Gd

BROADOAK ENT VILLAGE

Cromer's Wood

6

ROOKERY CL

PRIMROSE LA

PRIMROSE GR

THE STREET

MEDLAR CL

GORE RD

Bredgar

Sittingbourne Research Centre

BROADOAK RD

Gibbens Farm

Bredgar CE Prim Sch

Oakwood Orchard

Woodstock Cottage Farm

5

PARSONAGE COTTS

ME9

Broadoak

60

Parsonage Farm

Broadoak Farm

BEXON LA

Rawling Street Farm

Red Lion (PH)

4

BASHFORD BARN LA

Bexon

Bexon Manor Farm

Lion Farm

RAWLING ST

Bexon Manor Cottages

Milstead Wood

3

BOTTOM POND RD

MINTCHING WOOD LA

M2

59

HORN HILL

Robeshaw

Milstead

BECKMORTON LA

Bottom Pond Farm

Bottom Pond

FRINSTED RD

Manor Farm House

MANOR RD

2

Trundle Wood

High Wood

Woodmans

Norwood Farm

Stock Wood

Milstead Manor Farm

Milstead & Frinsted CE Prim Sch

1

58

88 **A** **B** **89** **C** **D** **90** **E** **F**

57
79

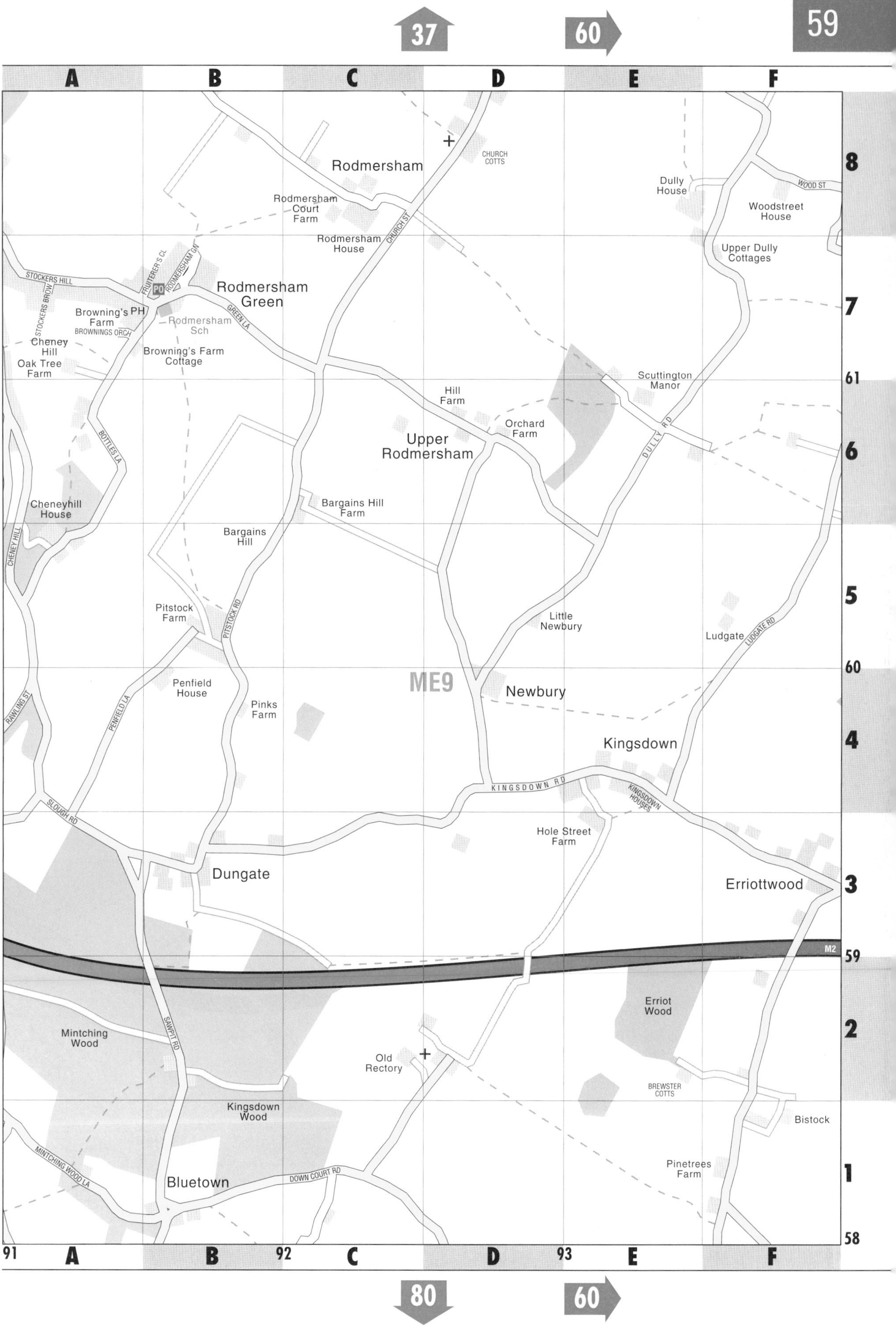
37
60
A
B
C
D
E
F
8
7
61
6
5
60
4
3
59
2
1
58
91
92
93
Rodmersham
CHURCH COTTS
Rodmersham Court Farm
Rodmersham House
CHURCH ST
Dully House
WOOD ST
Woodstreet House
Upper Dully Cottages
STOCKERS HILL
STOCKERS BROW
FRUITERER'S CL
RODMERSHAM GN
PO
Rodmersham Green
Browning's Farm
PH
BROWNINGS ORCH
Rodmersham Sch
GREEN LA
Cheney Hill
Oak Tree Farm
Browning's Farm Cottage
Scuttington Manor
Hill Farm
Orchard Farm
Upper Rodmersham
DULLY RD
BOTTLES LA
Cheneyhill House
Bargains Hill Farm
Bargains Hill
CHENEY HILL
Pitstock Farm
PITSTOCK RD
Little Newbury
Ludgate
LUDGATE RD
Penfield House
ME9
Newbury
RAWLING ST
PENFIELD LA
Pinks Farm
Kingsdown
KINGSDOWN RD
KINGSDOWN HOUSES
SLOUGH RD
Hole Street Farm
Dungate
Erriottwood
M2
Erriot Wood
Mintching Wood
SAWPIT RD
Old Rectory
BREWSTER COTTS
Kingsdown Wood
Bistock
MINTCHING WOOD LA
Pinetrees Farm
Bluetown
DOWN COURT RD
80
60

59
38

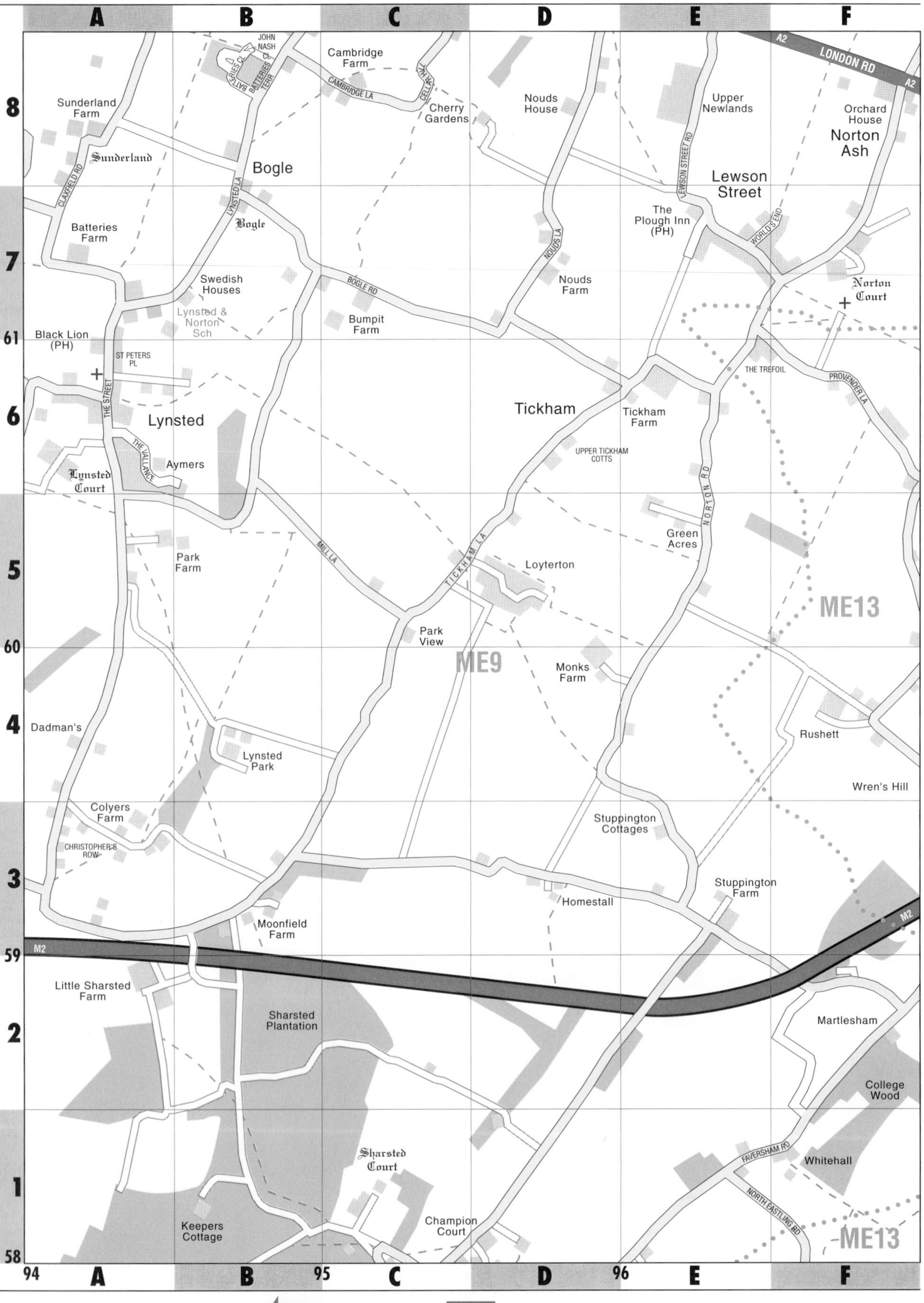
A
B
C
D
E
F
8
7
61
6
5
60
4
3
59
2
1
58
94
95
96
A2
LONDON RD
JOHN NASH CL
BATTERIES CL
BATTERIES TERR
Cambridge Farm
CAMBRIDGE LA
CELLAR HILL
Cherry Gardens
Nouds House
Upper Newlands
Orchard House
Norton Ash
Sunderland Farm
Sunderland
Bogle
LEWSON STREET RD
Lewson Street
CLAXFIELD RD
LYNSTED LA
Bogle
The Plough Inn (PH)
WORLD'S END
Batteries Farm
NOUDS LA
Swedish Houses
BOGLE RD
Nouds Farm
Norton Court
Lynsted & Norton Sch
Bumpit Farm
Black Lion (PH)
ST PETERS PL
THE TREFOIL
PROVENDER LA
THE STREET
Lynsted
Tickham
Tickham Farm
THE VALLANCE
Aymers
UPPER TICKHAM COTTS
Lynsted Court
NORTON RD
Green Acres
Park Farm
MILL LA
TICKHAM LA
Loyterton
ME13
Park View
ME9
Monks Farm
Dadman's
Rushett
Lynsted Park
Wren's Hill
Colyers Farm
Stuppington Cottages
CHRISTOPHER'S ROW
Stuppington Farm
Homestall
Moonfield Farm
M2
Little Sharsted Farm
Sharsted Plantation
Martlesham
College Wood
FAVERSHAM RD
Whitehall
Sharsted Court
NORTH EASTLING RD
Keepers Cottage
Champion Court
ME13

59
81

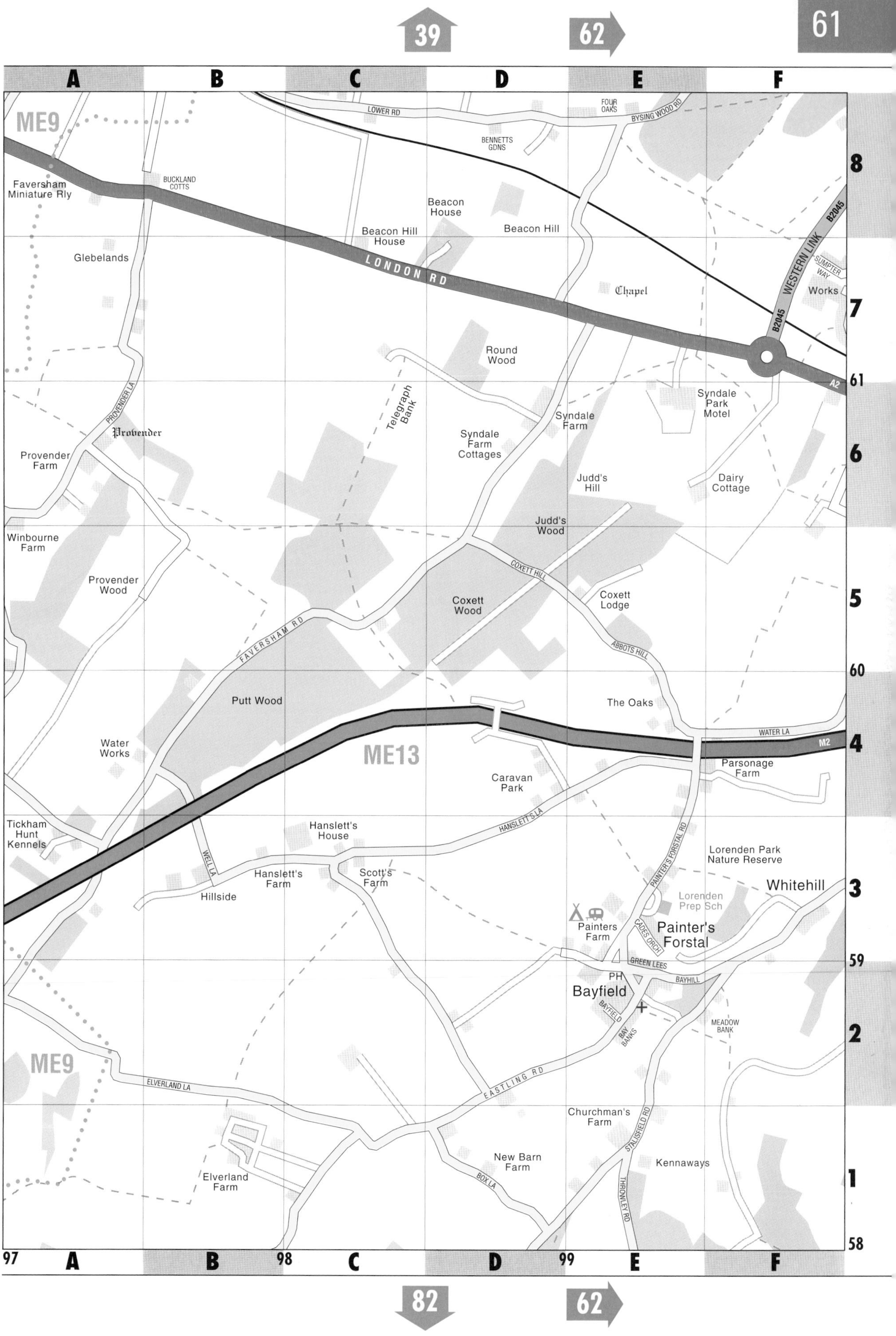
39
62
A
B
C
D
E
F
ME9
LOWER RD
FOUR OAKS
BYSING WOOD RD
BENNETTS GDNS
8
Faversham Miniature Rly
BUCKLAND COTTS
Beacon House
Beacon Hill House
Beacon Hill
B2045
WESTERN LINK
SUMPTER WAY
Glebelands
LONDON RD
Chapel
Works
7
B2045
Round Wood
A2
61
Telegraph Bank
Syndale Park Motel
Syndale Farm
PROVENDER LA
Provender
Syndale Farm Cottages
Provender Farm
6
Judd's Hill
Dairy Cottage
Judd's Wood
Winbourne Farm
COXETT HILL
Provender Wood
Coxett Lodge
5
Coxett Wood
FAVERSHAM RD
ABBOTS HILL
60
Putt Wood
The Oaks
WATER LA
Water Works
M2
4
ME13
Parsonage Farm
Caravan Park
Tickham Hunt Kennels
HANSLETT'S LA
Hanslett's House
Lorenden Park Nature Reserve
PAINTER'S FORSTAL RD
WELL LA
Hanslett's Farm
Scott's Farm
Whitehill
3
Hillside
Lorenden Prep Sch
Painters Farm
Painter's Forstal
CADES ORCH
GREEN LEES
59
PH
BAYHILL
Bayfield
BAYFIELD
BAY BANKS
MEADOW BANK
2
ME9
ELVERLAND LA
EASTLING RD
Churchman's Farm
STALISFIELD RD
New Barn Farm
Kennaways
Elverland Farm
BOX LA
THROWLEY RD
1
58
97
A
B
98
C
D
99
E
F
82
62

C7
1 CURTIS WAY
2 CASLOCKE ST
3 HATCH ST
4 BECKETT ST
5 MENDFIELD ST
6 WATER LA

C7
7 REEVES PAS
8 WESTBROOK WLK

D7
1 MARKET PL
2 MIDDLE ROW
3 GANGE MEWS
4 GARFIELD PL
5 HUGH PL
6 BACK LA
7 CROSS LA
8 JACOB YD
9 GATEFIELD LA
10 HERBERT DANE CT
11 JOHN ANDERSON CT
12 QUEENS PAR
13 ST MARY CT
14 WILLIAM GIBBS CT
15 LIMES PL

61
40

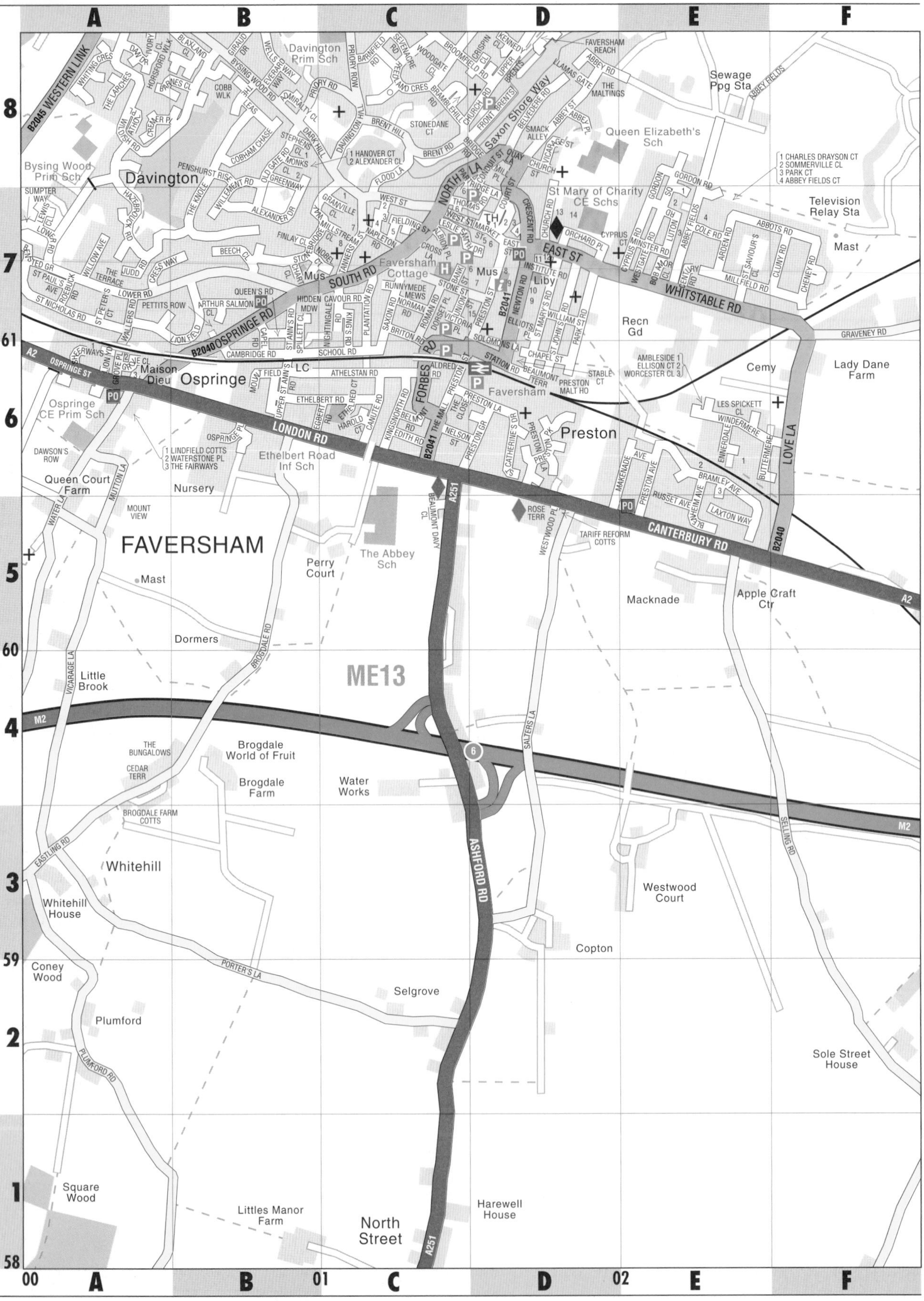

61
83

41
64

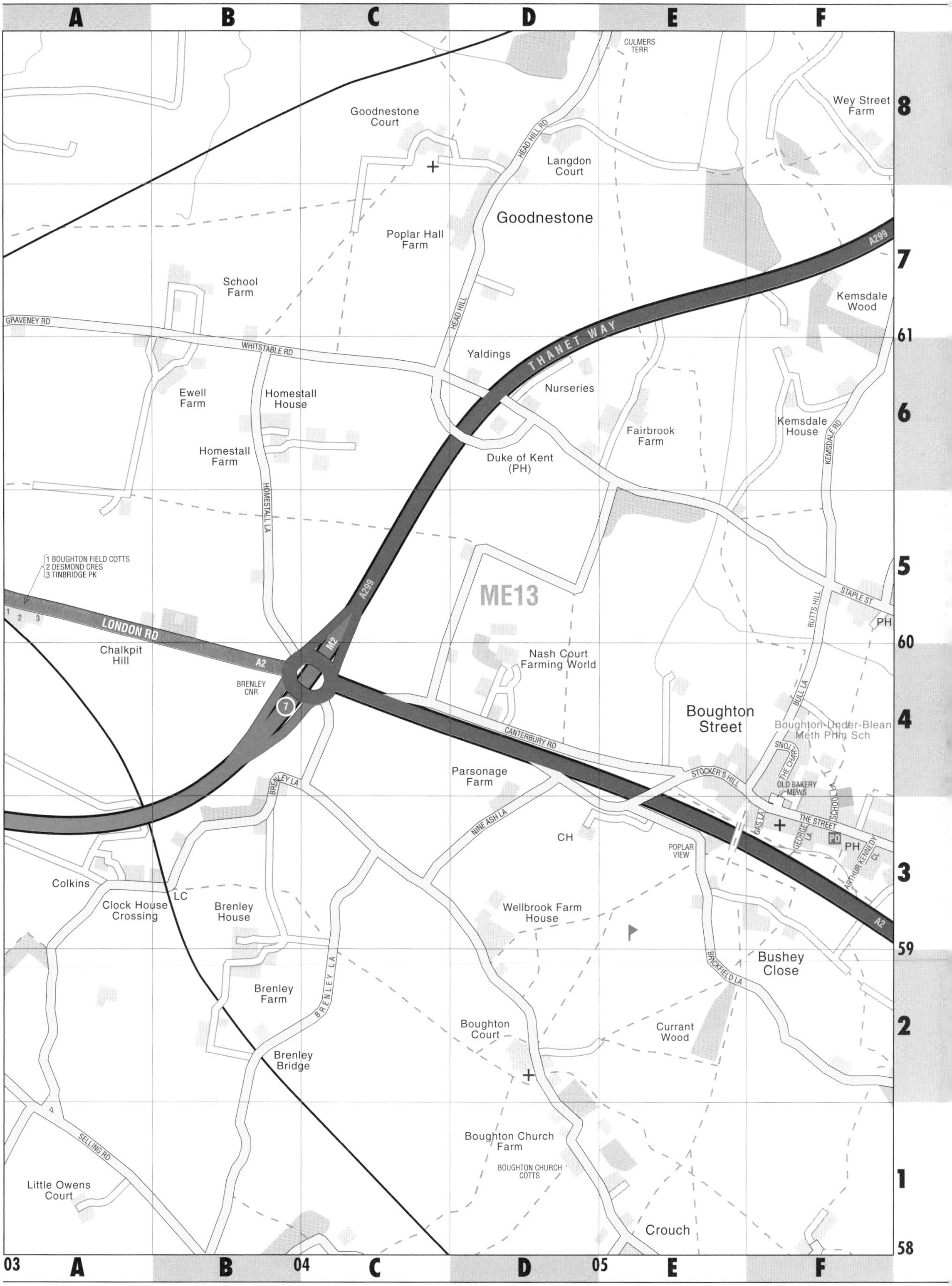
A
B
C
D
E
F
CULMERS TERR
Goodnestone Court
Wey Street Farm
HEAD HILL RD
Langdon Court
Goodnestone
Poplar Hall Farm
A299
School Farm
Kemsdale Wood
HEAD HILL
GRAVENEY RD
WHITSTABLE RD
THANET WAY
Yaldings
Ewell Farm
Homestall House
Nurseries
Kemsdale House
KEMSDALE RD
Fairbrook Farm
Homestall Farm
Duke of Kent (PH)
HOMESTALL LA
1 BOUGHTON FIELD COTTS
2 DESMOND CRES
3 TINBRIDGE PK
ME13
A299
STAPLE ST
BUTTS HILL
PH
LONDON RD
Chalkpit Hill
A2
M2
Nash Court Farming World
BRENLEY CNR
7
BULL LA
Boughton Street
Boughton-Under-Blean Meth Prim Sch
CANTERBURY RD
THE CHARLTONS
STOCKER'S HILL
Parsonage Farm
BRENLEY LA
OLD BAKERY MEWS
SCHOOL LA
NINE ASH LA
GAS LA
THE STREET
CH
GEORGE LA
PO
PH
POPLAR VIEW
ARTHUR KENNEDY CL
Colkins
LC
Clock House Crossing
Brenley House
Wellbrook Farm House
A2
Bushey Close
BRICKFIELD LA
Brenley Farm
BRENLEY LA
Boughton Court
Currant Wood
Brenley Bridge
SELLING RD
Boughton Church Farm
BOUGHTON CHURCH COTTS
Little Owens Court
Crouch
8
7
61
6
5
60
4
3
59
2
1
58
03
04
05

84
64

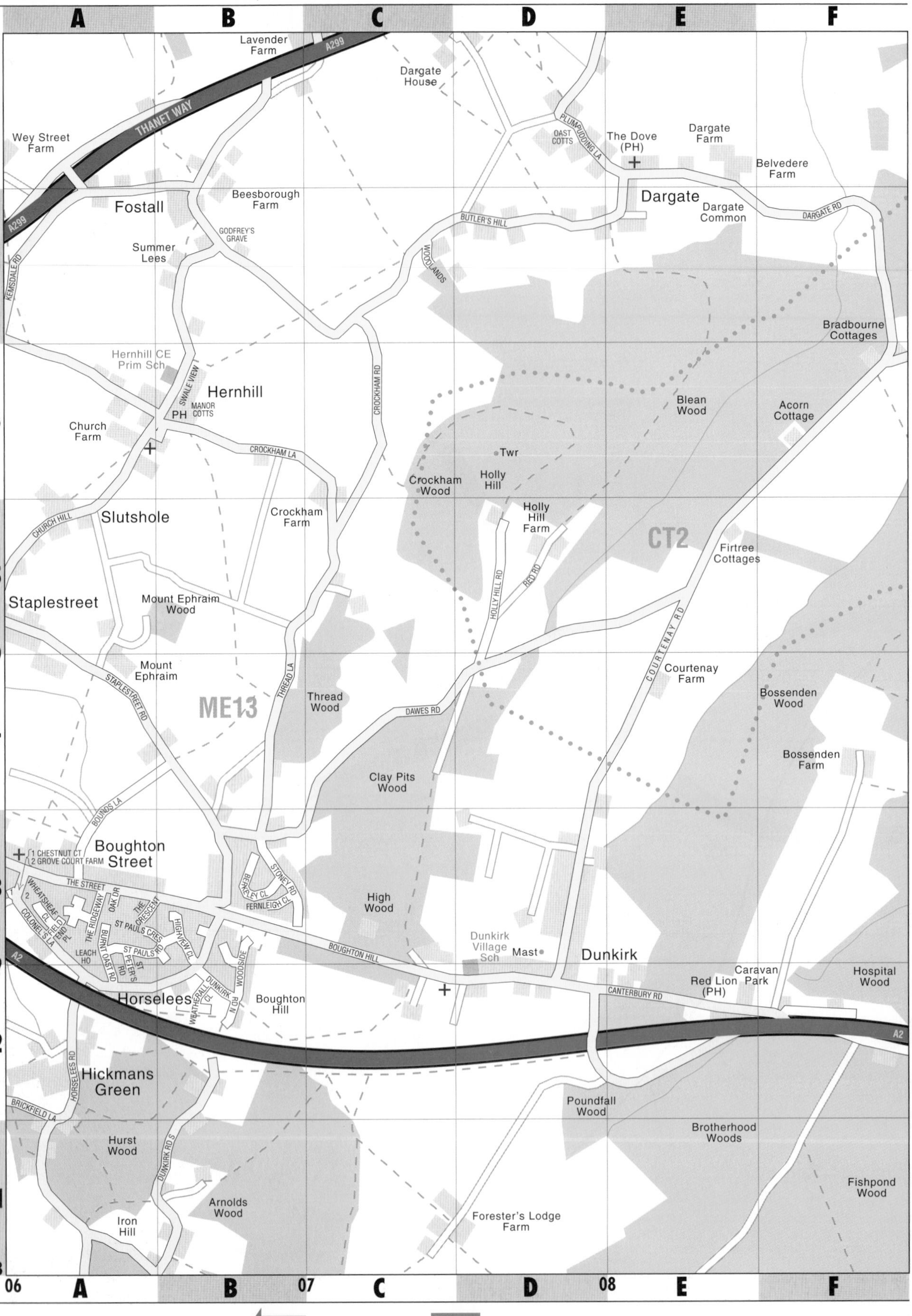

63 42

A B C D E F

8

Wey Street Farm
THANET WAY
A299
Lavender Farm
A299
Dargate House

Fostall
Beesborough Farm
Godfrey's Grave
OAST COTTS
PLUMPUDDING LA
The Dove (PH)
Dargate Farm
Belvedere Farm

7
Summer Lees
BUTLER'S HILL
Dargate
Dargate Common
DARGATE RD

61
Hernhill CE Prim Sch
SWALE VIEW
WOODLANDS
Bradbourne Cottages

6
Church Farm
Hernhill
PH MANOR COTTS
CROCKHAM LA
Twr
Crockham Wood
Holly Hill
Blean Wood
Acorn Cottage
CT2

Slutshole
Crockham Farm
CROCKHAM RD
Holly Hill Farm
HOLLY HILL RD
RED RD
Firtree Cottages

5
CHURCH HILL
Staplestreet
Mount Ephraim Wood

60
STAPLESTREET RD
Mount Ephraim
THREAD LA
Thread Wood
DAWES RD
COURTENAY RD
Courtenay Farm
Bossenden Wood

4
ME13
Clay Pits Wood
Bossenden Farm

Boughton Street
BOUNDS LA
SIDNEY RD
BERKELEY CL
FERNLEIGH CL
High Wood

3
1 Chestnut Ct
2 Grove Court Farm
THE STREET
WHEATSHEAM CL
COLONEL'S LA
THE RIDGEWAY
OAK RD
St Pauls Crs
HIGHVIEW CL
Dunkirk Village Sch
Mast
Dunkirk

59
A2
LEACH HO
St Pauls
ST PETER'S RD
DUNKIRK RD
WOODRIDGE
BOUGHTON HILL
Canterbury RD
Red Lion (PH)
Caravan Park
Hospital Wood

Horselees
WEATHERALL
Boughton Hill
CANTERBURY RD

2
HORSELEES RD
Hickmans Green
A2

BRICKFIELD LA
Poundfall Wood
Brotherhood Woods

1
DUNKIRK RD
Hurst Wood
Arnolds Wood
Forester's Lodge Farm
Fishpond Wood

58
Iron Hill
Iron Hill

06 A B 07 C D 08 E F

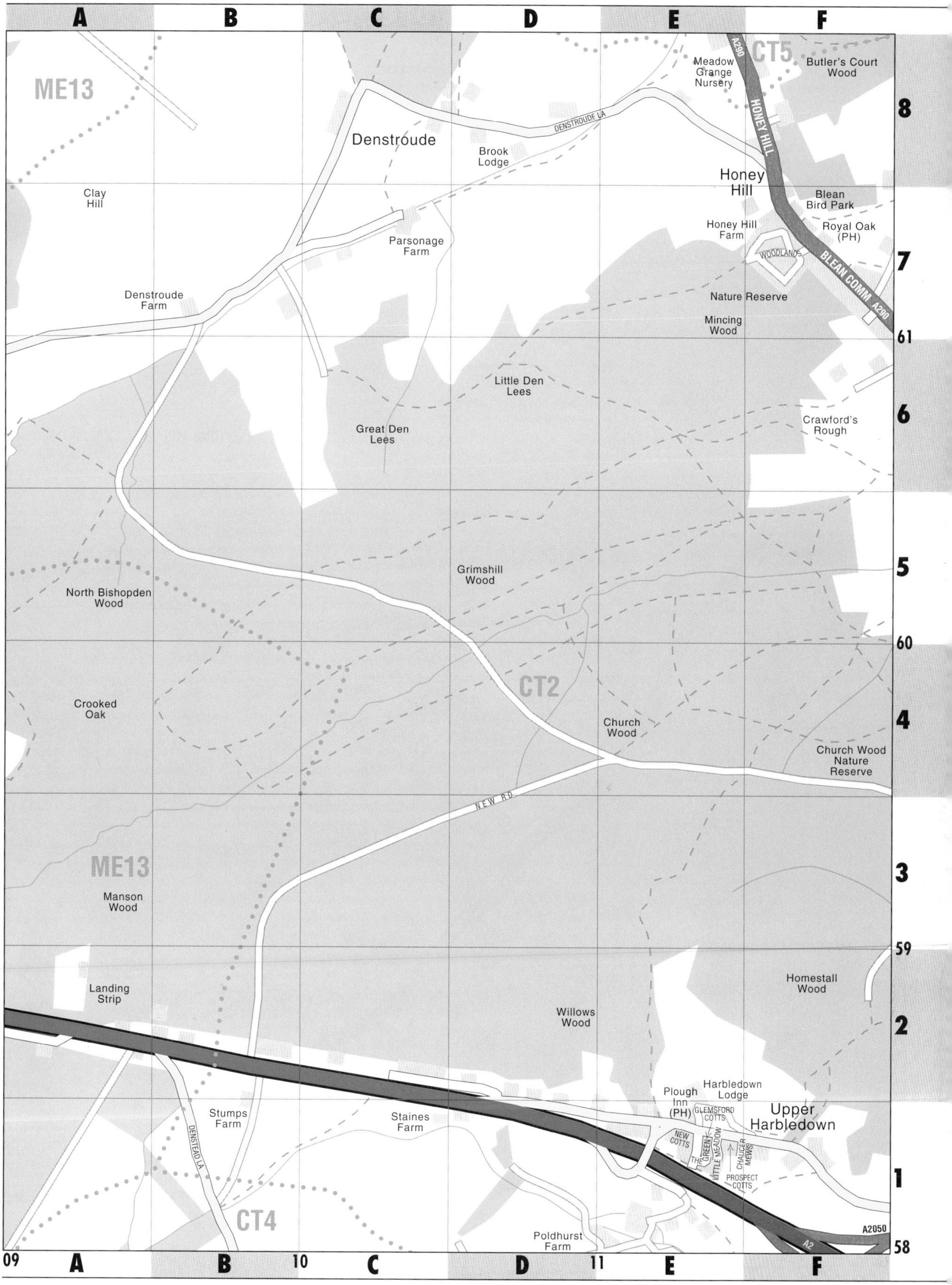

ME13

A   B   C   D   E   F

CT5

Meadow Grange Nursery

Butler's Court Wood

8

Denstroude

Brook Lodge

DENSTROUDE LA

HONEY HILL

Honey Hill

Clay Hill

Blean Bird Park

Parsonage Farm

Honey Hill Farm

Royal Oak (PH)

7

Denstroude Farm

WOODLANDS

Nature Reserve

BLEAN COMM A290

Mincing Wood

61

Little Den Lees

6

Great Den Lees

Crawford's Rough

North Bishopden Wood

Grimshill Wood

5

60

CT2

Crooked Oak

Church Wood

4

Church Wood Nature Reserve

NEW RD

ME13

Manson Wood

3

59

Landing Strip

Homestall Wood

Willows Wood

2

Plough Inn (PH)

Harbledown Lodge

GLEMSFORD COTTS

Upper Harbledown

Stumps Farm

Staines Farm

NEW COTTS

THE GREEN

LITTLE MEADOW

CHAUCER MEWS

DENSTEAD LA

PROSPECT COTTS

1

Poldhurst Farm

CT4

A2050

A2

58

09   A   B   10   C   D   11   E   F

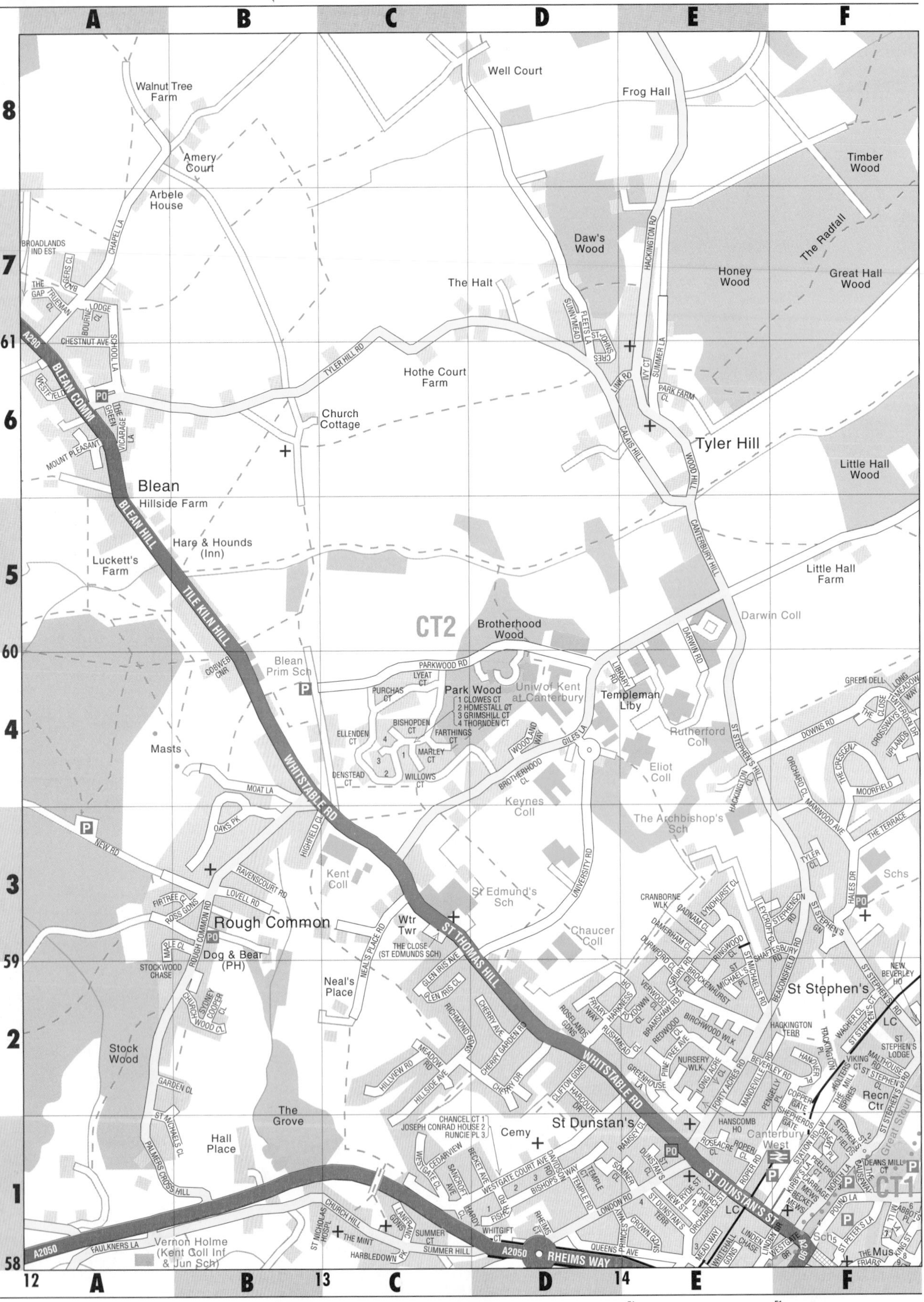

A B C D E F

8

7

61

6

5

60

4

3

59

2

1

58

12 A 13 B 14 C D E F

Walnut Tree Farm
Well Court
Frog Hall
Amery Court
Timber Wood
Arbele House
Daw's Wood
The Radfall
BROADLANDS IND EST
Honey Wood
Great Hall Wood
The Halt
Hothe Court Farm
Tyler Hill
Blean
Church Cottage
Little Hall Wood
Hillside Farm
Hare & Hounds (Inn)
Luckett's Farm
Little Hall Farm
CT2
Brotherhood Wood
Darwin Coll
Blean Prim Sch
Park Wood
Univ of Kent at Canterbury
Templeman Liby
PARKWOOD RD
LYEAT CT
PURCHAS CT
1 CLOWES CT
2 HOMESTALL CT
3 GRIMSHILL CT
4 THORNDEN CT
GREEN DELL
Rutherford Coll
ELLENDEN CT
BISHOPDEN CT
FARTHINGS CT
Masts
MARLEY CT
Eliot Coll
DENSTEAD CT
WILLOWS CT
Brotherhood Cl
MOAT LA
Keynes Coll
The Archbishop's Sch
OAKS PK
NEW RD
Kent Coll
St Edmund's Sch
RAVENSCOURT RD
Schs
FIRTREE CT
LOVELL RD
Rough Common
Wtr Twr
Chaucer Coll
ROSS GDNS
Dog & Bear (PH)
THE CLOSE (ST EDMUNDS SCH)
St Stephen's
STOCKWOOD CHASE
Neal's Place
NEW BEVERLEY HO
ST STEPHEN'S LODGE
Stock Wood
GARDEN CL
The Grove
St Dunstan's
Canterbury West
Recn Ctr
Hall Place
Cemy
PALMERS CROSS HILL
Vernon Holme (Kent Coll Inf & Jun Sch)
THE MINT
CHURCH HILL
SUMMER HILL
HARBLEDOWN
A2050 RHEIMS WAY
CT1
The Mus

BLEAN COMM
BLEAN HILL
TILE KILN HILL
WHITSTABLE RD
ST THOMAS HILL
WHITSTABLE RD
ST DUNSTAN'S ST
A2050
A290
A2050

E1
1 ROSIERS CT
2 CROSS ST
3 LIONARD HO
4 ST DUNSTANS CT

F1
1 THE MERCHANT STORE
2 BARTON MILL CT
3 RIVERSIDE CT
4 STOURSIDE STUDIOS
5 WESTGATE HALL RD
6 CHANTRY CT
7 BLACKFRIARS ST
8 ST ALPHEGE LA
9 THE CLOISTERS

45
68

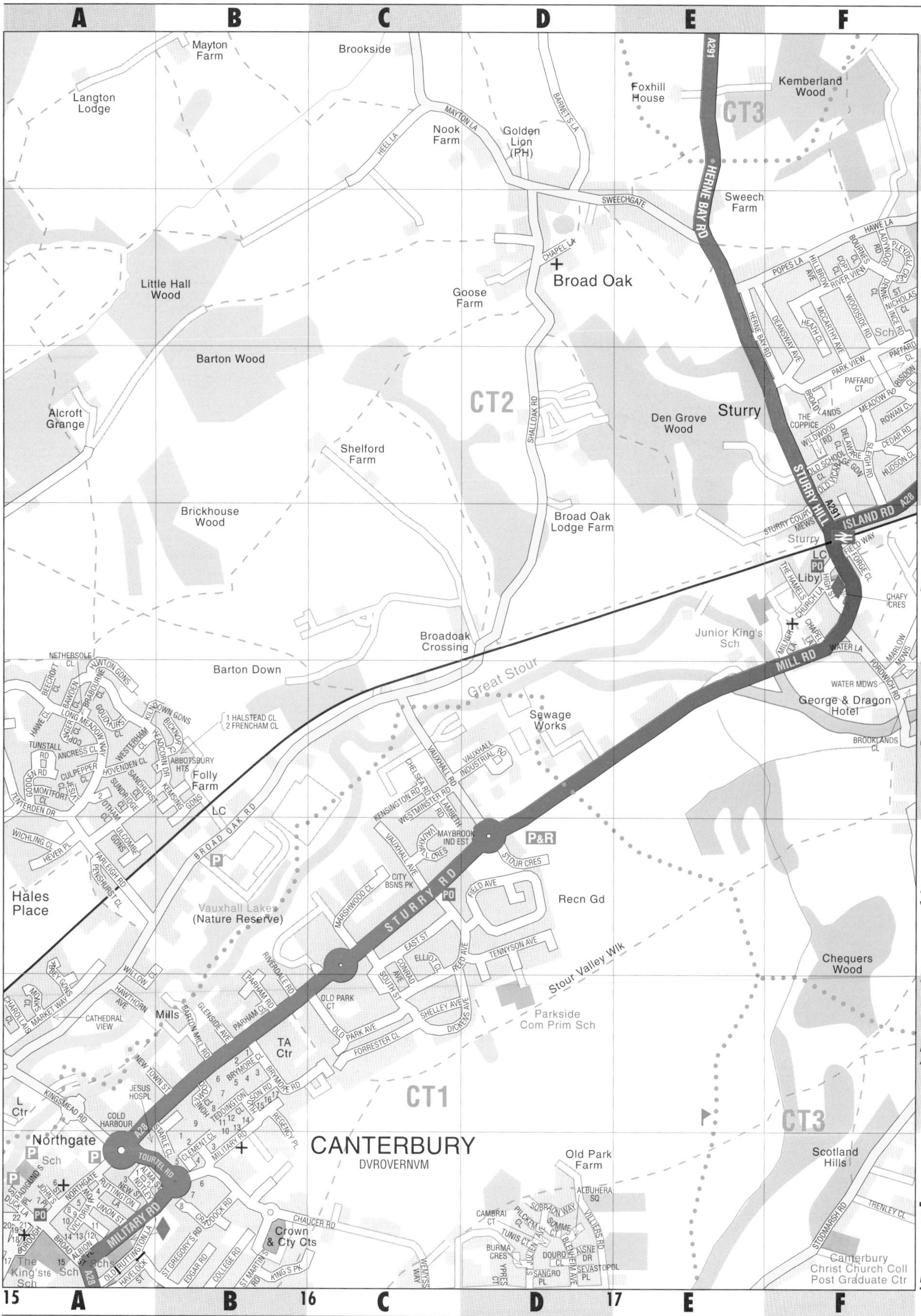

A1
1 CLYDE ST
2 ALMA PL
3 NOTLEY TERR
4 UNION PL
5 LANFRANC HO
6 ST JOHN'S HOSPL
7 KINGS MEWS
8 HIGH ST
9 ST GREGORY'S
10 DRAGOON HO
11 ARTILLERY ST
12 ARTILLERY GDNS
13 ARTILLERY HO
14 DEAN CT
15 THE FORRENS
16 THE PRECINCTS
17 PALACE ST
18 COBDEN PL
19 HOMESPIRE HO
20 KNOTT'S LA
21 CHURCH LA
22 ST RADIGUND ST

B1
1 KNOWLTON WLK
2 JESSICA MEWS
3 PYOTT MEWS
4 PAYTON MEWS
5 PLUMPTON WLK
6 MANNOCK HO
7 THE RIDINGS
8 CRADDOCK DR

B2
1 METCALFE MEWS
2 GREEN CLOTH MEWS
3 GORE MEWS
4 ARRAN MEWS
5 MARY GREEN WLK
6 CALCROFT MEWS
7 KEYWORTH MEWS
8 ANNE GREEN WLK
9 GILLON MEWS
10 HALLETT WLK
11 PETCHELL MEWS
12 REMSTON MEWS
13 WEMYSS CT
14 WEMYSS HO
15 ANZIO HO
16 CASSINO HO
17 MALTA HO

88
68

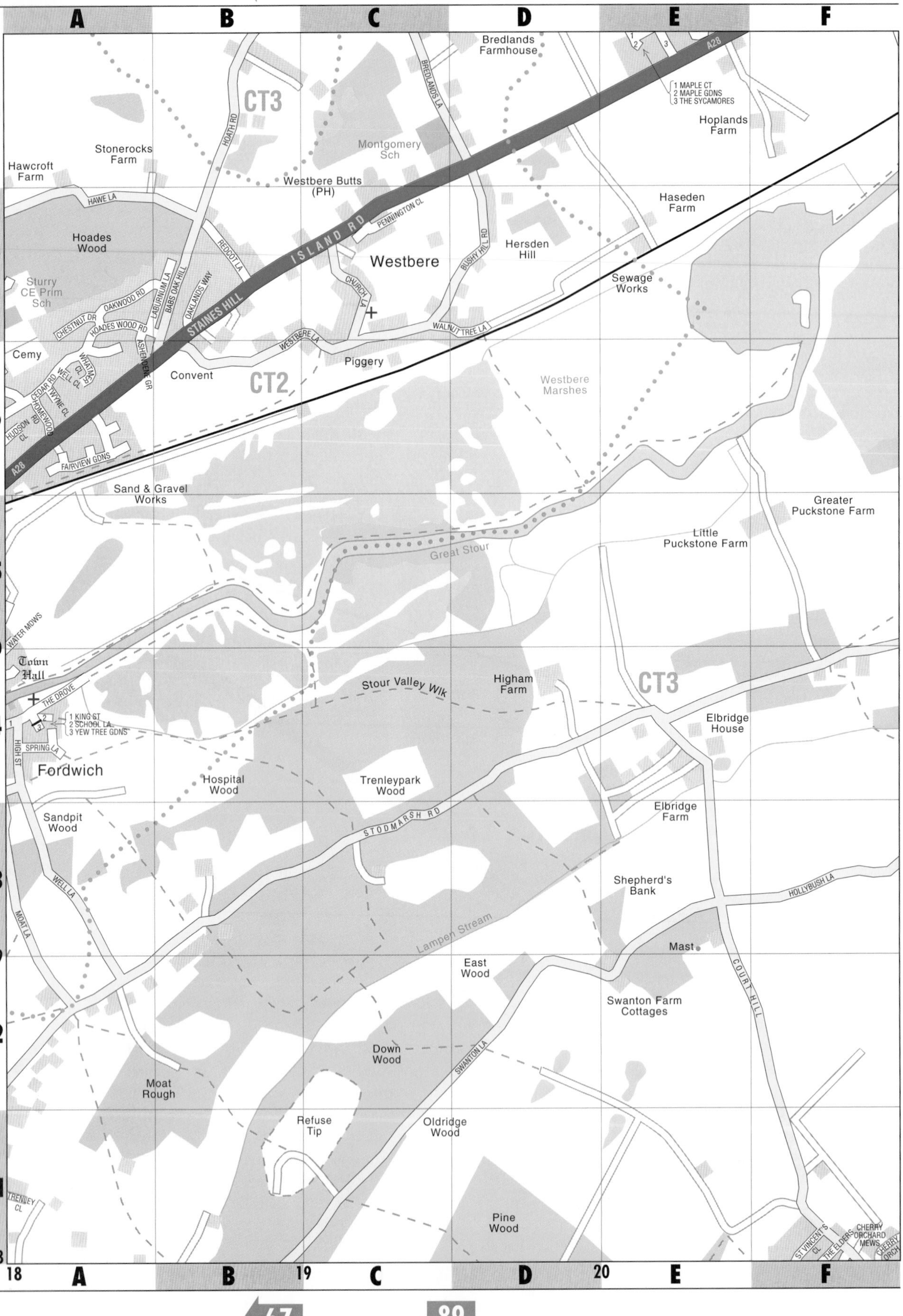
67
46
A
B
C
D
E
F
8
7
61
6
5
60
4
3
59
2
1
58
18
19
20
Bredlands Farmhouse
1 MAPLE CT
2 MAPLE GDNS
3 THE SYCAMORES
A28
CT3
Hoplands Farm
Stonerocks Farm
Hawcroft Farm
Montgomery Sch
Westbere Butts (PH)
HAWE LA
Haseden Farm
Hoades Wood
ISLAND RD
PENNINGTON CL
Westbere
Hersden Hill
STAINES HILL
Sturry CE Prim Sch
Sewage Works
OAKWOOD RD
CHESTNUT DR
HOADES WOOD RD
WALNUT TREE LA
Cemy
Convent
CT2
Piggery
Westbere Marshes
FAIRVIEW GDNS
Sand & Gravel Works
Greater Puckstone Farm
Little Puckstone Farm
Great Stour
WATER MDWS
Town Hall
Stour Valley Wlk
Higham Farm
CT3
THE DROVE
1 KING ST
2 SCHOOL LA
3 YEW TREE GDNS
Elbridge House
Fordwich
Hospital Wood
Trenleypark Wood
Elbridge Farm
Sandpit Wood
STODMARSH RD
Shepherd's Bank
HOLLYBUSH LA
WELL LA
MOAT LA
Lampen Stream
Mast
East Wood
COURT HILL
Swanton Farm Cottages
Down Wood
SWANTON LA
Moat Rough
Refuse Tip
Oldridge Wood
TRENLEY CL
Pine Wood
ST VINCENT'S CL
THE ELDERS
CHERRY ORCHARD MEWS
67
89

47
70

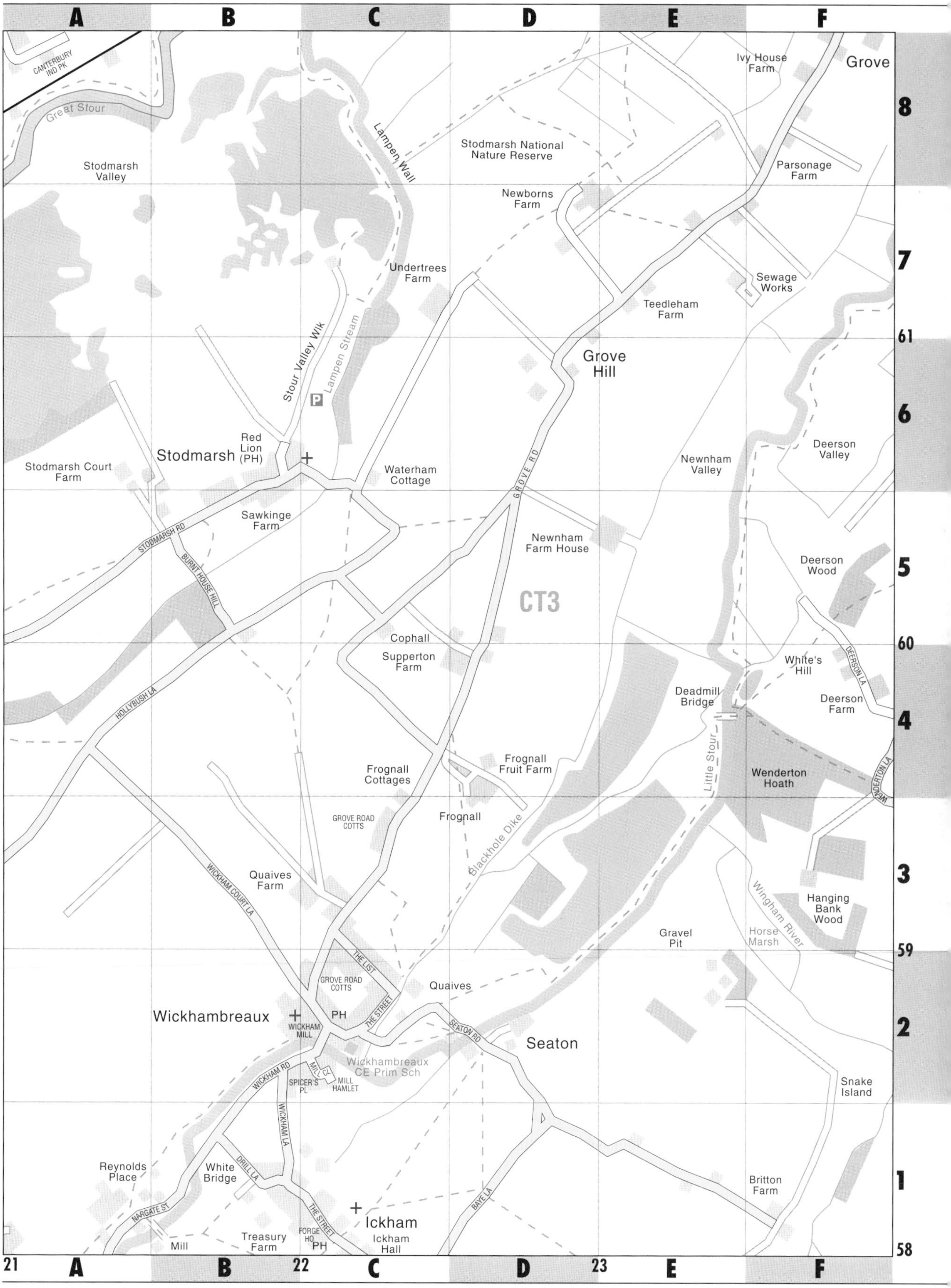
A
B
C
D
E
F
8
7
61
6
5
60
4
3
59
2
1
58
21
22
23
CANTERBURY IND PK
Great Stour
Stodmarsh Valley
Lampen Wall
Stodmarsh National Nature Reserve
Ivy House Farm
Grove
Parsonage Farm
Newborns Farm
Undertrees Farm
Sewage Works
Teedleham Farm
Grove Hill
Stour Valley Wlk
Lampen Stream
P
Red Lion (PH)
Stodmarsh
Stodmarsh Court Farm
Waterham Cottage
Newnham Valley
Deerson Valley
GROVE RD
Sawkinge Farm
STODMARSH RD
BURNT HOUSE HILL
Newnham Farm House
Deerson Wood
CT3
Cophall
Supperton Farm
White's Hill
DEERSON LA
HOLLYBUSH LA
Deadmill Bridge
Deerson Farm
Little Stour
Frognall Cottages
Frognall Fruit Farm
Wenderton Hoath
WENDERTON LA
GROVE ROAD COTTS
Frognall
Blackhole Dike
WICKHAM COURT LA
Quaives Farm
Wingham River
Hanging Bank Wood
Gravel Pit
Horse Marsh
THE LIST
GROVE ROAD COTTS
Quaives
Wickhambreaux
PH
THE STREET
WICKHAM MILL
SEATON RD
Seaton
Wickhambreaux CE Prim Sch
MILL CL
WICKHAM RD
SPICER'S PL
MILL HAMLET
Snake Island
WICKHAM LA
Reynolds Place
White Bridge
DRILL LA
Britton Farm
NARGATE ST
BAYE LA
THE STREET
Ickham
Mill
Treasury Farm
FORGE HO
PH
Ickham Hall

90
70

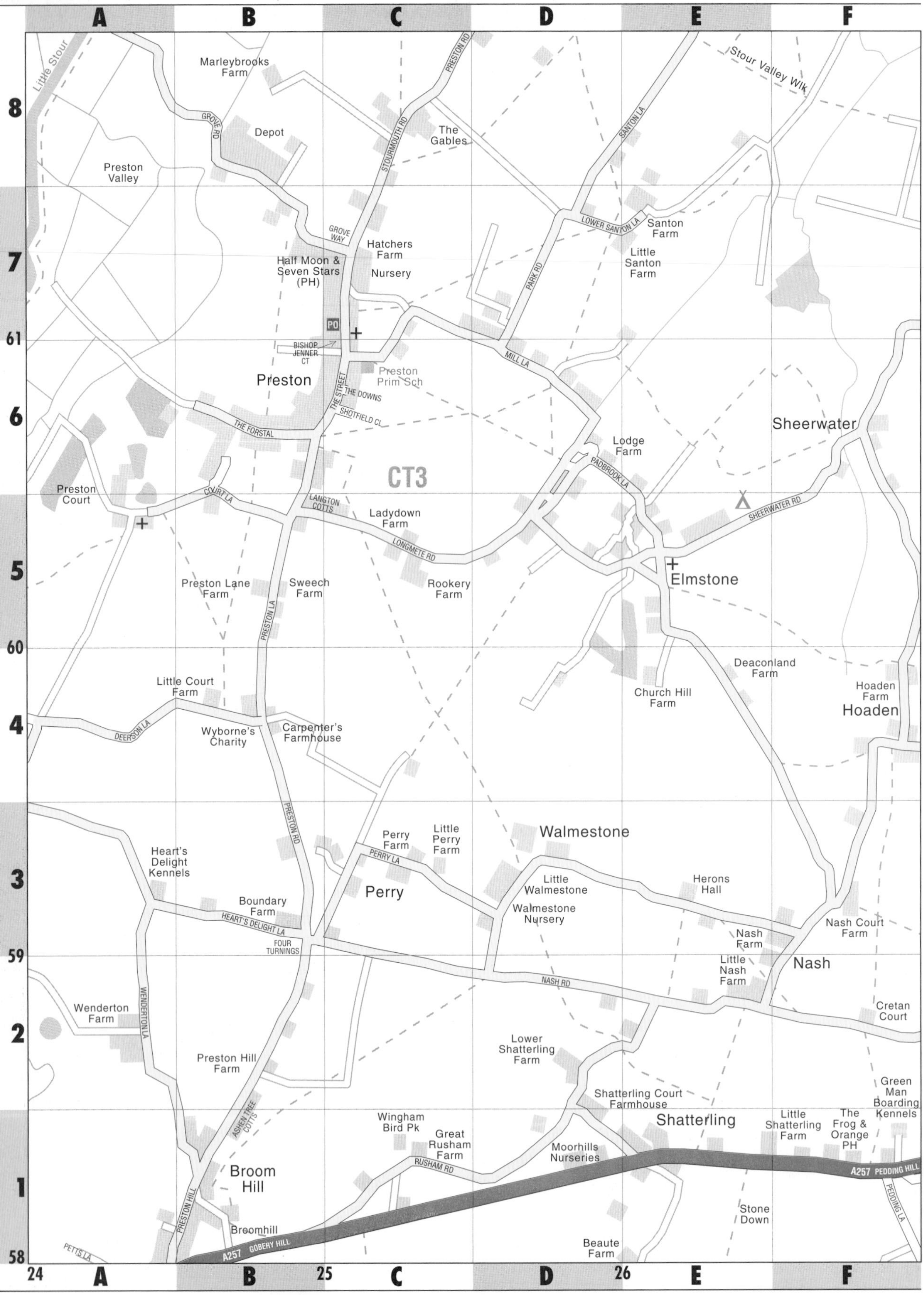

A B C D E F

8

Little Stour

Marleybrooks Farm

Preston Valley

Depot

GROVE RD

STOURMOUTH RD

PRESTON RD

The Gables

SANTON LA

Stour Valley Wlk

LOWER SANTON LA

Santon Farm

7

GROVE WAY

Half Moon & Seven Stars (PH)

Hatchers Farm

Nursery

PARK RD

Little Santon Farm

61

PO

BISHOP JENNER CT

Preston

THE STREET

THE DOWNS

Preston Prim Sch

MILL LA

6

THE FORSTAL

SHOTFIELD CL

Lodge Farm

PADBROOK LA

Sheerwater

CT3

Preston Court

COURT LA

LANGTON COTTS

Ladydown Farm

SHEERWATER RD

5

PRESTON LA

Preston Lane Farm

Sweech Farm

LONGMETE RD

Rookery Farm

Elmstone

60

Little Court Farm

DEERSON LA

Wyborne's Charity

Carpenter's Farmhouse

Deaconland Farm

Church Hill Farm

Hoaden Farm

Hoaden

4

3

PRESTON RD

Heart's Delight Kennels

Boundary Farm

HEART'S DELIGHT LA

Perry Farm

PERRY LA

Little Perry Farm

Perry

Walmestone

Little Walmestone

Walmestone Nursery

Herons Hall

Nash Farm

Nash Court Farm

59

FOUR TURNINGS

NASH RD

Little Nash Farm

Nash

2

WENDERTON LA

Wenderton Farm

Preston Hill Farm

Lower Shatterling Farm

Cretan Court

Green Man Boarding Kennels

ASHEN TREE COTTS

Shatterling Court Farmhouse

Shatterling

Little Shatterling Farm

The Frog & Orange PH

PEDDING LA

1

PRESTON HILL

Broom Hill

Wingham Bird Pk

Great Rusham Farm

RUSHAM RD

Moorhills Nurseries

A257 PEDDING HILL

Stone Down

58

PETTIS LA

Breomhill

A257 GOBERY HILL

Beaute Farm

24 A B 25 C D 26 E F

49
72

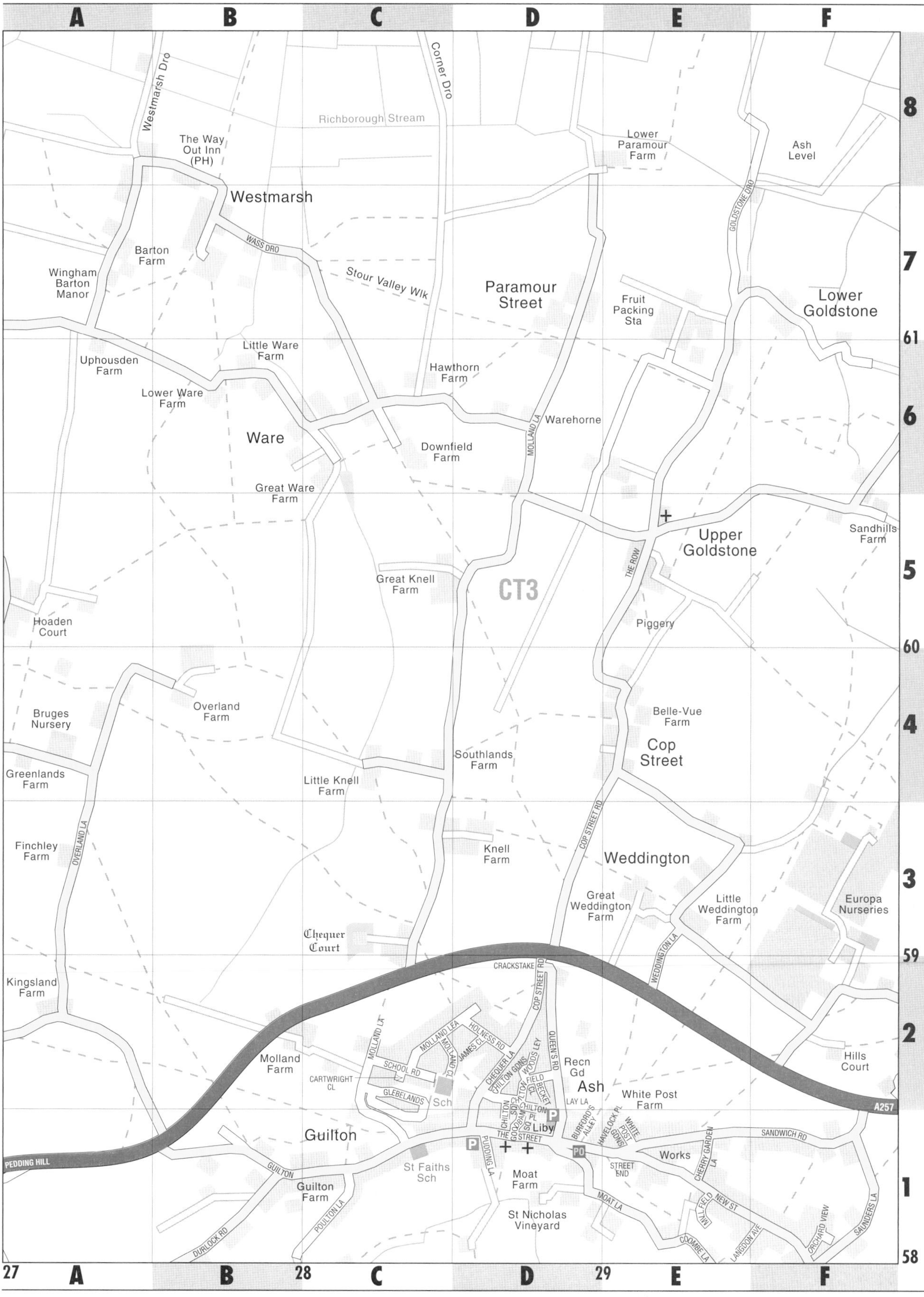
A
B
C
D
E
F
8
7
61
6
5
60
4
3
59
2
1
58
27
28
29
Westmarsh Dro
Corner Dro
Richborough Stream
The Way Out Inn (PH)
Westmarsh
Lower Paramour Farm
Ash Level
Barton Farm
WASS DRO
Wingham Barton Manor
Stour Valley Wlk
Paramour Street
Fruit Packing Sta
GOLDSTONE DRO
Lower Goldstone
Uphousden Farm
Little Ware Farm
Hawthorn Farm
Lower Ware Farm
Warehorne
Ware
Downfield Farm
MOLLAND LA
Great Ware Farm
Upper Goldstone
Sandhills Farm
THE ROW
Great Knell Farm
CT3
Hoaden Court
Piggery
Overland Farm
Bruges Nursery
Belle-Vue Farm
Cop Street
Southlands Farm
Greenlands Farm
Little Knell Farm
COP STREET RD
Finchley Farm
OVERLAND LA
Knell Farm
Weddington
Great Weddington Farm
Little Weddington Farm
Europa Nurseries
Chequer Court
WEDDINGTON LA
CRACKSTAKE
Kingsland Farm
COP STREET RD
MOLLAND LA
MOLLAND LEA
HOLNESS RD
JAMES CL
QUEEN'S RD
Molland Farm
SCHOOL RD
CHEQUER LA
CHILTON GDNS
WOODS LEY
Recn Gd
Hills Court
CARTWRIGHT CL
GLEBELANDS
Sch
FIELD CL
BECKET CL
Ash
White Post Farm
LAY LA
A257
CHILTON SQ
GOODBAN SQ
CHILTON PL
P
Liby
BURFORD'S ALLEY
HAVELOCK PL
POST GDNS
WHITE
SANDWICH RD
Guilton
THE STREET
P
PD
CHERRY GARDEN LA
PEDDING HILL
GUILTON
Works
St Faiths Sch
PUDDING LA
STREET END
Guilton Farm
Moat Farm
MOAT LA
MILL FIELD
NEW ST
POULTON LA
St Nicholas Vineyard
ORCHARD VIEW
SAUNDERS LA
DURLOCK RD
COOMBE LA
LANGDON AVE

92
72

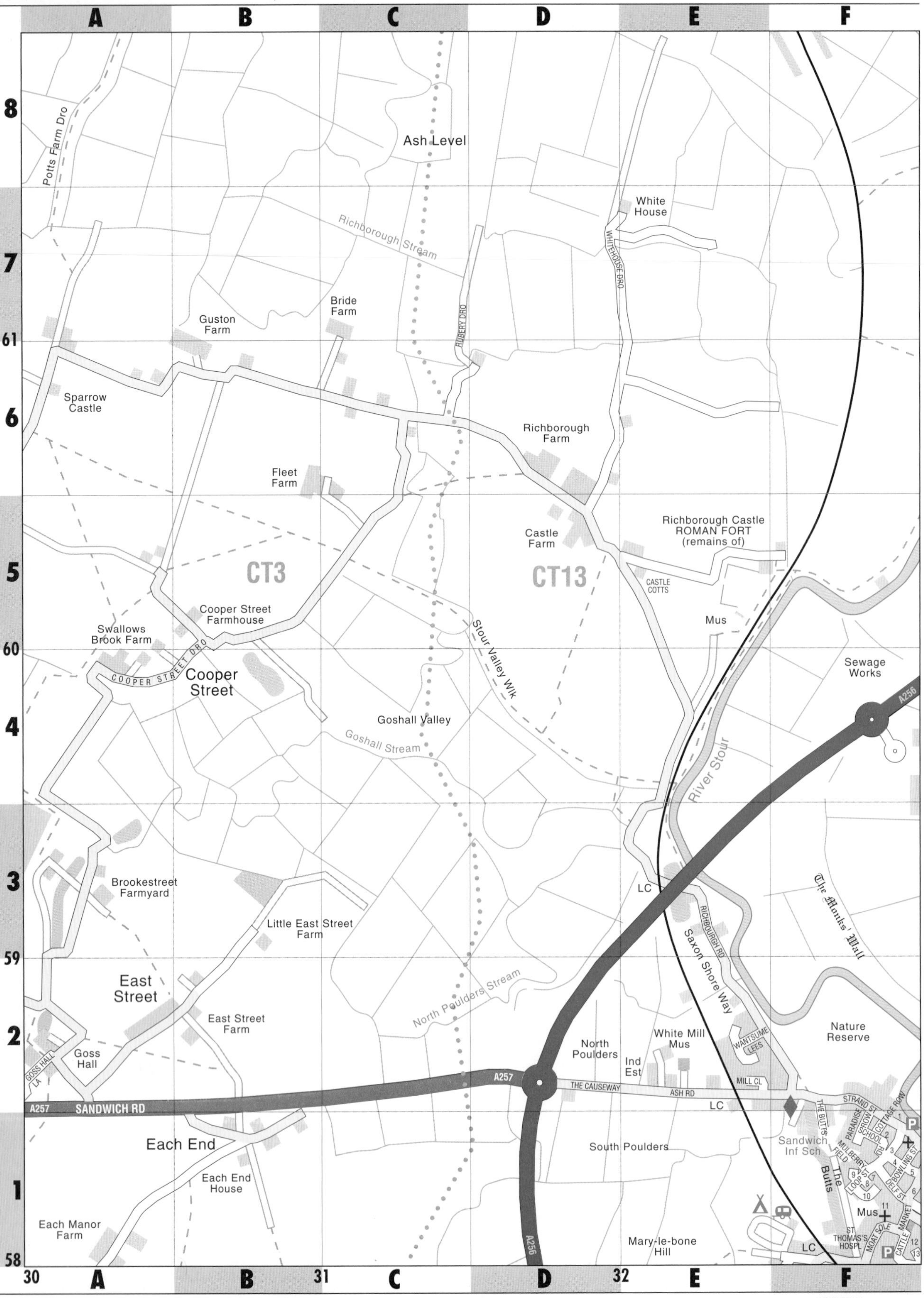

A B C D E F

8

7

61

6

5

60

4

3

59

2

1

58

30 A B 31 C D 32 E F

Potts Farm Dro

Ash Level

Richborough Stream

White House

WHITEHOUSE DRO

Guston Farm

Bride Farm

RUBERY DRO

Sparrow Castle

Richborough Farm

Fleet Farm

Castle Farm

Richborough Castle
ROMAN FORT
(remains of)

CT3

CT13

CASTLE COTTS

Mus

Cooper Street Farmhouse

Swallows Brook Farm

Stour Valley Wlk

Sewage Works

COOPER STREET DRO

Cooper Street

A256

Goshall Valley

Goshall Stream

River Stour

Brookestreet Farmyard

Little East Street Farm

The Monks Wall

North Poulders Stream

LC

RICHBOROUGH RD

East Street

Saxon Shore Way

East Street Farm

Goss Hall

GOSS HALL LA

North Poulders

Ind Est

White Mill Mus

WANTSUME LEES

Nature Reserve

MILL CL

A257

A257 SANDWICH RD

THE CAUSEWAY

ASH RD

LC

Each End

Sandwich Inf Sch

Each End House

Each Manor Farm

South Poulders

Mary-le-bone Hill

A256

LC

Mus

ST THOMAS'S HOSPL

F1
1 GUESTLING MILL CT
2 CRAIGHTON FLATS
3 CHURCH STREET ST MARY'S
4 VICARAGE LA
5 GUILDCOUNT LA
6 HARNET ST
7 WANTSUM MEWS
8 STOUR CT
9 LOOP COURT MEWS
10 TANNERY LA
11 ST JOHN'S COTTS
12 WATTS YD
13 WHITEFRIARS WAY

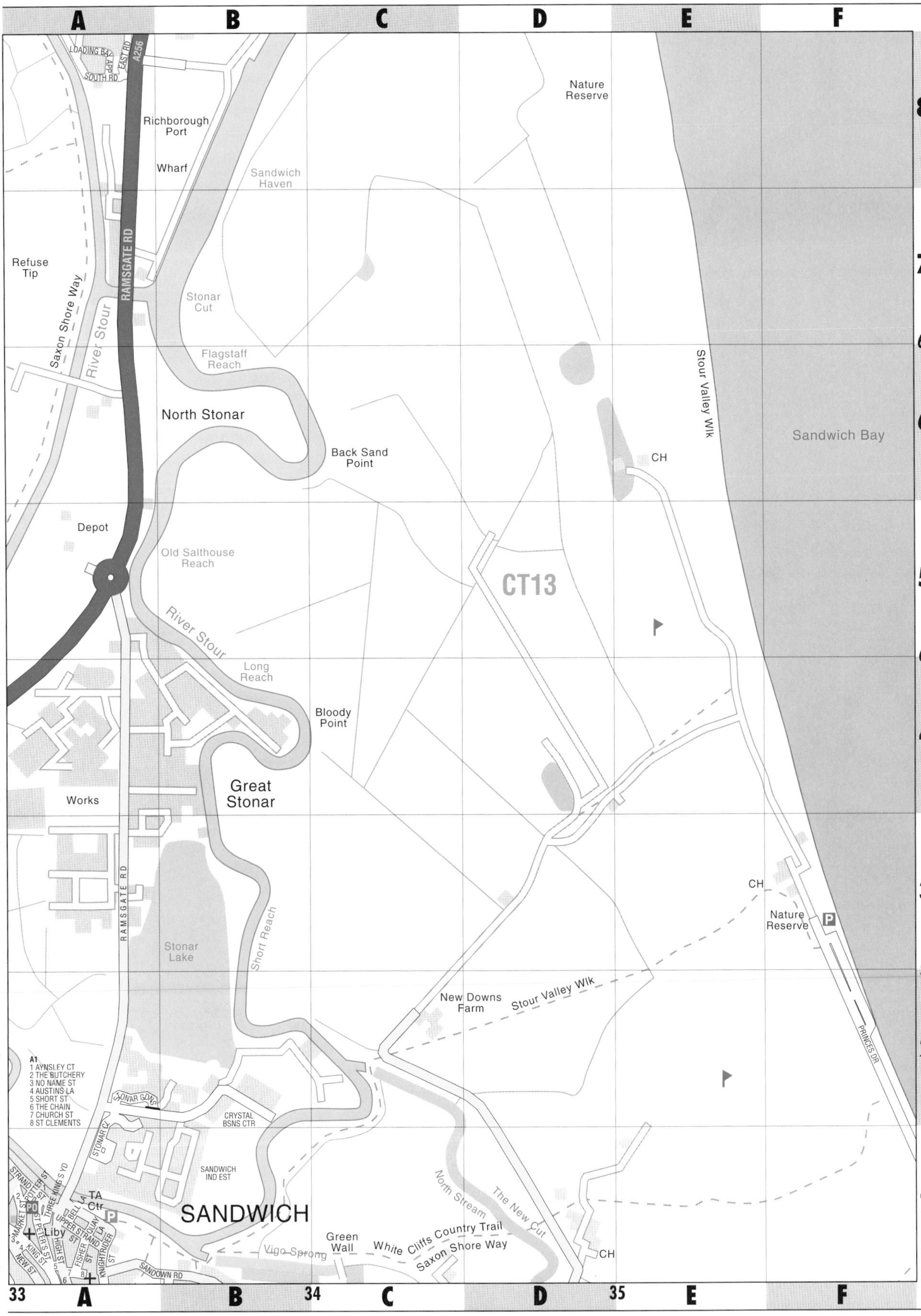

A B C D E F

8
7
61
6
5
60
4
3
59
2
1
58

LOADING BAY
SOUTH RD
EAST RD
A256
RAMSGATE RD

Richborough Port

Wharf

Sandwich Haven

Nature Reserve

Refuse Tip

Saxon Shore Way

River Stour

Stonar Cut

Flagstaff Reach

North Stonar

Back Sand Point

Stour Valley Wlk

Sandwich Bay

Depot

Old Salthouse Reach

CT13

CH

River Stour

Long Reach

Bloody Point

Works

Great Stonar

Short Reach

RAMSGATE RD

Stonar Lake

CH

Nature Reserve

P

PRINCES DR

A1
1 AYNSLEY CT
2 THE BUTCHERY
3 NO NAME ST
4 AUSTINS LA
5 SHORT ST
6 THE CHAIN
7 CHURCH ST
8 ST CLEMENTS

New Downs Farm

Stour Valley Wlk

STONAR GDNS

CRYSTAL BSNS CTR

SANDWICH IND EST

STONAR CT

THREE KING'S YD

STRAND ST

UPPER STRAND ST

FISHER ST

KING'S LA

HIGH ST

MARKET ST

NEW ST

KING ST

FISHER ST

SANDOWN RD

KNIGHTRIDER ST

TA Ctr

P

PO

Liby

SANDWICH

Green Wall

Vigo Sprong

White Cliffs Country Trail

Saxon Shore Way

North Stream

The New Cut

CH

33 34 35

53

F7
1 GAGETOWN TERR
2 GILBERT TERR
3 McPHIE HO
4 JARVIS HO

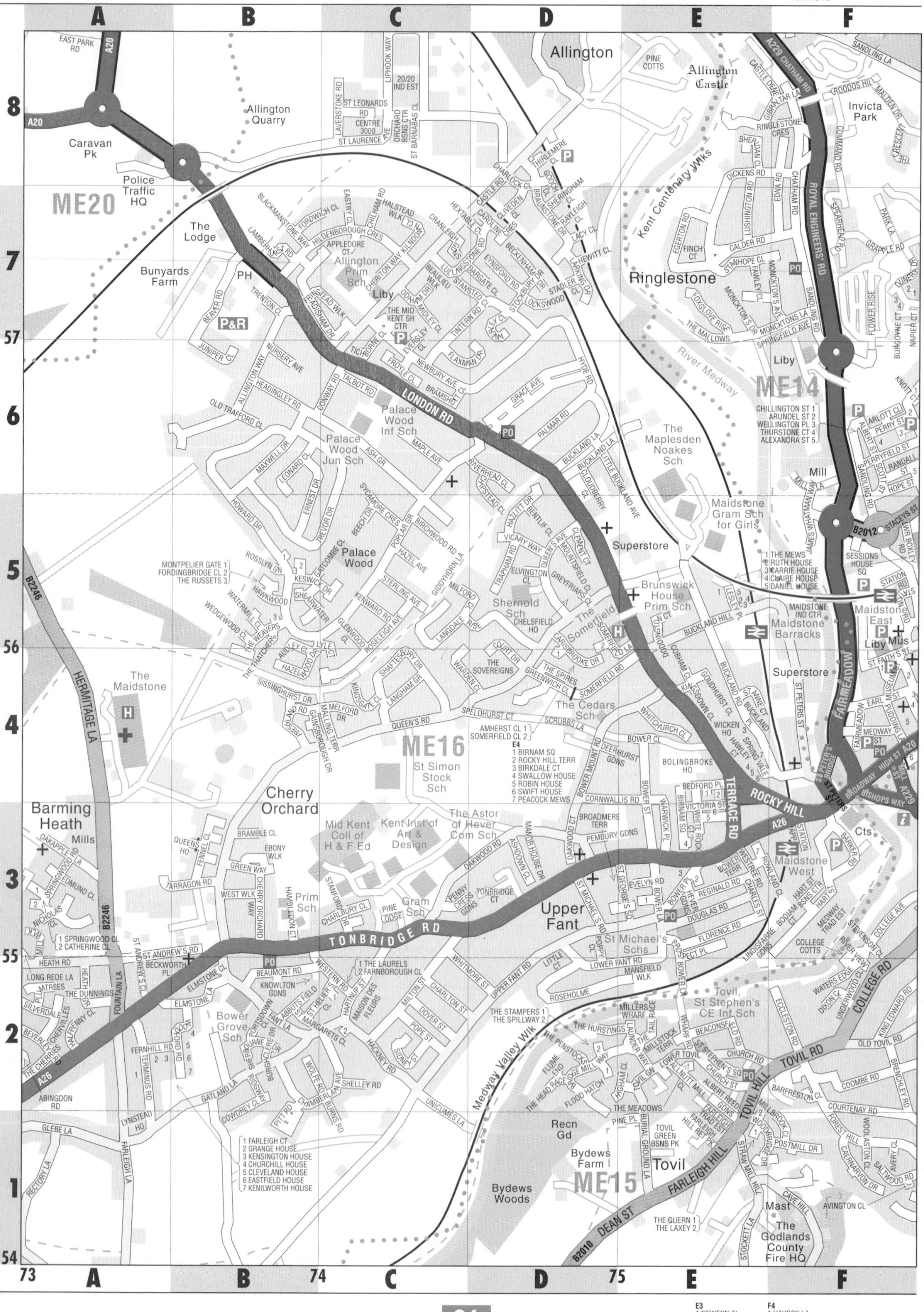

96

E3
1 NEWTON CL
2 ORCHARD PL
3 OLDCHURCH CT
4 RYECAULT CL
5 WHITE ROCK PL
6 VICTORIA CT
7 WESTREE CT

F4
1 HAVOCK LA
2 MARKET ST
3 MARKET COLONNADE
4 MARKET BLDGS
5 ROYAL STAR ARC
6 MIDDLE ROW

A5
1 MANDEVILLE CT
2 CRUNDALE
3 WALMER CT
4 PRIORY GATE
5 STARNES CT
6 KILBURN HO
7 LADBROOKE HO
8 LAMBARD HO
9 WINCHESTER PL
10 LOWER BOXLEY RD

A6
1 TELFORD HO
2 WALSHAW HO
3 WALSINGHAM HO

A7
1 ADEN TERR
2 BARBADOS TERR
3 CANADA TERR
4 NORWAY TERR
5 MALTA TERR
6 LIBYA TERR
7 KENYA TERR
8 HONDURAS TERR

54
76

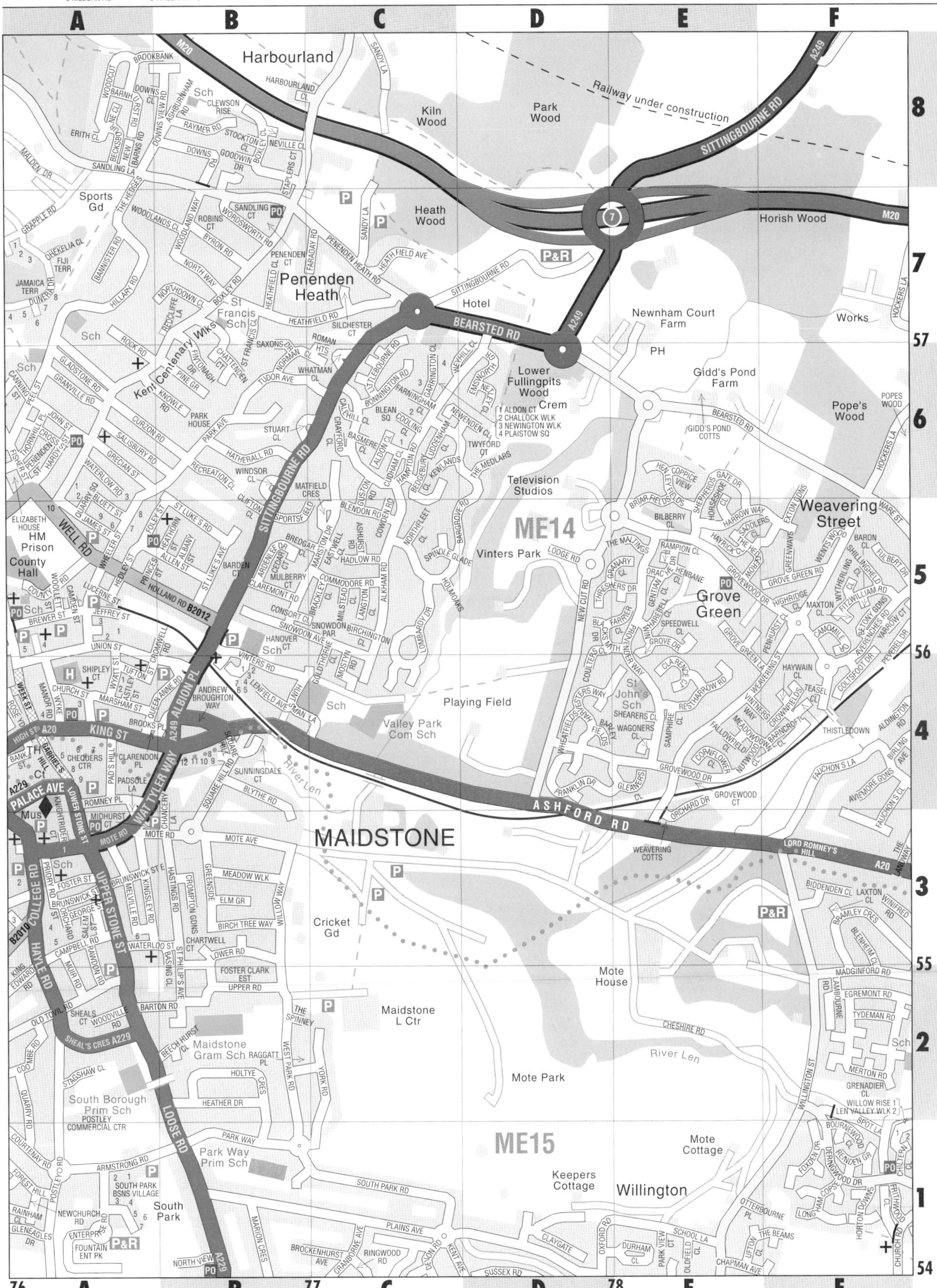

76
97

A1
1 KINGS ROW
2 NORTH CT
3 WEST CT
4 EAST CT
5 WORSFOLD CT
6 BASIL TERR
7 STONEACRE CT

A3
1 KNIGHTRIDER ST
2 CUTBUSH ALMSHOUSES
3 GREENHITHE
4 CORRALL ALMSHOUSES
5 COLLEGE CT
6 BYCHURCH PL

A4
1 NEWLYN CT
2 BLOOMSBURY WLK
3 CUTBUSH ALMSHOUSES
4 COLMAN HOUSE
5 EDGER PL
6 WATER LA
7 DUKES WLK
8 GRANADA HOUSE
9 GRANADA ST

B4
1 CUTBUSH AND CORRALL CT
2 DAY HO
3 HAYNES HO
4 GULLAND HO
5 PINE HO
6 CLIFFORD HO

B4
7 ELLIS HO
8 RIVER BANK CL
9 BELMONT CT
10 LENHAM CT
11 KINGFISHER CT
12 WILLOWBANK CT

97
76

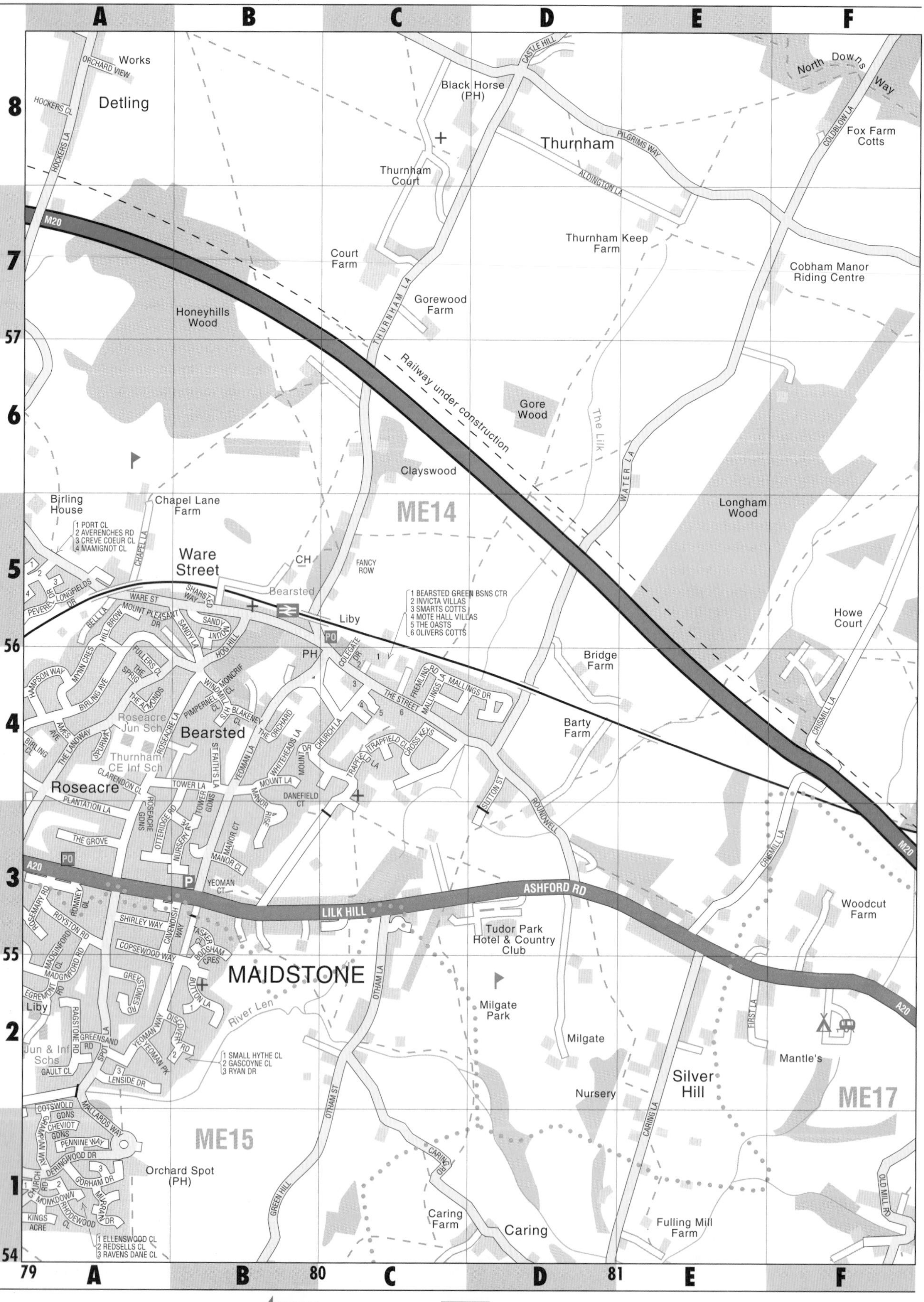
A   B   C   D   E   F

8   Detling
Works
ORCHARD VIEW
HOCKERS CL
HOCKERS LA

Black Horse (PH)
CASTLE HILL
Thurnham
North Downs Way
COLDBLOW LA
Fox Farm Cotts

Thurnham Court
ALDINGTON LA
PILGRIMS WAY

7   M20
Court Farm
Thurnham Keep Farm
Cobham Manor Riding Centre

Honeyhills Wood
Gorewood Farm
THURNHAM LA

57   Railway under construction
Gore Wood
WATER LA
The Lilk

6   Clayswood
Longham Wood

Birling House
Chapel Lane Farm
ME14
Howe Court

1 PORT CL
2 AVERENCHES RD
3 CREVE COEUR CL
4 MAMIGNOT CL

5   Ware Street
CH
FANCY ROW
CHAPEL LA

Bearsted
WARE ST
SHARSTED WAY
Liby
1 BEARSTED GREEN BSNS CTR
2 INVICTA VILLAS
3 SMARTS COTTS
4 MOTE HALL VILLAS
5 THE OASTS
6 OLIVERS COTTS

56   PH
PO
COLEGATE DR
Bridge Farm
CRISMILL LA

LONGFIELDS DR
PEVERELL
BELL LA
MOUNT PLEASANT
HILL BROW
SANDY LA
SANDS
HOG HILL
FREARINS RD
MALLINGS DR
MALLINGS LA

4   MYTHI CRES
BIRLING AVE
FULLERS CL
THE SPRIG
WINDMILL CL
PIMPERNEL CL
THE STREET
Barty Farm
M20

HAMPSON WAY
THE WOODS
BLAKENEY
Roseacre Jun Sch
Bearsted
THE ORCHARD
WHITEHEAD LA
CHURCH LA
TRAPFIELD CLOSS KEYS
SUTTON ST
RAMNOLL

SPURWAY
THE LANDWAY
Thurnham CE Inf Sch
ST FAITH ST
YEOMAN LA
MOUNT DR
TRAPFIELD LA

Roseacre
CLARENDON CL
TOWER LA
MANOR RD
MOUNT LA
DANEFIELD CT

PLANTATION LA
ROSEACRE GDNS
COTTERIDGE RD
NURSERY RD
MANOR CT

3   THE GROVE
A20
PO
MANOR CL
Ashford Rd
Woodcut Farm

P
YEOMAN CT
LILK HILL
CRISMILL LA

RASEMARY RD
ROMNEY
SHIRLEY WAY
BASKER CAVENDISH BDSHAM CRES
OTHAM LA
A20

ROYSTON RD
COPSEWOOD WAY
Tudor Park Hotel & Country Club

55   MADGINFORD RD
GREYSTONES
SUTTON LA
MAIDSTONE
River Len
Milgate Park
Silver Hill
Mantle's
FIRST LA

EGREMONT RD
RAGSTONE RD
YEOMAN WAY
GREENSAND WAY
DISCOVERY RD
Milgate
ME17

2   Liby
Jun & Inf Schs
GAULT CL
LENSIDE DR
1 SMALL HYTHE CL
2 GASCOYNE CL
3 RYAN DR
OTHAM ST
Nursery
CARING LA

COTSWOLD GDNS
CHEVIOT
PENNINE WAY
DERINGWOOD DR
MALLARDS WAY
GORHAM DR
ME15
Caring Farm
Fulling Mill Farm

1   CHURCH
MONKDOWN
RIDGEWOOD CL
Orchard Spot (PH)
GREEN HILL
CARING DR
Caring
OLD MILL RD

KINGS ACRE
1 ELLENSWOOD CL
2 REDSELLS CL
3 RAVENS DANE CL

54
79   A   B   80   C   D   81   E   F

56
78

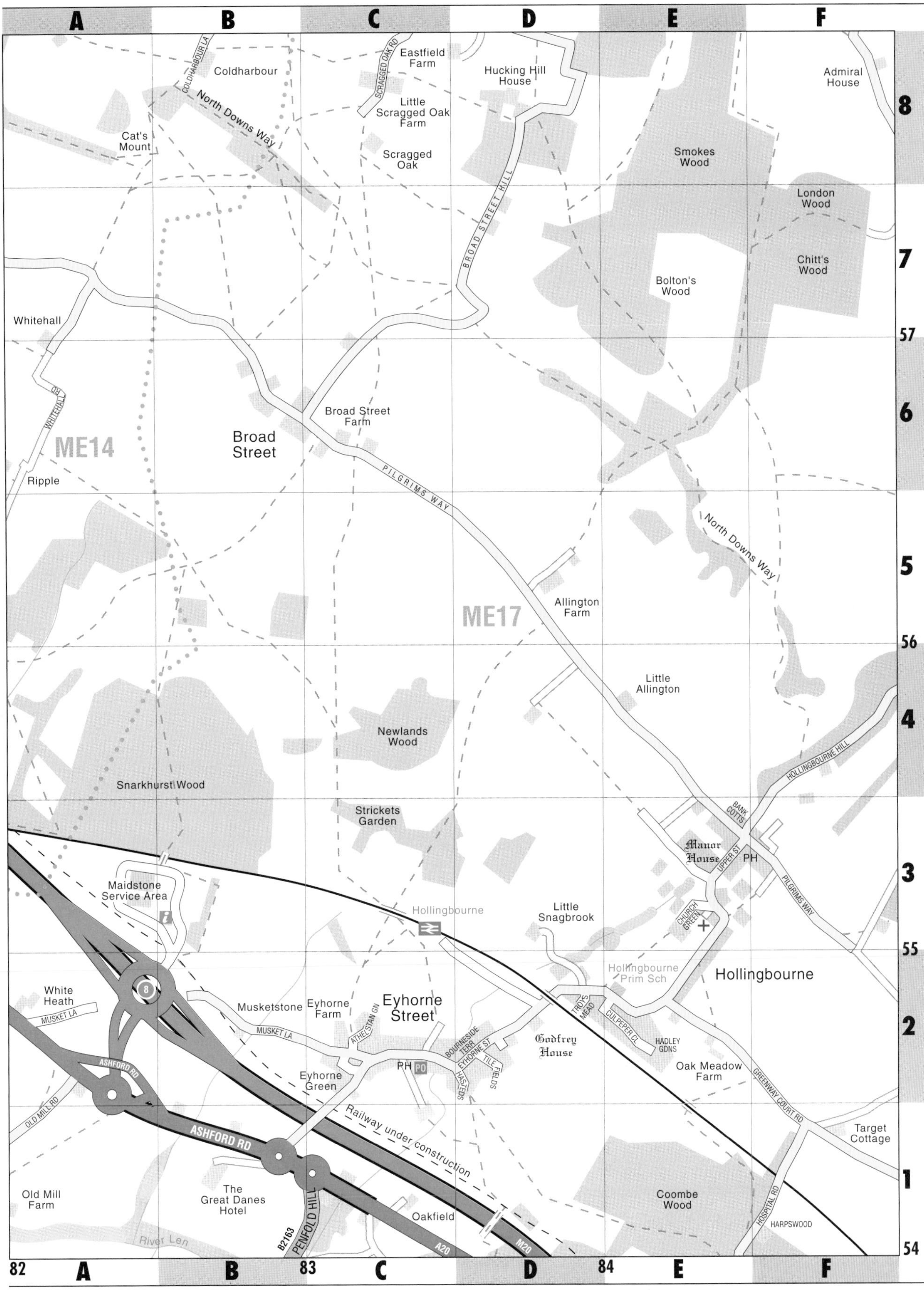
A
B
C
D
E
F
8
7
57
6
5
56
4
3
55
2
1
54
82
83
84
COLDHARBOUR LA
Coldharbour
SCRAGGED OAK RD
Eastfield Farm
Hucking Hill House
Admiral House
North Downs Way
Cat's Mount
Little Scragged Oak Farm
Scragged Oak
Smokes Wood
London Wood
BROAD STREET HILL
Chitt's Wood
Bolton's Wood
Whitehall
WHITEHALL RD
Broad Street Farm
ME14
Broad Street
Ripple
PILGRIMS WAY
North Downs Way
Allington Farm
ME17
Little Allington
Newlands Wood
HOLLINGBOURNE HILL
Snarkhurst Wood
Strickets Garden
BANK COTTS
Manor House
UPPER ST
PH
PILGRIMS WAY
Maidstone Service Area
Hollingbourne
Little Snagbrook
CHURCH GREEN
Hollingbourne Prim Sch
Hollingbourne
White Heath
8
MUSKET LA
Musketstone
Eyhorne Farm
Eyhorne Street
ATHELSTAN GN
MUSKET LA
BOURNESIDE TERR
EYHORNE ST
TROYS MEAD
CULPEPER CL
Godfrey House
HADLEY GDNS
Oak Meadow Farm
ASHFORD RD
PH
PO
TILE FIELDS
HASTEDS
Eyhorne Green
GREENWAY COURT RD
OLD MILL RD
Railway under construction
ASHFORD RD
Target Cottage
Old Mill Farm
The Great Danes Hotel
PENFOLD HILL
B2163
Oakfield
Coombe Wood
HOSPITAL RD
HARPSWOOD
River Len
A20
M20

77 57

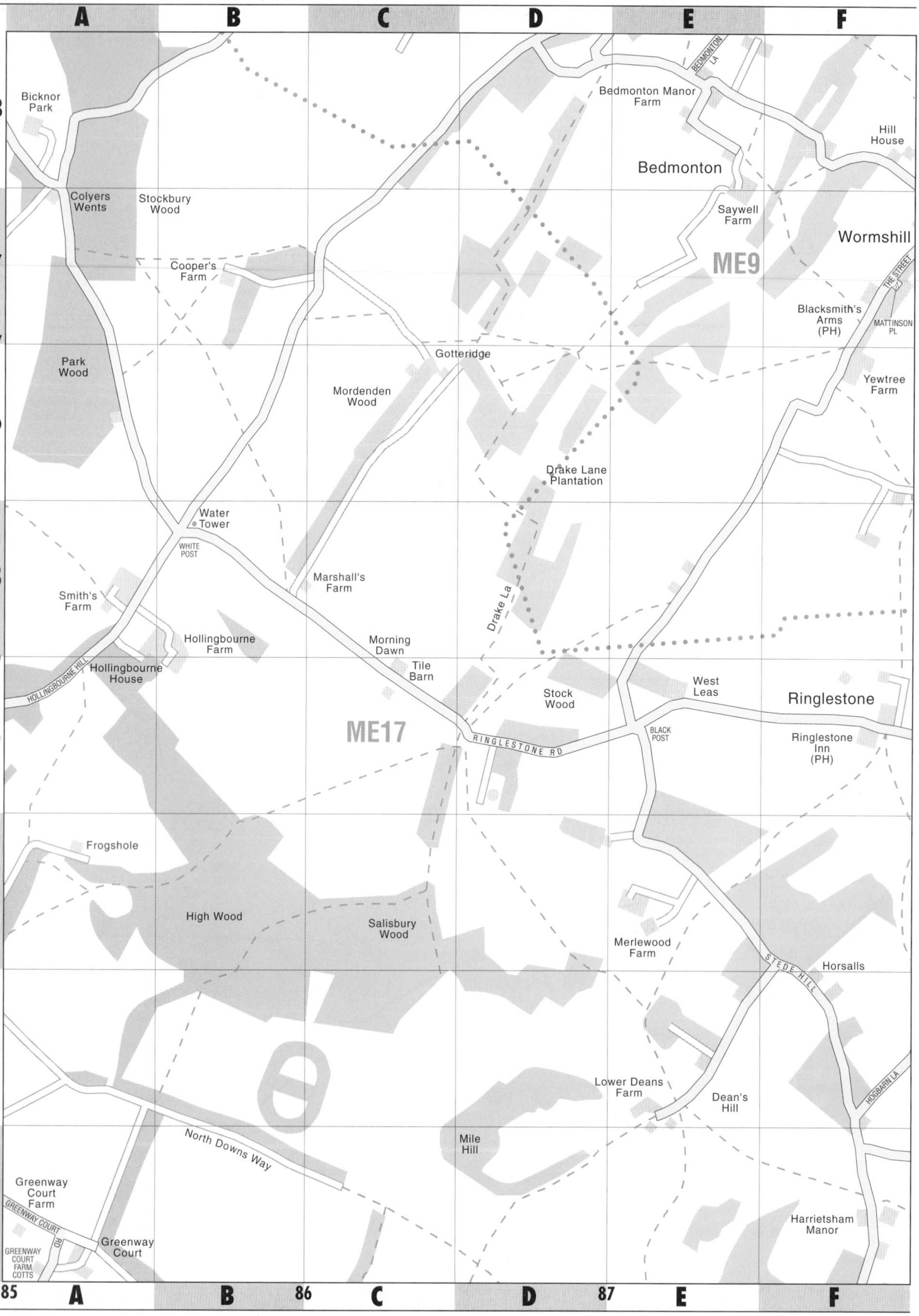

A **B** **C** **D** **E** **F**

8
Bicknor Park
Colyers Wents
Stockbury Wood
Bedmonton Manor Farm
Bedmonton
Hill House

7
Cooper's Farm
Saywell Farm
Wormshill
ME9

57
Park Wood
Gotteridge
Blacksmith's Arms (PH)
MATTINSON PL

6
Mordenden Wood
Drake Lane Plantation
Yewtree Farm
THE STREET

5
Water Tower
WHITE POST
Marshall's Farm
Drake La

Smith's Farm

56
Hollingbourne Farm
Morning Dawn
Tile Barn
Stock Wood
West Leas
Ringlestone

Hollingbourne House
HOLLINGBOURNE HILL

4
ME17
RINGLESTONE RD
BLACK POST
Ringlestone Inn (PH)

3
Frogshole
High Wood
Salisbury Wood
Merlewood Farm
STEDE HILL
Horsalls

55

2
Lower Deans Farm
Dean's Hill
HOGBARN LA

North Downs Way
Mile Hill

1
Greenway Court Farm
GREENWAY COURT RD
Greenway Court
GREENWAY COURT FARM COTTS
Harrietsham Manor

54
85 **A** **B** 86 **C** **D** 87 **E** **F**

77 100

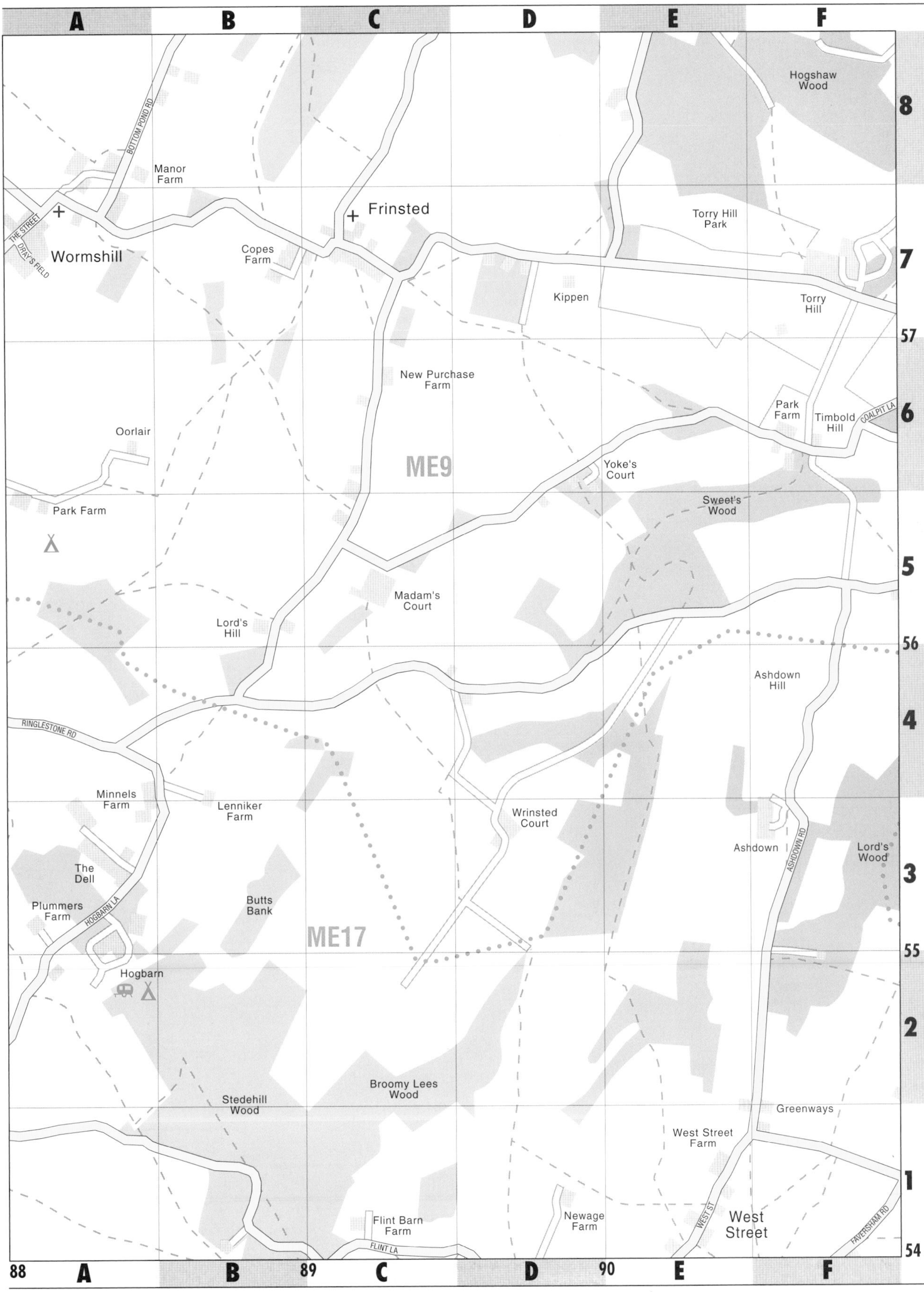

A B C D E F

8

Hogshaw
Wood

Manor
Farm

+ Frinsted

Torry Hill
Park

7

THE STREET
DRAY'S FIELD
BOTTOM POND RD
Copes
Farm

Wormshill

Kippen

Torry
Hill

57

New Purchase
Farm

Park
Farm

Timbold
Hill

COALPIT LA
6

Oorlair

ME9

Yoke's
Court

Sweet's
Wood

Park Farm

Madam's
Court

5

Lord's
Hill

Ashdown
Hill

56

RINGLESTONE RD

4

Minnels
Farm

Lenniker
Farm

Wrinsted
Court

Ashdown

ASHDOWN RD

Lord's
Wood

3

The
Dell

Butts
Bank

ME17

Plummers
Farm

HOGBARN LA

Hogbarn

55

2

Stedehill
Wood

Broomy Lees
Wood

Greenways

West Street
Farm

1

WEST ST

West
Street

TAVERSTIAM RD

Flint Barn
Farm

Newage
Farm

FLINT LA

54

88 A B 89 C D 90 E F

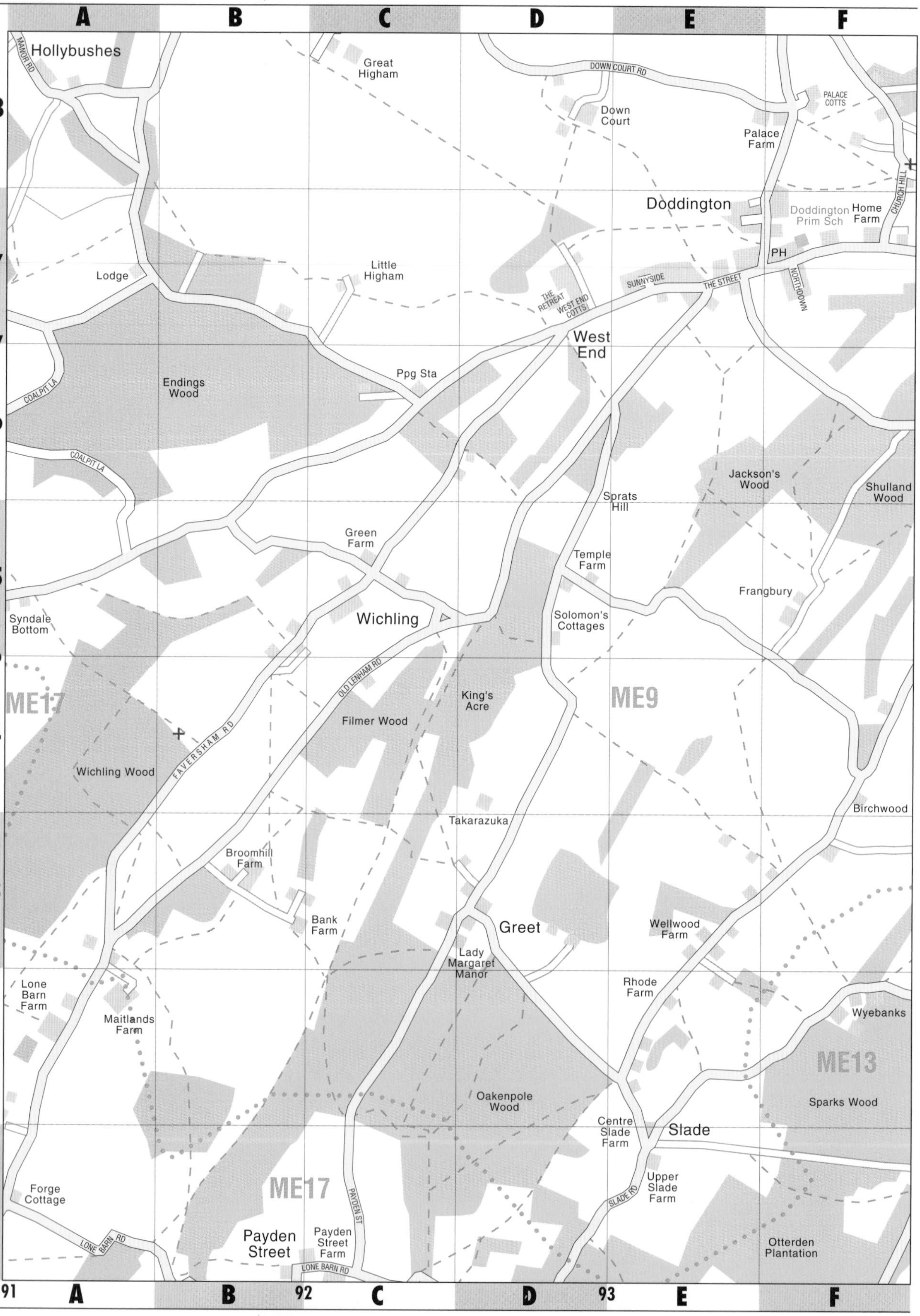

A B C D E F

8
7
57
6
5
56
4
3
55
2
1
54

Hollybushes

MANOR RD

Great Higham

DOWN COURT RD

Down Court

PALACE COTTS

Palace Farm

CHURCH HILL

Doddington

Doddington Prim Sch

Home Farm

PH

Lodge

Little Higham

THE RETREAT

WEST END COTTS

SUNNYSIDE

THE STREET

NORTHDOWN

West End

COALPIT LA

Endings Wood

Ppg Sta

Jackson's Wood

Shulland Wood

COALPIT LA

Sprats Hill

Green Farm

Temple Farm

Frangbury

Wichling

Solomon's Cottages

Syndale Bottom

ME17

King's Acre

ME9

Filmer Wood

FAVERSHAM RD

OLD LENHAM RD

Wichling Wood

Birchwood

Takarazuka

Broomhill Farm

Bank Farm

Greet

Wellwood Farm

Lone Barn Farm

Lady Margaret Manor

Rhode Farm

Wyebanks

Maitlands Farm

ME13

Oakenpole Wood

Sparks Wood

Centre Slade Farm

Slade

Forge Cottage

LONE BARN RD

ME17

PAYDEN ST

Upper Slade Farm

SLADE RD

Otterden Plantation

Payden Street

Payden Street Farm

LONE BARN RD

60
82

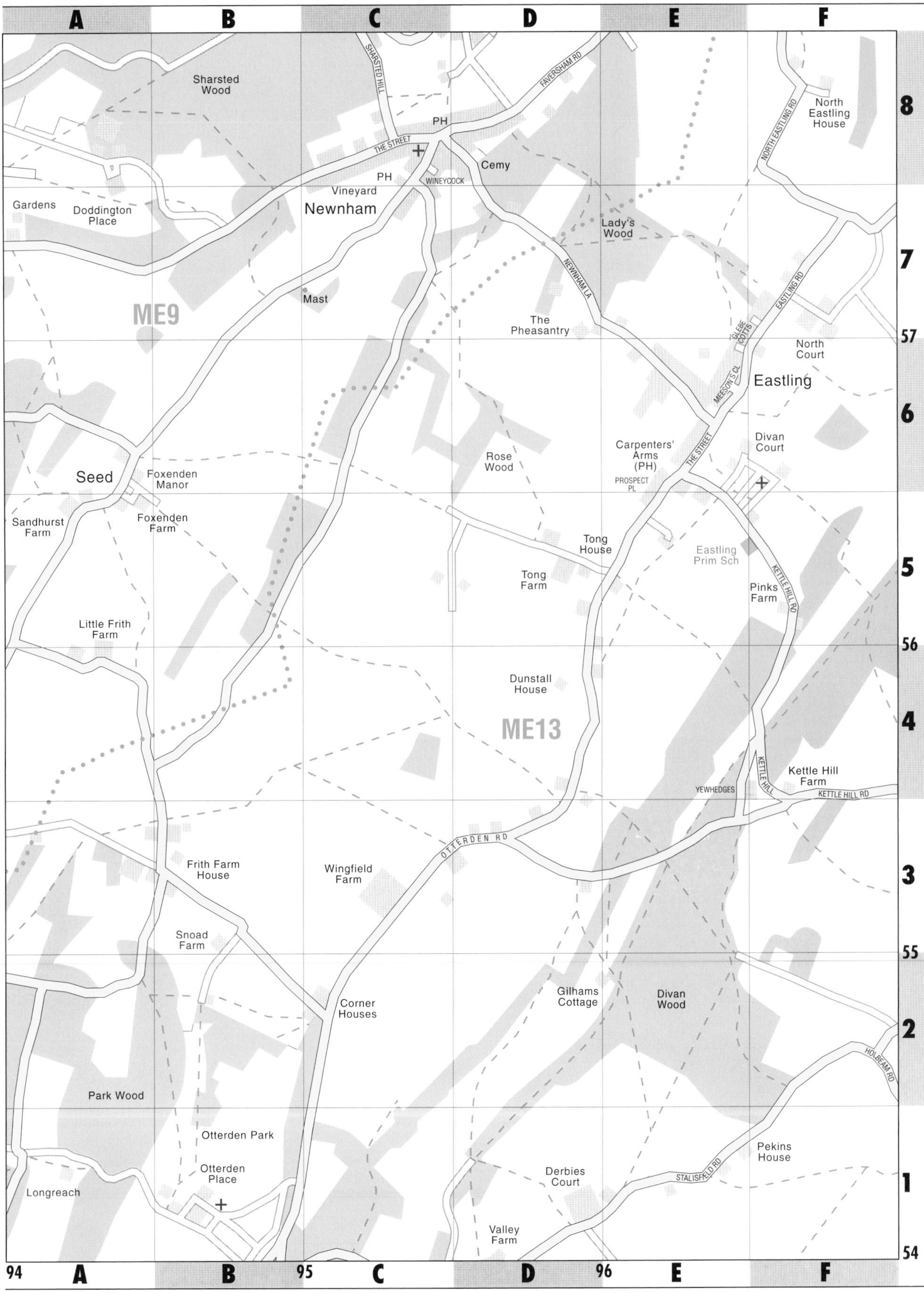
A
B
C
D
E
F
8
7
57
6
5
56
4
3
55
2
1
54
94
95
96
Sharsted Wood
SHARSTED HILL
FAVERSHAM RD
PH
THE STREET
PH
Cemy
WINEYCOCK
Vineyard
Newnham
Gardens
Doddington Place
North Eastling House
NORTH EASTLING RD
Lady's Wood
NEWNHAM LA
Mast
ME9
The Pheasantry
EASTLING RD
GLEBE COTTS
MEESON'S CL
North Court
Eastling
Carpenters' Arms (PH)
PROSPECT PL
THE STREET
Divan Court
Rose Wood
Seed
Foxenden Manor
Foxenden Farm
Sandhurst Farm
Tong House
Tong Farm
Eastling Prim Sch
KETTLE HILL RD
Pinks Farm
Little Frith Farm
Dunstall House
ME13
YEWHEDGES
KETTLE HILL
Kettle Hill Farm
KETTLE HILL RD
OTTERDEN RD
Frith Farm House
Wingfield Farm
Snoad Farm
Corner Houses
Gilhams Cottage
Divan Wood
HOLBEAM RD
Park Wood
Otterden Park
Otterden Place
Longreach
Pekins House
STALISFIELD RD
Derbies Court
Valley Farm

103
82

81
61

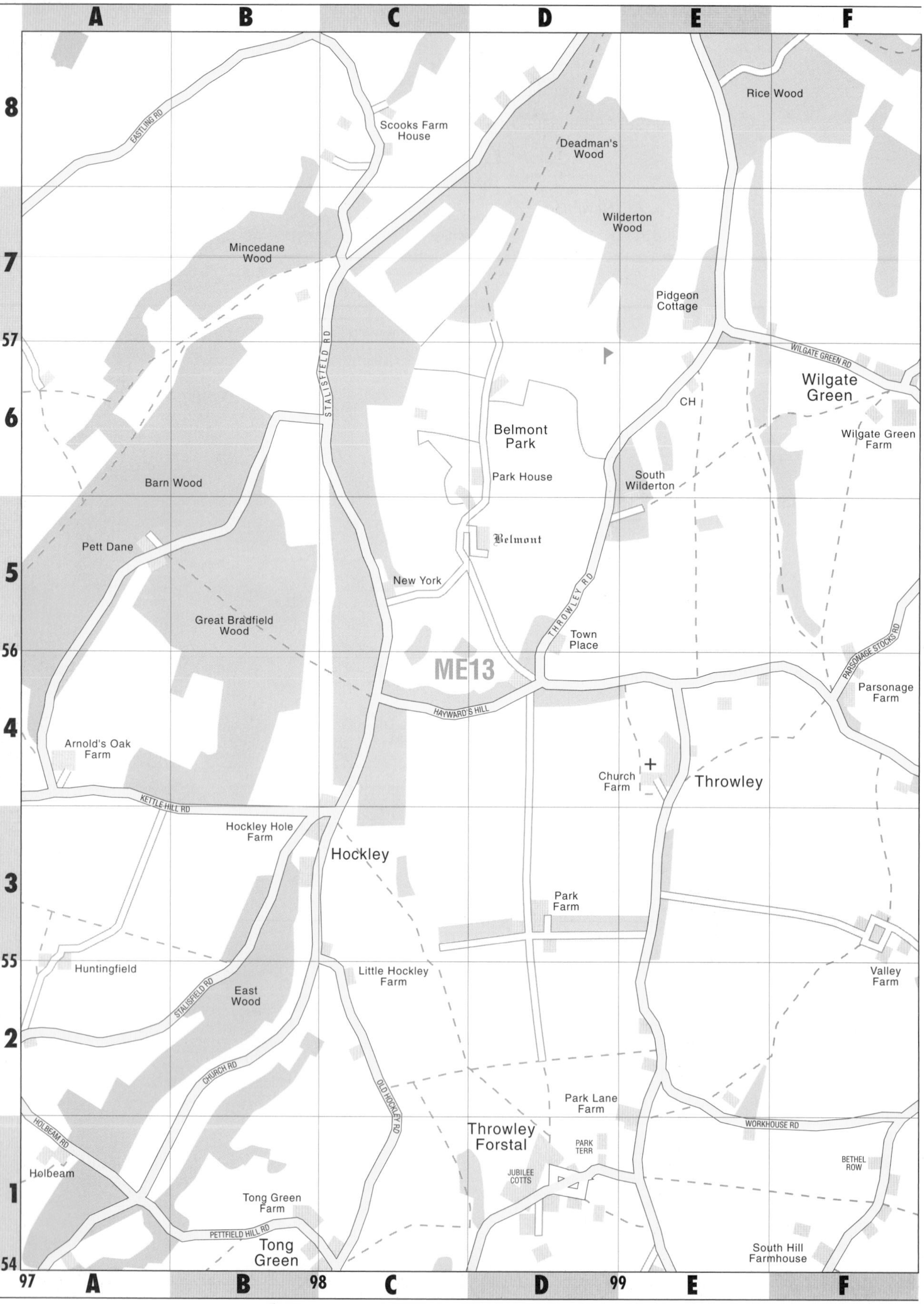

A | B | C | D | E | F

8

Rice Wood

Scooks Farm House

Deadman's Wood

Mincedane Wood

Wilderton Wood

7

Pidgeon Cottage

57

Wilgate Green Rd

CH

Wilgate Green

6

STALISFIELD RD

Belmont Park

Wilgate Green Farm

Barn Wood

Park House

South Wilderton

Pett Dane

Belmont

5

New York

THROWLEY RD

Great Bradfield Wood

56

Town Place

ME13

PARSONAGE STOCKS RD

HAYWARD'S HILL

Parsonage Farm

4

Arnold's Oak Farm

Church Farm

Throwley

KETTLE HILL RD

Hockley Hole Farm

3

Hockley

Park Farm

55

Huntingfield

STALISFIELD RD

Little Hockley Farm

Valley Farm

East Wood

2

CHURCH RD

OLD HOCKLEY RD

Park Lane Farm

WORKHOUSE RD

HOLBEAM RD

Throwley Forstal

PARK TERR

BETHEL ROW

Holbeam

JUBILEE COTTS

1

Tong Green Farm

PETTFIELD HILL RD

Tong Green

South Hill Farmhouse

54

81
104

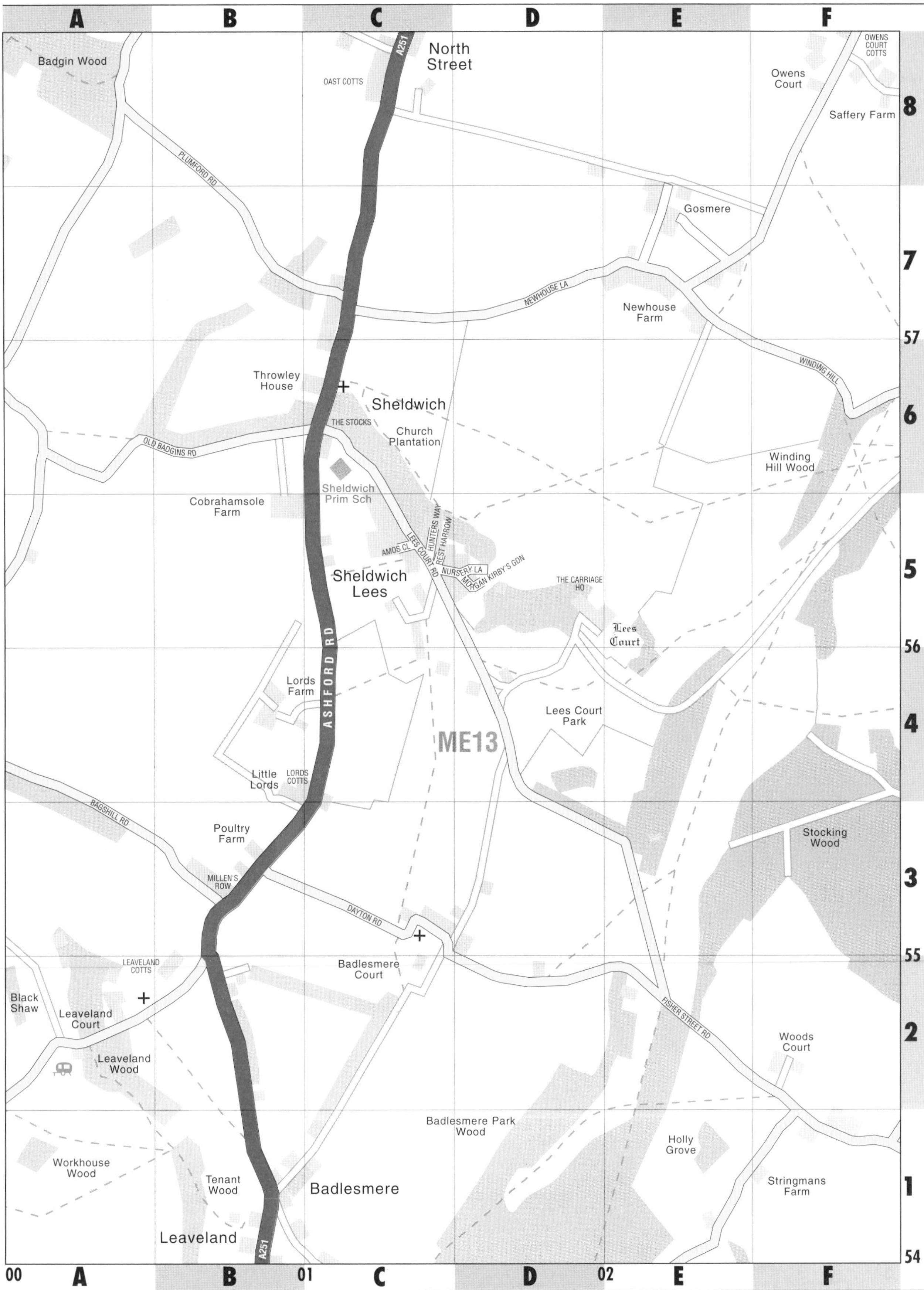

A B C D E F

North
Street

Badgin Wood

OAST COTTS

OWENS
COURT
COTTS

Owens
Court

8

Saffery Farm

PLUMFORD RD

Gosmere

NEWHOUSE LA

7

Newhouse
Farm

57

WINDING HILL

Throwley
House

Sheldwich

6

THE STOCKS

Church
Plantation

Winding
Hill Wood

OLD BADGINS RD

Sheldwich
Prim Sch

Cobrahamsole
Farm

HUNTERS WAY

LEES COURT RD

REST HARROW

AMOS CL

NURSERY LA

MORGAN KIRBY'S GDN

THE CARRIAGE
HO

5

Sheldwich
Lees

ASHFORD RD

Lees
Court

Lords
Farm

56

Lees Court
Park

ME13

4

Little
Lords

LORDS
COTTS

BAGSHILL RD

Poultry
Farm

Stocking
Wood

3

MILLEN'S
ROW

DAYTON RD

LEAVELAND
COTTS

55

FISHER STREET RD

Badlesmere
Court

Black
Shaw

Leaveland
Court

Woods
Court

2

Leaveland
Wood

Workhouse
Wood

Badlesmere Park
Wood

Holly
Grove

Tenant
Wood

Badlesmere

Stringmans
Farm

1

Leaveland

A251

54

83
63

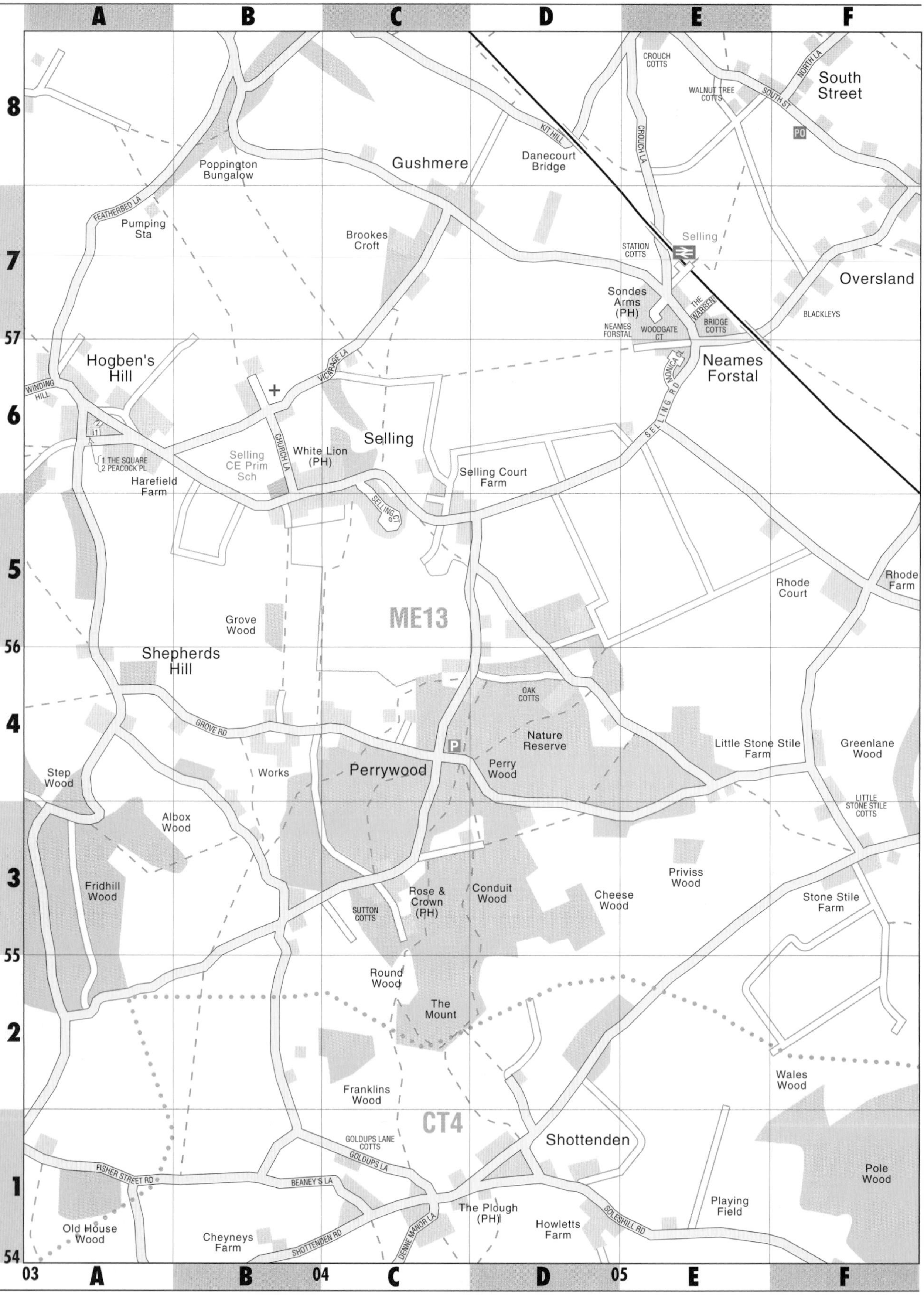

A   B   C   D   E   F

8

CROUCH COTTS

WALNUT TREE COTTS

South Street

NORTH LA

SOUTH ST

PO

Gushmere

KIT HILL

Danecourt Bridge

CROUCH LA

FEATHERBED LA

Poppington Bungalow

Pumping Sta

Brookes Croft

STATION COTTS

Selling

7

Sondes Arms (PH)

THE WARREN

Oversland

BLACKLEYS

VICARAGE LA

NEAMES FORSTAL

WOODGATE CT

BRIDGE COTTS

57

Hogben's Hill

WINDING HILL

Neames Forstal

SELLING RD

MONICA CT

6

1 THE SQUARE
2 PEACOCK PL

White Lion (PH)

Selling

CHURCH LA

Selling CE Prim Sch

Selling Court Farm

Harefield Farm

SELLING

Rhode Court

Rhode Farm

5

Grove Wood

ME13

56

Shepherds Hill

OAK COTTS

GROVE RD

4

Nature Reserve

Little Stone Stile Farm

Greenlane Wood

Step Wood

Works

Perrywood

Perry Wood

LITTLE STONE STILE COTTS

Albox Wood

3

Fridhill Wood

SUTTON COTTS

Rose & Crown (PH)

Conduit Wood

Cheese Wood

Priviss Wood

Stone Stile Farm

55

Round Wood

The Mount

2

Wales Wood

Franklins Wood

CT4

GOLDUPS LANE COTTS

GOLDUPS LA

Shottenden

Pole Wood

1

FISHER STREET RD

BEANEY'S LA

The Plough (PH)

Howletts Farm

SOLESHILL RD

Playing Field

Old House Wood

Cheyneys Farm

SHOTTENDEN RD

DENNE MANOR LA

54

03   A   B   04   C   D   05   E   F

83
106

64
86

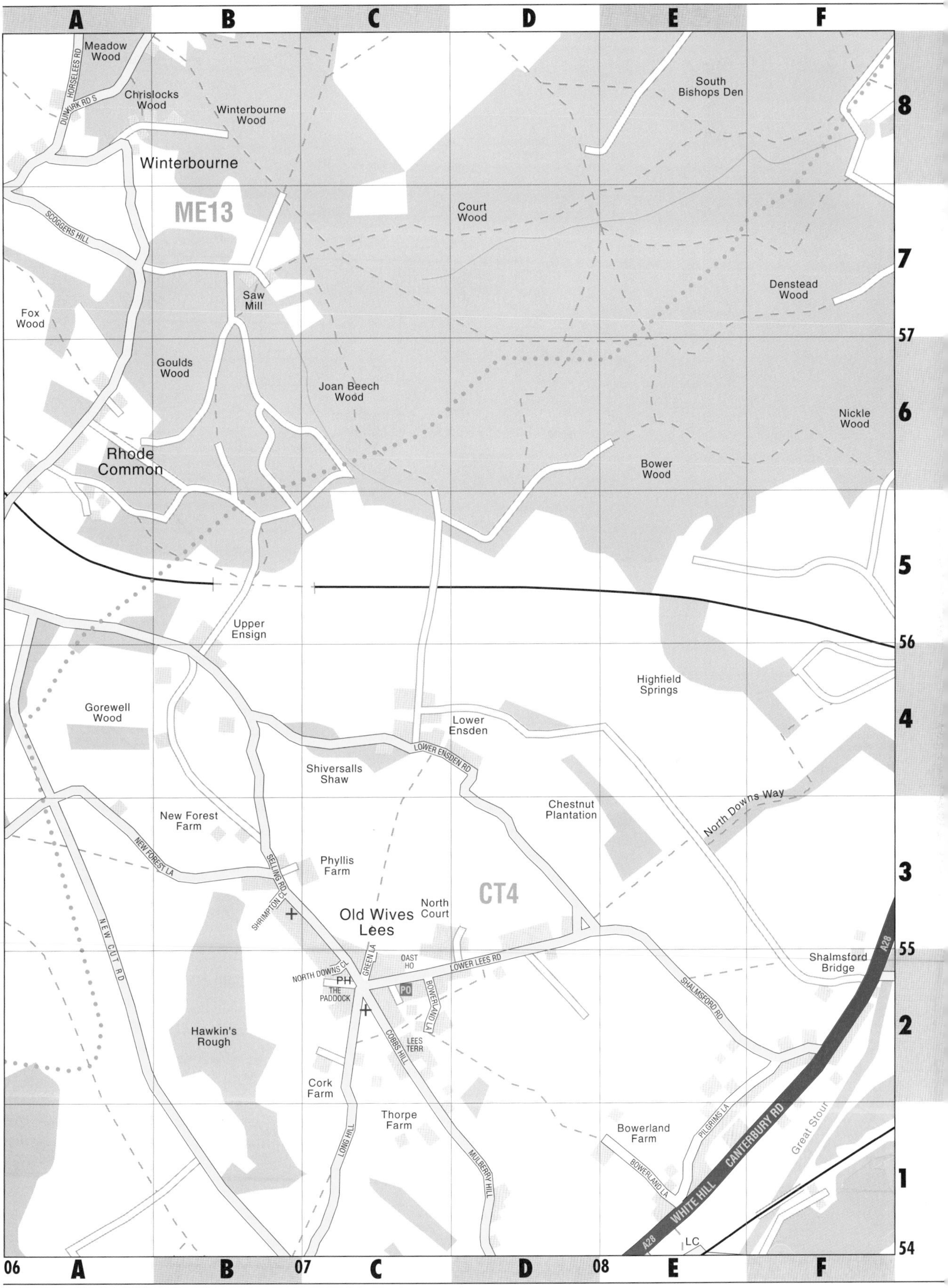
A
B
C
D
E
F
Meadow Wood
HORSELEES RD
DUNKIRK RD S
Chrislocks Wood
Winterbourne Wood
Winterbourne
South Bishops Den
ME13
SCOGGERS HILL
Court Wood
Saw Mill
Fox Wood
Denstead Wood
Goulds Wood
Joan Beech Wood
Nickle Wood
Rhode Common
Bower Wood
Upper Ensign
Highfield Springs
Gorewell Wood
Lower Ensden
LOWER ENSDEN RD
Shiversalls Shaw
Chestnut Plantation
North Downs Way
New Forest Farm
NEW FOREST LA
Phyllis Farm
SELLING RD
CT4
SHRIMPTON CL
North Court
Old Wives Lees
NEW CUT RD
GREEN LA
OAST HO
LOWER LEES RD
NORTH DOWNS CL
PH
THE PADDOCK
PO
BOWERLAND LA
SHALMSFORD RD
Shalmsford Bridge
A28
Hawkin's Rough
COBBS HILL
LEES TERR
Cork Farm
Thorpe Farm
Bowerland Farm
PILGRIMS LA
CANTERBURY RD
Great Stour
LONG HILL
MULBERRY HILL
BOWERLAND LA
WHITE HILL
A28
LC
8
7
57
6
5
56
4
3
55
2
1
54
06
07
08

107
86

A   B   C   D   E   F

ME13

8

7

57

6

56

5

4

56

CT4

3

55

2

1

54

09   A   B   10   C   D   11   E   F

Densted Cotts

Denstead Oast

Denstead Farm

DENSTEAD LA

Poldhurst Farm

A2050   A2

CT2

FAULKNER LA

Bigbury Camp

Howfield Wood

Bigbury House

Petty France

BIGBURY RD

Bigbury Wood

PRIMROSE HILL

North Downs Way

Bigberry Farm

Chartham Hatch

Howfield Wood Farm

Hunstead Wood

NIGHTINGALE CL

TOWN LA

The Royal Oak (PH)

NEW TOWN ST

HOWFIELD LA

Howfield Farm

Fright Wood

The Rough

Mast

Howfield LA

Langdane Wood

Works

Nickle Farm

HATCH LA

A28

Dunning Shaw

LC

NICKLE COTTS

Cemy

HORTON COTTS

HORTON GDNS

LC

Stour Valley Wlk

Sewage Works

Horton

ASHFORD RD

A28

Great Stour

RIVERSIDE

Deanery Farm

LC

STATION RD

LC

Chartham

1 APSLEY COTTS
2 DE L'ANGLE ROW
3 MILL TERR
4 DE L'ANGLE HO

THE GREEN

CHURCH LA

4 2

LC

3

STOUR CL

STOUR RD

Chartham

LC

PARISH RD

RIVER

Mill

OLD SCHOOL MEWS

THE HYDE

BOLTS HILL

RENTAIN RD

BABINGTON ST

COCKERING RD

The George (PH)

PO

ASHDOWN FIELD

PH

SHALMSFORD ST

BRUNDELL TERR

BOBBIN LODGE HILL

SHALMSFORD CT

ARNOLD RD

CREMER CL

BRICE AVE

HIGHLAND RD

WOODSIDE AVE

BAKER S LA

LAWSON CL

POMFRET HO

POMFRET RD

LARKEY VIEW

THRUXTED LA

Shalmsford Street

Chartham Prim Sch

Stour Valley Wlk

THE CRESCENT

PH

MYSTOLE LA

Chartham Downs

JASMINE CL

BEECH AVE

OLD GARDEN CT

LITTLE COPSE

OLD CHURCH RD

GARDENERS PL

UPDOWN WAY

CHESTNUT CL

LIME RD

ASPEN RD

LAUREL WAY

ALMOND

MAGNOLIA DR

THE DOWNS

SYCAMORE CL

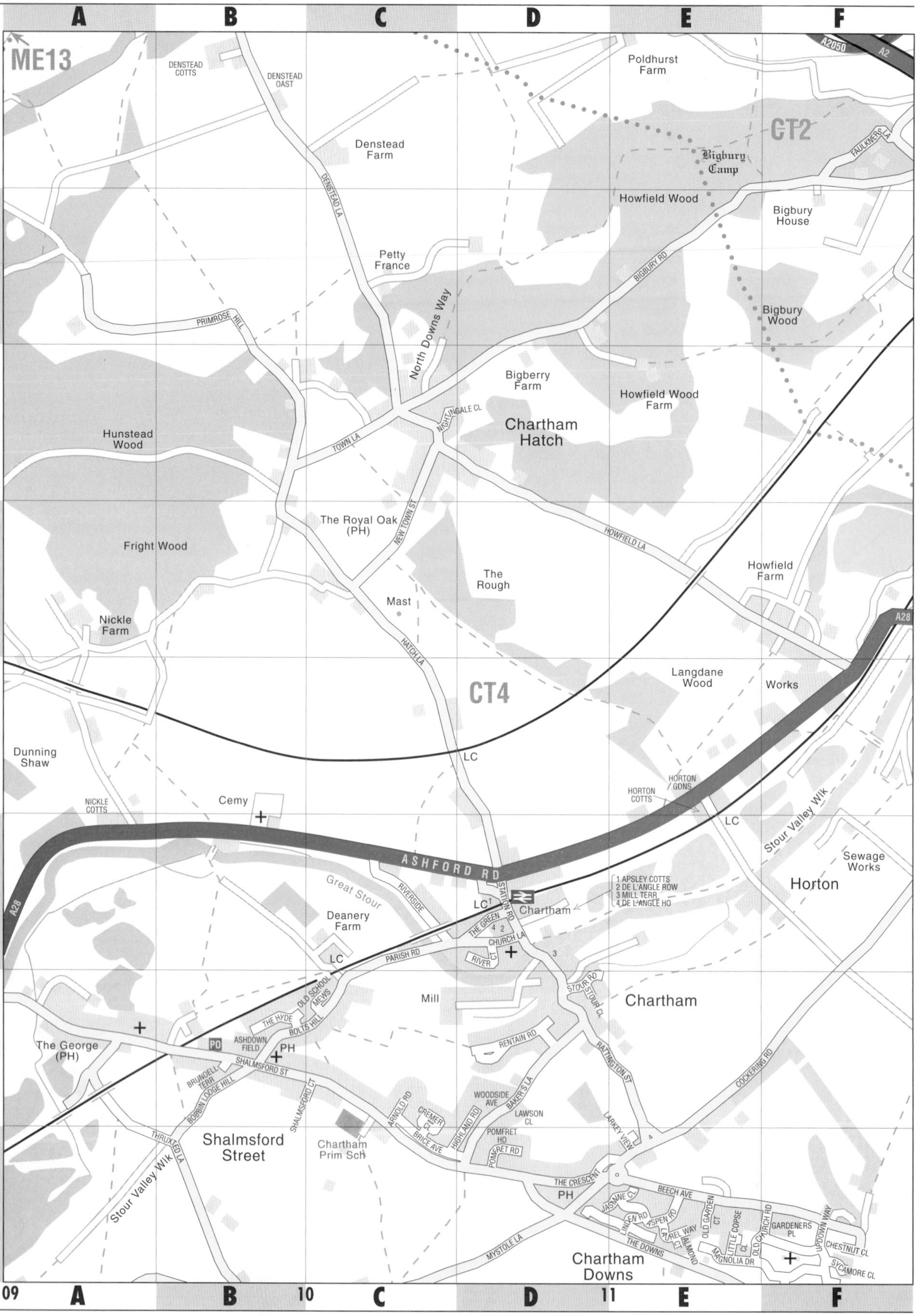

F7
1 DANE JOHN MEWS
2 WORTHGATE PL
3 DANE JOHN CT
4 WINCHEAP GN
5 CAREY HO
6 RUNCIE HO
7 COGGAN HO
8 RAMSEY HO
9 GREENFIELD COTTS
F8
1 TOWER WAY
2 ALL SAINTS LA

66

F8
3 TURNAGAIN LA
4 GUILDHALL ST
5 MERCERY LA
6 WHITE HORSE LA
7 STOUR CT
8 GREY FRIARS COTTS

88

F8
9 MAYNARD AND COTTON'S SPITAL
10 TEMPLE MEWS
11 MARLOWE ARC
12 GRAVEL WLK
13 MARLOWE CT
14 WILLOUGHBY CT
15 LULLINGSTONE CT
16 ROSEMARY LA
17 ST MARY'S CT
18 THE PRECINCTS

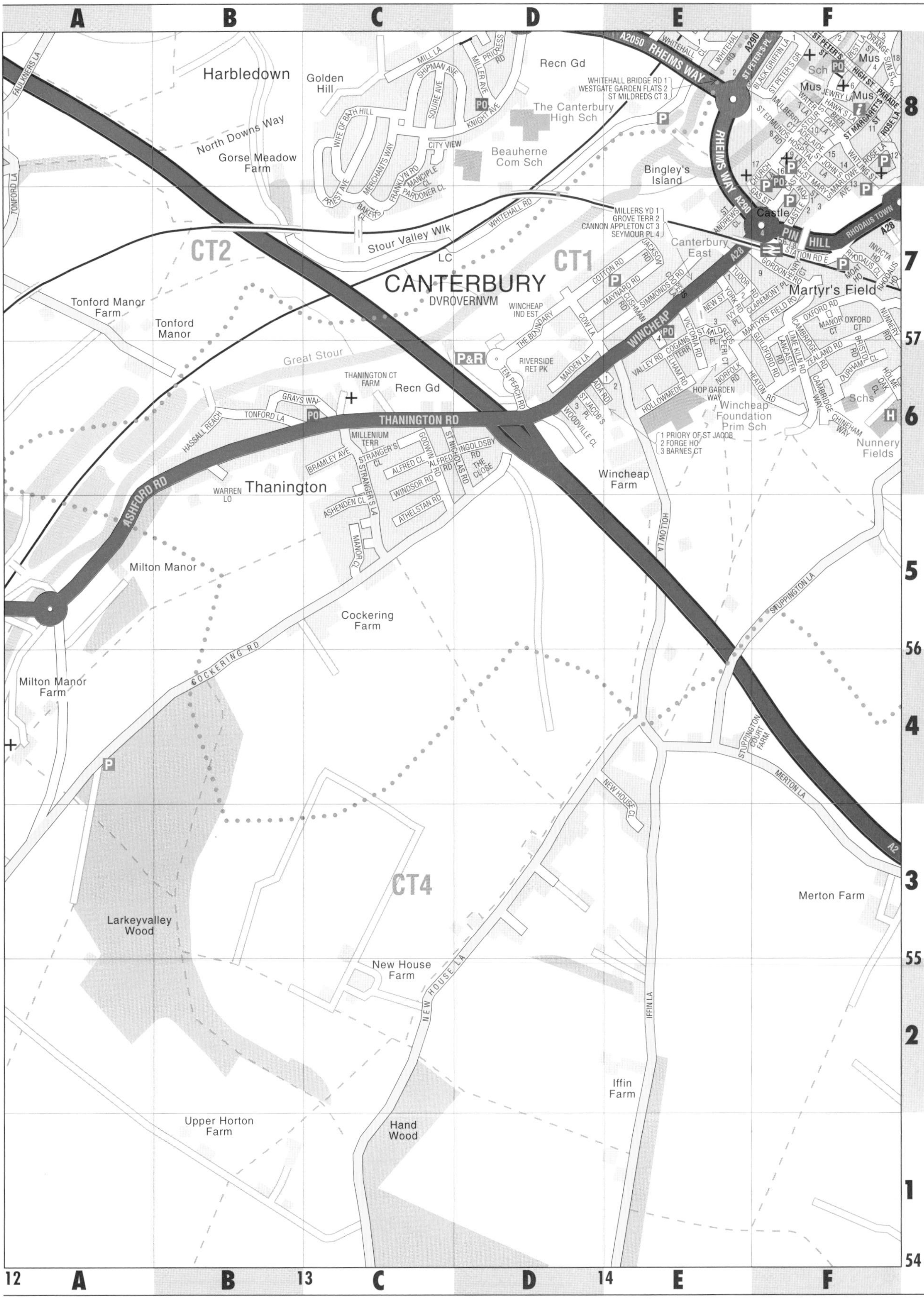

109
88

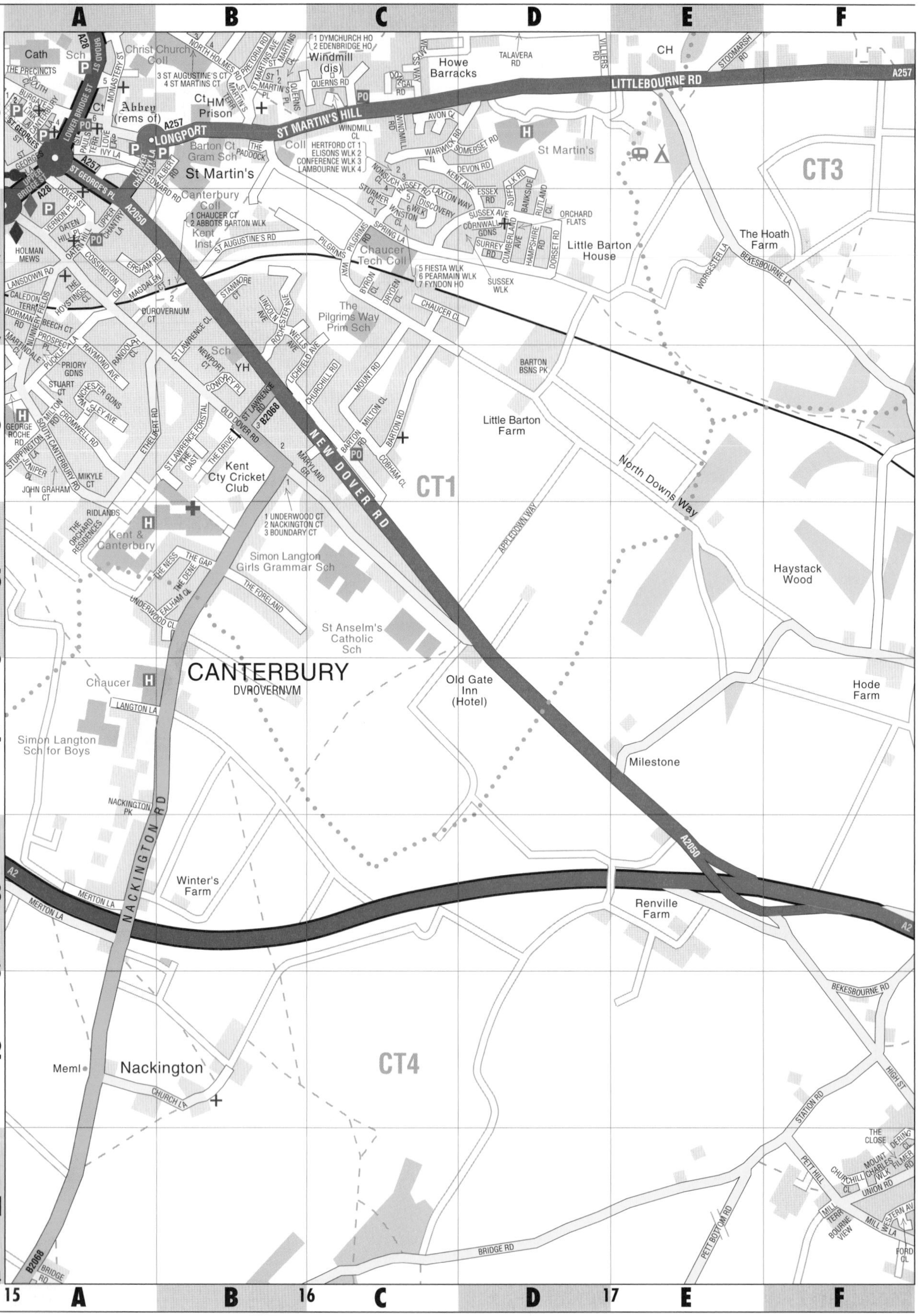

68
90

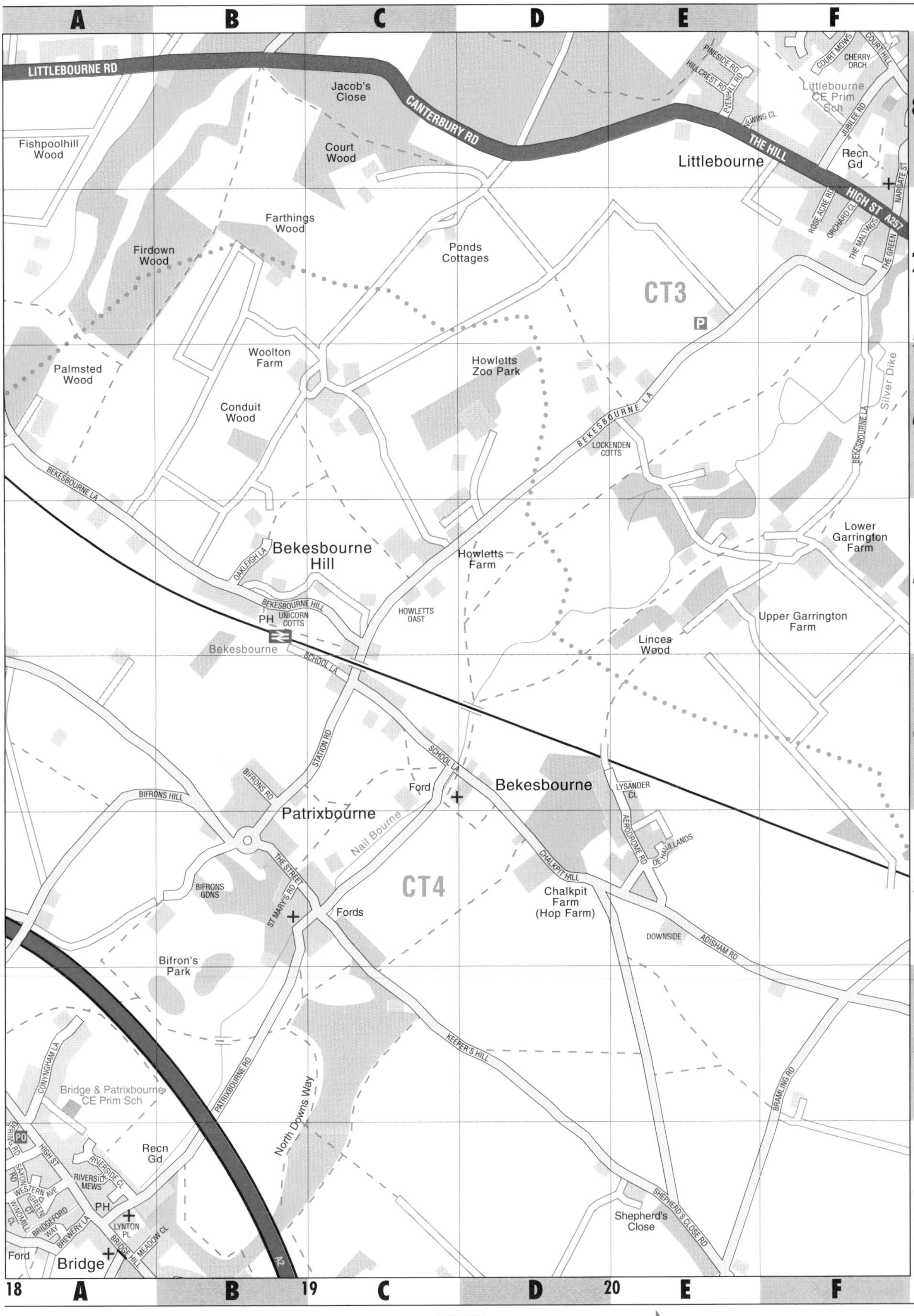
LITTLEBOURNE RD
Jacob's Close
CANTERBURY RD
Court Wood
Fishpoolhill Wood
Farthings Wood
Firdown Wood
Ponds Cottages
Littlebourne
Littlebourne CE Prim Sch
Recn Gd
THE HILL
HIGH ST
A257
CT3
Palmsted Wood
Woolton Farm
Conduit Wood
Howletts Zoo Park
BEKESBOURNE LA
LOCKENDEN COTTS
Silver Dike
Lower Garrington Farm
Bekesbourne Hill
Howletts Farm
HOWLETTS OAST
OAKLEIGH LA
BEKESBOURNE HILL
UNICORN COTTS
PH
Bekesbourne
SCHOOL LA
Upper Garrington Farm
Linces Wood
STATION RD
BIFRONS RD
BIFRONS HILL
Patrixbourne
Ford
Bekesbourne
LYSANDER CL
AERODROME RD
DE HAVILLANDS
Nail Bourne
CT4
CHALKPIT HILL
Chalkpit Farm (Hop Farm)
BIFRONS GDNS
THE STREET
ST MARY'S RD
Fords
DOWNSIDE
ADISHAM RD
Bifron's Park
KEEPER'S HILL
CONYNGHAM LA
PATRIXBOURNE RD
North Downs Way
Bridge & Patrixbourne CE Prim Sch
BRAMLING RD
Recn Gd
HIGH ST
RIVERSIDE CL
RIVERSIDE MEWS
WESTERN AVE
SAXON RD
SPRING RD
PO
GREEN CT
WINDMILL CL
BRIDGEFORD WAY
BREWERY LA
PH
LYNTON PL
MEADOW CL
BRIDGE HILL
Ford
Bridge
A2
SHEPHERD'S CLOSE RD
Shepherd's Close
A B C D E F
8 7 57 6 5 56 4 3 55 2 1 54
18 19 20

111
90

← 89   69 ↑

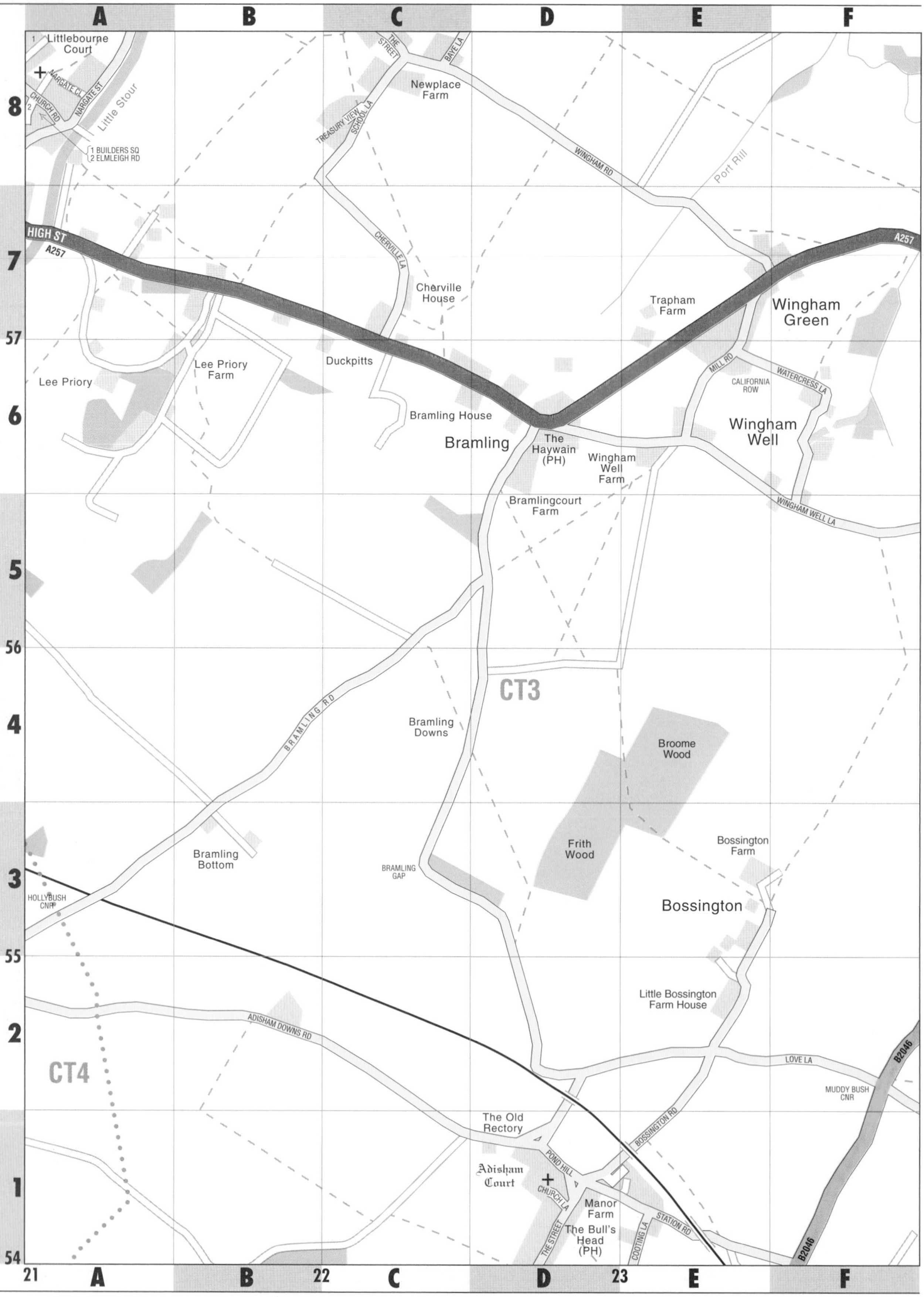

A   B   C   D   E   F

8

Littlebourne
Court

MARGATE CL
NARGATE ST
CHURCH RD
Little Stour

1 BUILDERS SQ
2 ELMLEIGH RD

THE STREET
BAKE LA
Newplace
Farm

TREASURY VIEW
SCHOOL LA

WINGHAM RD

Port Rill

7

HIGH ST
A257

A257

CHERVILLE LA

Charville
House

Trapham
Farm

Wingham
Green

57

Lee Priory

Lee Priory
Farm

Duckpitts

MILL RD

CALIFORNIA
ROW

WATERCRESS LA

6

Bramling House

Bramling

The
Haywain
(PH)

Wingham
Well
Farm

Wingham
Well

WINGHAM WELL LA

Bramlingcourt
Farm

5

CT3

56

Bramling Downs

BRAMLING RD

4

Broome
Wood

Bossington
Farm

Frith
Wood

Bramling
Bottom

3

HOLLYBUSH
CNR

BRAMLING
GAP

Bossington

55

Little Bossington
Farm House

2

ADISHAM DOWNS RD

LOVE LA

B2046

CT4

MUDDY BUSH
CNR

The Old
Rectory

BOSSINGTON RD

1

Adisham
Court

POND HILL
CHURCH LA

Manor
Farm

STATION RD

The Bull's
Head
(PH)

THE STREET

COOTING LA

B2046

54

21   A   B   22   C   D   23   E   F

70
92

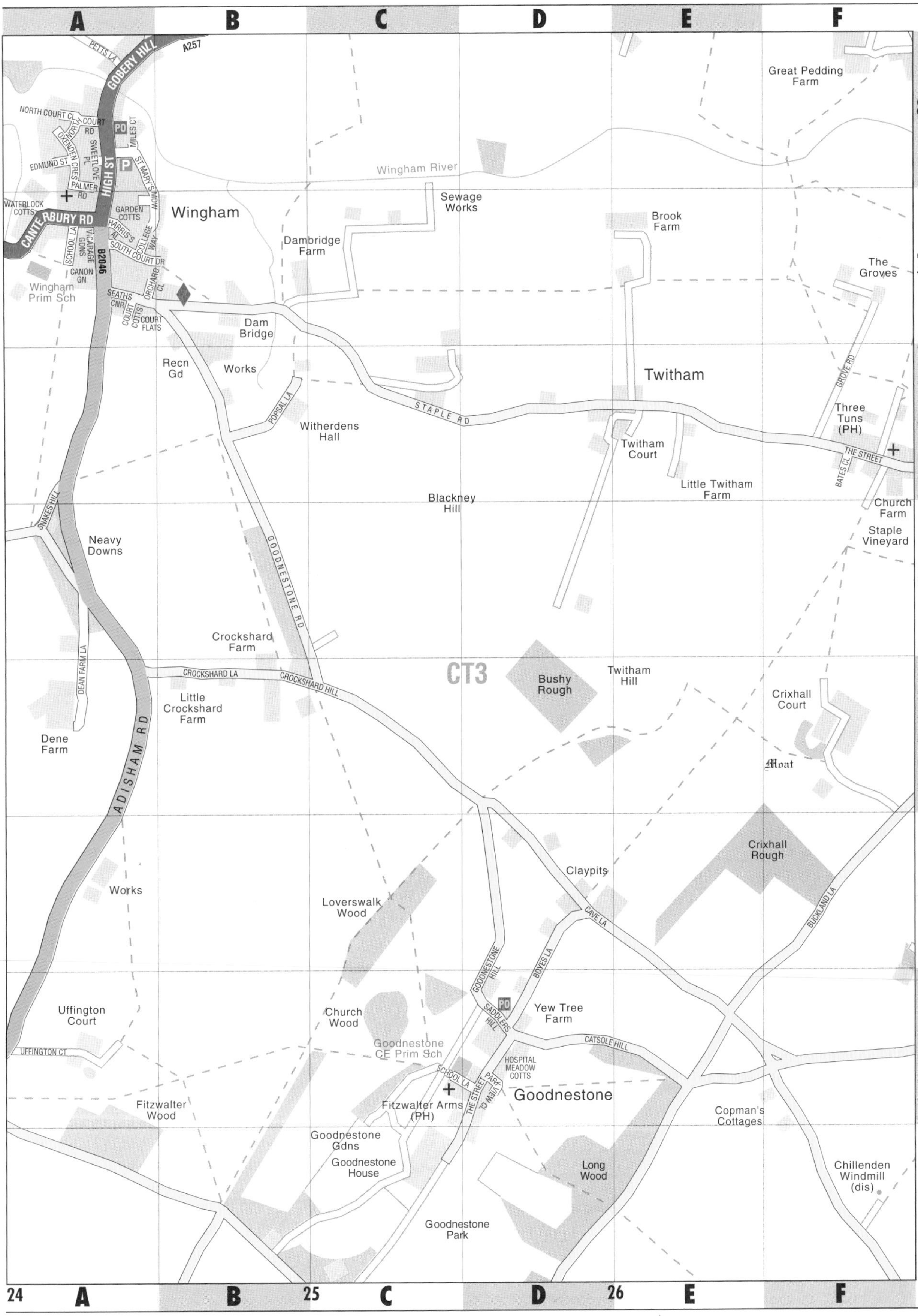
A
B
C
D
E
F
8
7
57
6
5
56
4
3
55
2
1
54
24
25
26
Great Pedding Farm
GOBERY HILL
A257
PETTS LA
NORTH COURT CL
NORTH COURT RD
OXENDEN CRES
SWEETLOVE PL
MILES CT
EDMUND ST
HIGH ST
ST MARY'S MDW
PALMER RD
WATERLOCK COTTS
CANTERBURY RD
GARDEN COTTS
Wingham
Wingham River
Sewage Works
Brook Farm
Dambridge Farm
SCHOOL LA
VICARAGE GDNS
HARRIS'S AL
COLLEGE WAY
SOUTH COURT DR
B2046
CANON GN
ORCHARD CL
The Groves
Wingham Prim Sch
SEATHS CNR
COURT COTTS
COURT FLATS
Dam Bridge
Recn Gd
Works
Twitham
GROVE RD
POPSAL LA
Witherdens Hall
STAPLE RD
Three Tuns (PH)
Twitham Court
THE STREET
BATES CL
Little Twitham Farm
Church Farm
Blackney Hill
SNAKES HILL
Neavy Downs
GOODNESTONE RD
Staple Vineyard
Crockshard Farm
CT3
Bushy Rough
Twitham Hill
CROCKSHARD LA
CROCKSHARD HILL
DEAN FARM LA
Little Crockshard Farm
Crixhall Court
Dene Farm
Moat
ADISHAM RD
Crixhall Rough
Claypits
Works
Loverswalk Wood
CAVE LA
BUCKLAND LA
GOODNESTONE HILL
BOYES LA
Uffington Court
Church Wood
SADDLERS HILL
Yew Tree Farm
CATSOLE HILL
UFFINGTON CT
Goodnestone CE Prim Sch
HOSPITAL MEADOW COTTS
SCHOOL LA
THE STREET
PARK VIEW CL
Fitzwalter Wood
Fitzwalter Arms (PH)
Goodnestone
Copman's Cottages
Goodnestone Gdns
Goodnestone House
Long Wood
Chillenden Windmill (dis)
Goodnestone Park

113
92

A　B　C　D　E　F

8

Nursery

Durlock

Durlock Bridge

Poulton Farm

POULTON LA

Ash Coombe Vineyard

Coombe

COOMBE LA

NEW ST

Coombe Farm

7

DURLOCK RD

The Rookery

Ringleton Manor

Radar Sta

57

Staple Farm

Nurseries

1 2
3

1 THE OAST
2 THE OAST PADDOCK
3 THE COURTYARD

Chapel Farm

Little Flemings Farm

FLEMING RD

Black Pond Farm

Christian Court

6

SCHOOL LA

FINN CL

LOWER RD

CHAPEL LA

Flemings

Ringlemere Farm

DRAINLESS RD

Nurseries

Mill Road Farm

Fernleigh

Barnsole

THE STREET

Staple

BARNSOLE RD

PH

Gander Court

Flemings House

Mushroom Farm

Onionbeds

MILL RD

5

Chalk Farm Lodge

CHALK PIT LA

Nurseries

Summerfield Farm

Summerfield Farm Pottery

CT13

Hammill Court

Denne Court Farm

56

BUCKLAND LA

CT3

Summerfield

Dix's Farm

The Hammill Brick Works

4

Hammill

Hammill Farm

3

Green La

GREEN LA

55

Lower Rowling Farm

Great Tickenhurst Farm

Rowling House

Upper Rowling Farm

MEADOW COTTS

Rowling Court

2

Tickenhurst

Little Tickenhurst Farm

Middle Heronden Farm

1

Heronden

HERONDEN RD

THORNTON LA

Tickenhurst Shave

Heronden Farm

54

27　A　B　28　C　D　29　E　F

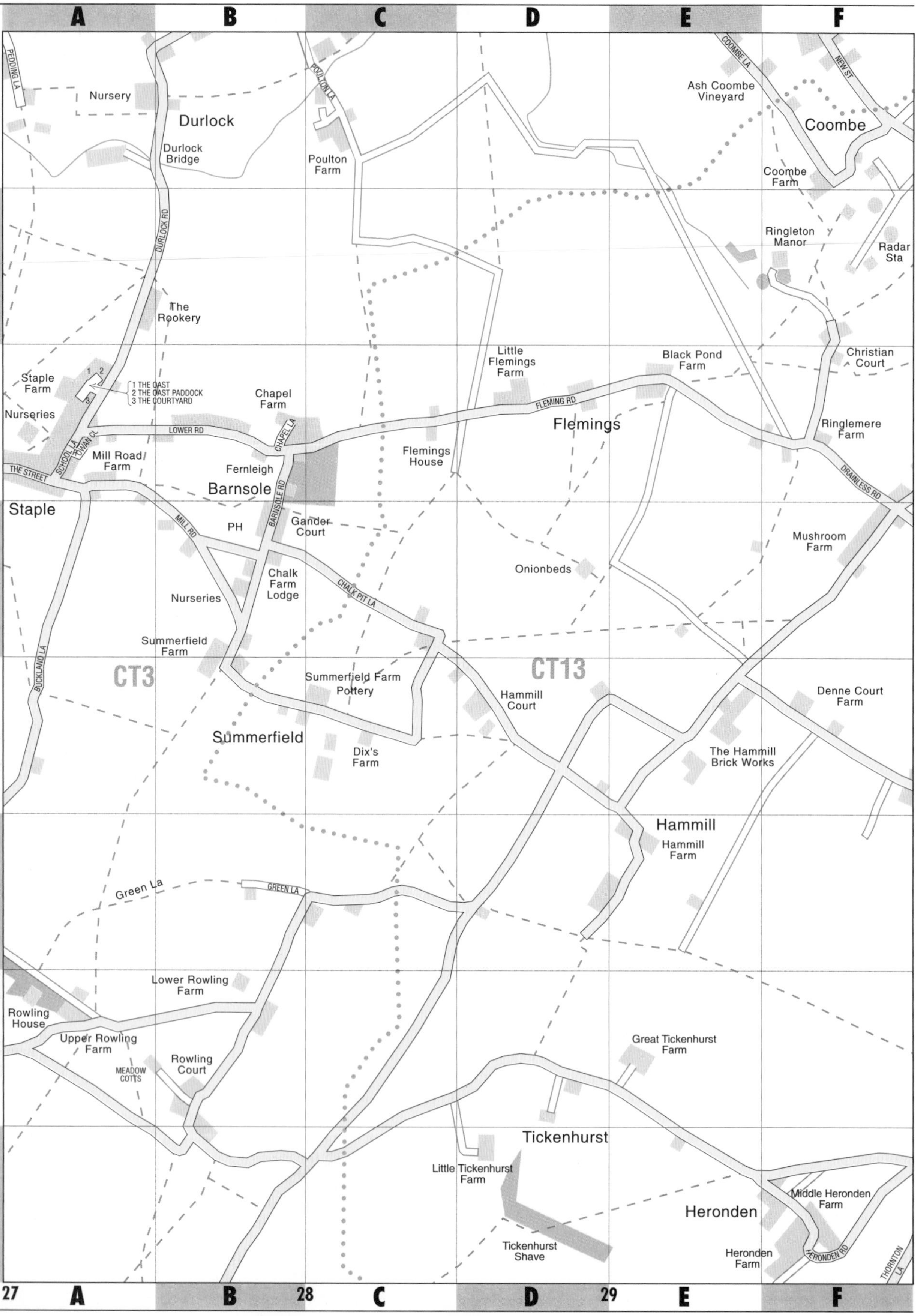

72
94

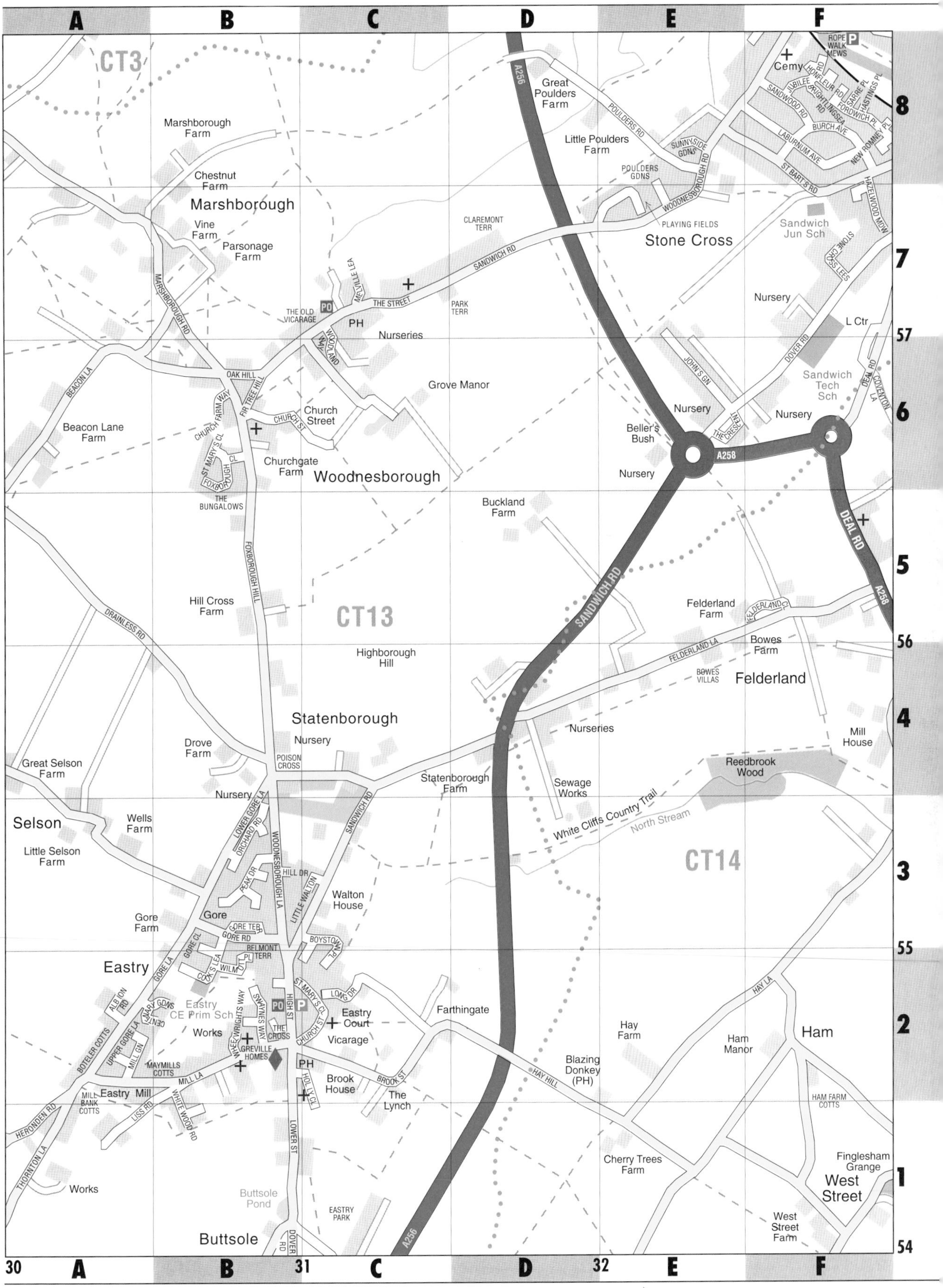
A
B
C
D
E
F
CT3
Marshborough Farm
Chestnut Farm
Marshborough
Vine Farm
Parsonage Farm
MARSHBOROUGH RD
BEACON LA
Beacon Lane Farm
OAK HILL
FIR TREE HILL
CHURCH FARM WAY
ST MARY'S CL
FOXBOROUGH CL
THE BUNGALOWS
CHURCH ST
Church Street
Churchgate Farm
Woodnesborough
THE OLD VICARAGE
PO
PH
WOODLAND WAY
MELVILLE LEA
THE STREET
Nurseries
Grove Manor
PARK TERR
CLAREMONT TERR
SANDWICH RD
A256
Great Poulders Farm
Little Poulders Farm
POULDERS RD
POULDERS GDNS
SUNNYSIDE GDNS
WOODNESBOROUGH RD
PLAYING FIELDS
Stone Cross
Cemy
ROPE WALK MEWS
P
HONFLEUR RD
JUBILEE RD
SANDWOOD RD
BRIGHTLINGSEA RD
SARRE PL
HASTINGS PL
FORDWICH PL
BURCH AVE
LABURNUM AVE
NEW ROMNEY PL
ST BART'S RD
HAZELWOOD MDW
Sandwich Jun Sch
STONE CROSS LEES
Nursery
L Ctr
DOVER RD
Sandwich Tech Sch
DEAL RD
COVERTON LA
JOHN'S GN
THE CRESCENT
Nursery
Beller's Bush
A258
Nursery
Buckland Farm
DEAL RD
A258
FOXBOROUGH HILL
Hill Cross Farm
DRAINLESS RD
CT13
Highborough Hill
SANDWICH RD
Felderland Farm
FELDERLAND CL
FELDERLAND LA
Bowes Farm
BOWES VILLAS
Felderland
Statenborough
Nursery
Drove Farm
Great Selson Farm
POISON CROSS
Nursery
Statenborough Farm
Nurseries
Sewage Works
Mill House
Reedbrook Wood
White Cliffs Country Trail
North Stream
Selson
Wells Farm
Little Selson Farm
LOWER GORE LA
ORCHARD RD
WOODNESBOROUGH LA
SANDWICH RD
HILL DR
PEAK DR
LITTLE WALTON
Walton House
CT14
Gore Farm
Gore
GORE TER
GORE RD
BOYSTOWN PL
BELMONT TERR
GORE CL
GORE LA
COOKS LEA
WILMOTT PL
Eastry
ALBION RD
Eastry CE Prim Sch
ST MARY'S GDNS
CENTRE
UPPER GORE LA
MILL GN
BOTELER COTTS
WRIGHTS WAY
WHEELWRIGHTS WAY
SWAYNES WAY
HIGH ST
THE CROSS
ST MARY'S CL
CHURCH ST
LONG DR
Eastry Court
Vicarage
Farthingate
HAY LA
Ham
Hay Farm
Ham Manor
Works
GREVILLE HOMES
MAYMILLS COTTS
MILL LA
PH
HOLLY CL
Brook House
BROOK ST
The Lynch
HAY HILL
Blazing Donkey (PH)
HAM FARM COTTS
MILL BANK COTTS
Eastry Mill
LISS RD
WHITE WOOD RD
HERONDEN RD
THORNTON LA
LOWER ST
Works
Buttsole Pond
EASTRY PARK
Cherry Trees Farm
Finglesham Grange
West Street
West Street Farm
Buttsole
DOVER RD
A256
8
7
57
6
5
56
4
3
55
2
1
54
30
31
32

115
94

A B C D E F

8

WHITE ROSS ROW
NEW ST
MILL WALL
WIGHTRIDER ST
WELLESLEY TERR
ST GEORGE'S LEES
MANWOOD RD
ST GEORGES PL
1 GALLIARD ST
2 BARNESENDE CT
ST GEORGE'S RD
St George's Lees
Sir Roger Manwood's Sch
Little Sandown Farm
Sandown Rd
Sandown Rd
Vigo Sprong
Old Haven
Toll
Guilford Rd
Newcut Bridge
HYTHE END
DELFSIDE
LC
ST ANDREW'S
Sandwich
CT13
Old Downs Farm
Sandwich Bay Bird Obsy
KING'S AVE
ST BART'S RD
DEAL RD
FOSTER'S CT
DOVER RD
St Bartholomew's Hospl
WALDERSHARE AVE
Toll

7
Delf Nursery

57
Little Downs Bridge

6
The Delf
Temptye Farmhouse
Little Temptye
LC
Blue Pigeons
Isle of Dogs
COVENTON LA
GORE TOP LA
Brewer's Bridge
North Stream

5
Links Farm
Worth Hill
St Crispin (PH)
Worth Prim Sch
MINNIS WAY
Minnis Farm
Great Wood
Pinnock Wall
White Cliffs Country Trail

56
DEAL RD
A258
THE STREET
CHURCH VIEW
Worth
CEIL VILLAS

4
MILL LA
CHESTNUT DR
TEMPLE WAY
Upton House
JUBILEE RD
JUBILEE COTTS
Cornfield Wood
Worth Minnis
Roaring Gutter

3
MILL LA
KING GEORGE VILLAS
Greenacres Bungalow
CT14
Lydden Valley
Old North Stream
Roaring Gutter Dike
Ring Sewer

55
Ham Brooks Wood
Ring Wall

2
HACKLINGE HILL
Hacklinge Farm
Hacklinge

1
WEST STREET COTTS
West Street
Westhill House
Mercer's Farm
South Stream
Brook Stream
A258
The Coach House (PH)
Foulmead Farm
Spoil Heap

54
33 A B 34 C D 35 E F

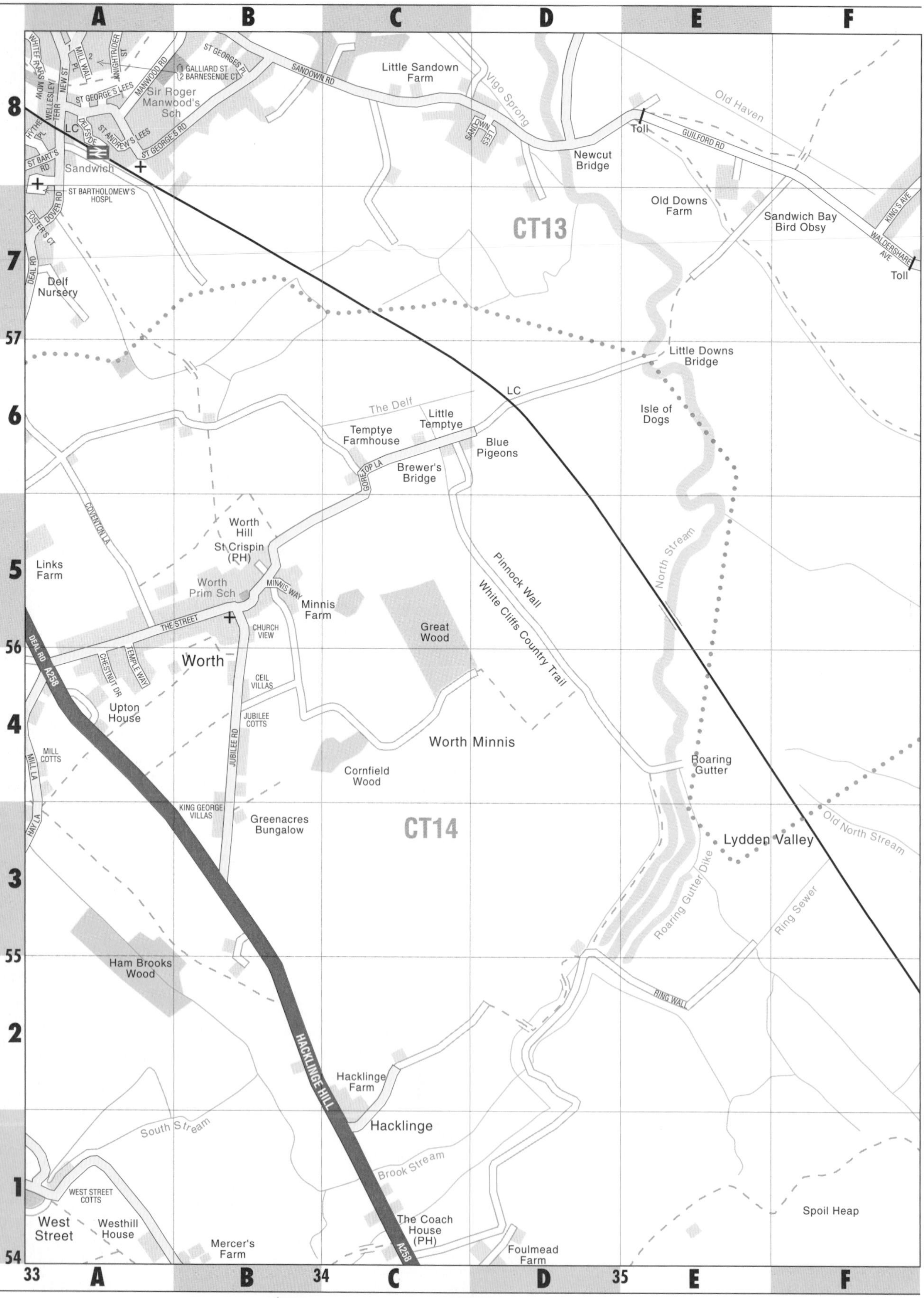

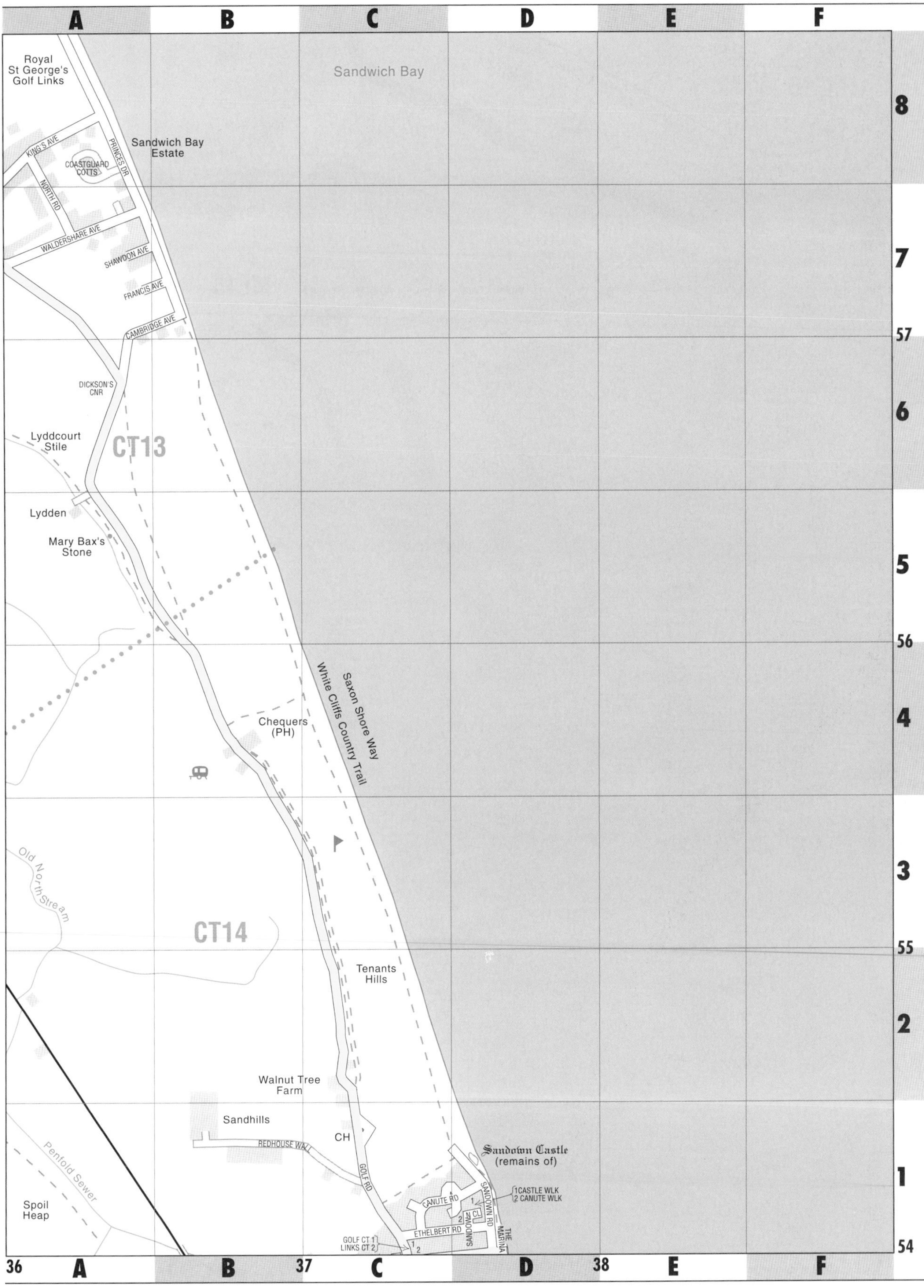

Sandwich Bay

Royal St George's Golf Links

Sandwich Bay Estate

KING'S AVE
COASTGUARD COTTS
PRINCES DR
NORTH RD
WALDERSHARE AVE
SHAWDON AVE
FRANCIS AVE
CAMBRIDGE AVE

DICKSON'S CNR

CT13

Lyddcourt Stile

Lydden

Mary Bax's Stone

CT14

Old North Stream

Chequers (PH)

Saxon Shore Way
White Cliffs Country Trail

Tenants Hills

Walnut Tree Farm

Sandhills

REDHOUSE WALK

CH

GOLF RD

Sandown Castle
(remains of)

1 CASTLE WLK
2 CANUTE WLK

CANUTE RD
SANDOWN
CLI
SANDOWN RD
THE MARINA
ETHELBERT RD

GOLF CT 1
LINKS CT 2
1
2

Penfold Sewer

Spoil Heap

8 7 57 6 5 56 4 3 55 2 1 54

36 A B 37 C 38 E F

74

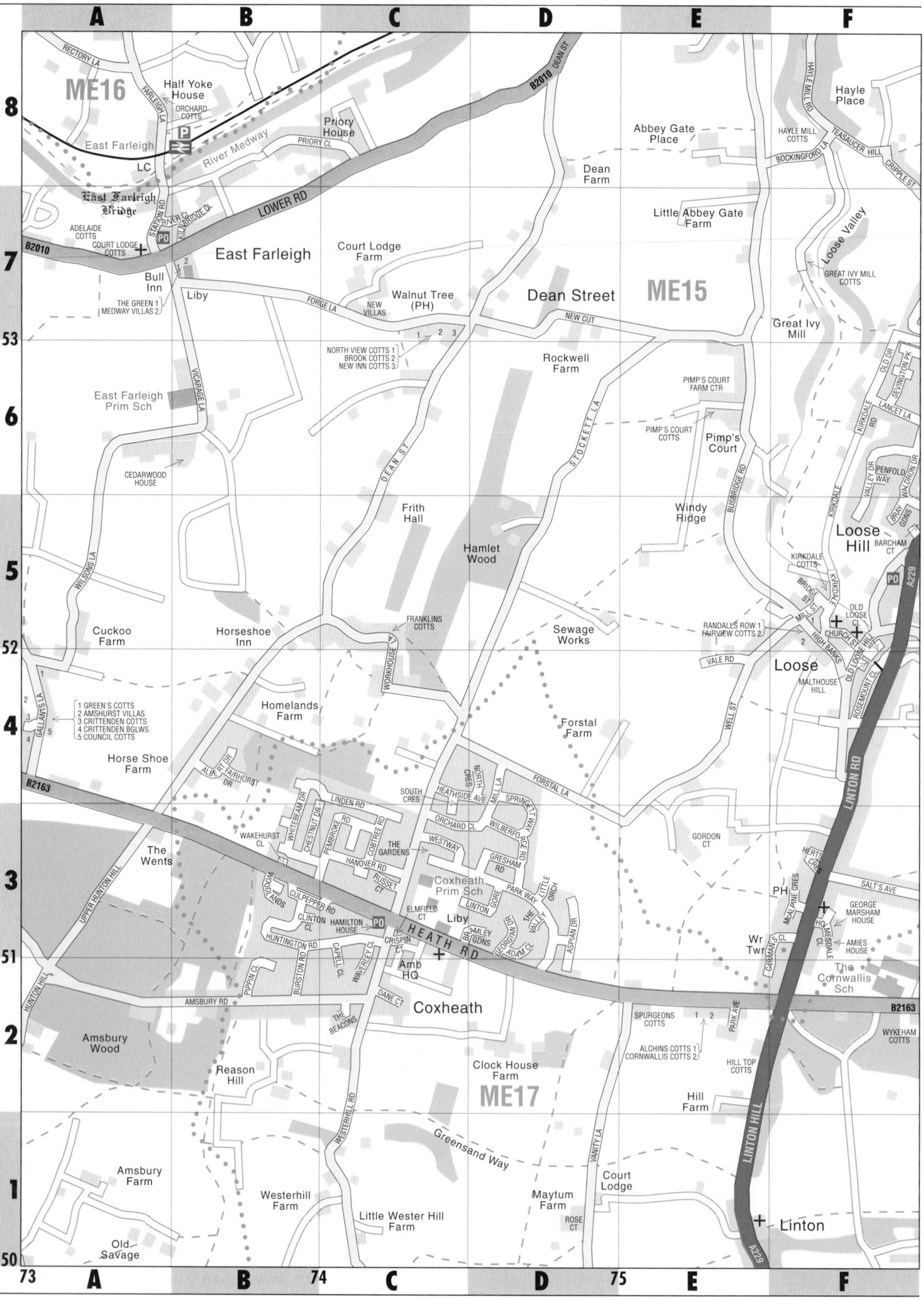
A
B
C
D
E
F
8
7
53
6
5
52
4
3
51
2
1
50
73
74
75
RECTORY LA
ME16
Half Yoke House
FARLEIGH LA
ORCHARD COTTS
Priory House
PRIORY CL
East Farleigh
River Medway
LC
B2010
DEAN ST
LOWER RD
East Farleigh Bridge
STATION RD
KILNBRIDGE CL
ADELAIDE COTTS
COURT LODGE COTTS
PO
B2010
East Farleigh
Court Lodge Farm
Bull Inn
Liby
THE GREEN 1
MEDWAY VILLAS 2
FORGE LA
NEW VILLAS
Walnut Tree (PH)
NORTH VIEW COTTS 1
BROOK COTTS 2
NEW INN COTTS 3
Abbey Gate Place
Dean Farm
Little Abbey Gate Farm
Dean Street
ME15
NEW CUT
Rockwell Farm
HAYLE MILL RD
Hayle Place
HAYLE MILL COTTS
BOCKINGFORD LA
TEASAUCER HILL
CRIPPLE ST
Loose Valley
GREAT IVY MILL COTTS
Great Ivy Mill
East Farleigh Prim Sch
VICARAGE LA
CEDARWOOD HOUSE
DEAN ST
STOCKETT LA
PIMP'S COURT FARM CTR
PIMP'S COURT COTTS
Pimp's Court
OLD DR
SEVINGTON PK
LANCET LA
KIRKDALE RD
PENFOLD WAY
VALLEY DR
WALDRON DR
BRAY GDNS
KIRKDALE
Frith Hall
Hamlet Wood
Windy Ridge
BUSBRIDGE RD
Loose Hill
BARCHAM CT
KIRKDALE COTTS
WILSONS LA
Cuckoo Farm
Horseshoe Inn
FRANKLINS COTTS
Sewage Works
RANDALLS ROW 1
FAIRVIEW COTTS 2
MILL ST
BRIDGE ST
CHURCH ST
OLD LOOSE CL
OLD LOOSE HILL
HIGH BANKS
A229
PO
VALE RD
Loose
MALTHOUSE HILL
ROSEMOUNT CL
WORKHOUSE LA
GALLANTS LA
1 GREEN'S COTTS
2 AMSHURST VILLAS
3 CRITTENDEN COTTS
4 CRITTENDEN BGLWS
5 COUNCIL COTTS
Homelands Farm
Forstal Farm
WELL ST
Horse Shoe Farm
B2163
ALBERT DR
FAIRHURST DR
LINDEN RD
SOUTH CRES
HEATHSIDE AVE
NORTH CRES
MILL LA
SPRINGETT WAY
FORSTAL LA
LINTON RD
WHITEBEAM DR
CHESTNUT DR
PEMBROKE RD
COBTREE RD
ORCHARD CL
WILBERFORCE RD
GORDON CT
WAKEHURST CL
THE GARDENS
WESTWAY
GRESHAM RD
HANOVER RD
RUSSET CT
HERTS CRES
The Wents
UPPER HUNTON HILL
WOODLANDS
CULPEPPER RD
Coxheath Prim Sch
PARK WAY
LITTLE ORCH
SALT'S AVE
PH
GEORGE MARSHAM HOUSE
McALPINE CRES
ELMFIELD CT
LINTON GORE
CLINTON CL
HAMILTON HOUSE
PO
Liby
HEATH RD
BRAMLEY GDNS
GEORGIAN DR
ADAM CL
THE VALLEY
ASPIAN DR
HOLMESDALE CL
AMIES HOUSE
HUNTINGTON RD
CAPELL CL
WAVERLEY CL
CRISPIN CT
Amb HQ
Wr Twr
CARMANS CL
The Cornwallis Sch
HUNTON HILL
PIPPIN CL
BURSTON RD
AMSBURY RD
DANE CT
Coxheath
THE BEACONS
SPURGEONS COTTS
PARK AVE
B2163
Amsbury Wood
ALCHINS COTTS 1
CORNWALLIS COTTS 2
WYKEHAM COTTS
Reason Hill
Clock House Farm
HILL TOP COTTS
ME17
Hill Farm
WESTERHILL RD
Greensand Way
VANITY LA
LINTON HILL
Amsbury Farm
Westerhill Farm
Court Lodge
Maytum Farm
Little Wester Hill Farm
ROSE CT
Linton
A229
Old Savage

D7
1 ROCHESTER HOUSE
2 CANTERBURY HOUSE
3 CAMBRIDGE HOUSE
4 WINCHESTER HOUSE
5 SALISBURY HOUSE

D8
1 KENDALL PL
2 RAYLEIGH HO
3 LAVENDER HO
4 CLOVER TERR
5 SHERINGHAM HO
6 BURDOCK HO

E7
1 SHROPSHIRE TERR
2 HUNTINGDON WLK
3 DERWENT HO
4 WINDERMERE HO
5 ULLSWATER HO
6 DUNKELD HO

7
7 INVERNESS HO
8 GLASGOW HO
9 ABERDEEN HO
10 PRIMROSE HO
11 WISTERIA HO
12 LICHFIELD HO
13 CHAUCER CL

14 BELFAST HO
15 LONDONDERRY HO
16 DUBLIN HO

E8
1 CHILHAM HO
2 DOVER HO
3 DUNSTER TERR

E8
4 WILTSHIRE WAY

F6
1 AINTREE HOUSE
2 ASCOT HOUSE
3 CHEPSTOW HOUSE
4 FOLKSTONE CL
5 TITCHFIELD CL
6 THIRSK HOUSE

7 DONCASTER CL
8 HAVANT WLK
9 PLUMPTON WLK
10 FAREHAM WLK
11 DENSTEAD WLK
12 ANDOVER WLK
13 GROOMBRIDGE SQ

75   98   97

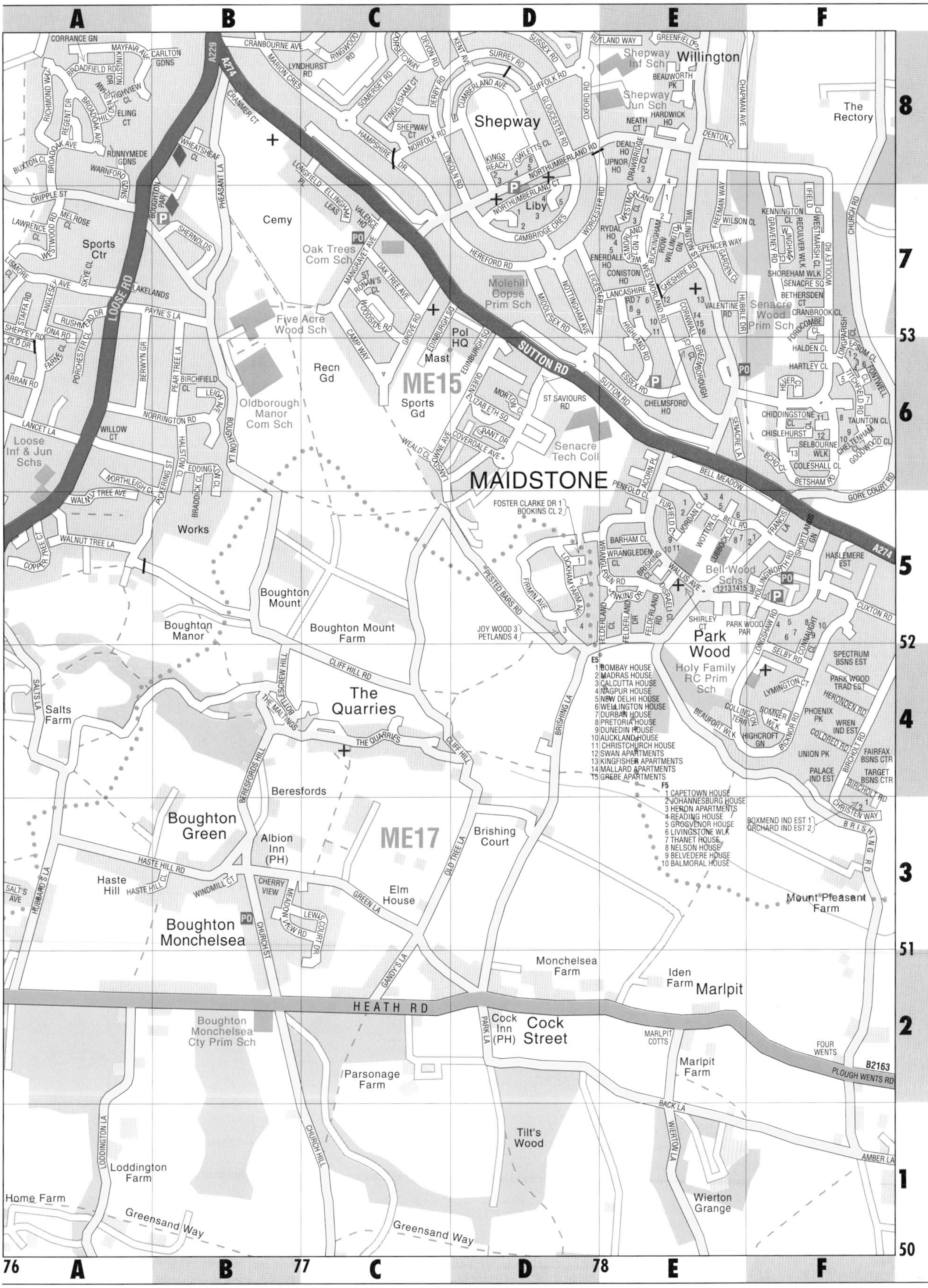

97
76

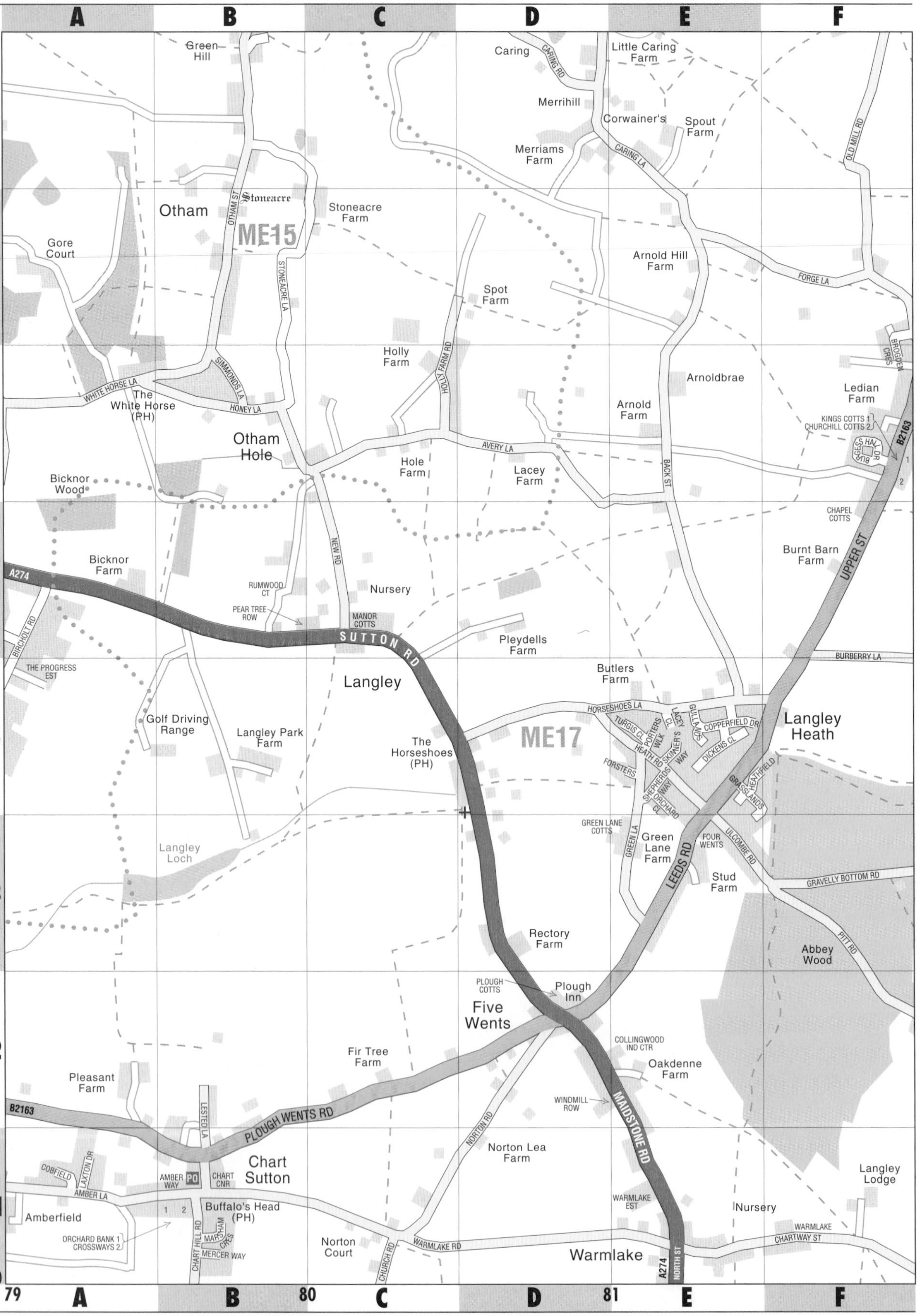
A B C D E F
8 7 53 6 5 52 4 3 51 2 1 50
79 80 81
Green Hill
Caring
Little Caring Farm
Merrihill
Corwainer's
Spout Farm
Merriams Farm
CARING RD
CARING LA
OLD MILL RD
Otham
OTHAM ST
Stoneacre
ME15
Stoneacre Farm
Gore Court
STONEACRE LA
Arnold Hill Farm
FORGE LA
Spot Farm
BROGDEN CRES
Holly Farm
HOLLY FARM RD
Arnoldbrae
Ledian Farm
WHITE HORSE LA
The White Horse (PH)
SIMMONDS LA
HONEY LA
Arnold Farm
KINGS COTTS 1
CHURCHILL COTTS 2
Otham Hole
AVERY LA
Hole Farm
Lacey Farm
BACK ST
BURGESS HALL DR
B2163
Bicknor Wood
CHAPEL COTTS
Bicknor Farm
NEW RD
Burnt Barn Farm
A274
RUMWOOD CT
Nursery
UPPER ST
PEAR TREE ROW
MANOR COTTS
SUTTON RD
Pleydells Farm
BIRCHOLT RD
BURBERRY LA
THE PROGRESS EST
Langley
Butlers Farm
HORSESHOES LA
Golf Driving Range
Langley Park Farm
ME17
Langley Heath
COPPERFIELD DR
DICKENS CL
TURGIS CL
PORTERS WLK
LACEY CL
GULLANDS
SKINNER'S WAY
HEATH RD
The Horseshoes (PH)
FORSTERS
HEATHFIELD
GRASSLANDS
SHEPHERDS WAY
ORCHARD CL
GREEN LANE COTTS
GREEN LA
Green Lane Farm
FOUR WENTS
ULCOMBE RD
Langley Loch
LEEDS RD
Stud Farm
GRAVELLY BOTTOM RD
Rectory Farm
PITT RD
Abbey Wood
PLOUGH COTTS
Plough Inn
Five Wents
COLLINGWOOD IND CTR
Fir Tree Farm
Oakdenne Farm
Pleasant Farm
WINDMILL ROW
MAIDSTONE RD
LESTED LA
B2163
PLOUGH WENTS RD
NORTON RD
Norton Lea Farm
COBFIELD
LAXTON DR
Chart Sutton
AMBER WAY
PO
CHART CNR
Langley Lodge
AMBER LA
Amberfield
1 2
Buffalo's Head (PH)
WARMLAKE EST
Nursery
ORCHARD BANK 1
CROSSWAYS 2
CHART HILL RD
MARSHAM CRES
MERCER WAY
Norton Court
CHURCH RD
WARMLAKE RD
Warmlake
WARMLAKE
CHARTWAY ST
A274
NORTH ST

97

77
100

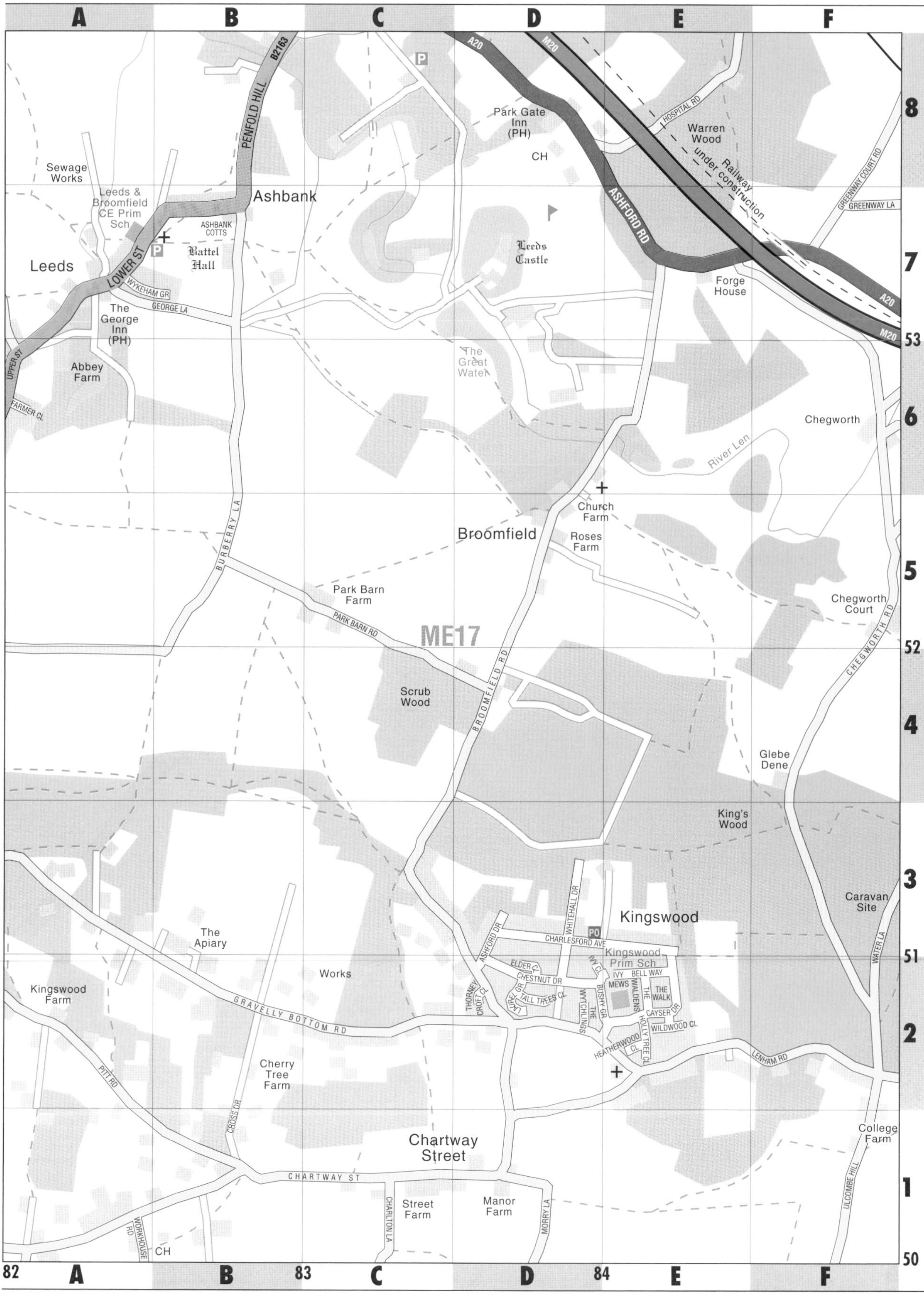
A
B
C
D
E
F
8
7
6
5
4
3
2
1
53
52
51
50
82
83
84
B2163
PENFOLD HILL
A20
M20
Park Gate
Inn
(PH)
CH
HOSPITAL RD
Warren
Wood
Railway
under construction
GREENWAY COURT RD
GREENWAY LA
Sewage
Works
Leeds &
Broomfield
CE Prim
Sch
Ashbank
ASHBANK
COTTS
Battel
Hall
Leeds
Castle
ASHFORD RD
Leeds
LOWER ST
WYKEHAM GR
GEORGE LA
The
George
Inn
(PH)
Forge
House
UPPER ST
Abbey
Farm
FARMER CL
The
Great
Water
Chegworth
River Len
Church
Farm
Broomfield
Roses
Farm
BURBERRY LA
Park Barn
Farm
PARK BARN RD
ME17
Chegworth
Court
CHEGWORTH RD
Scrub
Wood
BROOMFIELD RD
Glebe
Dene
King's
Wood
Caravan
Site
WHITEHALL DR
Kingswood
PO
ASHFORD DR
CHARLESFORD AVE
Kingswood
Prim Sch
The
Apiary
ELDER CL
IVY CL
IVY
MEWS
BELL WAY
CHESTNUT DR
THE
WALK
Works
WATER LA
Kingswood
Farm
LAUREL GR
TALL TREES CL
BUSHY GR
WALDENS
THE
THORNEY
CROFT CL
THE
WYTCHLINGS
CAYSER DR
GRAVELLY BOTTOM RD
HOLLY TREE CL
WILDWOOD CL
HEATHERWOOD
CL
PITT RD
LENHAM RD
Cherry
Tree
Farm
CROSS DR
Chartway
Street
College
Farm
CHARTWAY ST
ULCOMBE HILL
CHARLTON LA
Street
Farm
Manor
Farm
MORRY LA
WORKHOUSE
RD
CH

100

99
78

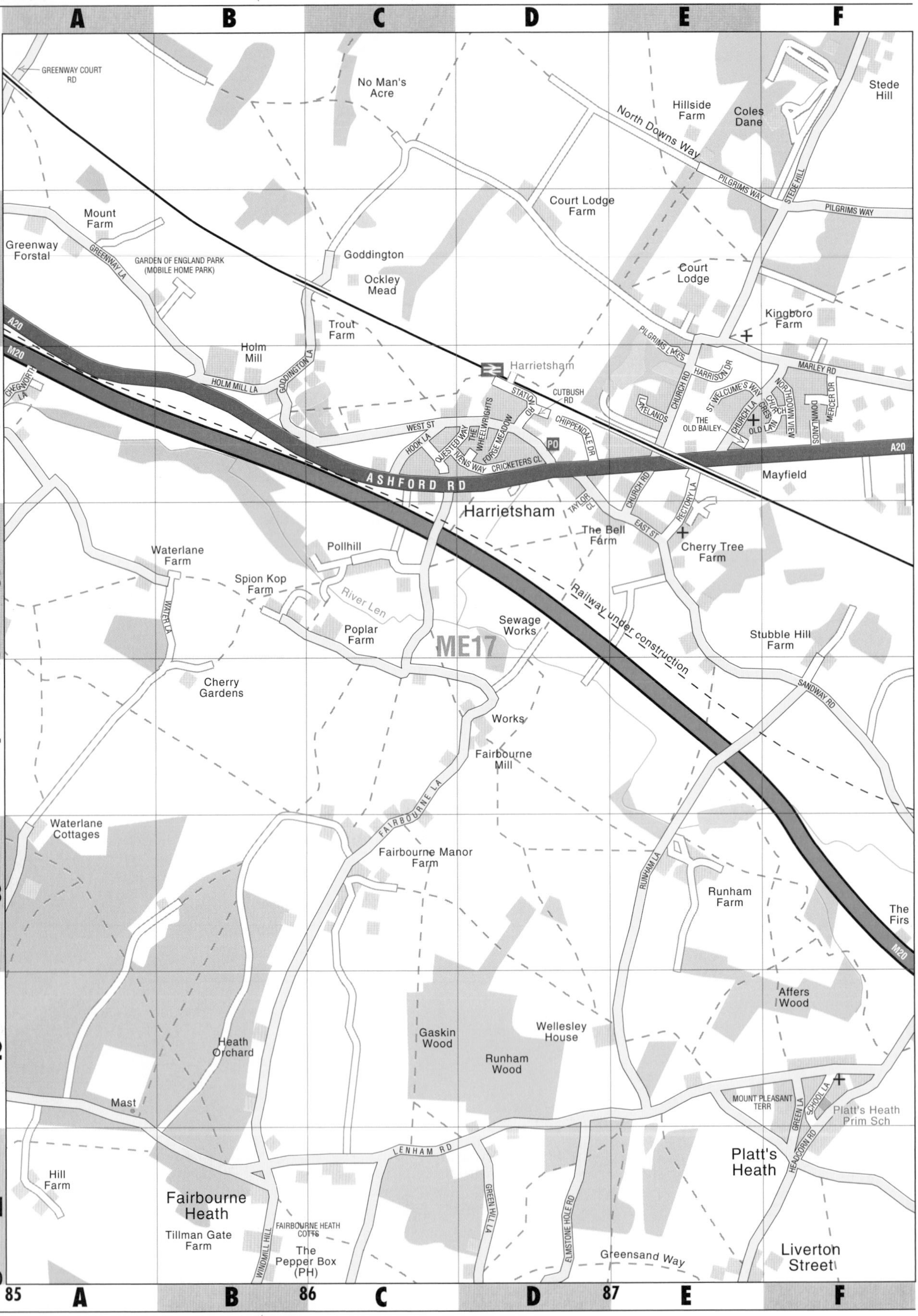

A | **B** | **C** | **D** | **E** | **F**

8

GREENWAY COURT RD

No Man's Acre

North Downs Way

Hillside Farm

Coles Dane

Stede Hill

Court Lodge Farm

Mount Farm

Greenway Forstal

GREENWAY LA

GARDEN OF ENGLAND PARK (MOBILE HOME PARK)

Goddington

7

Ockley Mead

Court Lodge

PILGRIMS WAY

STEDE HILL

PILGRIMS WAY

Kingsboro Farm

53

A20

M20

Holm Mill

Trout Farm

GODDINGTON LA

HOLM MILL LA

Harrietsham

PILGRIMS L MCS

CHURCH RD

HARRISON DR

ST WLCUME'S WAY

CHURCHILL A

MARLEY RD

NORTHDOWN VIEW

DOWNLANDS

MERCER DR

DREGGORTH LA

6

WEST ST

HOOK LA

QUESTED WAY

THE WHEELWRIGHTS

VENS WAY

FORGE MEADOW

CRICKETERS CL

STATION RD

CUTBUSH RD

CHIPPENDALE DR

PO

IRELANDS

THE OLD BAILEY

CHURCHILL A

OLD LA

CHURCH

A20

ASHFORD RD

Harrietsham

TAYLOR CL

CHURCH RD

EAST ST

RECTORY LA

Mayfield

The Bell Farm

Cherry Tree Farm

5

Waterlane Farm

Spion Kop Farm

Pollhill

River Len

WATER LA

Sewage Works

Stubble Hill Farm

Cherry Gardens

Poplar Farm

ME17

Railway under construction

SANDWAY RD

52

Works

4

Fairbourne Mill

FAIRBOURNE LA

Waterlane Cottages

Fairbourne Manor Farm

RUNHAM LA

Runham Farm

The Firs

M20

3

51

Affers Wood

Heath Orchard

Gaskin Wood

Wellesley House

Runham Wood

MOUNT PLEASANT TERR

GREEN LA

SCHOOL LA

Platt's Heath Prim Sch

2

Mast

LENHAM RD

HEADCORN RD

Platt's Heath

Hill Farm

WINDMILL HILL

GREEN HILL LA

ELMSTONE HOLE RD

Liverton Street

1

Fairbourne Heath

Tillman Gate Farm

FAIRBOURNE HEATH COTTS

The Pepper Box (PH)

Greensand Way

50

85 | **A** | **B** | 86 | **C** | **D** | 87 | **E** | **F**

99

79
102

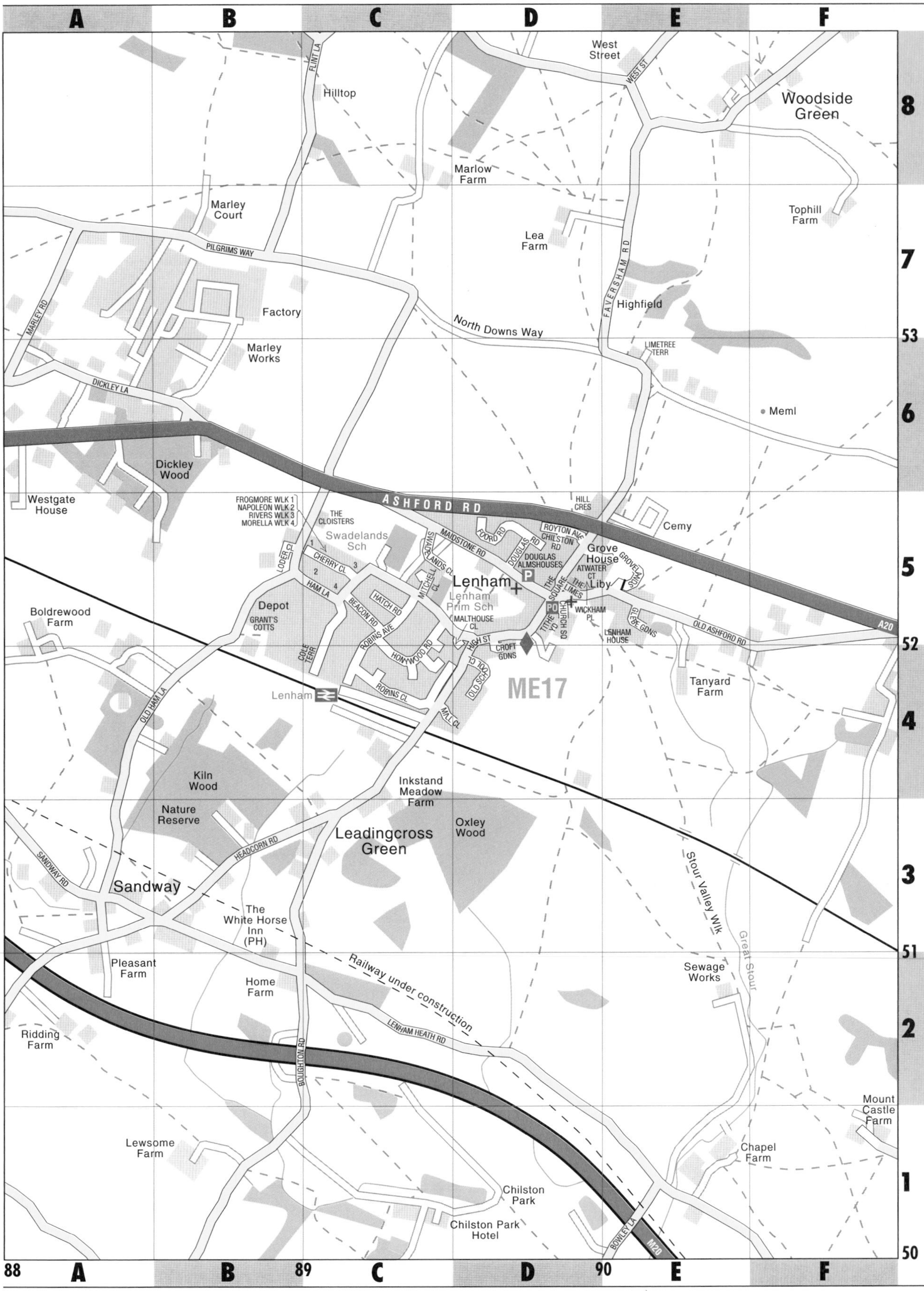
A
B
C
D
E
F
West Street
WEST ST
FLINT LA
Hilltop
Woodside Green
8
Marlow Farm
Marley Court
Tophill Farm
Lea Farm
PILGRIMS WAY
7
FAVERSHAM RD
Factory
Highfield
MARLEY RD
North Downs Way
Marley Works
53
LIMETREE TERR
DICKLEY LA
Meml
6
Dickley Wood
Westgate House
ASHFORD RD
HILL CRES
Cemy
FROGMORE WLK 1
NAPOLEON WLK 2
RIVERS WLK 3
MORELLA WLK 4
THE CLOISTERS
Swadelands Sch
MAIDSTONE RD
ROYTON AVE
CHILSTON RD
FFORD RD
DOUGLAS RD
DOUGLAS ALMSHOUSES
Grove House
GROVEL SQUARE
ATWATER CT
Liby
5
LODER CL
CHERRY CL
HAM LA
SWADELANDS CL
MITCHELL CL
Lenham
Lenham Prim Sch
THE SQUARE
THE LIMES
Depot
HATCH RD
BEACON RD
WICKHAM PL
GRANT'S COTTS
MALTHOUSE CL
CHURCH SQ
OLD ASHFORD RD
Boldrewood Farm
ROBINS AVE
HIGH ST
CROFT GDNS
TITHE YD
LENHAM HOUSE
A20
52
COLE TERR
HONYWOOD RD
OLD SCH CL
Tanyard Farm
ME17
Lenham
ROBINS CL
OLD HAM LA
MILL CL
4
Kiln Wood
Inkstand Meadow Farm
Nature Reserve
Leadingcross Green
Oxley Wood
HEADCORN RD
SANDWAY RD
Stour Valley Wlk
3
Sandway
The White Horse Inn (PH)
Great Stour
51
Pleasant Farm
Railway under construction
Sewage Works
Home Farm
LENHAM HEATH RD
2
Ridding Farm
BOUGHTON RD
Mount Castle Farm
Lewsome Farm
Chapel Farm
1
Chilston Park
Chilston Park Hotel
BOWLEY LA
M20
50
88
89
90

118
102

A B C D E F

Payden
Street

Bunker's
Hill

LONE BARN RD

PAYDEN ST

SLADE RD

ME9

Hurst
Farm

HURSTWOOD RD

Warren Lodge
Farm

ME13

8

Birch
Wood

Stubblefield
House

BUNCE COURT RD

Bunce
Court

7

Warren
Street

WARREN ST

Blue House
Farm

53

Little Pivington
Farm

Wr
Twr

The
Harrow Inn
(PH)

Middleton
Farm

Oak
Farm

COLD HARBOUR RD

Cold
Harbour

6

Great Pivington
Farm

HUBBARDS HILL

Glebe
Farm

RAYNERS HILL

HIGHBOURNE PK

Waterditch
Farm

WATERDITCH LA

Westbury
Farm

5

Pilgrims' Way

ME17

North Downs Way

Fair
View

A20

52

ASHFORD RD

4

New Shelve
Farm

Cobham
Farm

Wheatgratten
Farm

Old
Shelve

3

Old Shelve
Farm

COUNTRY WAY'S

51

Acton
Farm

TN27

2

MAIDSTONE RD

FORSTAL
COTTS

Sand
Pit

Shepherd's
Farm

Bolton
Farm

Lenham
Heath

HART HILL

The
Forstal

BULL HILL

CRABTREE LA

LENHAM FORSTAL RD

ROSE LA

HEATHFIELD
BGLWS

CHARING HEATH RD

A20

1

Lenham
Forstal

50

91 A B 92 C D 93 E F

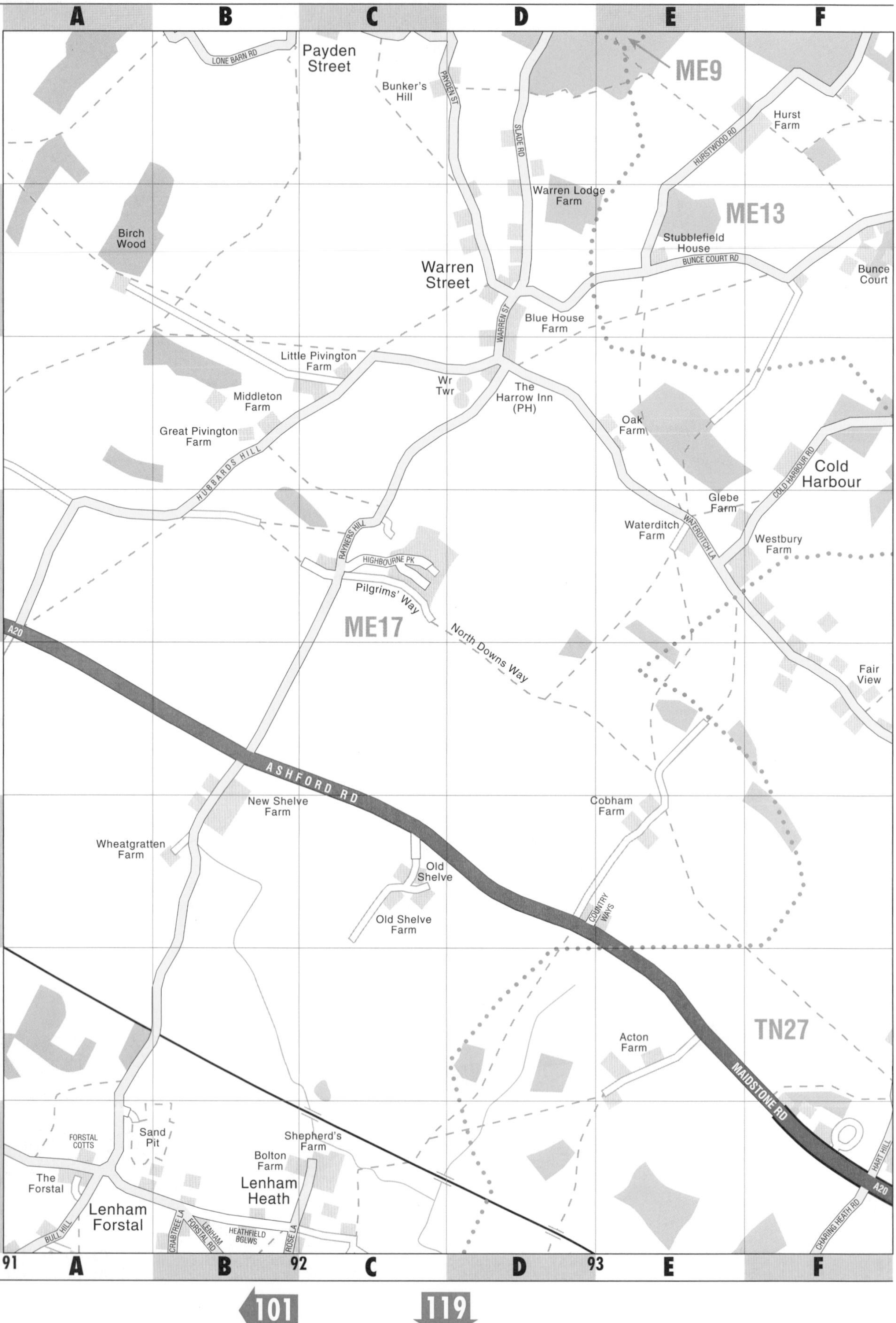

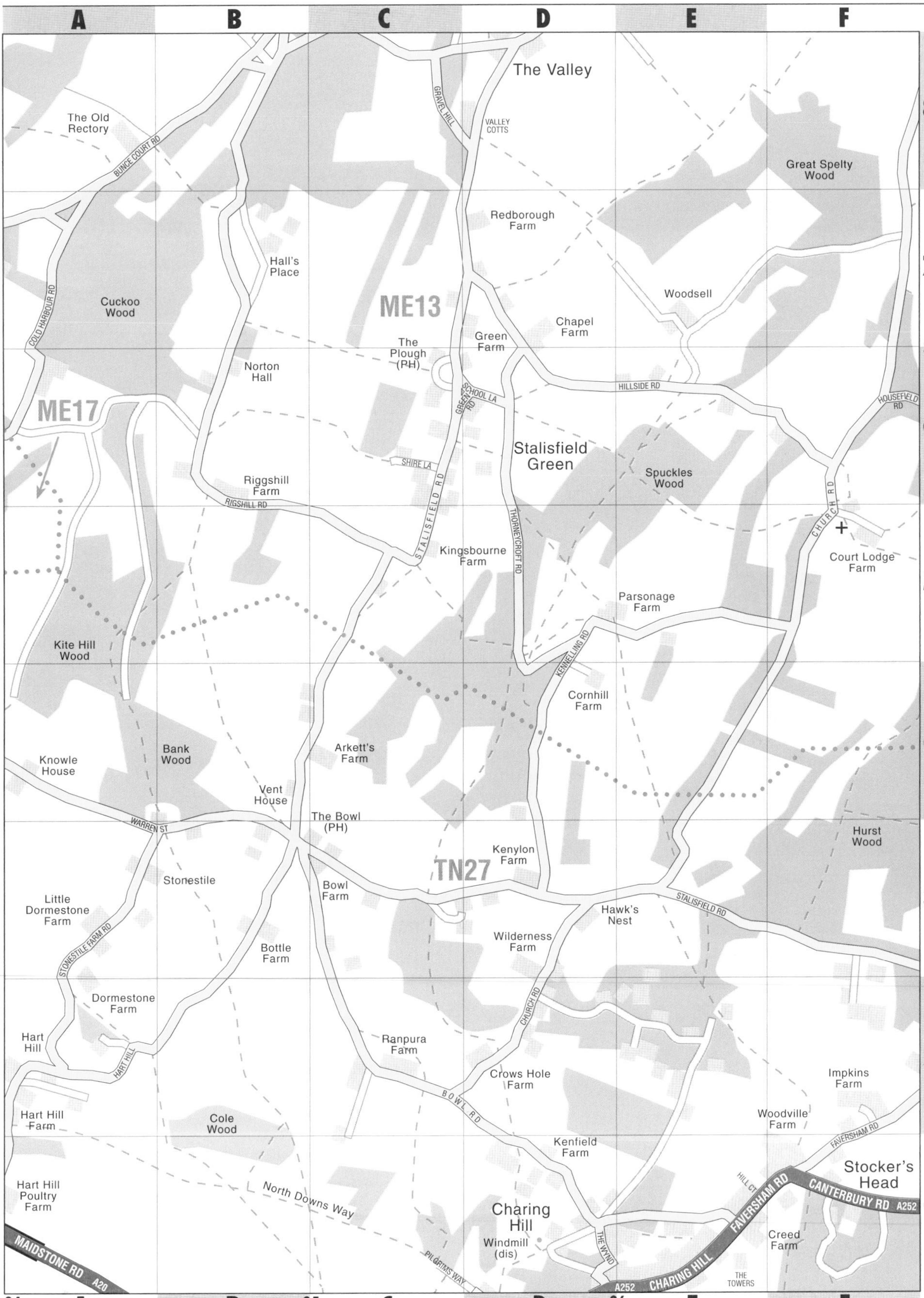

A B C D E F

The Valley

8

The Old
Rectory

BUNCE COURT RD

Valley
Cotts

Great Spelty
Wood

Redborough
Farm

7

Hall's
Place

ME13

Woodsell

COLD HARBOUR RD

Cuckoo
Wood

Chapel
Farm

53

Green
Farm

The Plough
(PH)

ME17

Norton
Hall

HILLSIDE RD

HOUSEFIELD RD

6

GREAT SCHOOL LA

Stalisfield
Green

SHIRE LA

Rigshill
Farm

Spuckles
Wood

CHURCH RD

RIGSHILL RD

STALISFIELD RD

THORNEYCROFT RD

Court Lodge
Farm

+

5

Kingsbourne
Farm

Parsonage
Farm

Kite Hill
Wood

52

KENNELLING RD

Cornhill
Farm

Knowle
House

Bank
Wood

Arkett's
Farm

4

Vent
House

Hurst
Wood

WARREN ST

The Bowl
(PH)

Kenylon
Farm

Stonestile

TN27

STALISFIELD RD

3

Little
Dormestone
Farm

Bowl
Farm

Hawk's
Nest

STONESTILE FARM RD

Bottle
Farm

Wilderness
Farm

51

HART HILL

Dormestone
Farm

CHURCH RD

Impkins
Farm

2

Hart
Hill

Ranpura
Farm

Crows Hole
Farm

Woodville
Farm

FAVERSHAM RD

Hart Hill
Farm

Cole
Wood

BOWL RD

Kenfield
Farm

Stocker's
Head

HILL CT

FAVERSHAM RD

CANTERBURY RD

A252

Hart Hill
Poultry
Farm

North Downs Way

Charing
Hill

THE WYND

Creed
Farm

1

Windmill
(dis)

MAIDSTONE RD A20

PILGRIMS WAY

A252

CHARING HILL

THE
TOWERS

50

94 A B 95 C D 96 E F

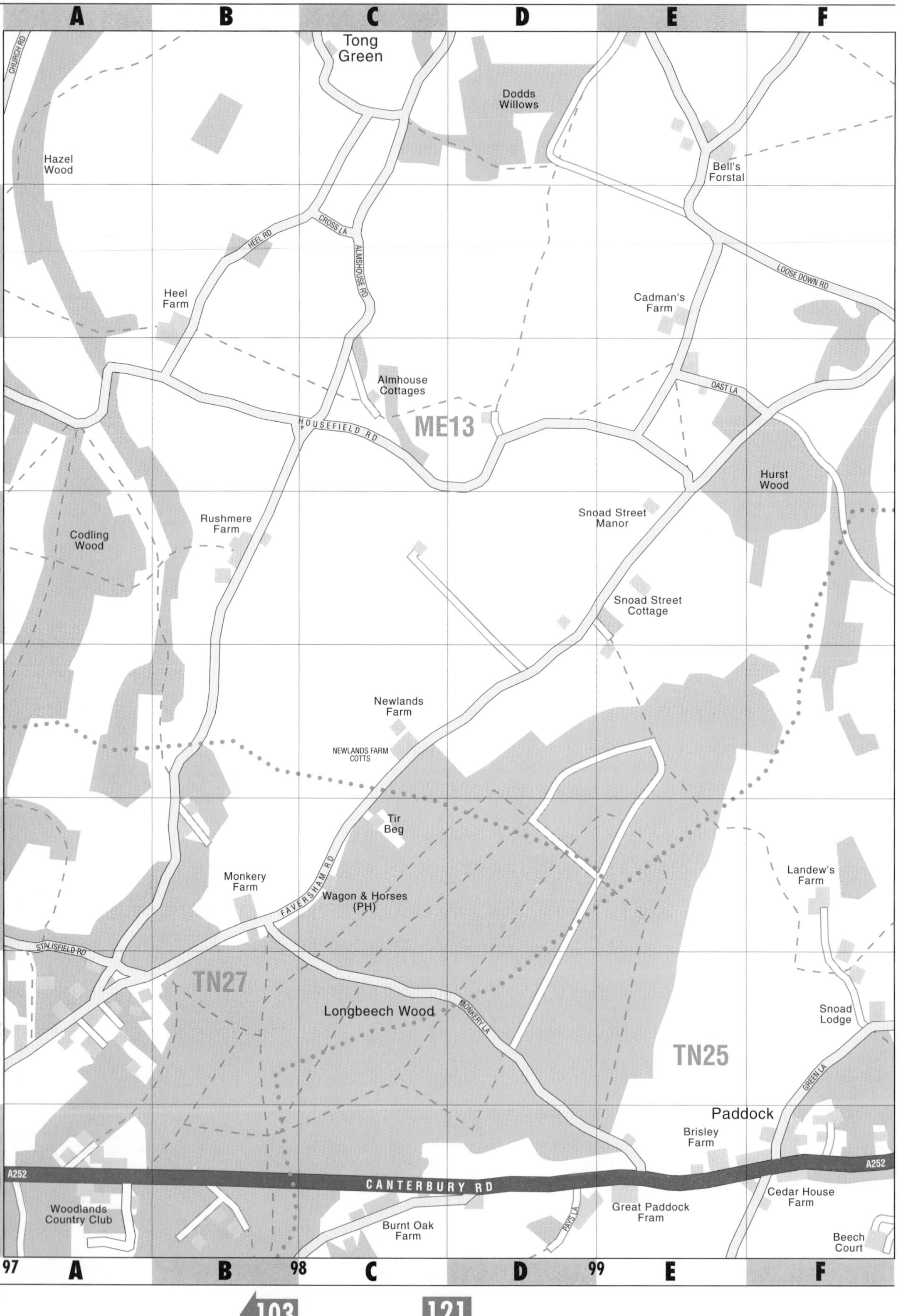

103
82

A B C D E F

8

Tong Green

Dodds Willows

Hazel Wood

Bell's Forstal

CROSS LA

HEEL RD

7

ALMSHOUSE RD

LOOSE DOWN RD

Heel Farm

Cadman's Farm

53

Almhouse Cottages

OAST LA

6

HOUSEFIELD RD

ME13

Hurst Wood

Rushmere Farm

Snoad Street Manor

Codling Wood

5

Snoad Street Cottage

52

Newlands Farm

4

NEWLANDS FARM COTTS

Landew's Farm

Tir Beg

FAVERSHAM RD

3

Monkery Farm

Wagon & Horses (PH)

51

STN ISFIELD RD

TN27

Snoad Lodge

Longbeech Wood

MONKERY LA

2

TN25

Paddock

Brisley Farm

A252

1

A252

CANTERBURY RD

Woodlands Country Club

Burnt Oak Farm

PKS LA

Great Paddock Fram

Cedar House Farm

50

Beech Court

97 A B 98 C D 99 E F

103
121

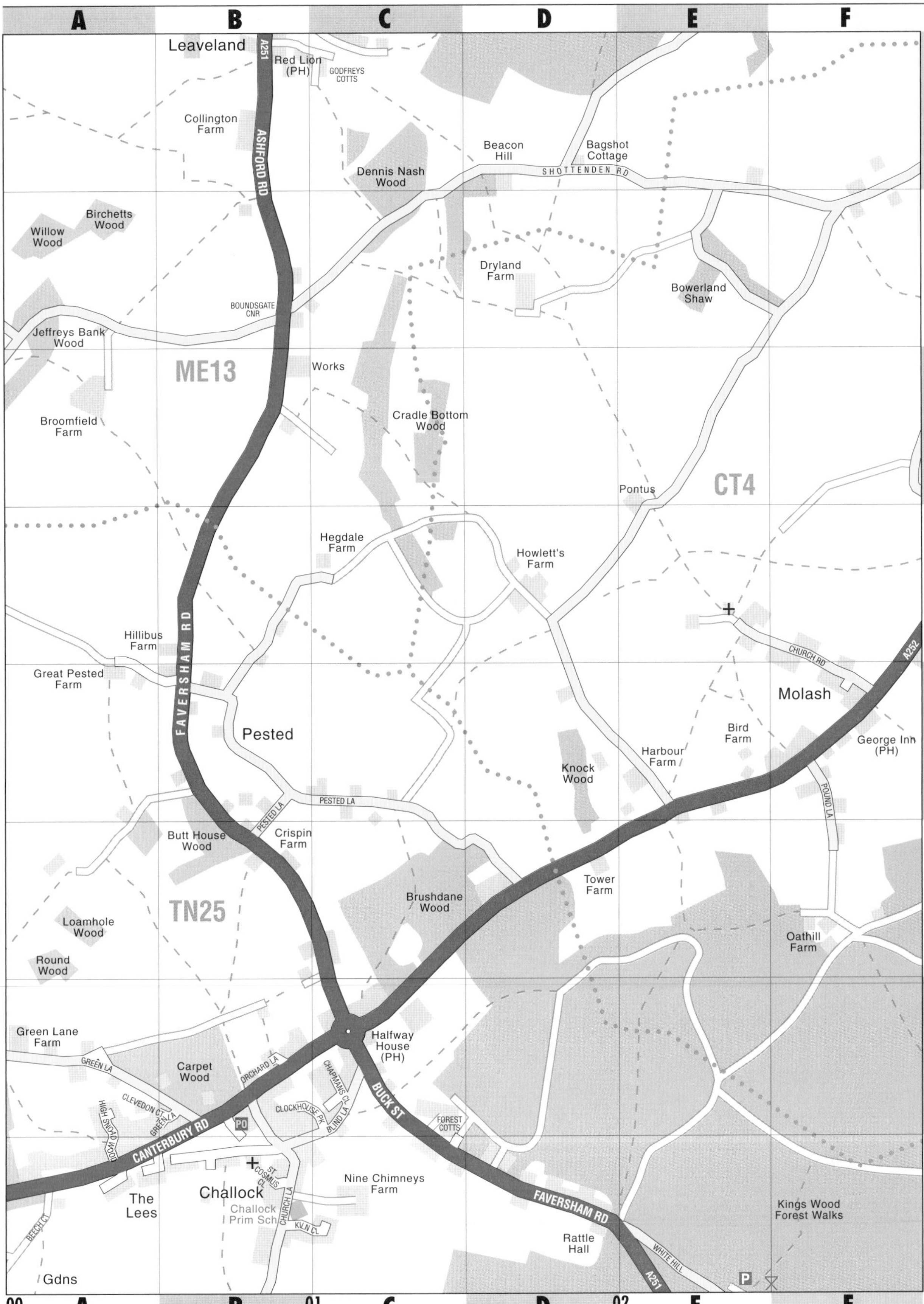

A B C D E F

Leaveland
Red Lion (PH)
GODFREYS COTTS
Collington Farm
ASHFORD RD
A251
Dennis Nash Wood
Beacon Hill
Bagshot Cottage
SHOTTENDEN RD
Birchetts Wood
Willow Wood
Dryland Farm
Bowerland Shaw
Jeffreys Bank Wood
BOUNDSGATE CNR
ME13
Works
Broomfield Farm
Cradle Bottom Wood
Pontus
CT4
Hegdale Farm
Howlett's Farm
Hillibus Farm
FAVERSHAM RD
CHURCH RD
A252
Great Pested Farm
Molash
Pested
Bird Farm
George Inn (PH)
Knock Wood
Harbour Farm
PESTED LA
POUND LA
Butt House Wood
Crispin Farm
PESTED LA
Loamhole Wood
TN25
Brushdane Wood
Tower Farm
Oathill Farm
Round Wood
Green Lane Farm
Halfway House (PH)
GREEN LA
Carpet Wood
ORCHARD LA
CHAPMANS CL
BUCK ST
CLEVEDON CT
CLOCKHOUSE PK
FOREST COTTS
HIGH SNOAD WOOD
CANTERBURY RD
PO
Kings Wood Forest Walks
ST COSMUS CL
Nine Chimneys Farm
The Lees
Challock
CHURCH LA
KILN CL
Challock Prim Sch
Rattle Hall
FAVERSHAM RD
WHITE HILL
A251
BECKETS LN
Gdns
P

00 01 02

8 7 53 6 5 52 4 3 51 2 1 50

105
84

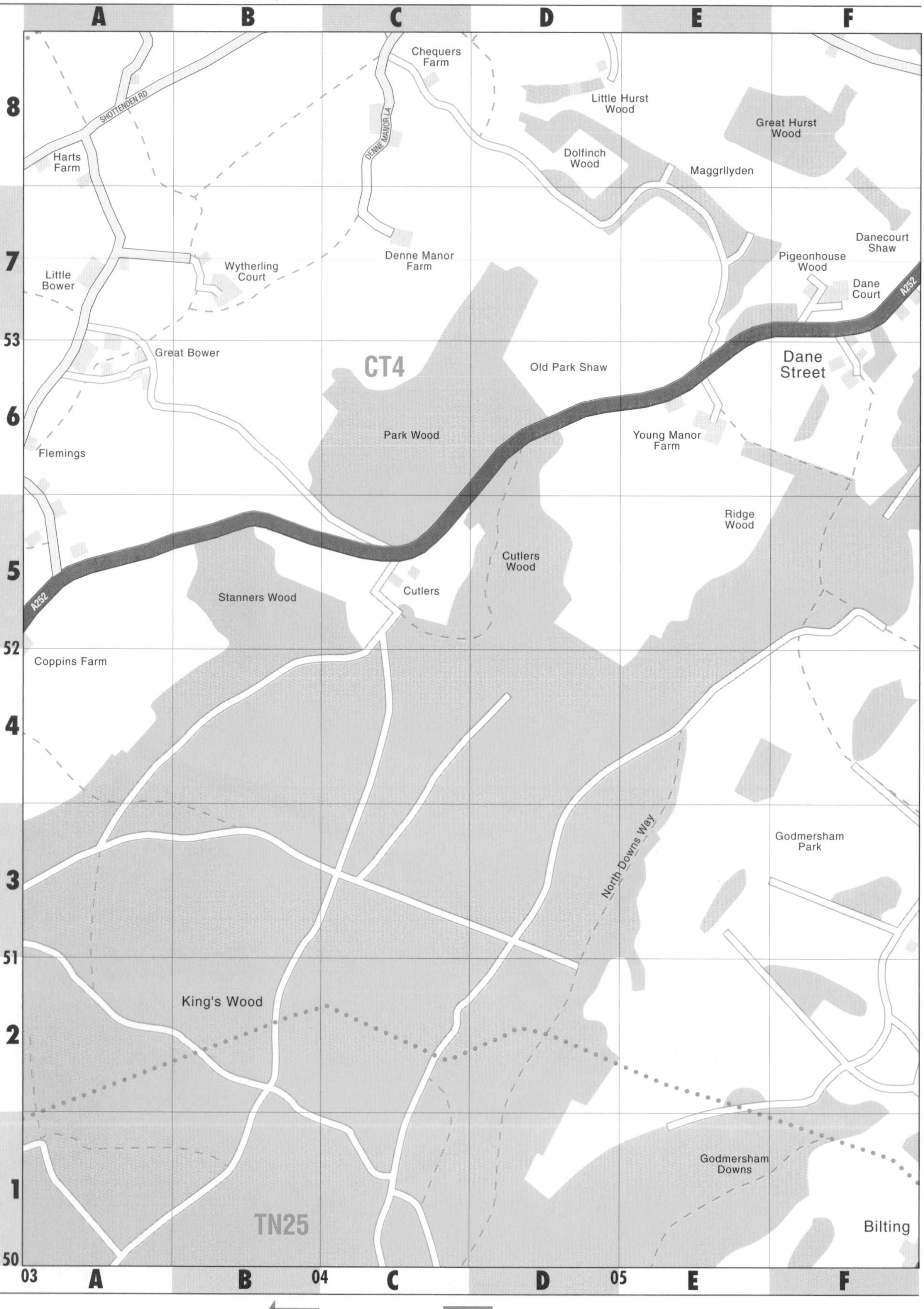
A B C D E F
8
7
53
6
5
52
4
3
51
2
1
50
03 04 05
Chequers Farm
SHOTTENDEN RD
DENNE MANOR LA
Little Hurst Wood
Great Hurst Wood
Harts Farm
Dolfinch Wood
Maggrllyden
Danecourt Shaw
Little Bower
Wytherling Court
Denne Manor Farm
Pigeonhouse Wood
Dane Court
A252
Great Bower
CT4
Old Park Shaw
Dane Street
Park Wood
Young Manor Farm
Flemings
Ridge Wood
Cutlers Wood
Stanners Wood
Cutlers
A252
Coppins Farm
North Downs Way
Godmersham Park
King's Wood
Godmersham Downs
TN25
Bilting

105
123

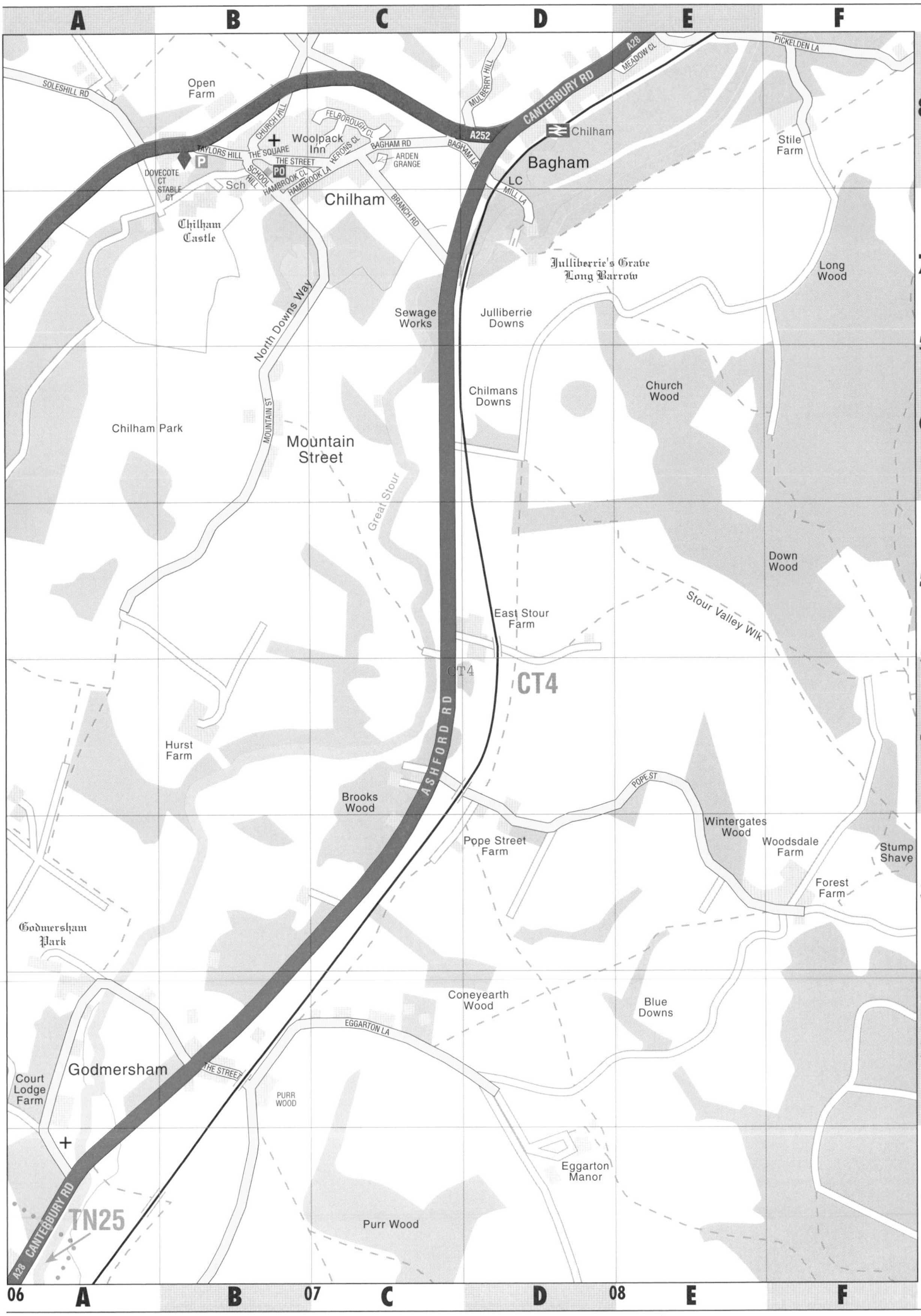

85
108

A B C D E F

8

SOLESHILL RD

Open
Farm

CHURCH HILL
FELBOROUGH CL

Woolpack
Inn

TAYLORS HILL
THE SQUARE
THE STREET
P
DOVECOTE
CT
STABLE
CT
Sch
SCHOOL
HILL
PO
HAMBROOK LA
HERONS CL
BAGHAM RD
ARDEN
GRANGE

MULBERRY HILL

A252
BAGHAM LA

CANTERBURY RD
A28
MEADOW CL

PICKELDEN LA

Chilham

Bagham

LC

MILL LA

Stile
Farm

Chilham
Castle

Chilham

BRANCH RD

Julliberrie's Grave
Long Barrow

Long
Wood

7

53

Sewage
Works

Julliberrie
Downs

NORTH DOWNS WAY

Chilmans
Downs

Church
Wood

6

Chilham Park

MOUNTAIN ST

Mountain
Street

Great Stour

Down
Wood

5

Stour Valley Wlk

East Stour
Farm

CT4

CT4

52

4

Hurst
Farm

ASHFORD RD

Brooks
Wood

POPE ST

Wintergates
Wood

Woodsdale
Farm

Stump
Shave

Pope Street
Farm

Forest
Farm

3

51

Godmersham
Park

Coneyearth
Wood

Blue
Downs

2

Court
Lodge
Farm

Godmersham

THE STREET

EGGARTON LA

PURR
WOOD

Eggarton
Manor

CANTERBURY RD
A28

TN25

Purr Wood

1

50

06 A B 07 C D 08 E F

124
108

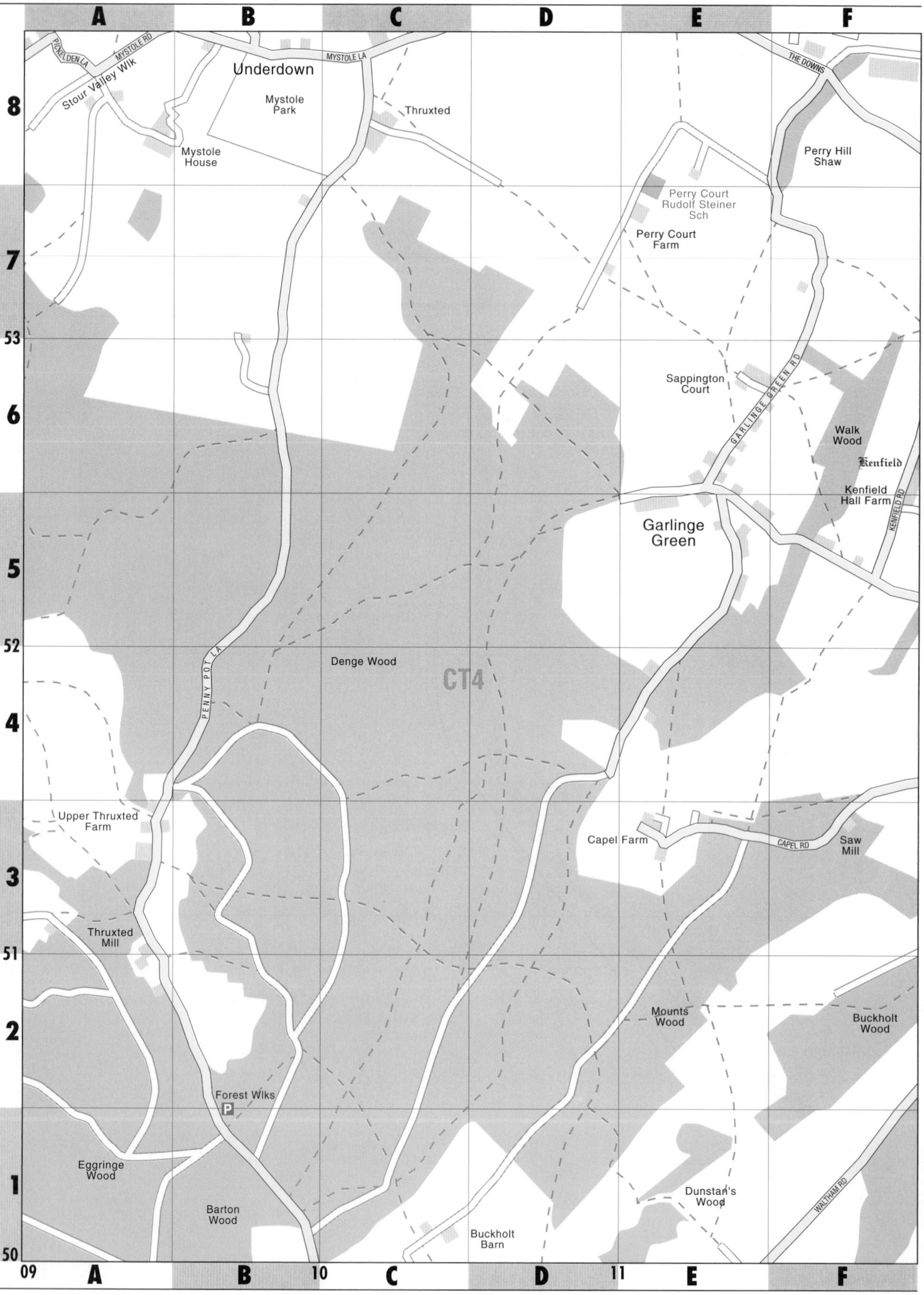

A B C D E F

8

Underdown

Mystole LA

Thruxted

Mystole Park

Mystole House

Stour Valley Wlk

FOXELDEN LA

MYSTOLE RD

THE DOWNS

Perry Hill Shaw

7

Perry Court Rudolf Steiner Sch

Perry Court Farm

53

Sappington Court

Walk Wood

6

Kenfield

Kenfield Hall Farm

GARLINGE GREEN RD

KENFIELD RD

5

Garlinge Green

52

Denge Wood

CT4

PENNY POT LA

4

Upper Thruxted Farm

Capel Farm

CAPEL RD

Saw Mill

3

Thruxted Mill

51

Mounts Wood

Buckholt Wood

2

Forest Wlks

P

1

Eggringe Wood

Dunstan's Wood

WALTHAM RD

Barton Wood

Buckholt Barn

50

09 A B 10 C D 11 E F

87
110

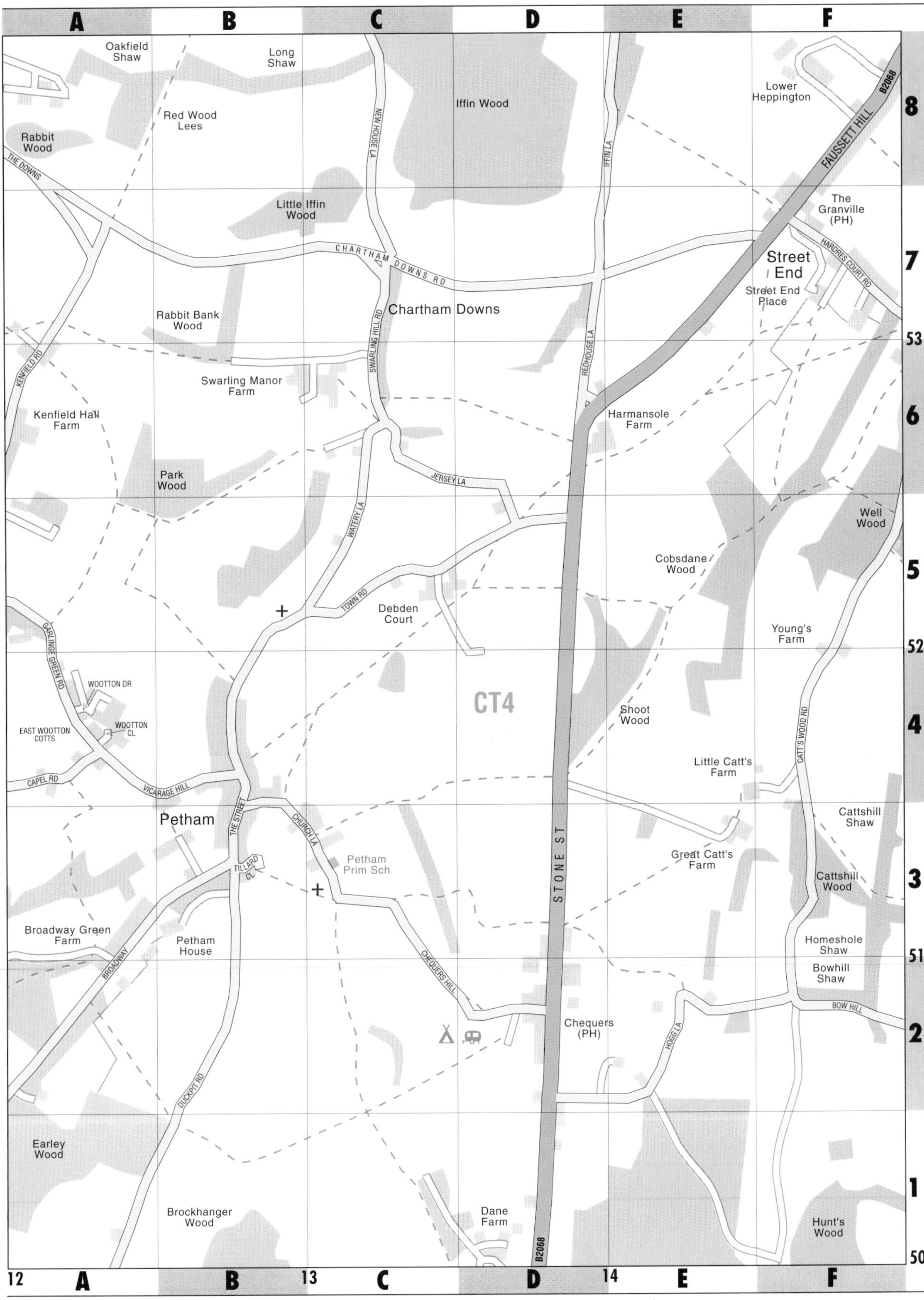
A
B
C
D
E
F
Oakfield Shaw
Long Shaw
Iffin Wood
Lower Heppington
B2068
FAUSSETT HILL
Rabbit Wood
Red Wood Lees
NEW HOUSE LA
IFFIN LA
THE DOWNS
Little Iffin Wood
The Granville (PH)
HARDRES COURT RD
CHARTHAM DOWNS RD
Street End
Street End Place
Chartham Downs
Rabbit Bank Wood
SWARLING HILL RD
REDHOUSE LA
KENFIELD RD
Swarling Manor Farm
Harmansole Farm
Kenfield Hall Farm
JERSEY LA
Park Wood
WATERY LA
Well Wood
Cobsdane Wood
TOWN RD
Debden Court
Young's Farm
GARLINGE GREEN RD
WOOTTON DR
CT4
Shoot Wood
EAST WOOTTON COTTS
WOOTTON CL
CATT'S WOOD RD
Little Catt's Farm
CAPEL RD
VICARAGE HILL
Cattshill Shaw
Petham
THE STREET
CHURCH LA
Great Catt's Farm
TILLARD CL
Petham Prim Sch
STONE ST
Cattshill Wood
Broadway Green Farm
Petham House
Homeshole Shaw
BROADWAY
CHEQUERS HILL
Bowhill Shaw
BOW HILL
Chequers (PH)
HOGG LA
DUCKPIT RD
Earley Wood
Brockhanger Wood
Dane Farm
B2068
Hunt's Wood
8
7
53
6
5
52
4
3
51
2
1
50
12
13
14

126
110

109
88

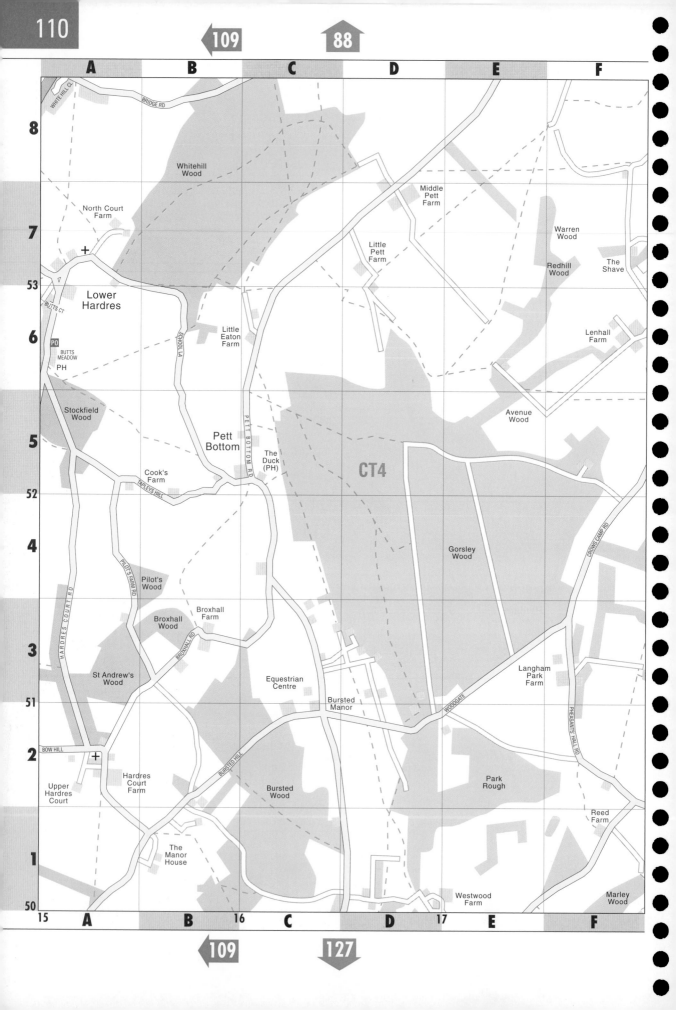
A
B
C
D
E
F
8
7
53
6
5
52
4
3
51
2
1
50
15
16
17
WHITE HILL CL
BRIDGE RD
Whitehill Wood
North Court Farm
Middle Pett Farm
Warren Wood
Little Pett Farm
Redhill Wood
The Shave
Lower Hardres
BUTTS CT
Little Eaton Farm
SCHOOL LA
Lenhall Farm
PO
BUTTS MEADOW
PH
Stockfield Wood
Avenue Wood
PETT BOTTOM RD
Pett Bottom
The Duck (PH)
CT4
Cook's Farm
TAPLEYS HILL
Gorsley Wood
CROWS CAMP RD
PILOTS FARM RD
Pilot's Wood
HARDRES COURT RD
Broxhall Farm
Broxhall Wood
BROXHALL RD
Langham Park Farm
St Andrew's Wood
Equestrian Centre
Bursted Manor
WOODGATE
PHEASANTS' HALL RD
BOW HILL
BURSTED HILL
Hardres Court Farm
Upper Hardres Court
Bursted Wood
Park Rough
Reed Farm
The Manor House
Westwood Farm
Marley Wood

109
127

89
112

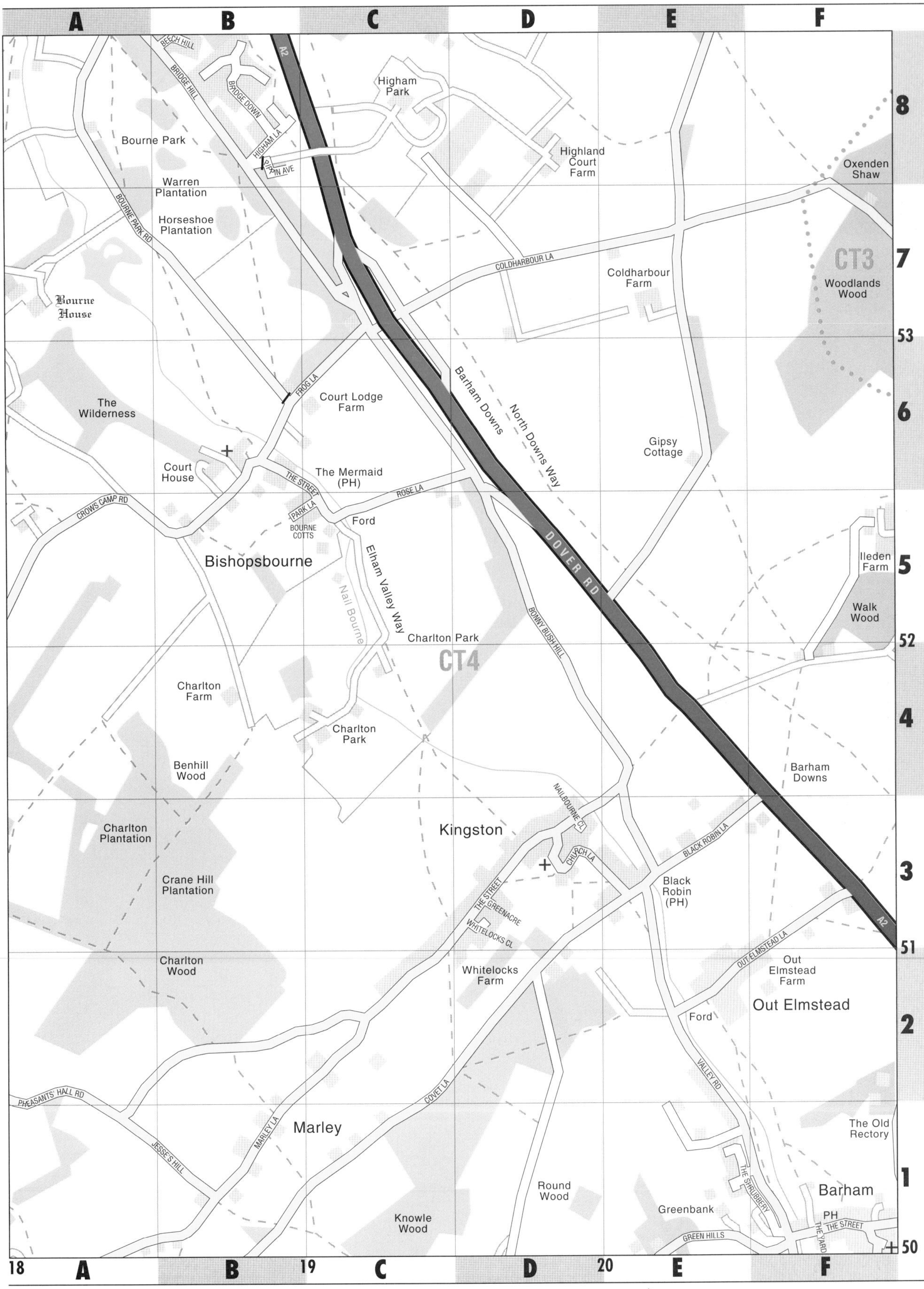
A
B
C
D
E
F
A2
BEECH HILL
BRIDGE HILL
BRIDGE DOWN
HIGHAM LA
GIPSY TN AVE
Higham Park
Highland Court Farm
Oxenden Shaw
Bourne Park
Warren Plantation
Horseshoe Plantation
BOURNE PARK RD
COLDHARBOUR LA
Coldharbour Farm
CT3
Woodlands Wood
Bourne House
The Wilderness
FROG LA
Court Lodge Farm
Barham Downs
North Downs Way
Court House
The Mermaid (PH)
THE STREET
ROSE LA
PARK LA
BOURNE COTTS
Ford
CROWS CAMP RD
Gipsy Cottage
DOVER RD
Ileden Farm
Bishopsbourne
Elham Valley Way
Nail Bourne
BONNY BUSH HILL
Walk Wood
Charlton Park
CT4
Charlton Farm
Charlton Park
Benhill Wood
Barham Downs
NAILBOURNE CL
Kingston
Charlton Plantation
CHURCH LA
BLACK ROBIN LA
Crane Hill Plantation
THE STREET
GREENACRE
WHITELOCKS CL
Black Robin (PH)
Charlton Wood
Whitelocks Farm
OUT ELMSTEAD LA
Out Elmstead Farm
Out Elmstead
Ford
VALLEY RD
PHEASANTS' HALL RD
COVET LA
Marley
MARLEY LA
JESSE'S HILL
The Old Rectory
THE SHRUBBERY
Round Wood
Barham
Knowle Wood
Greenbank
PH
THE STREET
THE YARD
GREEN HILLS
8
7
53
6
5
52
4
3
51
2
1
50
18
19
20

128
112

111
90

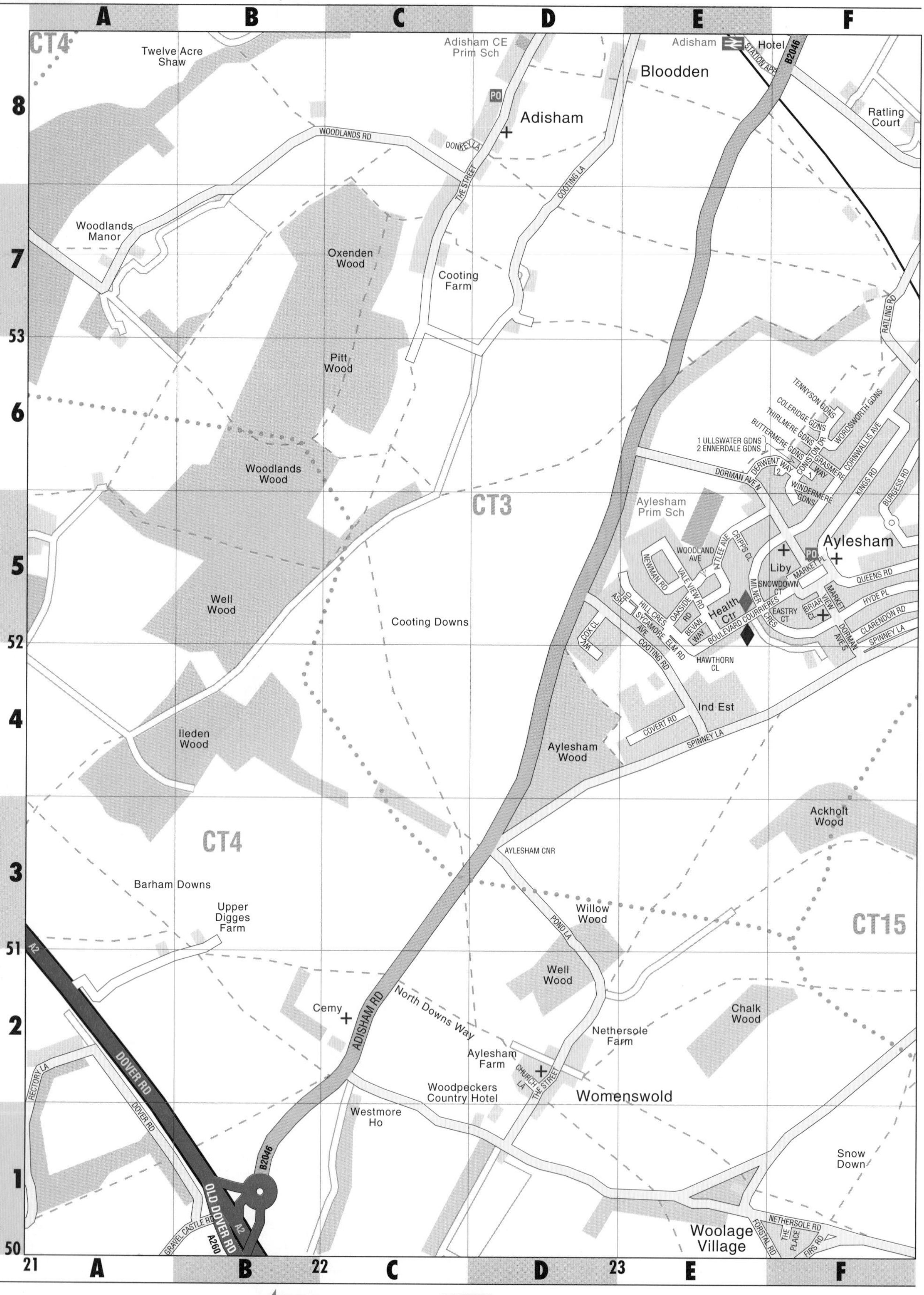

A **B** **C** **D** **E** **F**

CT4

Twelve Acre Shaw

Adisham CE Prim Sch

Bloodden

Adisham

Ratling Court

8

Woodlands Manor

WOODLANDS RD

DONKEY LA

THE STREET

COOTING LA

Station App

B2046

Hotel

7

Oxenden Wood

Cooting Farm

53

RATLING RD

Pitt Wood

6

Woodlands Wood

TENNYSON GDNS

COLERIDGE GDNS

THIRLMERE GDNS

BUTTERMERE GDNS

WORDSWORTH GDNS

GRASMERE

CONISTON

CORNWALLIS AVE

1 ULLSWATER GDNS
2 ENNERDALE GDNS

DERWENT WAY

WINDERMERE GDNS

KINGS RD

BURGESS RD

CT3

Aylesham Prim Sch

DORMAN AVE N

5

Well Wood

Woodland Ave

NEWMAN RD

VALE VIEW RD

CRIPPS CL

SNOWDOWN CT

Libry

PO

Aylesham

QUEENS RD

MARKET

HYDE PL

Cooting Downs

ASH

HILL CRES

SYCAMORE

ELM RD

OAKSIDE

DEVON

WAY

BRIAN

CL

VERN

EASTRY CT

CLARENDON RD

SPINNEY LA

52

COX CL

WK

Health Ctr

BOULEVARD COURTENAYS

DORMAN AVE S

Ileden Wood

COOTING RD

AVENUE

HAWTHORN CL

Ind Est

4

Aylesham Wood

COVERT RD

SPINNEY LA

Ackholt Wood

3

CT4

Barham Downs

AYLESHAM CNR

Willow Wood

CT15

Upper Digges Farm

POND LA

A2

51

Cemy

ADISHAM RD

North Downs Way

Well Wood

Nethersole Farm

Chalk Wood

2

RECTORY LA

DOVER RD

Aylesham Farm

CHURCH LA

THE STREET

Womenswold

Woodpeckers Country Hotel

Westmore Ho

Snow Down

1

B2046

NETHERSOLE RD

OLD DOVER RD

A2

GRAVEL CASTLE RD

A260

Woolage Village

FOSTALL RD

THE PLACE

FIRS RD

50

21 **A** **B** 22 **C** **D** 23 **E** **F**

91
114

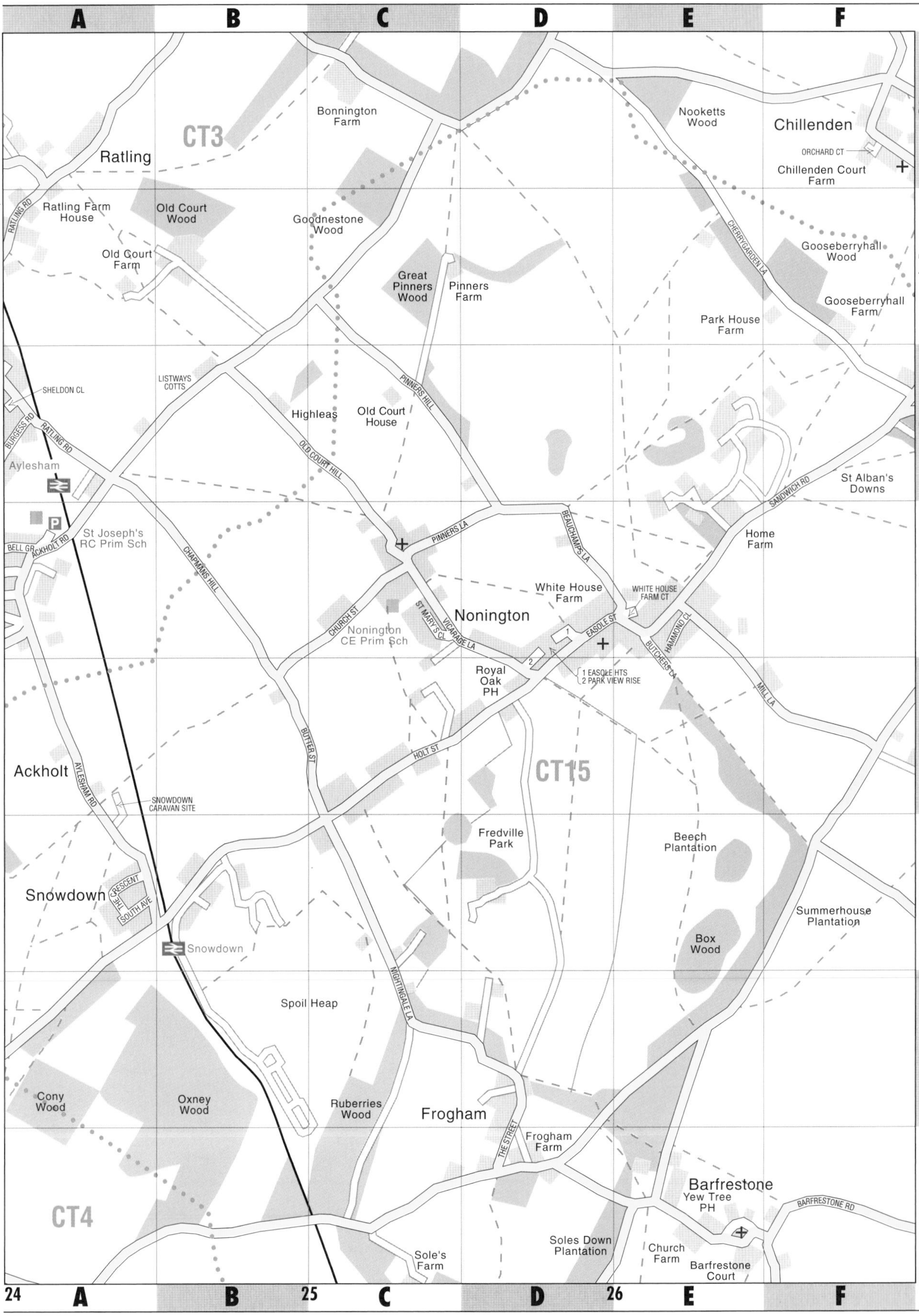
A
B
C
D
E
F
8
7
53
6
5
52
4
3
51
2
1
50
24
25
26
CT3
CT15
CT4
Bonnington Farm
Nooketts Wood
Chillenden
ORCHARD CT
Chillenden Court Farm
Ratling
Ratling Farm House
Old Court Wood
Goodnestone Wood
RATLING RD
Old Court Farm
Great Pinners Wood
Pinners Farm
CHERRYGARDEN LA
Gooseberryhall Wood
Gooseberryhall Farm
Park House Farm
LISTWAYS COTTS
SHELDON CL
PINNERS HILL
Highleas
Old Court House
BURGESS RD
RATLING RD
Aylesham
OLD COURT HILL
SANDWICH RD
St Alban's Downs
BEAUCHAMPS LA
PINNERS LA
Home Farm
BELL GR
ACKHOLT RD
St Joseph's RC Prim Sch
CHAPMANS HILL
White House Farm
WHITE HOUSE FARM CT
Nonington
CHURCH ST
ST MARY'S CL
VICARAGE LA
Nonington CE Prim Sch
EASOLE ST
HAMMOND CL
BUTCHERS LA
Royal Oak PH
1 EASOLE HTS
2 PARK VIEW RISE
MILL LA
BUTTER ST
HOLT ST
Ackholt
AYLESHAM RD
SNOWDOWN CARAVAN SITE
Fredville Park
Beech Plantation
Snowdown
THE CRESCENT
SOUTH AVE
Summerhouse Plantation
Box Wood
Snowdown
NIGHTINGALE LA
Spoil Heap
Cony Wood
Oxney Wood
Ruberries Wood
Frogham
THE STREET
Frogham Farm
Barfrestone
Yew Tree PH
BARFRESTONE RD
Soles Down Plantation
Church Farm
Sole's Farm
Barfrestone Court

130
114

113
92

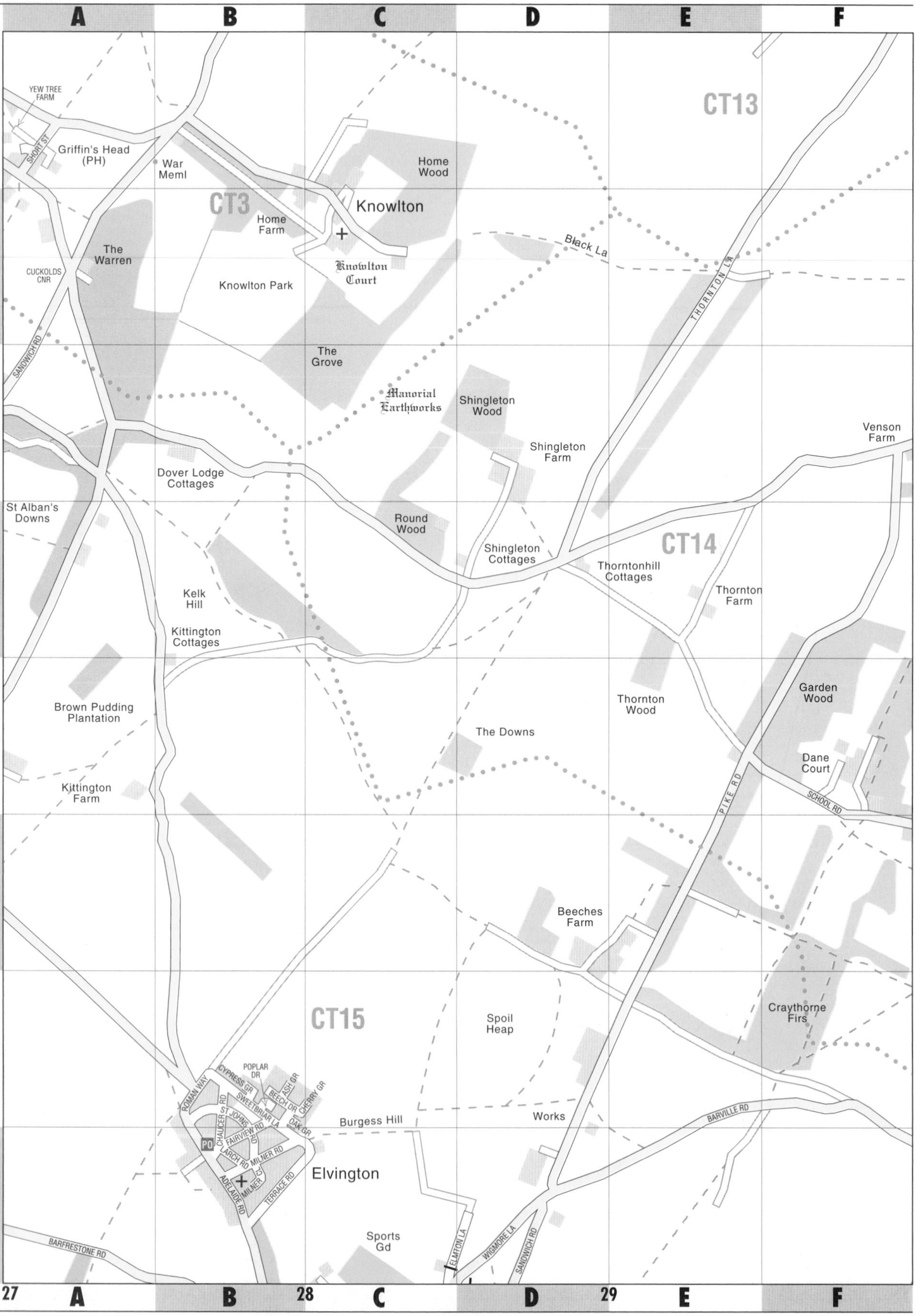

A B C D E F

8
7
53
6
5
52
4
3
51
2
1
50

27 28 29

CT13

CT3

YEW TREE FARM

Griffin's Head (PH)

War Meml

Home Wood

Knowlton

Home Farm

The Warren

CUCKOLDS CNR

Knowlton Park

Knowlton Court

SANDWICH RD

SHORT ST

The Grove

Manorial Earthworks

Black La

THORNTON LA

Shingleton Wood

Shingleton Farm

Venson Farm

Dover Lodge Cottages

St Alban's Downs

Round Wood

Shingleton Cottages

CT14

Thorntonhill Cottages

Thornton Farm

Kelk Hill

Kittington Cottages

Thornton Wood

Garden Wood

Brown Pudding Plantation

The Downs

Dane Court

PIKE RD

SCHOOL RD

Kittington Farm

Beeches Farm

CT15

Spoil Heap

Craythorne Firs

Burgess Hill

Works

BARVILLE RD

ROMAN WAY

POPLAR DR

CYPRESS GR

ST JOHNS RD

CHAUCER RD

SWEET BRIAR LA

BEECH DR

ASH GR

OAK GR

CHERRY GR

FAIRVIEW RD

LARCH RD

MILNER RD

ADELAIDE RD

MILNER

TERRACE RD

PO

Elvington

Sports Gd

Barfrestone Rd

ELMTON LA

WIGMORE LA

SANDWICH RD

113
131

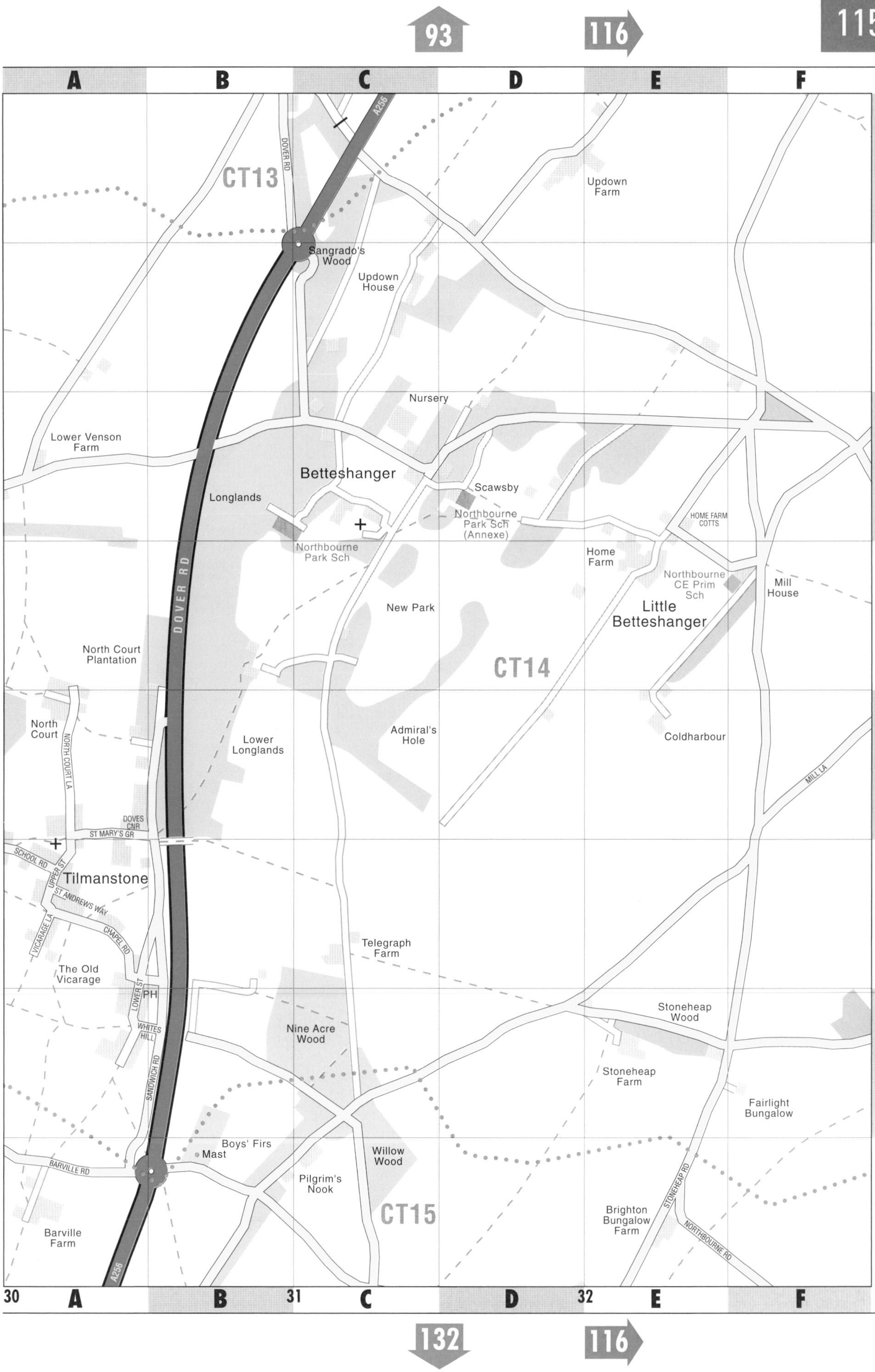
93
116
A
B
C
D
E
F
8
7
53
6
5
52
4
3
51
2
1
50
30
31
32
CT13
A256
DOVER RD
Updown Farm
Sangrado's Wood
Updown House
Nursery
Lower Venson Farm
Betteshanger
Scawsby
Longlands
Northbourne Park Sch (Annexe)
Northbourne Park Sch
HOME FARM COTTS
Home Farm
Northbourne CE Prim Sch
Mill House
New Park
Little Betteshanger
North Court Plantation
CT14
North Court
NORTH COURT LA
Lower Longlands
Admiral's Hole
Coldharbour
MILL LA
DOVES CNR
ST MARY'S GR
SCHOOL RD
UPPER ST
Tilmanstone
ST ANDREWS WAY
CHAPEL RD
VICARAGE LA
Telegraph Farm
The Old Vicarage
LOWER ST
PH
WHITES HILL
Nine Acre Wood
Stoneheap Wood
SANDWICH RD
Stoneheap Farm
Fairlight Bungalow
Boys' Firs
Mast
Willow Wood
BARVILLE RD
Pilgrim's Nook
STONEHEAP RD
CT15
Brighton Bungalow Farm
NORTHBOURNE RD
Barville Farm
132
116

115
94

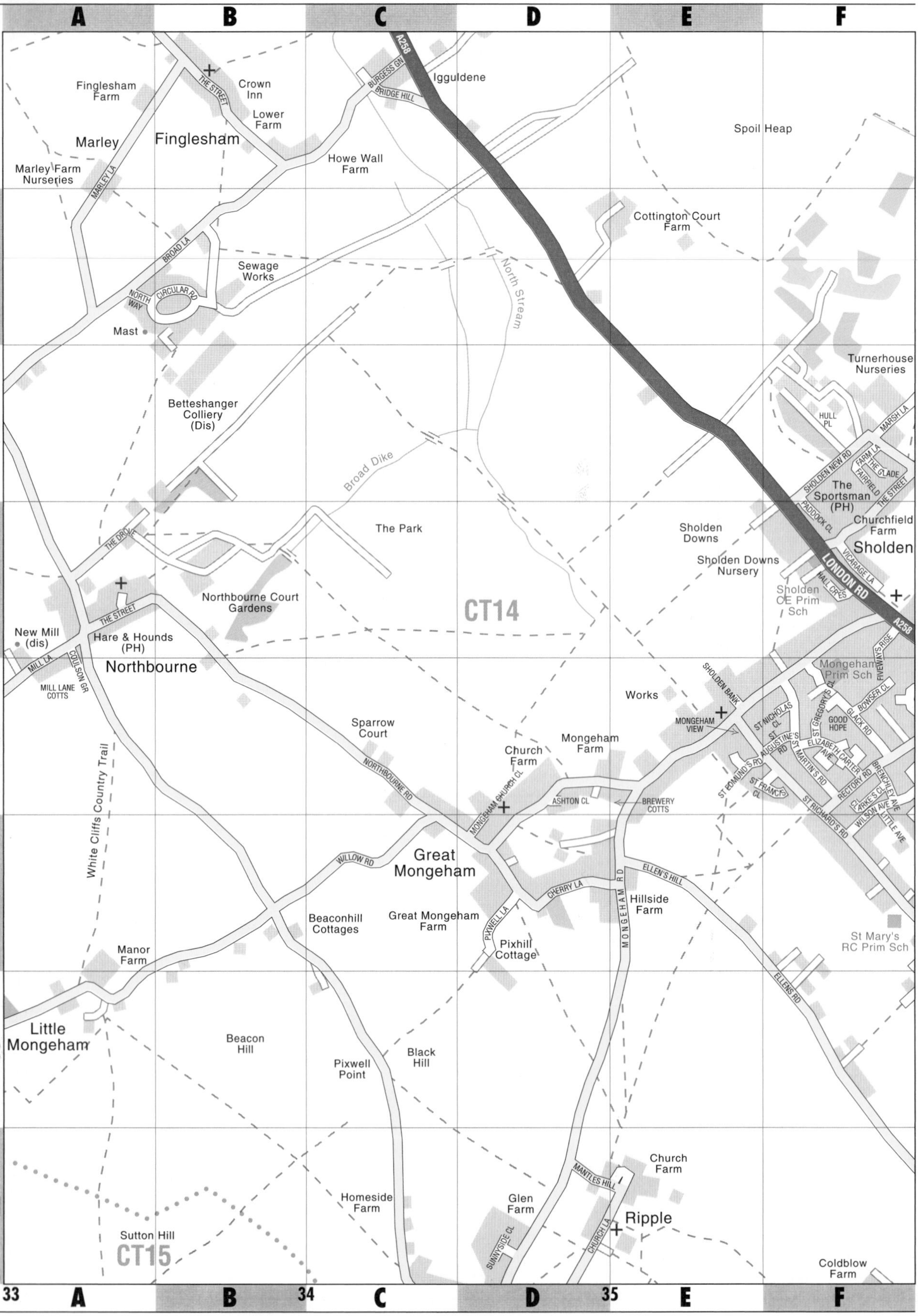

A B C D E F

8

Finglesham Farm

Marley

Marley Farm Nurseries

MARLEY LA

BROAD LA

THE STREET

Crown Inn

Lower Farm

Finglesham

Howe Wall Farm

BURGESS GN

BRIDGE HILL

A258

Igguldene

Spoil Heap

Cottington Court Farm

7

NORTH WAY

CIACULAR RD

Sewage Works

North Stream

Mast

53

Turnerhouse Nurseries

6

Betteshanger Colliery (Dis)

Broad Dike

The Sportsman (PH)

SHOLDEN NEW RD

FARM LA

THE GLADE

FAIRFIELD RD

THE STREET

HULL PL

MARSH LA

THE DROV

The Park

Sholden Downs

Churchfield Farm

Sholden

LONDON RD

PADDOCK CL

VICARAGE LA

A258

5

THE STREET

Northbourne Court Gardens

CT14

Sholden Downs Nursery

Sholden CE Prim Sch

HALL CRES

New Mill (dis)

Hare & Hounds (PH)

MILL LA

COLL SDN GR

52

Northbourne

MILL LANE COTTS

Works

Mongeham Prim Sch

SHOLDEN BANK

SAXON WAY

BOWSER CL

BLACK RD

4

White Cliffs Country Trail

Sparrow Court

NORTHBOURNE RD

Church Farm

Mongeham Farm

Mongeham View

ST NICHOLAS CL

ST AUGUSTINE S RD

ST GREGORY S

ST MARTIN S RD

ELIZABETH CARTER

GOOD HOPE

RECTORY RD

BRENCHLEY AVE

WILSON AVE

MONGEHAM CHURCH CL

ASHTON CL

BREWERY COTTS

ST EDMUND S RD

ST FRANCS CL

ST RICHARD S RD

PARKES CL

LITTLE AVE

WILLOW RD

Great Mongeham

Great Mongeham Farm

PIXWELL LA

CHERRY LA

Hillside Farm

MONGEHAM RD

ELLEN'S HILL

3

Manor Farm

Beaconhill Cottages

Pixhill Cottage

Pixwell Point

Black Hill

St Mary's RC Prim Sch

ELLENS RD

51

Little Mongeham

Beacon Hill

Homeside Farm

SUNNYSIDE CL

Glen Farm

MANTLES HILL

CHURCH LA

Church Farm

2

1

Ripple

Coldblow Farm

Sutton Hill

CT15

50

33 A B 34 C D 35 E F

95

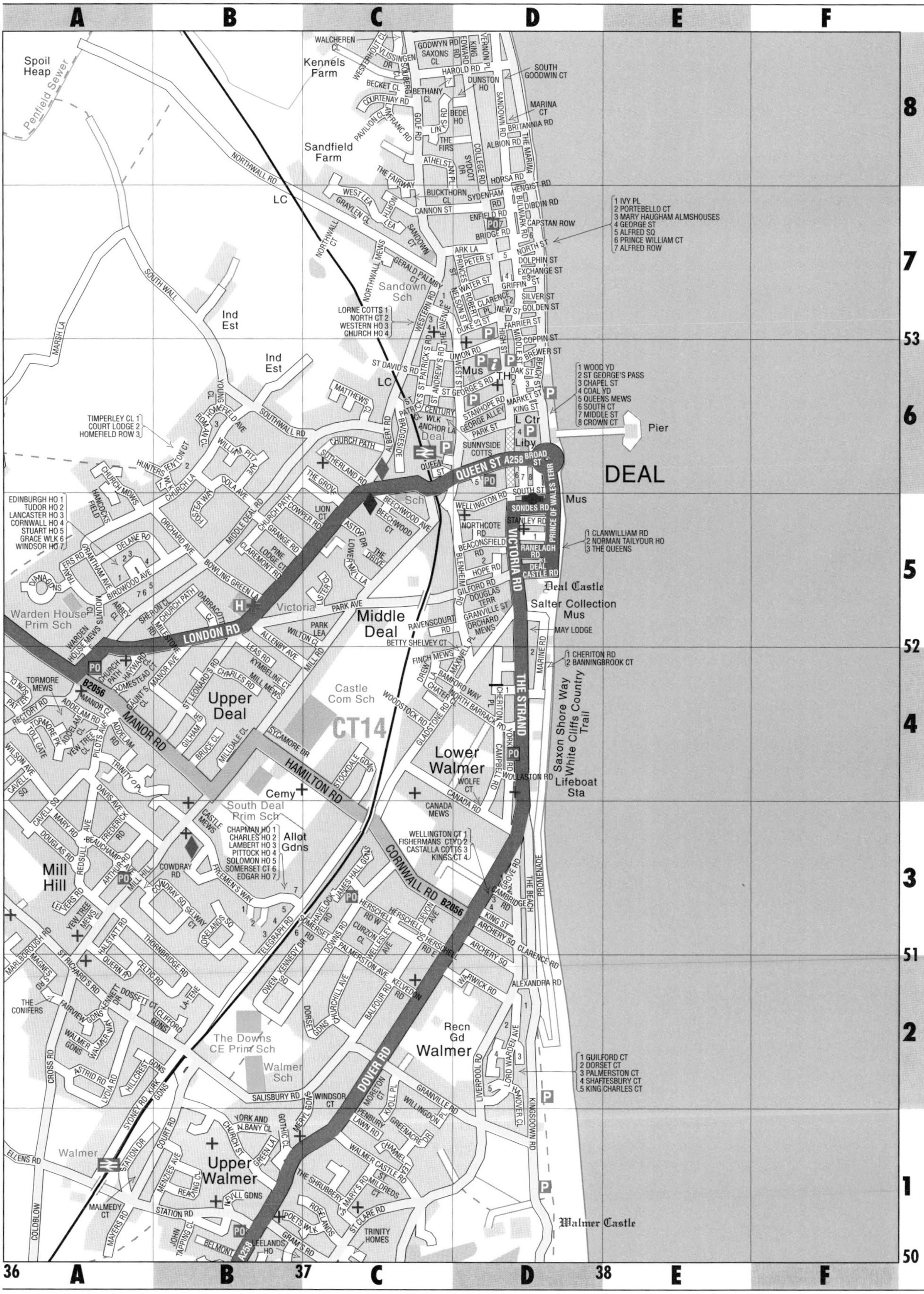
A
B
C
D
E
F
8
7
53
6
5
52
4
3
51
2
1
50
36
37
38
Spoil Heap
Penfield Sewer
Kennels Farm
Sandfield Farm
NORTHWALL RD
LC
SOUTH WALL
MARSH LA
Ind Est
Ind Est
NORTHWALL CT
NORTHWALL MEWS
Sandown Sch
WALCHEREN CL
WESTERHOUT CL
VLISSINGEN DR
SOLBERG
BECKET CL
COURTENAY RD
PAVILION CL
LANFRANC RD
GOLF RD
GODWYN RD
SAXONS CL
KING EDWARD RD
VERNON PL
HAROLD RD
SOUTH GOODWIN CT
BETHANY CL
DUNSTON HO
BEDE HO
LIN
THE FIRS
SANDOWN RD
MARINA CT
BRITANNIA RD
ALBION RD
THE MARINA
ATHELSTAN PL
SYDCOT DR
COLLEGE RD
HORSA RD
HENGIST RD
THE FAIRWAY
WEST LEA
GRAYLEN CL
NORTH LEA
SANDOWN CT
BUCKTHORN CL
CANNON ST
SYDENHAM RD
ENFIELD RD
DIBDIN RD
BULWARK RD
CAPSTAN ROW
BRIDGE RD
1 IVY PL
2 PORTEBELLO CT
3 MARY HAUGHAM ALMSHOUSES
4 GEORGE ST
5 ALFRED SQ
6 PRINCE WILLIAM CT
7 ALFRED ROW
GERALD PALMBY CT
ARK LA
PETER ST
PRINCES ST
NORTH ST
DOLPHIN ST
EXCHANGE ST
WATER ST
GRIFFIN ST
ROBERT ST
NELSON ST
CLARENCE PL
SILVER ST
GOLDEN ST
NEW ST
WESTERN RD
THE AVENUE
DUKE ST
FARRIER ST
LORNE COTTS 1
NORTH CT 2
WESTERN HO 3
CHURCH HO 4
COPPIN ST
BREWER ST
HIGH ST
MIDDLE ST
BEACH ST
UNION RD
ST PATRICK'S RD
ST ANDREW'S RD
WEST ST
ST DAVID'S RD
Mus
OAK ST
1 WOOD YD
2 ST GEORGE'S PASS
3 CHAPEL ST
4 COAL YD
5 QUEENS MEWS
6 SOUTH CT
7 MIDDLE ST
8 CROWN CT
ST GEORGE'S RD
TH
MATTHEWS CL
ALBERT RD
BRIDGESIDE
CENTURY WLK
STANHOPE RD
MARKET ST
KING ST
GEORGE ALLEY
ANCHOR LA
PARK ST
L Ctr
Liby
Pier
Deal
SUNNYSIDE COTTS
QUEEN ST
A258
BROAD ST
DEAL
CHURCH PATH
SOUTHWALL RD
SUTHERLAND RD
THE GROVE
LION CT
BEECHWOOD AVE
BEECHWOOD CT
Sch
WELLINGTON RD
SOUTH ST
SONDES RD
PRINCE OF WALES TERR
Mus
NORTHCOTE RD
STANLEY RD
BEACONSFIELD RD
RANELAGH RD
1 CLANWILLIAM RD
2 NORMAN TAILYOUR HO
3 THE QUEENS
HOPE RD
BLENHEIM RD
VICTORIA RD
DEAL CASTLE RD
Deal Castle
Salter Collection Mus
GILFORD RD
DOUGLAS TERR
GRANVILLE ST
ORCHARD MEWS
MAY LODGE
TIMPERLEY CL 1
COURT LODGE 2
HOMEFIELD ROW 3
YOUNG CL
HOMEFIELD AVE
ROMAN CL
WILLIAM PITT AVE
FENTON CT
HUNTERS WLK
CHURCH LA
DOLA AVE
FOSTER WAY
CHURCH MEWS
HANCOCKS FIELD
EDINBURGH HO 1
TUDOR HO 2
LANCASTER HO 3
CORNWALL HO 4
STUART HO 5
GRACE WLK 6
WINDSOR HO 7
DELANE RD
ORCHARD AVE
MIDDLE DEAL RD
CHURCH PATH
COWPER RD
GRANGE RD
PINE LODGE CT
CLAREMONT RD
ASTOR DR
LOWER MILL LA
THE DRIVE
BOWLING GREEN LA
GRANTHAM AVE
TRAVERS RD
DIANA GDNS
BIRDWOOD AVE
MOUNTS CL
ABBEY CL
SHERON CL
CHURCH PATH
DARRACOTT CL
MILESTONE
Victoria
PARK AVE
Middle Deal
RAVENSCOURT RD
Warden House Prim Sch
WARDEN HOUSE MEWS
LONDON RD
PARK LEA
WILTON CL
ALLENBY AVE
MILL RD
BETTY SHELVEY CT
FINCH MEWS
1 CHERITON RD
2 BANNINGBROOK CT
PO
CHURCH PATH
HAYWARD CL
HOMESTEAD CT
GAUNT'S CL
MANOR AVE
ST LEONARD'S RD
CHARLES RD
LEAS RD
KYMBELINE CT
MILL MEWS
Upper Deal
Castle Com Sch
CT14
WOODSTOCK RD
DREW LA
MAXWELL PL
BAMFORD WAY
CHATER CL
NORTH BARRACK RD
CHERITON PL
MARINE RD
THE STRAND
Saxon Shore Way
White Cliffs Country Trail
TORMORE MEWS
PATTERSON CL
RECTORY RD
ADDELAM RD
MANOR CL
B2056
MANOR RD
TOLL GATE
TORMORE PK
ADDELAM CL
YEW TREE CL
PILOTS AVE
ADDELAM RD
GILHAM GR
BRUCE CL
MILLDALE CL
SYCAMORE DR
STOCKDALE GDNS
GLADSTONE RD
Lower Walmer
CAMPBELL RD
YORK RD
WOLFE CT
WOLLASTON RD
Lifeboat Sta
WILSON AVE
CAVELL SQ
TRINITY PL
HAMILTON RD
Cemy
CANADA MEWS
CANADA RD
CAVELL SQ
MARY RD
DAVIS AVE
FREDERICK RD
CASTLE MEWS
South Deal Prim Sch
CHAPMAN HO 1
CHARLES HO 2
LAMBERT HO 3
PITTOCK HO 4
SOLOMON HO 5
SOMERSET CT 6
EDGAR HO 7
Allot Gdns
WELLINGTON CT 1
FISHERMANS CTYD 2
CASTALLA COTTS 3
KINGS CT 4
DOUGLAS RD
REDSULL AVE
BEAUCHAMP AVE
ARTHUR RD
COWDRAY RD
FREEMEN'S WAY
CORNWALL RD
Mill Hill
MILL HILL
COWDRAY SQ
SELWAY CT
ORELANDS SQ
TELEGRAPH RD
HAVELOCK RD
JAMES HALL GDNS
HERSCHELL RD W
HERSCHELL SQ
DEVON AVE
CAMBRIDGE RD
GROVE RD
THE BEACH
PROMENADE
LEFTERS RD
YEW TREE MEWS
HALSTATT RD
THORNBRIDGE RD
SOMERSET RD
KENNEDY DR
DOWNS RD
CURZON CL
WELLESLEY AVE
HERSCHELL RD E
KING ST
ARCHERY SQ
CLARENCE RD
MARLBOROUGH RD
MAGNESS RD
ST RICHARD'S RD
QUERN RD
CELTIC RD
OWEN SQ
PALMERSTON AVE
KELVEDON RD
WARWICK RD
ALEXANDRA RD
DOSSETT CT
LA-TENE
CLIFFORD GDNS
THE CONIFERS
FAIRVIEW GDNS
KENNETT DR
CHURCHILL AVE
BALFOUR RD
DORSET GDNS
WALMER GDNS
WALMER WAY
The Downs CE Prim Sch
Recn Gd
Walmer
DOVER RD
LIVERPOOL RD
LORD WARDEN AVE
1 GUILFORD CT
2 DORSET CT
3 PALMERSTON CT
4 SHAFTESBURY CT
5 KING CHARLES CT
CROSS RD
ASTRID RD
LYDIA RD
HILLCREST GDNS
Walmer Sch
SALISBURY RD
KIRK GDNS
SYDNEY RD
WINDSOR CT
MERYL GDNS
MORETON CT
KNOLL PL
GRANVILLE RD
WILLINGDON PL
HANOVER CL
KINGSDOWN RD
YORK AND ALBANY CL
GOTHIC CL
PENBURY LAWN RD
GREENACRE DR
CHURCH ST
GREEN LA
Walmer
ELLENS RD
STATION DR
COURT RD
MENZIES AVE
Upper Walmer
READING CL
NEVILL GDNS
THE SHRUBBERY
WALMER CASTLE RD
CHANNEL REST
ST MARY'S RD
ST MILDREDS CT
ST CLARE RD
Walmer Castle
MALMEDY CT
STATION RD
COLDBLOW
MAYERS RD
JOHN TAPPING CL
BELMONT RD
LEELANDS HO
POETS WLK
GRAM'S RD
ROSELANDS
TRINITY HOMES
A258

134

101

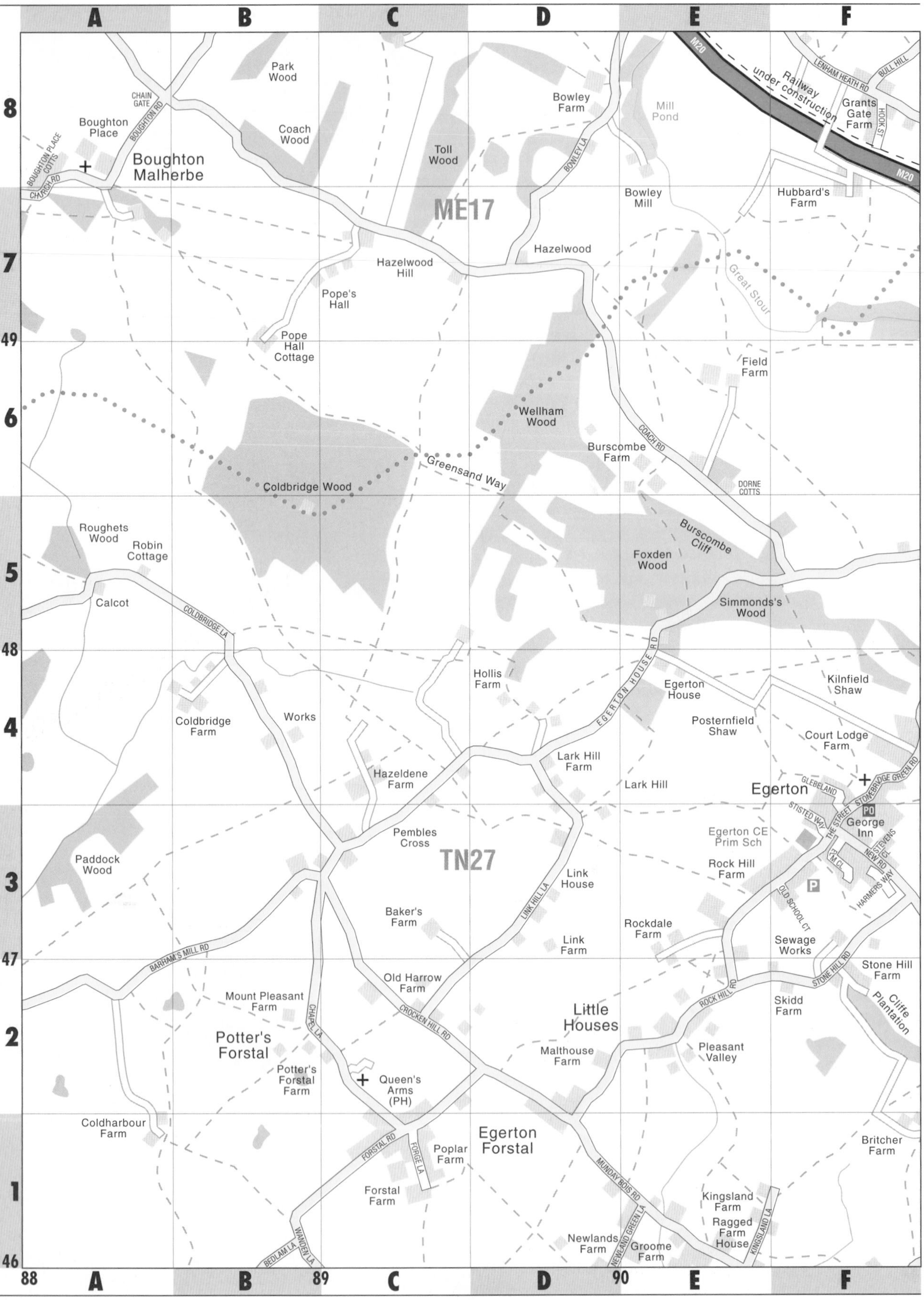
A
B
C
D
E
F
8
7
49
6
5
48
4
3
47
2
1
46
88
89
90
Park Wood
Coach Wood
Chain Gate
Boughton Rd
Boughton Place
Boughton Place Cotts
Church Rd
Boughton Malherbe
Toll Wood
ME17
Bowley Farm
Bowley La
Mill Pond
Bowley Mill
M20
Railway under construction
Lenham Heath Rd
Bull Hill
Grants Gate Farm
Hook St
Hubbard's Farm
Hazelwood
Hazelwood Hill
Pope's Hall
Pope Hall Cottage
Great Stour
Field Farm
Wellham Wood
Coach Rd
Burscombe Farm
Greensand Way
Coldbridge Wood
Dorne Cotts
Burscombe Cliff
Foxden Wood
Roughets Wood
Robin Cottage
Calcot
Coldbridge La
Simmonds's Wood
Hollis Farm
Egerton House Rd
Egerton House
Kilnfield Shaw
Coldbridge Farm
Works
Posternfield Shaw
Court Lodge Farm
Lark Hill Farm
Hazeldene Farm
Lark Hill
Egerton
Glebeland
Stonebridge Green Rd
PO
Stisted Way
The Street
George Inn
Pembles Cross
Egerton CE Prim Sch
Stevens Cl
New Rd
TN27
Paddock Wood
Link House
Rock Hill Farm
M Cl
Harmers Way
P
Link Hill La
Baker's Farm
Old School Ct
Rockdale Farm
Link Farm
Sewage Works
Stone Hill Rd
Stone Hill Farm
Barham's Mill Rd
Old Harrow Farm
Mount Pleasant Farm
Rock Hill Rd
Skidd Farm
Cliffe Plantation
Chapel La
Crocken Hill Rd
Little Houses
Potter's Forstal
Malthouse Farm
Pleasant Valley
Potter's Forstal Farm
Queen's Arms (PH)
Coldharbour Farm
Egerton Forstal
Forstal Rd
Forge La
Poplar Farm
Britcher Farm
Munday Bois Rd
Forstal Farm
Kingsland Farm
Ragged Farm House
Kingsland La
Newlands Farm
Newland Green La
Groome Farm
Bedlam La
Wanden La

135

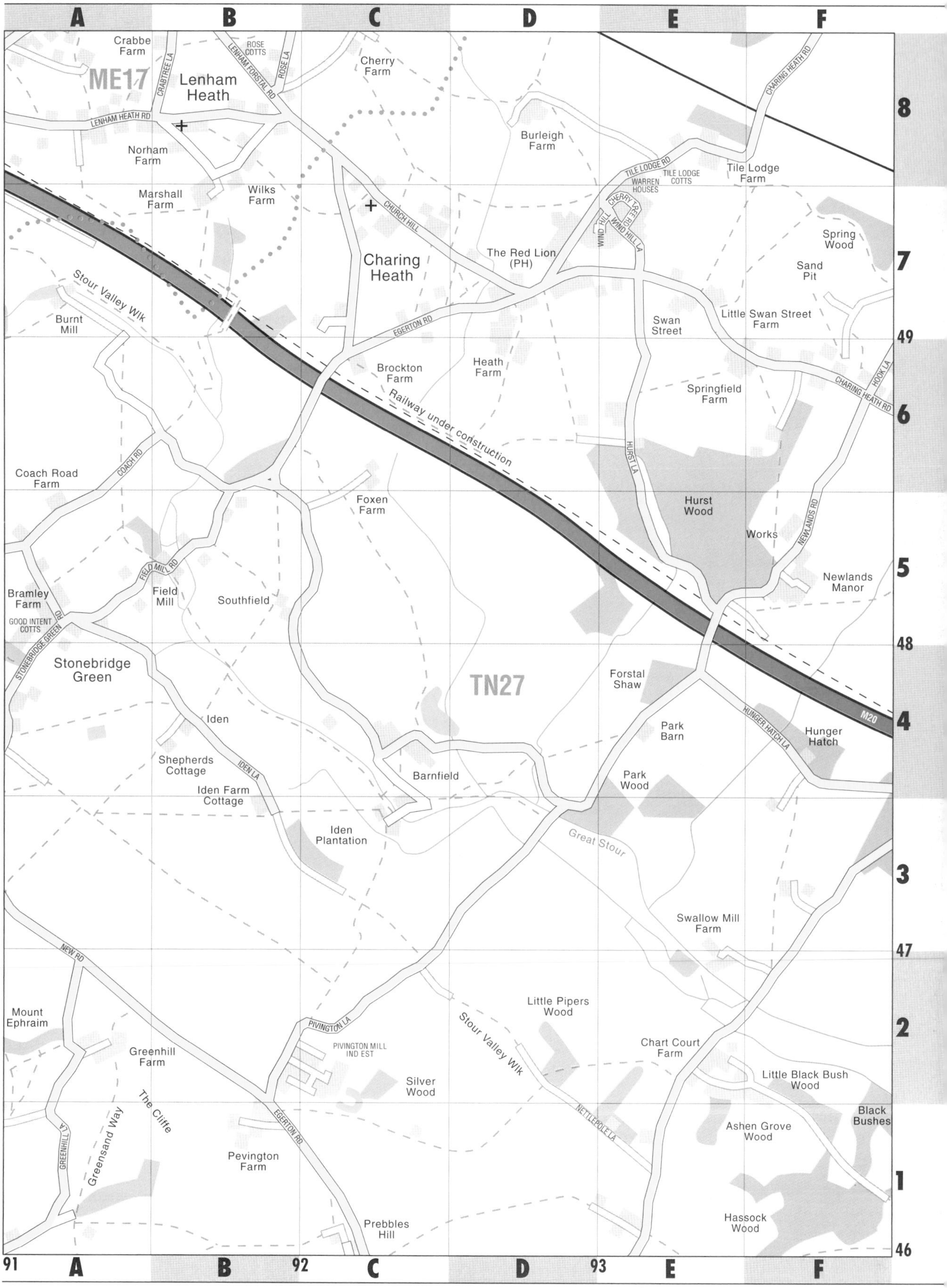
A
B
C
D
E
F
Crabbe Farm
ME17
ROSE COTTS
CRABTREE LA
LENHAM FORSTAL RD
ROSE LA
Lenham Heath
Cherry Farm
LENHAM HEATH RD
Norham Farm
Burleigh Farm
CHARING HEATH RD
Tile Lodge Farm
TILE LODGE RD
TILE LODGE COTTS
WARREN HOUSES
Marshall Farm
Wilks Farm
CHURCH HILL
CHERRY TREE RD
WIND HILL
WIND HILL LA
Spring Wood
The Red Lion (PH)
Sand Pit
Charing Heath
Stour Valley Wlk
Burnt Mill
EGERTON RD
Swan Street
Little Swan Street Farm
Brockton Farm
Heath Farm
Springfield Farm
HOOK LA
CHARING HEATH RD
Railway under construction
COACH RD
Coach Road Farm
HURST LA
Foxen Farm
Hurst Wood
NEWLANDS RD
Works
Newlands Manor
FIELD MILL RD
Bramley Farm
Field Mill
Southfield
GOOD INTENT COTTS
STONEBRIDGE GREEN RD
Stonebridge Green
Forstal Shaw
TN27
HUNGER HATCH LA
Hunger Hatch
M20
Iden
Park Barn
Shepherds Cottage
IDEN LA
Park Wood
Barnfield
Iden Farm Cottage
Iden Plantation
Great Stour
Swallow Mill Farm
NEW RD
Little Pipers Wood
Mount Ephraim
PIVINGTON LA
Stour Valley Wlk
Chart Court Farm
PIVINGTON MILL IND EST
Greenhill Farm
The Cliffe
Silver Wood
Little Black Bush Wood
NETTLEPOLE LA
Black Bushes
Ashen Grove Wood
GREENHILL LA
Greensand Way
EGERTON RD
Pevington Farm
Hassock Wood
Prebbles Hill
8
7
49
6
5
48
4
3
47
2
1
46
91
92
93

← 119   103

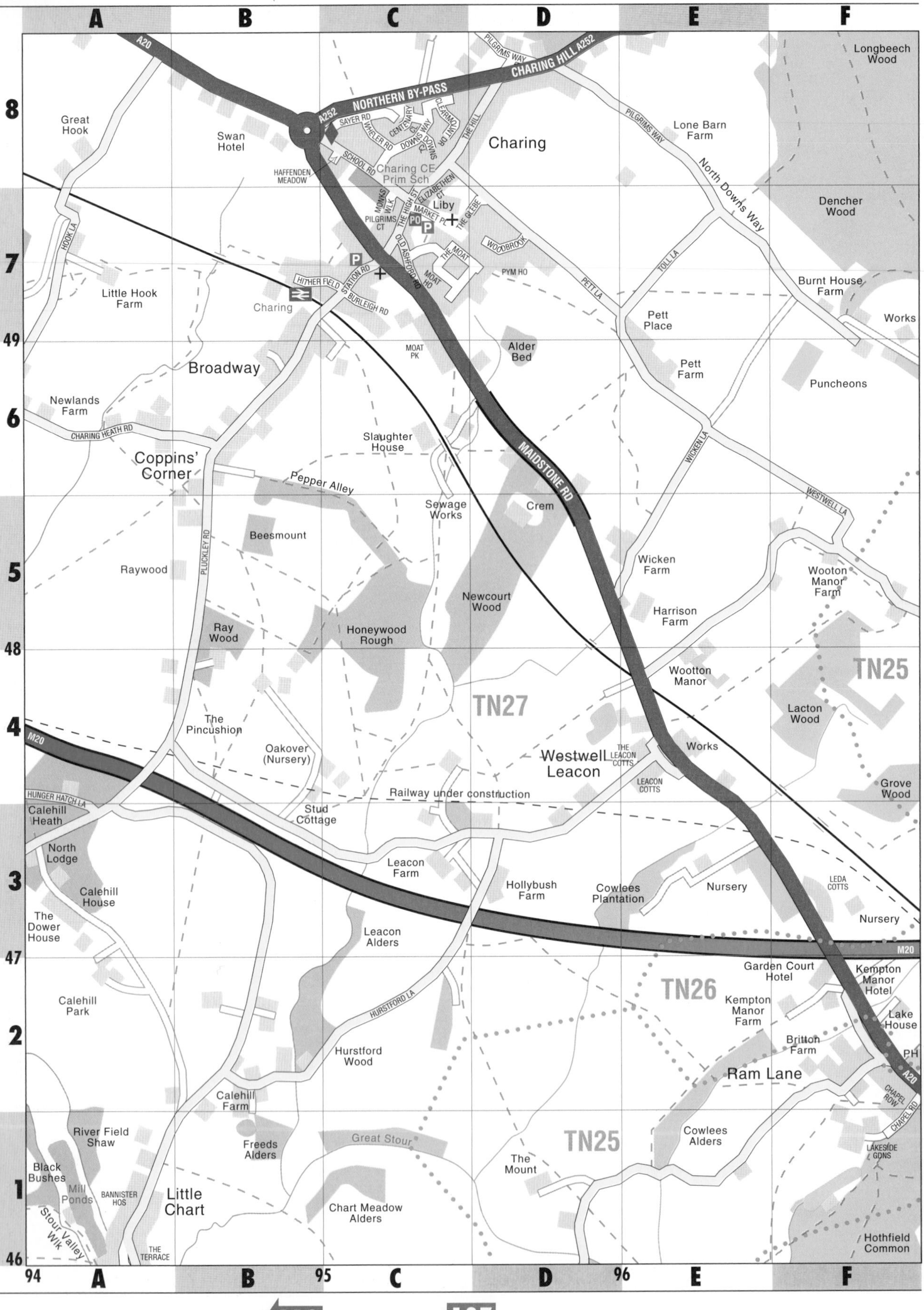

A   B   C   D   E   F

8

Great Hook

Swan Hotel

A20

A252 NORTHERN BY-PASS

CHARING HILL A252

PILGRIMS WAY

Charing

Lone Barn Farm

Longbeech Wood

North Downs Way

Dencher Wood

SAYER RD
WHEELER RD
CENTENARY WAY
DOWNS VIEW
SCHOOL RD
SWAN LANE
THE HILL
PILGRIMS WAY

HAFFENDEN MEADOW

Charing CE Prim Sch

MONKS WLK
THE HIGH ST
MARKET PL
ELIZABETHEN CT
PEARTREE LANE
Liby
PO P
PILGRIMS CT
OLD ASHFORD RD
THE GLEBE
WOODBROOK

7

Little Hook Farm

HOOK LA

P
HITHER FIELD
ST
BURLEIGH RD
Charing
STATION RD
THE MOAT
MOAT
PYM HO
PETT LA
TOLL LA

Burnt House Farm

Works

49

Broadway

MOAT PK

Alder Bed

Pett Place

Puncheons

6

Newlands Farm

CHARING HEATH RD

Coppins' Corner

Pepper Alley

Slaughter House

Sewage Works

Crem

Pett Farm

WICKEN LA

Wicken Farm

WESTWELL LA

Wooton Manor Farm

5

Raywood

PLUCKLEY RD

Beesmount

Honeywood Rough

Newcourt Wood

MAIDSTONE RD

Harrison Farm

Ray Wood

48

The Pincushion

Oakover (Nursery)

TN27

Wootton Manor

Works

Lacton Wood

TN25

4

M20

HUNGER HATCH LA

Calehill Heath

North Lodge

Calehill House

Stud Cottage

Railway under construction

Westwell Leacon

THE LEACON COTTS

LEACON COTTS

Grove Wood

3

The Dower House

Calehill Park

Leacon Farm

Leacon Alders

HURSTFORD LA

Hollybush Farm

Cowlees Plantation

Nursery

LEDA COTTS

Nursery

47

Garden Court Hotel

TN26

Kempton Manor Farm

Kempton Manor Hotel

Lake House

PH

A20

M20

2

Hurstford Wood

Calehill Farm

Britton Farm

Ram Lane

CHAPEL ROW

CHAPEL RD

1

River Field Shaw

Black Bushes

Mill Ponds

BANNISTER HOS

Little Chart

Freeds Alders

Great Stour

Chart Meadow Alders

The Mount

TN25

Cowlees Alders

LAKESIDE GDNS

Hothfield Common

46

Stour Valley Wlk

THE TERRACE

94   A   B   95   C   D   96   E   F

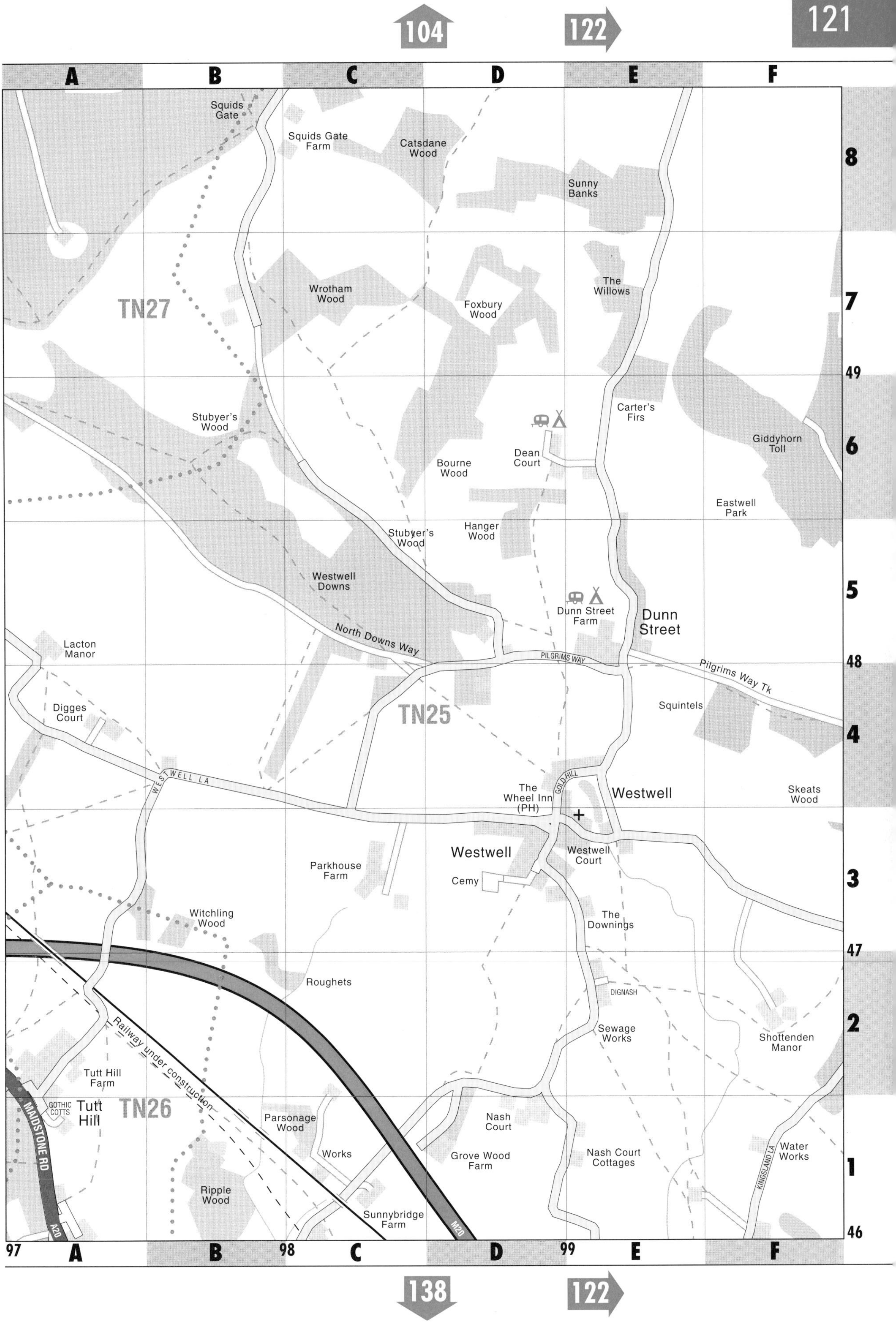

A B C D E F

8
7
49
6
5
48
4
3
47
2
1
46

97 98 99

Squids Gate
Squids Gate Farm
Catsdane Wood
Sunny Banks
TN27
Wrotham Wood
Foxbury Wood
The Willows
Stubyer's Wood
Carter's Firs
Dean Court
Giddyhorn Toll
Bourne Wood
Eastwell Park
Stubyer's Wood
Hanger Wood
Westwell Downs
Dunn Street Farm
Dunn Street
North Downs Way
PILGRIMS WAY
Pilgrims Way Tk
Lacton Manor
TN25
Squintels
Digges Court
WEST WELL LA
GOLD HILL
The Wheel Inn (PH)
Westwell
Skeats Wood
Parkhouse Farm
Westwell
Westwell Court
Cemy
The Downings
Witchling Wood
Railway under construction
Roughets
DIGNASH
Shottenden Manor
Sewage Works
Tutt Hill Farm
GOTHIC COTTS
Tutt Hill
TN26
Nash Court
Parsonage Wood
Works
Grove Wood Farm
Nash Court Cottages
Water Works
KINGSLAND LA
Ripple Wood
Sunnybridge Farm
MAIDSTONE RD
A20
M20

← 121
▲ 105

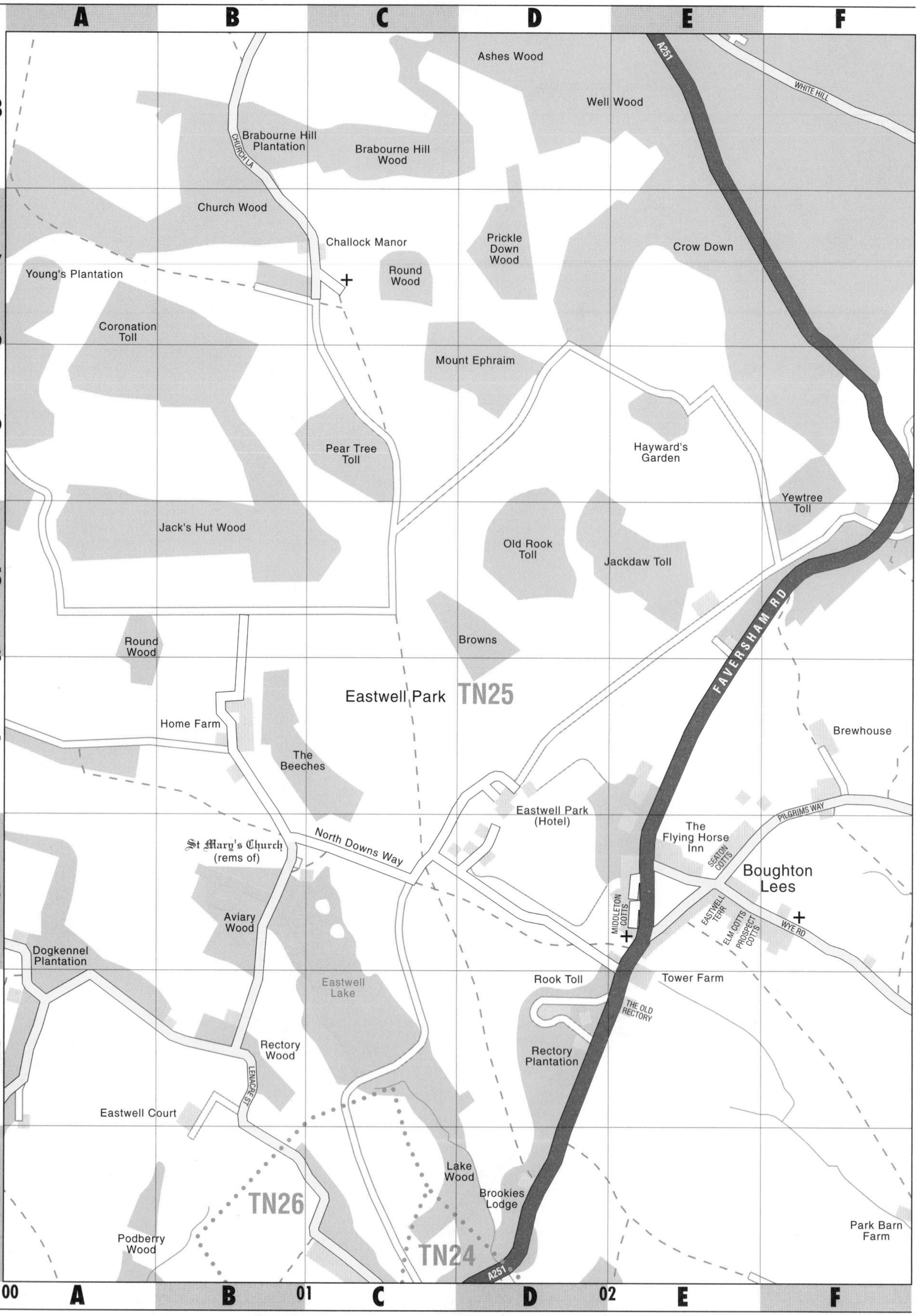

A B C D E F

8

Ashes Wood

Well Wood

A251

WHITE HILL

Brabourne Hill
Plantation

Brabourne Hill
Wood

CHURCH LA

Church Wood

7

Challock Manor

Round
Wood

Prickle
Down
Wood

Crow Down

Young's Plantation

Coronation
Toll

49

Mount Ephraim

6

Pear Tree
Toll

Hayward's
Garden

Yewtree
Toll

Jack's Hut Wood

Old Rook
Toll

Jackdaw Toll

FAVERSHAM RD

5

48

Round
Wood

Browns

Eastwell Park   TN25

4

Home Farm

Brewhouse

The
Beeches

Eastwell Park
(Hotel)

The
Flying Horse
Inn

PILGRIMS WAY

Boughton
Lees

SEATON COTTS

3

St Mary's Church
(rems of)

North Downs Way

MIDDLETON COTTS

EASTWELL TERR

ELM COTTS

PROSPECT COTTS

WYE RD

Aviary
Wood

Dogkennel
Plantation

47

Eastwell
Lake

Rook Toll

Tower Farm

THE OLD RECTORY

2

Rectory
Wood

Rectory
Plantation

LENACRE ST

Eastwell Court

Lake
Wood

Brookies
Lodge

Park Barn
Farm

1

TN26

Podberry
Wood

TN24

A251

46

00   A   01   B   C   02   D   E   F

← 121
▼ 139

106
124

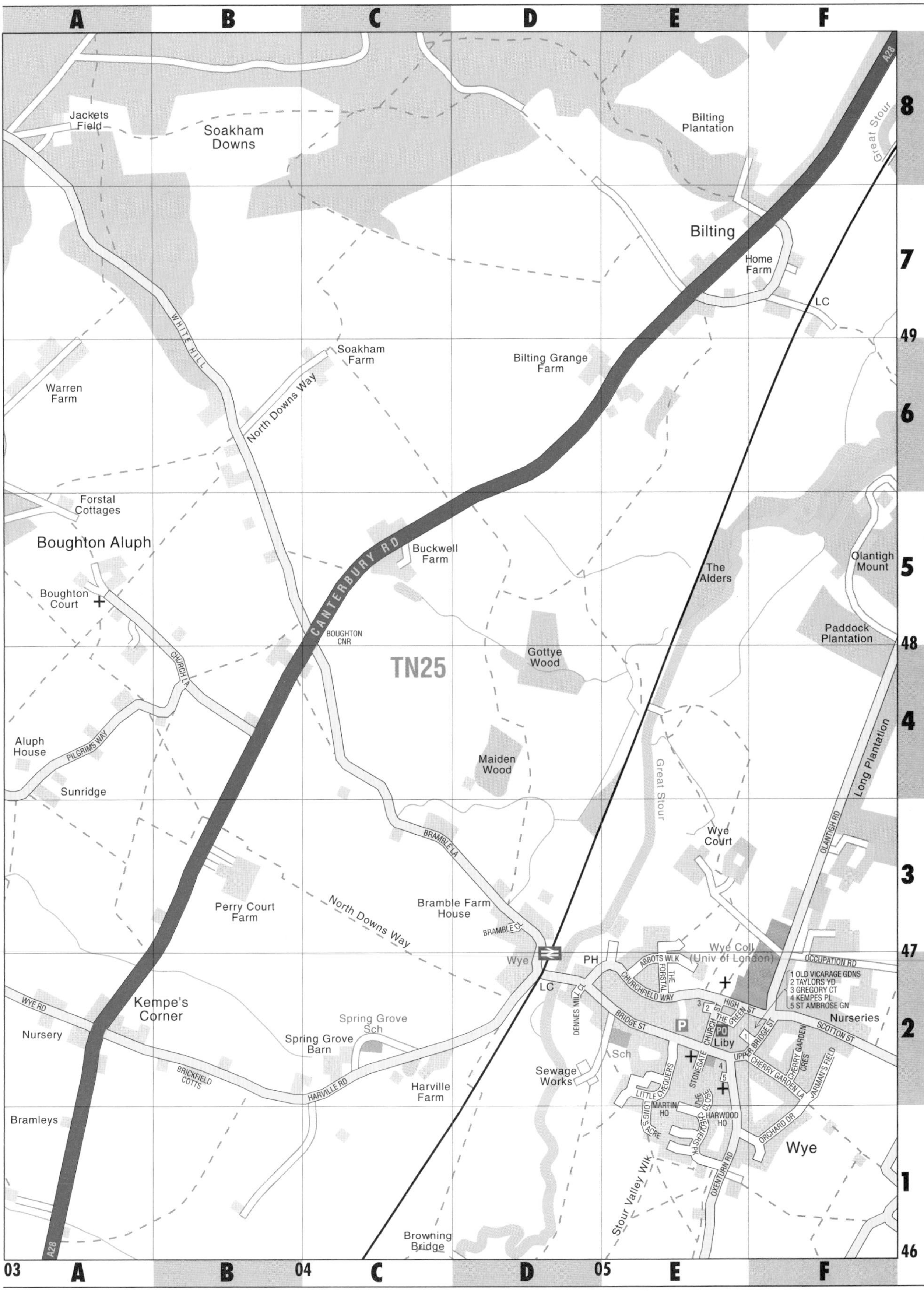
A
B
C
D
E
F
8
7
49
6
5
48
4
3
47
2
1
46
03
04
05
Jackets Field
Soakham Downs
Bilting Plantation
Great Stour
A28
Bilting
Home Farm
LC
WHITE HILL
Soakham Farm
North Downs Way
Bilting Grange Farm
Warren Farm
Forstal Cottages
Boughton Aluph
Buckwell Farm
CANTERBURY RD
The Alders
Olantigh Mount
Boughton Court
BOUGHTON CNR
Paddock Plantation
TN25
Gottye Wood
CHURCH LA
Aluph House
PILGRIMS WAY
Maiden Wood
Long Plantation
Sunridge
Great Stour
Wye Court
OLANTIGH RD
BRAMBLE LA
Perry Court Farm
North Downs Way
Bramble Farm House
BRAMBLE CL
Wye
PH
ABBOTS WLK
Wye Coll (Univ of London)
OCCUPATION RD
1 OLD VICARAGE GDNS
2 TAYLORS YD
3 GREGORY CT
4 KEMPES PL
5 ST AMBROSE GN
Kempe's Corner
LC
FORSTAL
THE
CHURCHFIELD WAY
WYE RD
DENNES MILL CL
BRIDGE ST
HIGH ST
CHURCH ST
THE GREEN
Nurseries
Spring Grove Sch
P
PO
Liby
UPPER BRIDGE ST
CHERRY GARDEN CRES
SCOTTON ST
Nursery
Spring Grove Barn
Sch
STONEGATE
CHERRY GARDEN LA
JARMAN'S FIELD
BRICKFIELD COTTS
Sewage Works
CHEQUERS
HARVILLE RD
Harville Farm
LITTLE CHEQUERS
MARTIN HO
THE CLOSE
HARWOOD HO
ORCHARD DR
Bramleys
LONG'S ACRE
CHEQUERS PK
Wye
Stour Valley Wlk
OXENTURN RD
Browning Bridge
A28

140
124

123
107

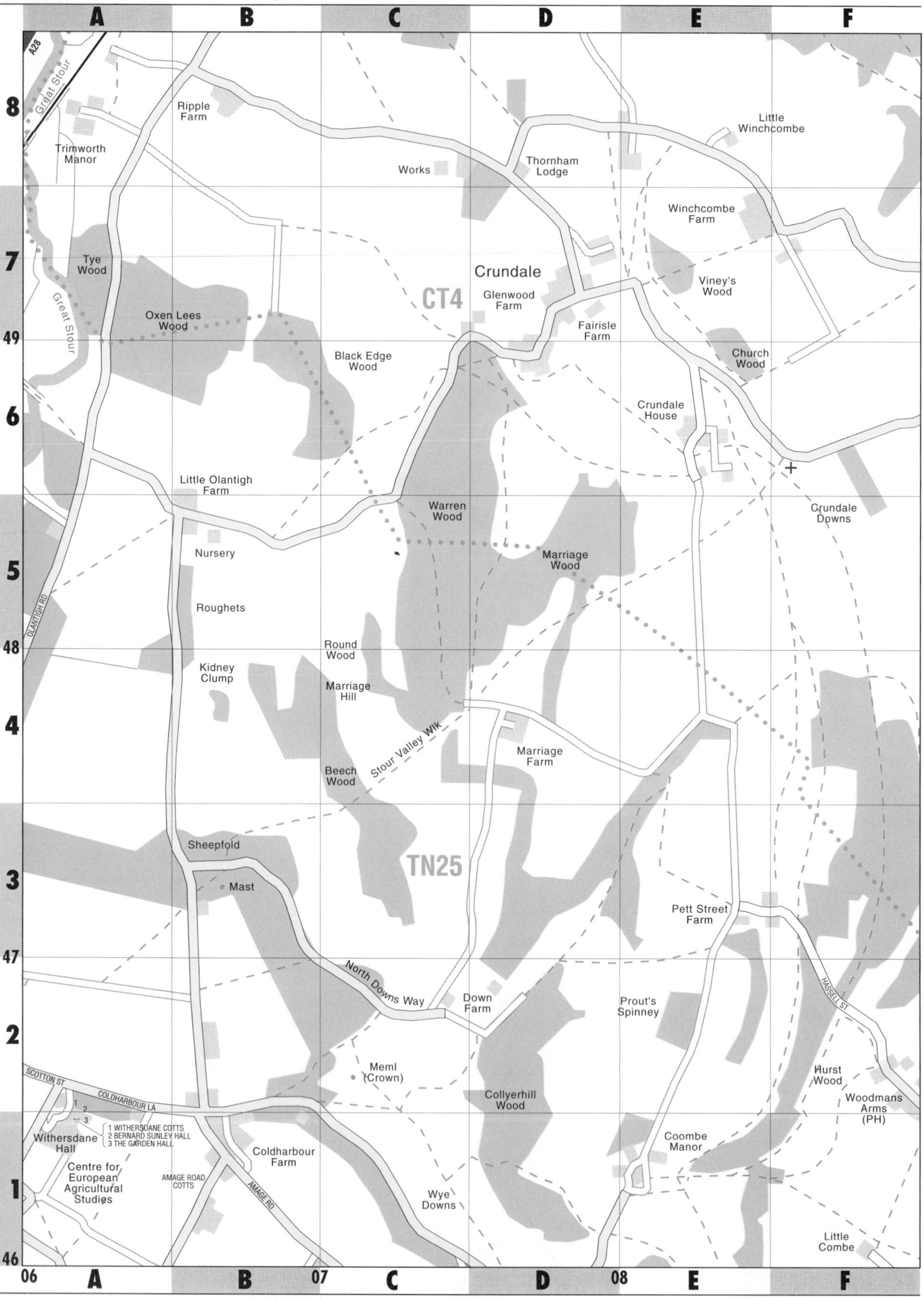

A B C D E F

8

Ripple
Farm

Trimworth
Manor

Little
Winchcombe

Works

Thornham
Lodge

Winchcombe
Farm

Tye
Wood

7

Crundale

Viney's
Wood

CT4

Glenwood
Farm

Oxen Lees
Wood

Fairisle
Farm

Church
Wood

49

Black Edge
Wood

6

Crundale
House

Little Olantigh
Farm

Warren
Wood

Crundale
Downs

Nursery

Marriage
Wood

5

Roughets

48

Round
Wood

Kidney
Clump

Marriage
Hill

4

Marriage
Farm

Beech
Wood

Stour Valley Wlk

Sheepfold

TN25

3

Mast

Pett Street
Farm

47

North Downs Way

Down
Farm

Prout's
Spinney

HASSELL ST

2

Meml
(Crown)

Hurst
Wood

SCOTTON ST

COLDHARBOUR LA

Woodmans
Arms
(PH)

1 WITHERSDANE COTTS
2 BERNARD SUNLEY HALL
3 THE GARDEN HALL

Collyerhill
Wood

Withersdane
Hall

Coombe
Manor

1

Centre for
European
Agricultural
Studies

AMAGE ROAD
COTTS

Coldharbour
Farm

AMAGE RD

Wye
Downs

Little
Combe

46

06 A B 07 C D 08 E F

Great Stour

Grdal Stour

A28

OLANTIGH RD

108
126

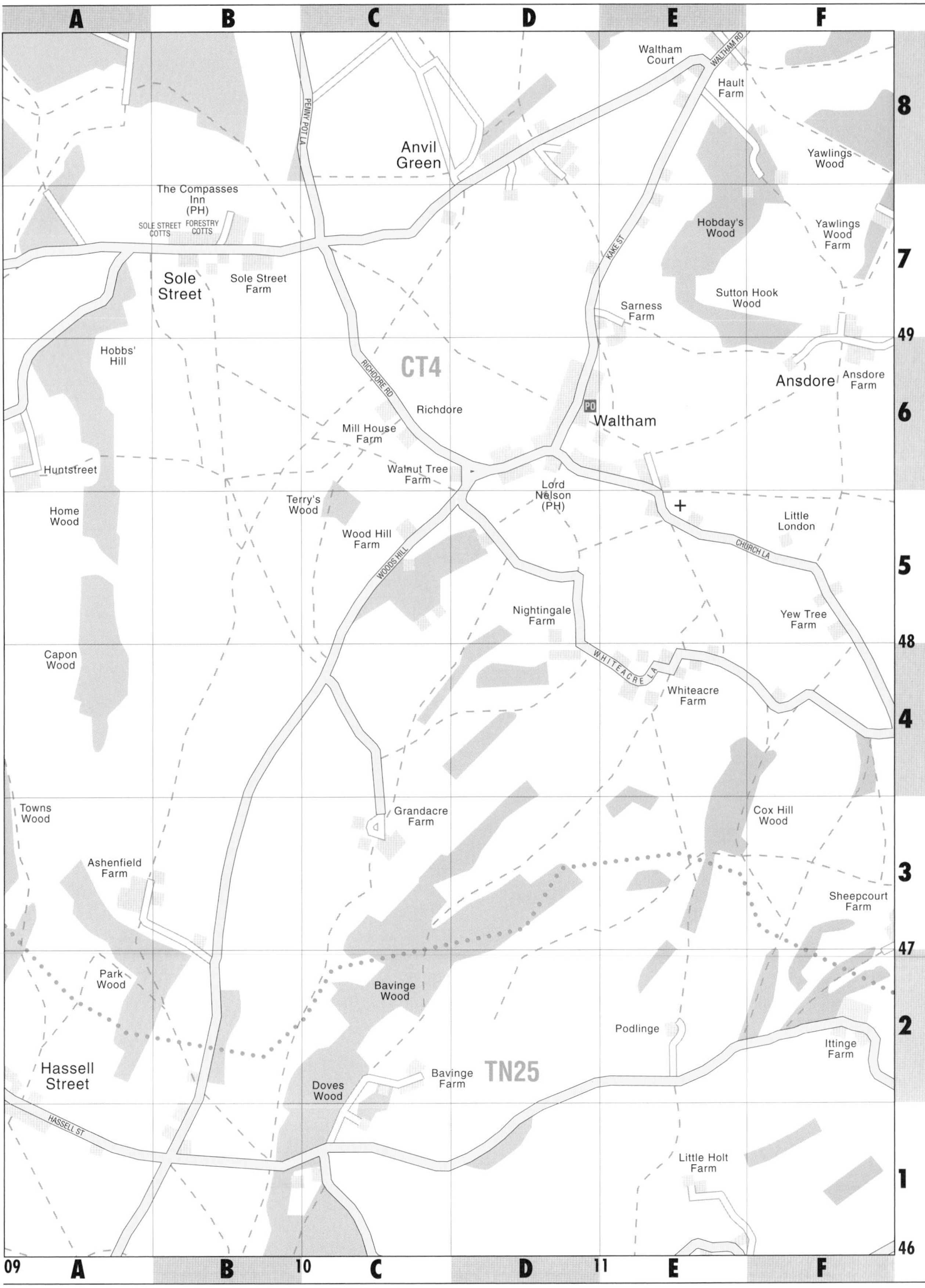
A
B
C
D
E
F
8
7
49
6
5
48
4
3
47
2
1
46
09
10
11
Waltham Court
WALTHAM RD
Hault Farm
PENNY POT LA
Anvil Green
Yawlings Wood
The Compasses Inn (PH)
SOLE STREET COTTS
FORESTRY COTTS
Hobday's Wood
Yawlings Wood Farm
KAKE ST
Sole Street
Sole Street Farm
Sutton Hook Wood
Sarness Farm
Hobbs' Hill
CT4
RICHDORE RD
Ansdore
Ansdore Farm
Richdore
PO
Waltham
Mill House Farm
Huntstreet
Walnut Tree Farm
Lord Nelson (PH)
Home Wood
Terry's Wood
Little London
Wood Hill Farm
CHURCH LA
WOODS HILL
Nightingale Farm
Yew Tree Farm
Capon Wood
WHITEACRE LA
Whiteacre Farm
Towns Wood
Grandacre Farm
Cox Hill Wood
Ashenfield Farm
Sheepcourt Farm
Park Wood
Bavinge Wood
Podlinge
Ittinge Farm
Hassell Street
Bavinge Farm
TN25
Doves Wood
HASSELL ST
Little Holt Farm

142
126

125
109

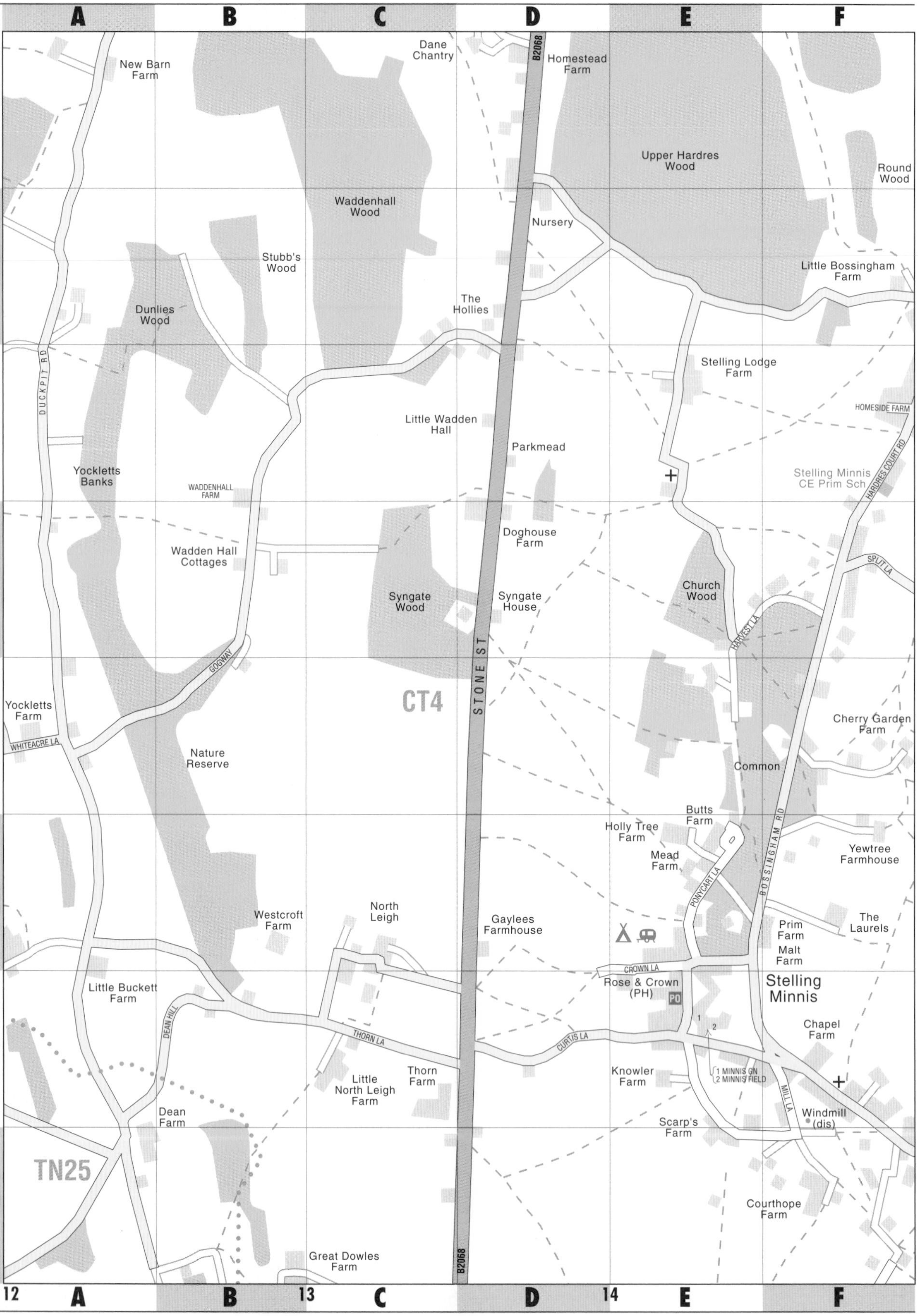

A B C D E F

8

New Barn Farm

Dane Chantry

Homestead Farm

B2068

Upper Hardres Wood

Round Wood

Waddenhall Wood

7

Stubb's Wood

Nursery

Little Bossingham Farm

Dunlies Wood

The Hollies

49

DUCKPIT RD

Stelling Lodge Farm

HOMESIDE FARM

6

Little Wadden Hall

Parkmead

Stelling Minnis CE Prim Sch

HARDRES COURT RD

Yockletts Banks

WADDENHALL FARM

Doghouse Farm

+

SPLIT LA

5

Wadden Hall Cottages

Syngate Wood

Syngate House

Church Wood

HARVEST LA

48

GODWAY

CT4

STONE ST

Common

Cherry Garden Farm

Yockletts Farm

4

WHITEACRE LA

Nature Reserve

Butts Farm

Holly Tree Farm

BOSSINGHAM RD

Yewtree Farmhouse

Mead Farm

3

Westcroft Farm

North Leigh

Gaylees Farmhouse

⛺ 🚐

Prim Farm

The Laurels

PONYCART LA

Malt Farm

47

Little Buckett Farm

CROWN LA

Rose & Crown (PH)

PO

Stelling Minnis

Chapel Farm

DEAN HILL

2

THORN LA

Thorn Farm

CURTIS LA

Knowler Farm

1 2

1 MINNIS GN
2 MINNIS FIELD

MILL LA

Little North Leigh Farm

Dean Farm

+

TN25

1

Scarp's Farm

Windmill (dis)

Courthope Farm

46

Great Dowles Farm

B2068

12 A B 13 C D 14 E F

110
128

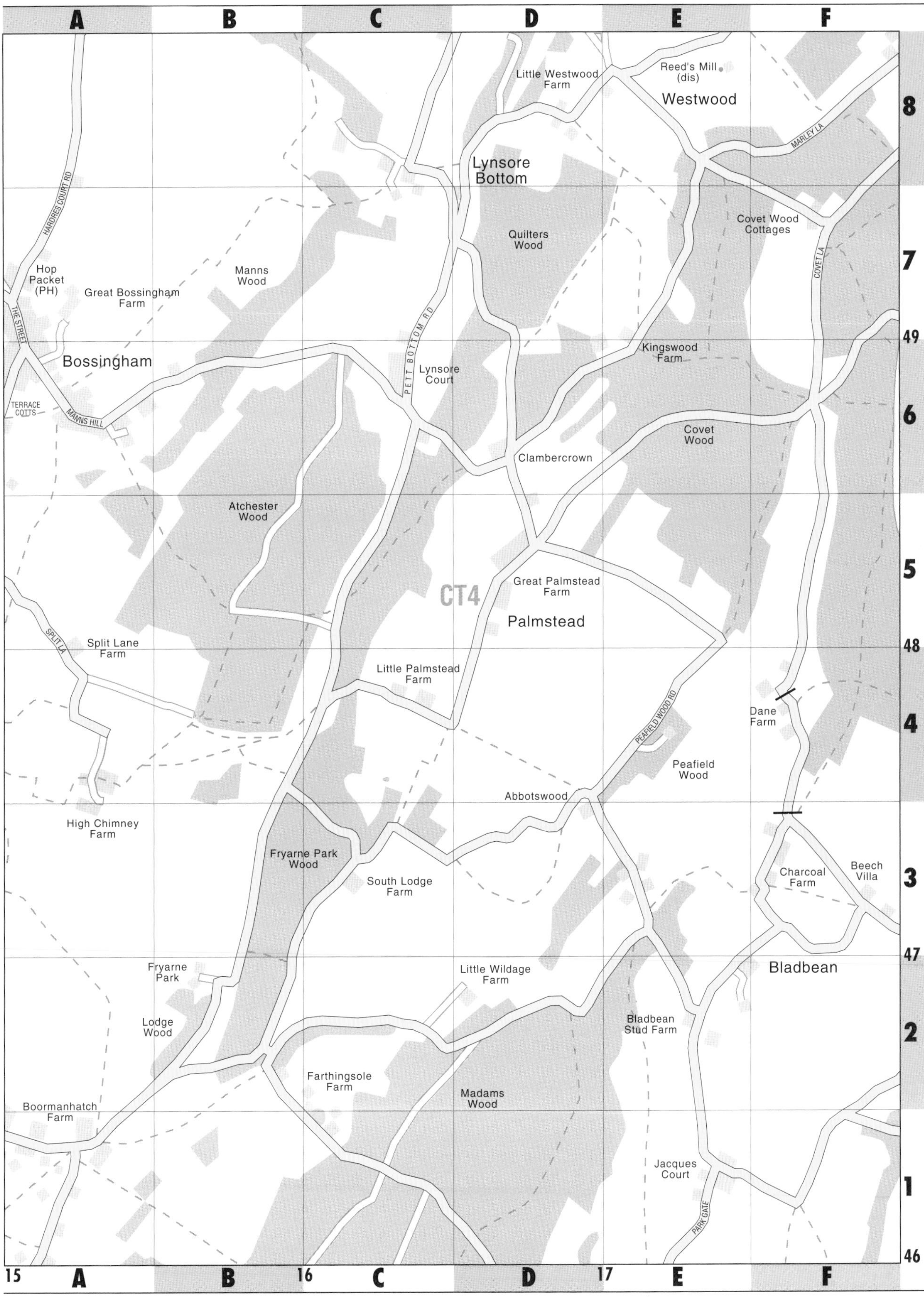
A
B
C
D
E
F
Little Westwood Farm
Reed's Mill (dis)
Westwood
MARLEY LA
Lynsore Bottom
HARDRES COURT RD
Quilters Wood
Covet Wood Cottages
COVET LA
Hop Packet (PH)
Great Bossingham Farm
Manns Wood
THE STREET
PETT BOTTOM RD
Bossingham
Lynsore Court
Kingswood Farm
TERRACE COTTS
MANNS HILL
Covet Wood
Clambercrown
Atchester Wood
CT4
Great Palmstead Farm
Palmstead
SPLIT LA
Split Lane Farm
Little Palmstead Farm
PEAFIELD WOOD RD
Dane Farm
Peafield Wood
Abbotswood
High Chimney Farm
Fryarne Park Wood
South Lodge Farm
Charcoal Farm
Beech Villa
Fryarne Park
Little Wildage Farm
Bladbean
Lodge Wood
Bladbean Stud Farm
Farthingsole Farm
Madams Wood
Boormanhatch Farm
Jacques Court
PARK GATE
8
7
49
6
5
48
4
3
47
2
1
46
15
16
17

144
128

127
111

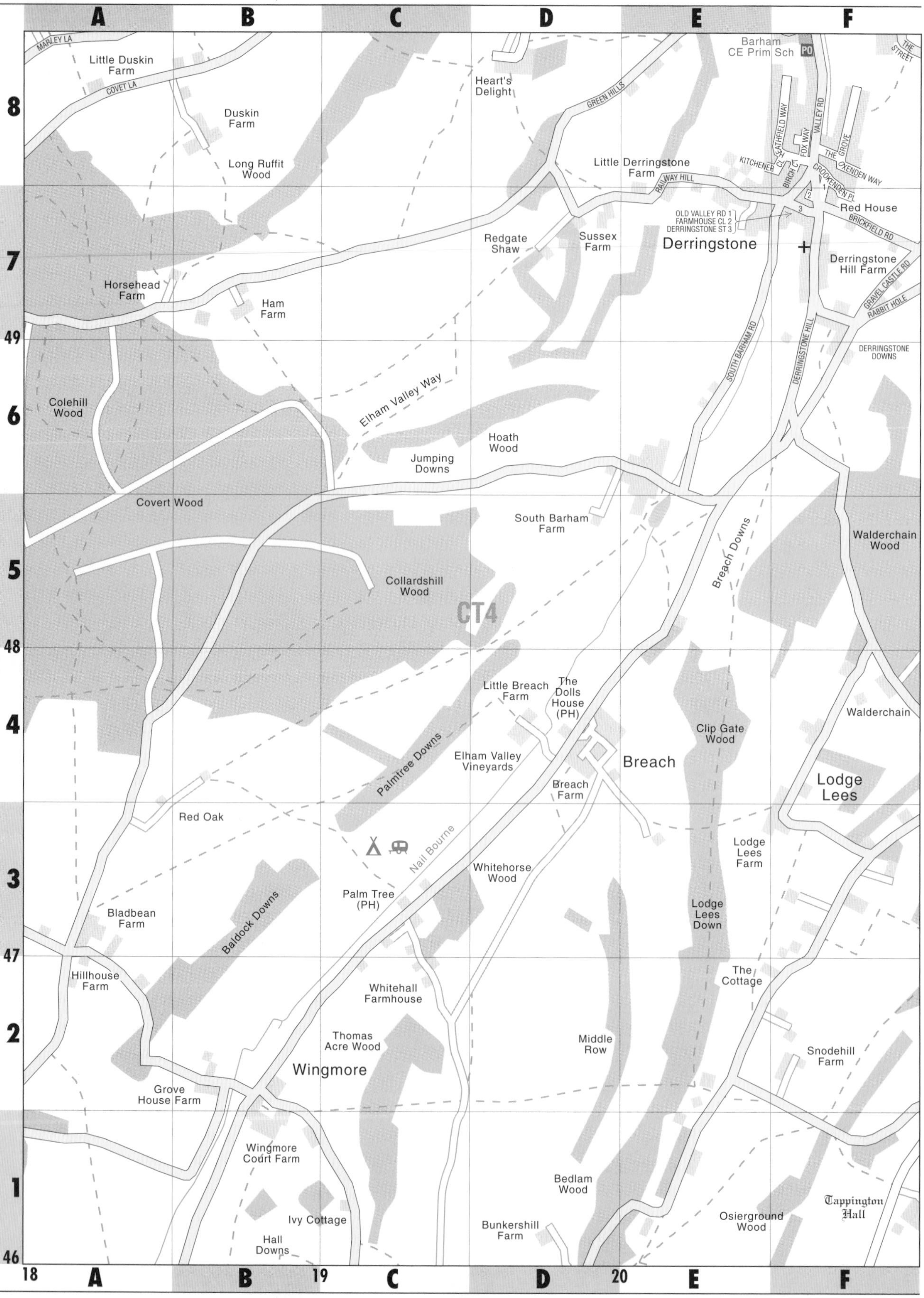
A
B
C
D
E
F
8
7
49
6
5
48
4
3
47
2
1
46
18
19
20
MARLEY LA
Little Duskin Farm
COVET LA
Duskin Farm
Long Ruffit Wood
Heart's Delight
GREEN HILLS
Barham CE Prim Sch
PO
THE STREET
Little Derringstone Farm
RAILWAY HILL
KITCHENER CL
HEATHFIELD WAY
FOX WAY
VALLEY RD
BIRCH CL
THE GROVE
THE OXENDEN WAY
CROCKENDEN PL
Red House
OLD VALLEY RD 1
FARMHOUSE CL 2
DERRINGSTONE ST 3
BRICKFIELD RD
Redgate Shaw
Sussex Farm
Derringstone
Derringstone Hill Farm
GRAVEL CASTLE RD
RABBIT HOLE
Horsehead Farm
Ham Farm
DERRINGSTONE DOWNS
SOUTH BARHAM RD
DERRINGSTONE HILL
Colehill Wood
Elham Valley Way
Hoath Wood
Jumping Downs
Covert Wood
South Barham Farm
Breach Downs
Walderchain Wood
Collardshill Wood
CT4
Little Breach Farm
The Dolls House (PH)
Walderchain
Clip Gate Wood
Palmtree Downs
Elham Valley Vineyards
Breach
Lodge Lees
Breach Farm
Red Oak
Nail Bourne
Lodge Lees Farm
Whitehorse Wood
Palm Tree (PH)
Bladbean Farm
Baldock Downs
Lodge Lees Down
Hillhouse Farm
The Cottage
Whitehall Farmhouse
Thomas Acre Wood
Middle Row
Snodehill Farm
Wingmore
Grove House Farm
Wingmore Court Farm
Bedlam Wood
Tappington Hall
Ivy Cottage
Bunkershill Farm
Osierground Wood
Hall Downs

127
145

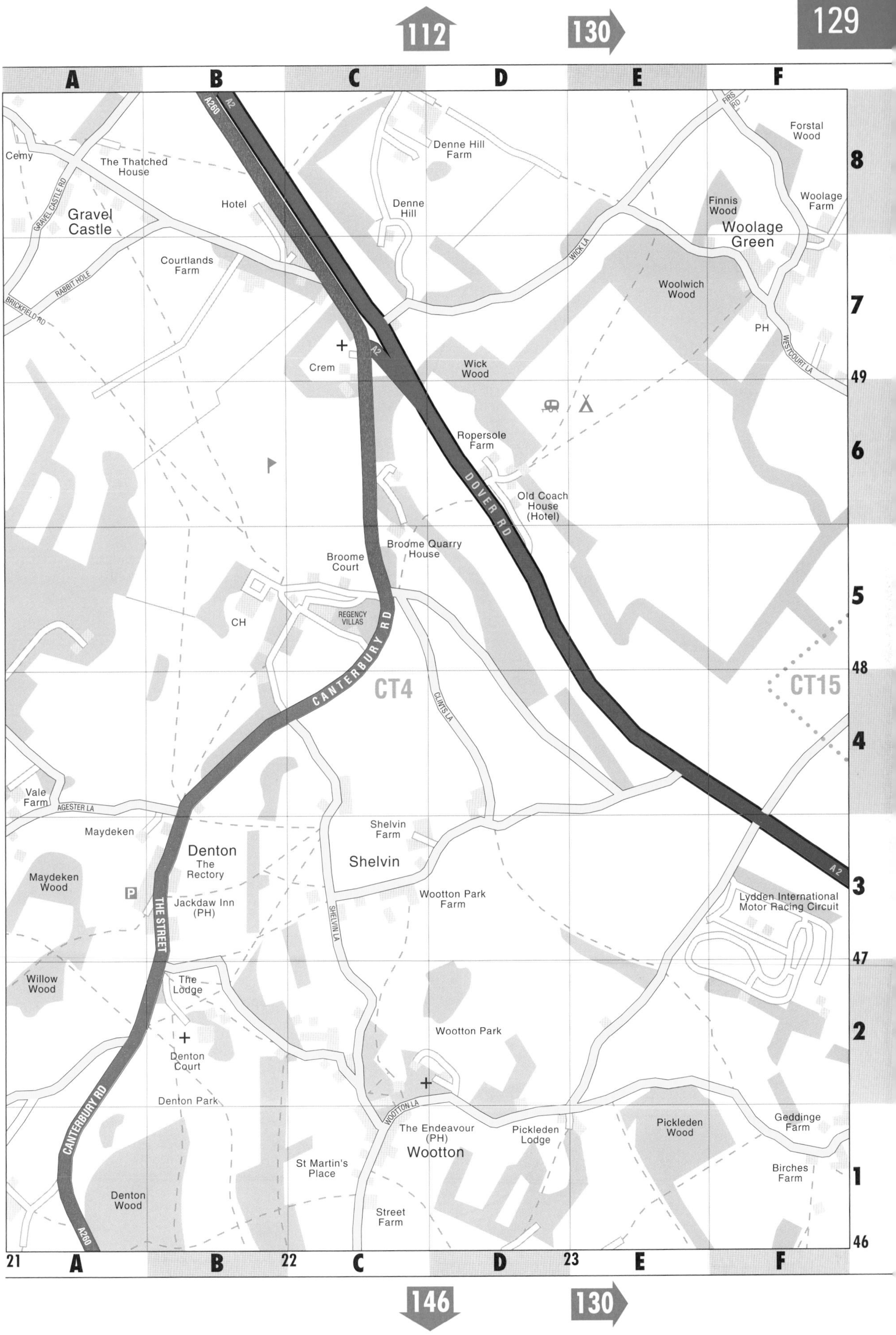
112
130
A
B
C
D
E
F
Cemy
The Thatched House
Gravel Castle
Hotel
Courtlands Farm
GRAVEL CASTLE RD
RABBIT HOLE
BRICKFIELD RD
A260
A2
Denne Hill Farm
Denne Hill
Forstal Wood
FIRS RD
Finnis Wood
Woolage Farm
Woolage Green
WICK LA
Woolwich Wood
PH
WESTCOURT LA
Crem
Wick Wood
Ropersole Farm
DOVER RD
Old Coach House (Hotel)
Broome Quarry House
Broome Court
REGENCY VILLAS
CH
CANTERBURY RD
CT4
CT15
CLIMTS LA
Vale Farm
AGESTER LA
Maydeken
Denton
The Rectory
Shelvin Farm
Shelvin
Maydeken Wood
Jackdaw Inn (PH)
THE STREET
SHELVIN LA
Wootton Park Farm
Lydden International Motor Racing Circuit
Willow Wood
The Lodge
Denton Court
Wootton Park
Denton Park
WOOTTON LA
The Endeavour (PH)
Wootton
Pickleden Lodge
Pickleden Wood
Geddinge Farm
Birches Farm
St Martin's Place
Street Farm
Denton Wood
8
7
49
6
5
48
4
3
47
2
1
46
21
22
23
146
130

129
113

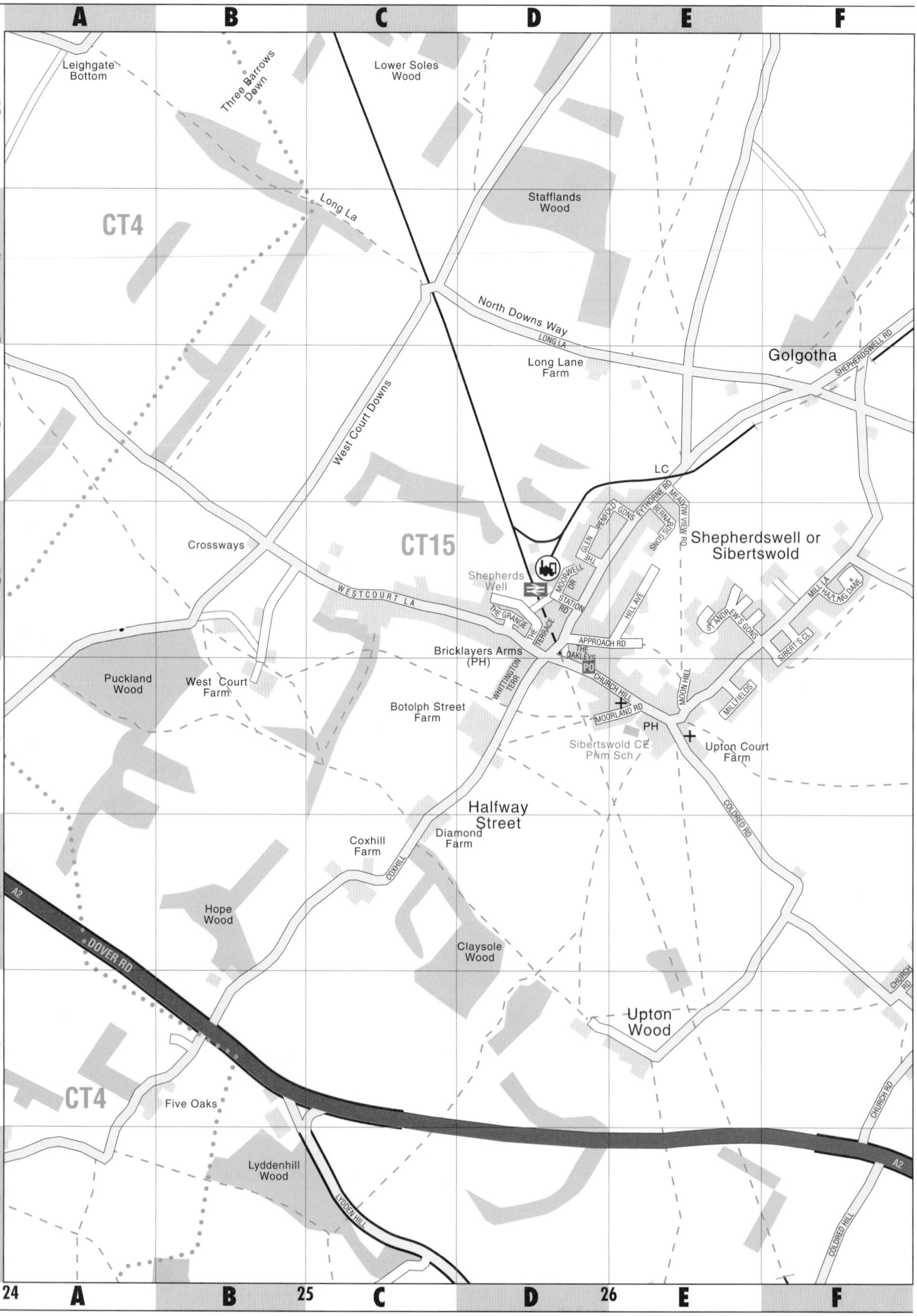

A B C D E F

8

Leighgate
Bottom

Three Barrows Down

Lower Soles
Wood

CT4

Long La

7

Stafflands
Wood

North Downs Way

49

LONG LA

Golgotha

SHEPHERDSWELL RD

Long Lane
Farm

West Court Downs

6

LC

Crossways

CT15

Shepherdswell or
Sibertswold

5

WESTCOURT LA

Shepherds
Well

GLEN
THE
OLD GDNS
EYTHORNE RD
BERNARD GDNS
MEADOW VIEW RD

HILL AVE

ST ANDREW'S GDNS

MILL LA

HAZLING DANE

MOORHELL DR
STATION RD

THE GRANGE

SIBERT'S CL

48

Puckland
Wood

West Court
Farm

THE TERRACE

APPROACH RD

THE
OAKLEYS

PO
CHURCH HILL

MILLFIELDS

Bricklayers Arms
(PH)

WHITTINGTON TERR

Botolph Street
Farm

MOORLAND RD

MOON HILL

Sibertswold CE
Prim Sch

PH

Upton Court
Farm

4

Halfway
Street

COLDRED RD

Coxhill
Farm

Diamond
Farm

COXHILL

A2

3

DOVER RD

Hope
Wood

Claysole
Wood

Upton
Wood

47

CHURCH RD

2

CT4

Five Oaks

COLDRED HILL

CHURCH RD

A2

Lyddenhill
Wood

LODGE HILL

1

46

24 A B 25 C D 26 E F

114
132

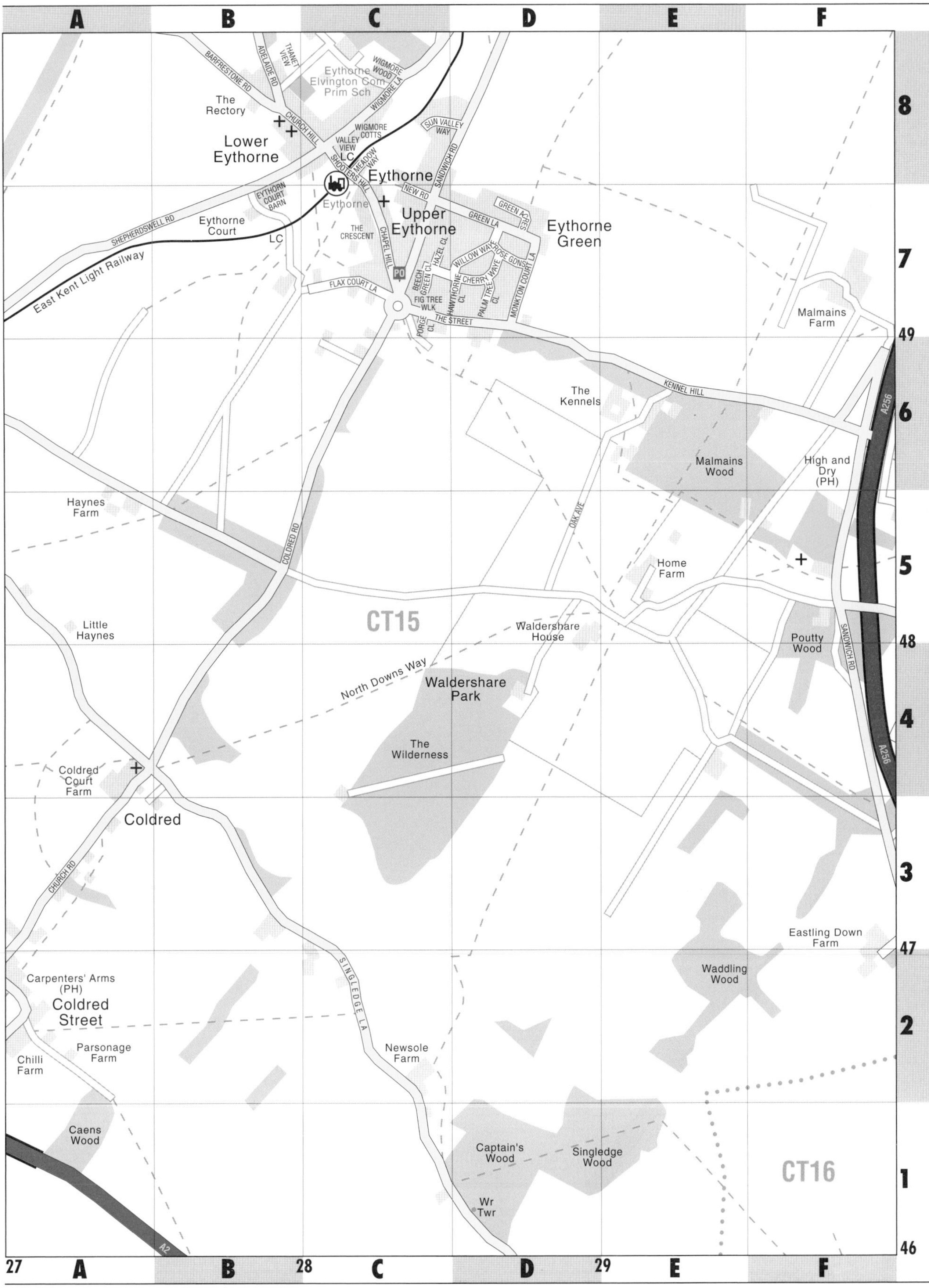
A
B
C
D
E
F
8
7
6
5
4
3
2
1
49
48
47
46
27
28
29
BARFRESTONE RD
ADELAIDE RD
THANET VIEW
Eythorne Elvington Com Prim Sch
WIGMORE WOOD
WIGMORE LA
The Rectory
CHURCH HILL
Lower Eythorne
WIGMORE COTTS
SUN VALLEY WAY
VALLEY VIEW
LC
MEADOW WAY
SHOOTERS HILL
Eythorne
NEW RD
SANDWICH RD
EYTHORN COURT BARN
Eythorne
Upper Eythorne
GREEN ACRES
GREEN LA
Eythorne Green
SHEPHERDSWELL RD
Eythorne Court
LC
THE CRESCENT
CHAPEL HILL
HAZEL CL
WILLOW WAY
ROSE GDNS
MONKTON COURT LA
East Kent Light Railway
PO
BEECH GREEN CL
CHERRY WAY
FLAX COURT LA
FIG TREE WLK
HAWTHORNE CL
PALM TREE CL
FORGE CL
THE STREET
Malmains Farm
The Kennels
KENNEL HILL
A256
Malmains Wood
High and Dry (PH)
Haynes Farm
COLDRED RD
OAK AVE
Home Farm
CT15
Little Haynes
Waldershare House
Poutty Wood
SANDWICH RD
North Downs Way
Waldershare Park
The Wilderness
A256
Coldred Court Farm
Coldred
CHURCH RD
Eastling Down Farm
SINGLEDGE LA
Waddling Wood
Carpenters' Arms (PH)
Coldred Street
Parsonage Farm
Chilli Farm
Newsole Farm
Caens Wood
Captain's Wood
Singledge Wood
CT16
Wr Twr
A2

148
132

131
115

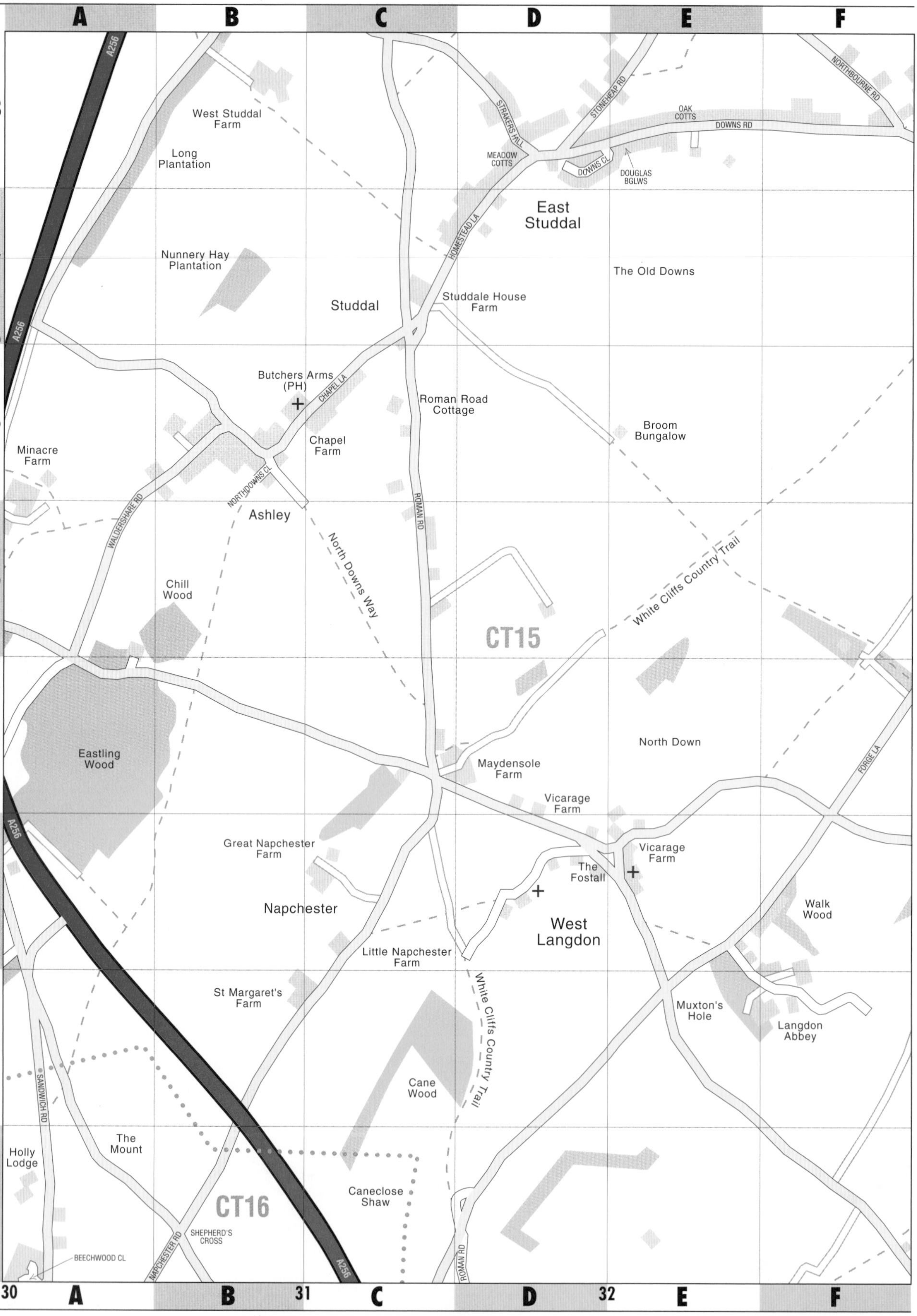
A
B
C
D
E
F
8
7
49
6
5
48
4
3
47
2
1
46
30
31
32
A256
West Studdal Farm
Long Plantation
Nunnery Hay Plantation
STRAKERS HILL
MEADOW COTTS
STONEHEAP RD
OAK COTTS
DOWNS RD
NORTHBOURNE RD
DOWNS CL
DOUGLAS BGLWS
East Studdal
HOMESTEAD LA
The Old Downs
Studdal
Studdale House Farm
Butchers Arms (PH)
CHAPEL LA
Roman Road Cottage
Broom Bungalow
Minacre Farm
Chapel Farm
NORTHDOWNS CL
WALDERSHARE RD
Ashley
ROMAN RD
North Downs Way
White Cliffs Country Trail
Chill Wood
CT15
Eastling Wood
North Down
Maydensole Farm
FORGE LA
Vicarage Farm
Great Napchester Farm
The Fostall
Napchester
Walk Wood
West Langdon
Little Napchester Farm
St Margaret's Farm
Muxton's Hole
Langdon Abbey
SANDWICH RD
Cane Wood
Holly Lodge
The Mount
Caneclose Shaw
CT16
SHEPHERD'S CROSS
NAPCHESTER RD
BEECHWOOD CL

131
149

116
134

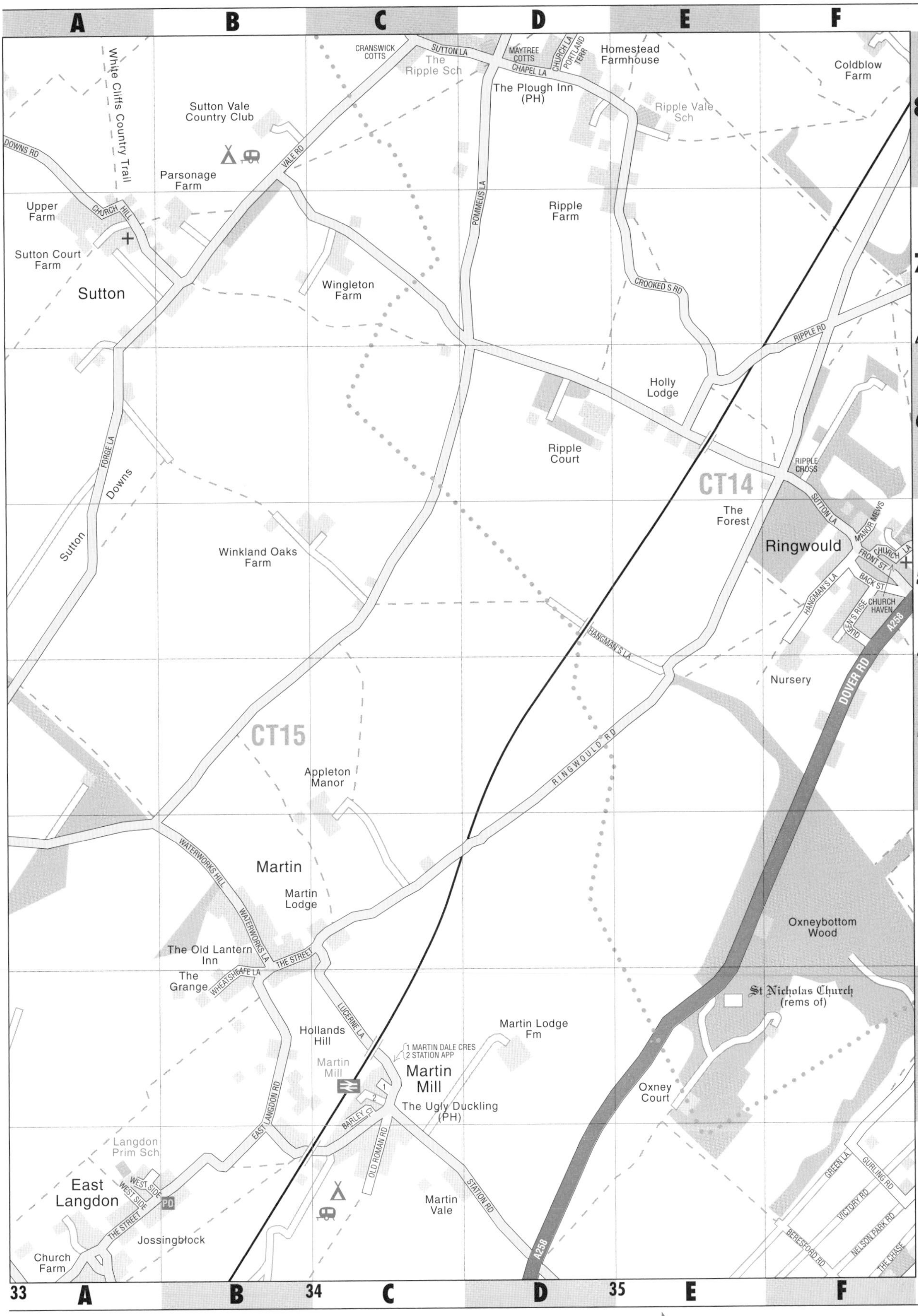
A
B
C
D
E
F
White Cliffs Country Trail
CRANSWICK COTTS
SUTTON LA
The Ripple Sch
MAYTREE COTTS
CHURCH LA
PORTLAND TERR
CHAPEL LA
Homestead Farmhouse
Coldblow Farm
The Plough Inn (PH)
Sutton Vale Country Club
Ripple Vale Sch
DOWNS RD
VALE RD
Parsonage Farm
Upper Farm
CHURCH HILL
POMMEUS LA
Ripple Farm
Sutton Court Farm
Sutton
Wingleton Farm
CROOKED S RD
RIPPLE RD
Holly Lodge
FORGE LA
Downs
Ripple Court
RIPPLE CROSS
CT14
The Forest
SUTTON LA
MANOR MEWS
Sutton
Winkland Oaks Farm
Ringwould
CHURCH LA
FRONT ST
BACK ST
HANGMAN'S LA
CHURCH HAVEN
QUEEN'S RISE
A258
HANGMAN'S LA
Nursery
DOVER RD
CT15
RINGWOULD RD
Appleton Manor
Martin
WATERWORKS HILL
Martin Lodge
WATERWORKS LA
Oxneybottom Wood
The Old Lantern Inn
THE STREET
The Grange
WHEATSHEAF LA
St Nicholas Church (rems of)
LUCERNE LA
Hollands Hill
Martin Lodge Fm
1 MARTIN DALE CRES
2 STATION APP
Martin Mill
Martin Mill
EAST LANGDON RD
The Ugly Duckling (PH)
Oxney Court
BARLEY CL
OLD ROMAN RD
Langdon Prim Sch
GREEN LA
GURLING RD
WEST SIDE
WEST SIDE
PO
East Langdon
THE STREET
Martin Vale
STATION RD
VICTORY RD
BERESFORD RD
NELSON PARK RD
Jossingblock
THE CHASE
Church Farm
A258
8
7
49
6
5
48
4
3
47
2
1
46
33
34
35

150
134

133
117

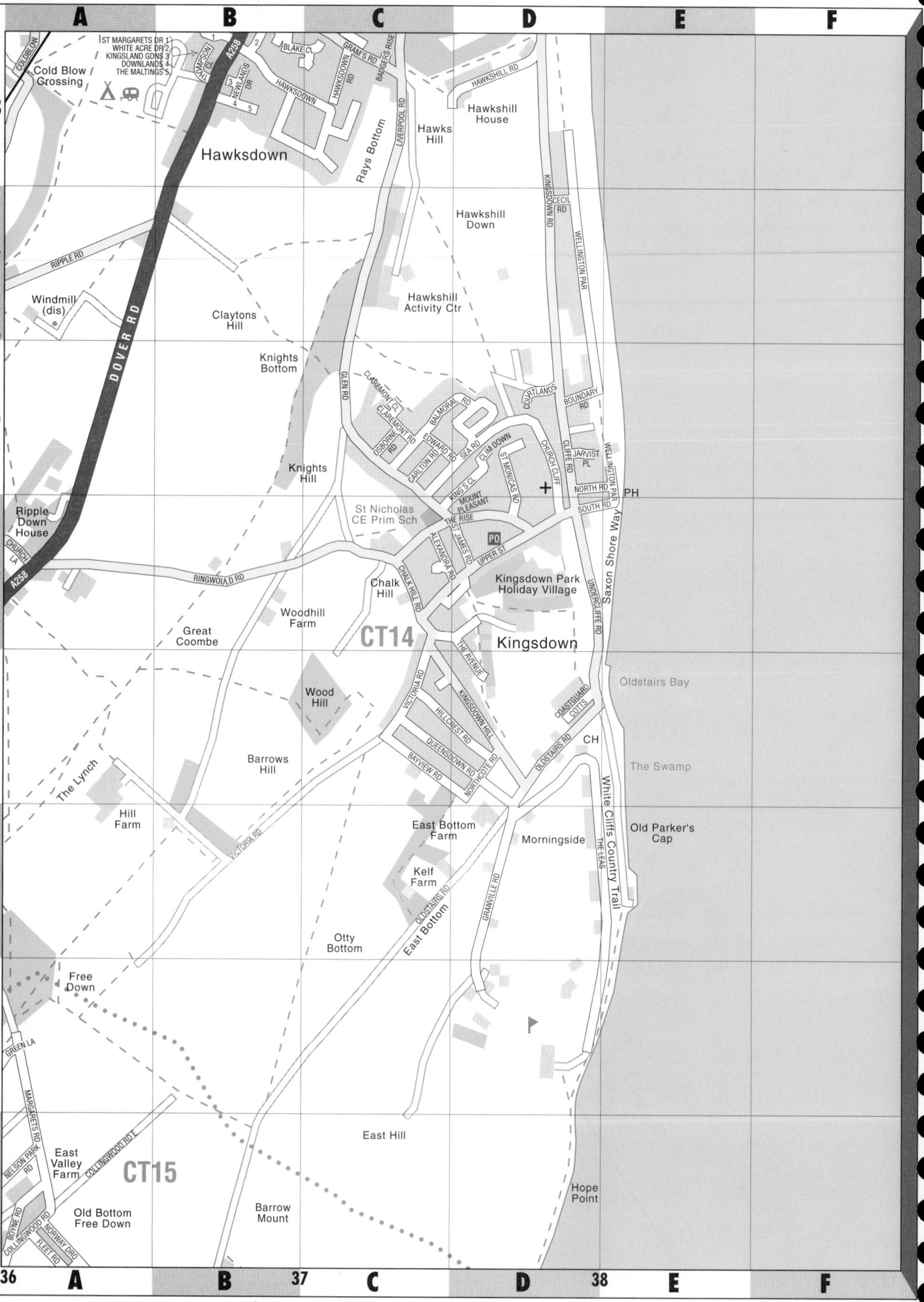
A
B
C
D
E
F
8
7
49
6
5
48
4
3
47
2
1
46
36
37
38
ST MARGARETS DR 1
WHITE ACRE DR 2
KINGSLAND GDNS 3
DOWNLANDS 4
THE MALTINGS 5
COLDBLOW
Cold Blow Crossing
THOMPSON CL
A258
NEWLANDS DR
BLAKE CL
GRAM'S RD
BADGERS RISE
HAWKSDOWN
HAWKSDOWN RD
LIVERPOOL RD
HAWKSHILL RD
Hawkshill House
Hawks Hill
Hawksdown
Rays Bottom
KINGSDOWN RD
CECIL RD
WELLINGTON PAR
Hawkshill Down
RIPPLE RD
Windmill (dis)
Hawkshill Activity Ctr
Claytons Hill
DOVER RD
Knights Bottom
GLEN RD
CLAREMONT CL
CLAREMONT RD
OSBORNE RD
BALMORAL RD
EDWARD RD
CARLTON RD
SEA RD
CLIM DOWN
ST MONICAS RD
KING'S CL
MOUNT PLEASANT
COURTLANDS
BOUNDARY RD
CHURCH CLIFF
CLIFFE RD
JARVIST PL
NORTH RD
SOUTH RD
PH
Knights Hill
St Nicholas CE Prim Sch
THE RISE
ALEXANDRA RD
ST JAMES RD
PO
UPPER ST
Ripple Down House
CHURCH LA
RINGWOULD RD
Chalk Hill
CHALK HILL RD
Kingsdown Park Holiday Village
UNDERCLIFFE RD
Saxon Shore Way
Woodhill Farm
Great Coombe
CT14
THE AVENUE
Kingsdown
Oldstairs Bay
Wood Hill
VICTORIA RD
KINGSDOWN HILL
HILLCREST RD
COASTGUARD COTTS
OLDSTAIRS RD
CH
The Swamp
QUEENSDOWN RD
BAYVIEW RD
NORTHCOTE RD
Barrows Hill
The Lynch
Hill Farm
East Bottom Farm
Morningside
White Cliffs Country Trail
THE LEAS
Old Parker's Cap
Kelf Farm
GRANVILLE RD
OLDSTAIRS RD
East Bottom
Otty Bottom
Free Down
GREEN LA
MARGARETS RD
East Hill
NELSON PARK RD
East Valley Farm
COLLINGWOOD RD E
CT15
Hope Point
BOYNE RD
COLLINGWOOD RD
NORWAY DRO
FLEET RD
Old Bottom Free Down
Barrow Mount

133
151

118
136
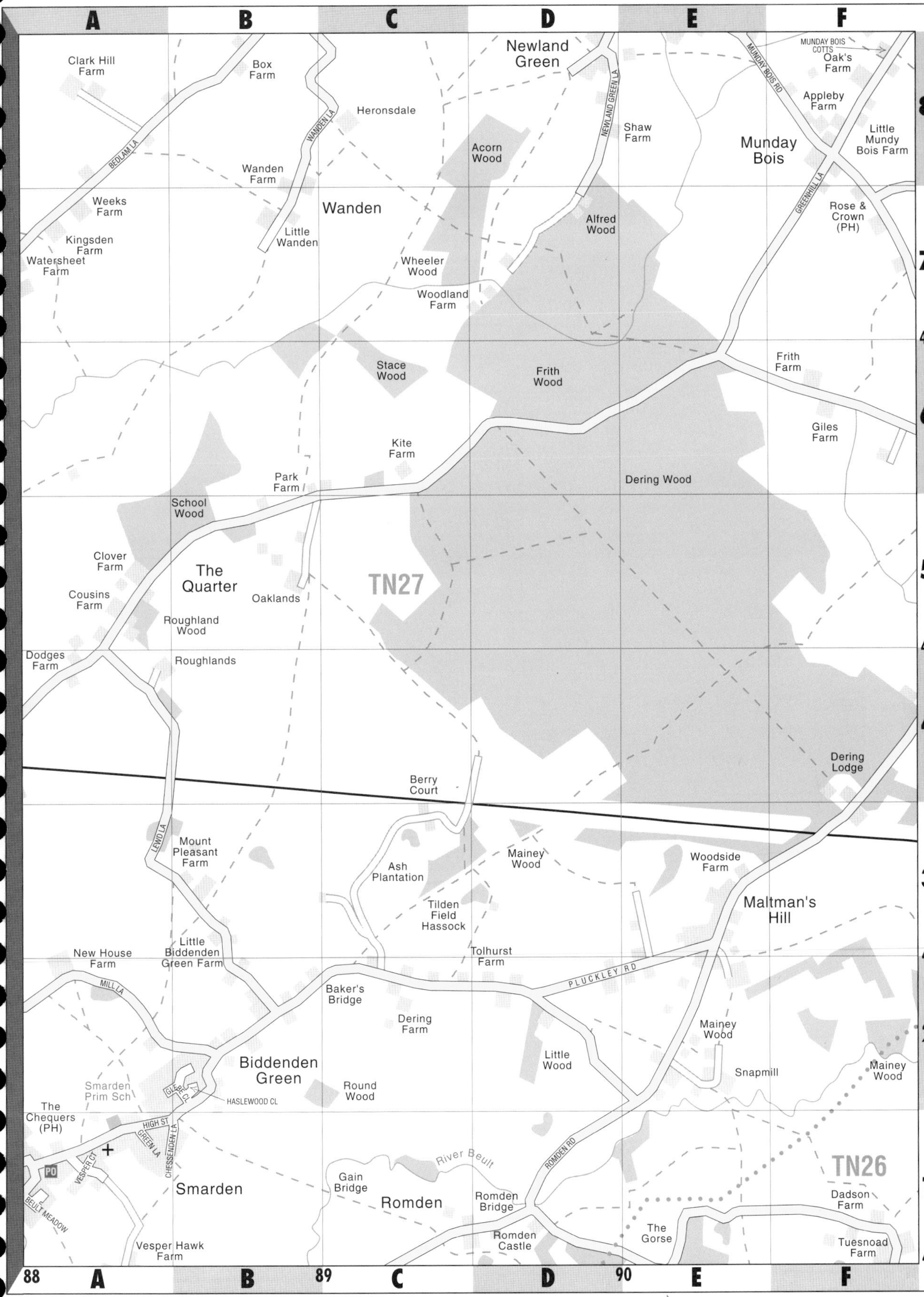
A
B
C
D
E
F
8
7
6
5
4
3
2
1
45
44
43
42
88
89
90
Clark Hill Farm
Box Farm
Heronsdale
Newland Green
MUNDAY BOIS COTTS
Oak's Farm
Appleby Farm
Shaw Farm
Munday Bois
Little Mundy Bois Farm
BEDLAM LA
WANDEN LA
NEWLAND GREEN LA
MUNDAY BOIS RD
GREENHILL LA
Acorn Wood
Wanden Farm
Weeks Farm
Wanden
Little Wanden
Alfred Wood
Rose & Crown (PH)
Kingsden Farm
Watersheet Farm
Wheeler Wood
Woodland Farm
Stace Wood
Frith Wood
Frith Farm
Giles Farm
Kite Farm
Park Farm
Dering Wood
School Wood
Clover Farm
The Quarter
TN27
Cousins Farm
Oaklands
Roughland Wood
Dodges Farm
Roughlands
Dering Lodge
Berry Court
LEWD LA
Mount Pleasant Farm
Ash Plantation
Mainey Wood
Woodside Farm
Tilden Field Hassock
Maltman's Hill
Little Biddenden Green Farm
New House Farm
Tolhurst Farm
PLUCKLEY RD
MILL LA
Baker's Bridge
Dering Farm
Mainey Wood
Little Wood
Snapmill
Mainey Wood
Biddenden Green
Smarden Prim Sch
GLEBE CL
HASLEWOOD CL
Round Wood
The Chequers (PH)
HIGH ST
GREEN LA
CHESSENDEN LA
VESPER CT
PO
River Beult
ROMDEN RD
TN26
BEULT MEADOW
Smarden
Gain Bridge
Romden
Romden Bridge
Dadson Farm
The Gorse
Romden Castle
Tuesnoad Farm
Vesper Hawk Farm
152
136

← 135
119

| A | B | C | D | E | F |

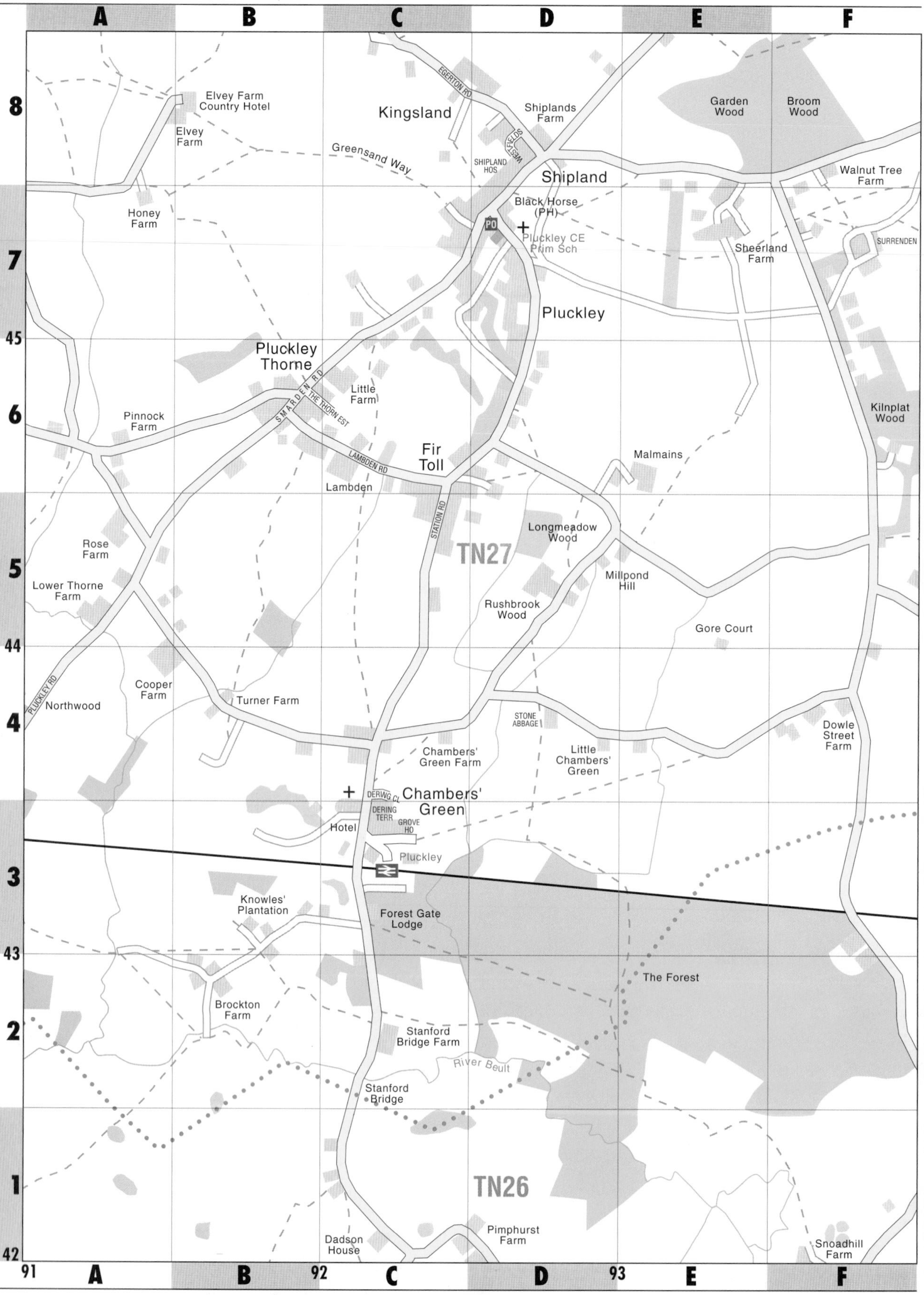

8 Elvey Farm Country Hotel
Kingsland
Shiplands Farm
Garden Wood
Broom Wood

Elvey Farm

Greensand Way
SHIPLAND HOS
Shipland
Walnut Tree Farm

Honey Farm
Black Horse (PH)
PO
Pluckley CE Prim Sch
Sheerland Farm
SURRENDEN

7

Pluckley

45

Pluckley Thorne
Kilnplat Wood

6
Pinnock Farm
Little Farm
Fir Toll
Malmains

SMARDEN RD THE THORN EST
LAMBDEN RD
Lambden
STATION RD

5
Rose Farm
TN27
Longmeadow Wood

Lower Thorne Farm
Millpond Hill

44
Rushbrook Wood
Gore Court

PLUCKLEY RD
Cooper Farm
Turner Farm
STONE ABBAGE
Little Chambers' Green
Dowle Street Farm

4
Northwood
Chambers' Green Farm

DERING CL
Chambers' Green
3
Knowles' Plantation
DERING TERR GROVE HO
Hotel
Pluckley
The Forest

Forest Gate Lodge

43
Brockton Farm

2
Stanford Bridge Farm

River Beult

Stanford Bridge

1
TN26

42
Dadson House
Pimphurst Farm
Snoadhill Farm

| 91 | A | B | 92 | C | D | 93 | E | F |

← 135
153 ↓

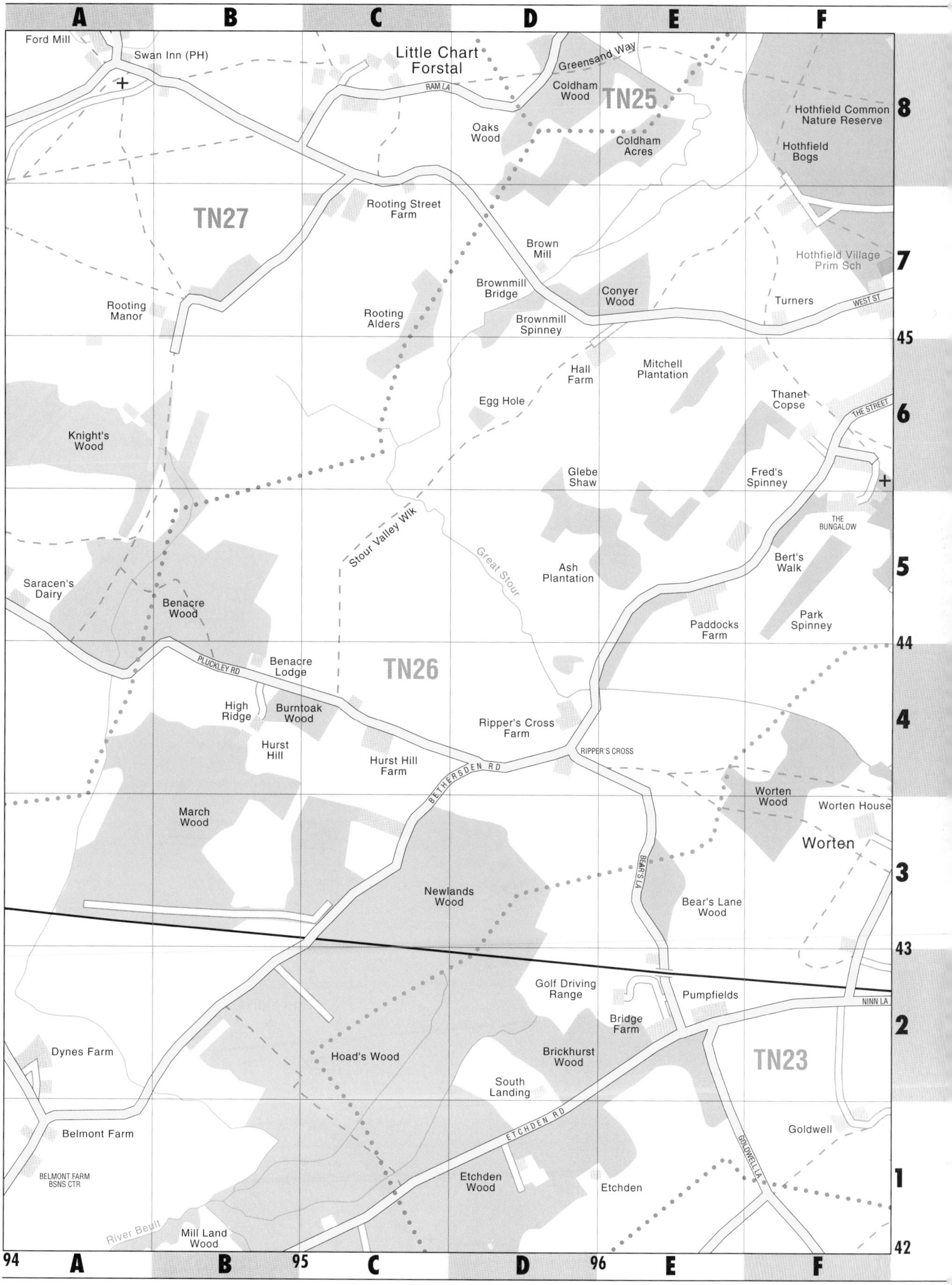

A B C D E F

8 7 45 6 5 44 4 3 43 2 1 42

Ford Mill
Swan Inn (PH)
Little Chart Forstal
RAM LA
Greensand Way
Coldham Wood
TN25
Oaks Wood
Coldham Acres
Hothfield Common Nature Reserve
Hothfield Bogs
TN27
Rooting Street Farm
Brown Mill
Hothfield Village Prim Sch
Brownmill Bridge
Conyer Wood
Turners
WEST ST
Rooting Manor
Rooting Alders
Brownmill Spinney
Hall Farm
Mitchell Plantation
Thanet Copse
Egg Hole
THE STREET
Knight's Wood
Glebe Shaw
Fred's Spinney
THE BUNGALOW
Stour Valley Wlk
Great Stour
Ash Plantation
Bert's Walk
Saracen's Dairy
Benacre Wood
Paddocks Farm
Park Spinney
PLUCKLEY RD
Benacre Lodge
TN26
High Ridge
Burntoak Wood
Ripper's Cross Farm
RIPPER'S CROSS
Worten Wood
Worten House
Hurst Hill
Hurst Hill Farm
BETHERSDEN RD
BEAR'S LA
Worten
March Wood
Newlands Wood
Bear's Lane Wood
Golf Driving Range
Pumpfields
NINN LA
Dynes Farm
Hoad's Wood
Bridge Farm
Brickhurst Wood
TN23
South Landing
Belmont Farm
ETCHDEN RD
GOLDWELL LA
Goldwell
BELMONT FARM BSNS CTR
Etchden Wood
Etchden
River Beult
Mill Land Wood

94   95   96

137
121

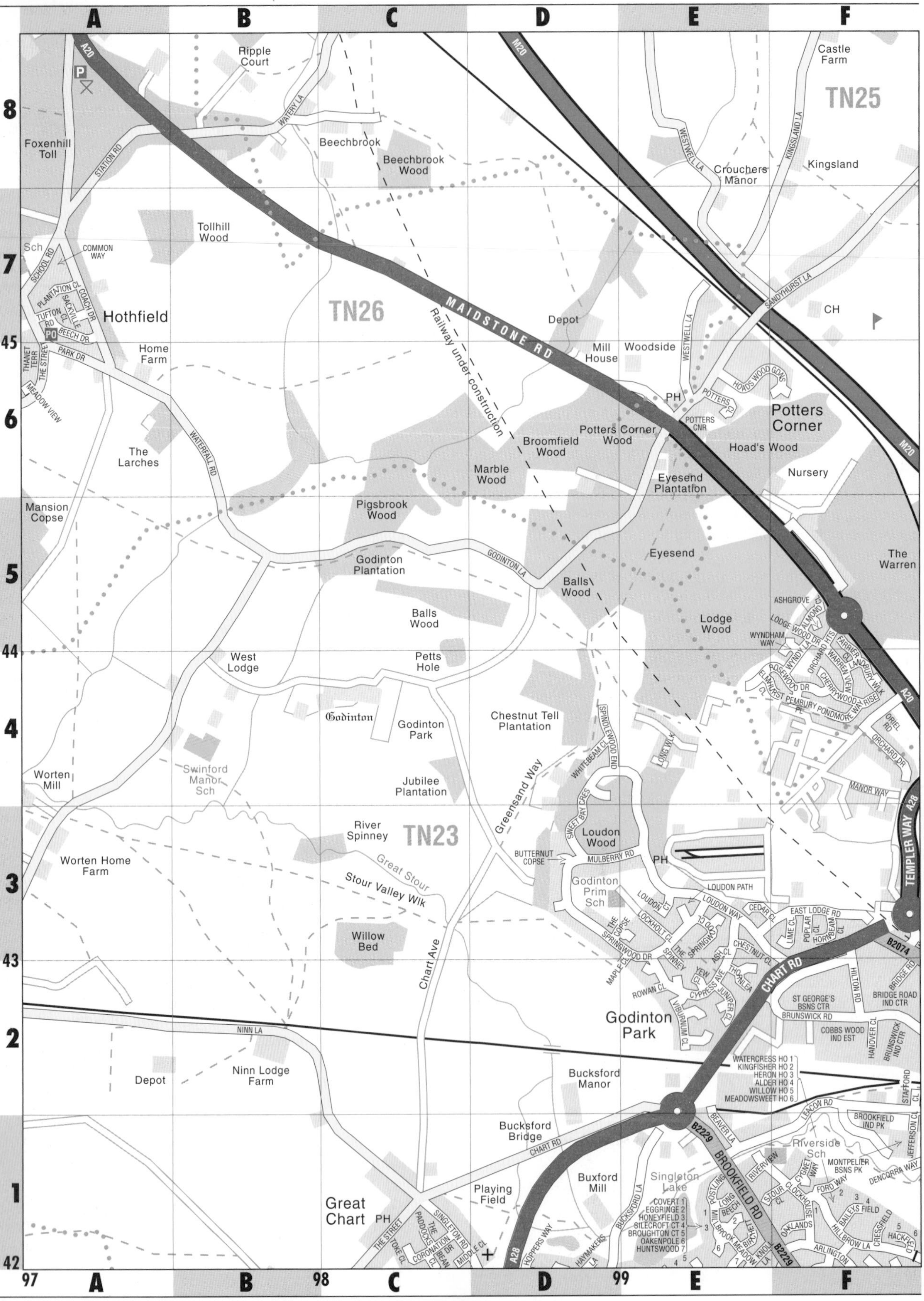
A
B
C
D
E
F
8
7
45
6
5
44
4
3
43
2
1
42
97
98
99
Ripple Court
Castle Farm
TN25
Foxenhill Toll
Beechbrook
Beechbrook Wood
Crouchers Manor
Kingsland
Tollhill Wood
Sch
COMMON WAY
Hothfield
TN26
CH
Depot
Home Farm
Mill House
Woodside
MAIDSTONE RD
Railway under construction
PH
Potters Corner
The Larches
Broomfield Wood
Potters Corner Wood
Hoad's Wood
Marble Wood
Eyesend Plantation
Nursery
Mansion Copse
Pigsbrook Wood
Eyesend
Godinton Plantation
Balls Wood
The Warren
Balls Wood
Lodge Wood
West Lodge
Petts Hole
Godinton
Godinton Park
Chestnut Tell Plantation
Worten Mill
Swinford Manor Sch
Jubilee Plantation
Greensand Way
Loudon Wood
River Spinney
TN23
Worten Home Farm
Great Stour
Stour Valley Wlk
Godinton Prim Sch
Willow Bed
Chart Ave
Godinton Park
Depot
Ninn Lodge Farm
Bucksford Manor
Bucksford Bridge
Riverside Sch
Buxford Mill
Singleton Lake
Playing Field
Great Chart
A20
M20
A28
B2229
B2074
STATION RD
WATERY LA
SCHOOL RD
PLANTATION CL
COACH DR
SACKVILLE
TUFTON RD
BEECH DR
PARK DR
THANET TERR
THE STREET
MEADOW VIEW
WATERFALL RD
WESTWELL LA
KINGSLAND LA
SANDYHURST LA
HOADS WOOD GDNS
POTTERS CL
POTTERS CNR
GODINTON LA
ASHGROVE
WYNDHAM WAY
LODGE WOOD DR
ORCHARD HTS
FARRIER CL
ROSEWOOD DR
ELMHURST
PEMBURY PL
PONDMORE WAY
ORIEL RD
ORCHARD DR
MANOR WAY
TEMPLER WAY
SPINDLEWOOD END
WHITEBEAM CL
SWEET BAY CRES
LONG WLK
BUTTERNUT COPSE
MULBERRY RD
LOUDON PATH
LOUDON CT
LOUDON WAY
CEDAR CL
EAST LODGE RD
LIME CL
POPLAR CL
HORNBEAM CL
THE COPSE
LOCKHOLT CL
SPRINGWOOD DR
THE SPINNEY
CHESTNUT CL
ASH CL
YEW CL
CYPRESS AVE
JUNIPER CL
MAPLE CL
ROWAN CL
VIBURNUM CL
CHART RD
HILTON RD
BRIDGE RD
ST GEORGE'S BSNS CTR
BRUNSWICK RD
BRIDGE ROAD IND CTR
COBBS WOOD IND EST
HANOVER CL
BRUNSWICK IND CTR
NINN LA
WATERCRESS HO 1
KINGFISHER HO 2
HERON HO 3
ALDER HO 4
WILLOW HO 5
MEADOWSWEET HO 6
STAFFORD CL
LEACON RD
BEAVER LA
BROOKFIELD IND PK
BROOKFIELD RD
RIVERVIEW
JEFFERSON
MONTPELIER BSNS PK
DENCORRA WAY
FORD WAY
BAILEYS FIELD
CRESSFIELD
HACKFIELD
HILLBROW LA
ARLINGTON
OAKLANDS
STOUR CL
CYGNET WAY
CLOCKHOUSE
COVERT 1
EGGRINGE 2
HONEYFIELD 3
SILECROFT CT 4
BROUGHTON CT 5
OAKENPOLE 6
HUNTSWOOD 7
BUCKSFORD LA
POSTLING
LONG BEECH
MILLBROOK MEADOW
HAYMAKERS LA
HOPPERS WAY
THE STREET
TOKE CL
THE PADDOCKS
CORONATION CL
BEAN CL
SINGLETON RD
MIDDLE CL

137
155

122
140

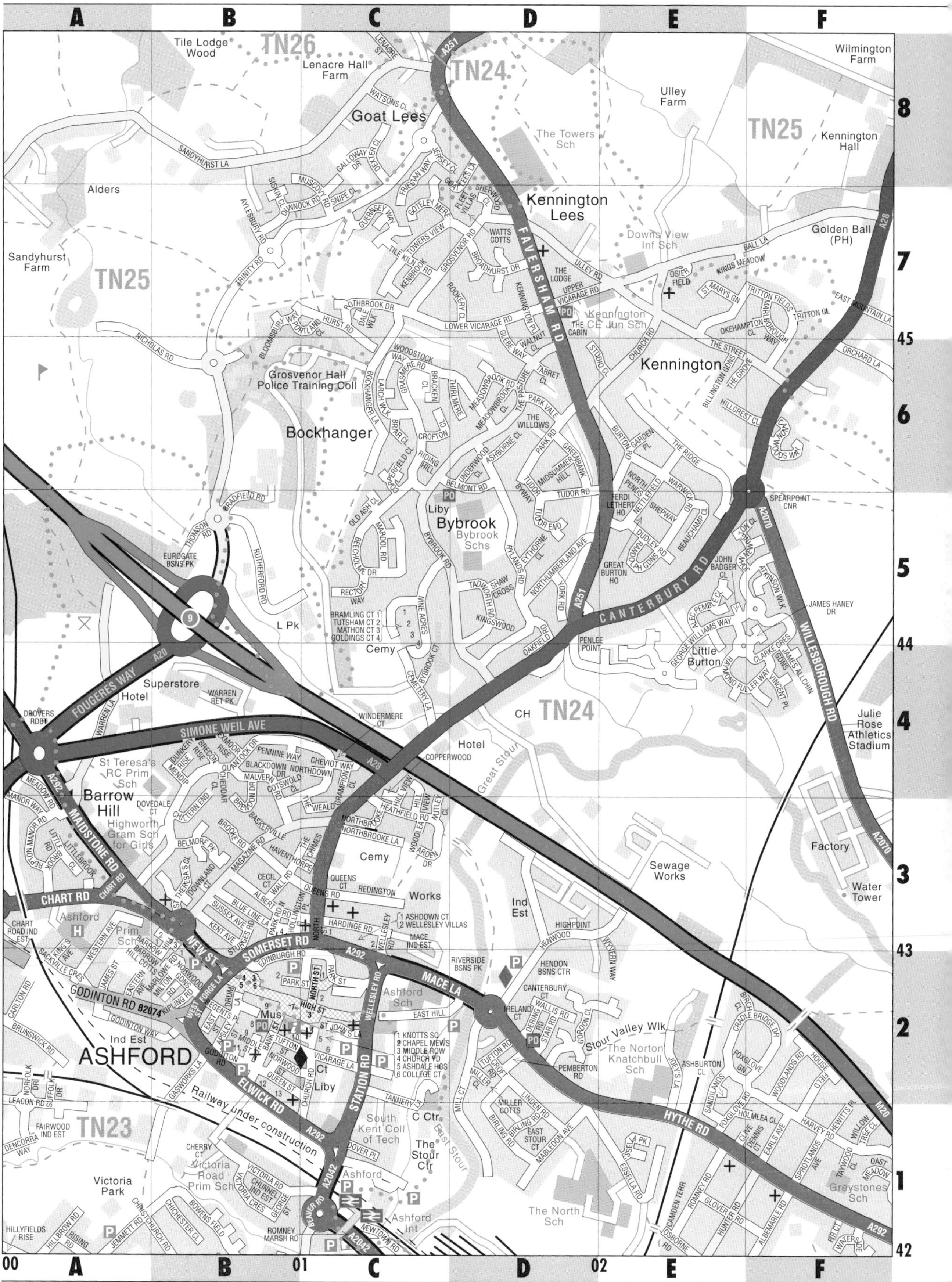

B2
1 ENGINEERS CT
2 PARK MALL
3 ST GEORGE'S SQ
4 GILBERT RD
5 NEW RENTS
6 CASTLE ST
7 KINGS PAR
8 COUNTY SQ
9 TUFTON WLK
10 CHURCH YARD PAS
11 HEMPSTED ST
12 MARKET LA
13 ELWICK LA
B3
1 BARROW HILL TERR
2 BARROW HILL PL
3 GRAVEL WLK
4 WOLSELEY PL

156
140

139
123

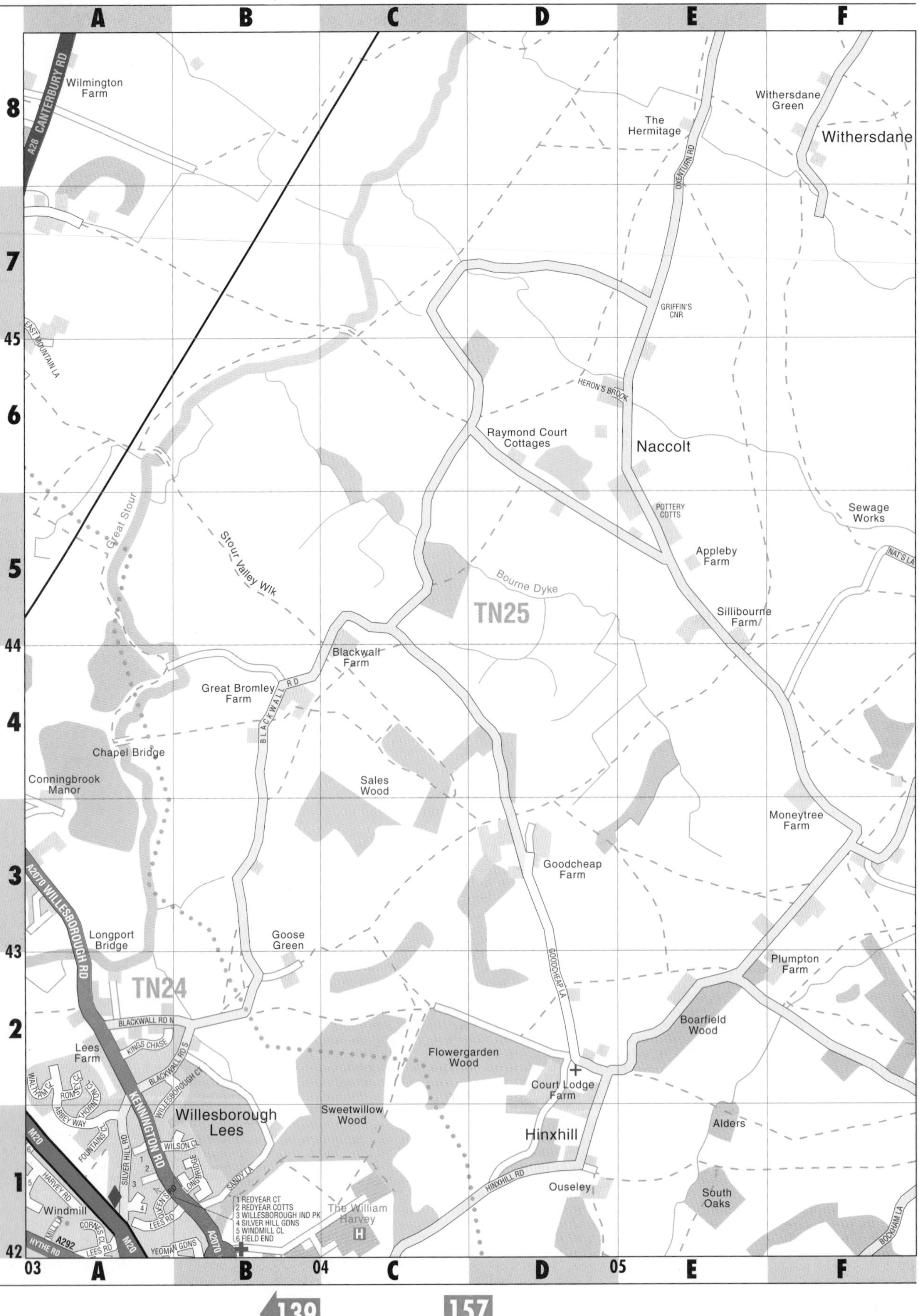
A
B
C
D
E
F
8
7
45
6
5
44
4
3
43
2
1
42
03
04
05
Wilmington Farm
CANTERBURY RD
A28
EAST MOUNTAIN LA
The Hermitage
Withersdane Green
Withersdane
OXENTURN RD
GRIFFIN'S CNR
HERON'S BROOK
Raymond Court Cottages
Naccolt
POTTERY COTTS
Sewage Works
Appleby Farm
NAT'S LA
Great Stour
Stour Valley Wlk
Bourne Dyke
TN25
Sillibourne Farm
Blackwall Farm
Great Bromley Farm
BLACKWALL RD
Chapel Bridge
Conningbrook Manor
Sales Wood
Moneytree Farm
Goodcheap Farm
A2070 WILLESBOROUGH RD
Longport Bridge
Goose Green
GOODCHEAP LA
Plumpton Farm
TN24
BLACKWALL RD N
Boarfield Wood
Lees Farm
KINGS CHASE
BLACKWALL RD S
Flowergarden Wood
Court Lodge Farm
WILLESBOROUGH CT
KENNINGTON RD
Willesborough Lees
Sweetwillow Wood
Hinxhill
Alders
ABBEY WAY
FOUNTAINS CL
SILVER HILL RD
WILSON CL
M20
HARVEY RD
SANDY LA
HINXHILL RD
Ouseley
South Oaks
1 REDYEAR CT
2 REDYEAR COTTS
3 WILLESBOROUGH IND PK
4 SILVER HILL GDNS
5 WINDMILL CL
6 FIELD END
Windmill
The William Harvey
A292
HYTHE RD
LEES RD
YEOMAN GDNS
A2070
BOCKHAM LA

139
157

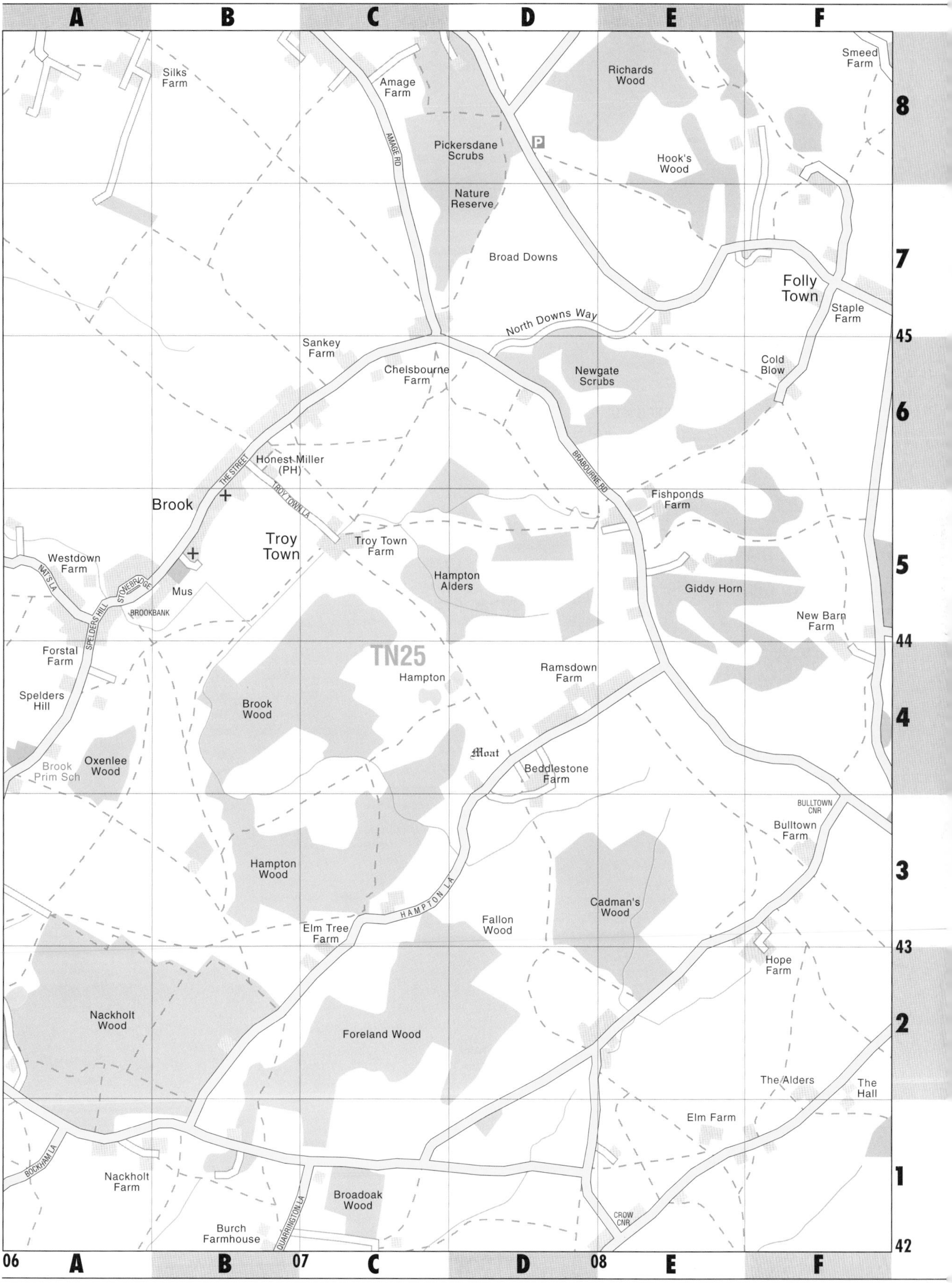

A B C D E F

8
7
45
6
5
44
4
3
43
2
1
42

Silks Farm
Amage Farm
Richards Wood
Smeed Farm
AMAGE RD
Pickersdane Scrubs
P
Hook's Wood
Nature Reserve
Broad Downs
Folly Town
Staple Farm
North Downs Way
Sankey Farm
Chelsbourne Farm
Newgate Scrubs
Cold Blow
Honest Miller (PH)
THE STREET
Brook
TROY TOWN LA
BRABOURNE RD
Fishponds Farm
Westdown Farm
Troy Town
Troy Town Farm
Hampton Alders
Giddy Horn
NATS LA
STONEBRIDGE RD
SPELDERS HILL
Mus
New Barn Farm
BROOKBANK
Forstal Farm
TN25
Hampton
Ramsdown Farm
Spelders Hill
Brook Wood
Brook Prim Sch
Oxenlee Wood
Moat
Beddlestone Farm
BULLTOWN CNR
Bulltown Farm
Hampton Wood
HAMPTON LA
Cadman's Wood
Hope Farm
Elm Tree Farm
Fallon Wood
BOOKHAM LA
Nackholt Wood
Foreland Wood
The Alders
The Hall
Elm Farm
QUARRINGTON LA
Nackholt Farm
Broadoak Wood
CROW CNR
Burch Farmhouse

06
07
08

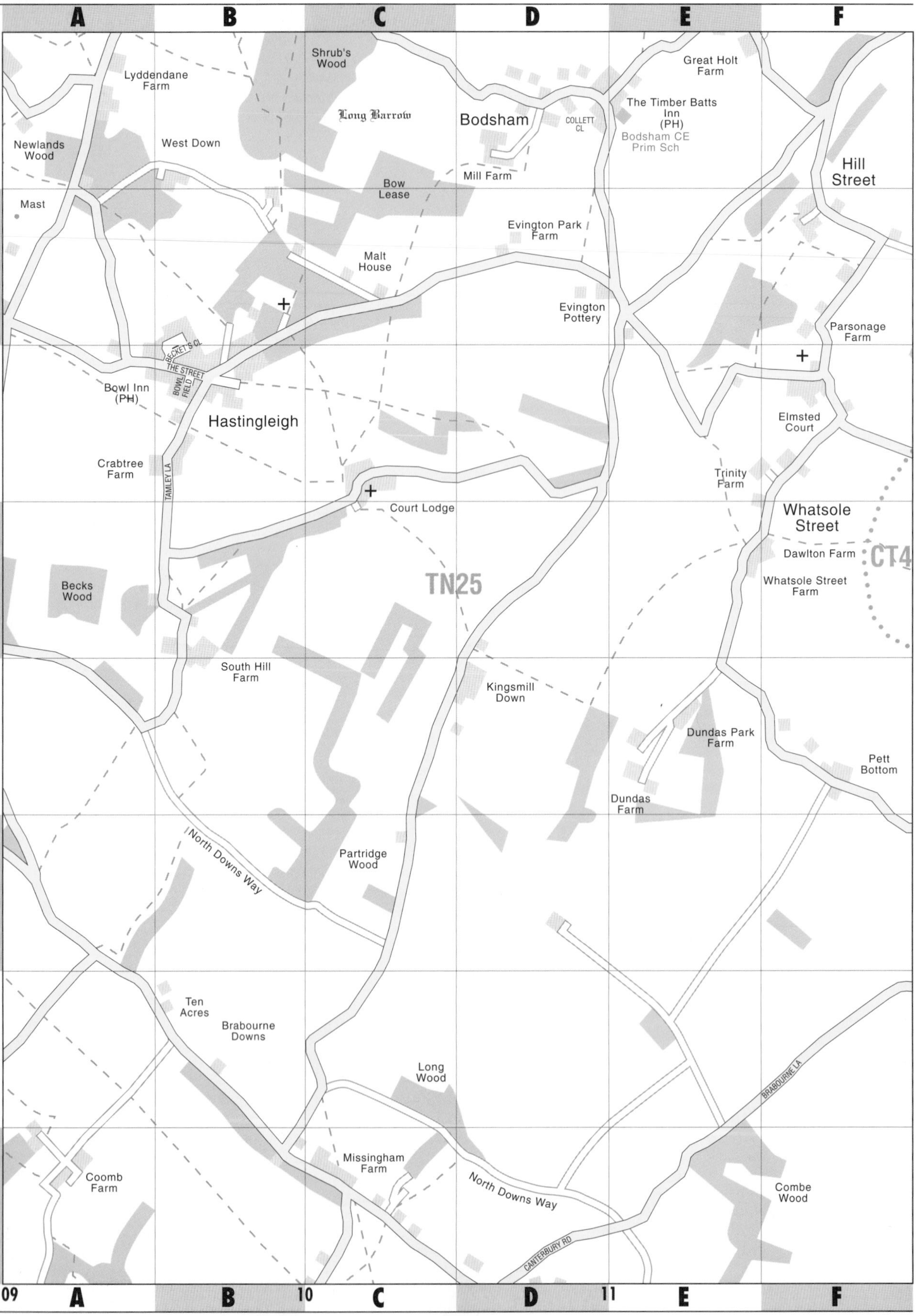

A   B   C   D   E   F

8

Lyddendane Farm

Shrub's Wood

Long Barrow

Bodsham

Great Holt Farm

The Timber Batts Inn (PH)

COLLETT CL

Bodsham CE Prim Sch

Newlands Wood

West Down

Hill Street

Mast

Bow Lease

Mill Farm

7

Malt House

Evington Park Farm

+

45

Evington Pottery

Parsonage Farm

BECKET'S CL

THE STREET

BOWL FIELD

Bowl Inn (PH)

+

6

Hastingleigh

Elmsted Court

TAMLEY LA

Crabtree Farm

+

Court Lodge

Trinity Farm

Whatsole Street

Becks Wood

TN25

Dawlton Farm

CT4

5

Whatsole Street Farm

44

South Hill Farm

Kingsmill Down

4

Dundas Park Farm

Pett Bottom

Dundas Farm

North Downs Way

Partridge Wood

3

43

Ten Acres

Brabourne Downs

BRABOURNE LA

2

Long Wood

Missingham Farm

1

Coomb Farm

North Downs Way

Combe Wood

42

CANTERBURY RD

09   A   B   10   C   D   11   E   F

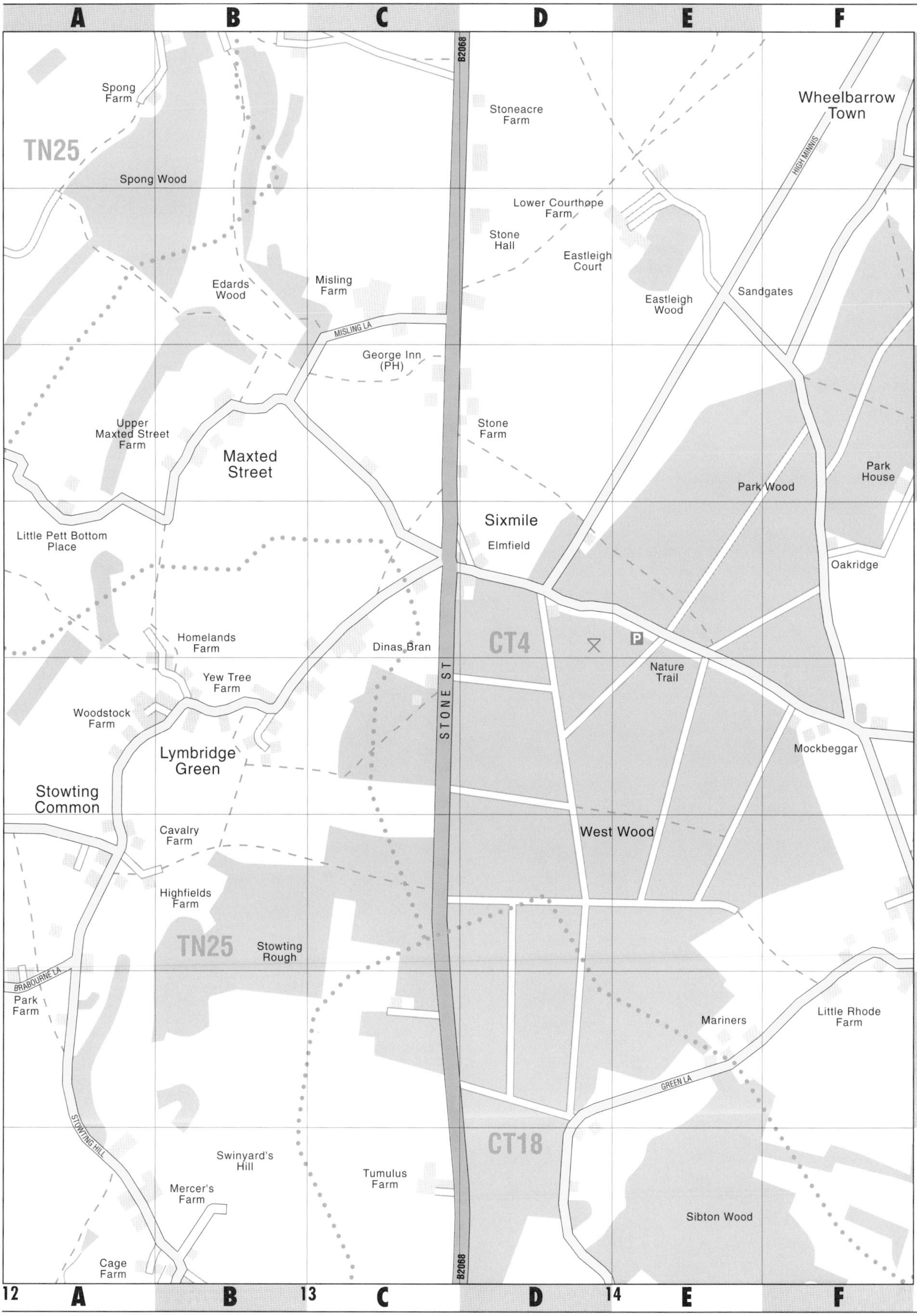

A　B　C　D　E　F

126
144 ▶
160
144 ▶

Spong Farm

TN25

Spong Wood

Stoneacre Farm

Wheelbarrow Town

Lower Courthope Farm

Stone Hall

Eastleigh Court

Edards Wood

Misling Farm

Eastleigh Wood

Sandgates

MISLING LA

George Inn (PH)

Upper Maxted Street Farm

Maxted Street

Stone Farm

Park Wood

Park House

Little Pett Bottom Place

Sixmile

Elmfield

Oakridge

Homelands Farm

Dinas Bran

CT4

Nature Trail

Yew Tree Farm

Woodstock Farm

Lymbridge Green

Mockbeggar

STONE ST

Stowting Common

West Wood

Cavalry Farm

Highfields Farm

TN25

Stowting Rough

BRABOURNE LA

Park Farm

43

Mariners

Little Rhode Farm

GREEN LA

STOWTING HILL

Swinyard's Hill

Tumulus Farm

CT18

Sibton Wood

Mercer's Farm

Cage Farm

B2068

12　A　13　B　C　D　14　E　F

143
127

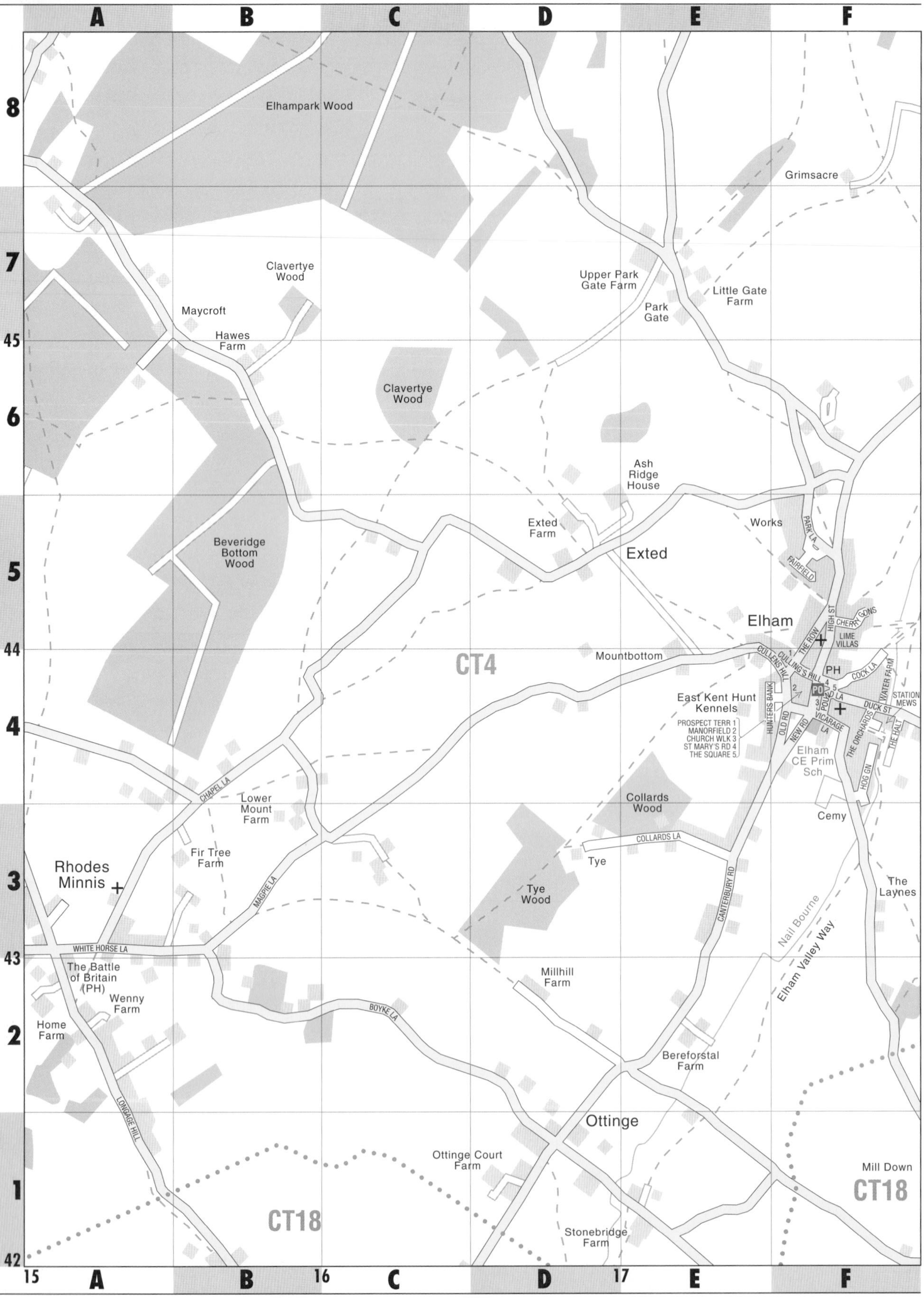

A **B** **C** **D** **E** **F**

8

Elhampark Wood

Grimsacre

7

Clavertye
Wood

Upper Park
Gate Farm

Little Gate
Farm

Maycroft

Park
Gate

45

Hawes
Farm

Clavertye
Wood

6

Ash
Ridge
House

Beveridge
Bottom
Wood

Exted
Farm

Works

Exted

5

Park La

Fairfield

Elham

High St

Cherrys Cons

Lime
Villas

44

Mountbottom

The Row

Culling's Hill

CT4

Cullens Hill

PH

Cock La

Station
Mews

Water Farm

East Kent Hunt
Kennels

Hunters Bank

Old Rd

New Rd

Pond La

Vicarage
La

The Orchards

Duck St

The Halt

PROSPECT TERR 1
MANORFIELD 2
CHURCH WLK 3
ST MARY'S RD 4
THE SQUARE 5.

Elham
CE Prim
Sch

4

Chapel La

Collards
Wood

Cemy

Hog Gn

Lower
Mount
Farm

Collards La

Fir Tree
Farm

Tye

Canterbury Rd

The
Laynes

3

Rhodes
Minnis

Magpie La

Tye
Wood

Nail Bourne

Elham Valley Way

White Horse La

43

The Battle
of Britain
(PH)

Wenny
Farm

Millhill
Farm

Home
Farm

Boyke La

2

Longage Hill

Bereforstal
Farm

Ottinge

Ottinge Court
Farm

Mill Down

1

CT18

CT18

42

A 15 **B** 16 **C** **D** 17 **E** **F**

Stonebridge
Farm

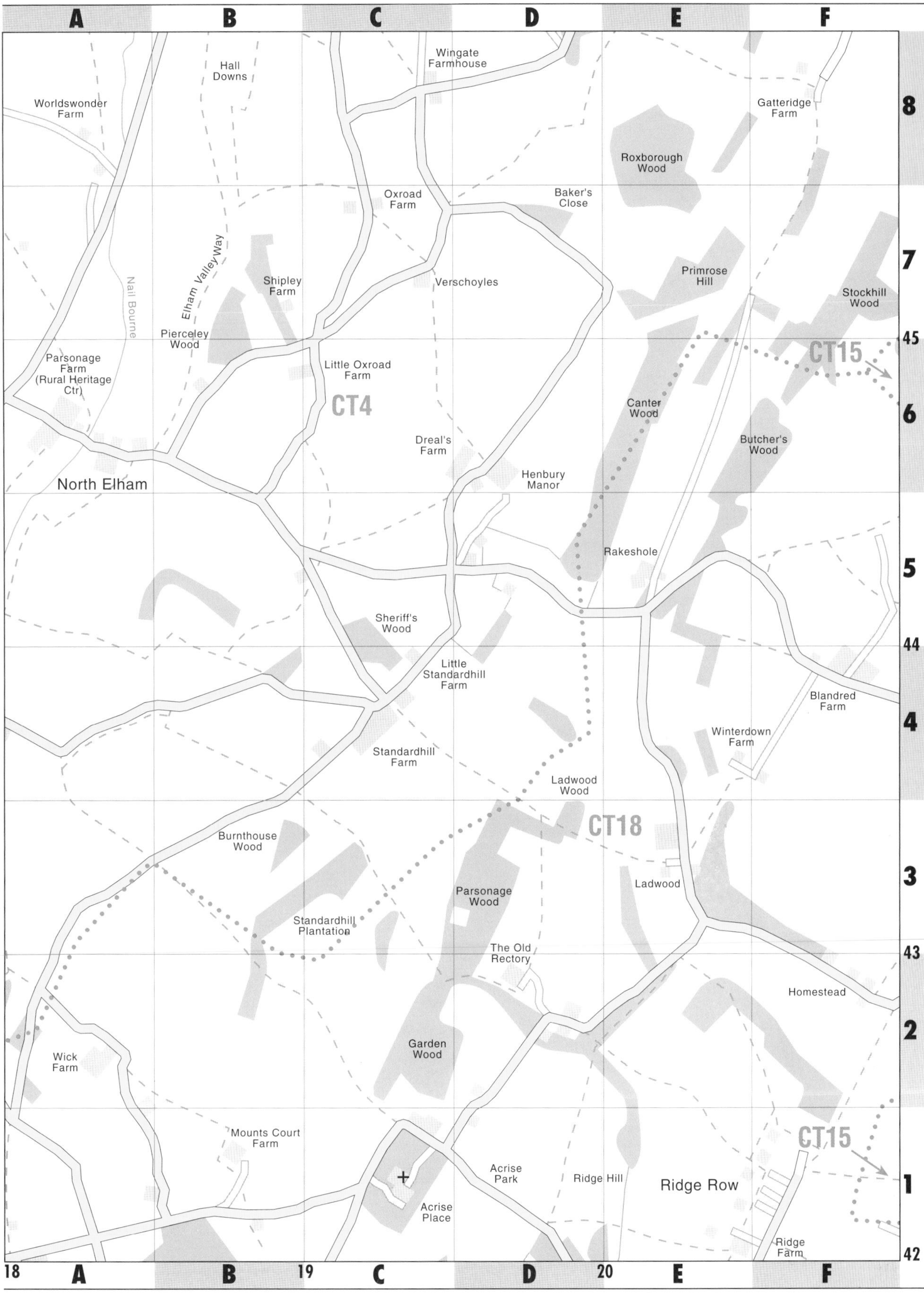

A B C D E F

8

Worldswonder Farm

Hall Downs

Wingate Farmhouse

Gatteridge Farm

Roxborough Wood

Oxroad Farm

Baker's Close

7

Elham Valley Way

Shipley Farm

Verschoyles

Primrose Hill

Stockhill Wood

Nail Bourne

Pierceley Wood

45

CT15

Parsonage Farm (Rural Heritage Ctr)

Little Oxroad Farm

CT4

Canter Wood

6

Butcher's Wood

Dreal's Farm

North Elham

Henbury Manor

Rakeshole

5

Sheriff's Wood

44

Little Standardhill Farm

Blandred Farm

4

Winterdown Farm

Standardhill Farm

Ladwood Wood

CT18

Burnthouse Wood

Ladwood

3

Standardhill Plantation

Parsonage Wood

43

The Old Rectory

Homestead

2

Garden Wood

Wick Farm

Mounts Court Farm

CT15

Acrise Park

Ridge Hill

Ridge Row

1

Acrise Place

Ridge Farm

42

18 A B 19 C D 20 E F

145
129

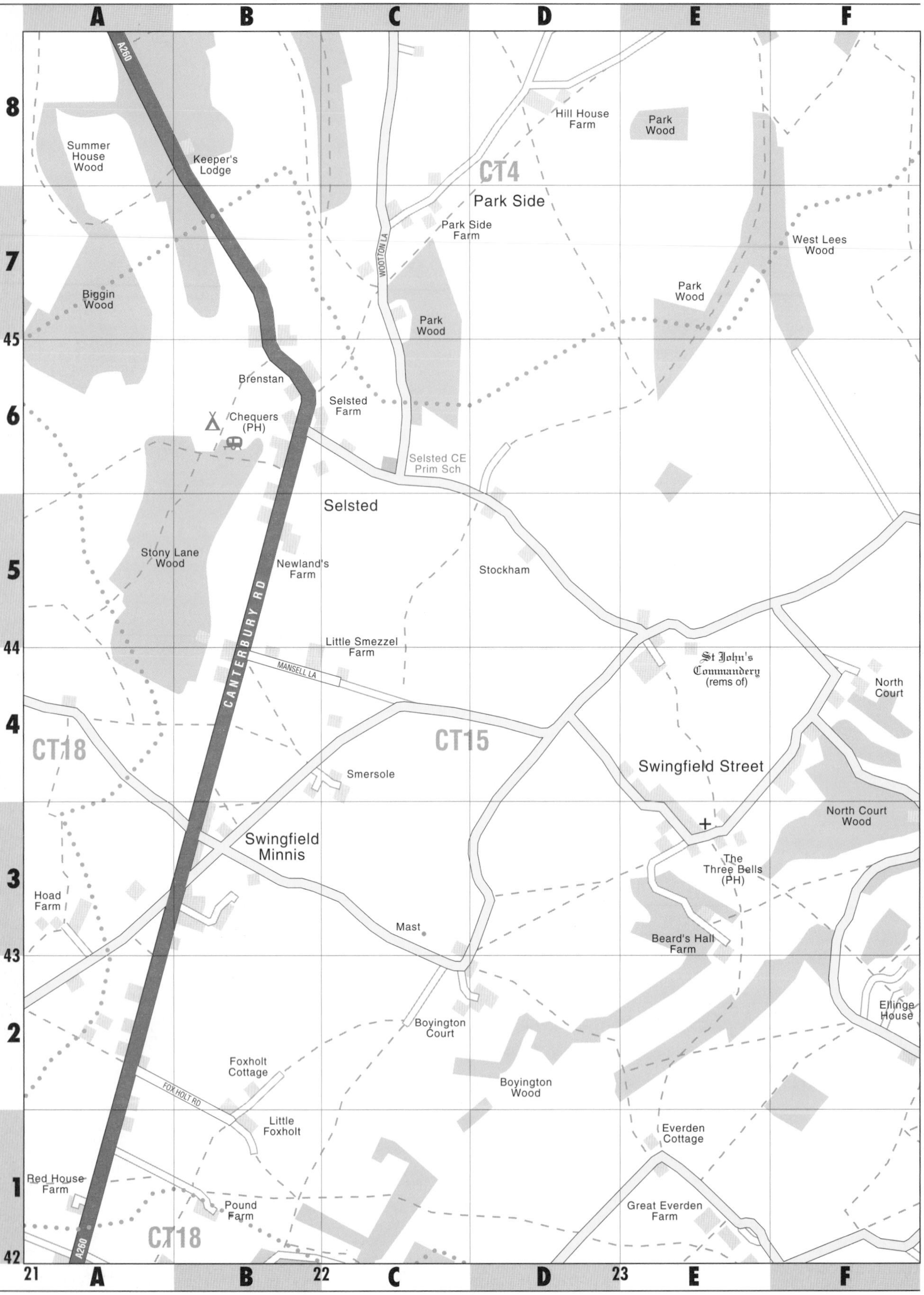
A B C D E F
8
7
45
6
5
44
4
3
43
2
1
42
21
22
23
A260
Summer House Wood
Keeper's Lodge
Hill House Farm
Park Wood
CT4
Park Side
Park Side Farm
WOOTTON LA
West Lees Wood
Park Wood
Biggin Wood
Park Wood
Brenstan
Selsted Farm
Chequers (PH)
Selsted CE Prim Sch
Selsted
Stony Lane Wood
Newland's Farm
Stockham
CANTERBURY RD
Little Smezzel Farm
MANSELL LA
St John's Commandery (rems of)
North Court
CT18
CT15
Smersole
Swingfield Street
Swingfield Minnis
North Court Wood
The Three Bells (PH)
Hoad Farm
Mast
Beard's Hall Farm
Ellinge House
Boyington Court
Foxholt Cottage
Boyington Wood
FOX HOLT RD
Little Foxholt
Everden Cottage
Red House Farm
Pound Farm
Great Everden Farm
CT18
A260
A B C D E F

145
163

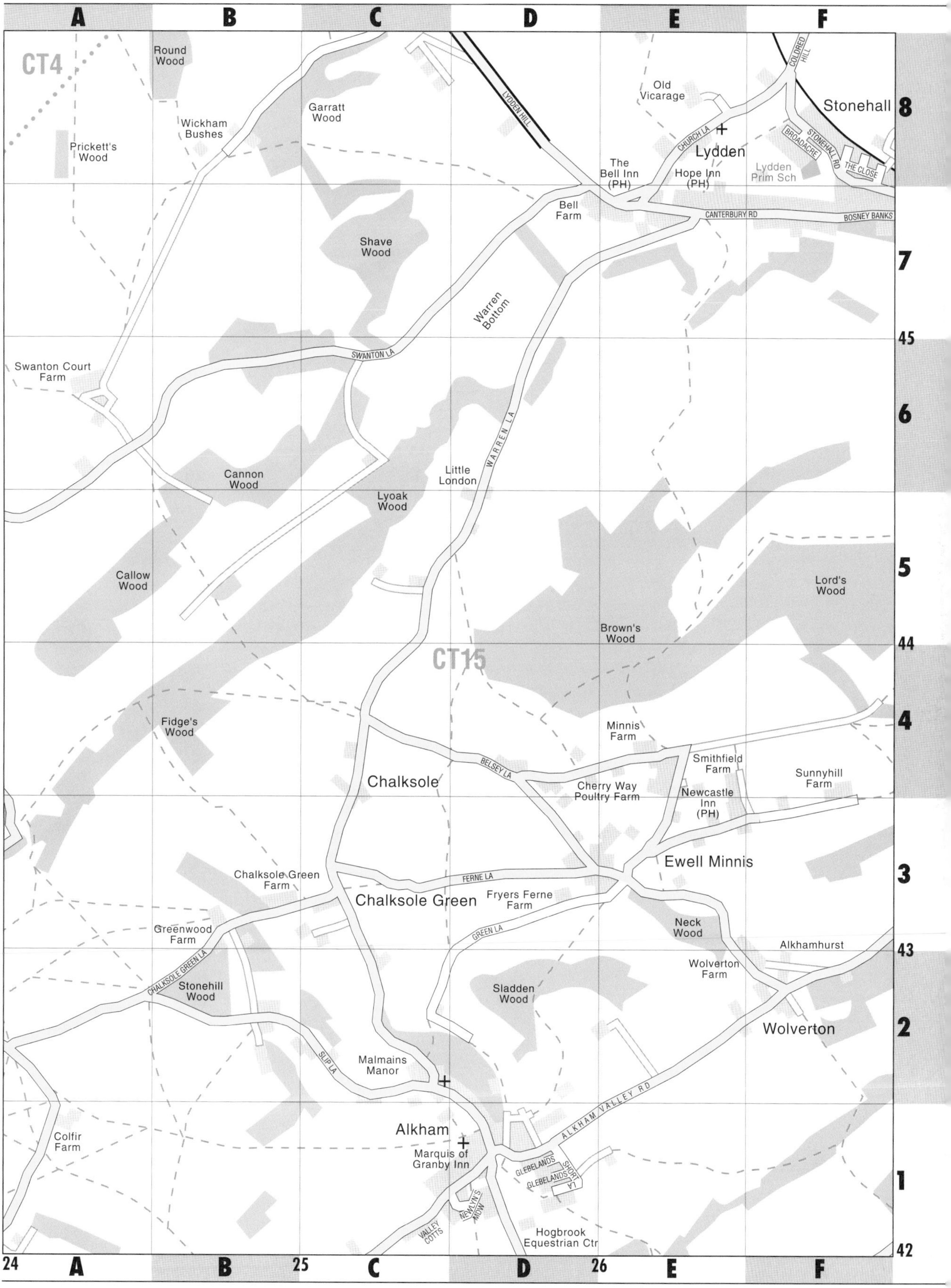

130
148

A **B** **C** **D** **E** **F**

CT4

Round Wood

Prickett's Wood

Wickham Bushes

Garratt Wood

Old Vicarage

Stonehall **8**

Shave Wood

Church La

Lydden

The Bell Inn (PH)

Hope Inn (PH)

Lydden Prim Sch

Bell Farm

Bosney Banks

CANTERBURY RD

7

Warren Bottom

SWANTON LA

45

Swanton Court Farm

WARREN LA

6

Cannon Wood

Little London

Lyoak Wood

Lord's Wood

5

Callow Wood

Brown's Wood

44

CT15

Fidge's Wood

Minnis Farm

4

BELSEY LA

Smithfield Farm

Sunnyhill Farm

Chalksole

Cherry Way Poultry Farm

Newcastle Inn (PH)

Ewell Minnis

Chalksole Green Farm

FERNE LA

Neck Wood

Alkhamhurst

43

Chalksole Green

Fryers Ferne Farm

Wolverton Farm

Greenwood Farm

GREEN LA

CHALKSOLE GREEN LA

Stonehill Wood

Sladden Wood

Wolverton **2**

SLIP LA

Malmains Manor

ALKHAM VALLEY RD

Colfir Farm

Alkham

Marquis of Granby Inn

GLEBELANDS

GLEBELANDS LA

1

VALLEY COTTS

REWINS MDW

Hogbrook Equestrian Ctr

42

24 **A** **B** **25** **C** **D** **26** **E** **F**

164
148

147
131

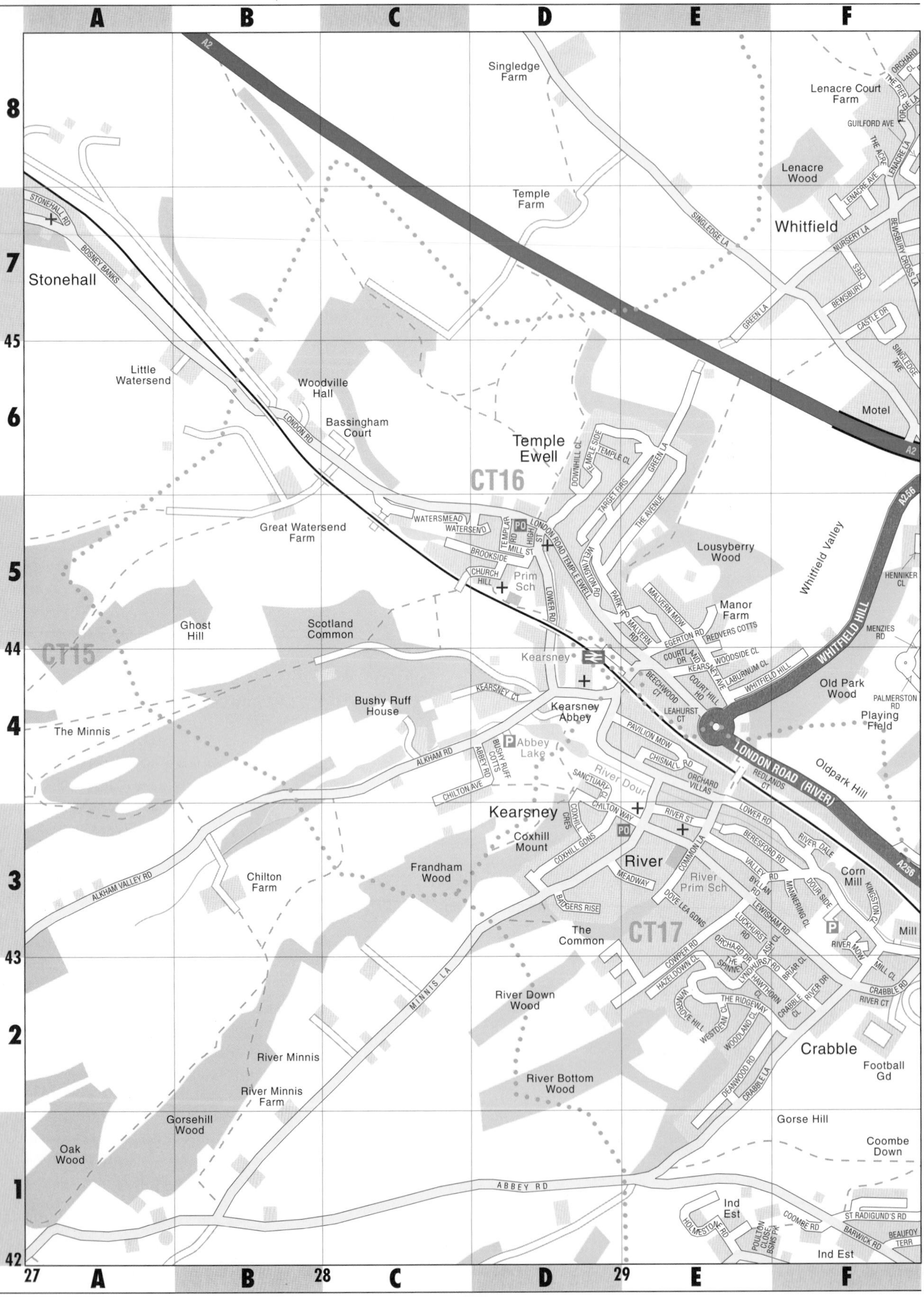
A
B
C
D
E
F
8
7
45
6
5
44
4
3
43
2
1
42
27
28
29
A2
Singledge Farm
Lenacre Court Farm
ORCHARD CL
THE PIER
FORGE LA
GUILFORD AVE
THE ACRE
LENACRE LA
Lenacre Wood
LENACRE AVE
Temple Farm
SINGLEDGE LA
Whitfield
NURSERY LA
BEWSBURY CROSS LA
BEWSBURY CRES
CASTLE DR
SINGLEDGE AVE
GREEN LA
STONEHALL RD
BOSNEY BANKS
Stonehall
Little Watersend
Woodville Hall
Bassingham Court
LONDON RD
Temple Ewell
DOWNHILL CL
TEMPLE SIDE
TEMPLE CL
TARGET FIRS
GREEN LA
THE AVENUE
Motel
A2
CT16
A256
Whitfield Valley
WATERSMEAD
WATERSEND
TEMPLAR RD
HIGH ST
LONDON ROAD TEMPLE EWELL
MILL ST
BROOKSIDE
CHURCH HILL
Prim Sch
WELLINGTON RD
PARK RD
Great Watersend Farm
Lousyberry Wood
HENNIKER CL
WHITFIELD HILL
Ghost Hill
Scotland Common
LOWER RD
MALVERN MDW
MALVERN RD
Manor Farm
EGERTON RD
REDVERS COTTS
COURTLAND DR
WOODSIDE CL
KEARSNEY AVE
LABURNUM CL
WHITFIELD HILL
MENZIES RD
CT15
Kearsney
BEECHWOOD CT
COURT HILL HO
Old Park Wood
KEARSNEY CT
Bushy Ruff House
Kearsney Abbey
LEAHURST CT
PALMERSTON RD
Playing Field
The Minnis
PAVILION MDW
Abbey Lake
ALKHAM RD
ABBEY RD
BUSHY RUFF COTTS
CHISNALL RD
LONDON ROAD (RIVER)
Oldpark Hill
SANCTUARY CL
River Dour
ORCHARD VILLAS
REDLANDS CT
CHILTON AVE
Kearsney
COXHILL CRES
CHILTON WAY
RIVER ST
LOWER RD
Coxhill Mount
BERESFORD RD
RIVER DALE
COXHILL GDNS
River
COMMON LA
Chilton Farm
Frandham Wood
VALLEY RD
BYLLAN
River Prim Sch
MANNERING CL
DOUR SIDE
Corn Mill
KINGSTON CL
A256
ALKHAM VALLEY RD
MEADWAY
BADGERS RISE
DOVE LEA GDNS
LEWISHAM RD
The Common
CT17
LUCKHURST RD
ASH CL
ORCHARD DR
RIVER MDW
Mill
COWPER RD
THE SPINNEY
LYNDHURST RD
BRIAR CL
HAZELDOWN CL
HAWTHORN CL
RIVER DR
MILL CL
CRABBLE RD
RIVER CT
MINNIS LA
River Down Wood
HAWTHORN CL
GROVE HILL
THE RIDGEWAY
CRABBLE CL
WESTDEAN CL
WOODLAND CL
Crabble
River Minnis
Football Gd
River Minnis Farm
River Bottom Wood
DEANWOOD RD
CRABBLE LA
Gorsehill Wood
Gorse Hill
Oak Wood
Coombe Down
ABBEY RD
Ind Est
COOMBE RD
ST RADIGUND'S RD
HOLMESTONE RD
POULTON CLOSE BSNS PK
BARWICK RD
BEAUFOY TERR
Ind Est

147
165

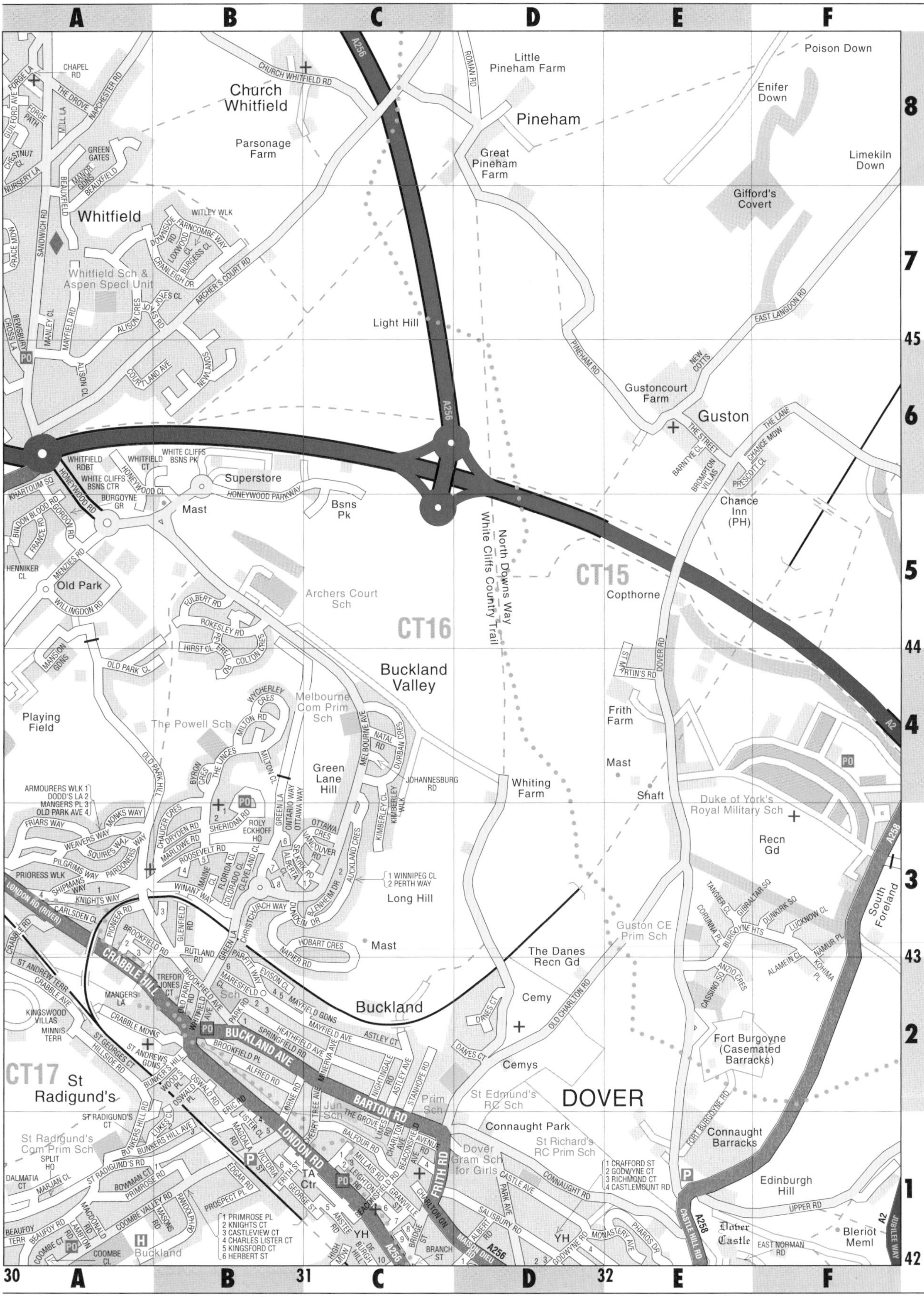

B2
1 ST ANNE'S CT
2 OSPREY CT
3 MAYFIELD CT
4 MAGPIE LODGE
5 CHAFFINCH LODGE
6 HERON LODGE

B3
1 FITZWALTER CT
2 WELLINGTON GDNS
3 BRUNSWICK GDNS
4 WASHINGTON CL
5 BOSTON CL
6 TORONTO CL
7 HUDSON CL
8 MONTREAL CL

C1
1 ALEXANDRA PL
2 BARTON VIEW TERR
3 LEIGHTON CT
4 ST ALPHEGE HILL
5 SHOOTER'S HILL
6 BARTHOLOMEW ST
7 CHURCHILL ST
8 PAUL'S PL
9 MATTHEW'S PL

10 WARDEN CT

149
133

A · B · C · D · E · F

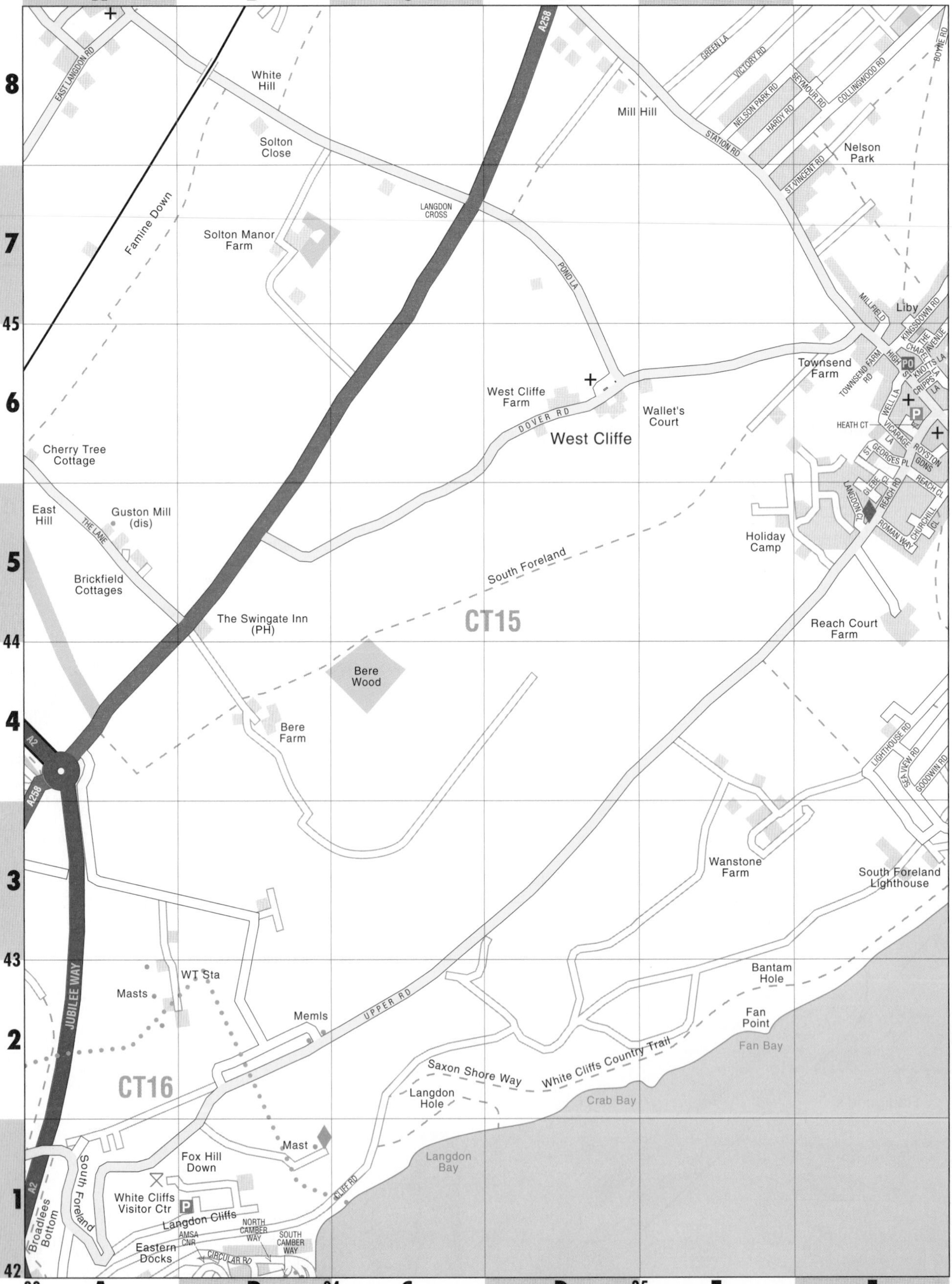

8

EAST LANGDON RD

White Hill

Solton Close

Mill Hill

GREEN LA

VICTORY RD

NELSON PARK RD

SEYMOUR RD

HARDY RD

COLLINGWOOD RD

BOWLE RD

STATION RD

ST VINCENT RD

Nelson Park

Famine Down

Solton Manor Farm

Langdon Cross

7

MILLFIELD

Liby

KINGSDOWN RD

THE CHASE

THE AVENUE

KNOTTS LA

CRIPPS LA

45

POND LA

Townsend Farm

TOWNSEND FARM RD

WELL LA

CRIPPS LA

PO

West Cliffe Farm

Wallet's Court

HEATH CT

P

VICARAGE RD

ST GEORGES PL

ROYSTON GDNS

REACH CL

6

DOVER RD

West Cliffe

Cherry Tree Cottage

LANGDON CL

REACH RD

ROMAN WAY

CHURCHILL

UPHILL

East Hill

THE LANE

Guston Mill (dis)

Holiday Camp

South Foreland

5

Brickfield Cottages

The Swingate Inn (PH)

CT15

Reach Court Farm

44

Bere Wood

A2

4

Bere Farm

A258

LIGHTHOUSE RD

SEA VIEW RD

GOODWIN RD

3

Wanstone Farm

South Foreland Lighthouse

43

JUBILEE WAY

Masts

WT Sta

Bantam Hole

Fan Point

UPPER RD

Memls

Fan Bay

2

CT16

Saxon Shore Way

White Cliffs Country Trail

Crab Bay

Langdon Hole

SOUTH FORELAND

Mast

CLIFF RD

Langdon Bay

Fox Hill Down

1

White Cliffs Visitor Ctr

P

Langdon Cliffs

NORTH CAMBER WAY

AMSA CNR

SOUTH CAMBER WAY

Eastern Docks

CIRCULAR RD

Broadlees Bottom

A2

42

33 · A · B · 34 · C · D · 35 · E · F

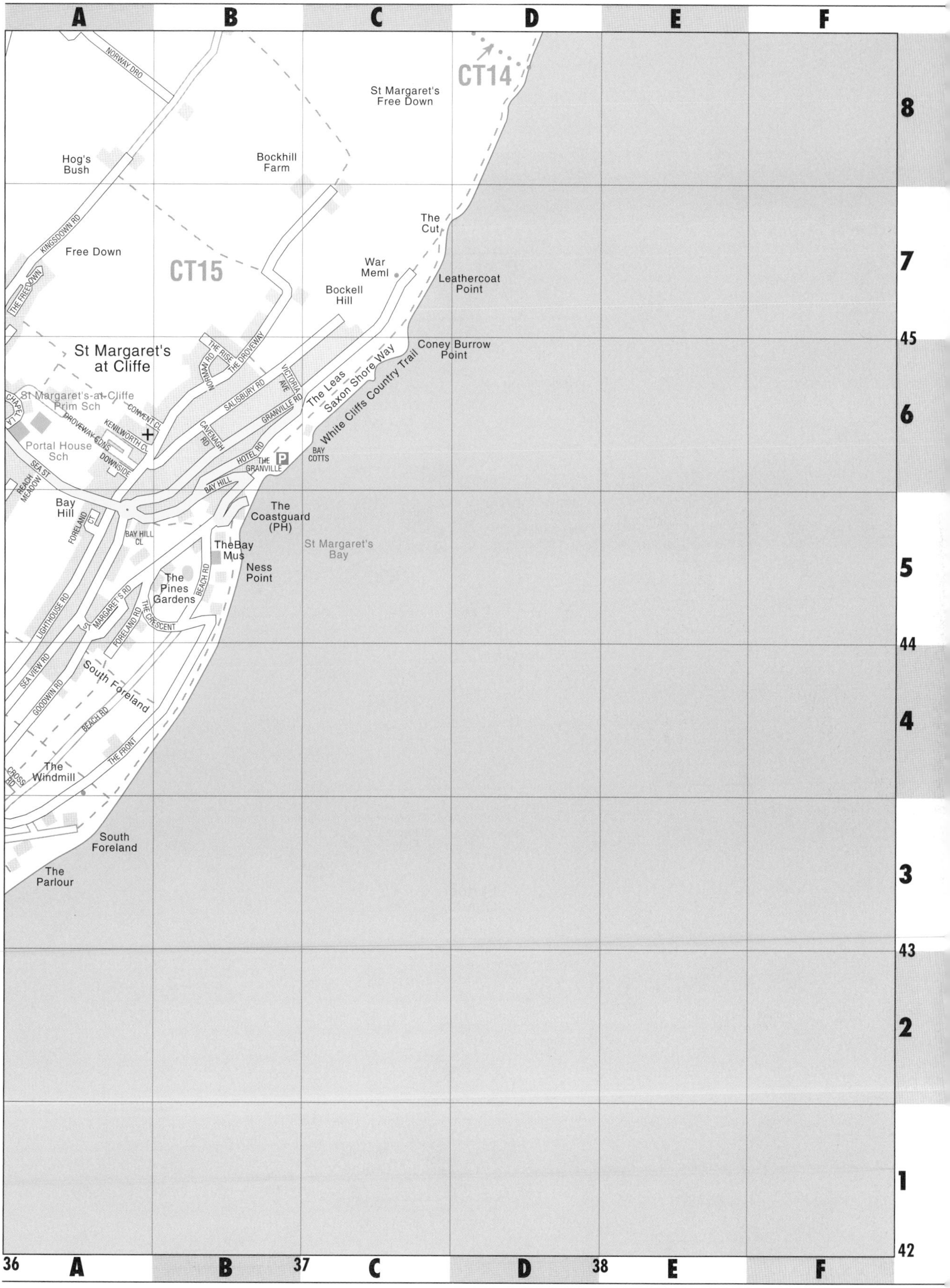

A   B   C   D   E   F

8

CT14

St Margaret's
Free Down

Hog's
Bush

Bockhill
Farm

The
Cut

7

NORWAY DRO

Free Down

CT15

War
Meml

Leathercoat
Point

Bockell
Hill

KINGSDOWN RD

THE FREEDOWN

45

St Margaret's
at Cliffe

Coney Burrow
Point

The Leas

Saxon Shore Way

St Margaret's-at-Cliffe
Prim Sch

THE RISE

THE DROVEWAY

White Cliffs Country Trail

6

MYRTON RD

VICTORIA AVE

SALISBURY RD

CONVENT CL

GRANVILLE RD

CHAPEL LA

Portal House
Sch

KENILWORTH CL

DROVEWAY GDNS

DOWNSIDE

CAVELAGH RD

HOTEL RD

BAY HILL

THE
GRANVILLE   P

BAY
COTTS

SEA ST

BEACH
MEADOW

Bay
Hill

FORELAND CT

BAY HILL
CL

The
Coastguard
(PH)

TheBay
Mus

St Margaret's
Bay

5

LIGHTHOUSE RD

MARGARET'S RD

FORELAND RD

BEACH RD

THE CRESCENT

The
Pines
Gardens

Ness
Point

44

SEA VIEW RD

GOODWIN RD

South Foreland

BEACH RD

4

THE FRONT

The
Windmill

CROSS RD

South
Foreland

3

The
Parlour

43

2

1

36   A   37   B   C   37   D   38   E   F   42

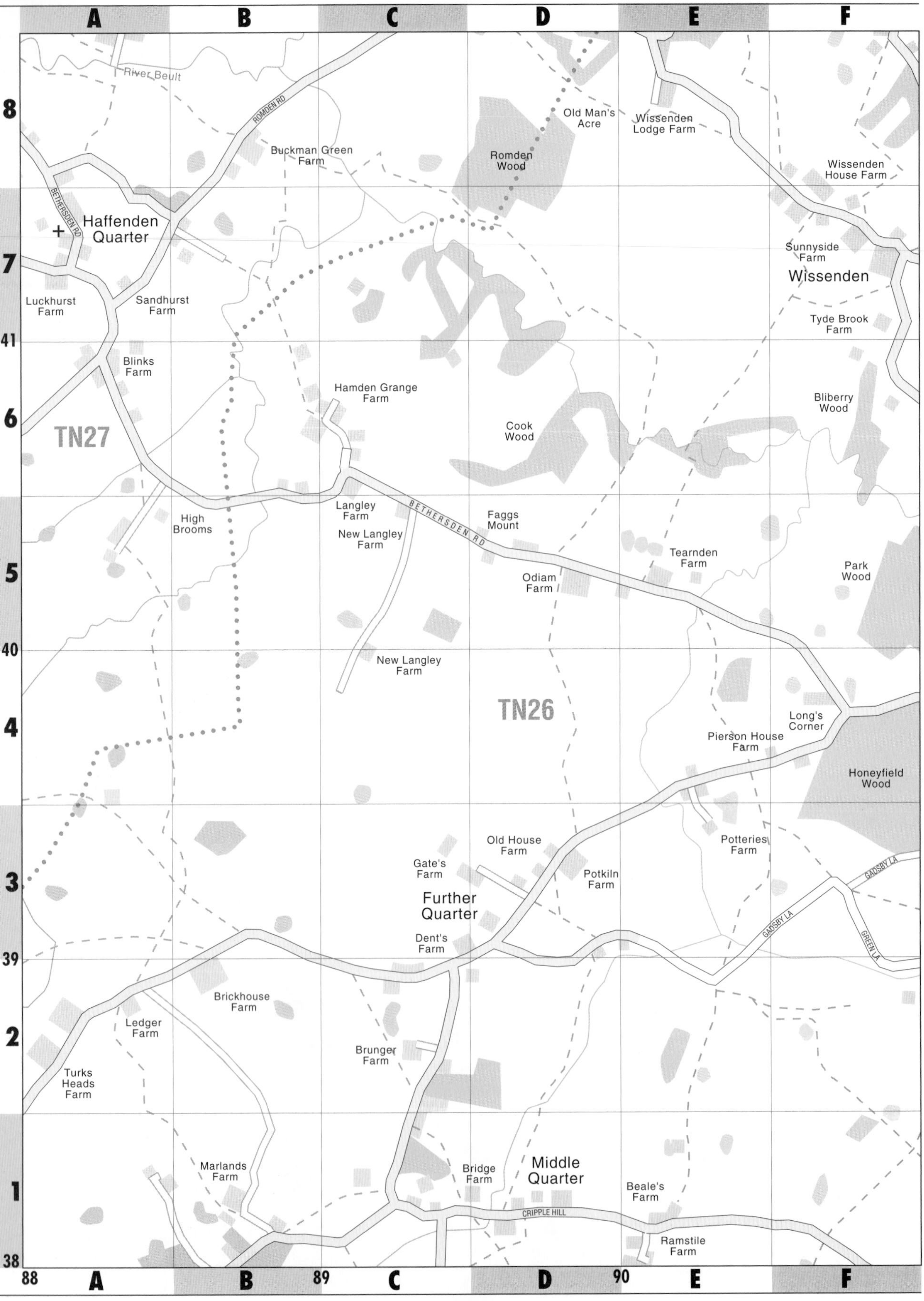

A B C D E F

8

Old Man's Acre

Wissenden Lodge Farm

Romden Wood

Wissenden House Farm

River Beult

ROMDEN RD

Buckman Green Farm

BETHERSDEN RD

Haffenden Quarter

7

Sunnyside Farm

Wissenden

Luckhurst Farm

Sandhurst Farm

Tyde Brook Farm

41

Blinks Farm

Hamden Grange Farm

Bliberry Wood

6

TN27

Cook Wood

Langley Farm

High Brooms

New Langley Farm

BETHERSDEN RD

Faggs Mount

Tearnden Farm

Park Wood

5

Odiam Farm

40

New Langley Farm

TN26

Long's Corner

4

Pierson House Farm

Honeyfield Wood

Potteries Farm

GADSBY LA

Old House Farm

3

Gate's Farm

Potkiln Farm

GADSBY LA

GREEN LA

Dent's Farm

39

Further Quarter

Brickhouse Farm

2

Ledger Farm

Brunger Farm

Turks Heads Farm

Marlands Farm

Middle Quarter

Bridge Farm

1

Beale's Farm

CRIPPLE HILL

Ramstile Farm

38

88 A B 89 C D 90 E F

136
154

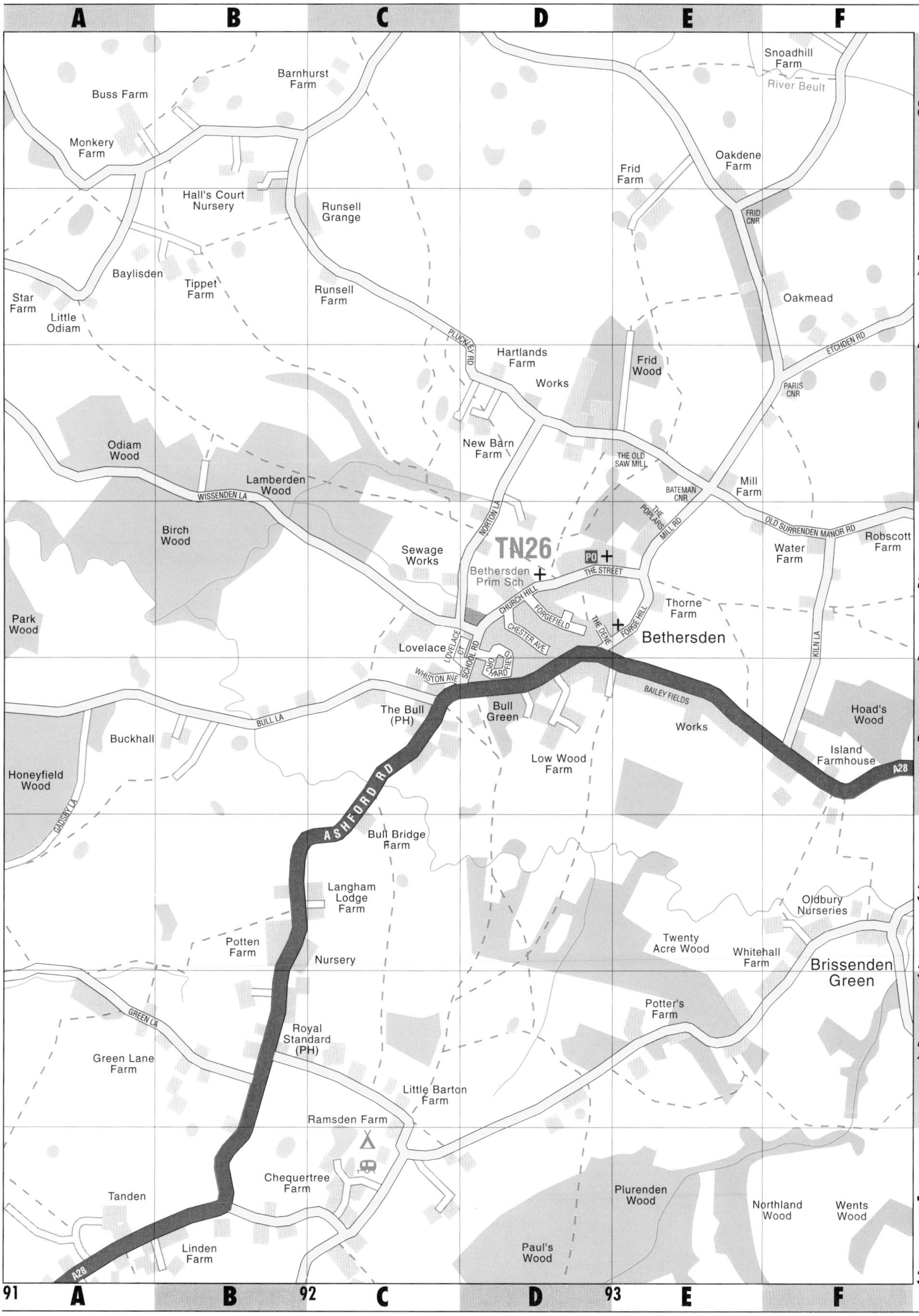
A
B
C
D
E
F
8
7
41
6
5
40
4
3
39
2
1
38
91
92
93
Snoadhill Farm
River Beult
Barnhurst Farm
Buss Farm
Monkery Farm
Oakdene Farm
Frid Farm
Hall's Court Nursery
Runsell Grange
FRID CNR
Baylisden
Tippet Farm
Runsell Farm
Star Farm
Little Odiam
Oakmead
PLUCKLEY RD
ETCHDEN RD
Hartlands Farm
Frid Wood
Works
PARIS CNR
Odiam Wood
New Barn Farm
THE OLD SAW MILL
Lamberden Wood
WISSENDEN LA
BATEMAN CNR
Mill Farm
THE POPLARS
MILL RD
Birch Wood
NORTON LA
OLD SURRENDEN MANOR RD
TN26
Robscott Farm
Water Farm
Sewage Works
PO
Bethersden Prim Sch
THE STREET
CHURCH HILL
Thorne Farm
FORGEFIELD
Park Wood
THE DENE
FORGE HILL
CHESTER AVE
Bethersden
Lovelace
LOVELACE CT
SCHOOL RD
ORCHARD FIELD
KILN LA
WHISTON AVE
BAILEY FIELDS
The Bull (PH)
Bull Green
Hoad's Wood
BULL LA
Works
Buckhall
Island Farmhouse
Low Wood Farm
A28
Honeyfield Wood
ASHFORD RD
GADSBY LA
Bull Bridge Farm
Langham Lodge Farm
Oldbury Nurseries
Twenty Acre Wood
Potten Farm
Whitehall Farm
Nursery
Brissenden Green
Potter's Farm
GREEN LA
Royal Standard (PH)
Green Lane Farm
Little Barton Farm
Ramsden Farm
Chequertree Farm
Plurenden Wood
Tanden
Northland Wood
Wents Wood
Linden Farm
Paul's Wood
A28

153
137

| A | B | C | D | E | F |

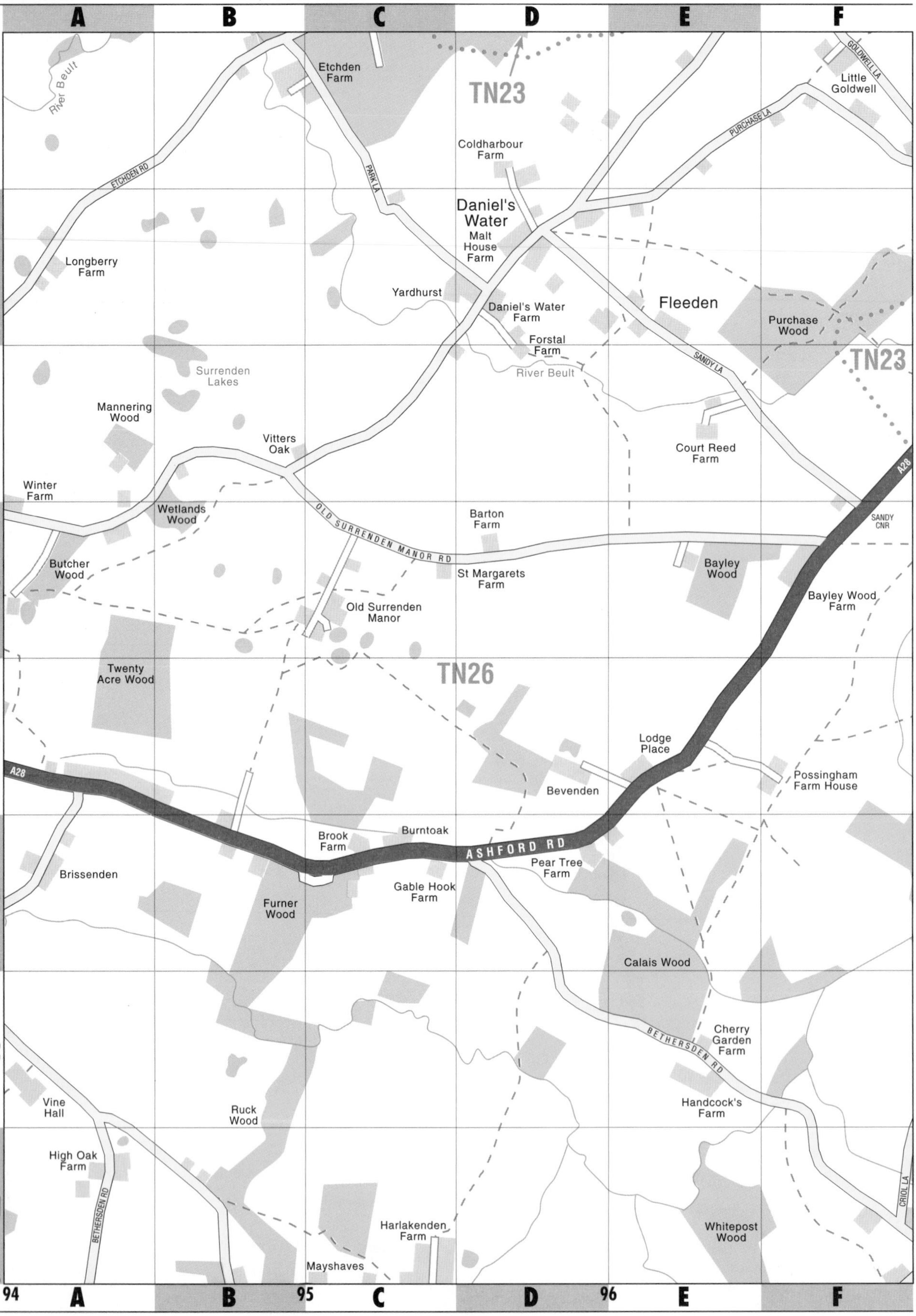

TN23

Etchden
Farm

ETCHDEN RD

River Beult

Longberry
Farm

PARK LA

Coldharbour
Farm

PURCHASE LA

GOLDWELL LA

Little
Goldwell

**Daniel's
Water**

Malt
House
Farm

Yardhurst

Daniel's Water
Farm

Fleeden

Purchase
Wood

TN23

Surrenden
Lakes

Forstal
Farm

River Beult

SANDY LA

Mannering
Wood

Vitters
Oak

Court Reed
Farm

A28

Winter
Farm

Wetlands
Wood

OLD SURRENDEN MANOR RD

Barton
Farm

Bayley
Wood

SANDY
CNR

Butcher
Wood

St Margarets
Farm

Bayley Wood
Farm

Old Surrenden
Manor

TN26

Twenty
Acre Wood

Lodge
Place

Possingham
Farm House

A28

Bevenden

Burntoak

Brook
Farm

ASHFORD RD

Pear Tree
Farm

Brissenden

Furner
Wood

Gable Hook
Farm

Calais Wood

BETHERSDEN RD

Cherry
Garden
Farm

Vine
Hall

Ruck
Wood

Handcock's
Farm

BETHERSDEN RD

High Oak
Farm

CRIOL LA

Harlakenden
Farm

Whitepost
Wood

Mayshaves

| A | B | C | D | E | F |

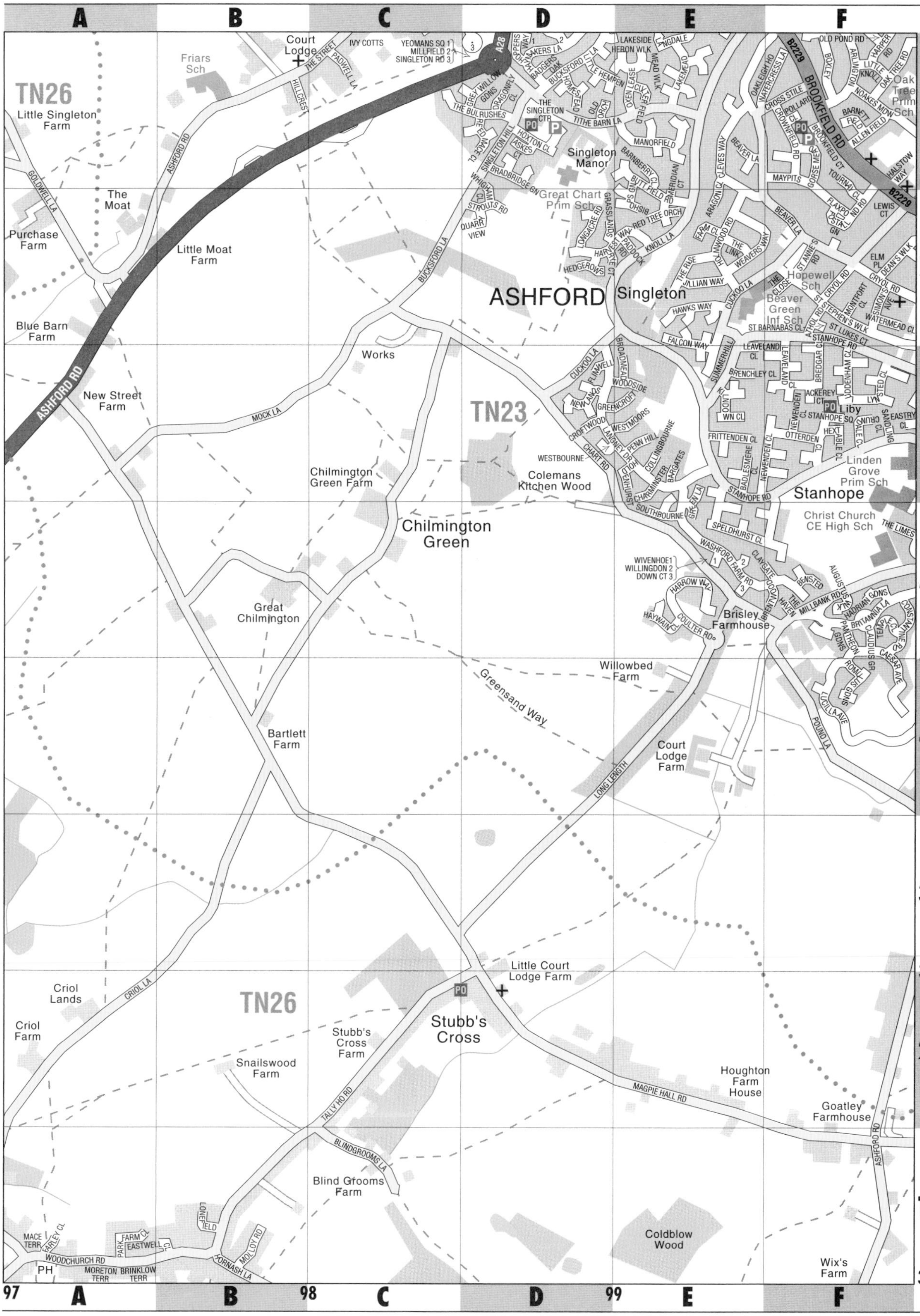
A B C D E F
8
7
41
6
5
40
4
3
39
2
1
38
97 98 99
TN26
Little Singleton Farm
Friars Sch
Court Lodge
IVY COTTS
YEOMANS SQ 1
MILLFIELD 2
SINGLETON RD 3
A28
The Moat
Purchase Farm
Little Moat Farm
Blue Barn Farm
New Street Farm
ASHFORD RD
ASHFORD
Singleton
Singleton Manor
Great Chart Prim Sch
Works
TN23
MOCK LA
BUCKSFORD LA
Chilmington Green Farm
Colemans Kitchen Wood
Chilmington Green
Great Chilmington
Bartlett Farm
Greensand Way
Willowbed Farm
Court Lodge Farm
LONG LENGTH
Brisley Farmhouse
Hopewell Sch
Beaver Green Inf Sch
Oak Tree Prim Sch
Linden Grove Prim Sch
Stanhope
Christ Church CE High Sch
Liby
BROOKFIELD RD
B2229
WIVENHOE 1
WILLINGDON 2
DOWN CT 3
Little Court Lodge Farm
Stubb's Cross
Stubb's Cross Farm
TN26
Criol Lands
Criol Farm
CRIOL LA
Snailswood Farm
MAGPIE HALL RD
Houghton Farm House
Goatley Farmhouse
TALLY HO RD
BLINDGROOMS LA
Blind Grooms Farm
Coldblow Wood
Wix's Farm
WOODCHURCH RD
PH

155
139

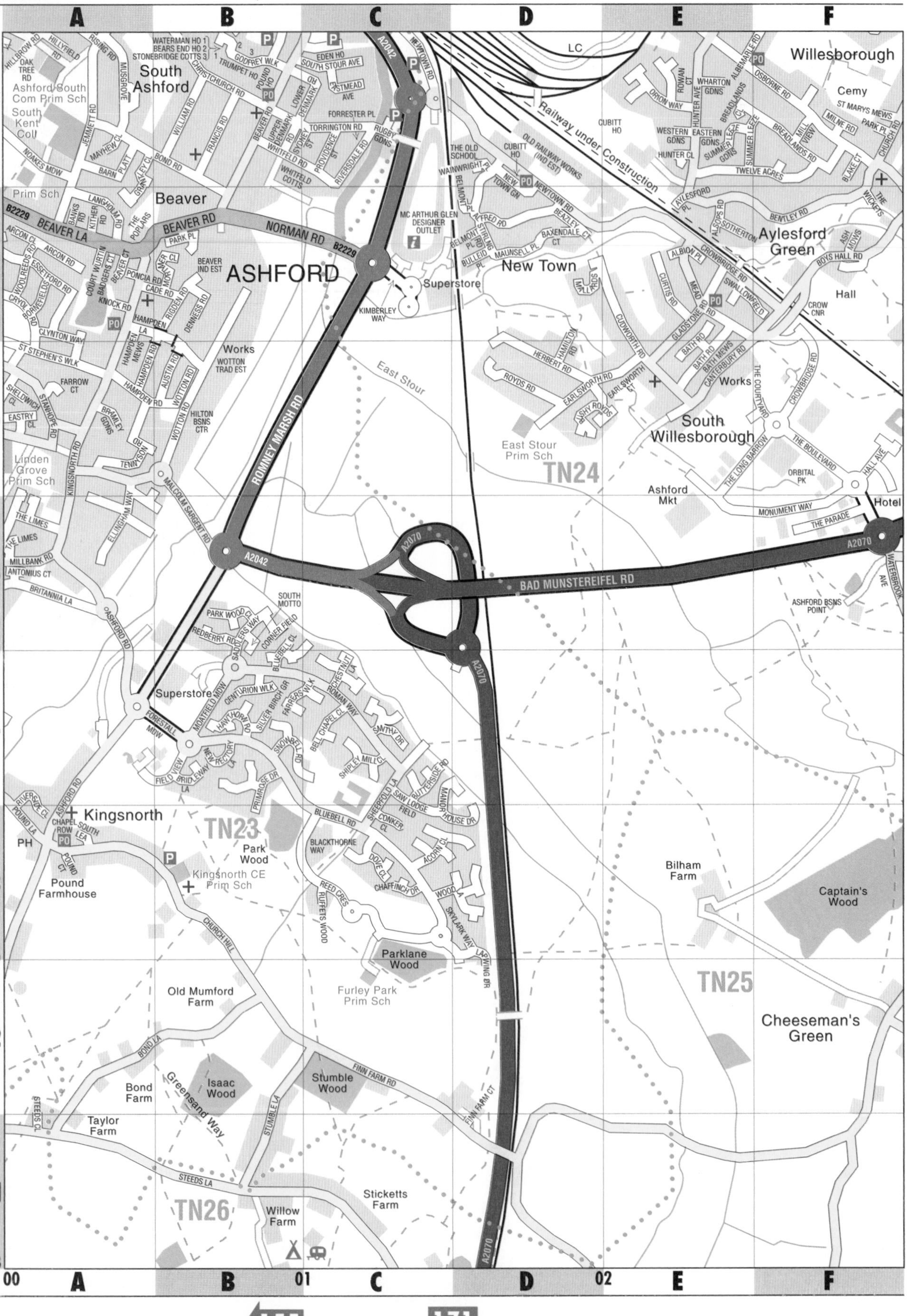
A
B
C
D
E
F
8
7
41
6
5
40
4
3
39
2
1
38
00
01
02
South Ashford
Ashford South Com Prim Sch
South Kent Coll
Prim Sch
Beaver
ASHFORD
B2229
BEAVER LA
BEAVER RD
NORMAN RD
A2042
NEWTOWN RD
Works
WOTTON TRAD EST
HILTON BSNS CTR
BEAVER IND EST
MC ARTHUR GLEN DESIGNER OUTLET
Superstore
KIMBERLEY WAY
LC
Railway under Construction
CUBITT HO
THE OLD SCHOOL
OLD RAILWAY WORKS (IND EST)
New Town
Willesborough
Cemy
Aylesford Green
Hall
CROW CNR
Works
South Willesborough
East Stour
East Stour Prim Sch
TN24
Ashford Mkt
ORBITAL PK
MONUMENT WAY
THE PARADE
Hotel
A2070
BAD MUNSTEREIFEL RD
ROMNEY MARSH RD
MALCOLM SARGENT RD
Linden Grove Prim Sch
KINGSNORTH RD
ASHFORD RD
BRITANNIA LA
SOUTH MOTTO
ASHFORD BSNS POINT
Superstore
FORESTALL MDW
Kingsnorth
PH
TN23
Park Wood
Kingsnorth CE Prim Sch
Pound Farmhouse
CHURCH HILL
Bilham Farm
Captain's Wood
Parklane Wood
Furley Park Prim Sch
TN25
Cheeseman's Green
Old Mumford Farm
BOND LA
Bond Farm
Isaac Wood
Greensand Way
Stumble Wood
FINN FARM RD
FINN FARM CT
STUMBLE LA
Taylor Farm
STEEDS CL
STEEDS LA
TN26
Willow Farm
Sticketts Farm

155
171

140
158

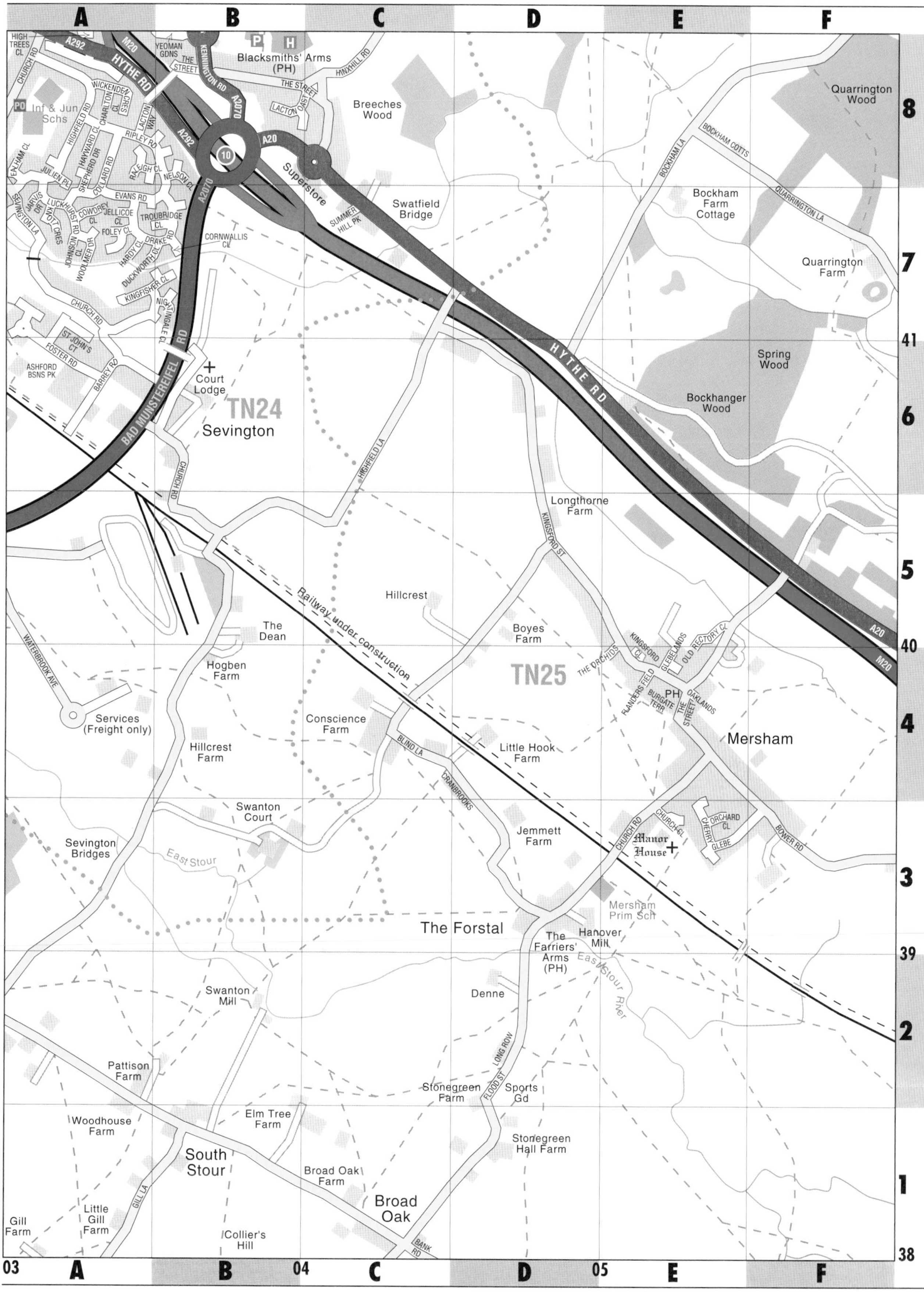
A
B
C
D
E
F
8
7
41
6
5
40
4
3
39
2
1
38
03
04
05
Blacksmiths' Arms (PH)
Breeches Wood
Quarrington Wood
Inf & Jun Schs
HYTHE RD
A292
M20
A2070
A20
KENNINGTON RD
THE STREET
HINXHILL RD
LACTON OAST
Superstore
SUMMER HILL PK
Swatfield Bridge
BOCKHAM LA
BOCKHAM COTTS
QUARRINGTON LA
Bockham Farm Cottage
Quarrington Farm
Spring Wood
Bockhanger Wood
CORNWALLIS CL
KINGFISHER CL
NIGHTINGALE CL
CHURCH RD
ST JOHN'S CT
FOSTER RD
ASHFORD BSNS PK
BARREY RD
BAD MUNSTEREIFEL RD
Court Lodge
TN24
Sevington
HIGHFIELD LA
Longthorne Farm
KINGSFORD ST
Hillcrest
Boyes Farm
Railway under construction
The Dean
Hogben Farm
WATERBROOK AVE
Services (Freight only)
TN25
THE ORCHIDS
KINGSFORD CL
GLEBELANDS
OLD RECTORY CL
FLANDERS FIELD
BURGATE TERR
THE STREET
OAKLANDS
PH
Mersham
Conscience Farm
Hillcrest Farm
BLIND LA
CRANBROOKS
Little Hook Farm
Swanton Court
Jemmett Farm
CHURCH RD
CHURCH CL
CHERRY GLEBE
ORCHARD CL
BOWER RD
Manor House
Sevington Bridges
East Stour
Mersham Prim Sch
The Forstal
The Farriers' Arms (PH)
Hanover Mill
East Stour River
Swanton Mill
Denne
LONG ROW
FLOOD ST
Pattison Farm
Stonegreen Farm
Sports Gd
Woodhouse Farm
Elm Tree Farm
Stonegreen Hall Farm
South Stour
Broad Oak Farm
Broad Oak
GILL LA
Gill Farm
Little Gill Farm
Collier's Hill
BANK RD

172
158

157 141

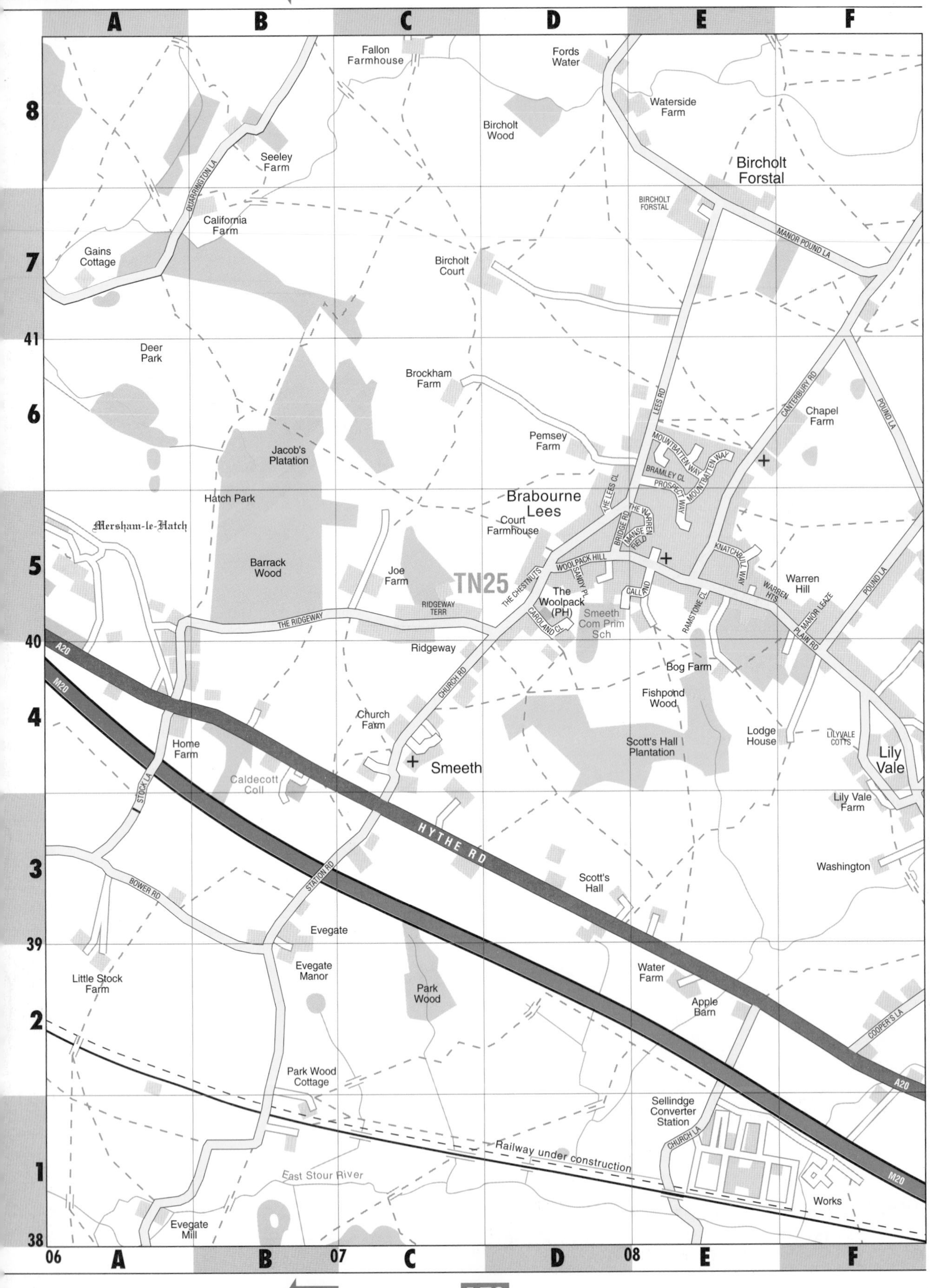

A B C D E F

8
7
41
6
5
40
4
3
39
2
1
38

06 A B 07 C D 08 E F

Fallon Farmhouse
Fords Water
Waterside Farm
Bircholt Forstal
BIRCHOLT FORSTAL
MANOR POUND LA
Seeley Farm
Bircholt Wood
California Farm
Gains Cottage
Bircholt Court
Chapel Farm
POUND LA
CANTERBURY RD
Deer Park
Brockham Farm
Jacob's Platation
Pemsey Farm
MOUNTBATTEN WAY
BRAMLEY CL
PROSPECT WAY
Hatch Park
Brabourne Lees
THE LEES CL
THE WARREN
Mersham-le-Hatch
Court Farmhouse
BRIDGE RD
GRANGE FIELD
Warren Hill
Barrack Wood
Joe Farm
WOOLPACK HILL
KNATCHBULL WAY
WARREN HTS
TN25
THE CHESTNUTS
The Woolpack (PH)
CALL RD
RAMSTONE CL
MANOR LEAZE
LEES RD
RIDGEWAY TERR
Smeeth Com Prim Sch
PLAIN RD
THE RIDGEWAY
Ridgeway
CAROLAND CL
Bog Farm
POUND LA
CHURCH RD
Fishpond Wood
Lodge House
LILYVALE COTTS
Lily Vale
A20
Church Farm
Scott's Hall Plantation
M20
Home Farm
Smeeth
Lily Vale Farm
STOCK LA
Caldecott Coll
HYTHE RD
BOWER RD
STATION RD
Evegate
Scott's Hall
Washington
Little Stock Farm
Evegate Manor
Park Wood
Water Farm
Apple Barn
COOPER'S LA
A20
Park Wood Cottage
Sellindge Converter Station
CHURCH LA
M20
East Stour River
Railway under construction
Works
Evegate Mill

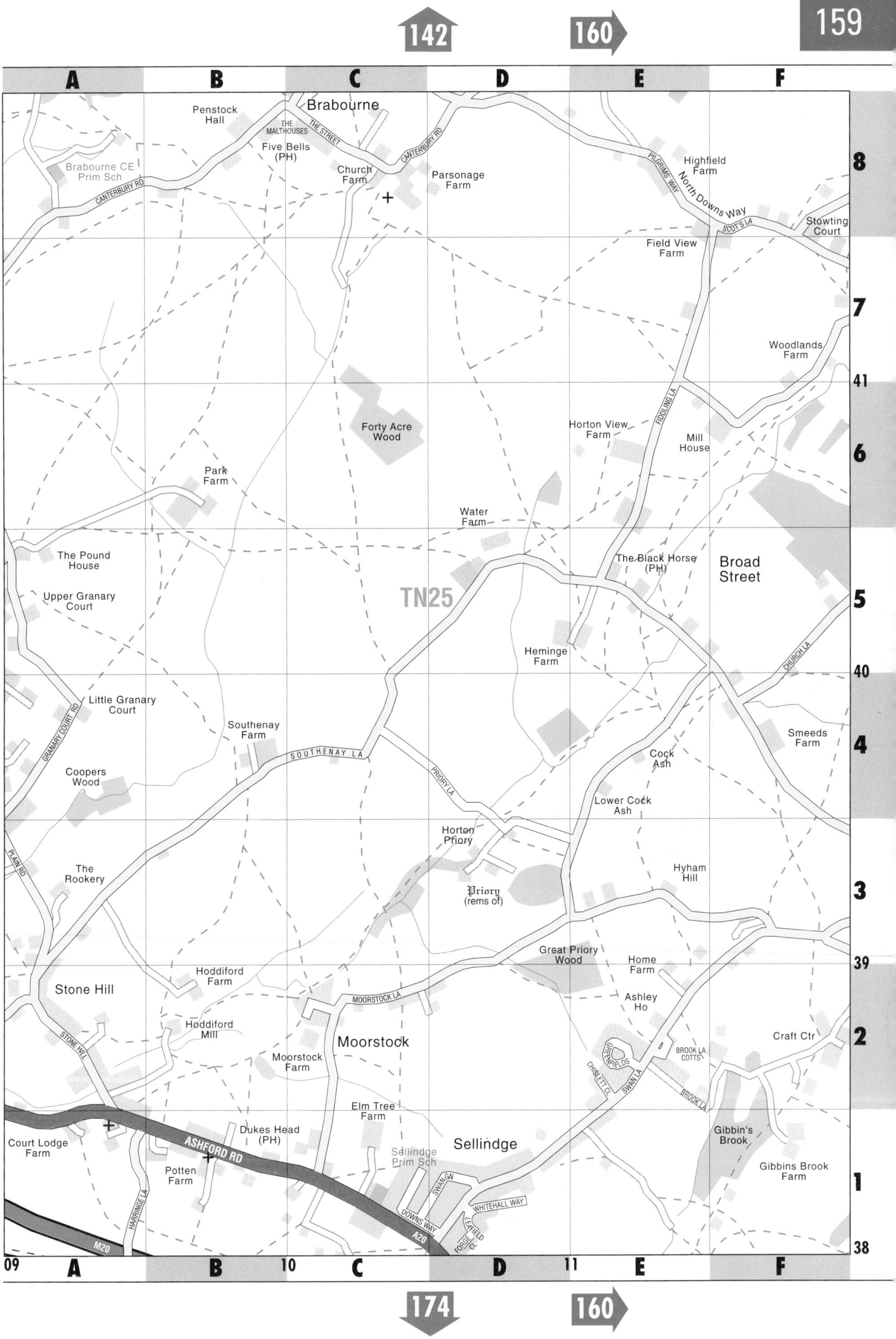
142
160
A
B
C
D
E
F
Brabourne
Penstock Hall
THE MALTHOUSES
THE STREET
Five Bells (PH)
Church Farm
CANTERBURY RD
Parsonage Farm
Highfield Farm
PILGRIMS' WAY
North Downs Way
SCOT'S LA
Stowting Court
Brabourne CE Prim Sch
Field View Farm
Woodlands Farm
Forty Acre Wood
Horton View Farm
FIDDLING LA
Mill House
Park Farm
Water Farm
The Pound House
The Black Horse (PH)
Broad Street
Upper Granary Court
TN25
Heminge Farm
CHURCH LA
Little Granary Court
GRANARY COURT RD
Southenay Farm
SOUTHENAY LA
Smeeds Farm
Cock Ash
Coopers Wood
PRIORY LA
Lower Cock Ash
Horton Priory
PLAIN RD
The Rookery
Hyham Hill
Priory (rems of)
Great Priory Wood
Home Farm
Stone Hill
Hoddiford Farm
MOORSTOCK LA
Ashley Ho
Hoddiford Mill
Moorstock
Craft Ctr
STONE HILL
GREENFIELDS
BROOK LA COTTS
Moorstock Farm
CHISLETT CL
SWAN LA
BROOK LA
Elm Tree Farm
Gibbin's Brook
Court Lodge Farm
Dukes Head (PH)
ASHFORD RD
Sellindge
Sellindge Prim Sch
Gibbins Brook Farm
Potten Farm
SWAN GN
WHITEHALL WAY
HARRINGE LA
DOWNS WAY
LEAFIELD
FORGE CL
A20
M20
8
7
41
6
5
40
4
3
39
2
1
38
09
10
11
174
160

159 143

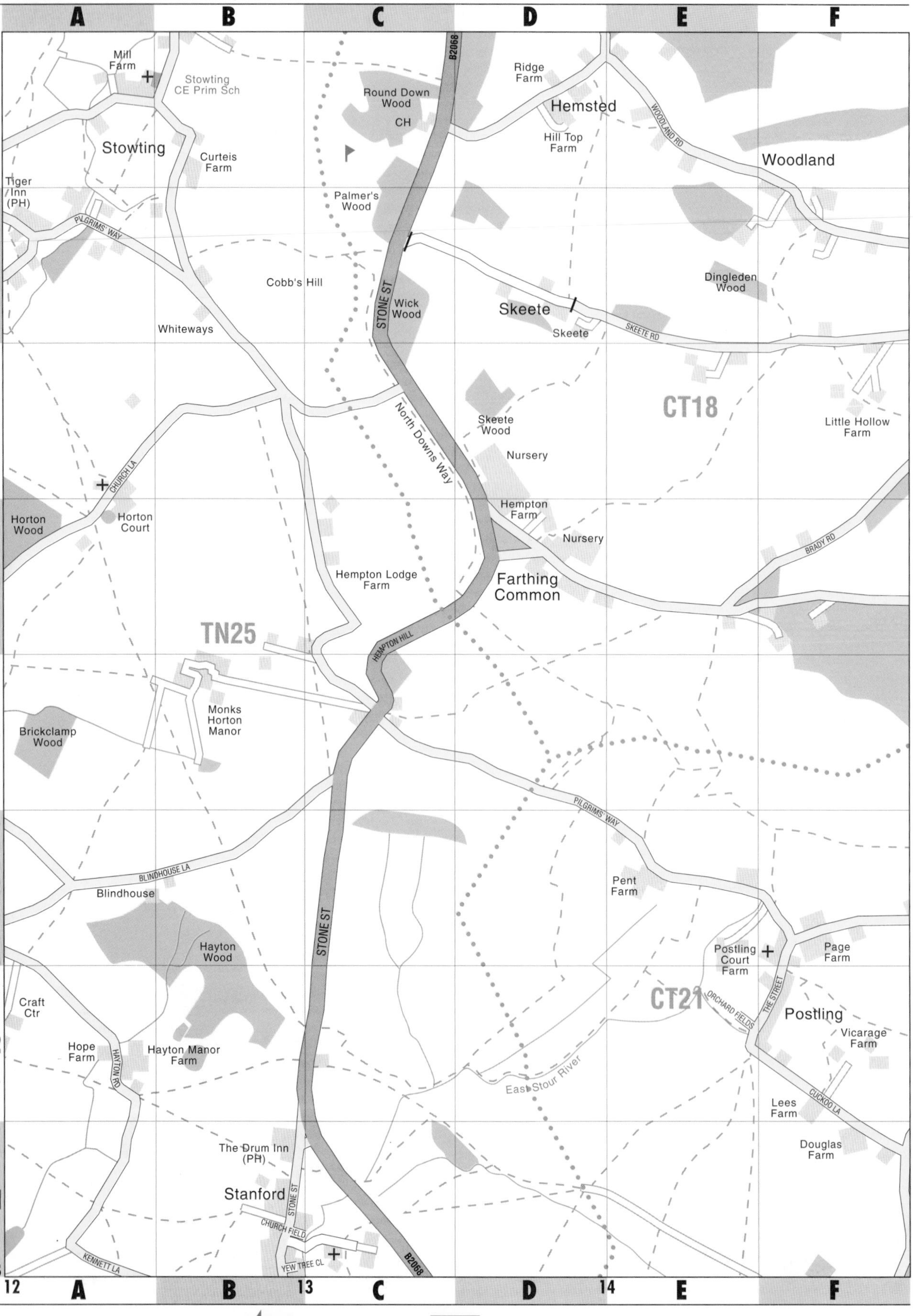

A B C D E F

8

Mill Farm
Stowting CE Prim Sch
Stowting
Curteis Farm
Round Down Wood
CH
Ridge Farm
Hemsted
Hill Top Farm
Woodland
WOODLAND RD

Tiger Inn (PH)
PILGRIMS WAY
Cobb's Hill
Palmer's Wood

7

STONE ST
Wick Wood
Skeete
Skeete
SKEETE RD
Dingleden Wood

41

Whiteways

Little Hollow Farm

6

CHURCH LA
North Downs Way
Skeete Wood
Nursery
CT18

Horton Wood
Horton Court
Hempton Farm
Nursery
BRADY RD

5

Hempton Lodge Farm
Farthing Common

40

TN25
HEMPTON HILL

Brickclamp Wood
Monks Horton Manor

4

PILGRIMS WAY

BLINDHOUSE LA
Blindhouse
Pent Farm

3

Hayton Wood
Postling Court Farm
Page Farm
THE STREET

39

Craft Ctr
CT21
ORCHARD FIELDS
Postling
Vicarage Farm

2

Hope Farm
HAYTON RD
Hayton Manor Farm
STONE ST
East Stour River
Lees Farm
CUCKOO LA

The Drum Inn (PH)
Douglas Farm

1

Stanford
STONE ST
CHURCH FIELD
B2068

38

12
KENNETT LA
YEW TREE CL
13
14

A B C D E F

159 175

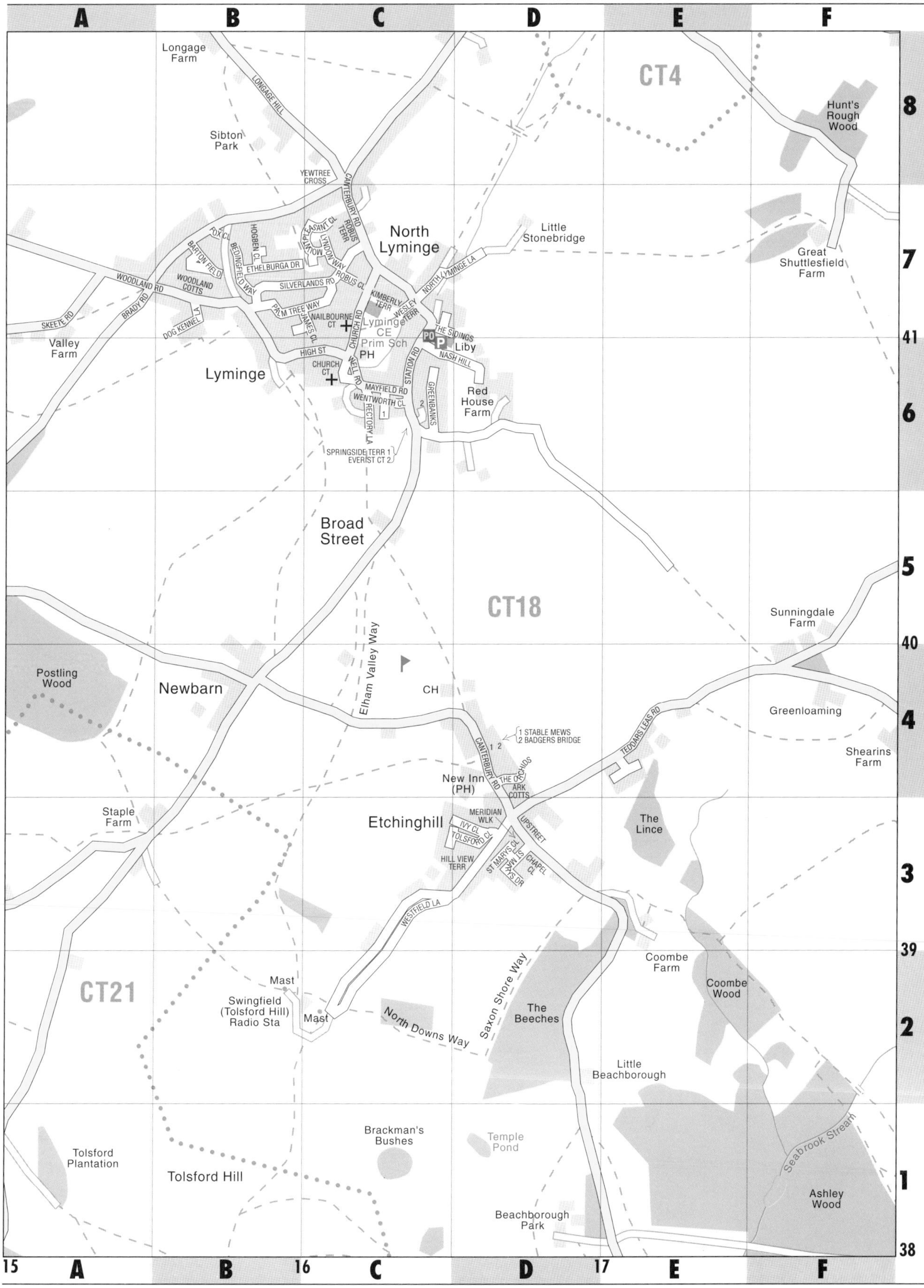

144
162
162

CT4

Longage Farm

Hunt's Rough Wood

Sibton Park

YEWTREE CROSS

Little Stonebridge

Great Shuttlesfield Farm

LONGAGE HILL

CANTERBURY RD

FOX CL

HOBBEN CL

PLEASANT CL

ROBUS TERR

North Lyminge

NORTH LYMINGE LA

BEDDINGFIELD WAY

ETHELBURGA DR

LYNDON WAY

ROBUS CL

WOODLAND RD

BARTON FIELD

WOODLAND COTTS

PALM TREE WAY

SILVERLANDS RD

JANE'S CL

NAILBOURNE CT

KIMBERLY TERR

WESLEY TERR

Lyminge CE Prim Sch

THE SIDINGS

SKEET RD

BRADY RD

DOG KENNEL

Valley Farm

HIGH ST

CHURCH CT

WELL RD

RECTORY LA

MAYFIELD RD

WENTWORTH CL

STATION RD

GREENBANKS

NASH HILL

P.O.
P Liby

PH

Lyminge

Red House Farm

1

2

SPRINGSIDE TERR 1
EVERIST CT 2

Broad Street

CT18

Sunningdale Farm

Postling Wood

Elham Valley Way

CH

40

Greenloaming

Newbarn

Shearins Farm

CANTERBURY RD

1 STABLE MEWS
2 BADGERS BRIDGE

1 2

TEDDARS LEAS RD

Staple Farm

New Inn (PH)

THE ORCHIDS

ARK COTTS

UP STREET

The Lince

MERIDIAN WLK

Etchinghill

IVY CL

TOLSFORD CL

ST MARYS CL

MAY CL

TAYLOR

CHAPEL CL

Coombe Farm

CT21

HILL VIEW TERR

Coombe Wood

39

Mast

Swingfield (Tolsford Hill) Radio Sta

Mast

WESTFIELD LA

North Downs Way

Saxon Shore Way

The Beeches

Little Beachborough

Tolsford Plantation

Brackman's Bushes

Temple Pond

Seabrook Stream

Tolsford Hill

Beachborough Park

Ashley Wood

15   A   B   16   C   D   17   E   F
38 1 2 39 3 40 4 5 41 6 7 8

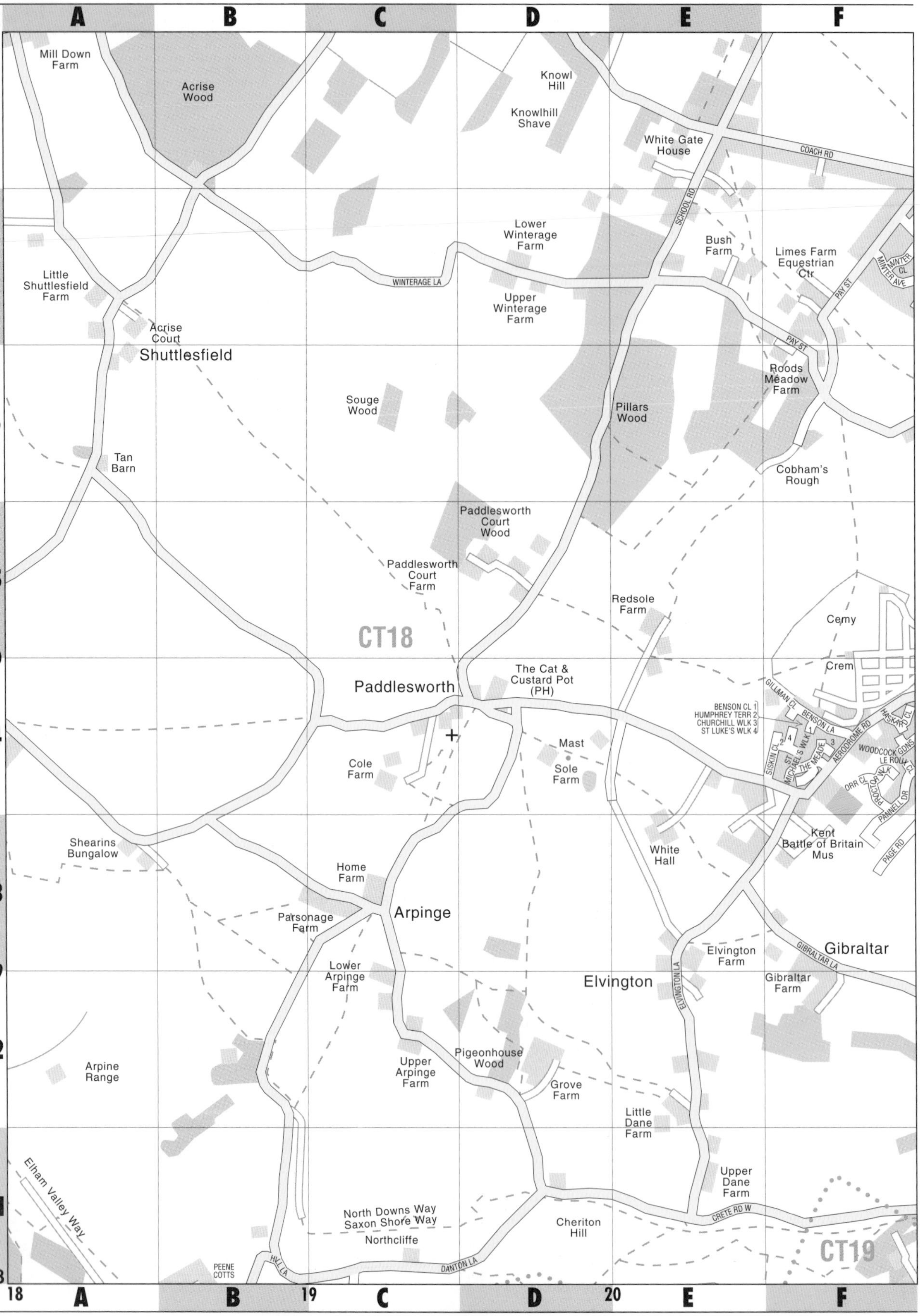

161
145

A B C D E F

8

7

41

6

5

40

4

3

39

2

1

38

18   A   B   19   C   D   20   E   F

Mill Down Farm
Acrise Wood
Knowl Hill
Knowlhill Shave
White Gate House
COACH RD
Lower Winterage Farm
Bush Farm
Limes Farm Equestrian Ctr
WINTER CL
WINTER AVE
Little Shuttlesfield Farm
WINTERAGE LA
Upper Winterage Farm
SCHOOL RD
PAY ST
PAY ST
Acrise Court
Shuttlesfield
Roods Meadow Farm
Souge Wood
Pillars Wood
Cobham's Rough
Tan Barn
Paddlesworth Court Wood
CT18
Paddlesworth Court Farm
Redsole Farm
Cemy
Crem
Paddlesworth
The Cat & Custard Pot (PH)
BENSON CL 1
HUMPHREY TERR 2
CHURCHILL WLK 3
ST LUKE'S WLK 4
GILLMAN CL
BENSON LA
HASKARD
ARDENROME RD
Mast
Sole Farm
Cole Farm
SUSKIN CL
MICHAEL S WLK
THE MEADE
WOODCOCK GDNS
LE ROU
ORR CL
GRANT CL
PANNELL CH
PAGE RD
Shearins Bungalow
White Hall
Kent Battle of Britain Mus
Home Farm
Parsonage Farm
Arpinge
Elvington Farm
GIBRALTAR LA
Gibraltar
Lower Arpinge Farm
Elvington
Gibraltar Farm
39
ELVINGTON LA
Arpine Range
Upper Arpinge Farm
Pigeonhouse Wood
Grove Farm
Little Dane Farm
Elham Valley Way
Upper Dane Farm
North Downs Way
Saxon Shore Way
Northcliffe
Cheriton Hill
CRETE RD W
CT19
PEENE COTTS
HV LA
DANTON LA

146
164

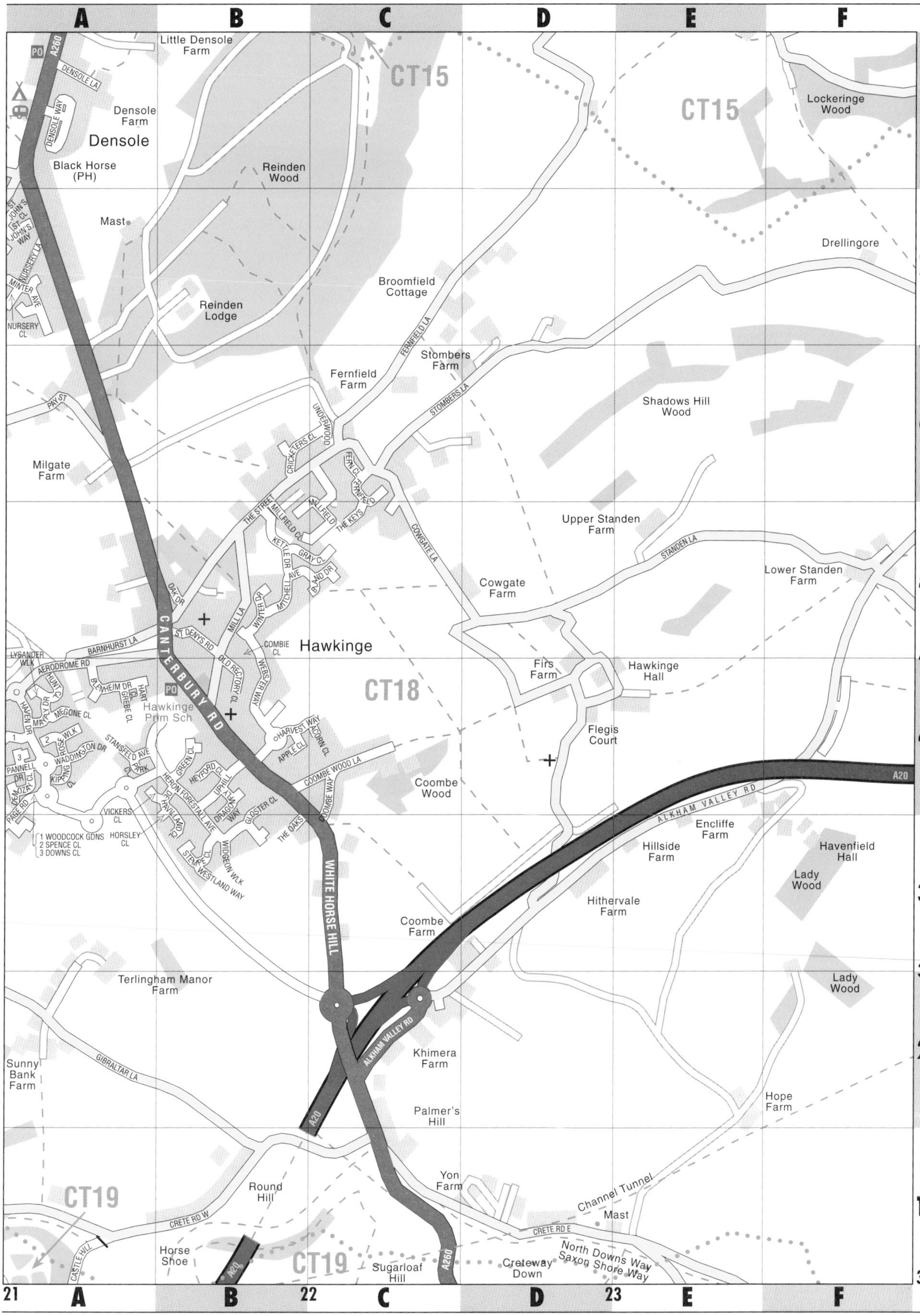
A
B
C
D
E
F
8
7
41
6
5
40
4
3
39
2
1
38
21
22
23
A260
A20
CT15
CT18
CT19
Little Densole Farm
DENSOLE LA
DENSOLE WAY
Densole Farm
Densole
Black Horse (PH)
Reinden Wood
Mast
ST JOHN'S CL
ST JOHN'S WAY
NURSERY LA
MINTER AVE
NURSERY CL
Reinden Lodge
Broomfield Cottage
Lockeringe Wood
Drellingore
FERNFIELD LA
Stombers Farm
Fernfield Farm
STOMBERS LA
PAY ST
UNDERWOOD
CRICKETERS CL
FERN CL
FERNFIELD
Shadows Hill Wood
Milgate Farm
THE STREET
MILLFIELD
MILLFIELD CL
THE KEYS
COWGATE LA
Upper Standen Farm
STANDEN LA
Lower Standen Farm
KETTLE DR
GRAY CL
MITCHELL AVE
BLAND DR
OAK DR
Cowgate Farm
WINTER DR
MILL LA
ST DENYS RD
COMBIE CL
Hawkinge
BARNHURST LA
LYSANDER WLK
AERODROME RD
CANTERBURY RD
Firs Farm
Hawkinge Hall
OLD RECTORY CL
WEBSTER WAY
BLENHEIM DR
HART CL
GREBE CL
Hawkinge Prim Sch
HUNT CL
MAYFLY DR
MEGONE CL
HAVEN DR
CT18
HARVEST WAY
ACORN CL
APPLE CL
Flegis Court
ROSE WLK
WADDINGTON DR
STANSFELD AVE
PARK
GREEN CL
HEYFORD CL
UPHILL
PANNELL DR
KIPPING CL
COOMBE WOOD LA
COOMBE WAY
Coombe Wood
HERON FORESTALL AVE
HAVILL CL
DRAGON WAY
GLOSTER CL
THE OAKS
VICKERS CL
HORSLEY CL
1 WOODCOCK GDNS
2 SPENCE CL
3 DOWNS CL
STEMPE CL
WIDGEON WLK
WESTLAND WAY
ALKHAM VALLEY RD
Encliffe Farm
Hillside Farm
Havenfield Hall
Lady Wood
WHITE HORSE HILL
Hithervale Farm
Coombe Farm
Terlingham Manor Farm
Lady Wood
ALKHAM VALLEY RD
Khimera Farm
GIBRALTAR LA
Sunny Bank Farm
Palmer's Hill
Hope Farm
Yon Farm
Round Hill
Channel Tunnel
CT19
Mast
CRETE RD W
CRETE RD E
North Downs Way
Saxon Shore Way
Horse Shoe
CASTLE HILL
CT19
Sugarloaf Hill
Creteway Down
PO

178
164

163 147

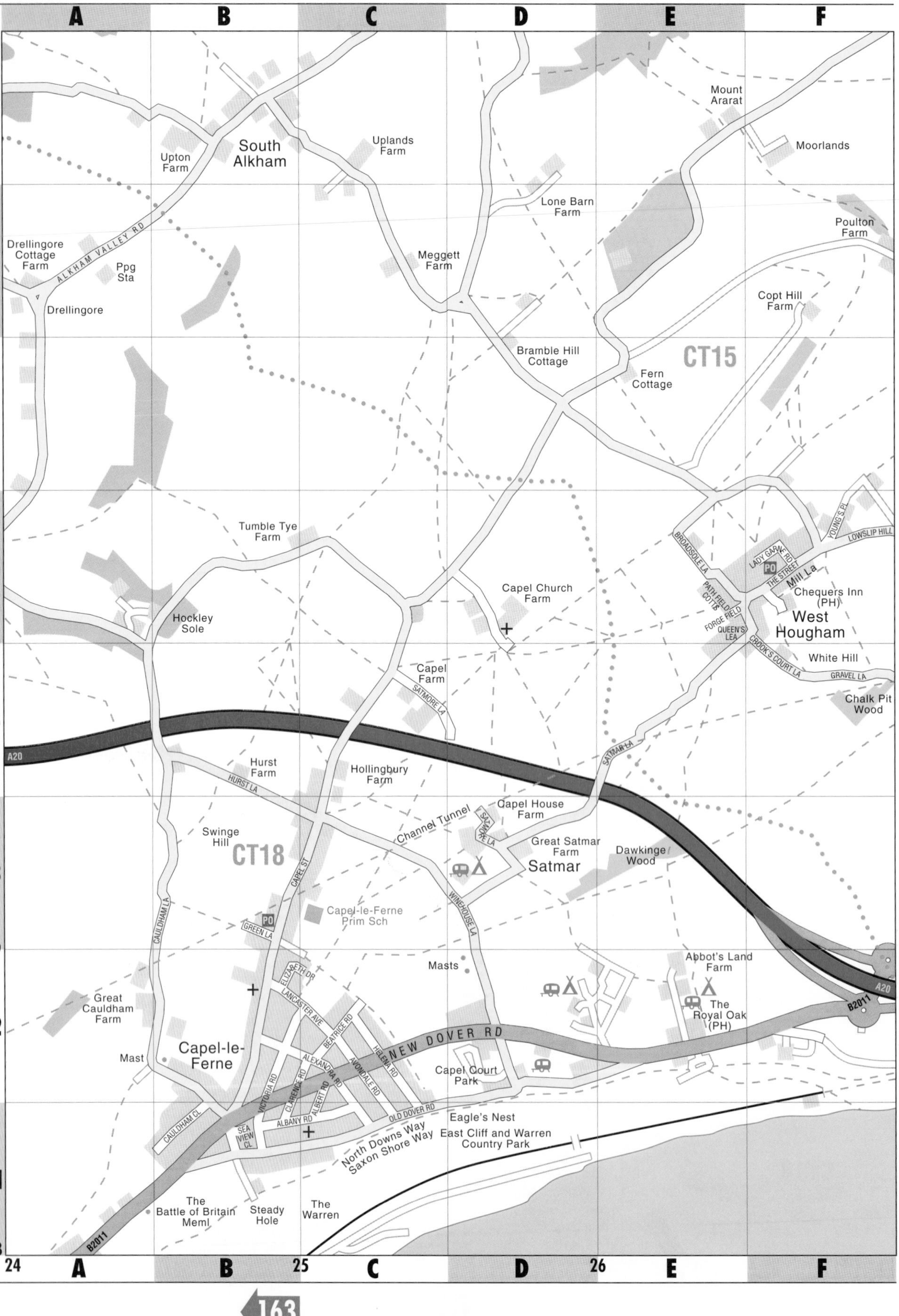

A B C D E F

8

Mount Ararat

Upton Farm

South Alkham

Uplands Farm

Moorlands

Lone Barn Farm

Drellingore Cottage Farm

7

Ppg Sta

ALKHAM VALLEY RD

Meggett Farm

Poulton Farm

Drellingore

Copt Hill Farm

41

Bramble Hill Cottage

CT15

6

Fern Cottage

Tumble Tye Farm

BROADSOLE LA

YOUNG'S PL

LOWSLIP HILL

5

PATHFIELD COTS

LADY GARTH

THE STREET

Mill La

Capel Church Farm

Chequers Inn (PH)

Hockley Sole

FORGE FIELD

QUEEN'S LEA

West Hougham

40

White Hill

Capel Farm

CROOK'S COURT LA

GRAVEL LA

SATMORE LA

Chalk Pit Wood

4

A20

SATMAR LA

Hurst Farm

HURST LA

Hollingbury Farm

Capel House Farm

Swinge Hill

CT18

CAPEL ST

Channel Tunnel

SLACK LA

Great Satmar Farm

Dawkinge Wood

CAULDHAM LA

Satmar

3

Capel-le-Ferne Prim Sch

PO

GREEN LA

WINEHOUSE LA

39

Masts

Abbot's Land Farm

SETH DR

LANCASTER AVE

LIZZIE RD

Great Cauldham Farm

A20

B2011

The Royal Oak (PH)

2

BEATRICE RD

TRENN RD

NEW DOVER RD

Mast

VICTORIA RD

ALEXANDRA RD

CLARENCE RD

ALBERT RD

AVONDALE RD

OLD DOVER RD

Capel Court Park

Capel-le-Ferne

ALBANY RD

SEA VIEW CL

Eagle's Nest

North Downs Way

East Cliff and Warren Country Park

Saxon Shore Way

1

The Battle of Britain Meml

Steady Hole

The Warren

B2011

38

163

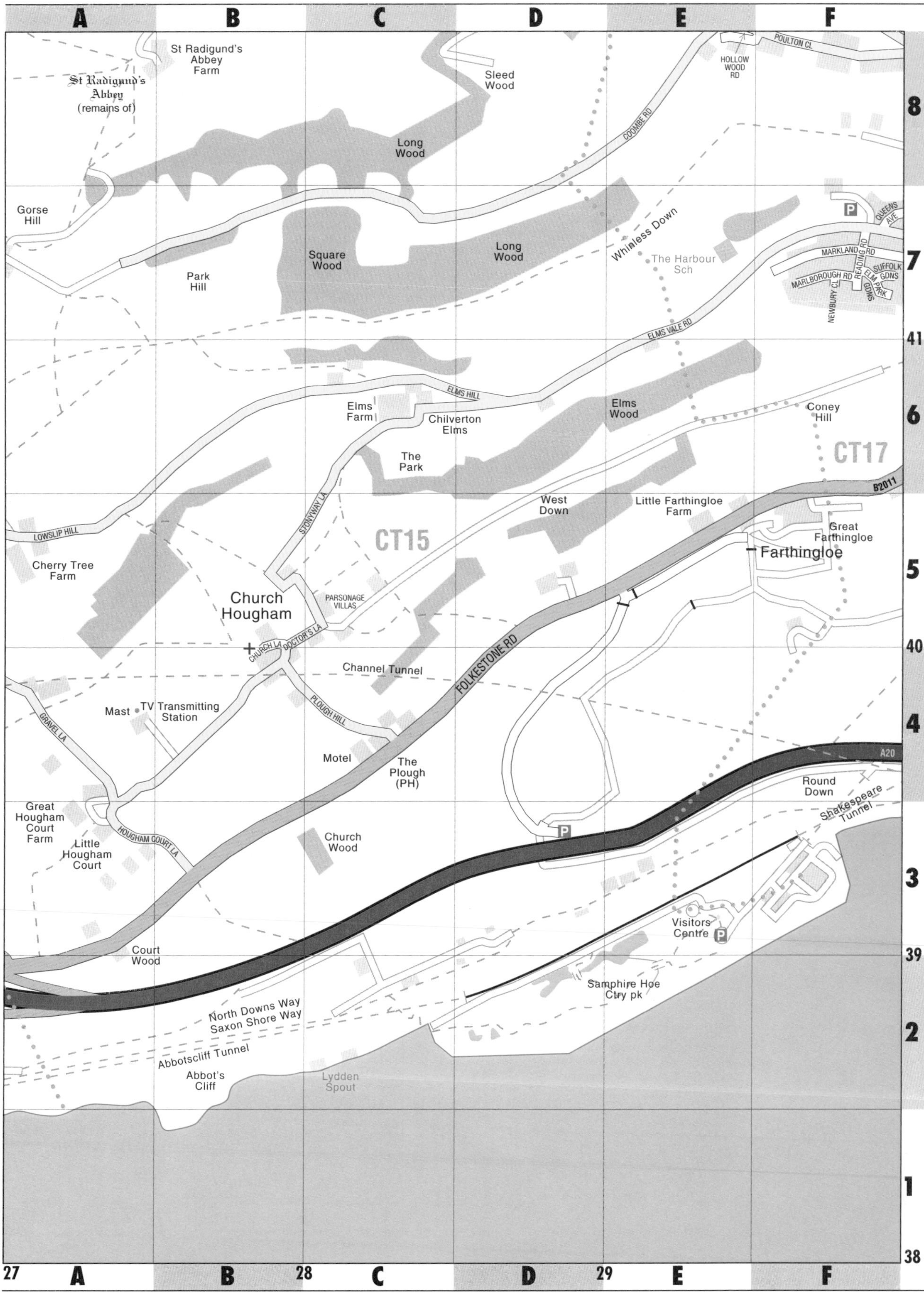

A   B   C   D   E   F

8

St Radigund's
Abbey Farm

Sleed
Wood

St Radigund's
Abbey
(remains of)

HOLLOW
WOOD
RD

POULTON CL

Long
Wood

Gorse
Hill

7

Square
Wood

Long
Wood

Whinless Down

The Harbour
Sch

MARKLAND
READING RD
QUEENS
AVE
SUFFOLK
ELMS PARK
GDNS

Park
Hill

MARLBOROUGH RD
NEWBURY
SINGLEDGE

41

ELMS VALE RD

Elms Hill

Elms
Farm

6

Chilverton
Elms

Elms
Wood

Coney
Hill

The
Park

CT17

B2011

LOWSLIP HILL

West
Down

Little Farthingloe
Farm

Great
Farthingloe

Cherry Tree
Farm

CT15

Farthingloe

5

STONYWAY LA

Church
Hougham

PARSONAGE
VILLAS

40

CHURCH LA
DOCTOR'S LA

Channel Tunnel

FOLKESTONE RD

GRAVEL LA

Mast
TV Transmitting
Station

PLOUGH HILL

4

A20

Motel

The
Plough
(PH)

Round
Down

Shakespeare
Tunnel

Great
Hougham
Court Farm

HOUGHAM COURT LA

Little
Hougham
Court

Church
Wood

3

Visitors
Centre

Court
Wood

39

North Downs Way
Saxon Shore Way

Samphire Hoe
Ctry pk

2

Abbotscliff Tunnel

Abbot's
Cliff

Lydden
Spout

1

38

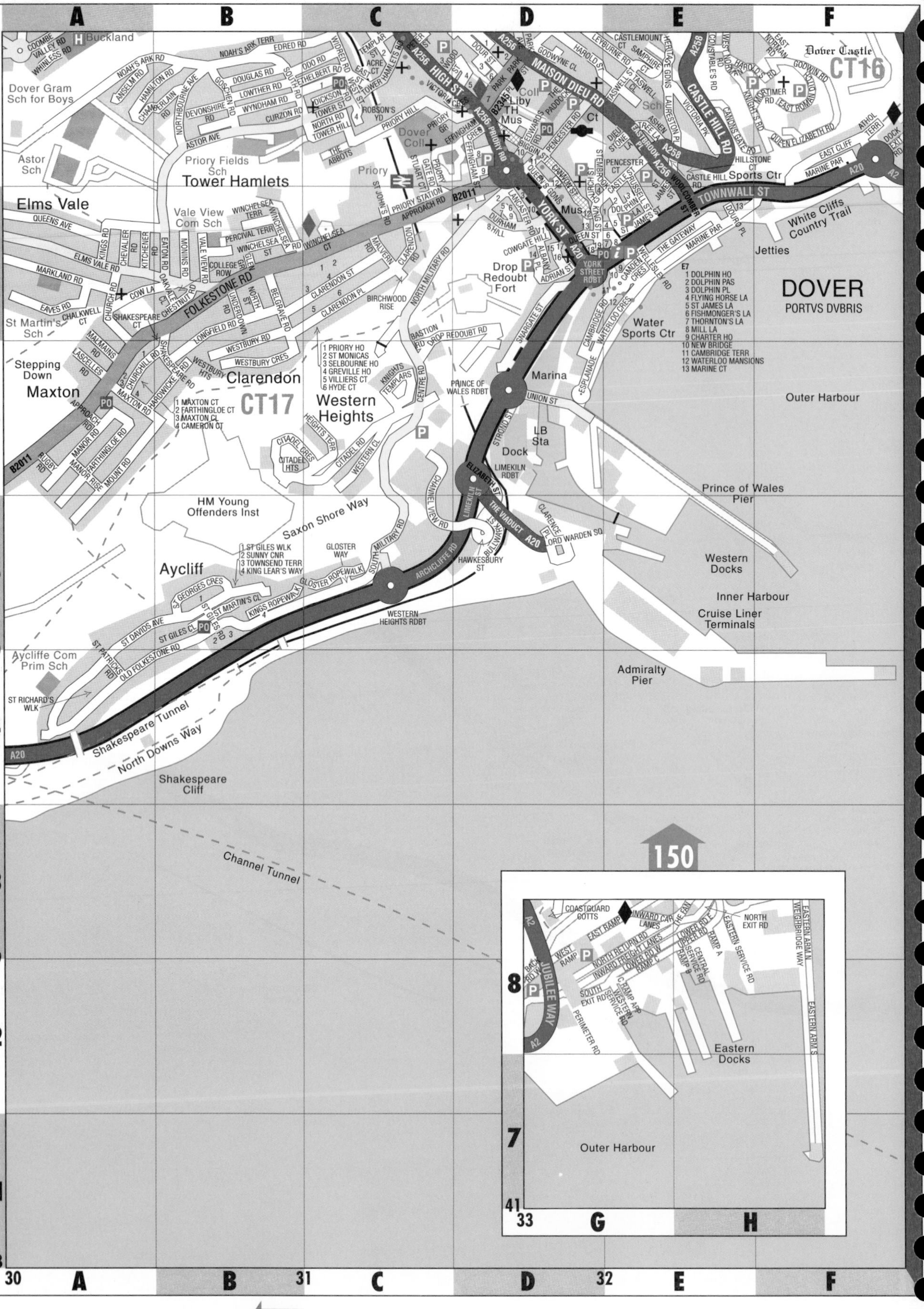

165
149
150

C8
1 TOWER HAMLETS ST
2 DE BURGH ST
3 CHARLTON CTR
4 ST BARTHOLEMEWS CL
D7
1 CHRISTCHURCH CT

D7
2 MILITARY RD
3 LANCASTER HO
4 STEMBROOK CT
5 CORNWALL HO
6 WINDSOR HO
7 EDINBURGH HO

8 BOWLING GREEN TERR
9 DURHAM CL
10 YORK HO
11 PRINCES ST
12 MARKET SQ
13 GAOL LA
14 GORELY HO

15 ALBANY HO
16 CHAPEL PL
17 BATTLE OF BRITAIN HOMES
18 CHAPEL LA
19 BENCH ST
D8
1 HEWITT RD

2 LADYWELL HO
3 MAISON DIEU PL
4 GOODFELLOW WAY
5 ROYAL VICTORIA PL
6 PARK MEWS
7 LADYWELL
8 NORMAN ST

9 SAXON ST
10 PRIORY ST
11 WORTHINGTON ST
12 NEW ST

E7
1 DOLPHIN HO
2 DOLPHIN PAS
3 DOLPHIN PL
4 FLYING HORSE LA
5 ST JAMES LA
6 FISHMONGER'S LA
7 THORNTON'S LA
8 MILL LA
9 CHARTER HO
10 NEW BRIDGE
11 CAMBRIDGE TERR
12 WATERLOO MANSIONS
13 MARINE CT

152
168

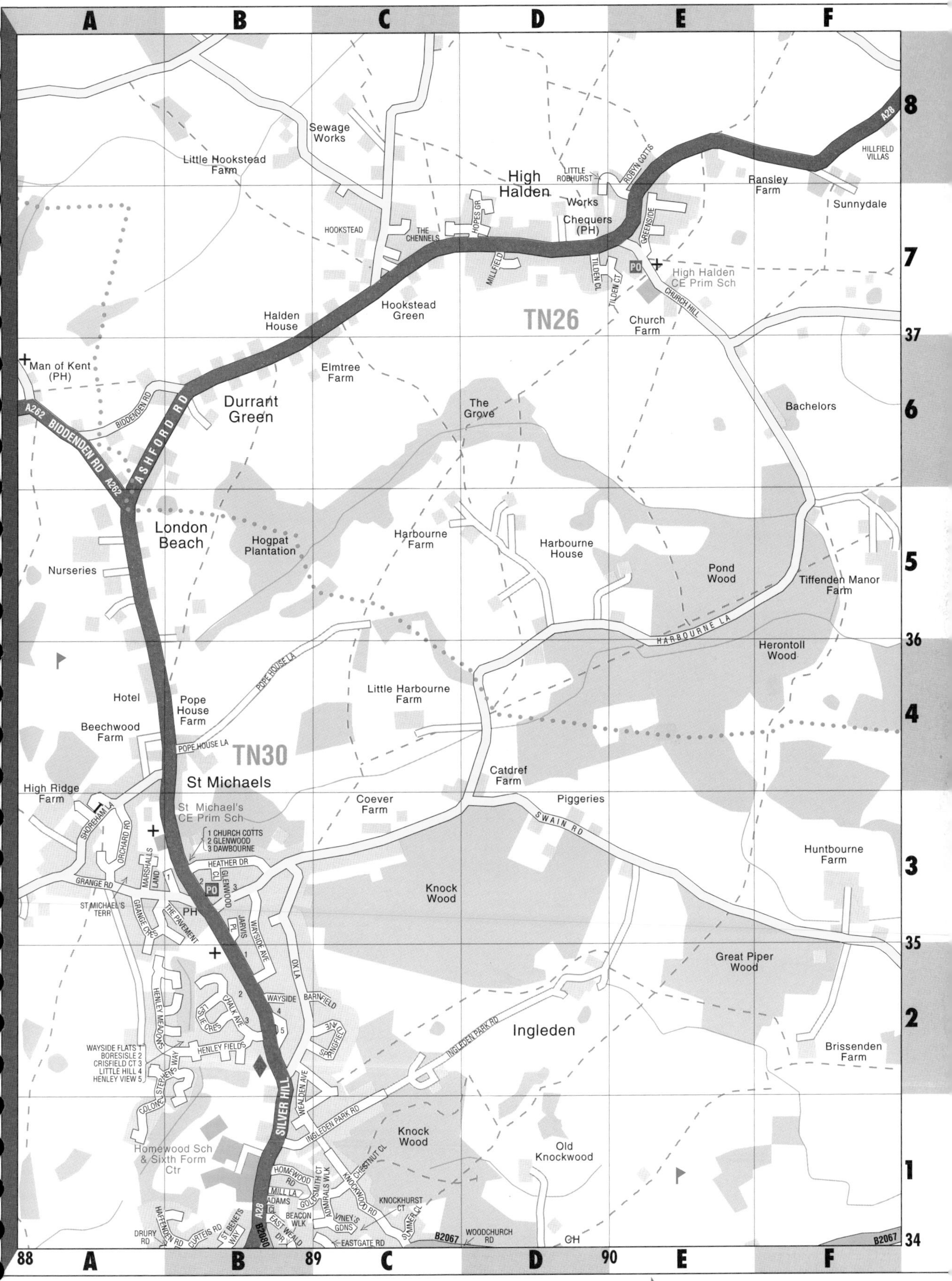
A
B
C
D
E
F
8
7
37
6
5
36
4
3
35
2
1
34
88
89
90
A28
HILLFIELD VILLAS
Sewage Works
Little Hookstead Farm
High Halden
LITTLE ROBHURST
ROBYN GOTTS
Works
Ransley Farm
Sunnydale
HOOKSTEAD
THE CHENNELS
HOPES GR
Chequers (PH)
GREENSIDE
MILLFIELD
TILDEN CL
TILDEN CT
PO
High Halden CE Prim Sch
CHURCH HILL
Halden House
Hookstead Green
TN26
Church Farm
Man of Kent (PH)
Elmtree Farm
A262
BIDDENDEN RD
ASHFORD RD
Durrant Green
The Grove
Bachelors
London Beach
Hogpat Plantation
Harbourne Farm
Harbourne House
Pond Wood
Tiffenden Manor Farm
Nurseries
HARBOURNE LA
Herontoll Wood
POPE HOUSE LA
Hotel
Pope House Farm
Little Harbourne Farm
Beechwood Farm
TN30
Catdref Farm
High Ridge Farm
St Michaels
St Michael's CE Prim Sch
Coever Farm
Piggeries
SWAIN RD
SHOREHAM LA
ORCHARD RD
1 CHURCH COTTS
2 GLENWOOD
3 DAWBOURNE
HEATHER DR
MARSHALLS LAND
GLENWOOD CL
GRANGE RD
Knock Wood
Huntbourne Farm
ST MICHAEL'S TERR
GRANGE CRS
THE PAVEMENT
PH
JARVIS PL
WAYSIDE AVE
OX LA
Great Piper Wood
WAYSIDE
BARNFIELD
HENLEY MEADOWS
CHALK AVE
Ingleden
INGLEDEN PARK RD
SPRINGFIELD
WAYSIDE FLATS 1
BORESISLE 2
CRISFIELD CT 3
LITTLE HILL 4
HENLEY VIEW 5
HENLEY FIELDS
STEPHENS WAY
Brissenden Farm
COLONEL'S WAY
SILVER HILL
WEALDEN AVE
INGLEDEN PARK RD
Knock Wood
Old Knockwood
Homewood Sch & Sixth Form Ctr
CHESTNUT CL
HOMEWOOD RD
MILL LA
ADAMS CL
GOLDSMITH CT
ADMIRALS WLK
KNOCKWOOD RD
KNOCKHURST CT
BEACON WLK
EAST WEALD DR
VINEY'S GDNS
SUMMER CL
HARTFENDEN RD
CURTEIS RD
ST BENETS WAY
DRURY RD
B2080
EASTGATE RD
B2067
WOODCHURCH RD
CH

179
168

167
153

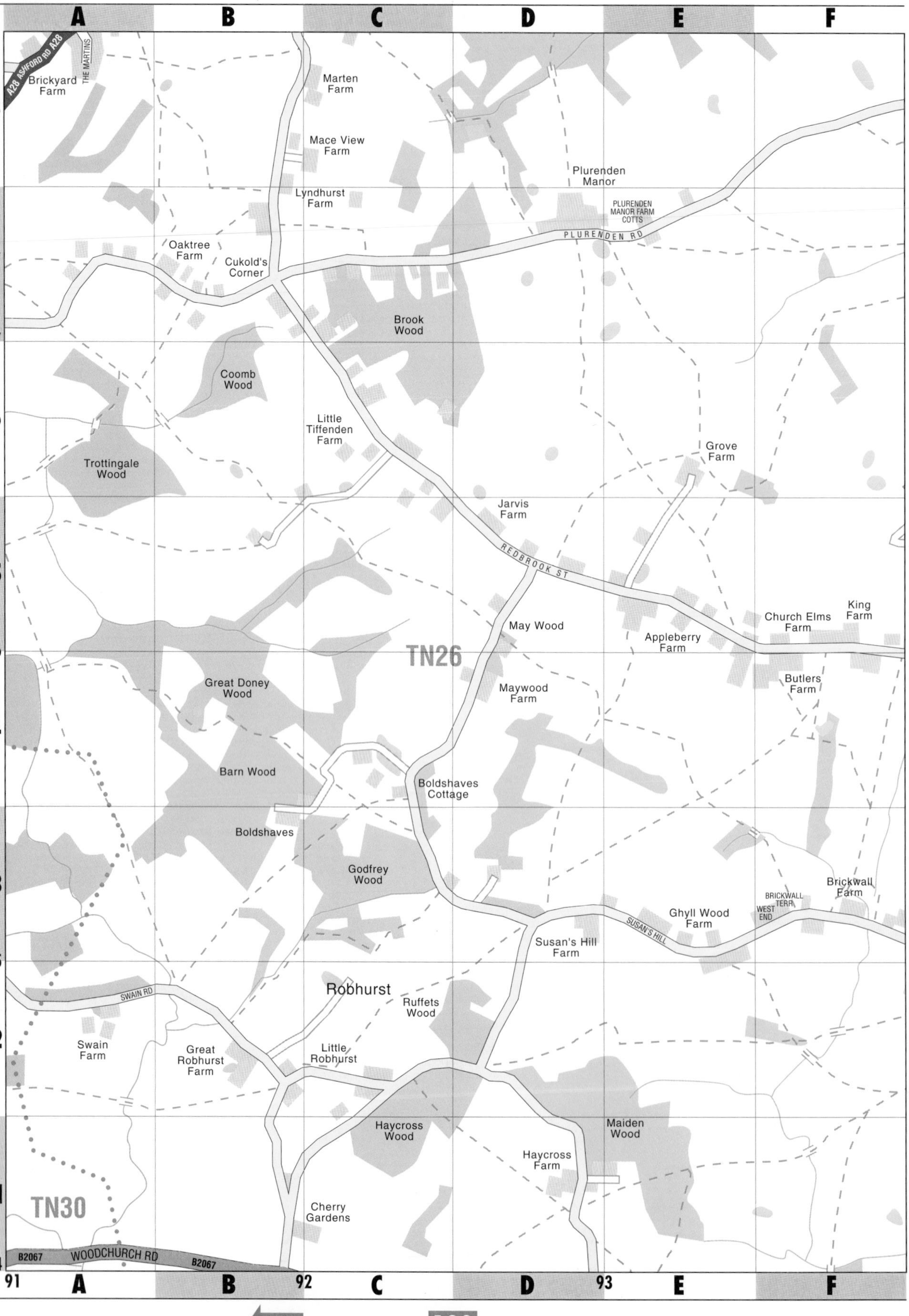

A   B   C   D   E   F

8

A28 ASHFORD RD A28

THE MARTINS

Brickyard Farm

Marten Farm

Mace View Farm

Plurenden Manor

Lyndhurst Farm

PLURENDEN MANOR FARM COTTS

PLURENDEN RD

7

Oaktree Farm

Cukold's Corner

Brook Wood

37

Coomb Wood

6

Little Tiffenden Farm

Grove Farm

Trottingale Wood

Jarvis Farm

REDBROOK ST

5

May Wood

Church Elms Farm

King Farm

36

Appleberry Farm

TN26

Butlers Farm

Great Doney Wood

Maywood Farm

4

Barn Wood

Boldshaves Cottage

Boldshaves

Brickwall TERR

Brickwall Farm

3

Godfrey Wood

Ghyll Wood Farm

WEST END

SUSAN'S HILL

Susan's Hill Farm

35

Robhurst

Ruffets Wood

SWAIN RD

2

Swain Farm

Great Robhurst Farm

Little Robhurst

Haycross Wood

Maiden Wood

Haycross Farm

1

TN30

Cherry Gardens

34

B2067

WOODCHURCH RD

B2067

91   A   B   92   C   D   93   E   F

167
180

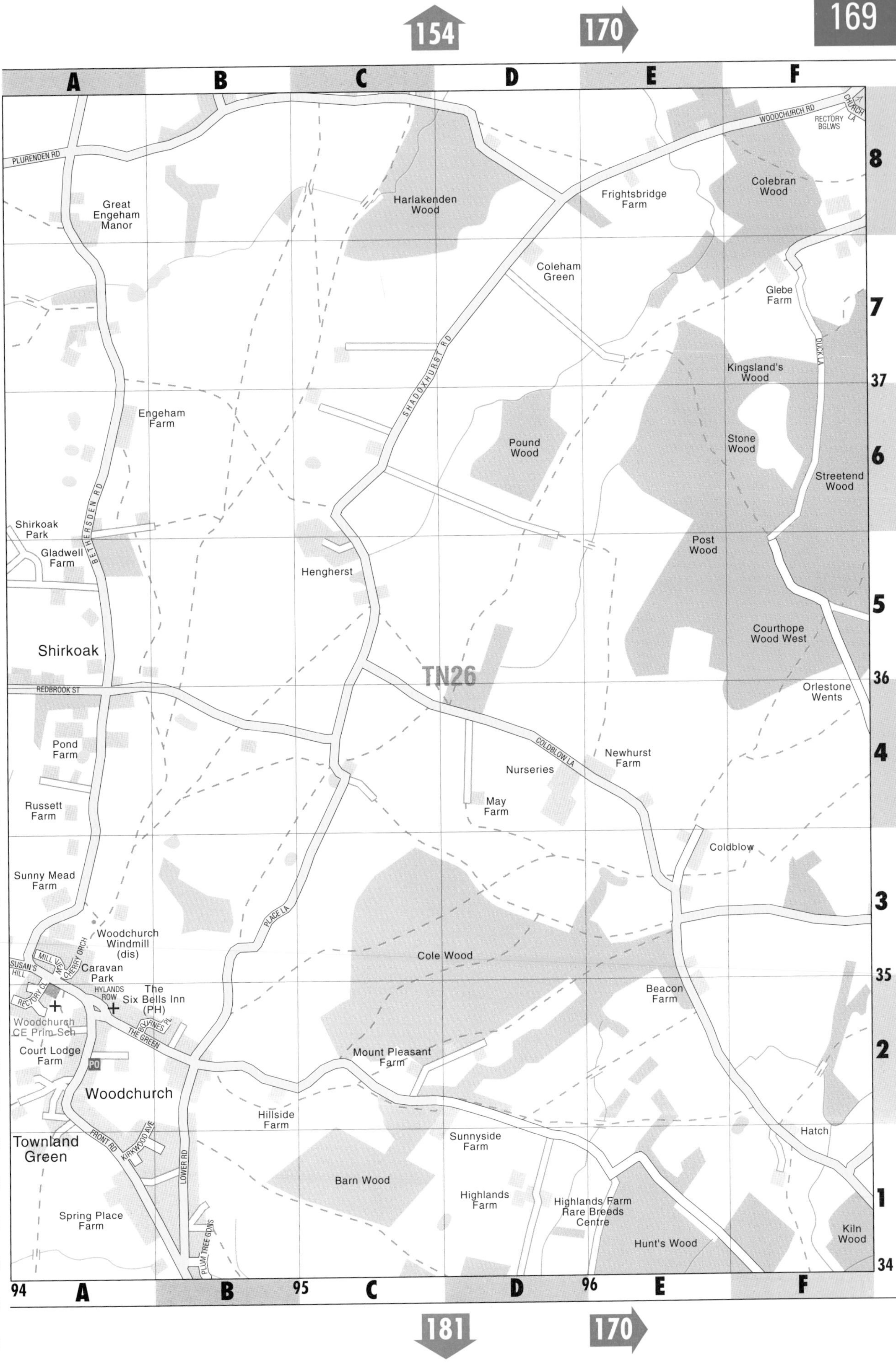
154
170
A
B
C
D
E
F
8
7
37
6
5
36
4
3
35
2
1
34
94
95
96
PLURENDEN RD
WOODCHURCH RD
CHURCH LA
RECTORY BGLWS
Great Engeham Manor
Harlakenden Wood
Frightsbridge Farm
Colebran Wood
Coleham Green
Glebe Farm
SHADOXHURST RD
DUCK LA
Kingsland's Wood
Engeham Farm
Pound Wood
Stone Wood
Streetend Wood
BETHERSDEN RD
Shirkoak Park
Gladwell Farm
Hengherst
Post Wood
Courthope Wood West
Shirkoak
TN26
REDBROOK ST
Orlestone Wents
Pond Farm
COLDBLOW LA
Newhurst Farm
Nurseries
Russett Farm
May Farm
Coldblow
Sunny Mead Farm
PLACE LA
Woodchurch Windmill (dis)
Cole Wood
SUSAN'S HILL
MILL VIEW
CHERRY ORCH
Caravan Park
HYLANDS ROW
The Six Bells Inn (PH)
RECTORY CL
Beacon Farm
Woodchurch CE Prim Sch
BYLANES PL
THE GREEN
Court Lodge Farm
PO
Mount Pleasant Farm
Woodchurch
Hillside Farm
Townland Green
FRONT RD
KIRKWOOD AVE
Sunnyside Farm
Hatch
LOWER RD
Barn Wood
Highlands Farm
Highlands Farm Rare Breeds Centre
Spring Place Farm
PLUM TREE GDNS
Hunt's Wood
Kiln Wood
181
170

A B C D E F

St Peter's Way
Shadoxhurst
8

THE STREET
Nursery
DUCK LA

Alex
Farm

7

Upper Toke's
Wood

37

6

Moat
Farm

Courthope
Wood East

5

36

4

3

Spot House
Farm

35

Parsonage
Farm

2

Tucker
Farm

1

34

97   98   99

Kenilworth
Farm

Woodside
Farm

Coxland
Wood

HORNASH LA

Hillcrest
Farm

Great Turrels
Wood

Manor
Farm

Forty Acre
Wood

Nursery
CHURCH LA

Nickley
Wood

NICKLEY WOOD RD

Bambridge Wood

Kennels

Dering
Wood

Jenkey
Farm

Poplar
Farm

Bromley
Green

Little
Hurst

Bromley Green
Farm

Long Hurst

BROMLEY GREEN RD

Bayland
Wood

TN26

Birchett
Wood

HAMSTREET RD

Capel Wood

Longrope
Wood

Capel
House

Sugarloaf

CAPEL RD

St Edward Street's
Wood

ST THOMAS'
CROSS

BIRCHETT LA

Faggs Wood
Forest Wlks

P

Orlestone

Burnt
Oak

Court
Lodge

ASHFORD RD

Fifty Acre Wood

Faggs
Wood

MALTHOUSE LA

Lord's Wood

Apsley
Wood

Adams Wood

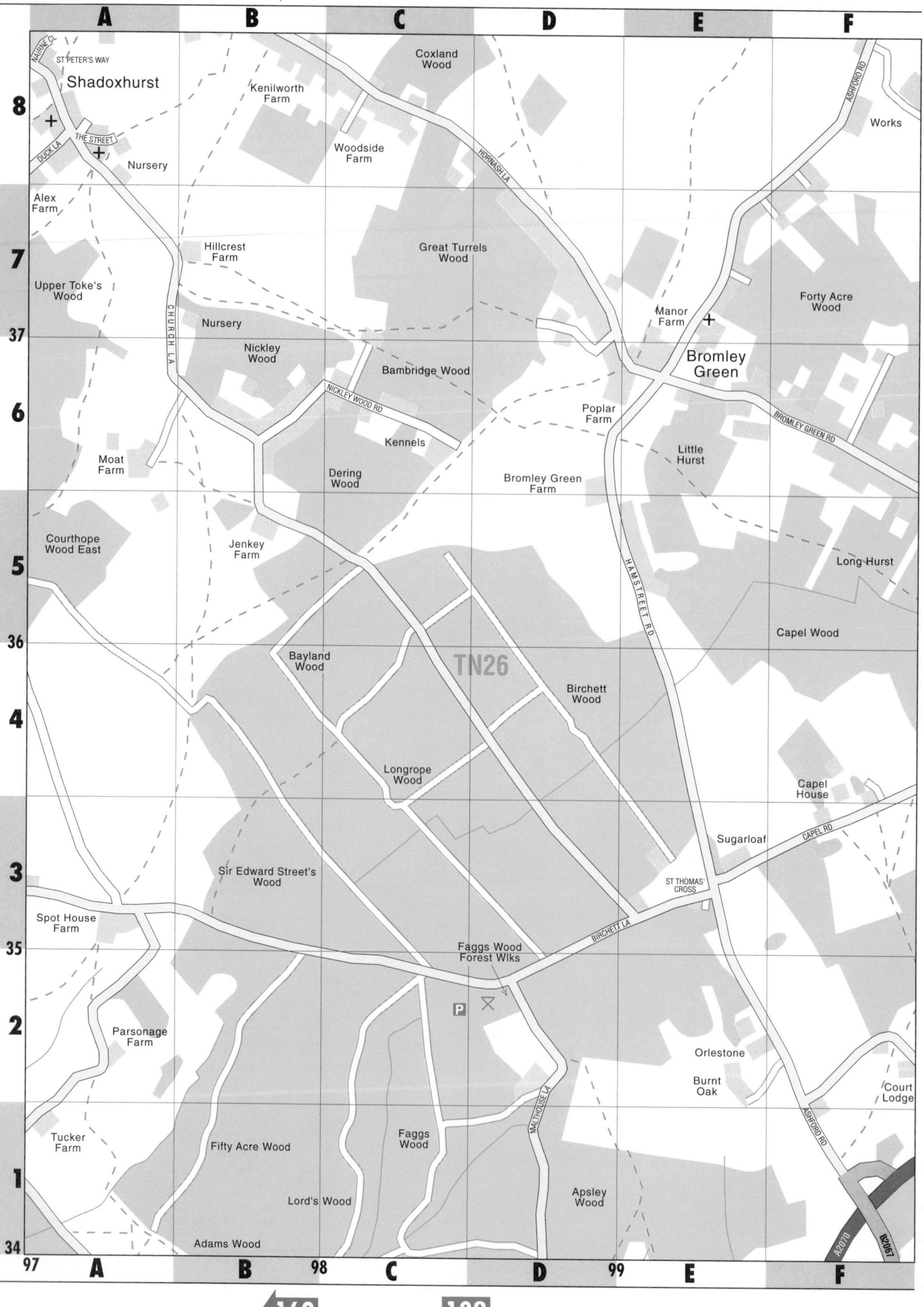

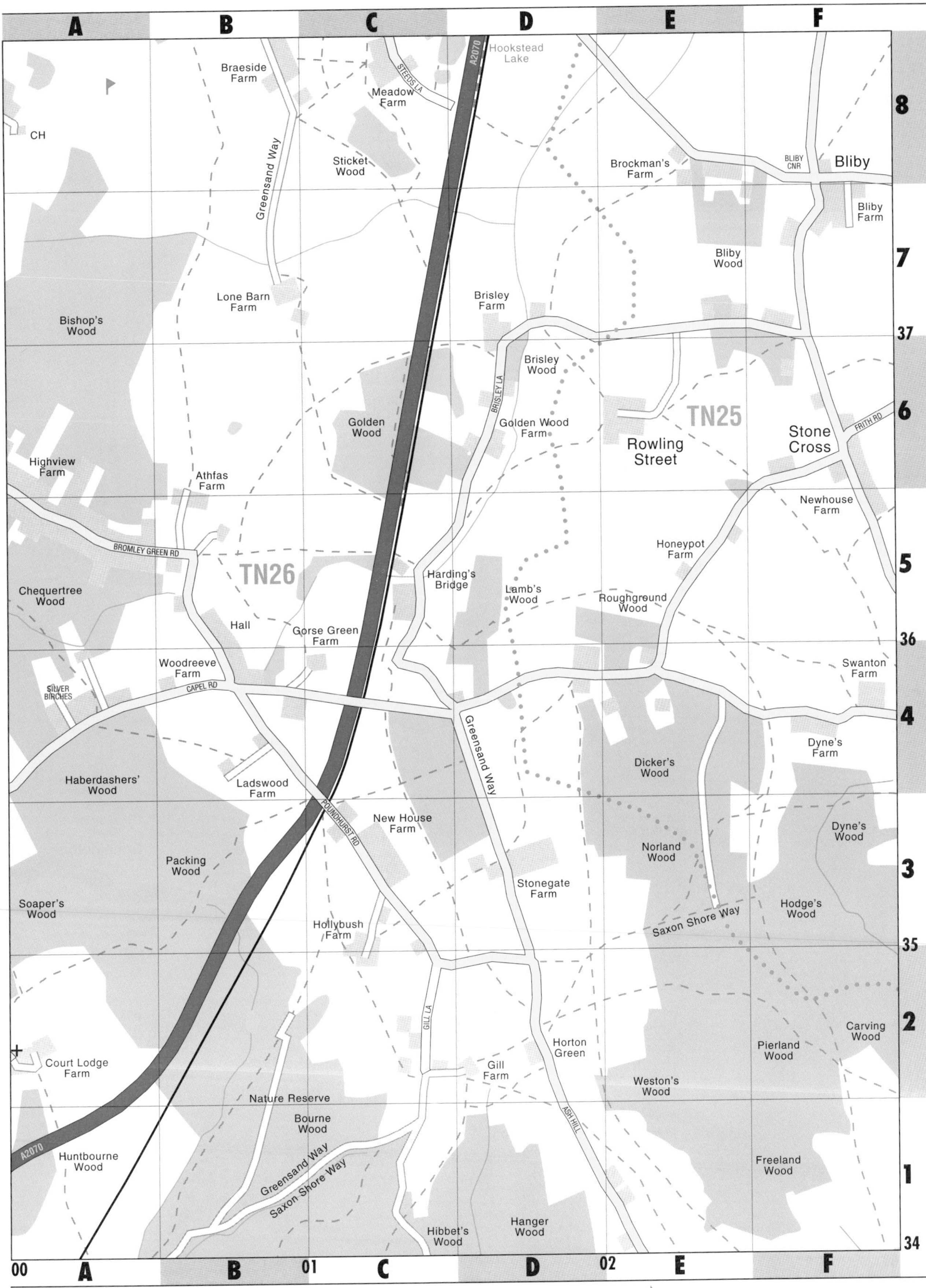

A B C D E F

8

CH

Braeside
Farm

Meadow
Farm

Hookstead
Lake

Bliby

BLIBY
CNR

Bliby
Farm

Sticket
Wood

Greensand Way

STEEDS LA

A2070

Brockman's
Farm

Bliby
Wood

7

Lone Barn
Farm

Brisley
Farm

37

Bishop's
Wood

Brisley
Wood

TN25

6

Golden
Wood

BRISLEY LA

Golden Wood
Farm

Rowling
Street

Stone
Cross

FRITH RD

Highview
Farm

Athfas
Farm

Newhouse
Farm

TN26

Honeypot
Farm

5

Chequertree
Wood

BROMLEY GREEN RD

Harding's
Bridge

Lamb's
Wood

Roughground
Wood

Hall

Gorse Green
Farm

36

Woodreeve
Farm

CAPEL RD

Swanton
Farm

SILVER
BIRCHES

Greensand Way

4

Haberdashers'
Wood

Ladswood
Farm

New House
Farm

Dicker's
Wood

Dyne's
Farm

ROUNDHURST RD

Packing
Wood

Norland
Wood

Dyne's
Wood

3

Soaper's
Wood

Hollybush
Farm

Stonegate
Farm

Saxon Shore Way

Hodge's
Wood

35

GILL LA

Carving
Wood

2

Court Lodge
Farm

Gill
Farm

Horton
Green

Pierland
Wood

Nature Reserve

Weston's
Wood

ASH HILL

A2070

Huntbourne
Wood

Bourne
Wood

Greensand Way

Saxon Shore Way

Hibbet's
Wood

Hanger
Wood

Freeland
Wood

1

34

00 A B 01 C D 02 E F

171 157

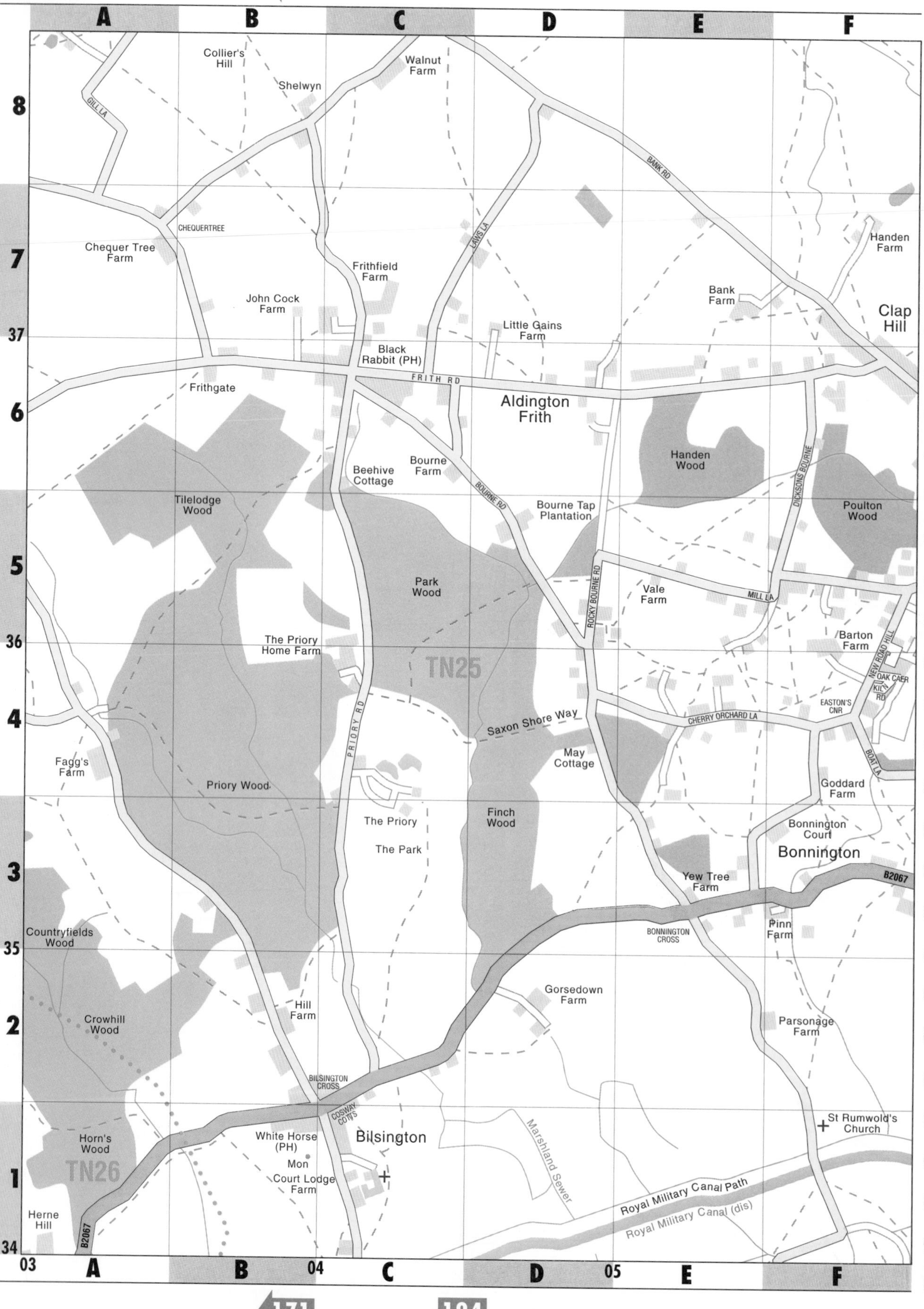

A B C D E F

8

CHEQUERTREE

Collier's Hill
Shelwyn
Walnut Farm

BILL LA

7

Chequer Tree Farm
Frithfield Farm
John Cock Farm
Little Gains Farm
LAUG LA
BANK RD
Bank Farm
Handen Farm

37

Black Rabbit (PH)
Clap Hill

6

Frithgate
FRITH RD
Aldington Frith

Beehive Cottage
Bourne Farm
BOURNE RD
Handen Wood

Tilelodge Wood
Bourne Tap Plantation
DICKSONS BOURNE
Poulton Wood

5

Park Wood
ROCKY BOURNE RD
Vale Farm
MILL LA

36

The Priory Home Farm
TN25
Barton Farm
NEW ROAD HILL
OAK CAER
KIL RD

4

Fagg's Farm
Saxon Shore Way
CHERRY ORCHARD LA
EASTON'S CNR
BOLT LA

Priory Wood
PRIORY RD
May Cottage
Goddard Farm

The Priory
Finch Wood
Bonnington Court

The Park
Bonnington

3

Countryfields Wood
Yew Tree Farm
B2067

35

BONNINGTON CROSS
Pinn Farm

2

Crowhill Wood
Hill Farm
Gorsedown Farm
Parsonage Farm

BILSINGTON CROSS

COSWAY COT'S

1

Horn's Wood
TN26
White Horse (PH)
Mon
Court Lodge Farm
Bilsington
Marshland Sewer
St Rumwold's Church

Herne Hill
B2067
Royal Military Canal Path
Royal Military Canal (dis)

34

03 **A** **B** 04 **C** **D** 05 **E** **F**

158
174

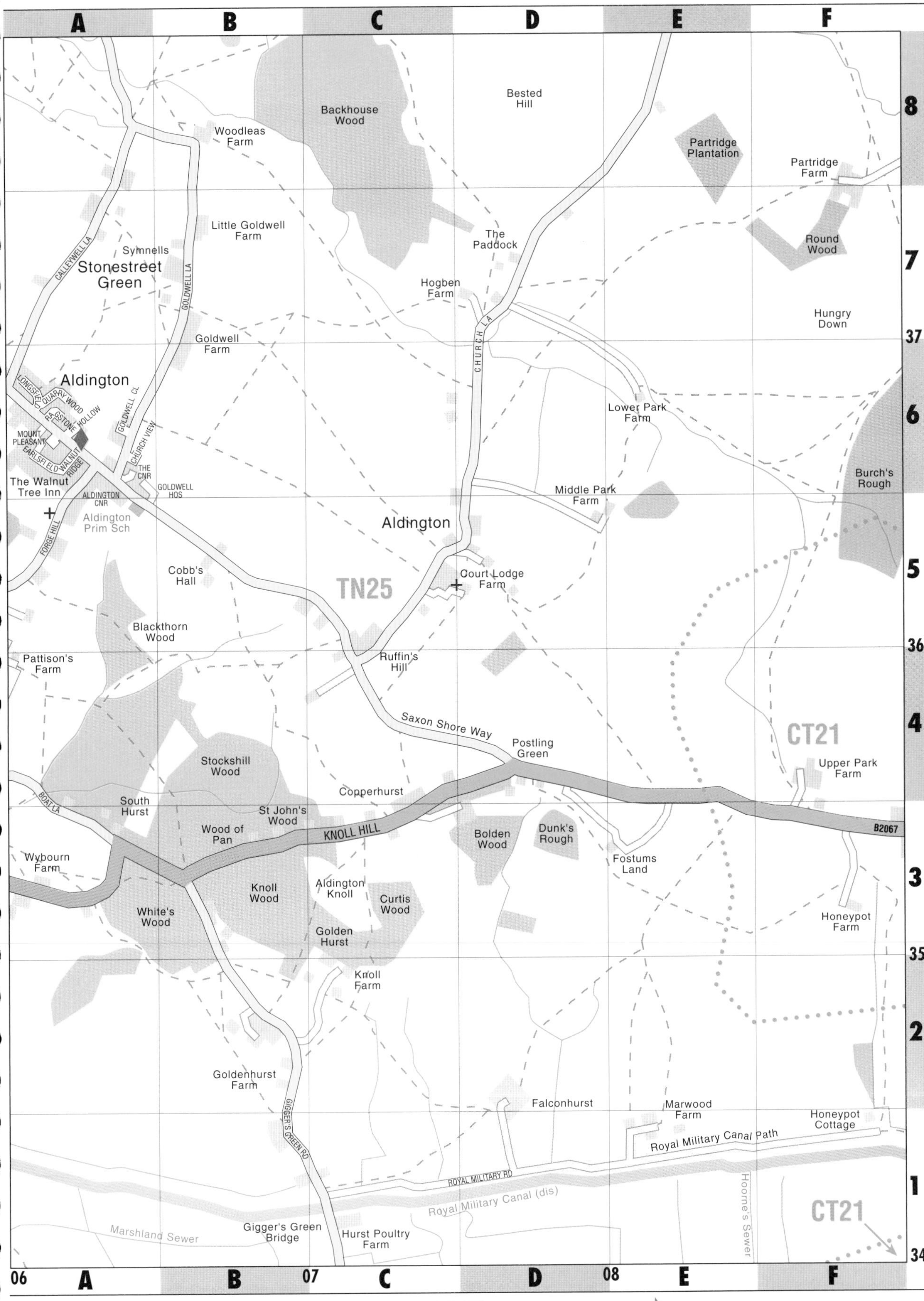
A
B
C
D
E
F
8
7
37
6
5
36
4
3
35
2
1
34
06
07
08
Bested Hill
Backhouse Wood
Woodleas Farm
Partridge Plantation
Partridge Farm
Little Goldwell Farm
The Paddock
Round Wood
Symnells
Stonestreet Green
CALLEYWELL LA
GOLDWELL LA
Hogben Farm
Hungry Down
CHURCH LA
Goldwell Farm
Aldington
LONGSFIELD
QUARRY WOOD
RAGSTONE HOLLOW
MOUNT PLEASANT
EARLSFIELD
WALNUT RIDGE
GOLDWELL CL
CHURCH VIEW
THE CNR
GOLDWELL HOS
ALDINGTON CNR
Lower Park Farm
Burch's Rough
The Walnut Tree Inn
Aldington Prim Sch
FORGE HILL
Middle Park Farm
Aldington
Cobb's Hall
TN25
Court Lodge Farm
Blackthorn Wood
Pattison's Farm
Ruffin's Hill
Saxon Shore Way
Postling Green
CT21
Upper Park Farm
Stockshill Wood
Copperhurst
South Hurst
BOAT LA
St John's Wood
Wood of Pan
KNOLL HILL
Bolden Wood
Dunk's Rough
B2067
Wybourn Farm
Fostums Land
Knoll Wood
Aldington Knoll
Curtis Wood
White's Wood
Honeypot Farm
Golden Hurst
Knoll Farm
Goldenhurst Farm
GIGGER'S GREEN RD
Falconhurst
Marwood Farm
Honeypot Cottage
Royal Military Canal Path
ROYAL MILITARY RD
Royal Military Canal (dis)
Hoorne's Sewer
CT21
Marshland Sewer
Gigger's Green Bridge
Hurst Poultry Farm

185
174

173
159

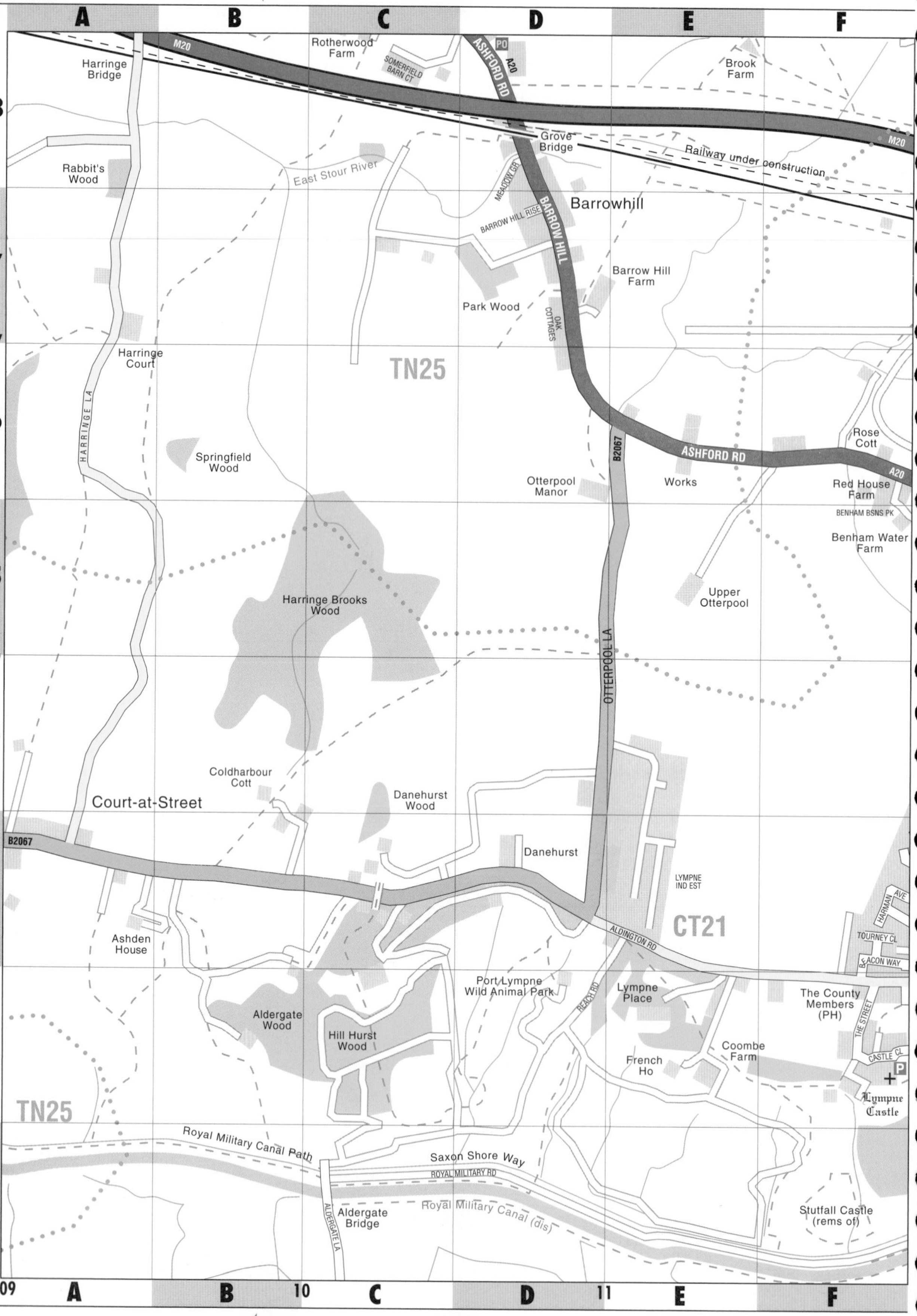
A
B
C
D
E
F
8
7
37
6
5
36
4
3
35
2
1
34
09
10
11
M20
Rotherwood Farm
Harringe Bridge
SOMERFIELD BARN CT
ASHFORD RD
A20
PO
Brook Farm
Grove Bridge
Railway under construction
Rabbit's Wood
East Stour River
MEADOW GR
Barrowhill
BARROW HILL RISE
BARROW HILL
Barrow Hill Farm
Park Wood
OAK COTTAGES
Harringe Court
TN25
HARRINGE LA
Rose Cott
B2067
ASHFORD RD
Springfield Wood
Otterpool Manor
Works
Red House Farm
BENHAM BSNS PK
Benham Water Farm
Harringe Brooks Wood
Upper Otterpool
OTTERPOOL LA
Coldharbour Cott
Danehurst Wood
Court-at-Street
B2067
Danehurst
LYMPNE IND EST
CT21
HARMAN AVE
Ashden House
ALDINGTON RD
TOURNEY CL
BEACON WAY
Port Lympne Wild Animal Park
REACH RD
Lympne Place
The County Members (PH)
Aldergate Wood
Hill Hurst Wood
THE STREET
Coombe Farm
French Ho
CASTLE CL
P
Lympne Castle
TN25
Royal Military Canal Path
Saxon Shore Way
ROYAL MILITARY RD
Royal Military Canal (dis)
Aldergate Bridge
ALDERGATE LA
Stutfall Castle (rems of)

173
186

160
176

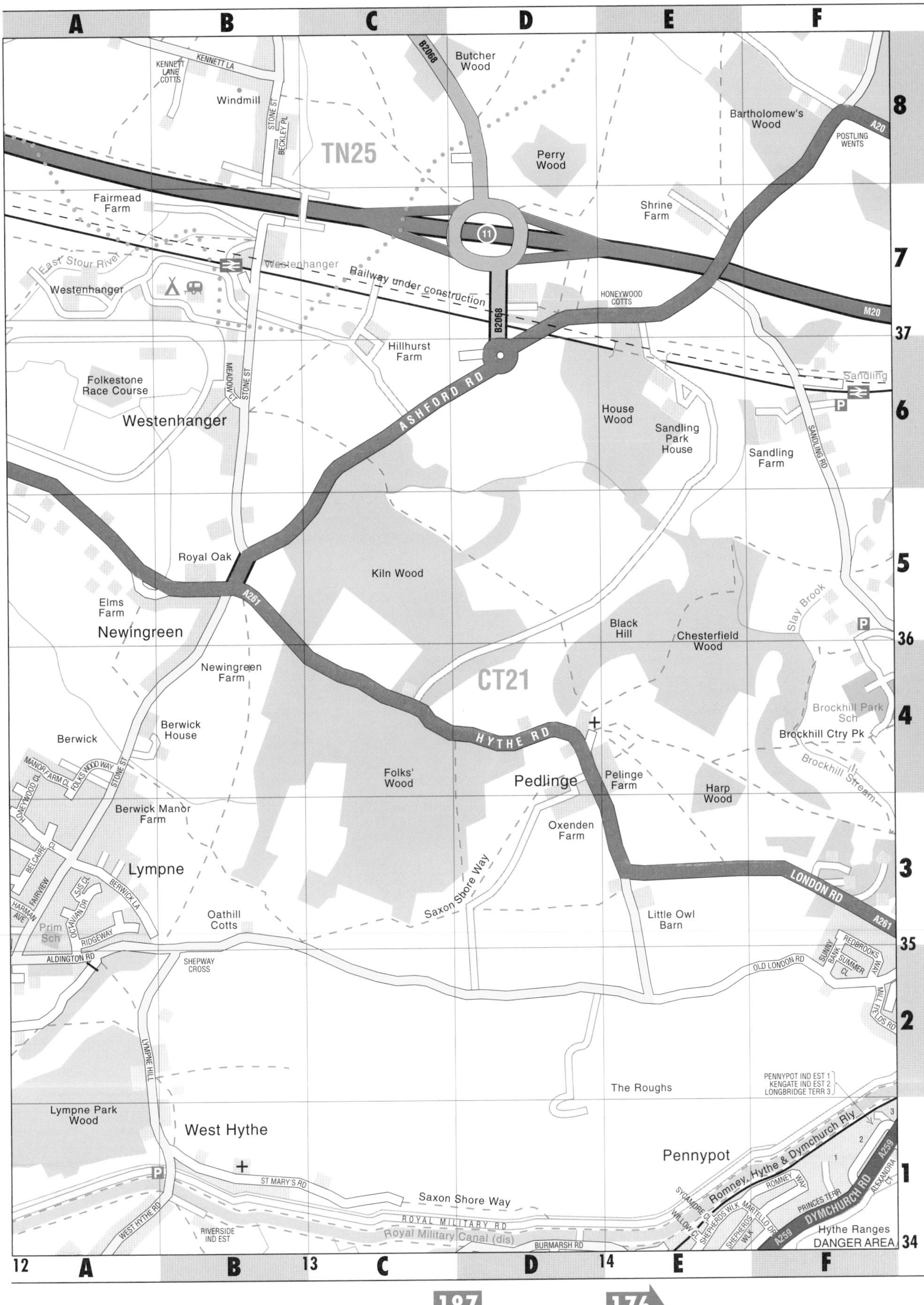
A
B
C
D
E
F
8
7
37
6
5
36
4
3
35
2
1
34
12
13
14
B2068
Butcher Wood
KENNETT LA
KENNETT LANE COTTS
Windmill
STONE ST
BECKLEY PL
TN25
Perry Wood
Bartholomew's Wood
A20
POSTLING WENTS
Fairmead Farm
Shrine Farm
11
East Stour River
Westenhanger
Westenhanger
Railway under construction
HONEYWOOD COTTS
M20
Hillhurst Farm
Sandling
MEADOW CL
Folkestone Race Course
Westenhanger
ASHFORD RD
House Wood
Sandling Park House
Sandling Farm
SANDLING RD
Royal Oak
Kiln Wood
Elms Farm
A261
Newingreen
Black Hill
Chesterfield Wood
Slay Brook
Newingreen Farm
CT21
Brockhill Park Sch
Berwick House
Brockhill Ctry Pk
Berwick
HYTHE RD
MANOR FARM CL
FOLKS WOOD WAY
HONEYWOOD CL
Folks' Wood
Pedlinge
Pelinge Farm
Harp Wood
Brockhill Stream
Berwick Manor Farm
Oxenden Farm
BELCAIRE CL
Lympne
Saxon Shore Way
FAIRVIEW
SJS CL
BERWICK LA
LONDON RD
HARMAN AVE
OCTAVIAN DR
Oathill Cotts
Little Owl Barn
Prim Sch
RIDGEWAY
A261
ALDINGTON RD
SHEPWAY CROSS
OLD LONDON RD
SUNNY BANK
REDBROOKS WAY
SUMMER CL
MILL FIELDS RD
LYMPNE HILL
PENNYPOT IND EST 1
KENGATE IND EST 2
LONGBRIDGE TERR 3
The Roughs
Lympne Park Wood
West Hythe
Romney, Hythe & Dymchurch Rly
Pennypot
A259
ALEXANDRA CT
ST MARY'S RD
ROMNEY WAY
PRINCES TERR
DYMCHURCH RD
Saxon Shore Way
SYCAMORE CL
WILLOW CL
SHEPHERDS WLK
MARTELLO DR
WEST HYTHE RD
ROYAL MILITARY RD
Royal Military Canal (dis)
A259
Hythe Ranges
DANGER AREA
RIVERSIDE IND EST
BURMARSH RD

187
176

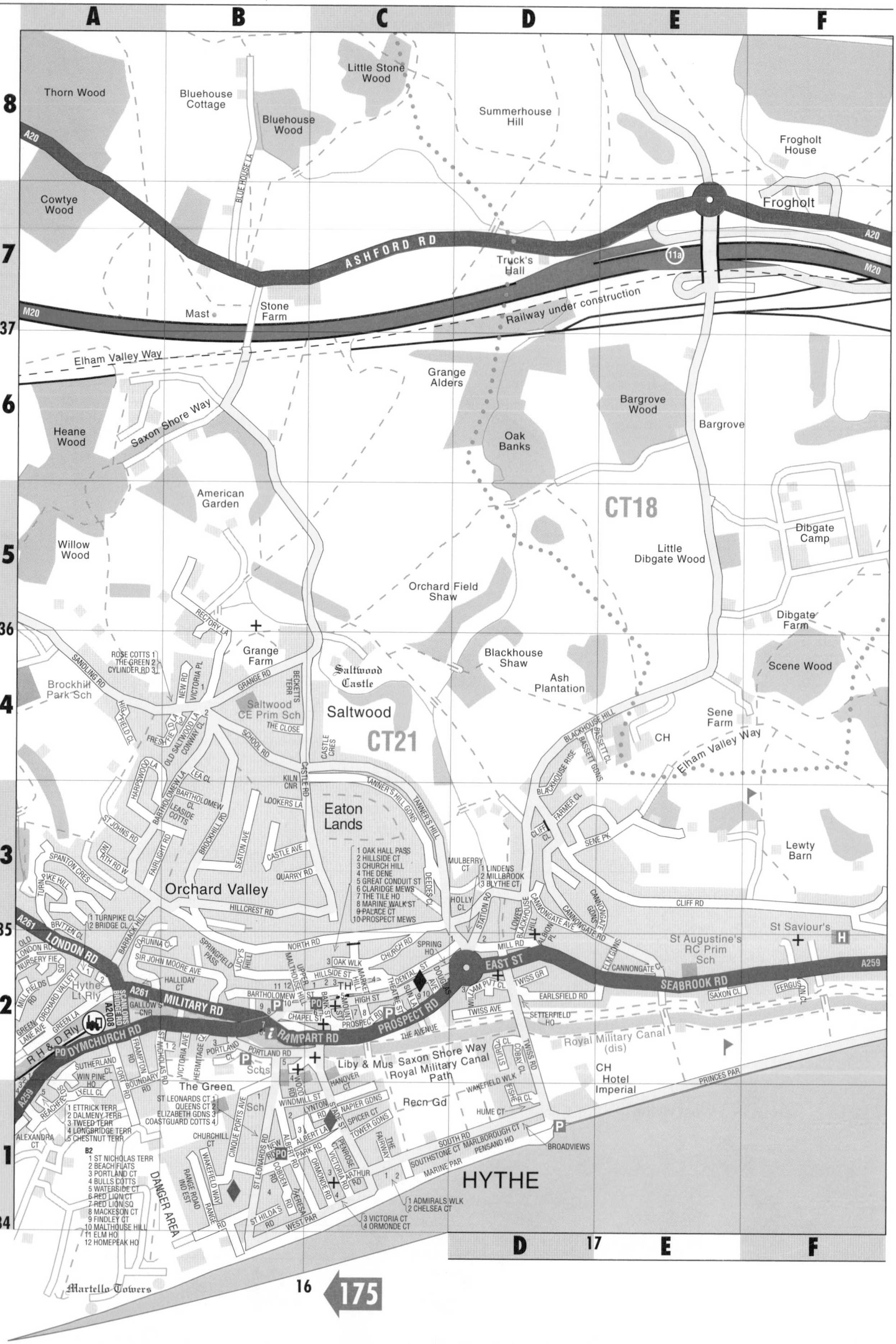

A   B   C   D   E   F

Thorn Wood

Bluehouse
Cottage

Little Stone
Wood

Bluehouse
Wood

Summerhouse
Hill

Frogholt
House

8

A20

Cowtye
Wood

Frogholt

7

ASHFORD RD

A20

M20

11a

Truck's
Hall

M20

Stone
Farm

Mast

Railway under construction

37

Elham Valley Way

Grange
Alders

6

Heane
Wood

Saxon Shore Way

Oak
Banks

Bargrove
Wood

Bargrove

American
Garden

CT18

5

Willow
Wood

Little
Dibgate Wood

Dibgate
Camp

Orchard Field
Shaw

36

RECTORY LA

Grange
Farm

Dibgate
Farm

ROSE COTTS 1
THE GREEN 2
CYLINDER RD 3

Blackhouse
Shaw

Scene Wood

Brockhill
Park Sch

Saltwood
Castle

Ash
Plantation

Sene
Farm

CH

4

SANDLING RD

HILLFIELD CL

GRANGE RD

BECKETT'S TERR

Saltwood
CE Prim Sch

THE CLOSE

Saltwood

CT21

FRESH FIELD

OLD SALTWOOD LA

DONWAY CL

SCHOOL RD

KILN
CNR

CASTLE
CRES

LANNER'S HILL GDNS

TANNER'S HILL

BLACKHOUSE HILL

BASSETT CL

BASSETT GDNS

Elham Valley Way

Lewty
Barn

3

HARPS WOOD LA

ST JOHN'S RD

BARTHOLOMEW LA

LEASIDE
COTTS

BROCKHILL RD

LEA CL

BARTHOLOMEW

CASTLE AVE

SEATON AVE

QUARRY RD

Eaton
Lands

1 OAK HALL PASS
2 HILLSIDE CT
3 CHURCH HILL
4 THE DENE
5 GREAT CONDUIT ST
6 CLARIDGE MEWS
7 THE TILE HO
8 MARINE WALK ST
9 PALACE CT
10 PROSPECT MEWS

Mulberry
CT

DEEDES CL

HOLLY
CL

CLIFF
CL

FARMER CL

SENE PK

CLIFF RD

St Saviour's

H

35

A261

TURN CL

LAKE HILL

SPANTON CRES

FAIRLIGHT RD

PINE RD W

RTH RD W

HILLCREST RD

Orchard Valley

1 TURNPIKE CL
2 BRIDGE CL

LONDON RD

OLD
LONDON RD

NURSERY FIELD

GRUNNA CT

SIR JOHN MOORE AVE

SPRINGFIELD
PASS

LUCY'S HILL

NORTH RD

UPPER HILLSIDE ST

MALTHOUSE RD

OAK WLK

CHURCH RD

SPRING
LA

3

SEABROOK RD

A259

St Augustine's
RC Prim Sch

CANNONGATE AVE

CANNONGATE RD

CANNONGATE GDNS

LOWER BLACKHOUSE HILL

STATION RD

1 LINDENS
2 MILLBROOK
3 BLYTHE CT

Cannongate

ELY GDNS

CLIFF RD

FERGUS RD

ION CL

2

Hythe
Lt Rly

A261

A2008

MILITARY RD

GALLOW'S
CNR

BARTHOLOMEW

HALLIDAY
CT

HIGH ST

MARKET
SQ

3 OAK WLK

P

PO

CHAPEL ST

PROSPECT RD

THE AVENUE

DENTAL ST

EAST ST

EARLSFIELD RD

TWISS GR

TWISS AVE

SETTERFIELD RD

SAXON CL

Royal Military Canal
(dis)

PRINCES PAR

RH&D RLY

PO

DYMCHURCH RD

RAMPART RD

Liby & Mus Saxon Shore Way
Royal Military Canal
Path

CH
Hotel
Imperial

P

Broadviews

Alexandra
CT

SUTHERLAND
RD

WIN PINE
HO

WELL CL

1 ETTRICK TERR
2 DALMENY TERR
3 TWEED TERR
4 LONGBRIDGE TERR
5 CHESTNUT TERR

B2
1 ST NICHOLAS TERR
2 BEACH FLATS
3 PORTLAND CT
4 BULLS COTTS
5 WATERSIDE CT
6 RED LION CT
7 RED LION SQ
8 MACKESON CT
9 FINDLEY CT
10 MALTHOUSE HILL
11 ELM HO
12 HOMEPEAK HO

THE GREEN

ST LEONARDS CT 1
ELIZABETH GDNS 2
COASTGUARD COTTS 4

PORTLAND RD

VICTORIA AVE

NICHOLAS RD

HERMITAGE CT

FORT RD

Schs

WINDMILL ST

NAPIER GDNS

SPICER RD

TOWER GDNS

HANOVER

Recn Gd

WAKEFIELD WLK

HUME CT

FR CL

1

ST LEONARDS RD

CINQUE PORTS AVE

WAKEFIELD WAY

RANGE ROAD IND EST

CHURCHILL
AVE

PO

ST HILDA'S
RD

ALBERT LA

NEW RD

PENROSE

LYNTON

VICTORIA
RD

ROBERT ST

ORMONDE RD

ARTHUR RD

WEST PAR

THE
FAIRWAY

SOUTH RD

SOUTHSTONE CT
MARLBOROUGH CT 1
PENSAND HO

HYTHE

DANGER
AREA

Martello Towers

34

1 ADMIRALS WLK
2 CHELSEA CT

3 VICTORIA CT
4 ORMONDE CT

D   17   E   F

16   175

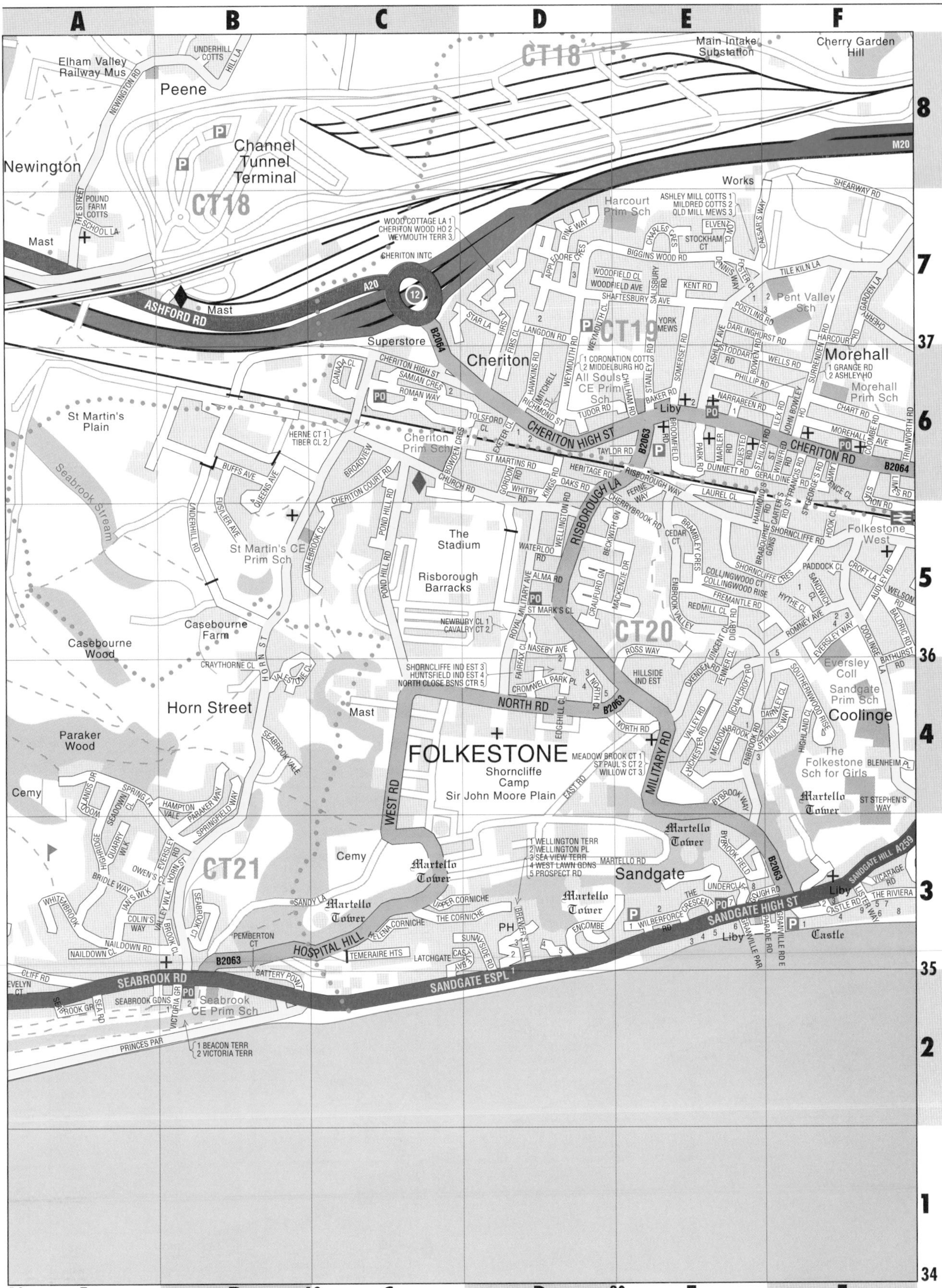

178
E3
1 HILLSIDE
2 SOUTHOVER CT
3 HOMEVALE HO
4 TOWER CT
5 SIR JOHN MOORE CT
6 RIVIERA CT
7 NORTH LA
8 WHITE CT

F3
1 MARTELLO TERR
2 LACHLAN WAY
3 JAMES MORRIS CT
4 CASTLE CL
5 VARNE LODGE
6 VARNE CT
7 BEACH MARINE
8 ZARENA CT
9 CASTLE GLEN

A7
1 PAPWORTH CL
2 BERKELEY CL
3 NORRINGTON MEAD
4 SUNNINGDALE AVE

B5
1 ST MARGARETS CT
2 KINGSNORTH CT
3 KINGSTONE CT

177

C4
1 GRANGE CT
2 COBBS MEWS
3 INGLES MEWS
4 CLIFTON MANSIONS
5 LANGHORNE GDNS
6 JARRETT HO

163

C4
7 GEORGE COOPER HO
8 SHAKESPEARE TERR
9 ST MALO CT

D4
1 BOUVERIE SQ
2 BOUVERIE PL
3 ALBION MEWS RD
4 WESTCLIFF HO
5 ASPEN HO
6 ALBION VILLAS
7 MARINE CRES
8 PRIOR'S LEES
9 LONGFORD TERR
10 LONGFORD WAY
11 WHITE CLIFFS
12 PLAYDELL CT
13 RADNOR CHAMBERS
14 HOLMESDALE TERR

D6
1 RUSSELL RD
2 ALLENDALE ST
3 JESMOND ST
4 PALMERSTON ST
5 SUSSEX RD

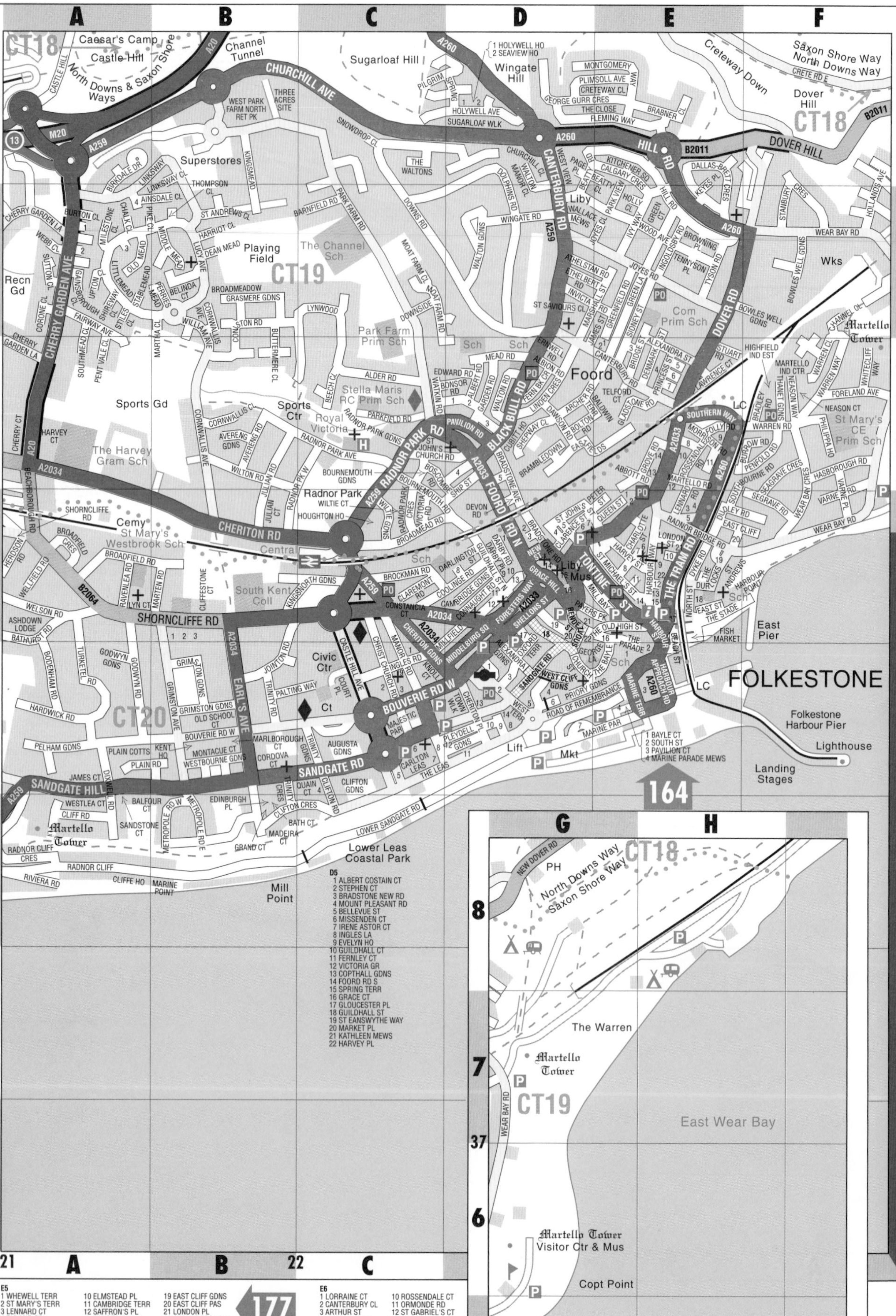

D5
1 ALBERT COSTAIN CT
2 STEPHEN CT
3 BRADSTONE NEW RD
4 MOUNT PLEASANT RD
5 BELLEVUE ST
6 MISSENDEN CT
7 IRENE ASTOR CT
8 INGLES LA
9 EVELYN HO
10 GUILDHALL CT
11 FERNLEY CT
12 VICTORIA GR
13 COPTHALL GDNS
14 BENNETT CT
15 SPRING TERR
16 GRACE CT
17 GLOUCESTER PL
18 GUILDHALL ST
19 ST EANSWYTHE WAY
20 MARKET PL
21 KATHLEEN MEWS
22 HARVEY PL

164

E5
1 WHEWELL TERR
2 ST MARY'S TERR
3 LENNARD CT
4 RYLAND CT
5 RYLAND PL
6 ST MICHAEL'S CT
7 HARVEY PL
8 MARGARET ST
9 KINGSBRIDGE CT
10 ELMSTEAD PL
11 CAMBRIDGE TERR
12 SAFFRON'S PL
13 RANDOLPH HO
14 BENNETT CT
15 BOULOGNE CT
16 BAYLE ST
17 RADNOR ST
18 CHANNEL VIEW
19 EAST CLIFF GDNS
20 EAST CLIFF PAS
21 LONDON PL
22 GEORGE STONE HO

177

E6
1 LORRAINE CT
2 CANTERBURY CL
3 ARTHUR ST
4 WALMSLEY HO
5 MYRTLE RD
6 ASH TREE RD
7 ELM RD
8 ROSSENDALE GDNS
9 EDWARD TERR
10 ROSSENDALE CT
11 ORMONDE RD
12 ST GABRIEL'S CT
13 ABBOTT CT
14 CHILTON CT

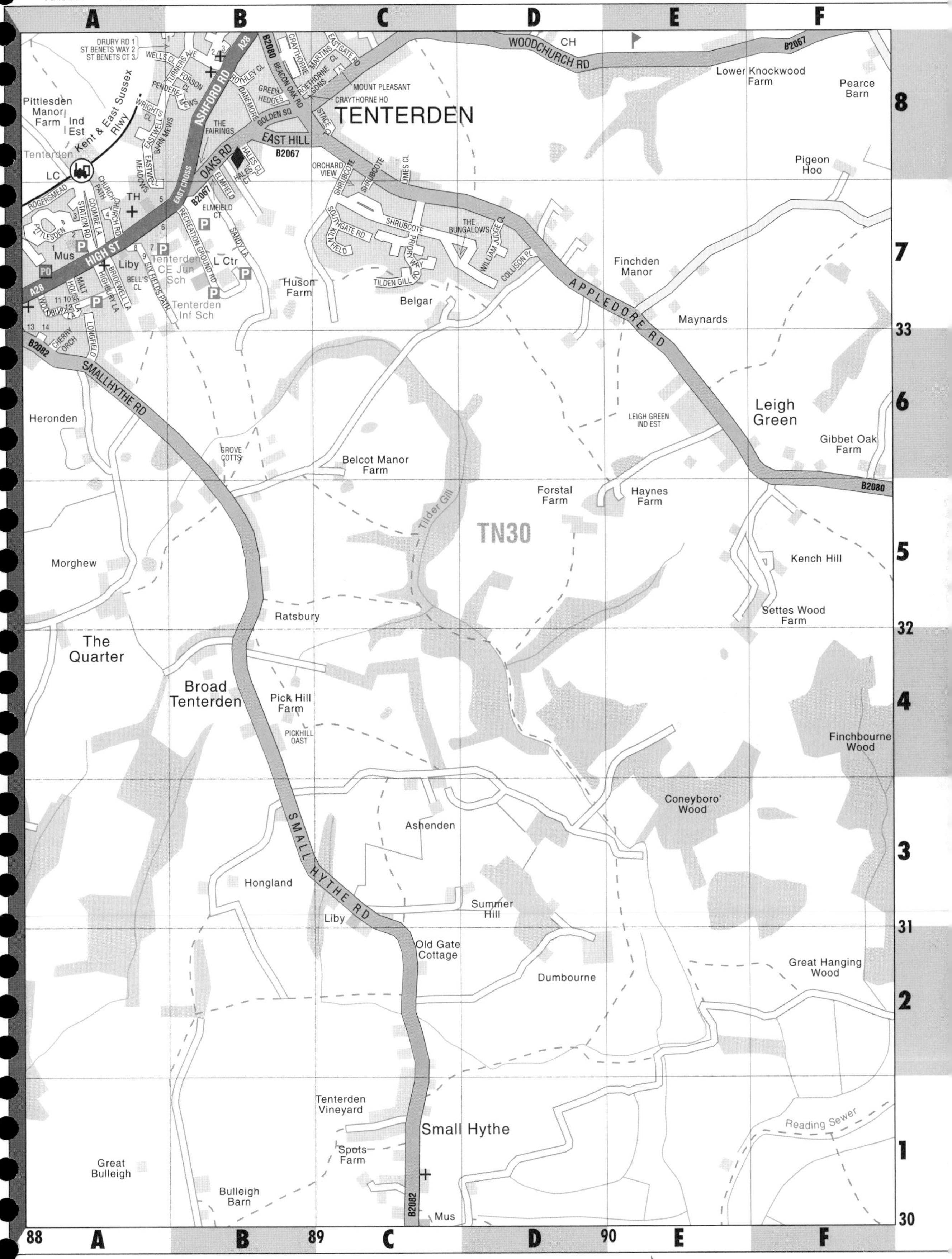

A B C D E F

8

The Dandy

Bourne
Farm

B2067

Cott
Farm

Bower Farm

Berridge
Farm

Oakhurst
Farm

Ditton
Farm

BROOK ST

Brook Street

B2067

Diamond
House

Orange
Farm

Malt House
Farm

7

33

6

Glover
Farm

MOOR LA

Highbank
Farm

B2080

Shirley
Farm

Nurseries

Frenchay
Wood

Tenterden Sewer

TN26

Shirley Moor

5

New
Bridge

Frenchay
Farm

32

APPLEDORE RD

Fleet Petty Sewer

4

TN30

Finchbourne
Wood

Barrack
Farm

3

The Century
Farm

31

Little
Ramsden

2

Willow
Farm

Reading
Street

READING ST

TENTERDEN RD

Nurseries

Reading Sewer

Rother Levels

Chapel Bank
Farm

1

Redhill
Bridge

Red Hill

Barrowsland
Farm

B2080

30

91 A B 92 C D 93 E F

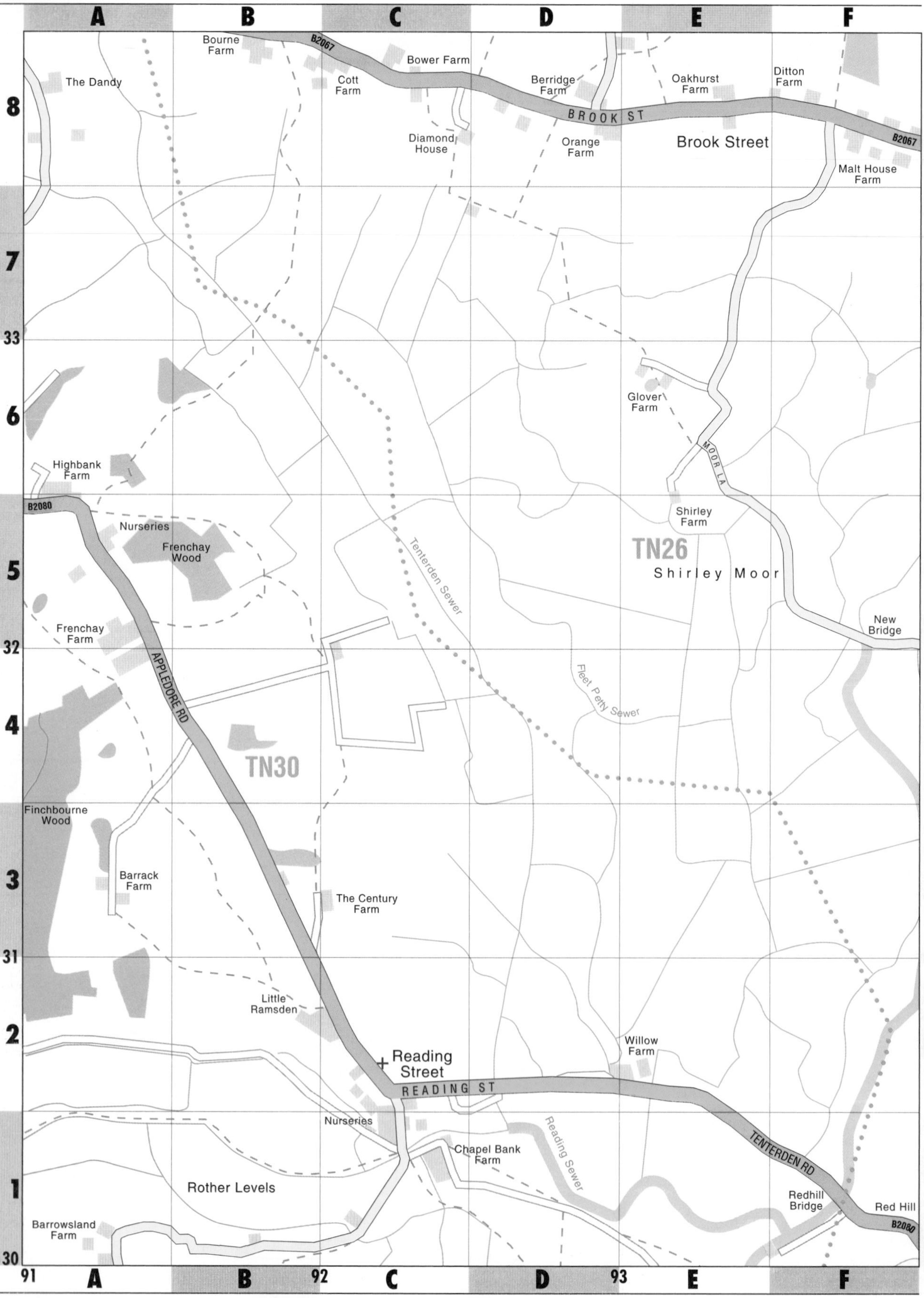

169
182

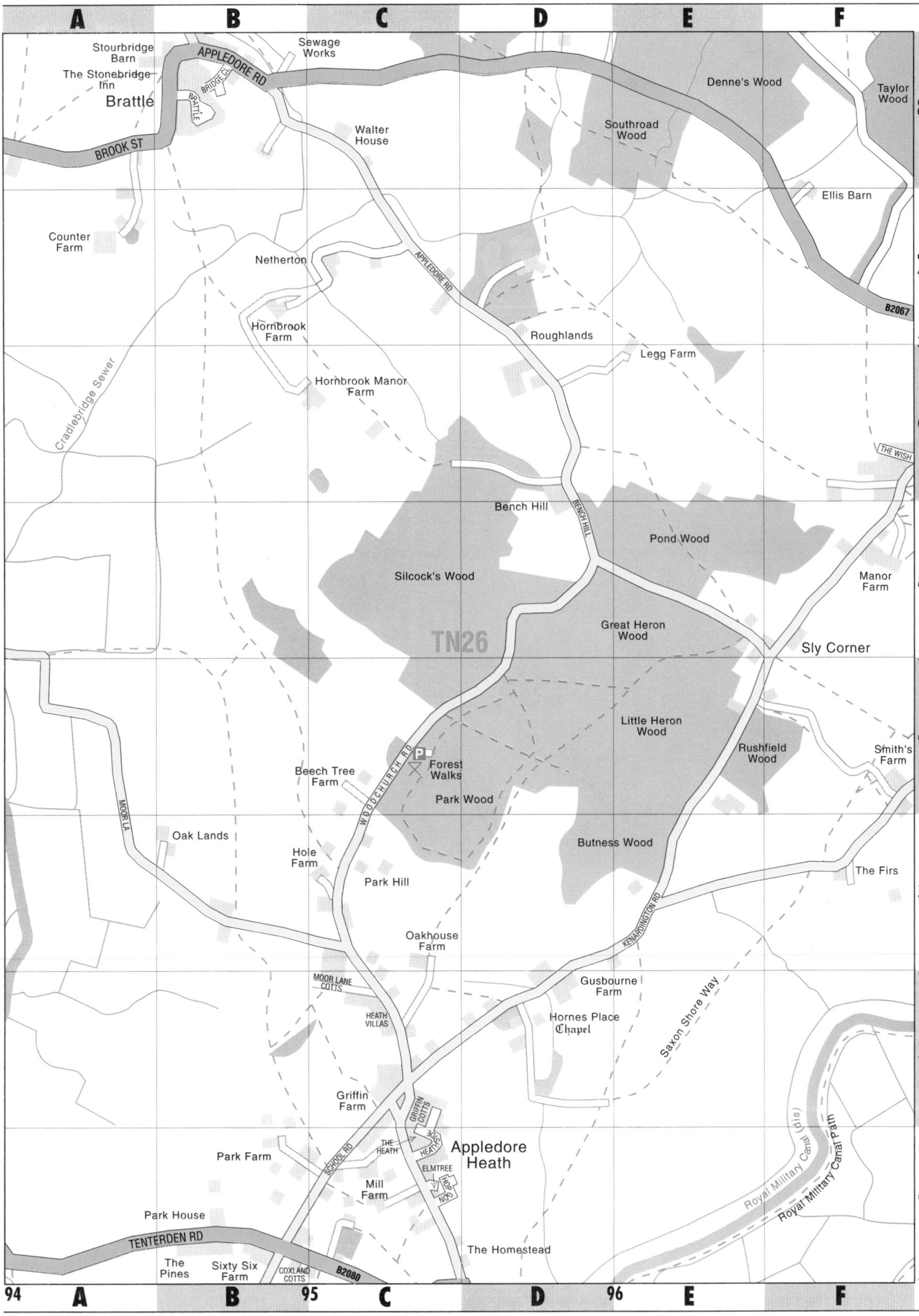
A
B
C
D
E
F
Stourbridge Barn
The Stonebridge Inn
Brattle
APPLEDORE RD
BRIDGE CL
BRATTLE
BROOK ST
Sewage Works
Walter House
Denne's Wood
Southroad Wood
Taylor Wood
Ellis Barn
Counter Farm
Netherton
APPLEDORE RD
B2067
Hornbrook Farm
Roughlands
Legg Farm
Hornbrook Manor Farm
Cradlebridge Sewer
THE WISH
Bench Hill
BENCH HILL
Pond Wood
Silcock's Wood
Manor Farm
Great Heron Wood
TN26
Sly Corner
Little Heron Wood
Rushfield Wood
Smith's Farm
Forest Walks
Beech Tree Farm
WOODCHURCH RD
Park Wood
MOOR LA
Oak Lands
Hole Farm
Butness Wood
The Firs
Park Hill
KENARDINGTON RD
Oakhouse Farm
MOOR LANE COTTS
Gusbourne Farm
HEATH VILLAS
Hornes Place Chapel
Saxon Shore Way
Griffin Farm
GRIFFIN COTTS
THE HEATH
HEATHSIDE
Appledore Heath
Park Farm
SCHOOL RD
ELMTREE
HOP CON
Mill Farm
Royal Military Canal (dis)
Royal Military Canal Path
Park House
TENTERDEN RD
The Homestead
The Pines
Sixty Six Farm
COXLAND COTTS
B2080
8
7
33
6
5
32
4
3
31
2
1
30
94
95
96

190
182

←181
170↑

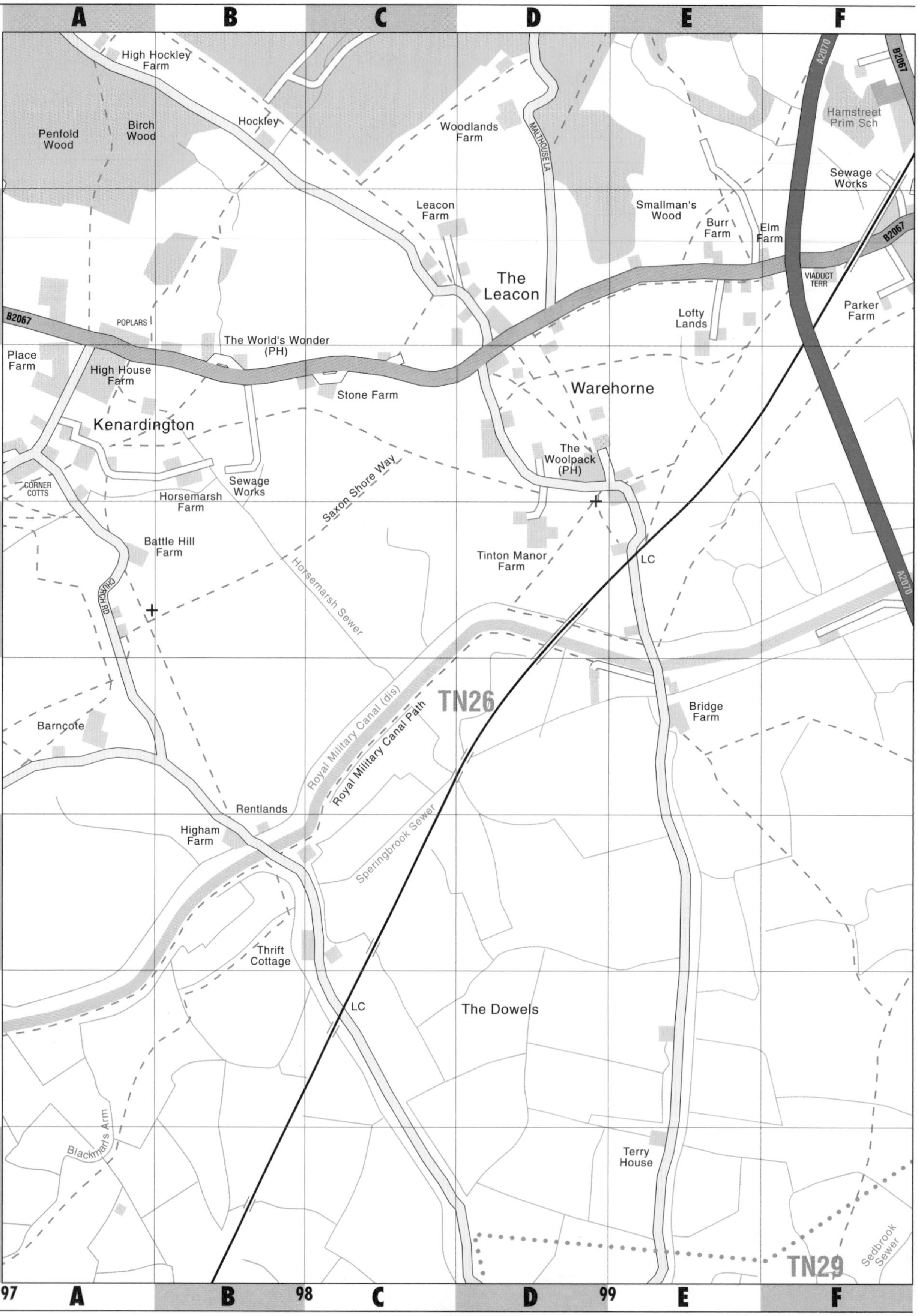

A B C D E F

8

High Hockley Farm

Hockley

Penfold Wood

Birch Wood

Woodlands Farm

MALTHOUSE LA

Hamstreet Prim Sch

Sewage Works

B2067

A2070

Leacon Farm

Smallman's Wood

Burr Farm

Elm Farm

7

The Leacon

B2067

VIADUCT TERR

Parker Farm

B2067

33

POPLARS

The World's Wonder (PH)

Lofty Lands

Place Farm

High House Farm

Stone Farm

Warehorne

6

Kenardington

Sewage Works

The Woolpack (PH)

CORNER COTTS

Horsemarsh Farm

Saxon Shore Way

Battle Hill Farm

Tinton Manor Farm

LC

CHURCH RD

Horsemarsh Sewer

A2070

5

32

Royal Military Canal (dis)

TN26

Bridge Farm

4

Barncote

Royal Military Canal Path

Speringbrook Sewer

Rentlands

Higham Farm

3

31

Thrift Cottage

LC

The Dowels

2

Blackman's Arm

Terry House

1

Sedbrook Sewer

TN29

30

97 A B 98 C D 99 E F

←181
191↓

171
184

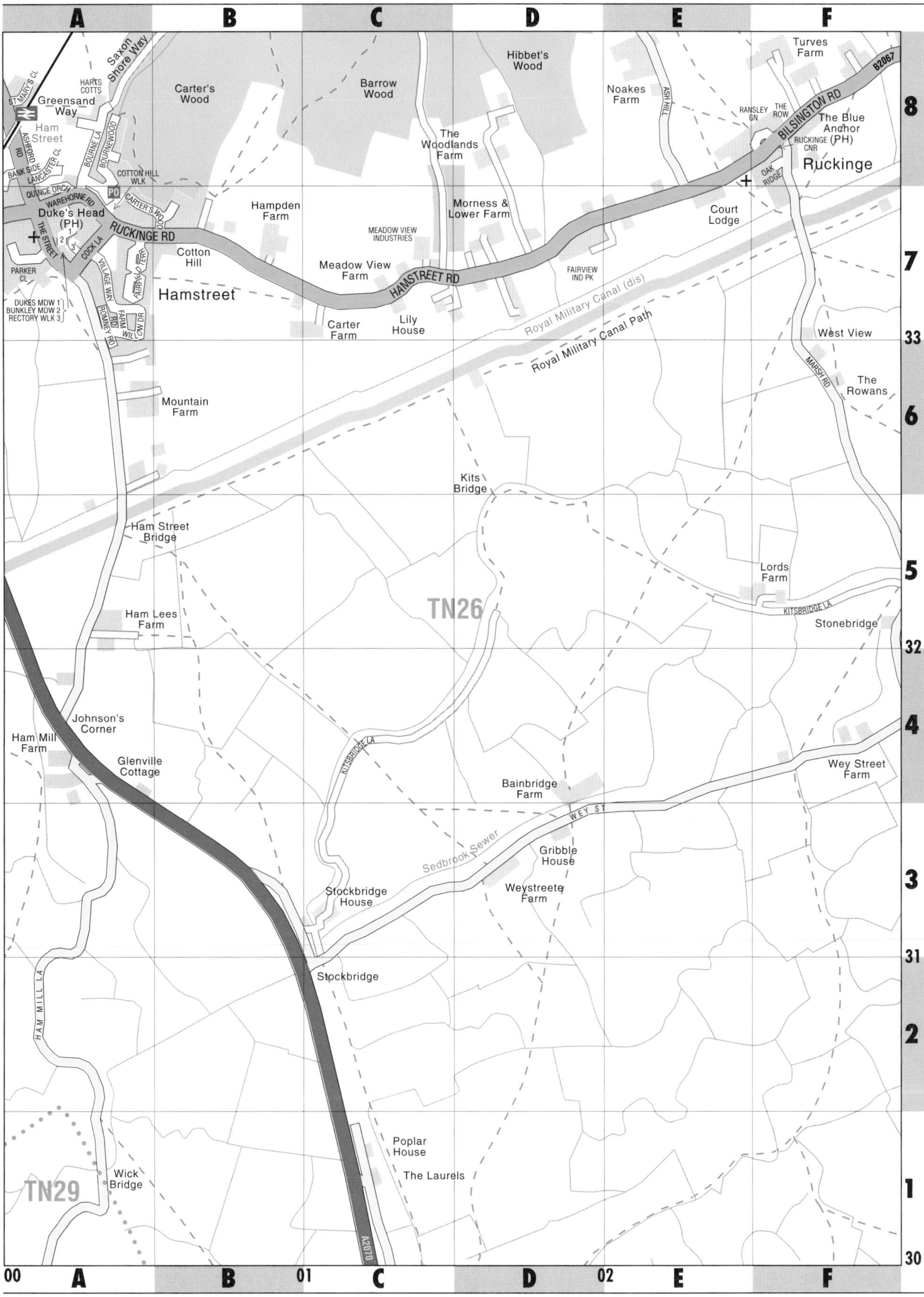
A
B
C
D
E
F
8
7
33
6
5
32
4
3
31
2
1
30
00
01
02
Saxon Shore Way
HARTS COTTS
ST MARY'S CL
Greensand Way
Ham Street
ASHFORD RD
BANK SIDE
LANCASTER CL
BOURNE LA
BOURNEWOOD
COTTON HILL WLK
QUINCE ORCH
WAREHORNE RD
PO
CARTER'S WOOD
Duke's Head (PH)
THE STREET
COCK LA
RUCKINGE RD
PARKER CL
VILLAGE WAY
FAIRVIEW TERR
DUKES MDW 1
BUNKLEY MDW 2
RECTORY WLK 3
ROMNEY RD
FARM RD
WILLOW DR
Carter's Wood
Barrow Wood
Hibbet's Wood
Noakes Farm
ASH HILL
Turves Farm
B2067
BILSINGTON RD
RANSLEY GN
THE ROW
The Blue Anchor (PH)
RUCKINGE CNR
Ruckinge
OAK RIDGE
The Woodlands Farm
Hampden Farm
Morness & Lower Farm
Court Lodge
Cotton Hill
MEADOW VIEW INDUSTRIES
Meadow View Farm
HAMSTREET RD
FAIRVIEW IND PK
Hamstreet
Carter Farm
Lily House
Royal Military Canal (dis)
Royal Military Canal Path
West View
MARSH RD
The Rowans
Mountain Farm
Kits Bridge
Ham Street Bridge
Lords Farm
KITSBRIDGE LA
Stonebridge
TN26
Ham Lees Farm
Johnson's Corner
Ham Mill Farm
Glenville Cottage
KITSBRIDGE LA
Bainbridge Farm
Wey Street Farm
WEY ST
Sedbrook Sewer
Gribble House
Stockbridge House
Weystreete Farm
Stockbridge
HAM MILL LA
Poplar House
The Laurels
Wick Bridge
TN29
A2070

192
184

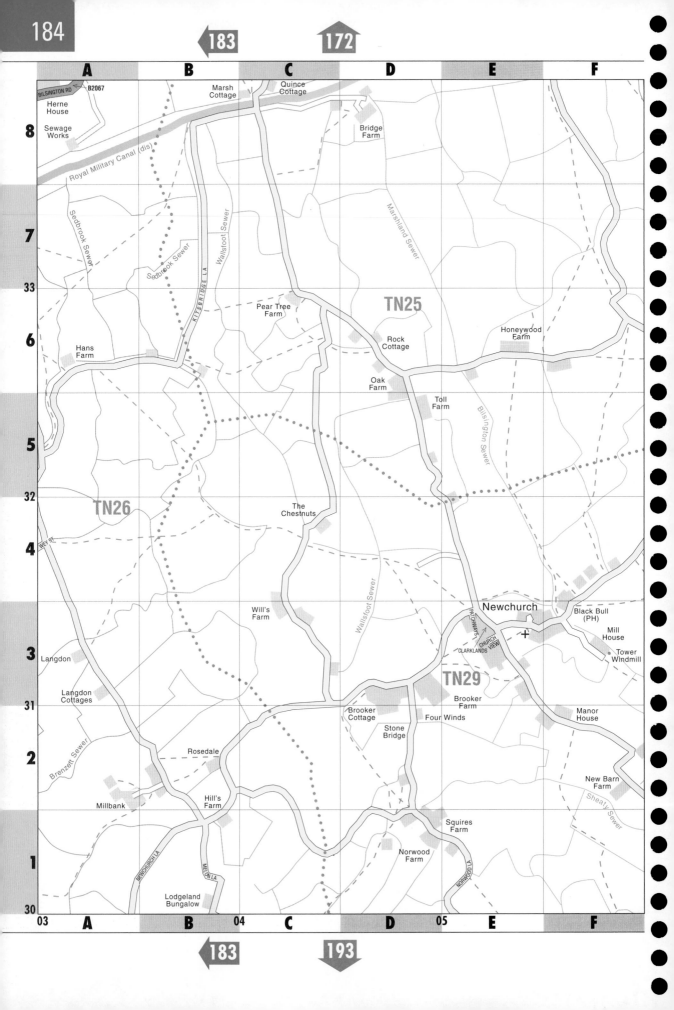

183
172

A   B   C   D   E   F

BILSINGTON RD
B2067
Herne House
Sewage Works

8

Royal Military Canal (dis)

Marsh Cottage
Quince Cottage

Bridge Farm

7

Sedbrook Sewer
Wallstoot Sewer
Sedbrook Sewer
KILSBRIDGE LA

Marshland Sewer

33

Pear Tree Farm

TN25

6

Hans Farm

Rock Cottage

Honeywood Farm

Oak Farm

Toll Farm

Bilsington Sewer

5

32

TN26

The Chestnuts

4

WEY ST

Wallstoot Sewer

Will's Farm

Newchurch

Black Bull (PH)

Mill House

3

Langdon

PATCHWAYS
CHURCH VIEW
CLARKLANDS

TN29

Tower Windmill

Langdon Cottages

31

Brooker Farm

Brooker Cottage

Four Winds

Manor House

2

Brenzett Sewer

Rosedale

Stone Bridge

Millbank

Hill's Farm

New Barn Farm

Sheaty Sewer

1

Squires Farm

NEWCHURCH LA
MELN LA
NORWOOD LA

Norwood Farm

Lodgeland Bungalow

30

03   A   B   04   C   D   05   E   F

183
193

173
186

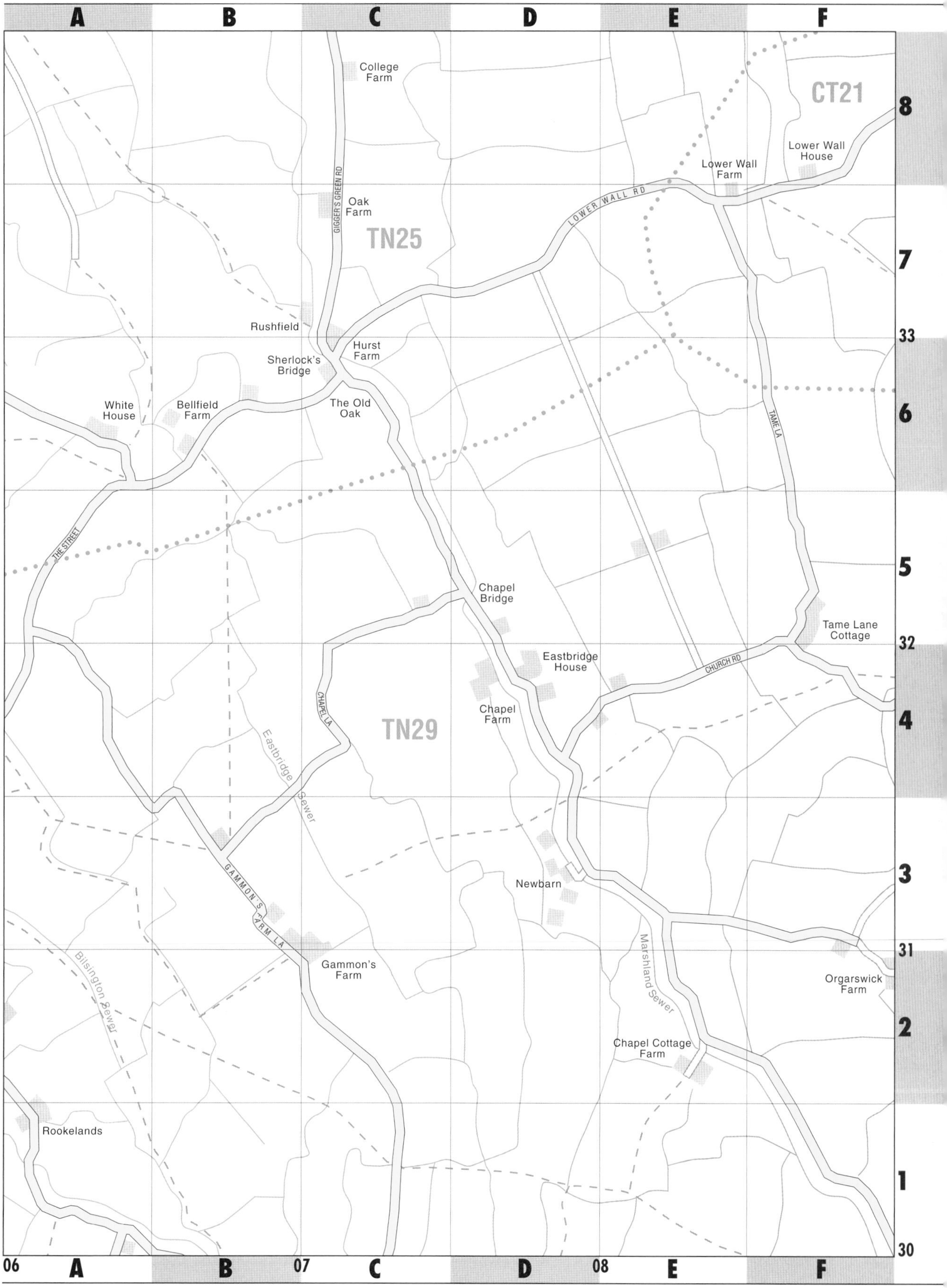
A
B
C
D
E
F
College Farm
CT21
8
Lower Wall House
Lower Wall Farm
LOWER WALL RD
GIGGER'S GREEN RD
Oak Farm
TN25
7
Rushfield
Hurst Farm
33
Sherlock's Bridge
White House
Bellfield Farm
The Old Oak
TAME LA
6
THE STREET
5
Chapel Bridge
Tame Lane Cottage
32
Eastbridge House
CHURCH RD
CHAPEL LA
TN29
Chapel Farm
4
Eastbridge Sewer
GAMMON'S FARM LA
Newbarn
3
Marshland Sewer
31
Gammon's Farm
Orgarswick Farm
Bilsington Sewer
2
Chapel Cottage Farm
Rookelands
1
30
06
07
08

194
186

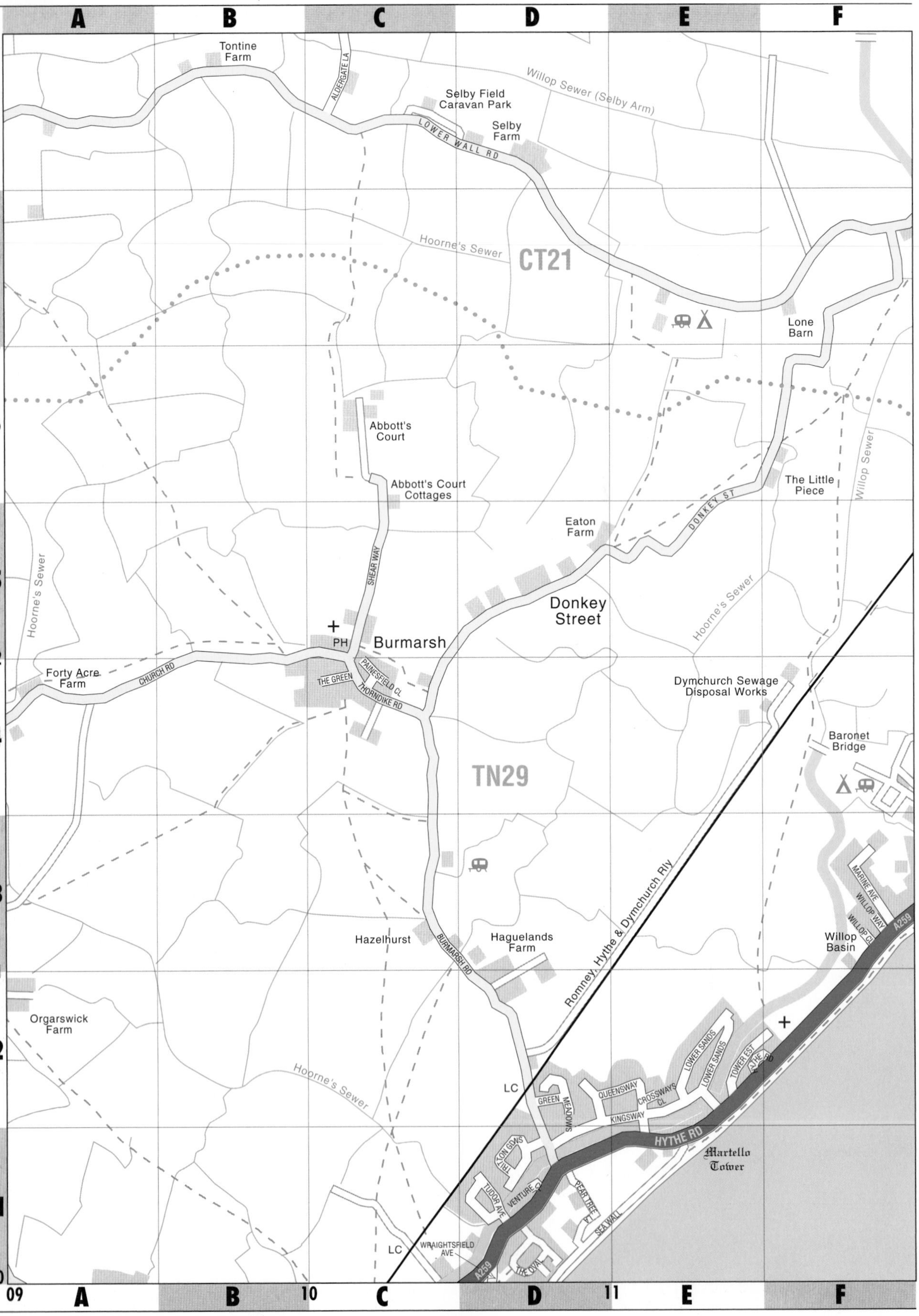

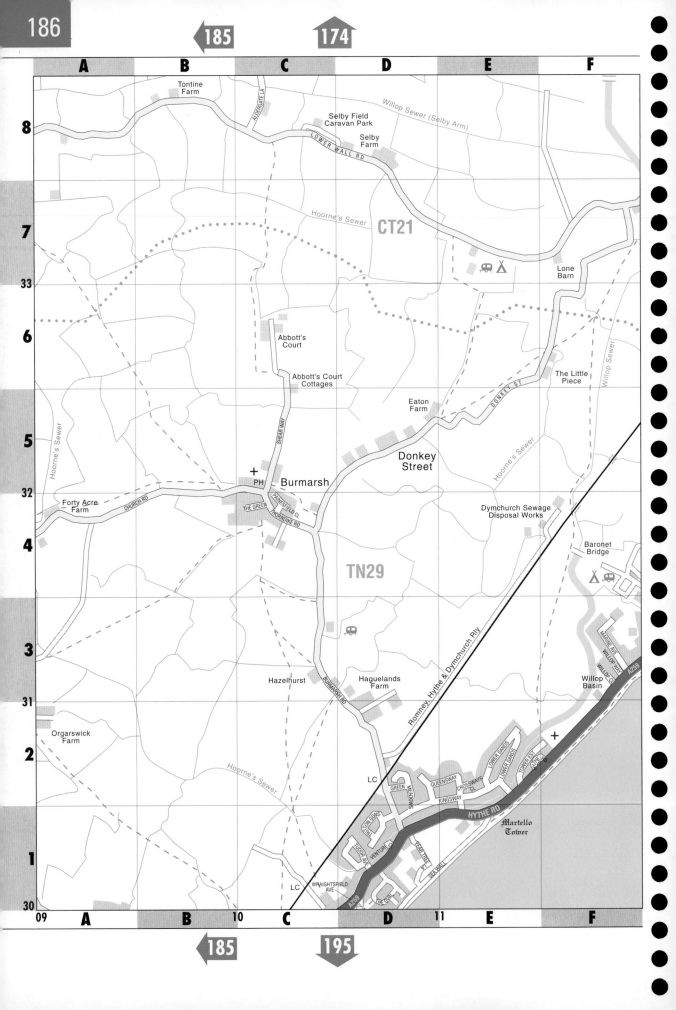

A B C D E F

8

7

33

6

5

32

4

3

31

2

1

30

Tontine
Farm

ALLERGATE LA

LOWER WALL RD

Selby Field
Caravan Park

Selby
Farm

Willop Sewer (Selby Arm)

Hoorne's Sewer

CT21

Lone
Barn

Abbott's
Court

Abbott's Court
Cottages

SHEAR WAY

DONKEY ST

The Little
Piece

Willop Sewer

Eaton
Farm

Donkey
Street

Hoorne's Sewer

Hoorne's Sewer

+
PH

Burmarsh

Forty Acre
Farm

CHURCH RD

THE GREEN

PAINESFIELD CL

THORNDIKE RD

Dymchurch Sewage
Disposal Works

Baronet
Bridge

TN29

Orgarswick
Farm

Hazelhurst

BURMARSH RD

Haguelands
Farm

Hoorne's Sewer

Romney, Hythe & Dymchurch Rly

Willop
Basin

MARINE AVE

WILLOP WAY

WILLOP CL

A259

LC

GREEN
MEADOWS

QUEENSWAY

KINGSWAY

CROSSWAYS
CL

LOWER SANDS

LOWER SANDS

TOWER EST

TYDE ROAD

+

LC

WRAIGHTSFIELD
AVE

TREVES WAY

TUDOR AVE

VENTURE CL

PEAR TREE

SEA WALL

A259

THE DOWN

HYTHE RD

Martello
Tower

09 A B 10 C D 11 E F 30

175

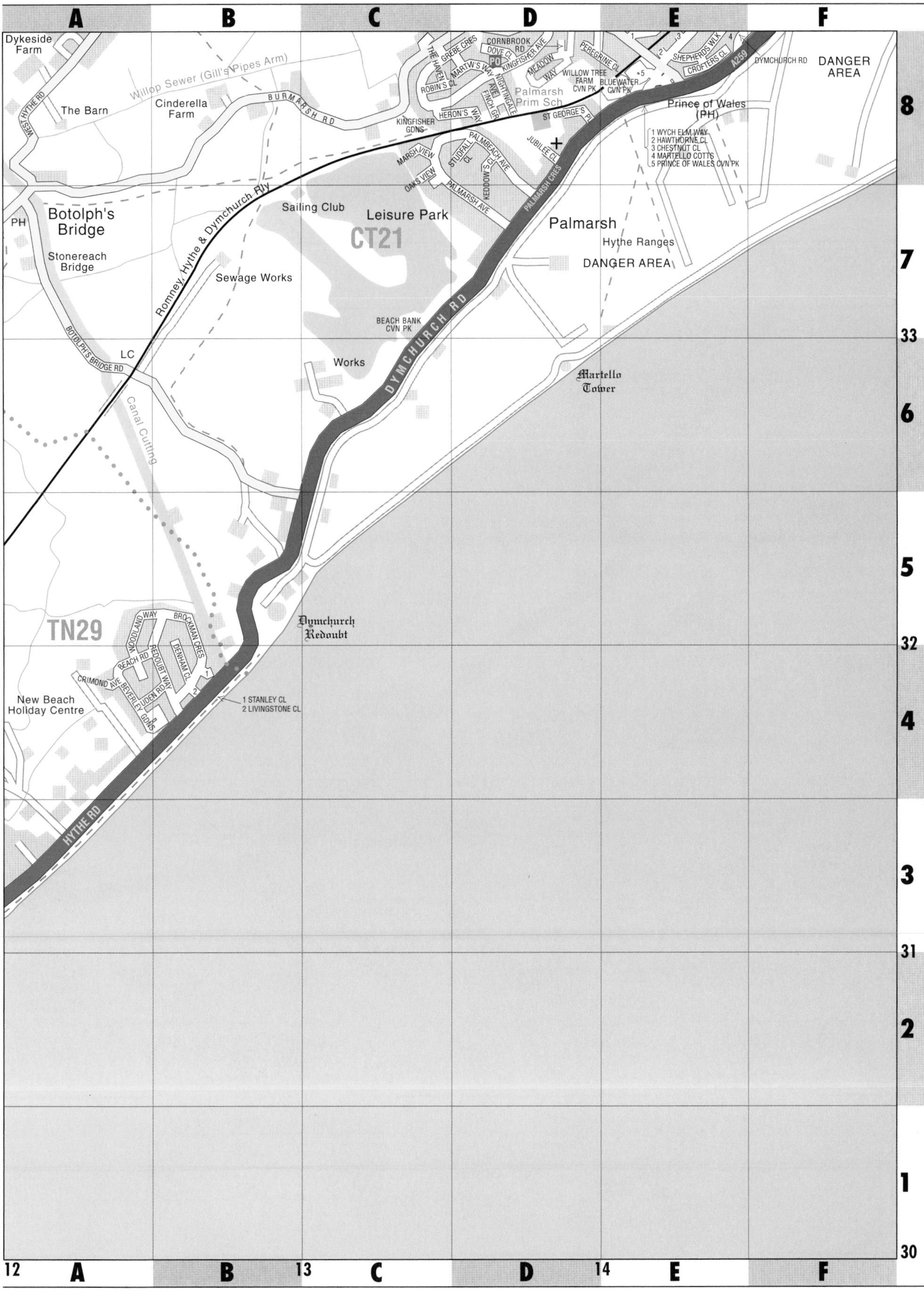

A
B
C
D
E
F
Dykeside Farm
The Barn
Cinderella Farm
Willop Sewer (Gill's Pipes Arm)
WEST HYTHE RD
BURMARSH RD
Botolph's Bridge
PH
Stonereach Bridge
Romney, Hythe & Dymchurch Rly
Sailing Club
Leisure Park
CT21
Sewage Works
BOTOLPH'S BRIDGE RD
LC
Canal Cutting
BEACH BANK CVN PK
Works
DYMCHURCH RD
PALMARSH CRES
A259
DYMCHURCH RD
DANGER AREA
Palmarsh
Hythe Ranges
DANGER AREA
Prince of Wales (PH)
1 WYCH ELM WAY
2 HAWTHORNE CL
3 CHESTNUT CL
4 MARTELLO COTTS
5 PRINCE OF WALES CVN PK
Palmarsh Prim Sch
ST GEORGE'S PL
JUBILEE CL
WILLOW TREE FARM CVN PK
BLUEWATER CVN PK
PEREGRINE CL
SHEPHERDS WLK
CROFTERS CL
CORNBROOK RD
DOVE CL
PO
KINGFISHER AVE
GREBE CRES
THE HAVEN
MARTIN'S WAY
ROBIN'S CL
MEADOW WAY
NIGHTINGALE AVE
FINCH GR
HERON'S WAY
KINGFISHER GDNS
MARSH VIEW
OAKS VIEW
STUDFALL CL
PALMBEACH AVE
KEDDOW'S CL
PALMARSH AVE
Martello Tower
Dymchurch Redoubt
TN29
WOODLAND WAY
BROCKMAN CRES
BEACH RD
REDOUBT WAY
DENHAM CL
CRIMOND AVE
BEVERLEY GDNS
UDEN RD
1 STANLEY CL
2 LIVINGSTONE CL
New Beach Holiday Centre
HYTHE RD
8
7
33
6
5
32
4
3
31
2
1
30
12
13
14

179

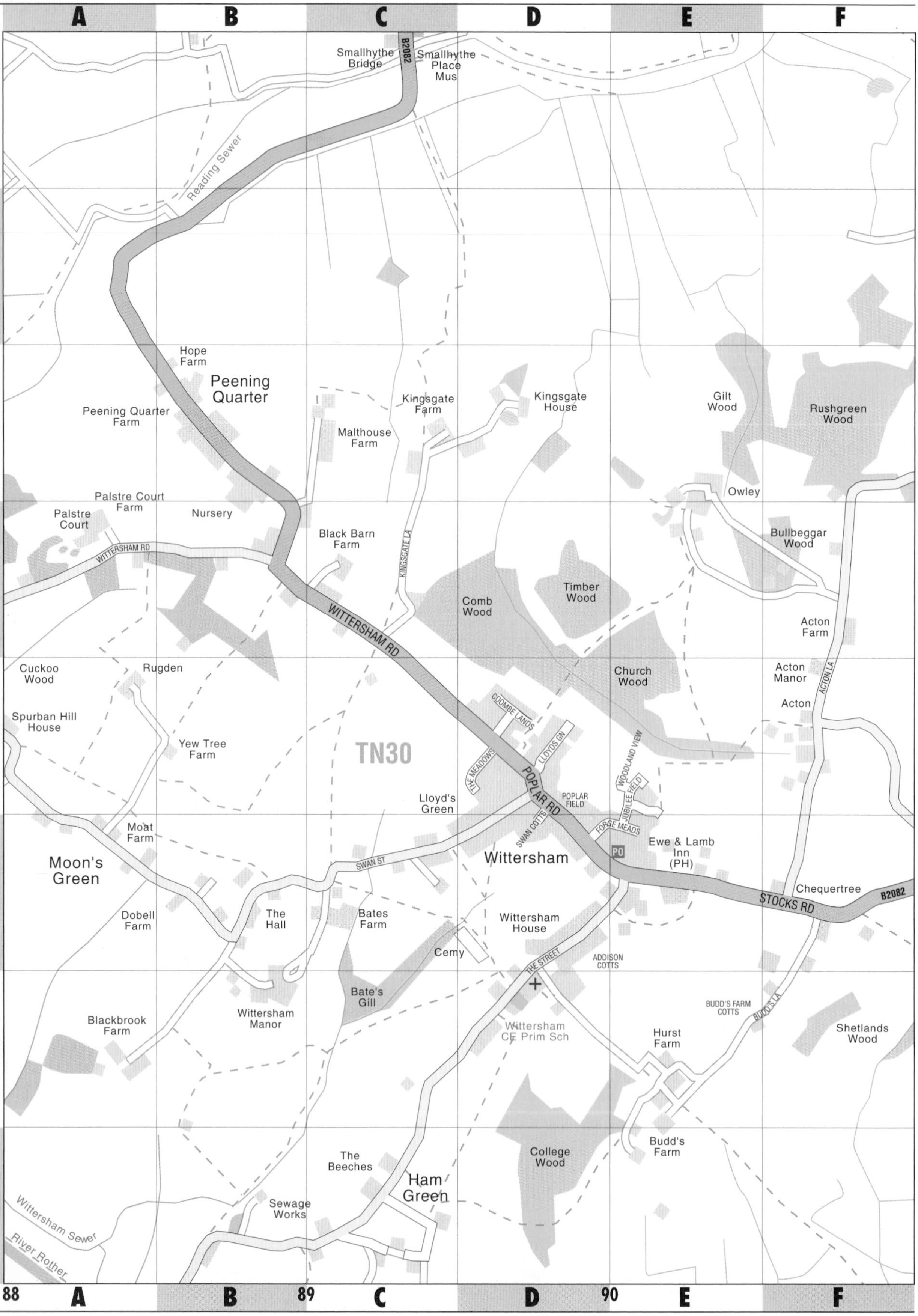
A
B
C
D
E
F
8
7
29
6
5
28
4
3
27
2
1
26
88
89
90
Smallhythe Bridge
B2082
Smallhythe Place Mus
Reading Sewer
Hope Farm
Peening Quarter
Peening Quarter Farm
Kingsgate Farm
Malthouse Farm
Kingsgate House
Gilt Wood
Rushgreen Wood
Owley
Palstre Court Farm
Palstre Court
Nursery
Black Barn Farm
Bullbeggar Wood
WITTERSHAM RD
KINGSGATE LA
Comb Wood
Timber Wood
Acton Farm
Cuckoo Wood
Rugden
Church Wood
Acton Manor
Acton
ACTON LA
Spurban Hill House
Yew Tree Farm
TN30
COOMBE LANDS
LLOYDS GN
THE MEADOWS
POPLAR RD
WOODLAND VIEW
JUBILEE FIELD
POPLAR FIELD
Lloyd's Green
Moat Farm
SWAN COTTS
FORGE MEADS
PO
Ewe & Lamb Inn (PH)
Moon's Green
SWAN ST
Wittersham
Chequertree
STOCKS RD
Dobell Farm
The Hall
Bates Farm
Wittersham House
Cemy
THE STREET
ADDISON COTTS
Bate's Gill
BUDD'S FARM COTTS
BUDD'S LA
Blackbrook Farm
Wittersham Manor
Wittersham CE Prim Sch
Hurst Farm
Shetlands Wood
College Wood
Budd's Farm
The Beeches
Ham Green
Sewage Works
Wittersham Sewer
River Rother

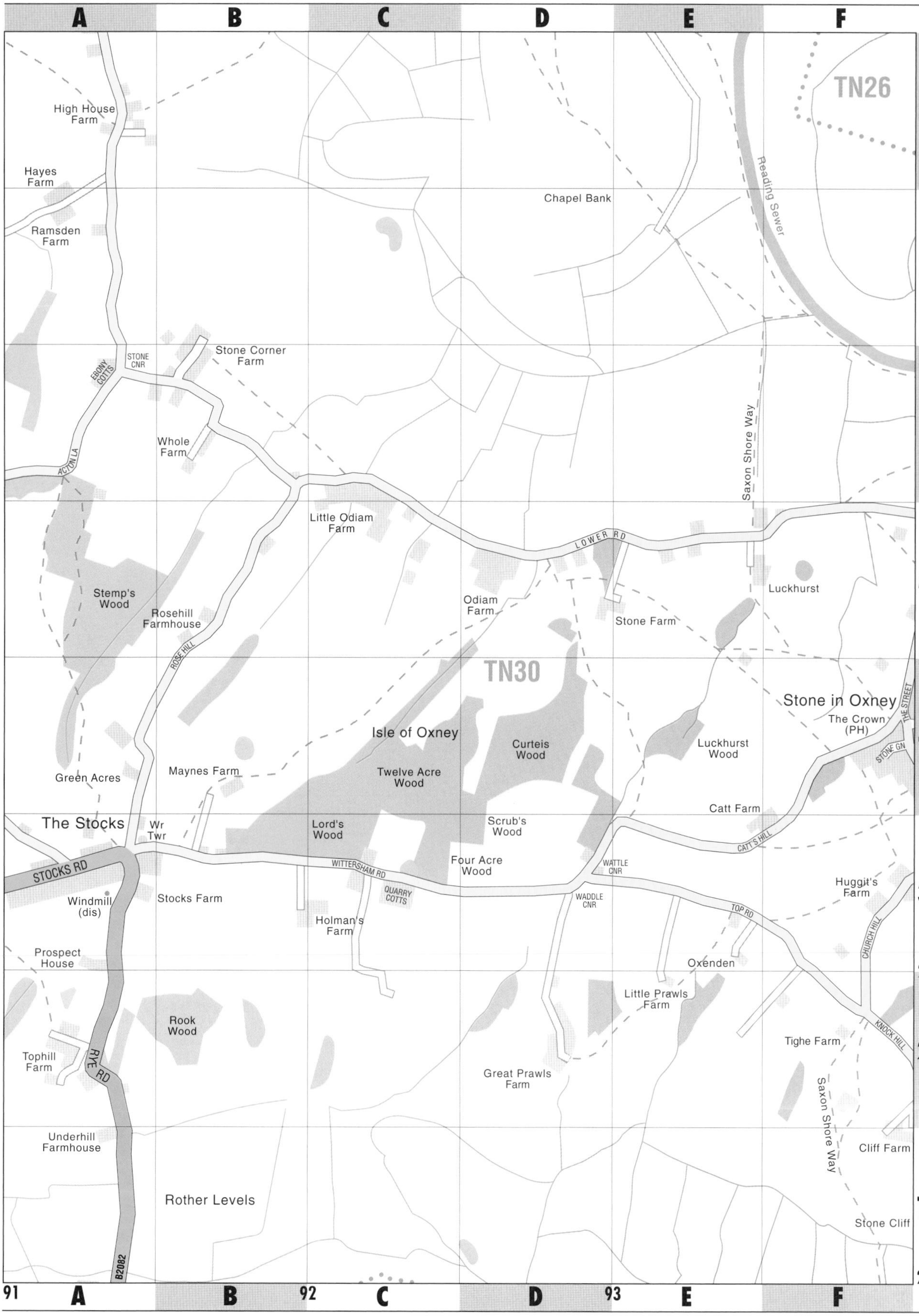
A
B
C
D
E
F
8
7
29
6
5
28
4
3
27
2
1
26
91
92
93
TN26
Reading Sewer
High House Farm
Hayes Farm
Ramsden Farm
Chapel Bank
Stone Corner Farm
STONE CNR
EBONY COTTS
Whole Farm
ACTON LA
Saxon Shore Way
Little Odiam Farm
LOWER RD
Luckhurst
Stemp's Wood
Rosehill Farmhouse
Odiam Farm
Stone Farm
ROSE HILL
TN30
Stone in Oxney
THE STREET
The Crown (PH)
Isle of Oxney
Curteis Wood
Luckhurst Wood
STONE GN
Green Acres
Maynes Farm
Twelve Acre Wood
Catt Farm
The Stocks
Wr Twr
Lord's Wood
Scrub's Wood
CATT'S HILL
STOCKS RD
WITTERSHAM RD
Four Acre Wood
WATTLE CNR
QUARRY COTTS
WADDLE CNR
Huggit's Farm
Windmill (dis)
Stocks Farm
TOP RD
Holman's Farm
CHURCH HILL
Prospect House
Oxenden
Little Prawls Farm
Rook Wood
KNOCK HILL
Tighe Farm
Tophill Farm
RYE RD
Great Prawls Farm
Underhill Farmhouse
Cliff Farm
Rother Levels
Stone Cliff
B2082

189
181

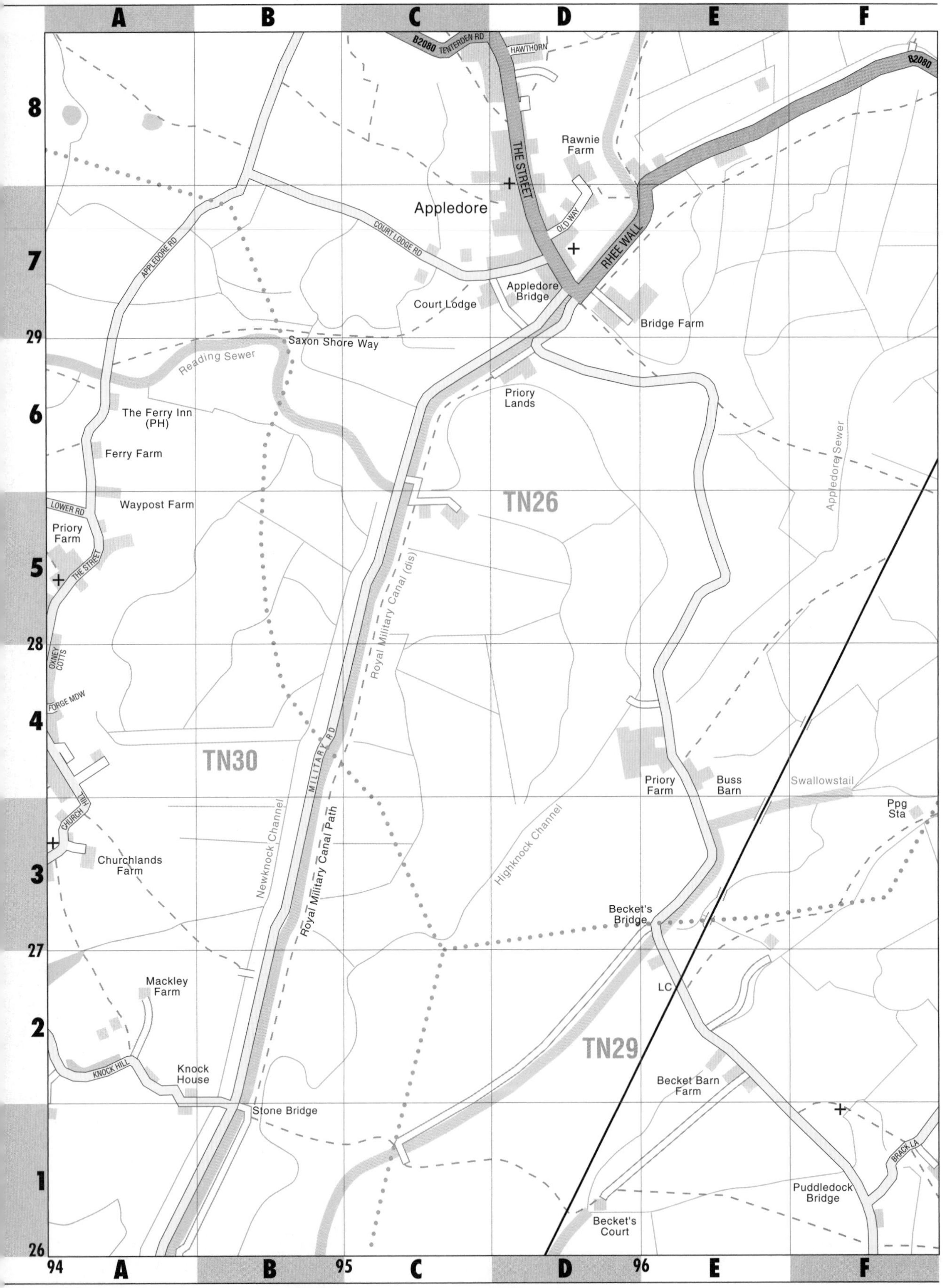
A
B
C
D
E
F
8
7
29
6
5
28
4
3
27
2
1
26
94
95
96
B2080
TENTERDEN RD
HAWTHORN
THE STREET
Rawnie Farm
Appledore
COURT LODGE RD
OLD WAY
RHEE WALL
APPLEDORE RD
Appledore Bridge
Court Lodge
Bridge Farm
Saxon Shore Way
Reading Sewer
Priory Lands
The Ferry Inn (PH)
Ferry Farm
Waypost Farm
LOWER RD
TN26
Appledore Sewer
Priory Farm
THE STREET
Royal Military Canal (dis)
OXNEY COTTS
FORGE MDW
TN30
MILITARY RD
Priory Farm
Buss Barn
Swallowstail
Ppg Sta
CHURCH HILL
Churchlands Farm
Newknock Channel
Royal Military Canal Path
Highknock Channel
Becket's Bridge
LC
Mackley Farm
TN29
KNOCK HILL
Knock House
Becket Barn Farm
Stone Bridge
BRACK LA
Puddledock Bridge
Becket's Court

189
196

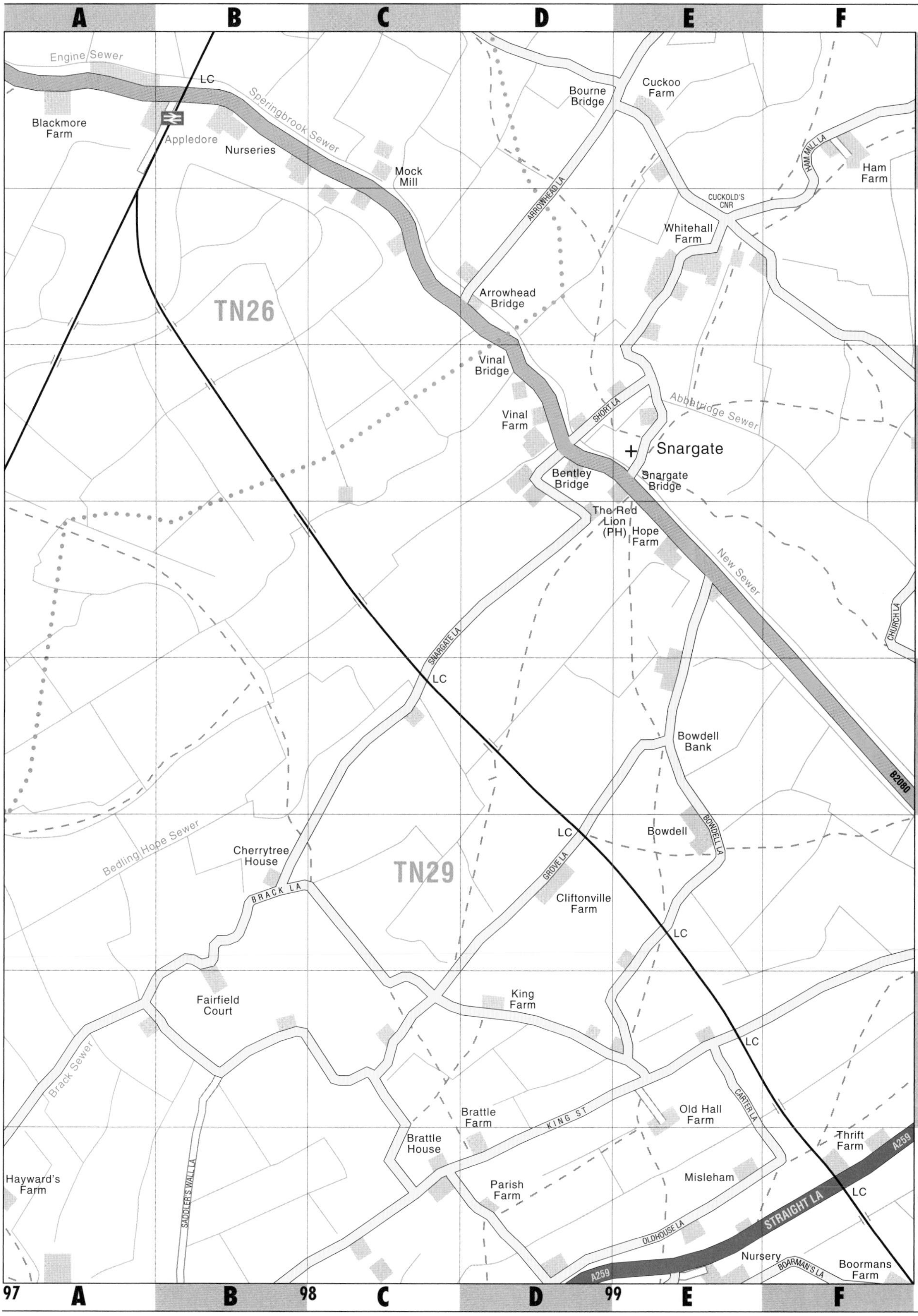
A
B
C
D
E
F
Engine Sewer
LC
Blackmore Farm
Appledore
Springbrook Sewer
Nurseries
Mock Mill
Bourne Bridge
Cuckoo Farm
HAM MILL LA
Ham Farm
CUCKOLD'S CNR
Whitehall Farm
ARROWHEAD LA
Arrowhead Bridge
TN26
Vinal Bridge
Vinal Farm
SHORT LA
Abbotridge Sewer
Snargate
Bentley Bridge
Snargate Bridge
The Red Lion (PH)
Hope Farm
New Sewer
CHURCH LA
SNARGATE LA
LC
Bowdell Bank
B2080
LC
Bowdell
BOWDELL LA
Bedling Hope Sewer
Cherrytree House
TN29
GROVE LA
BRACK LA
Cliftonville Farm
LC
Fairfield Court
King Farm
LC
Brack Sewer
Brattle Farm
KING ST
Old Hall Farm
CARTER LA
Brattle House
Thrift Farm
A259
Hayward's Farm
SADDLER'S WALL LA
Parish Farm
Misleham
STRAIGHT LA
LC
OLDHOUSE LA
Nursery
BOARMAN'S LA
Boormans Farm
A259
8
7
29
6
5
28
4
3
27
2
1
26
97
98
99

191
183

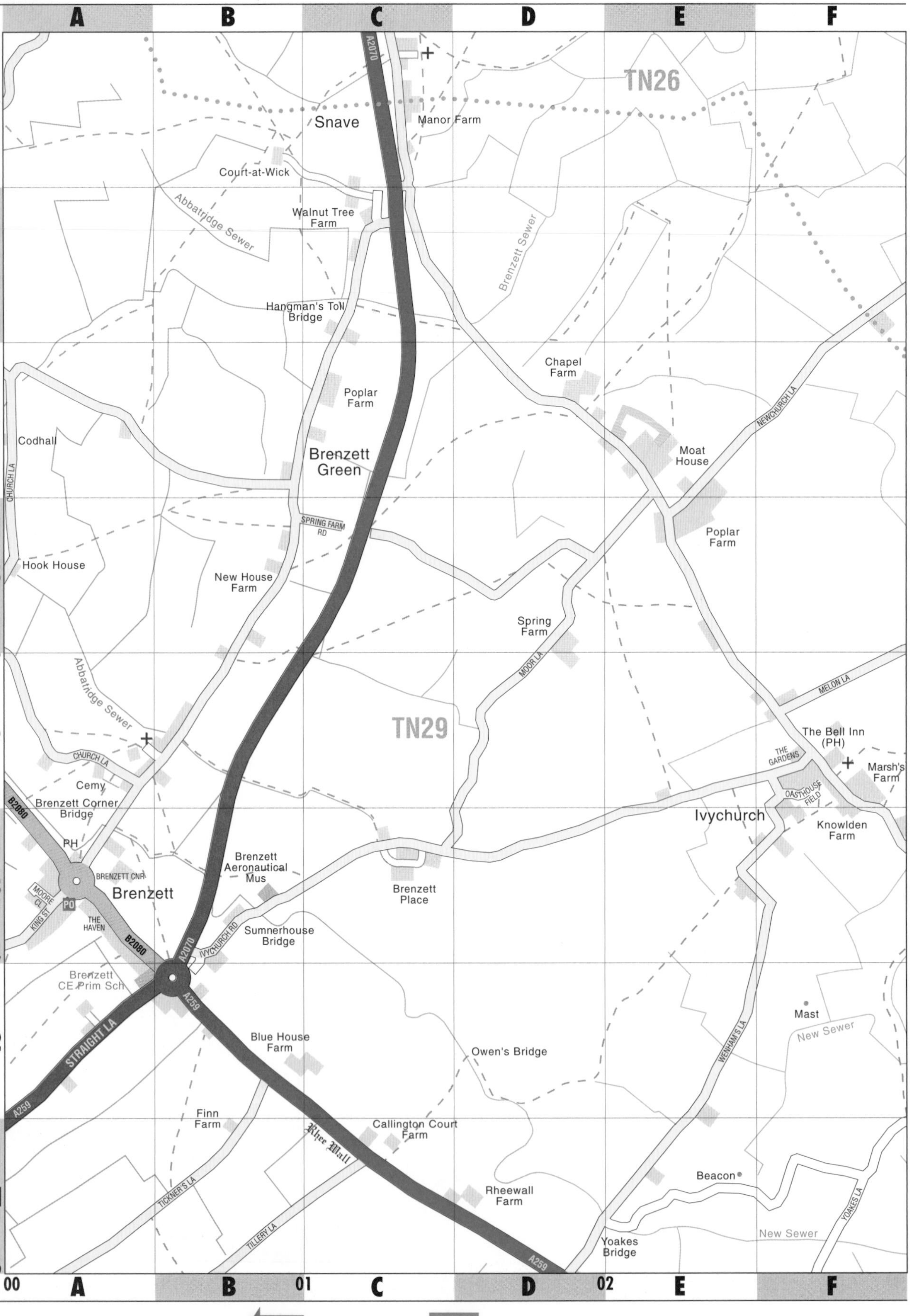
A B C D E F
8
7
29
6
5
28
4
3
27
2
1
26
00
01
02
TN26
Snave
Manor Farm
Court-at-Wick
Abbatridge Sewer
Walnut Tree Farm
Brenzett Sewer
Hangman's Toll Bridge
Chapel Farm
Poplar Farm
Codhall
Brenzett Green
Moat House
NEWCHURCH LA
CHURCH LA
SPRING FARM RD
Poplar Farm
Hook House
New House Farm
Spring Farm
MOOR LA
TN29
MELON LA
The Bell Inn (PH)
THE GARDENS
Marsh's Farm
CHURCH LA
Cemy
OASTHOUSE FIELD
Brenzett Corner Bridge
Ivychurch
Knowlden Farm
B2080
PH
Brenzett Aeronautical Mus
BRENZETT CNR
MOORE CL
PO
Brenzett
Brenzett Place
KING ST
THE HAVEN
Sumnerhouse Bridge
IVYCHURCH RD
A2070
Brenzett CE Prim Sch
A259
Mast
New Sewer
STRAIGHT LA
Blue House Farm
Owen's Bridge
WENHAM'S LA
Finn Farm
Callington Court Farm
Rhee Wall
Beacon
Rheewall Farm
TICKNER'S LA
YOAKES LA
New Sewer
TILLERY LA
Yoakes Bridge

191
198

184
194

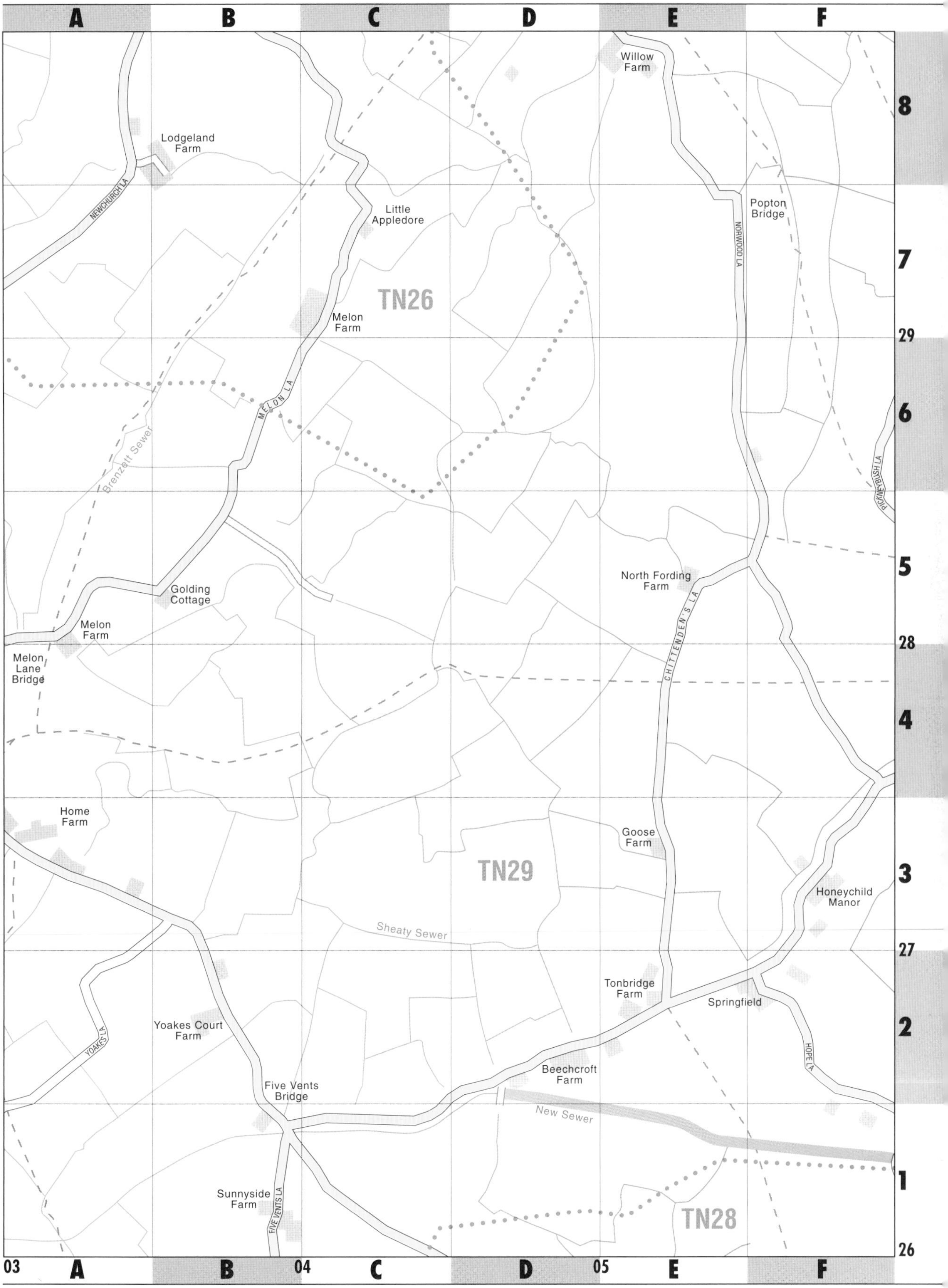
A
B
C
D
E
F
Willow Farm
Lodgeland Farm
NEWCHURCH LA
Little Appledore
Popton Bridge
NORWOOD LA
TN26
Melon Farm
MELON LA
Brenzett Sewer
PICKNEYBUSH LA
North Fording Farm
Golding Cottage
Melon Farm
Melon Lane Bridge
CHITTENDEN'S LA
Home Farm
Goose Farm
TN29
Honeychild Manor
Sheaty Sewer
Tonbridge Farm
Springfield
Yoakes Court Farm
YOAKES LA
HOPE LA
Beechcroft Farm
Five Vents Bridge
New Sewer
Sunnyside Farm
FIVE VENTS LA
TN28
8
7
29
6
5
28
4
3
27
2
1
26
03
04
05

199
194

193
185

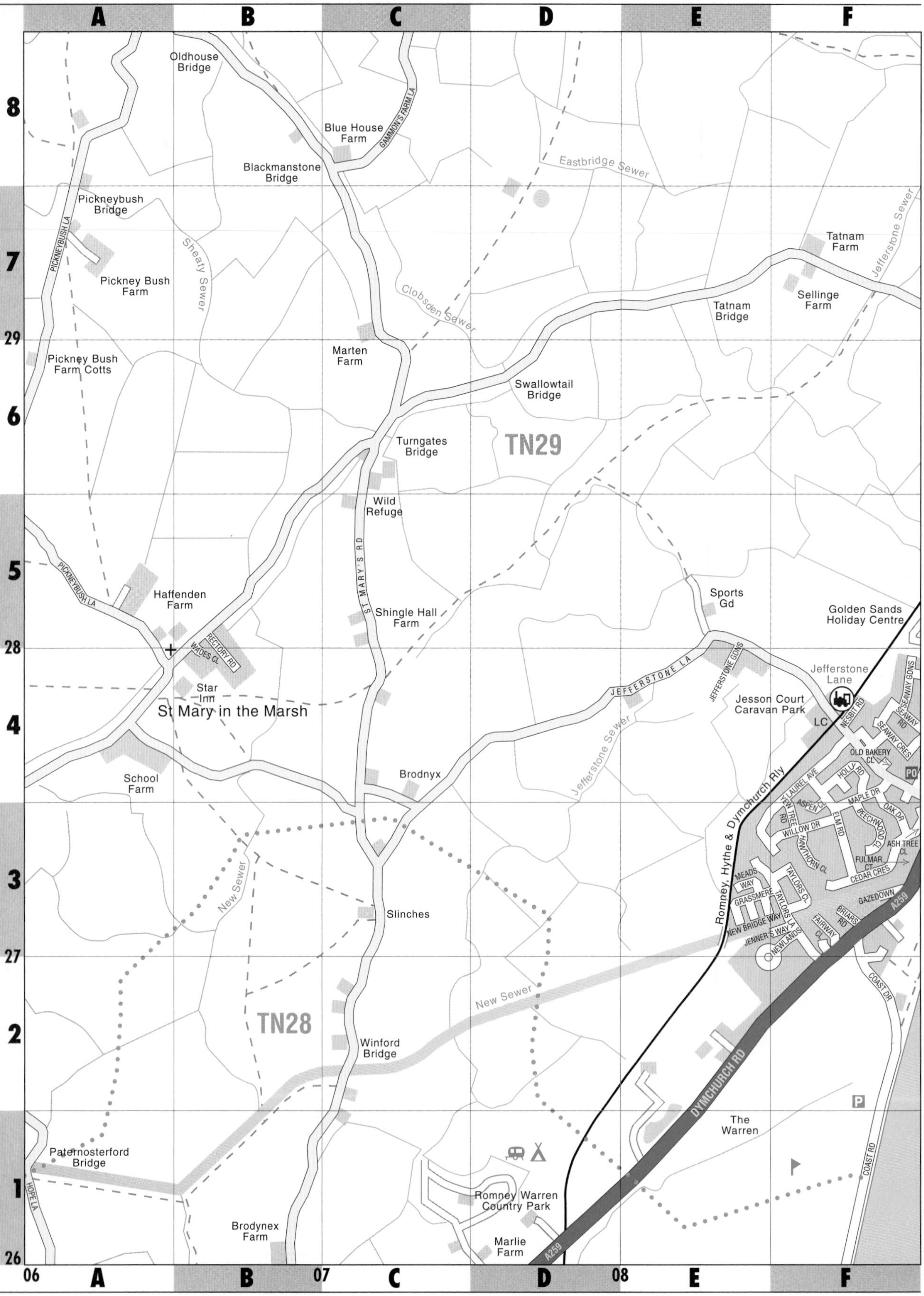

A B C D E F

8

Oldhouse
Bridge

Blue House
Farm

GAMMON'S FARM LA

Blackmanstone
Bridge

Pickneybush
Bridge

7

Eastbridge Sewer

Jefferstone Sewer

Tatnam
Farm

PICKNEYBUSH LA

Sheaty Sewer

Pickney Bush
Farm

Clobsden Sewer

Tatnam
Bridge

Sellinge
Farm

29

Pickney Bush
Farm Cotts

Marten
Farm

Swallowtail
Bridge

6

Turngates
Bridge

TN29

Wild
Refuge

PICKNEY BUSH LA

ST MARY'S RD

5

Haffenden
Farm

Shingle Hall
Farm

Sports
Gd

Golden Sands
Holiday Centre

28

RECTORY RD
WADES CL

Star
Inn

JEFFERSTONE LA

JEFFERSTONE GDNS

Jefferstone
Lane

Jesson Court
Caravan Park

SEAWAY GDNS
WESBO RD
SEAWAY CRES
SEAWAY RD

4

St Mary in the Marsh

Jefferstone Sewer

LC

OLD BAKERY CL

PO

School
Farm

Brodnyx

Romney, Hythe & Dymchurch Rly

LAUREL AVE
FERN TREE RD
ASPEN CL
WILLOW DR
HAWTHORN CL
HOLLY RD
BEECHWOOD
ELM RD
MAPLE DR
OAK DR
ASH TREE CL
FULMAR CT
CEDAR CRES

3

New Sewer

Slinches

MEADS
WAY
GRASSMERE
NEW BRIDGE WAY
TAYLORS CL
TAYLORS LA
JENNER'S WAY
NEWLANDS
FAIRWAY CL
BRIARS RD
GAZEDOWN
A259

27

2

TN28

Winford
Bridge

New Sewer

DYMCHURCH RD

COAST DR

HOPE LA

Paternosterford
Bridge

The
Warren

P

1

Romney Warren
Country Park

COAST RD

Brodynex
Farm

Marlie
Farm

A259

26

06 A B 07 C D 08 E F

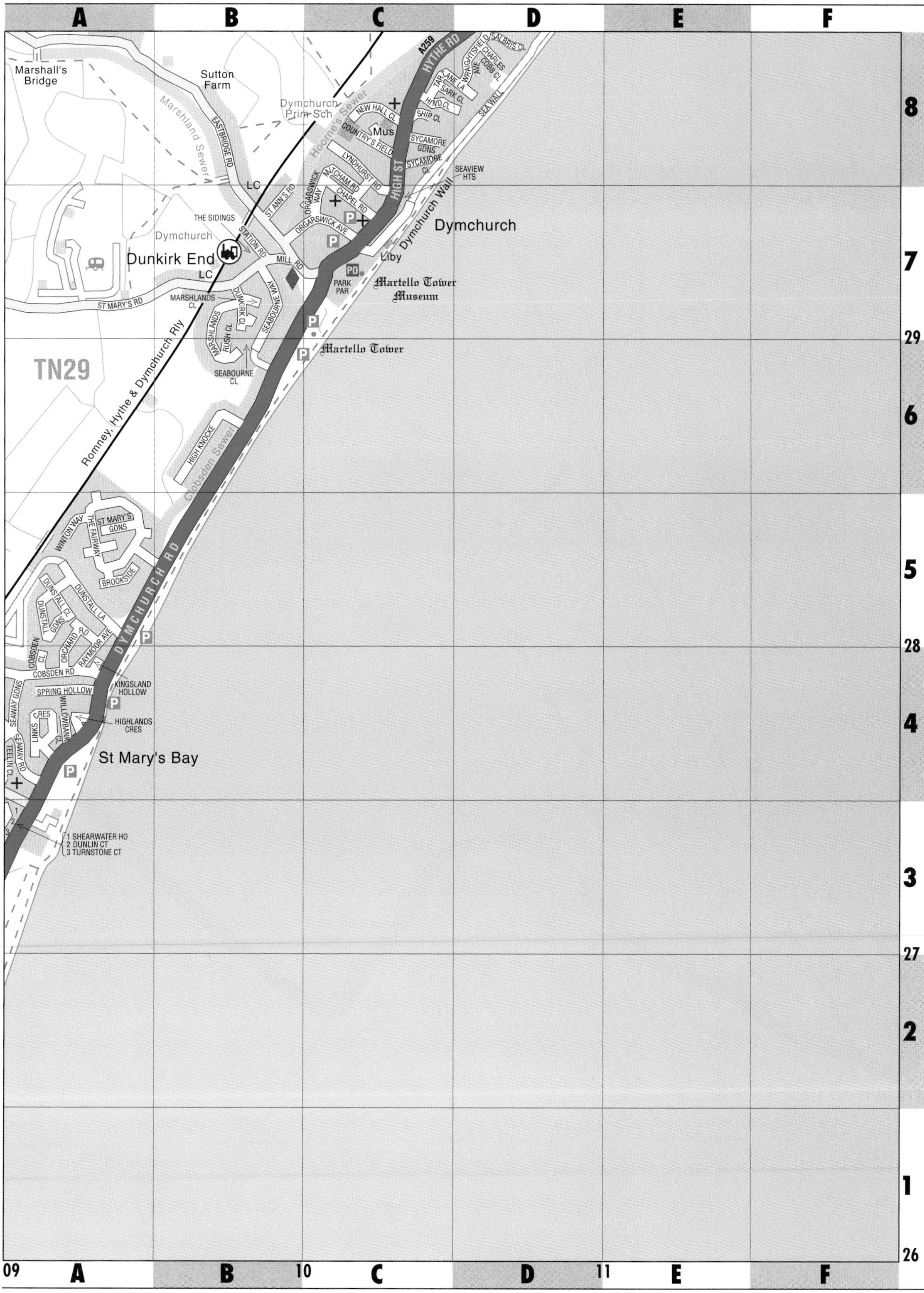
A
B
C
D
E
F
8
7
29
6
5
28
4
3
27
2
1
26
09
10
11
Marshall's Bridge
Sutton Farm
Marshland Sewer
EASTBRIDGE RD
Dymchurch Prim Sch
Hoorne's Sewer
A259
HYTHE RD
SALBRIS CL
WRAIGHTSFIELD AVE
CHARLES COBB CL
TARLANE LA
SARK CL
HIND CL
NEW HALL CL
SHIP CL
SEA WALL
COUNTRY'S FIELD
Mus
SYCAMORE GDNS
SYCAMORE CL
SEAVIEW HTS
LYNDHURST RD
HIGH ST
MITCHAM RD
CHAPEL RD
ORGARSWICK WAY
ORGARSWICK AVE
ST ANN'S RD
LC
THE SIDINGS
STATION RD
Dymchurch
Dymchurch Wall
Dymchurch
Dunkirk End
LC
MILL RD
Liby
PO
PARK PAR
Martello Tower Museum
ST MARY'S RD
MARSHLANDS CL
DUNKIRK CL
SEABOURNE WAY
MARSHLANDS
RUSH CL
SEABOURNE CL
Martello Tower
TN29
Romney, Hythe & Dymchurch Rly
HIGH KNOCKE
Clobsden Sewer
WINTON WAY
THE FAIRWAY
ST MARY'S GDNS
BROOKSIDE
DYMCHURCH RD
DUNSTALL CL
DUNSTALL GDNS
DUNSTALL LA
ORCHARD RD
RAYMOOR AVE
COBSDEN CL
COBSDEN RD
KINGSLAND HOLLOW
SPRING HOLLOW
SEAWAY GDNS
WILLOWBANK CL
CRES
LINKS
HIGHLANDS CRES
SEAWAY RD
TEELIN CL
St Mary's Bay
1 SHEARWATER HO
2 DUNLIN CT
3 TURNSTONE CT

190

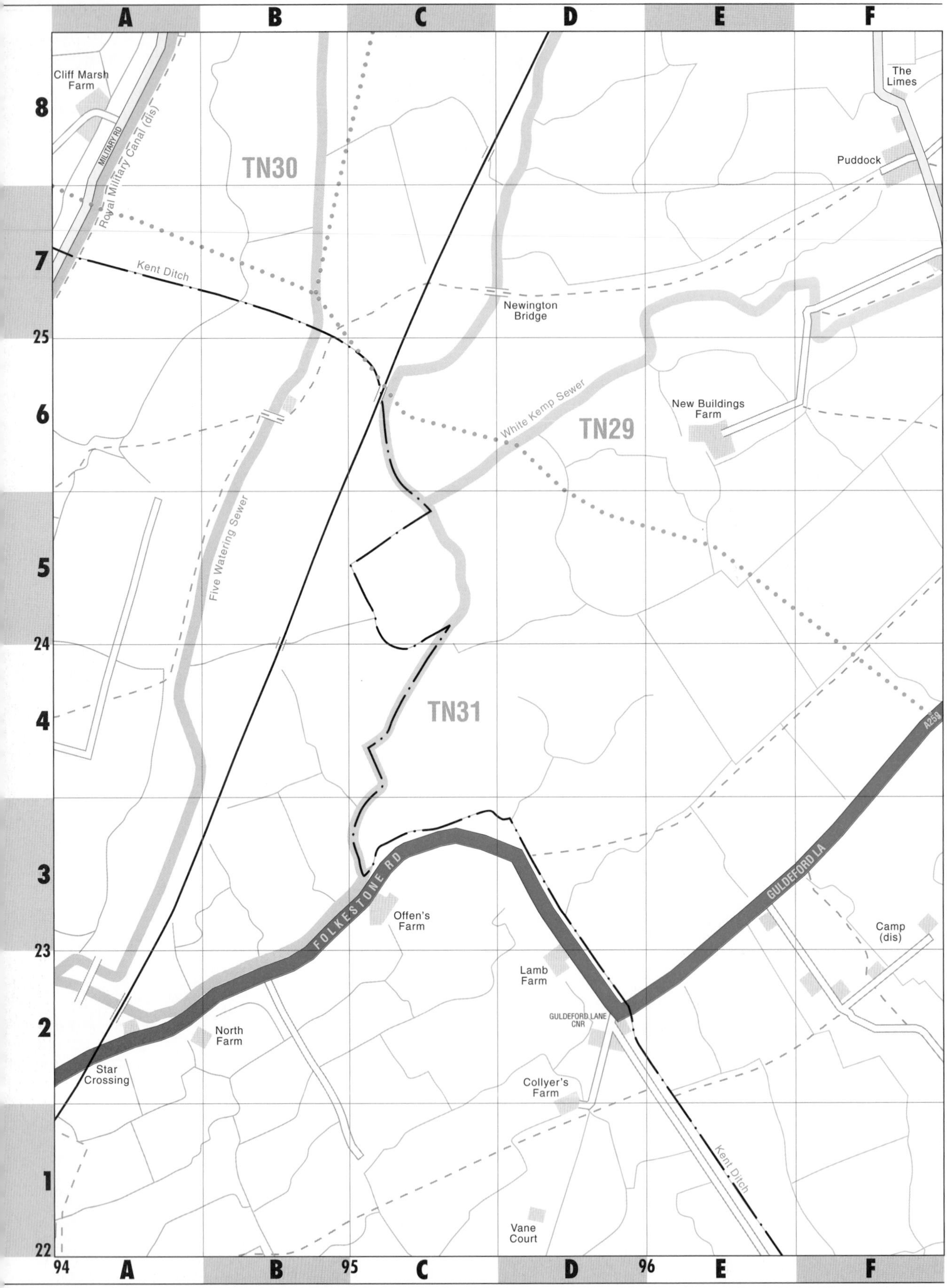
A
B
C
D
E
F
8
7
25
6
5
24
4
3
23
2
1
22
94
95
96
Cliff Marsh Farm
MILITARY RD
Royal Military Canal (dis)
TN30
The Limes
Puddock
Kent Ditch
Newington Bridge
White Kemp Sewer
New Buildings Farm
TN29
Five Watering Sewer
TN31
A259
FOLKESTONE RD
GULDEFORD LA
Offen's Farm
Camp (dis)
Lamb Farm
GULDEFORD LANE CNR
North Farm
Star Crossing
Collyer's Farm
Kent Ditch
Vane Court

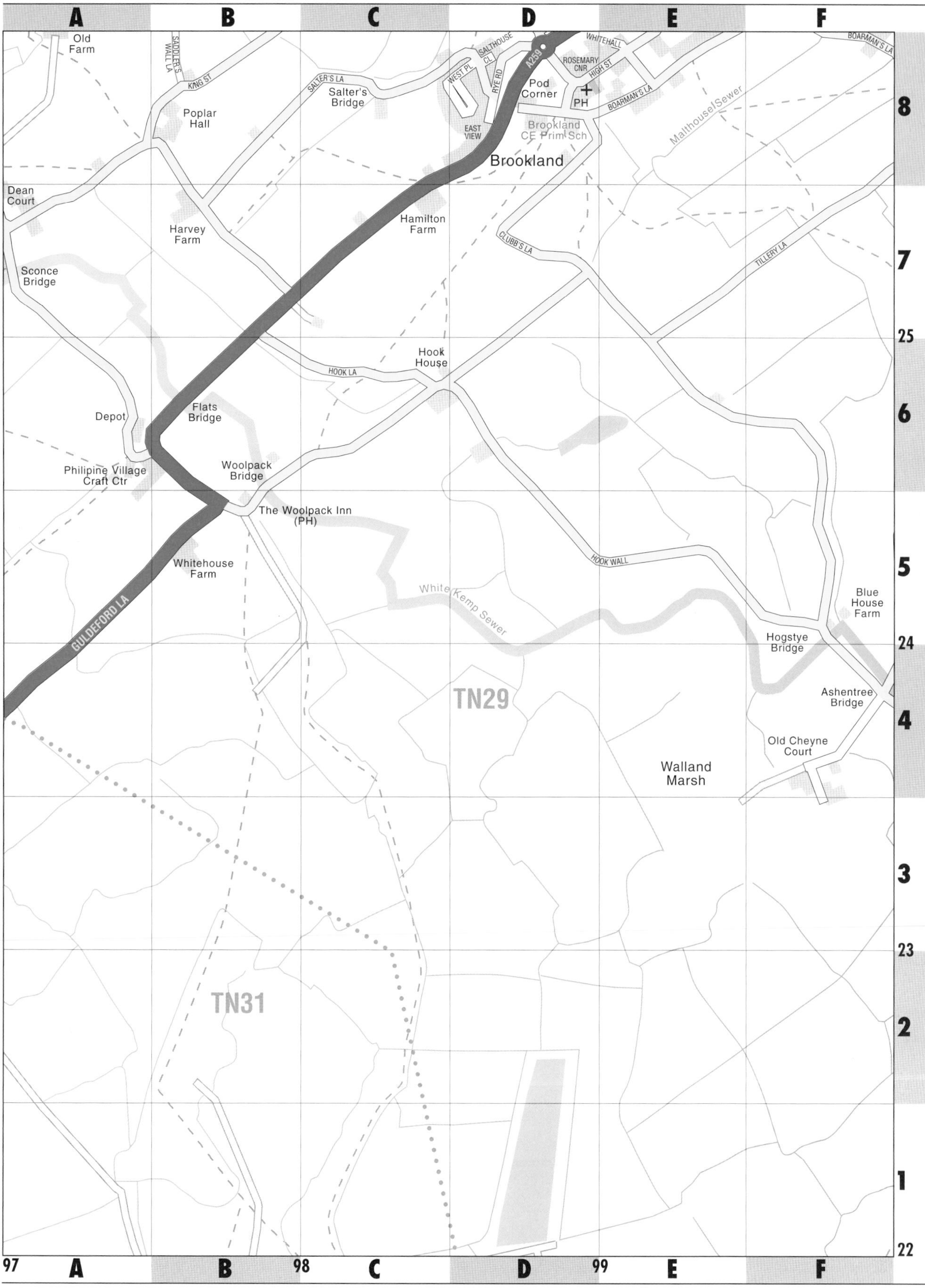

191
198

A B C D E F

8

7

25

6

5

24

4

3

23

2

1

22

Old Farm

SADDLER'S WALL LA

KING ST

Poplar Hall

SALTER'S LA

Salter's Bridge

Dean Court

Harvey Farm

Sconce Bridge

Depot

Flats Bridge

Philipine Village Craft Ctr

Woolpack Bridge

The Woolpack Inn (PH)

Whitehouse Farm

GULDEFORD LA

WEST PL

EAST VIEW

SALTHOUSE

CL

RYE RD

A259

Pod Corner

WHITEHALL

ROSEMARY CNR

HIGH ST

BOARMAN'S LA

Brookland CE Prim Sch

PH

BOARMAN'S LA

Brookland

Malthouse Sewer

Hamilton Farm

CLUBB'S LA

TILLERY LA

Hook House

HOOK LA

Hook Wall

Blue House Farm

White Kemp Sewer

Hogstye Bridge

Ashentree Bridge

TN29

Old Cheyne Court

Walland Marsh

TN31

97 A B 98 C D 99 E F

201
198

197 192

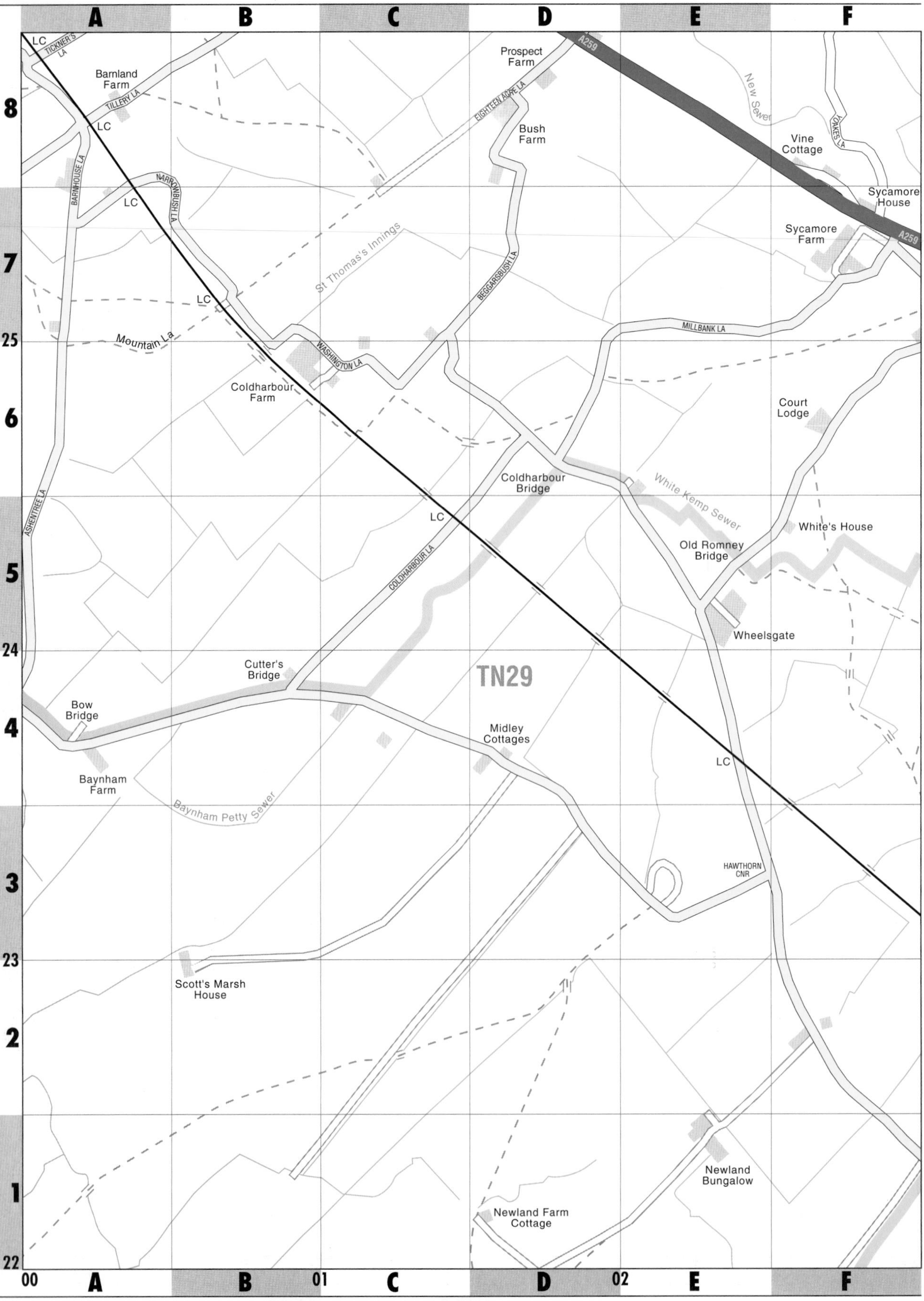

A B C D E F

8

LC
TICKNER'S LA
Barnland Farm
TILLERY LA
LC
BARNHOUSE LA
NARROWBUSH LA
LC
LC
Mountain La
EIGHTEEN ACRE LA
Prospect Farm
A259
New Sewer
Bush Farm
Vine Cottage
Sycamore House
A259
Sycamore Farm

7

St Thomas's Innings
BEGGARSBUSH LA
WASHINGTON LA
MILLBANK LA

25

Coldharbour Farm

6

Court Lodge

Coldharbour Bridge

White Kemp Sewer

White's House

Old Romney Bridge

LC

5

ASHENTREE LA

COLDHARBOUR LA

Wheelsgate

24

Cutter's Bridge

TN29

4

Bow Bridge

Midley Cottages

LC

Baynham Farm

Baynham Petty Sewer

HAWTHORN CNR

3

23

Scott's Marsh House

2

Newland Bungalow

1

Newland Farm Cottage

22

00 A B 01 C D 02 E F

197 202

193
200

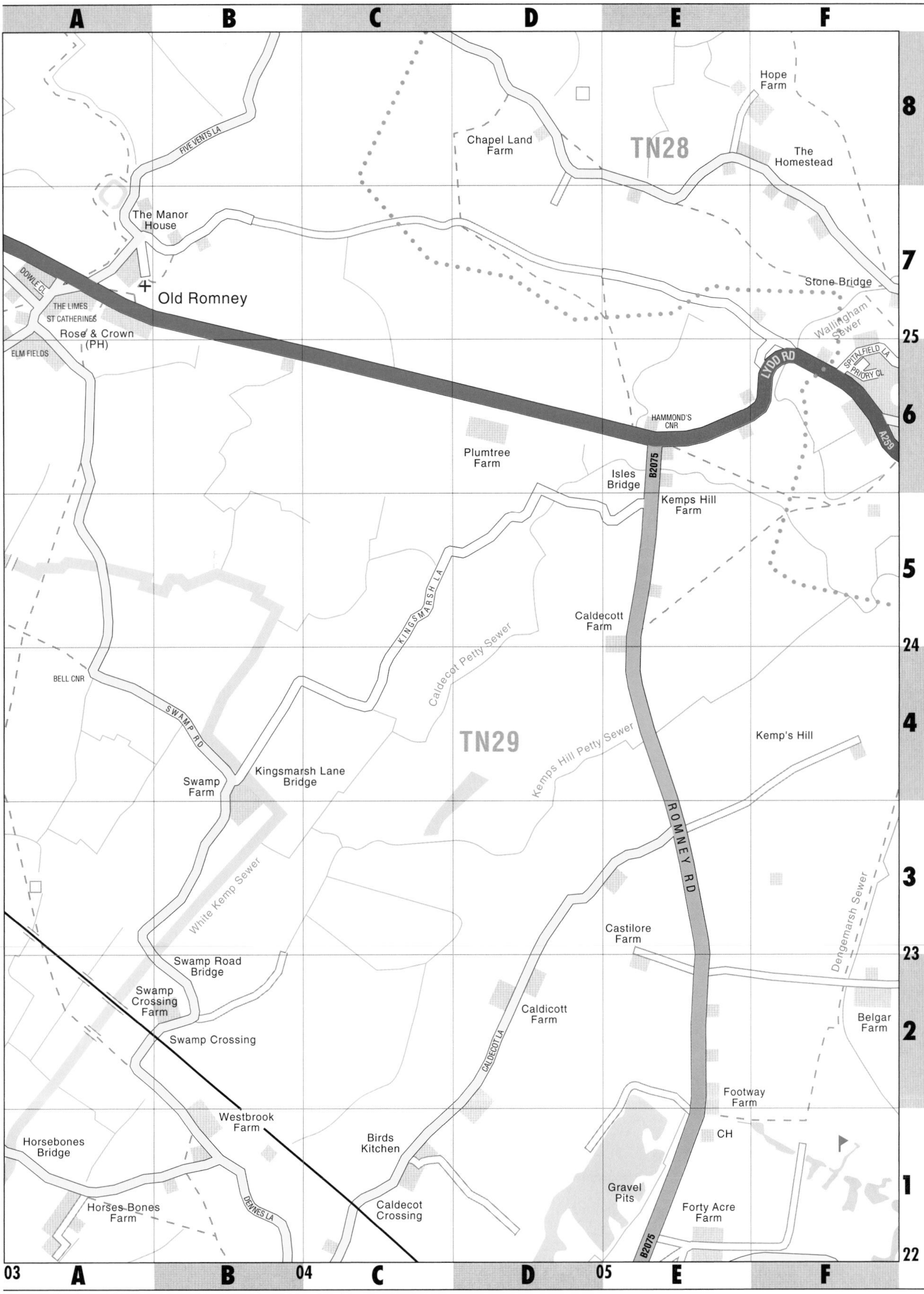
A
B
C
D
E
F
8
7
25
6
5
24
4
3
23
2
1
22
03
04
05
Hope Farm
Chapel Land Farm
TN28
The Homestead
FIVE VENTS LA
The Manor House
Old Romney
DOWLE CL
THE LIMES
ST CATHERINES
Rose & Crown (PH)
ELM FIELDS
Stone Bridge
Wallingham Sewer
LYDD RD
SPITALFIELD LA
PRIORY CL
A259
HAMMOND'S CNR
B2075
Plumtree Farm
Isles Bridge
Kemps Hill Farm
KINGSMARSH LA
Caldecott Farm
Caldecot Petty Sewer
BELL CNR
SWAMP RD
TN29
Kemps Hill Petty Sewer
Kemp's Hill
Swamp Farm
Kingsmarsh Lane Bridge
ROMNEY RD
White Kemp Sewer
Castilore Farm
Dengemarsh Sewer
Swamp Road Bridge
Swamp Crossing Farm
Caldicott Farm
Belgar Farm
Swamp Crossing
CALDECOT LA
Footway Farm
Westbrook Farm
CH
Horsebones Bridge
Birds Kitchen
Gravel Pits
Forty Acre Farm
Horses Bones Farm
DENNES LA
Caldecot Crossing

203
200

199
194

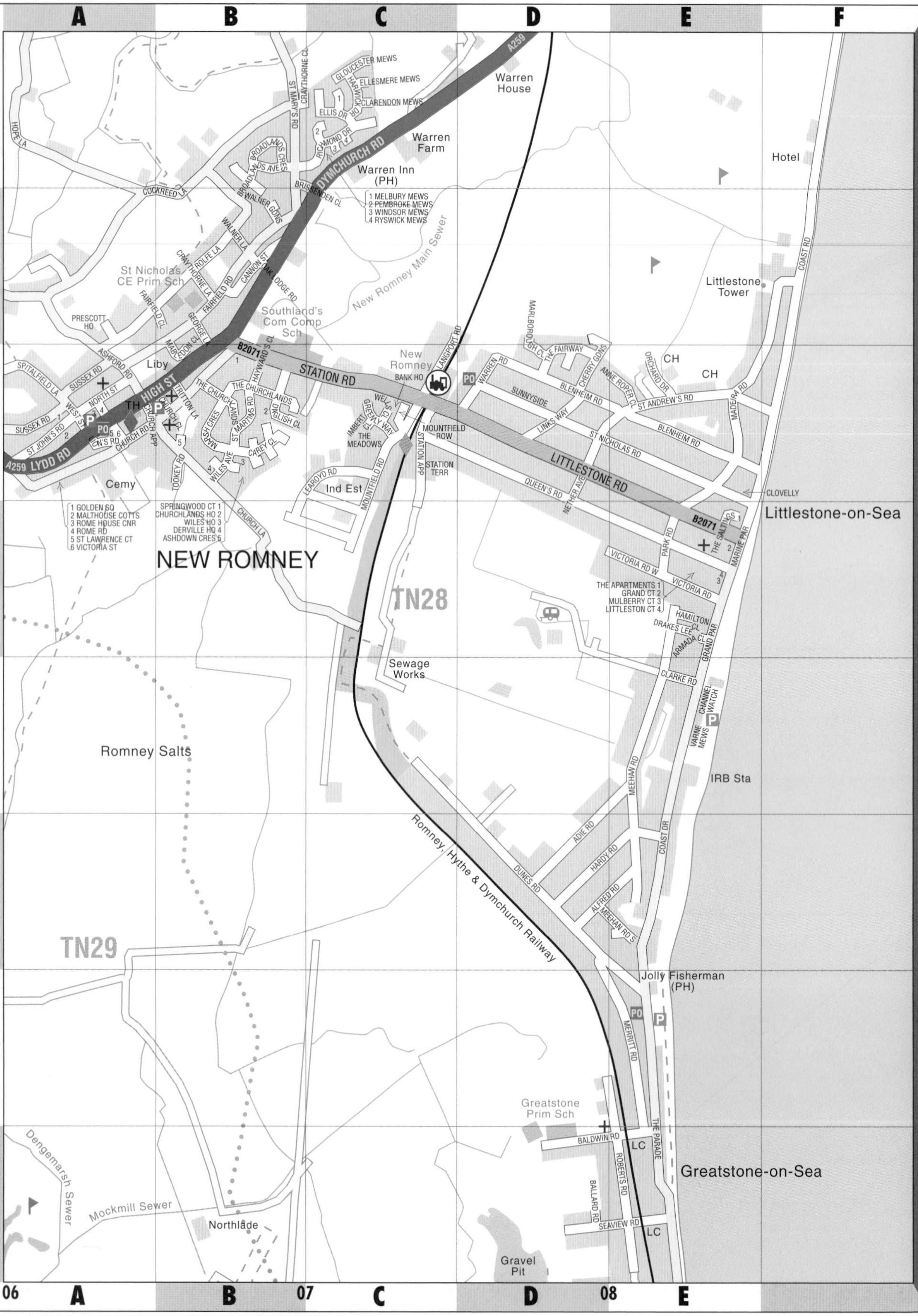
A B C D E F
8 7 25 6 5 24 4 3 23 2 1 22
06 07 08
NEW ROMNEY
Littlestone-on-Sea
Greatstone-on-Sea
TN28
TN29
Romney Salts
DYMCHURCH RD
STATION RD
LITTLESTONE RD
LYDD RD
HIGH ST
Warren House
Warren Farm
Warren Inn (PH)
1 MELBURY MEWS
2 PEMBROKE MEWS
3 WINDSOR MEWS
4 RYSWICK MEWS
New Romney Main Sewer
St Nicholas CE Prim Sch
Southland's Com Comp Sch
PRESCOTT HO
Liby
TH
Cemy
1 GOLDEN SQ
2 MALTHOUSE COTTS
3 ROME HOUSE CNR
4 ROME RD
5 ST LAWRENCE CT
6 VICTORIA ST
SPRINGWOOD CT 1
CHURCHLANDS HO 2
WILES HO 3
DERVILLE HO 4
ASHDOWN CRES 5
New Romney
Ind Est
Sewage Works
Hotel
Littlestone Tower
CH
CLOVELLY
THE APARTMENTS 1
GRAND CT 2
MULBERRY CT 3
LITTLESTON CT 4
IRB Sta
Romney, Hythe & Dymchurch Railway
Jolly Fisherman (PH)
Greatstone Prim Sch
LC
Gravel Pit
Northlade
Mockmill Sewer
Dengemarsh Sewer

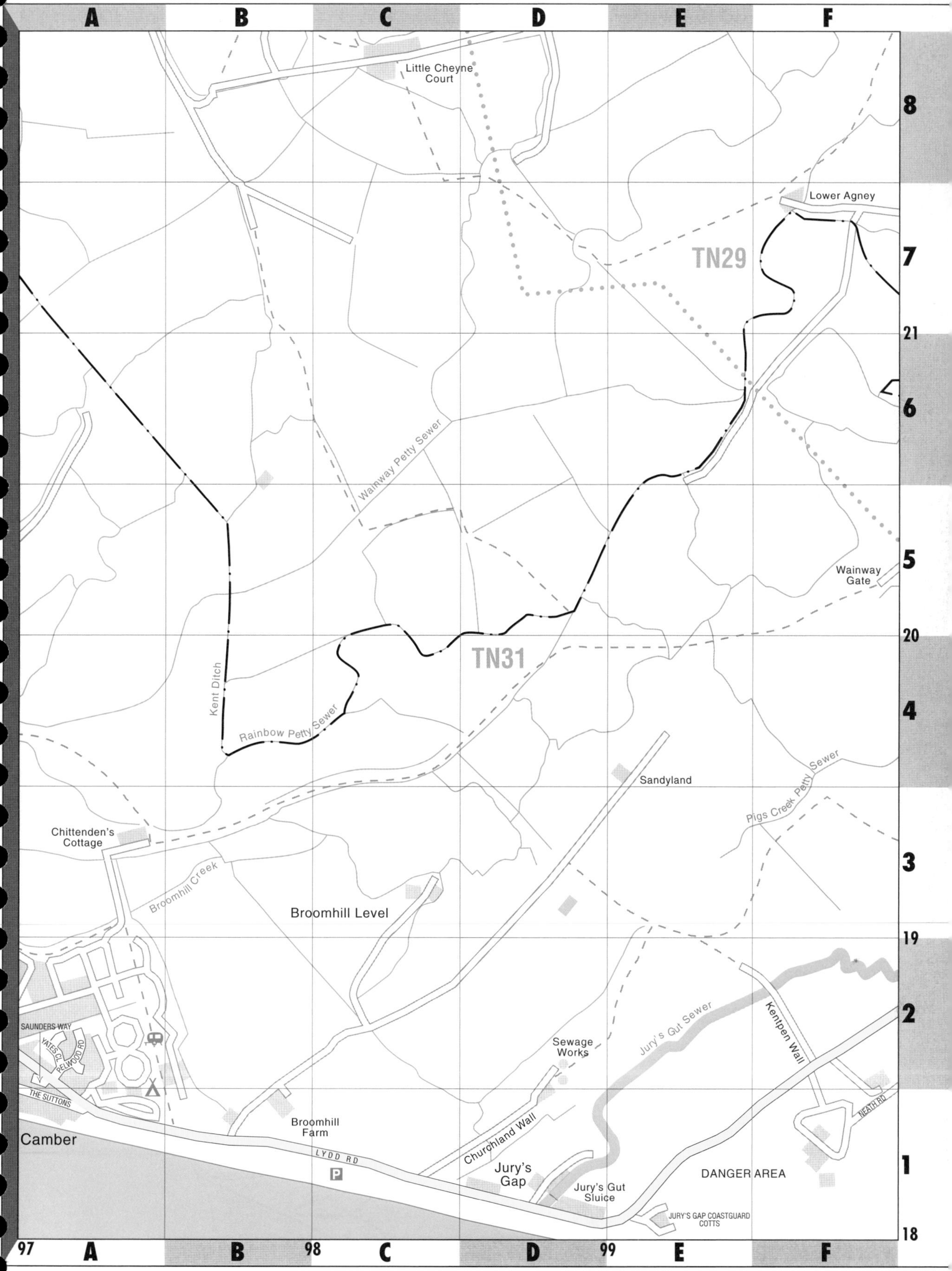

197
202

A   B   C   D   E   F

Little Cheyne
Court

Lower Agney

TN29

8

7

21

6

Wainway Petty Sewer

Wainway
Gate

5

Kent Ditch

TN31

20

Rainbow Petty Sewer

4

Pigs Creek Petty Sewer

Sandyland

Chittenden's
Cottage

3

Broomhill Creek

Broomhill Level

19

SAUNDERS WAY

Jury's Gut Sewer

Kentpen Wall

2

YATES ?
BELWOOD RD

Sewage
Works

THE SUTTONS

Churchland Wall

NEATH RD

Camber

LYDD RD

Broomhill
Farm

Jury's
Gap

Jury's Gut
Sluice

DANGER AREA

1

JURY'S GAP COASTGUARD
COTTS

18

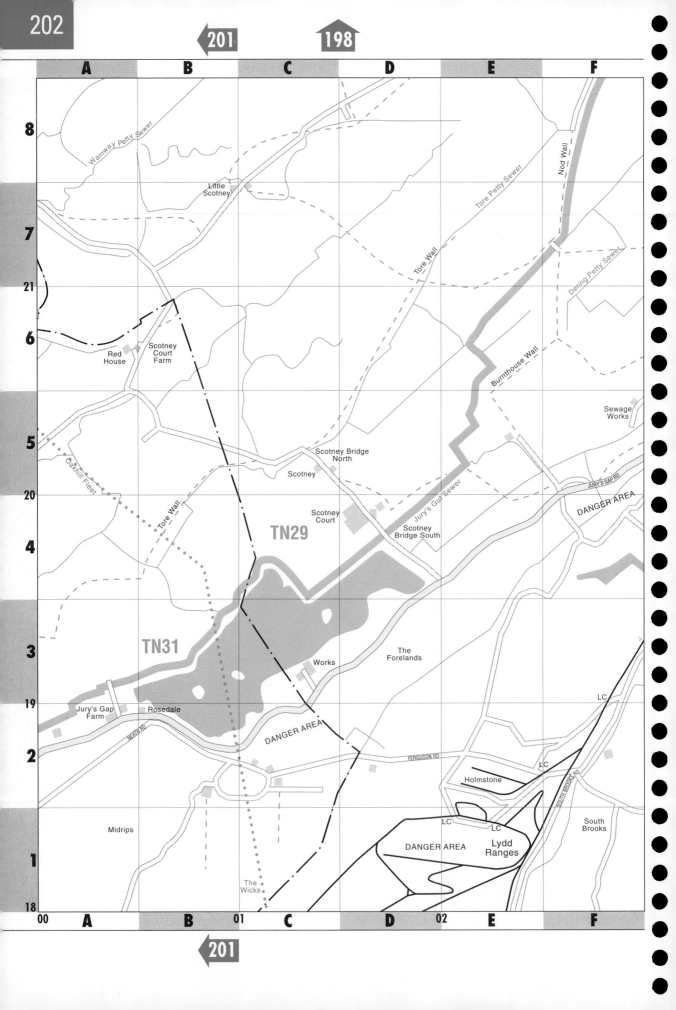

201
198

A B C D E F

8

7

21

6

Wainway Petty Sewer

Little Scotney

Tore Petty Sewer

Nod Wall

Tore Wall

Dering Petty Sewer

Red House

Scotney Court Farm

Burnthouse Wall

Sewage Works

5

20

4

Oakhill Fleet

Tore Wall

Scotney Bridge North

Scotney

Scotney Court

Scotney Bridge South

Jury's Gut Sewer

JURY'S GAP RD

DANGER AREA

TN29

3

19

2

1

18

TN31

Works

The Forelands

LC

Jury's Gap Farm

Rosedale

NEATH RD

DANGER AREA

FERGUSON RD

LC

Holmstone

SOUTH BROOKS RD

LC

Midrips

LC LC

DANGER AREA

Lydd Ranges

South Brooks

The Wicks

199
204

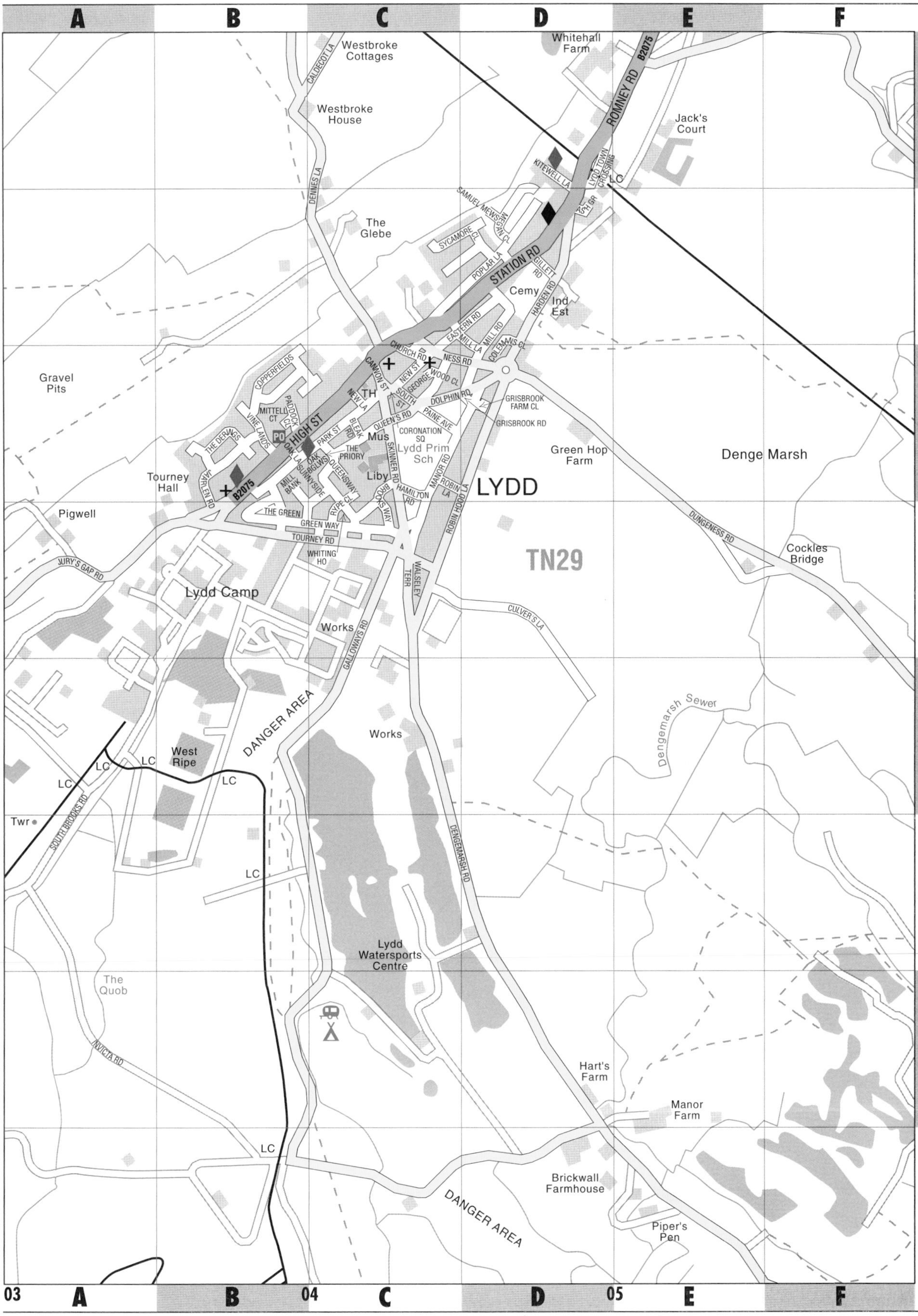
A
B
C
D
E
F
Westbroke Cottages
Whitehall Farm
B2075
ROMNEY RD
CALDECOT LA
Westbroke House
Jack's Court
KITEWELL LA
LYDD TOWN CROSSING
LC
DENNES LA
SAMUEL MEWS
The Glebe
SYCAMORE CL
POPLAR LA
STATION RD
GILLETT RD
Cemy
HARDEN RD
Ind Est
EASTERN RD
MILL LA
MILL RD
COLEMAN'S CL
CHURCH RD
NESS RD
CANNON ST
NEW ST
ST GEORGE
WOOD CL
COPPERFIELDS
Gravel Pits
TH
NEW LA
SOUTH ST
DOLPHIN RD
GRISBROOK FARM CL
GRISBROOK RD
MITTELL CT
PADDOCK CL
QUEEN'S RD
PAINE AVE
VINE LANDS
HIGH ST
CORONATION SQ
THE DERINGS
PO
PARK ST
BLEAK RD
Mus
Lydd Prim Sch
Green Hop Farm
Denge Marsh
THE PRIORY
Tourney Hall
OAK LA
OAK BGLWS
SKINNER RD
MANOR RD
QUEENSWAY
Liby
ROBIN LA
ROBIN HOOD LA
LYDD
JARLEN RD
B2075
MILL BANK
SUNNYSIDE
HAMILTON RD
BROOKS WAY
Pigwell
RYPE CL
THE GREEN
GREEN WAY
TOURNEY RD
DUNGENESS RD
TN29
Cockles Bridge
WHITING HO
JURY'S GAP RD
WALSELEY TERR
Lydd Camp
CULVER'S LA
Works
GALLOWAYS RD
DANGER AREA
Dengemarsh Sewer
Works
West Ripe
LC
LC
LC
LC
Twr
SOUTH BROOKS RD
DENGEMARSH RD
LC
Lydd Watersports Centre
The Quob
INVICTA RD
Hart's Farm
Manor Farm
LC
Brickwall Farmhouse
DANGER AREA
Piper's Pen
8
7
21
6
5
20
4
3
19
2
1
18
03
04
05

204

203

200

A B C D E F

8

TN28

Romney Sands
Holiday Village

LC

Romney Sands

Caravan
Park

1
2
3

LA ROCCO 1
LA TAUSCO 2
LA GALAMINA 3

BEACHMONT CL

PRIOR RD

CHANNON RD

Mockmill Sewer

Lydd
Airport

7

DERVILLE RD

WALLER RD

LEONARD RD

THE PARADE

COLEVILLE CRES

BEATRICE
MEWS

21

HULL RD

TOBY RD

LCs

P

6

The Ship
(PH)

TAYLOR RD

FORT CL

Lade

RYE FORT CRES

LADE FORT
COTTS

LC

Romney, Hythe & Dymchurch Railway

LYDDS CL

WILLIAMSON RD

SAXTON RD

PLEASANCE RD N

COAST DR

5

20

Works

Gravel
Pits

Gravel
Pits

4

Boulderwall
Farm

TN29

Works

PLEASANCE ROAD CENTRAL

3

DUNGENESS RD

KERTON RD

Lydd-on-Sea

19

2

PLEASANCE RD

Mast

BATTERY RD

Denge
Marsh

Coastguard
Cottages

1

Walkers Outland
(RSPB Reserve)

18

06 A B 07 C D 08 E F

203

205

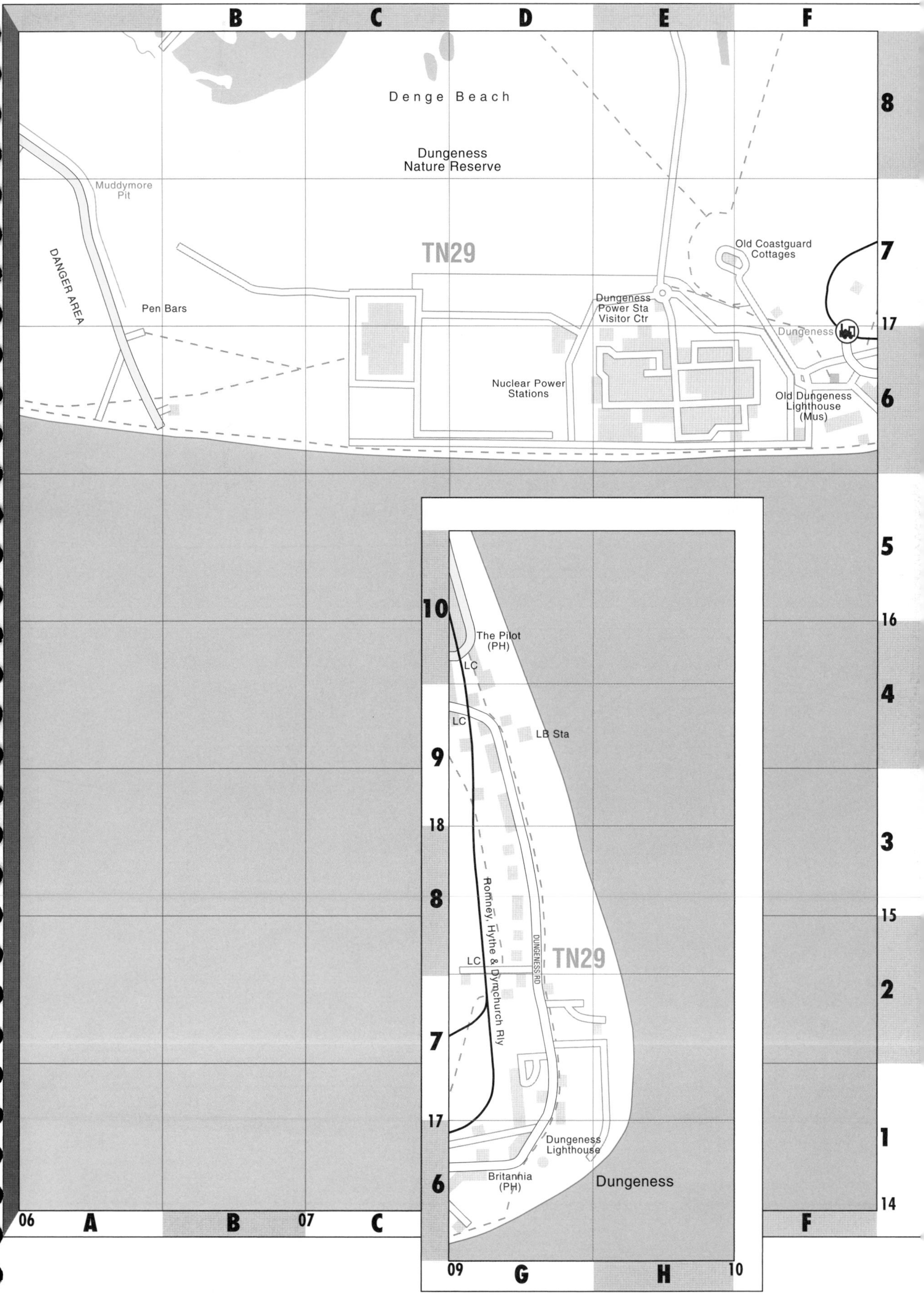

B C D E F

8

Denge Beach

Dungeness
Nature Reserve

Muddymore
Pit

7

DANGER AREA

TN29

Old Coastguard
Cottages

Dungeness
Power Sta
Visitor Ctr

17

Pen Bars

Dungeness

Nuclear Power
Stations

6

Old Dungeness
Lighthouse
(Mus)

5

10

16

The Pilot
(PH)

LC

4

LC

9

LB Sta

18

8

15

Romney, Hythe & Dymchurch Rly

DUNGENESS RD

TN29

3

LC

7

2

17

Dungeness
Lighthouse

1

6

Britannia
(PH)

Dungeness

14

06   A   B   07   C   F

09   G   H   10

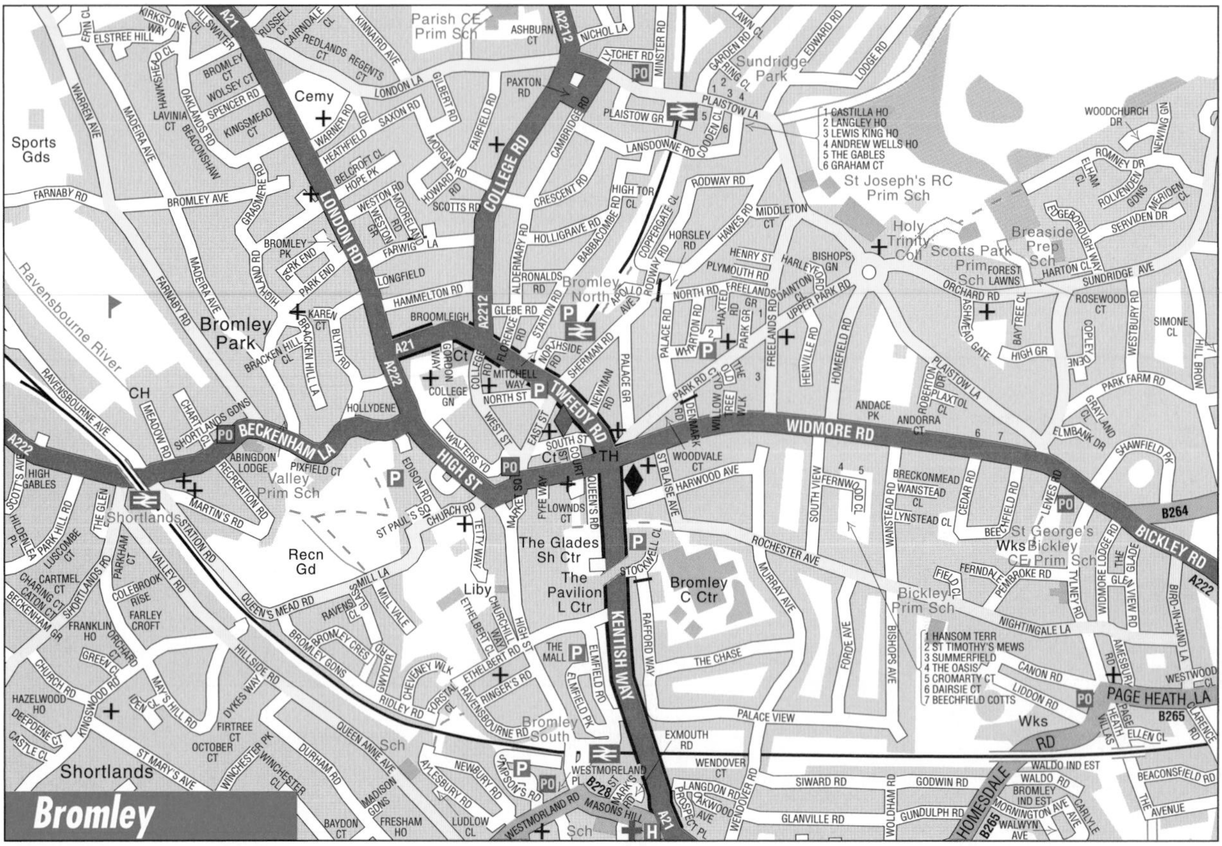
Parish CE Prim Sch
Sundridge Park
Cemy
Sports Gds
1 CASTILLA HO
2 LANGLEY HO
3 LEWIS KING HO
4 ANDREW WELLS HO
5 THE GABLES
6 GRAHAM CT
St Joseph's RC Prim Sch
Holy Trinity Coll
Scotts Park Prim Sch
Breaside Prep Sch
Bromley North
Bromley Park
Ravensbourne River
CH
LONDON RD
COLLEGE RD
HIGH ST
TWEEDY RD
WIDMORE RD
BECKENHAM LA
BICKLEY RD
KENTISH WAY
TH
Valley Prim Sch
Shortlands
Recn Gd
The Glades Sh Ctr
The Pavilion L Ctr
Liby
Bromley C Ctr
St George's Bickley CE Prim Sch
Wks
Bickley Prim Sch
1 HANSOM TERR
2 ST TIMOTHY'S MEWS
3 SUMMERFIELD
4 THE OASIS
5 CROMARTY CT
6 DAIRSIE CT
7 BEECHFIELD COTTS
PAGE HEATH LA
Bromley South
Sch
HOMESDALE RD
FARNABY RD
BROMLEY AVE
MASONS HILL
WESTMORELAND RD
PALACE VIEW
GODWIN RD
GLANVILLE RD
QUEEN ANNE AVE
ROCHESTER AVE
NIGHTINGALE LA
A21
A222
A2212
B228
B264
B265
Bromley

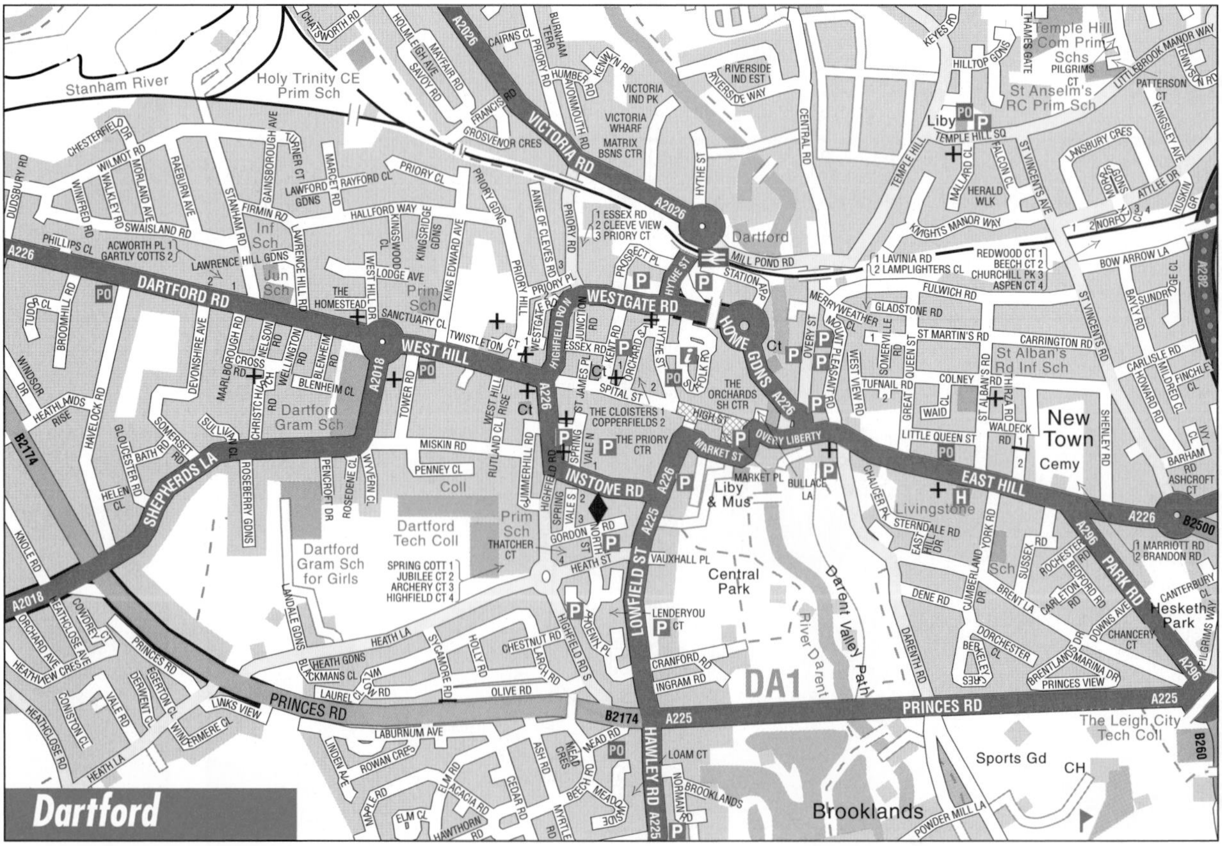
Stanham River
Holy Trinity CE Prim Sch
VICTORIA RD
VICTORIA IND PK
VICTORIA WHARF
MATRIX BSNS CTR
RIVERSIDE IND EST
Temple Hill Com Prim Schs
St Anselm's RC Prim Sch
Liby
1 ESSEX RD
2 CLEEVE VIEW
3 PRIORY CT
Dartford
Inf Sch
Jun Sch
Prim Sch
DARTFORD RD
WEST HILL
WESTGATE RD
HOME GDNS
1 LAVINIA RD
2 LAMPLIGHTERS CL
REDWOOD CT 1
BEECH CT 2
CHURCHILL PK 3
ASPEN CT 4
St Alban's Rd Inf Sch
New Town
Cemy
Dartford Gram Sch
THE CLOISTERS 1
COPPERFIELDS 2
THE PRIORY CTR
THE ORCHARDS SH CTR
OVERY LIBERTY
EAST HILL
SHEPHERDS LA
INSTONE RD
Coll
Dartford Tech Coll
Liby & Mus
Livingstone
Dartford Gram Sch for Girls
SPRING COTT 1
JUBILEE CT 2
ARCHERY CT 3
HIGHFIELD CT 4
Central Park
Darent Valley Path
River Darent
DA1
PARK RD
Hesketh Park
1 MARRIOTT RD
2 BRANDON RD
PRINCES RD
LOWFIELD ST
HAWLEY RD
The Leigh City Tech Coll
Sports Gd
CH
Brooklands
POWDER MILL LA
A226
A2026
A2018
A225
A296
A282
B2174
B2500
B260
Dartford

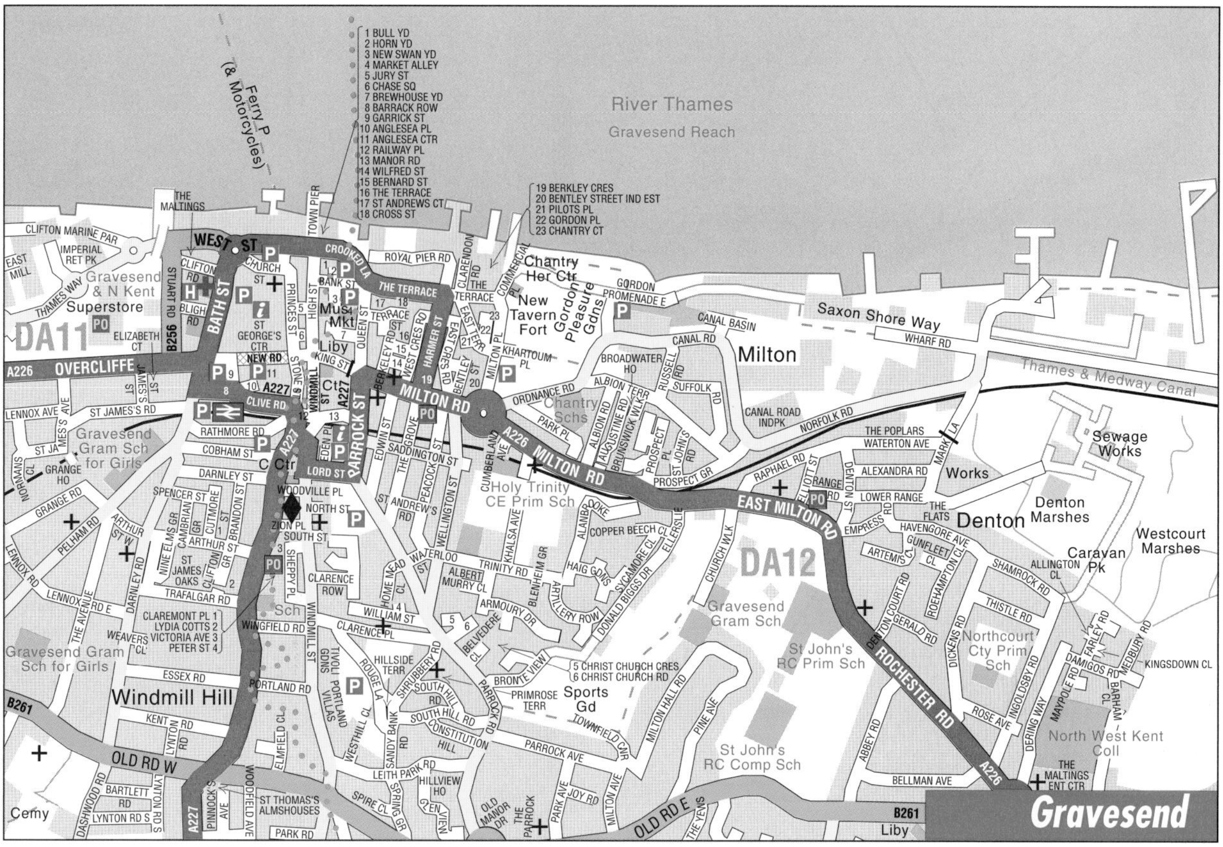
Gravesend
River Thames
Gravesend Reach
Ferry P (& Motorcycles)
1 BULL YD
2 HORN YD
3 NEW SWAN YD
4 MARKET ALLEY
5 JURY ST
6 CHASE SQ
7 BREWHOUSE YD
8 BARRACK ROW
9 GARRICK ST
10 ANGLESEA PL
11 ANGLESEA CTR
12 RAILWAY PL
13 MANOR RD
14 WILFRED ST
15 BERNARD ST
16 THE TERRACE
17 ST ANDREWS CT
18 CROSS ST
19 BERKLEY CRES
20 BENTLEY STREET IND EST
21 PILOTS PL
22 GORDON PL
23 CHANTRY CT
5 CHRIST CHURCH CRES
6 CHRIST CHURCH RD
CLAREMONT PL 1
LYDIA COTTS 2
VICTORIA AVE 3
PETER ST 4
DA11
DA12
Gravesend & N Kent
Superstore
Saxon Shore Way
Thames & Medway Canal
Milton
Denton
Denton Marshes
Westcourt Marshes
Sewage Works
Works
Chantry Her Ctr
New Tavern Fort
Gordon Pleasure Gdns
Chantry Schs
Holy Trinity CE Prim Sch
Gravesend Gram Sch
Gravesend Gram Sch for Girls
St John's RC Prim Sch
St John's RC Comp Sch
Northcourt Cty Prim Sch
North West Kent Coll
Caravan Pk
Sports Gd
Windmill Hill
C Ctr
Mus Mkt
Liby
Cemy
OVERCLIFFE
MILTON RD
EAST MILTON RD
ROCHESTER RD
OLD RD W
OLD RD E
WEST ST
BATH ST
PARROCK ST
CLIVE RD
THE TERRACE
CROOKED LA
HARMER ST
A226
A227
B261
B256

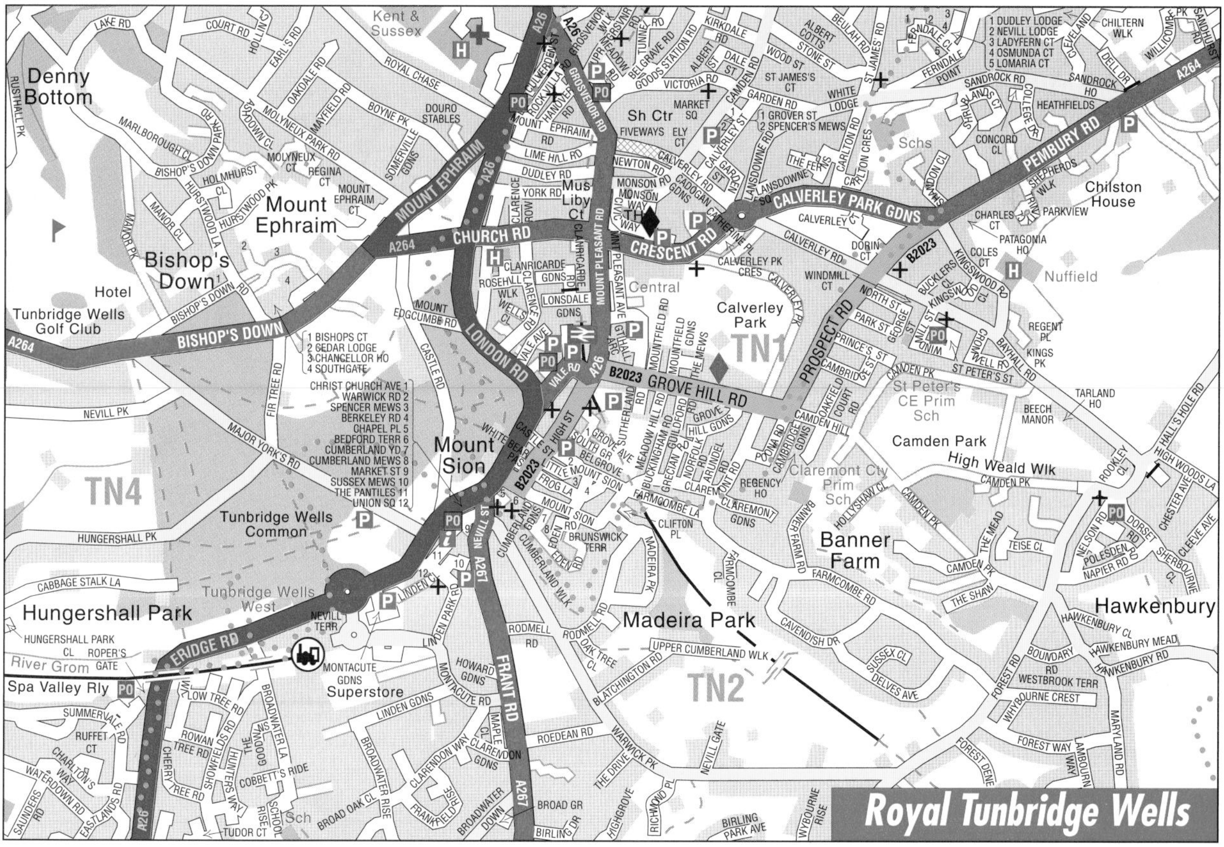
Royal Tunbridge Wells
1 DUDLEY LODGE
2 NEVILL LODGE
3 LADYFERN CT
4 OSMUNDA CT
5 LOMARIA CT
1 GROVER ST
2 SPENCER'S MEWS
1 BISHOPS CT
2 CEDAR LODGE
3 CHANCELLOR HO
4 SOUTHGATE
CHRIST CHURCH AVE 1
WARWICK RD 2
SPENCER MEWS 3
BERKELEY RD 4
CHAPEL PL 5
BEDFORD TERR 6
CUMBERLAND YD 7
CUMBERLAND MEWS 8
MARKET ST 9
SUSSEX MEWS 10
THE PANTILES 11
UNION SQ 12
TN1
TN2
TN4
Denny Bottom
Mount Ephraim
Bishop's Down
Hotel
Tunbridge Wells Golf Club
Kent & Sussex
Sh Ctr
Central
Calverley Park
Mount Sion
Tunbridge Wells Common
Tunbridge Wells West
Hungershall Park
River Grom
Spa Valley Rly
Superstore
Madeira Park
Banner Farm
Camden Park
High Weald Wlk
Hawkenbury
Chilston House
Nuffield
St Peter's CE Prim Sch
Claremont Cty Prim Sch
MOUNT EPHRAIM
CHURCH RD
BISHOP'S DOWN
LONDON RD
CRESCENT RD
CALVERLEY PARK GDNS
PEMBURY RD
GROVE HILL RD
PROSPECT RD
ERIDGE RD
FRANT RD
NEVILL ST
A26
A264
A267
B2023

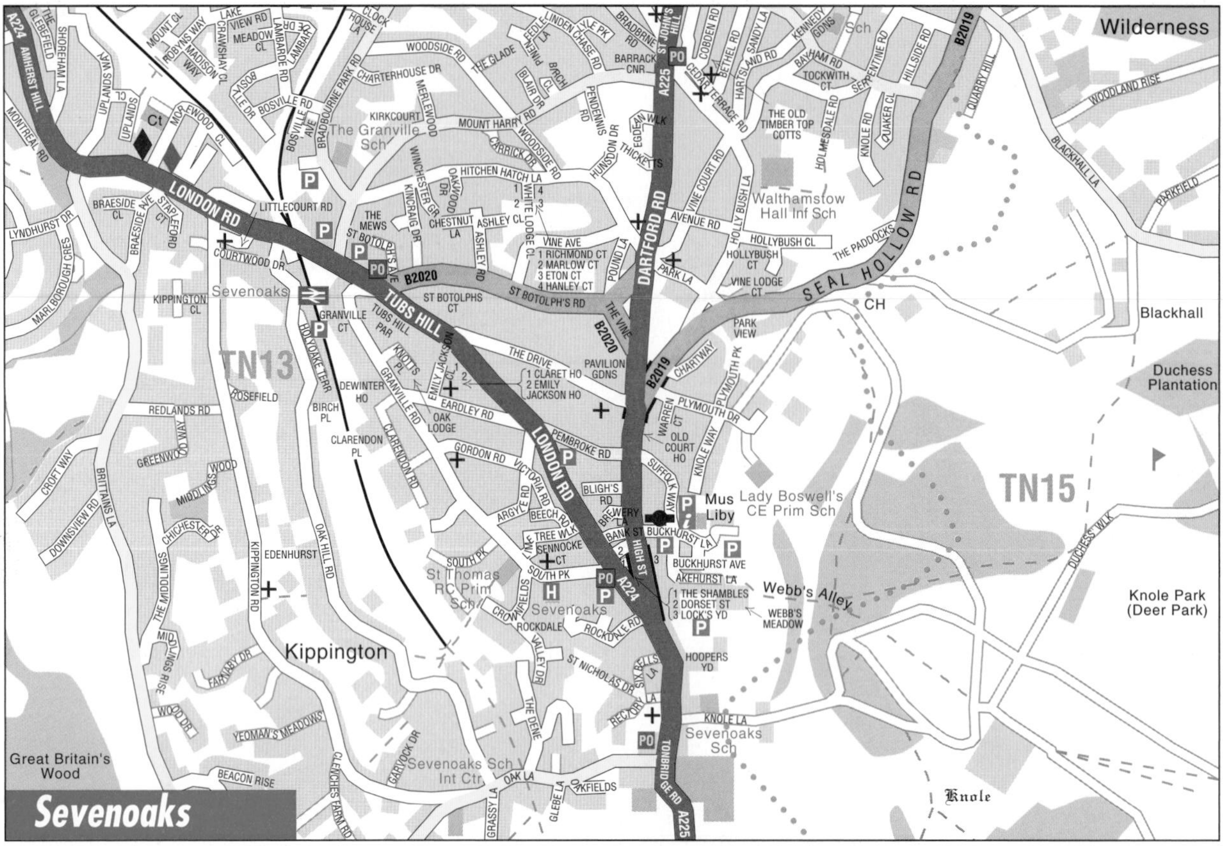
Sevenoaks
Wilderness
TN13
TN15
London Rd
Tubs Hill
Dartford Rd
Seal Hollow Rd
St Botolph's Rd
B2020
B2019
A224
A225
High St
Tonbridge Rd
Knole La
Kippington
Kippington Rd
Oak Hill Rd
Sevenoaks
The Granville Sch
Walthamstow Hall Inf Sch
Lady Boswell's CE Prim Sch
Mus Liby
St Thomas RC Prim Sch
Sevenoaks Sch
Sevenoaks Sch Int Ctr
Webb's Alley
Blackhall
Duchess Plantation
Knole Park (Deer Park)
Great Britain's Wood
Knole

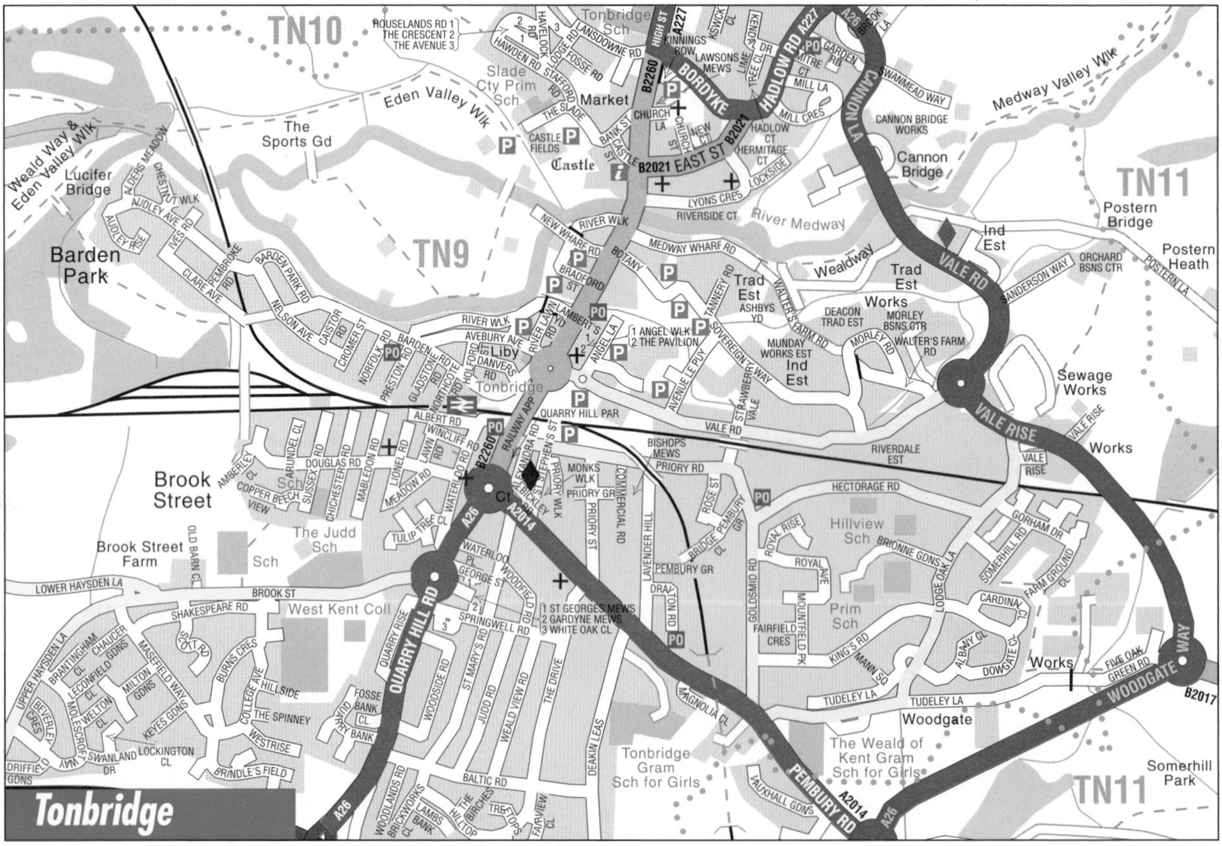
Tonbridge
TN10
TN9
TN11
Tonbridge Sch
Slade Cty Prim Sch
Market
Castle
East St
Bordyke
Hadlow Rd
Cannon La
Cannon Bridge
River Medway
Eden Valley Wlk
Medway Valley Wlk
Weald Way & Eden Valley Wlk
The Sports Gd
Lucifer Bridge
Barden Park
Postern Bridge
Postern Heath
Vale Rd
Vale Rise
Sewage Works
Brook Street
Brook Street Farm
The Judd Sch
West Kent Coll
Quarry Hill Rd
Pembury Rd
Woodgate Way
Tudeley La
Woodgate
Hillview Sch
The Weald of Kent Gram Sch for Girls
Tonbridge Gram Sch for Girls
Somerhill Park
A26
A2014
B2017
B2260
A227
B2021

Index

Archway Ct **4** Medway ME2.........**9** B8

Place name
May be abbreviated on the map

Location number
Present when a number indicates the place's position in a crowded area of mapping

Locality, town or village
Shown when more than one place has the same name

Postcode district
District for the indexed place

Page and grid square
Page number and grid reference for the standard mapping

Public and commercial buildings are highlighted in magenta   **Places of interest** are highlighted in blue with a star★

Abbreviations used in the index

App	**Approach**	Cl	**Close**	Espl	**Esplanade**	Orch	**Orchard**	Sq	**Square**
Arc	**Arcade**	Comm	**Common**	Est	**Estate**	Par	**Parade**	Strs	**Stairs**
Ave	**Avenue**	Cnr	**Corner**	Gdns	**Gardens**	Pk	**Park**	Stps	**Steps**
Bvd	**Boulevard**	Cotts	**Cottages**	Gn	**Green**	Pas	**Passage**	St	**Street, Saint**
Bldgs	**Buildings**	Ct	**Court**	Gr	**Grove**	Pl	**Place**	Terr	**Terrace**
Bglws	**Bungalows**	Ctyd	**Courtyard**	Hts	**Heights**	Prec	**Precinct**	Trad	**Trading Est**
Bsns Ctr	**Business Centre**	Cres	**Crescent**	Ind Est	**Industrial Estate**	Prom	**Promenade**	Wlk	**Walk**
Bsns Pk	**Business Park**	Dr	**Drive**	Intc	**Interchange**	Ret Pk	**Retail Park**	W	**West**
Cswy	**Causeway**	Dro	**Drove**	Junc	**Junction**	Rd	**Road**	Yd	**Yard**
Ctr	**Centre**	E	**East**	La	**Lane**	Rdbt	**Roundabout**		
Cir	**Circus**	Emb	**Embankment**	N	**North**	S	**South**		

Index of localities, towns and villages

Acol 27 B3	Chillenden 113 F8	Hernhill 64 B6	Otham 98 A6	Stockbury 56 D8
Adisham 112 C8	Chislet 47 A5	Hersden 46 E1	Park Wood 97 E5	Stone in Oxney 189 C3
Aldington 173 A6	Church Hougham 165 B5	High Halden 167 A6	Patrixbourne 89 B3	Stourmouth 48 D1
Alkham 147 C1	Cliffs End 51 C2	Hoath 46 E5	Pedlinge 175 D4	Stowting 160 A6
Appledore 190 A7	Coldred 131 A3	Hollingbourne 77 E2	Pested 105 B4	Stubb's Cross 155 E2
Ash 71 C2	Conyer 38 E6	Hothfield 138 A6	Petham 109 A2	Sturry 67 F4
Ashford 139 A1	Coxheath 96 A2	Hythe 176 A1	Platt's Heath 100 C1	Sutton 133 A6
Aylesford 53 A1	Daniel's Water 154 E6	Ickham 69 C1	Pluckley 136 C4	Temple Ewell 148 C4
Aylesham 112 E4	Dargate 64 D8	Ivychurch 192 D4	Postling 160 F2	Tenterden 179 E7
Barham 111 E2	Deal 117 A1	Iwade 14 C2	Potter's Forstal 118 B2	Teynham 38 A4
Bayfield 61 B3	Densole 163 A7	Kearsney 148 D4	Potters Corner 138 E7	The Quarries 97 B4
Bekesbourne 89 C4	Denton 129 A1	Kenardington 182 A5	Pratling Street 53 B4	Throwley 82 A4
Bethersden 153 A2	Detling 55 A1	Kingsdown 134 B5	Preston 70 B5	Throwley Forstal 82 C7
Biddenden Green 135 B2	Doddington 80 D7	Kingsnorth 156 A3	Queenborough 3 A4	Thurnham 76 D1
Birchington 26 D8	Dover 166 A6	Kingston 111 B1	Ram Lane 120 F1	Tilmanstone 115 A2
Bishopsbourne 111 C5	Dunkirk 64 E2	Kingswood 99 A1	Ramsgate 52 A7	Tyler Hill 66 E6
Blean 66 A6	Dymchurch 195 B6	Kit's Coty 53 C7	Reculver 24 B5	Upchurch 12 D2
Borden 36 A2	East Farleigh 96 A7	Langley Heath 98 C5	Rhodes Minnis 144 A3	Upstreet 47 D2
Bossingham 127 A7	East Langdon 133 A1	Leeds 99 A6	Ringwould 133 D4	Waltham 125 F5
Boughton Aluph 123 A4	East Studdal 132 B6	Lenham 101 B7	Ripple 116 D1	Warden 6 A6
Boughton Lees 122 E3	Eastchurch 5 D1	Lenham Heath 119 B8	River 148 D1	Warmlake 98 E1
Boughton Monchelsea .97 B2	Eastling 81 E6	Leysdown-on-S 6 C1	Rochester 9 A2	Warren Street 102 D7
Boughton Street 64 A3	Eastry 93 A2	Littlebourne 89 C8	Rodmersham 59 B7	Waterham 42 D2
Boxley 54 C2	Eccles 53 A6	Littlestone-on-S 200 D3	Rough Common 66 A2	West Hougham 164 F5
Boyden Gate 47 C7	Egerton 118 E1	Loose 96 E2	Ruckinge 183 F6	West Hythe 175 B1
Brabourne 159 C8	Egerton Forstal 118 C1	Lower Halstow 13 B2	Rushenden 2 F3	West Minster 3 A8
Brabourne Lees 158 D5	Elham 144 E3	Lower Hardres 110 A3	St Margaret's at Cliffe .151 A4	Westbere 68 C7
Bramling 90 E6	Elvington 114 B1	Lydd 203 A2	St Mary in the Marsh . .194 B4	Westenhanger 175 B6
Brattle 181 C7	Etchinghill 161 D3	Lydd-on-S 204 E6	St Mary's Bay 195 A5	Westfield Sole 54 B7
Bredgar 58 A5	Eyhorne Street 77 B2	Lydden 28 C4	St Michaels 167 C2	Westgate-on-S 27 D6
Bredhurst 33 A1	Eythorne 131 B8	Lyminge 161 C6	St Nicholas at Wade . . .25 E2	Westmarsh 71 D6
Brenzett 192 A3	Faversham 62 A4	Lympne 175 A3	Sandway 101 F4	Westwell 121 B4
Bridge 89 A1	Finglesham 116 A7	Lynsted 60 A6	Sandwich 73 A1	Whitfield 149 A5
Broad Oak 67 D7	Five Wents 98 D1	Maidstone 75 B4	Sarre 48 E7	Whitstable 20 C1
Broad Street 77 A6	Folkestone 178 A3	Manston 28 D1	Sellindge 159 B1	Wichling 80 B4
Broadstairs 30 A1	Fordwich 68 A3	Margate 7 E1	Selling 84 A6	Wickhambreaux 69 C1
Bromley Green 170 E5	Gillingham 10 A1	Martin Mill 133 B2	Sevington 157 A4	Wingham 91 A4
Brook 141 A5	Godmersham 107 B2	Mersham 157 C4	Shadoxhurst 170 A7	Wittersham 188 D4
Brookland 197 C6	Goodnestone 91 D2	Milstead 58 E2	Sheerness 1 B1	Womenswold 112 C2
Burham 53 A8	Great Chart 138 C1	Minster (Sheppey) 4 A4	Sheldwich 83 C4	Woodchurch 169 A2
Burmarsh 186 C3	Great Mongeham 116 C3	Minster (Thanet) 50 B5	Shepherdswell 130 D4	Woodnesborough 93 B5
Camber 201 A1	Greatstone-on-S 200 D1	Molash 105 F4	Shottenden 84 D8	Woodside Green 101 E8
Canterbury 87 B6	Guston 149 E4	Monkton 49 A8	Silver Hill 76 F1	Woolage Green 129 D6
Capel-le-F 164 B2	Halfway Houses 3 C5	New Romney 200 A6	Silver Street 57 F5	Woolage Village 112 E1
Challock 105 A1	Hamstreet 183 A7	Newchurch 184 E3	Sittingbourne 36 B5	Wormshill 79 A7
Charing 120 A6	Harbledown 87 A7	Newington 35 B6	Smarden 135 A1	Worth 94 A4
Charing Heath 119 C7	Harrietsham 100 B5	Newnham 81 C8	Smeeth 158 B3	Wye 123 D3
Chart Sutton 98 B1	Hartlip 34 C3	Nonington 113 C5	Snargate 191 B8	Yelsted 34 A1
Chartham 86 B2	Hastingleigh 142 B6	Northbourne 116 A5	Stalisfield Green 103 A3	Yorklets 42 E2
Chatham 10 A1	Hawkinge 163 A2	Oare 40 B2	Stanford 160 B1	
Chestnut Street 35 D4	Herne 46 A8	Old Romney 199 A7	Staple 92 A4	
Chilham 107 B7	Herne Bay 22 A1	Old Wives Lees 85 B3	Stelling Minnis 126 D4	

Ashley Cl
Halfway Houses ME12 3 C5
Ramsgate CT12 29 B2
Ashley Dr CT5 43 A7
Ashley Ho CT19 177 E6
Ashley Mill Cotts CT19 177 E7
Ashley Rd ME8 11 C2
Ashmead Cl ME5 32 C3
Ashtead Dr ME9 37 D2
Ashton Cl CT14 116 D4
Ashton Ct 4 CT10 29 E5
Ashton Mews 20 CT10 30 B4
Ashtree Ho ME10 37 B3
Ashtrees CT6 23 B3
Ashurst Ave CT5 43 C6
Ashurst Gdns CT9 8 E3
Ashurst Rd ME14 75 C5
Askes Ct TN23 155 D8
Aspen Cl TN29 194 F3
Aspen Ho 5 CT20 178 D4
Aspen Rd Chartham CT4 86 E1
Herne CT6 45 E7
Aspen Way 2 ME5 31 E4
Aspian Dr ME17 96 D3
Asquith Rd ME8 33 C6
Association Wlk ME1 31 C7
Astley Ave CT16 149 C2
Astley Ct CT16 149 C2
Astley St ME14 75 A4
Aston Cl ME5 32 A2
Astor Ave CT17 166 B8
Astor Dr CT14 117 C5
Astor of Hever Com Sch The ME16 74 C3
Astor Rd CT10 29 F8
Astor Sch CT17 166 A8
Astrid Rd CT14 117 A2
Athelstan Gn ME17 77 C2
Athelstan Pl CT14 117 C8
Athelstan Rd
Canterbury CT1 87 C5
Chatham ME4 9 F2
Faversham ME13 62 C6
Folkestone CT19 178 D7
Margate CT9 8 A3
Athol Pl ME13 62 A8
Athol Rd Ashford TN23 155 F7
Whitstable CT5 20 F2
Athol Terr CT16 166 F8
Atkinson Wlk TN24 139 F5
Atlanta Ct ME4 9 D3
Attlee Ave CT3 112 E5
Attlee Way ME10 36 E8
Atwater Ct ME17 101 D5
Aubretia Wlk ME10 37 A3
Auckland Ave CT12 52 A8
Auckland Cres CT16 149 C3
Auckland Dr ME10 36 C3
Auckland House 10 ME15 97 E5
Audley Ave
Gillingham ME7 10 E1
Margate CT9 7 E1
Audley Cl ME16 74 B5
Audley Rd CT20 177 F5
Auger Cl ME9 34 E5
Augusta Cl 1 ME7 10 C7
Augusta Gdns CT20 178 C4
Augusta Pl 12 CT11 52 F7
Augusta Rd CT11 52 F7
Augustine Rd
Minster (Sheppey) ME12 4 B8
Minster (Thanet) CT12 50 B6
Augustus Wlk TN23 155 F5
Austell Manor 5 ME7 10 C6
Austens Orch 14 TN30 179 A7
Austin Ave CT6 21 F4
Austin Cl Gillingham ME5 10 E2
Sittingbourne ME10 37 A8
Austin Rd TN23 156 B6
Austins La 4 CT13 73 A1
Autumn Glade ME5 54 D8
Avebury Ave CT11 52 G8
Aveling Ct 2 ME2 9 B7
Avent Wlk ME9 37 E2
Avenue Gdns CT9 8 C3
Avenue of Remembrance ME10 36 F3
Avenue Rd Dover CT16 149 C1
Herne Bay CT6 22 E5
Ramsgate CT11 52 F7
Avenue The Deal CT14 117 C7
Hersden CT3 46 E1
Hythe CT21 176 C2
Kingsdown CT14 134 D4
Margate CT9 8 A1
St Margaret's at Cliffe CT15 150 F6
Temple Ewell CT16 148 E5
Averenches Rd ME14 75 F5
Avereng Gdns CT19 178 B6
Avereng Rd CT19 178 B6
Avery Cl ME15 74 F1
Avery La ME15, ME17 98 D6
Aviation Ct ME12 5 E3
Aviemore Gdns ME14 75 F4
Avington Cl ME15 74 F1
Avocet Wlk ME5 32 D2
Avon Cl CT1 88 C8
Avondale Cl CT5 44 A8
Avondale Rd
Capel-le-F CT18 164 C2
Gillingham ME7 10 D5
Axford Ct ME8 34 A8
Aycliffe Com Prim Sch CT17 166 A4
Aylesbury Rd TN25 139 B7
Aylesford Cres ME8 11 B4
Aylesford Pl TN24 156 E7
Aylesham Cnr CT3 112 D3
Aylesham Prim Sch CT3 112 E5
Aylesham Rd CT15,CT3 113 A4
Aylesham Sta CT3 113 A5
Aylewyn Gn ME10 36 F8
Aynsley Ct 1 CT13 73 A1
Ayton Rd CT11 52 C6

B

Babs Oak Hill CT2 68 B7
Back La
6 Faversham ME13 62 D7
Maidstone ME17 97 E1
Minster (Sheppey) ME12 4 D6
Back Rd W CT16 166 G8
Back St
Langley Heath ME17 98 E6
Ringwould CT14 133 F5
Backfields ME1 9 B4
Bad Munstereifel Rd TN23,TN24 156 D5
Baddlesmere Rd CT5 21 A2
Baden Rd ME7 10 D7
Bader Cres ME5 32 A7
Badger Rd ME5 32 C1
Badgers Bridge CT18 161 D4
Badgers Cl CT2 66 A7
Badgers Ct TN23 156 A7
Badgers Oak TN23 155 D8
Badgers Rise Deal CT14 134 C8
River CT17 148 D3
Badlesmere Cl TN23 155 E6
Baffin Cl ME4 9 F2
Bagham La CT4 107 D8
Bagham Rd CT4 107 C8
Bagshill Rd ME13 83 A3
Bailey Dr ME7 11 A1
Bailey Fields TN26 153 E4
Baileys Field TN23 138 F1
Baird's Hill CT10 29 F6
Bairdsley Cl CT10 29 F6
Bakenham Ho 1 ME1 9 C1
Baker Cl ME9 38 C2
Baker Rd CT19 177 E6
Baker St ME1 9 C3
Baker's La CT4 86 D2
Baker's Wlk ME1 9 C6
Bakers Cl CT2 87 C7
Balas Dr ME10 36 C7
Balcomb Cres CT9 29 C8
Baldric Rd CT20 177 F5
Baldwin Rd
Greatstone-on-S TN28 200 D1
Minster (Sheppey) ME12 4 D7
Baldwin Terr CT19 178 D6
Balfour Ct CT20 178 B3
Balfour Inf Sch ME1 9 E1
Balfour Jun Sch ME4 9 E2
Balfour Rd Chatham ME4 9 E2
Deal CT14 117 C2
Dover CT16 149 C1
Baliol Rd CT5 20 E2
Ball La TN24 139 F7
Ballard Ind Est ME5 54 C8
Ballard Rd TN28 200 D1
Ballens Rd ME5 32 C3
Balliemoor Ct CT11 29 F1
Balliol Rd CT10 29 F8
Balmer Cl ME8 33 D7
Balmoral House 10 ME15 97 F5
Balmoral Pl 10 CT11 52 F7
Balmoral Rd
Gillingham ME7 10 D5
Kingsdown CT14 134 C6
4 Margate CT9 28 B8
Balmoral Terr ME10 36 D4
Bamford Way CT14 117 C4
Bank Cotts ME17 77 E3
Bank Ho TN28 200 C6
Bank Rd TN25 172 E8
Bank Side TN26 183 A8
Bank St Ashford TN23 139 B2
Chatham ME4 10 B3
Faversham ME13 62 C7
Herne Bay CT6 22 F5
Hythe CT21 176 C2
Maidstone ME14 75 A4
Banks Rd Ashford TN23 156 A7
Rochester ME2 9 C8
Banks The CT10 29 F6
Banks Yd 6 ME10 36 F4
Bankside Canterbury CT1 88 D7
Chatham ME4 32 B8
Banky Fields Cl ME8 12 B1
Banner Way ME12 3 E6
Banning St ME2 9 B8
Banningbrook Ct CT14 117 D4
Bannister Hill ME9 36 B2
Bannister Hos TN26 120 A1
Bannister Rd ME14 75 A7
Bapchild & Tonge CE Prim Sch ME9 37 D3
Barbados Terr 2 ME14 75 A7
Barberry Ave ME5 31 E5
Barcham Ct ME15 96 F5
Barclay Ct CT7 7 C1
Bardell Terr ME1 9 D5
Barden Ct ME14 75 B5
Barfleur Manor 3 ME7 10 A6
Barfreston Cl ME15 74 F2
Barfrestone Rd CT15 114 A1
Bargates TN23 155 E6
Bargrove Rd ME14 75 C5
Barham CE Prim Sch CT4 128 F8
Barham Cl ME15 97 E5
Barham's Mill Rd TN27 118 B3
Barker Rd ME16 74 F3
Barkers Ct ME10 36 D4
Barkis Cl ME1 31 D7
Barler Pl ME11 3 A5
Barley Cl Herne Bay CT6 23 D2
Martin Mill CT15 133 C2
Barley Fields ME14 75 D4
Barleycorn Dr ME8 33 E6
Barleymow Cl ME5 32 C7
Barling Cl ME5 31 D1
Barlow Cl ME8 33 E5
Barn Cl Borden ME9 36 A2
Hoath CT3 46 E5
Yorklets CT5 43 A3
Barn Cres CT9 7 F1
Barn Platt TN23 156 A8
Barn The ME9 36 A2
Barnaby Terr ME1 9 D2
Barnard Ct ME4 10 A2
Barnberry Cl TN23 155 E8
Barncroft Cl ME14 75 F4
Barncroft Dr ME7 32 F4
Barnes Ave CT9 7 F1
Barnes Cl ME13 62 B8
Barnes Ct CT1 87 D6
Barnesende Ct CT13 94 A8
Barnet's La CT2 67 D8
Barnett Ct CT12 29 B1
Barnett Field TN23 155 F8
Barnfield Chatham ME5 32 A8
Herne Bay CT6 22 C2
St Michaels TN30 167 C2
Barnfield Rd
Faversham ME13 62 C8
Folkestone CT19 178 C7
Barnhouse La TN29 198 A8
Barnhurst La CT18 163 A5
Barnhurst Rd ME14 75 A8
Barnsley Cl ME12 1 F2
Barnsole Inf Sch ME7 10 E4
Barnsole Jun Sch ME7 10 E4
Barnsole Rd
Gillingham ME7 10 E3
Staple CT3 92 B5
Barntye Cl CT15 149 E6
Barnwell Pl ME7 10 C5
Barnwood Cl ME1 31 B8
Baron Cl Gillingham ME7 10 E7
Maidstone ME14 75 F5
Barrack Hill CT21 176 A2
Barrack Rd ME4 10 B8
Barrey Rd TN24 157 A6
Barrier Rd ME4 9 F5
Barrington Cl ME5 31 F5
Barrington Cres CT7 27 B7
Barrow Gr ME10 36 D3
Barrow Grove Jun Sch ME10 36 D3
Barrow Hill
Ashford TN23 139 B2
Sellindge TN25 174 D7
Barrow Hill Cotts TN23 139 A2
Barrow Hill Pl 2 TN23 139 B3
Barrow Hill Rise TN25 174 D7
Barrow Hill Terr 1 TN23 139 B3
Barrowfields ME5 32 D1
Barrows Cl CT7 27 A6
Bartholomew Cl CT21 176 B3
Bartholomew La CT21 176 B3
Bartholomew St
6 Dover CT16 149 C1
Hythe CT21 176 B2
Bartlett Cl ME5 32 C1
Bartlett Dr CT5 21 A1
Bartletts Cl ME12 3 C5
Barton Bsns Pk CT1 88 D6
Barton Court Gram Sch CT1 88 B8
Barton Field CT18 161 B7
Barton Hill Dr ME12 4 A5
Barton Jun Sch CT16 149 C2
Barton Mill Ct 2 CT2 66 F1
Barton Mill Rd CT1 67 B2
Barton Rd Canterbury CT1 88 C6
Dover CT16 149 C2
Maidstone ME15 75 A2
Rochester ME2 9 A7
Barton View Terr 2 CT17 149 C1
Barton's Point Coastal Pk* ME12 1 G2
Barville Rd CT15 114 E2
Barwick Rd CT17 148 F1
Bashford Barn La ME9 58 A4
Basil Terr ME15 75 A1
Basing Cl ME15 75 B3
Baskerville TN24 139 B3
Basmere Cl ME14 75 C6
Bassett Cl CT21 176 E4
Bassett Gdns CT21 176 D4
Bassett Rd ME10 36 D4
Bastion Rd CT17 166 C6
Batchelor St ME4 10 A4
Bateman Cnr TN26 153 E6
Bates Cl CT3 91 F6
Bath Ct CT20 178 B3
Bath Hard ME1 9 D5
Bath Mews TN24 156 E6
Bath Pl CT9 7 J2
Bath Rd Ashford TN24 156 E6
Margate CT9 7 J2
Bathurst Cl CT12 29 B1
Bathurst Rd CT20 178 A5
Batteries Cl ME9 60 B8
Batteries Terr ME9 60 B8
Battery Point CT21 177 B2
Battery Rd TN29 204 F2
Battle of Britain Homes 17 CT17 166 D7
Bawden Cl CT2 67 A4
Baxendale Ct TN24 156 D7
Bay Banks ME13 61 E2
Bay Cotts CT15 151 C6
Bay Hill CT15 151 B6
Bay Hill Cl CT15 151 A5
Bay Mus The* CT15 151 B5
Bay View Gdns ME12 6 D2
Bay View Hts CT7 26 D8
Bay View Rd CT10 30 A2
Baye La CT3 69 D1
Bayfield ME13 61 E2
Bayford Rd ME10 37 A4
Bayhill ME13 61 E2
Bayle Ct CT20 178 E4
Bayle St 16 CT20 178 E5
Bayle The CT20 178 E4
Bayswater Dr ME8 33 E4
Bayview Rd
Kingsdown CT14 134 C4
Whitstable CT5 43 D7
Beach Alley 9 CT5 20 D2
Beach App ME12 6 E3
Beach Ave CT7 26 F8
Beach Bank Cvn Pk CT21 187 C7
Beach Flats 2 CT21 176 B2
Beach Ho's CT9 7 G2
Beach House Mews CT8 7 D1
Beach Marine 7 CT20 177 F3
Beach Rd
Dymchurch TN29 187 A4
St Margaret's at Cliffe CT15 151 B5
Westgate-on-S CT8,CT9 7 D1
Beach Rise CT9 7 D1
Beach St Deal CT14 117 D6
Folkestone CT20 178 E4
Herne Bay CT6 22 F5
Sheerness ME12 1 C3
Beach Terr ME12 1 C2
Beach The CT14 117 D3
Beach Wlk CT5 20 E3
Beachborough Rd CT19, CT20 178 A5
Beachfield Lodge ME12 1 D2
Beachmont Cl TN28 204 E8
Beacon Ave CT6 23 B5
Beacon Cl ME8 33 D7
Beacon Hill Chatham ME5 10 D2
Herne Bay CT6 23 B5
Beacon La CT13 93 A6
Beacon Oak Rd TN30 179 B8
Beacon Rd
Broadstairs CT10 29 F7
Chatham ME5 10 C2
Herne Bay CT6 23 A5
Lenham ME17 101 C5
Beacon Terr CT21 177 B2
Beacon Way CT21 174 F3
Beacon Wlk
Herne Bay CT6 23 A5
Tenterden TN30 167 B1
Beacons The ME17 96 C2
Beaconsfield CT5 42 F6
Beaconsfield Ave
Dover CT16 149 C1
Gillingham ME7 10 E5
Beaconsfield Gdns CT10 29 F5
Beaconsfield Rd
Canterbury CT2 66 F2
Chatham ME4 9 F3
Deal CT14 117 D5
Dover CT16 149 C1
Maidstone ME15 74 E2
Sittingbourne ME10 37 C4
Beamont Cl CT12 27 F2
Beams The ME15 75 F1
Bean Cl TN23 138 C1
Beaney's La CT4 84 C1
Bear's La TN23,TN26 137 E3
Bears End Ho TN23 156 B8
Bearsted ME14 76 B5
Bearsted Cl ME8 11 B3
Bearsted Green Bsns Ctr ME14 76 C4
Bearsted Rd ME14 75 E6
Beatrice Mews TN28 204 E7
Beatrice Rd
Capel-le-F CT18 164 C2
Margate CT9 28 E8
Beatty Ave ME7 10 F4
Beatty Cl CT19 178 E8
Beatty Rd Chatham ME1 31 D8
Folkestone CT19 178 D8
Beauchamp Ave CT14 117 A3
Beauchamp Cl TN24 139 E5
Beauchamps La CT15 113 D5
Beaufort Ave CT12 52 B8
Beaufort Ct ME2 9 E6
Beaufort Wlk ME15 97 E4
Beaufoy Rd CT17 149 A1
Beaufoy Terr CT17 148 F1
Beauherne Com Sch CT2 87 D8
Beaulieu Rise ME1 9 D1
Beaulieu Wlk ME16 74 C7
Beaumanor CT6 23 A3
Beaumont Davy Cl ME13 62 C5
Beaumont Rd ME16 74 B2
Beaumont St CT6 22 C4
Beaumont Terr ME13 62 D6
Beauvoir Dr ME10 37 A8
Beauworth Pk ME15 97 E8
Beauxfield CT16 149 A7
Beaver Ct TN23 156 A7
Beaver Green Inf Sch TN23 155 E7
Beaver Ind Est TN23 156 B7
Beaver La Ashford TN23 138 E1
Ashford, Beaver TN23 156 A7
Ashford,Singleton TN23 155 F7
Beaver Rd Ashford TN23 156 B8
Maidstone ME16 74 B7
Beazley Ct TN24 156 D7
Beckenham Dr ME16 74 D7
Becket Ave CT2 66 D1
Becket Cl Ash CT3 71 D2
Deal CT14 117 C8
Whitstable CT5 21 B1
Becket Mews CT2 66 F1
Becket's Cl TN25 142 B6
Beckett St 4 ME13 62 C7
Becketts Terr CT21 176 B4
Becketts Wood CT3 47 E3
Beckley Mews ME5 31 F5
Beckley Pl TN25 175 B8
Beckley Rd ME12 1 F2
Becksbourne Cl ME14 75 A8
Beckwith Gn CT20 177 E5
Beckworth Pl ME16 74 B2
Beddow Way ME20 53 B3
Bede Ho CT14 117 D8
Bedford Ave ME8 11 D1
Bedford Pl ME16 74 E4
Bedford Sq CT12 29 B2
Bedford Way CT7 25 F1
Bedgebury Cl
Chatham ME1 31 D8
Maidstone ME14 75 C6
Bedingfield Way CT18 161 B7
Bedlam Court La CT12 50 C6
Bedlam La TN27 135 A8
Bedson Wlk ME8 12 B1
Bedwin Cl ME1 31 D7
Beech Ave CT4 86 E1
Beech Cl Faversham ME13 62 B7
Folkestone CT19 178 C6
Beech Ct Canterbury CT1 88 A7
Challock TN25 105 A1
Beech Dr Broadstairs CT10 29 D4
Elvington CT15 114 B2
Hothfield TN26 138 A7
Maidstone ME16 74 C5
Beech Gr CT12 51 C5
Beech Green Cl CT15 131 C7
Beech Hill CT4 111 B8
Beech Hurst Cl ME15 75 B2
Beechcroft CT5 21 D1
Beechcroft Gdns CT11 52 F8
Beechen Bank Rd ME5 32 A1
Beeches The ME5 32 A4
Beeching Rd ME5 32 B3
Beechings Gn ME8 11 C3
Beechings Way ME8 11 C3
Beechings Way Ind Ctr ME8 11 B4
Beechmore Dr ME5 32 A2
Beecholme Dr TN24 139 C5
Beechwood Ave
Chatham ME5 10 D2
Deal CT14 117 C5
Sittingbourne ME10 36 E6
Beechwood Cl
St Mary's Bay TN29 194 F3
Whitfield CT16 132 A1
Beechwood Ct
Deal CT14 117 C5
River CT16 148 E4
Beecroft Cl CT2 67 A4
Beer Cart La CT1 87 F8
Beggars Cnr CT3 48 D1
Beggarsbush La TN29 198 D7
Begonia Ave ME8 11 C2
Beke Rd ME8 33 D4
Bekesbourne Hill CT4 89 B5
Bekesbourne La
Bekesbourne CT3,CT4 89 E6
Canterbury CT3 88 F7
Littlebourne CT3 89 F6
Bekesbourne Rd CT4 88 F2
Bekesbourne Sta CT4 89 B5
Belcaire Cl CT21 175 A3
Belfast Ho 14 ME15 97 E7
Belgrave Cl CT11 52 D7
Belgrave Rd Dover CT17 166 B7
Halfway Houses ME12 3 C5
Margate CT9 7 I2
Belinda Ct CT19 178 B7
Bell Chapel Cl TN23 156 C4
Bell Cnr TN29 199 A4
Bell Cotts ME9 13 B3
Bell Cres ME1 53 A8
Bell Farm La ME12 5 A6
Bell Gr CT3 113 A5
Bell La Burham ME1 53 A8
Maidstone ME14 76 A5
Sandwich CT13 73 A1
Westfield Sole ME14 54 B7
Bell Meadow ME15 97 E6
Bell Rd Park Wood ME15 97 E5
Sittingbourne ME10 36 F3
Bell Sh Ctr ME10 36 F4
Bell Way ME17 99 E2
Bell Wood Com Sch ME15 97 E5
Bell Wood Inf Sch ME15 97 E5
Bell's Cl TN30 179 A7
Bell-Davies Dr CT12 28 A1
Belle Friday Cl ME9 38 C2
Belle Vue Rd CT6 23 B5

Cherrygarden La CT15, CT3 113 E7
Cherville La CT3 90 C7
Chervilles ME16 74 A2
Chesham Dr ME8 33 E6
Cheshire Rd
Maidstone,Shepway ME15 97 E7
Maidstone,Willington ME15 75 E2
Chessenden La TN27 135 A1
Chester Ave TN26 153 D5
Chester Rd
Gillingham ME7 10 D2
Westgate-on-S CT8 27 F8
Chestfield & Swalecliffe Sta CT5 21 D2
Chestfield Cl ME8 11 E2
Chestfield Rd CT5 44 C7
Chestnut Ave Blean CT2 66 A7
Chatham ME5 31 F3
Chestnut Cl
Ashford TN23 138 E3
Hythe CT21 187 E8
Tenterden TN30 167 C1
Whitfield CT16 149 A8
Chartham CT4 86 F1
Chestnut Ct ME13 64 A3
Chestnut Dr
Broadstairs CT10 29 D4
Coxheath ME17 96 B3
Herne Bay CT6 22 D3
Kingswood ME17 99 D2
Sturry CT2 68 A7
Worth CT14 94 A4
Chestnut La TN23 156 C4
Chestnut Rd CT17 166 B7
Chestnut St ME9 35 E4
Chestnut Terr CT21 176 A1
Chestnut Wood La ME9 35 E3
Chestnuts The TN25 158 D5
Chevalier Rd CT17 166 A7
Chevening Cl ME5 32 A5
Cheviot Ct CT10 30 B5
Cheviot Gdns ME15 76 A1
Cheviot Way TN24 139 C4
Cheyne Cl ME10 36 F8
Cheyne Mid Sch The ME12 1 E2
Cheyne Rd ME12 5 D3
Chicago Ave ME7 10 F5
Chichester Cl
Ashford TN23 139 B1
Gillingham ME8 34 A8
Chichester Rd
Folkestone CT20 177 E4
Ramsgate CT12 29 B1
Chickfield Gdns [4] ME5 10 C2
Chiddingfold Cl ME12 4 D6
Chiddingstone Cl ME15 97 F6
Chieftain Cl ME7 11 B1
Childgate Rd CT5 42 F2
Childscroft Rd ME8 11 F2
Chilham Ave CT8 27 D7
Chilham Castle & Gdns★ CT4 107 B7
Chilham Cl Chatham ME4 9 E3
West Minst ME12 3 B8
Chilham Ho [1] ME15 97 E8
Chilham Rd
Folkestone CT19 177 E6
Gillingham ME8 11 A3
Maidstone ME16 74 C7
Chilham Sta CT4 107 D8
Chillenden Windmill (dis)★ CT3 91 F1
Chillington St ME14 74 F6
Chilston Rd ME17 101 D5
Chiltern Cl ME15 75 F1
Chiltern End TN24 139 B3
Chilton Ave
Kearsney CT16 148 C4
Sittingbourne ME10 37 A3
Chilton Ct
[14] Folkestone CT20 178 E6
Gillingham ME8 11 E1
Chilton Field CT3 71 D2
Chilton Gdns CT3 71 D2
Chilton La CT11 52 A6
Chilton Pl CT3 71 D2
Chilton Prim Sch CT11 52 A6
Chilton Sq CT3 71 D2
Chilton Way CT17 148 D3
Chimes The
Ashford TN24 139 C3
Rochester ME1 9 C5
Chineham Way CT1 87 F6
Chippendale Cl ME5 31 F1
Chippendale Dr ME17 100 D6
Chipstead Cl ME16 74 D6
Chipstead Rd ME8 33 D4
Chislehurst Cl ME15 97 F6
Chislet CE Prim Sch CT3 47 C5
Chislet Ct CT6 22 E5
Chislet Park Cotts CT3 46 F1
Chislet Wlk ME8 33 D5
Chislett Cl TN25 159 E2
Chisnall Rd CT17 148 E4
Chittenden's La TN29 193 E5
Chitty La CT3 47 D6
Christ Church Cath CT1 88 A8
Christ Church CE High Sch TN23 155 F5
Christ Church CE Jun Sch CT11 52 C6
Christ Church CE Prim Sch CT20 178 C5
Christ Church Coll CT1 88 B8
Christ Church Coll Post Graduate Ctr CT3 67 F1
Christ Church Rd CT20 178 C4
Christchurch Ct
[3] Chatham ME5 10 C2
[1] Dover CT17 166 D7
Christchurch House [11] ME15 97 E5
Christchurch Rd TN23 156 B8
Christchurch Way CT16 149 B3
Christen Way ME15,ME17 97 F3
Christian Ct [3] ME2 9 C8
Christie Cl ME5 32 B6
Christmas St ME7 10 E7
Christopher's Row ME9 60 A3
Chrysler Ave CT6 22 B4
Chunnel Ind Est TN23 139 B1
Church App TN28 200 A6
Church Cl Mersham TN25 157 E3
New Romney TN28 200 B6
Church Cliff CT14 134 D6
Church Cotts
Rodmersham ME9 59 D8
St Michaels TN30 167 B3
Church Court Gr CT10 29 E6
Church Cres ME17 100 F6
Church Ct CT18 161 C6
Church Farm Rd ME9 12 E3
Church Farm Way CT13 93 B6
Church Field TN25 160 B1
Church Gn
Hollingbourne ME17 77 E3
Rochester ME2 9 C8
Church Haven CT14 133 F5
Church Hill
Bethersden TN26 153 D5
Boughton Monchelsea ME17 97 C1
Boughton Street ME13 64 A5
Canterbury CT2 66 C1
Charing Heath ME17,TN27 119 C7
Chatham ME5 10 C2
Chilham CT4 107 B8
Doddington ME9 80 F8
Eythorne CT15 131 C8
High Halden TN26 167 E7
Hythe CT21 176 C2
Kingsnorth TN23 156 B3
Ramsgate CT11 52 E7
Shepherdswell CT15 130 D4
Stockbury ME9 56 F7
Stone in Oxney TN30 189 F3
Sutton CT15 133 A7
Temple Ewell CT16 148 D5
Church Ho CT14 117 C7
Church La Adisham CT3 90 D1
Aldington TN25 173 D7
Boughton Aluph TN25 123 B4
Boyden Gate CT3 47 C7
Brenzett TN29 191 F5
Canterbury CT1 87 F8
[21] Canterbury,Northgate CT1 67 A1
Challock TN25 122 B8
Chartham CT4 86 D3
Chatham ME4 9 F6
Church Hougham CT15 165 B5
Deal CT14 117 B6
Harrietsham ME17 100 E6
Kingston CT4 111 D3
Lower Hardres CT4 88 B2
Maidstone ME14 76 C4
New Romney TN28 200 B5
Newington ME9 35 B6
Petham CT4 109 C3
Ringwould CT14 133 F5
Ripple CT14 116 D1
River,Lydden CT15 147 E8
Selling ME13 84 B6
Shadoxhurst TN26 170 A7
Stockbury ME9 56 E8
Stowting TN25 160 A6
Sturry CT2 67 F5
Waltham CT4 125 F5
Westbere CT2 68 C7
Whitstable CT5 43 A6
Womenswold CT4 112 D2
Church Mdws CT14 117 A6
Church Mews ME8 33 F8
Church Path Deal CT14 117 B5
Gillingham ME7 10 E6
Lower Halstow ME9 13 C3
Church Rd Ashford TN23 139 C2
Ashford, Kennington TN24 139 E6
Ashford,Aylesford Green TN24 157 A7
Ashford,Willesborough TN24 157 A8
[1] Broadstairs CT10 30 B4
Burmarsh TN29 185 E4
Charing TN27 103 D2
Chart Sutton ME17 98 C1
Coldred CT15 131 A3
Dover CT17 166 A7
Eastchurch ME12 5 D2
Eastling ME13 82 B2
Faversham ME13 62 D7
Faversham,The Brents ME13 62 D8
Folkestone CT20 177 C6
Harrietsham ME17 100 E6
Hoath CT3 46 E5
Hollingbourne ME17 56 E1
Hythe CT21 176 C2
Kenardington TN26 182 A5
Lenham ME17 118 A8
Littlebourne CT3 90 A8
Lydd TN29 203 C6
Lyminge CT18 161 C7
Maidstone,Shepway ME15 97 F7
Maidstone,Tovil ME15 74 E2
Church Rd *continued*
Margate CT9 7 J1
Mersham TN25 157 E3
Molash CT4 105 F5
New Romney TN28 200 A6
Oare ME13 40 B3
Ramsgate CT11 52 E7
Sevington TN24 157 B6
Sittingbourne ME9 37 E5
Sittingbourne, Murston ME10 37 B5
Smeeth TN25 158 C4
Stalisfield Green ME13 103 F5
Tenterden TN30 179 A7
Church Sq
[2] Broadstairs CT10 30 B4
Lenham ME17 101 D5
Church St
Boughton Monchelsea ME17 97 B2
Broadstairs CT10 29 E6
Canterbury CT2 66 E1
Chatham ME4 10 A4
Deal CT14 117 B1
Dover CT16 166 D7
Eastry CT13 93 C2
Faversham ME13 62 D8
Folkestone CT20 178 D4
Gillingham ME7 10 E6
Loose ME15 96 F5
Maidstone ME14 75 A4
Maidstone,Tovil ME15 74 E2
Margate CT9 7 J1
Minster (Thanet) CT12 50 C5
Nonington CT15 113 C5
Rochester ME1 9 D4
Rodmersham ME9 59 C8
[7] Sandwich CT13 73 A1
[5] Sittingbourne ME10 36 E4
Sittingbourne,Milton Regis ME10 36 E5
Whitstable CT5 20 F1
Woodnesborough CT13 93 B6
Wye TN25 123 E2
Church Street (St Pauls) [6] CT1 88 A8
Church Street St Mary's [3] CT13 72 F1
Church Terr Chatham ME5 10 C2
Minster (Sheppey) ME12 4 C7
Church View
Aldington TN25 173 A6
Herne Bay CT6 23 C4
Newchurch TN29 184 E3
Worth CT14 94 B5
Church Way CT5 21 D3
Church Whitfield Rd CT16 149 B8
Church Wlk CT4 144 F4
Church Wood Cl CT2 66 B2
Church Wood Nature Reserve★ CT2 65 F4
Church Yard Pas [10] TN23 139 B2
Church Yd TN23 139 C2
Churchfield Pl CT9 7 I2
Churchfield Way TN25 123 E2
Churchfields
Broadstairs CT10 29 F7
Margate CT9 7 J1
Churchfields Terr ME1 9 B4
Churchill Ave
Chatham ME5 32 A7
Deal CT14 117 C2
Folkestone CT19 178 C8
Herne Bay CT6 23 D4
Churchill Cl Bridge CT4 88 F1
Folkestone CT19 178 D8
St Margaret's at Cliffe CT15 150 F5
Churchill Cotts ME17 98 F6
Churchill Ct Hythe CT21 176 B1
Ramsgate CT11 52 D7
Churchill Ho
[2] Folkestone CT20 177 F5
Maidstone ME16 74 B2
Sittingbourne ME10 37 C4
Teynham ME9 38 C3
Churchill Rd
Canterbury CT1 88 C6
Dover CT17 166 A6
Minster (Sheppey) ME12 4 D6
Churchill St [7] CT16 149 C1
Churchill Way ME13 40 B1
Churchill Wlk CT18 162 F4
Churchlands Ho TN28 200 B6
Churchlands The TN28 200 B6
Churchwood Dr CT5 21 D1
Chute Cl ME8 33 D4
Cinder Path CT10 30 A4
Cinnabar Cl ME5 32 A1
Cinnabar Dr ME10 36 C6
Cinque Ports Ave CT21 176 B1
Circular Rd Dover CT16 150 B1
Finglesham CT14 116 B7
Circus The CT6 22 E4
Citadel Cres CT17 166 B6
Citadel Hts CT17 166 B6
Citadel Rd CT17 166 C6
Citroen Cl CT6 22 B4
City Bsns Pk CT1 67 C3
City View CT2 87 C8
City Way ME1 9 D2
Claire Ct Birchington CT7 26 F7
Broadstairs CT10 30 B5
Claire House ME16 74 E5
Clandon Rd ME5 32 D2
Clanwilliam Rd CT14 117 D5
Clapham Hill CT5 43 D5
Clapton Ct ME8 33 D8
Clare Dr CT6 22 C2
Clare Rd CT5 20 E2
Claremont Cl CT14 134 C6
Claremont Gdns CT11 52 C7
Claremont Pl CT1 87 F7
Claremont Rd Deal CT14 117 B5
Folkestone CT20 178 C5
Kingsdown CT14 134 C6
Maidstone ME14 75 B5
Claremont St CT6 22 C4
Claremont Terr CT13 93 D7
Claremont Way [2] ME4 9 F3
Clarence Ave Margate CT9 8 D2
Rochester ME1 9 C4
Clarence Ct ME14 75 E4
Clarence Gdns ME12 6 E3
Clarence Pl Deal CT14 117 D7
Dover CT17 166 D5
Clarence Rd
Capel-le-F CT18 164 B2
Chatham ME4 10 B2
Deal CT14 117 D3
Herne Bay CT6 22 D5
Ramsgate CT11 52 C6
Clarence Row ME12 1 C2
Clarence St
Folkestone CT20 178 D5
Herne Bay CT6 22 E5
Clarendon Cl
Maidstone ME14 76 A4
Sittingbourne ME10 36 F1
Clarendon Gdns [7] CT11 52 D6
Clarendon House Gram Sch CT11 52 E6
Clarendon Mews
[1] Broadstairs CT10 30 A4
New Romney TN28 200 C8
Clarendon Pl
Dover CT17 166 C7
Maidstone ME14 75 A4
Clarendon Rd
Aylesham CT3 112 F5
Broadstairs CT10 30 A4
Dover CT17 166 C7
Margate CT9 8 A2
Clarendon St
Dover CT17 166 C7
Herne Bay CT6 22 C4
Claridge Ct ME7 32 F4
Claridge Mews CT21 176 C2
Clarke Cres TN24 139 F4
Clarke Rd TN28 200 E4
Clarke's Cl CT14 116 F4
Clarklands TN29 184 E3
Claudius Gr TN23 155 F5
Clavell Cl ME8 33 E4
Claxfield Cotts ME9 38 A2
Claxfield Rd ME9 60 A8
Claygate Ashford TN23 155 F5
Maidstone ME15 75 D1
Clearmount Dr TN27 120 C8
Cleave Rd ME7 10 E3
Cleaver La CT11 52 E7
Clematis Ave ME8 33 B5
Clement Cl
Canterbury CT1 67 B1
Sittingbourne ME10 36 E8
Clement Ct ME16 74 D5
Clement's Rd CT12 29 C2
Clementine Cl CT6 23 D4
Clerke Dr ME10 37 A8
Clermont Cl ME7 33 A4
Clevedon Ct TN25 105 B2
Cleveland Cl CT16 149 B3
Cleveland Ho ME16 74 B2
Cleveland Rd ME7 10 D6
Cleveley Lo CT11 29 E2
Cleven Lo CT7 48 D6
Cleves Way TN23 155 E8
Clewson Rise ME14 75 B8
Cliff Ave CT6 23 C5
Cliff Cl CT21 176 D3
Cliff Dr Herne Bay CT6 22 C4
Warden ME12 6 E4
Cliff Field CT8 27 C8
Cliff Gdns ME12 4 E7
Cliff Hill ME17 97 D4
Cliff Hill Rd ME17 97 C4
Cliff Prom CT10 30 C7
Cliff Rd Birchington CT7 26 F8
Broadstairs CT10 30 B7
Dover CT15,CT16 150 C1
Folkestone CT20 178 A3
Hythe CT21 176 E3
Whitstable CT5 20 F3
Cliff Sea Gr CT6 22 C4
Cliff St CT11 52 E6
Cliff Terr CT9 7 J3
Cliff View Gdns
Leysdown-on-S ME12 6 D1
Warden ME12 6 E4
Cliff View Rd CT12 51 D6
Cliffe Ave CT9 7 F1
Cliffe Ho CT20 178 A3
Cliffe Rd
Kingsdown CT14 134 D6
Rochester ME2 9 B8
Cliffestone Ct CT20 178 B5
Clifford Gdns CT14 117 B2
Clifford Ho [6] ME14 75 B4
Clifford Rd CT5 43 F8
Cliffs End Gr CT12 51 D5
Cliffs End Rd CT12 51 E5
Cliffside Dr CT10 30 A1
Clifftown Gdns CT6 22 B4
Clifton Cl ME14 75 B5
Clifton Cres CT20 178 B3
Clifton Gdns
Canterbury CT2 66 D2
Folkestone CT20 178 C4
Margate CT9 7 J3
Clifton Lawn CT11 52 D5
Clifton Mansions [4] CT20 178 C4
Clifton Pl CT9 8 A3
Clifton Rd
Folkestone CT20 178 C4
Gillingham ME7 10 C7
Margate CT9 8 A2
Ramsgate CT11 52 B8
Whitstable CT5 20 D1
Clifton St CT9 7 J3
Cliftonville Ave
Margate CT9 8 A2
Ramsgate CT12 29 B1
Cliftonville Ct CT9 8 A3
Cliftonville Mews CT9 8 A3
Cliftonville Prim Sch CT9 8 C2
Clim Down CT14 134 D6
Clinton Cl ME17 96 B3
Clints La CT4 129 D4
Clipper Cl ME2 9 E7
Clipper Ct ME2 9 E7
Clive Ct CT9 8 B2
Clive Dennis Ct TN24 139 E1
Clive Rd Cliffs End CT12 51 D6
Margate CT9 29 A5
Rochester ME1 9 C3
Sittingbourne ME10 36 B5
Cliveden Cl ME16 74 D7
Clockhouse TN23 138 F1
Clockhouse Pk TN25 105 C2
Cloisterham Rd ME1 31 D7
Cloisters The
[9] Canterbury CT1 66 F1
Lenham ME17 101 C5
Ramsgate CT11 52 D5
[8] Sittingbourne ME10 36 E4
Close The Ashford TN23 155 F7
Bridge CT4 88 F1
Canterbury,Hales Place CT2 66 F4
Canterbury,Thanington CT1 87 D6
Faversham ME13 62 C6
Folkestone CT19 178 E8
Hythe CT21 176 B4
River,Lydden CT15 147 F8
Rochester ME1 9 C4
Wye TN25 123 E2
Close The (St Edmunds Sch) CT2 66 C3
Cloudberry Cl ME16 74 D6
Cloudesley Cl ME1 9 B1
Clovelly TN28 200 E6
Clovelly Dr ME12 4 B8
Clovelly Rd CT5 43 D7
Clover Bank View ME5 32 B6
Clover Ct ME10 37 B5
Clover La ME8 12 B2
Clover Rise CT5 21 B1
Clover St [3] ME4 9 F4
Clover Terr [4] ME15 97 D8
Clowes Ct CT2 66 C4
Clubb's La TN29 197 D7
Cluny Rd ME13 62 F7
Clyde Cotts ME12 1 E2
Clyde St
[1] Canterbury CT1 67 A1
Sheerness ME12 1 E2
Clynton Way TN23 156 A7
Coach Dr TN26 138 A7
Coach Rd Densole CT18 162 F8
Egerton ME17, TN27 118 E6
Coalpit La ME9 80 A6
Coast Dr
Littlestone-on-S TN28 200 E3
Lydd-on-S TN29 204 F4
St Mary's Bay TN29 194 F2
Coast Rd TN28,TN29 200 F7
Coastguard Alley CT5 20 C1
Coastguard Cotts
Conyer ME9 38 E6
Dover CT16 166 G8
Herne Bay CT6 21 F4
Hythe CT21 176 B1
Kingsdown CT14 134 D4
Leysdown-on-S ME12 19 E4
Minster (Sheppey) ME12 5 C5
[18] Ramsgate,East Cliff CT11 52 F7
Ramsgate,Pegwell CT11 52 A5
Sandwich CT13 95 B7
Birchington CT7 26 D8
Coastguard Cotts The ME12 1 I1
Coastguard Hos ME12 6 C5
Coats Ave ME12 3 A8
Cobay Cl CT21 176 D2
Cobb Ct CT9 7 I3
Cobb Wlk ME13 62 B8
Cobblers Bridge Rd CT6 22 D3
Cobblestones ME7 32 F5
Cobbs Hill CT4 85 C2
Cobbs Mews [2] CT20 178 C4
Cobbs Pl CT9 7 I3
Cobbs Wood Ind Est TN23 138 F2
Cobden Pl [13] CT1 67 A1
Cobden Rd
[4] Gillingham ME4 10 B2
Hythe CT21 176 B1
Cobdown Gr ME8 12 A2
Cobfield ME17 98 A1

Cobham Ave ME10 .....36 E1
Cobham Chase ME13 ....62 B8
Cobham Cl
Canterbury CT1 ....88 C6
Maidstone ME16 ....74 E4
Cobham Rise ME7 ....10 F5
Cobsden Cl TN29 ......195 A4
Cobsden Rd TN29 ......195 A4
Cobtree Cl ME5 ....32 C8
Cobtree Rd ME17 ....96 C3
Cobtree Wharf ME20 ....53 C2
Cobweb Cnr CT2 ....66 B4
Cock La Elham CT4 ......144 F4
Hamstreet TN26 ....183 A7
Cockering Rd CT1,CT4 ...87 B4
Cockreed La TN28 .....200 B7
Codrington Rd CT11 ....52 D7
Cogans Terr CT1 ....87 E6
Coggan Ho 7 CT1 ....87 F7
Coinston Ave CT11 ......52 A7
Colburn Rd CT10 ....30 A2
Colchester Cl ME5 ......32 A7
Cold Harbour CT1 ......67 A2
Cold Harbour La ME9 ...35 F6
Cold Harbour Rd ME13 .103 A7
Coldblow CT14 ....117 A1
Coldblow La
Maidstone ME14 ....56 A2
Woodchurch TN26 ......169 D4
Coldbridge La TN27 ....118 B5
Coldharbour La
Aylesford ME20 ....53 A1
Bekesbourne CT4,CT3 ...111 D7
Hollingbourne ME14,ME9 ...56 B1
Old Romney TN29 ....198 C5
Sittingbourne ME10 ....14 F1
Wye TN25 ....124 A2
Coldred Hill CT15 ......130 F1
Coldred Rd Coldred CT15 131 B5
Park Wood ME15 ....97 F4
Shepherdswell CT15 .....130 E3
Coldswood Rd CT12 .....28 F2
Cole Rd ME13 ....62 E7
Cole Terr ME17 ....101 C4
Colegate Dr ME14 ....76 C4
Colegates Cl ME13 ......40 B2
Colegates Ct ME13 ......40 B2
Colegates Rd ME13 ......40 A2
Coleman Cres CT12 .....29 C1
Coleman Dr ME10 ....14 F1
Coleman's Stairs Rd CT7 27 A8
Coleman's Yd 3 CT11 ...52 E6
Colemans Cl TN29 .....203 D7
Coleridge Gdns CT3 ....112 F6
Coleshall Cl ME15 ....97 F6
Coleshall Cotts ME9 .....14 D3
Colette Cl CT10 ....8 G2
Coleville Cres TN28 ....204 E7
Colewood Rd CT5 ....21 E3
Colfe Way ME10 ....37 A8
Colin's Way CT21 ......177 A3
Collard Cl CT6 ....23 A4
Collard Rd TN24 ....157 A8
Collards Cl CT12 ....49 D7
Collards La CT4 ....144 E3
College Ave
Gillingham ME7 ....10 B4
Maidstone ME15 ....74 F3
College Cotts ME16 ......74 F3
College Ct Ashford TN23 .139 C2
5 Maidstone ME15 ......75 A3
College Rd Canterbury CT1 67 B1
Chatham ME4 ....10 A7
Deal CT14 ....117 D8
Maidstone ME15 ....74 F2
Margate CT9 ....8 A1
Ramsgate CT11 ....29 E1
Sittingbourne ME10 ......36 D3
College Row CT17 ......166 B7
College Sq 2 CT9 ....7 J2
College Way CT3 ....91 A7
College Wlk 3 CT9 ....7 J2
College Yd ME1 ....9 C6
Collet Wlk ME8 ....33 D4
Collett Cl TN25 ....142 D8
Collingbourne TN23 ....155 E6
Collings Wlk ME8 ....33 D4
Collington Terr ME15 ....97 E4
Collingwood Cl
Broadstairs CT10 ....29 E4
Westgate-on-S CT8 ....27 D7
Collingwood Ct
Folkestone CT20 ....177 E5
Ramsgate CT11 ....52 D7
Collingwood Ind Ctr
ME17 ....98 E2
Collingwood Rd
Kit's Coty ME20 ....53 C7
St Margaret's at Cliffe
CT15 ....150 F8
Whitstable CT5 ....20 C1
Collingwood Rd E CT15 134 A1
Collingwood Rise CT20 .177 E5
Collingwood Wlk ME10 ..36 B5
Collins Rd CT6 ....22 C2
Collis St ME2 ....9 A8
Collison Pl TN30 ....179 D7
Colman House 4 ME14 ..75 A4
Colombo Sq CT12 ....29 A1
Colonel Stephens Way
TN30 ....167 B2
Colonel's La ME13 ......64 A3
Colorado Cl CT16 ......149 B3
Colton Cres CT16 ......149 B4
Coltsfoot Dr ME14 ....75 F4
Columbia Ave CT5 ......43 B7
Columbine Cl CT5 ......43 C6
Columbus Ave CT12 .....27 D1
Com Coll Whitstable The
CT5 ....43 F8
Combie Cl CT18 ....163 B5
Command Rd ME14 .....74 F8
Commercial Rd ME2 ......9 A7
Commissioner's Rd ME2 ..9 C8
Commodore Rd ME14 ...75 C5
Common La CT17 ......148 E3
Common Rd ME5 ....31 B1
Common The ME1 ....9 C6
Common Way TN26 ....138 A7
Commonwealth Cl ME10 .37 B3
Compass Cl ME1 ....9 C1
Compass Ctr ME4 ....10 B8
Compton Cl ME5 ....32 D2
Concord Ave ME5 ....31 E5
Condor Cl ME12 ....6 E3
Conduit St ME13 ....62 D8
Coney Mews ME4 ....10 A1
Conference Wlk CT1 ....88 C8
Conifer Ct CT8 ....7 D1
Conifer Dr ME5 ....32 D1
Conifers The CT14 .....117 A2
Coniston Cl ME7 ....11 A6
Coniston Dr CT3 ....112 F6
Coniston Rd CT19 ......178 B7
Conker Cl TN23 ....156 C3
Connaught Barracks
CT16 ....149 E1
Connaught Cl ME15 .....97 F4
Connaught Gdns 9 CT9 ..7 J1
Connaught Mews 2 ME4 10 C2
Connaught Rd
Chatham ME4 ....10 C2
Dover CT16 ....149 D1
Folkestone CT20 ....178 D5
Gillingham ME7 ....10 D5
Margate CT9 ....7 J1
Sittingbourne ME10 ......36 E3
Conquest Ind Est ME2 ....9 A6
Conrad Ave CT1 ....67 C3
Conrad Cl ME8 ....33 D4
Consort Cl ME14 ....75 B5
Constable Rd CT7 ....27 A8
Constable's Rd CT16 ...166 E8
Constancia Ct CT20 ....178 C5
Constantine Rd TN23 ...155 F5
Constitution Hill 8 ME5 .10 B3
Constitution Rd ME5 ....10 B2
Consul Cl CT6 ....22 B4
Continental App CT9 ....28 F6
Convent Cl CT15 ....151 B6
Convent Rd CT10 ....8 G1
Convent Wlk CT11 ....52 B5
Conway Cl Birchington CT7 26 E7
Hythe CT21 ....176 B4
Conway Mews ME7 ......10 A6
Conway Rd ME16 ....74 C6
Conyer Rd ME9 ....38 F4
Conyers Wlk ME8 ....33 D4
Conyngham Cl CT12 .....29 B2
Conyngham La CT4 ......89 A2
Conyngham Rd
Herne Bay CT6 ....23 D5
Minster (Thanet) CT12 ....50 C5
Cooden Cl ME8 ....12 A2
Cook Cl ME5 ....32 C6
Cook's Lea CT13 ....93 B2
Cookham Hill ME1 ....9 A2
Cookham Wood Rd ME1 .31 B8
Cooks La ME10 ....36 F6
Cooks Wharf ME1 ....9 E4
Cooling Cl ME14 ....75 C6
Coolinge La CT20 ......177 F4
Coolinge Rd CT20 ......178 D5
Coombe Cl Chatham ME5 .32 B3
Dover CT17 ....149 A1
Coombe Ct CT17 ....149 A1
Coombe Dr ME10 ....37 C4
Coombe La Ash CT13,CT3 .92 E8
Tenterden TN30 ....179 A7
Coombe Lands TN30 ...188 D4
Coombe Rd
Dover CT15,CT17 ....165 E8
Dover,St Radigund's CT17 .148 F1
Folkestone CT19 ....177 F6
Maidstone ME15 ....74 F2
Coombe Valley Rd CT17 149 A1
Coombe Way CT18 .....163 C4
Coombe Wlk CT5 ....43 A2
Coombe Wood La CT18 .163 C4
Cooper Rd ME5 ....32 B3
Cooper Street Dro CT3 ..72 B4
Cooper's Hill CT6 ....22 F5
Cooper's La TN25 ......158 F2
Coopers La CT1 ....87 E7
Cooting La CT3 ....112 D8
Cooting Rd CT3 ....112 E4
Cop Street Rd CT3 ....71 D3
Copenhagen Rd ME7 ....10 C4
Copinger Cl CT2 ....67 A4
Copland Ave ME12 ....4 C6
Copper Tree Ct ME15 ....97 A5
Copper Tree Wlk ME5 ....32 C1
Copperfield ME12 ....5 F6
Copperfield Cl TN24 ...139 C6
Copperfield Ct CT10 .....30 B5
Copperfield Dr ME17 ....98 E4
Copperfield Ho 6 ME4 ...9 F4
Copperfield Rd ME1 ......9 C2
Copperfields TN29 .....203 B6
Copperfields The ME1 ....9 B4
Coppergate
Canterbury CT2 ....66 F2
Gillingham ME7 ....32 F5
Copperhouse La ME7 ....11 B6
Copperhurst Wlk CT9 .....8 F2
Copperpenny Dr ME7 ....33 B3
Copperwood TN24 .....139 C4
Coppice Ct ME7 ....33 B4
Coppice Rd ME5 ....32 C2
Coppice The CT2 ....67 F6
Coppice View ME14 .....75 E6
Coppin St CT14 ....117 D6
Coppins La ME9 ....36 B2
Copse Cl ME1 ....9 E1
Copse The TN23 ....138 D3
Copsewood Way ME15 ..76 A3
Copt Cl CT2 ....67 F7
Copthall Gdns 13 CT20 .178 D5
Cordelia Cres ME1 ....9 A2
Cordingham Rd CT5 .....43 A6
Cordova Ct CT20 ....178 B4
Corkwell St ME4 ....9 E3
Cornbrook Rd CT21 ....187 D8
Cornelis Dr CT12 ....50 B5
Corner Cotts TN26 .....182 A6
Corner Field TN23 .....156 B5
Corner The TN25 ......173 A6
Cornes Cl TN24 ....140 A1
Cornflower Cl ME14 .....75 E4
Cornford Rd CT7 ....27 A7
Cornhill 12 CT11 ....52 E6
Corniche The CT20 .....177 C3
Cornwall Ave CT11 ......52 F8
Cornwall Cl ME15 ....97 E7
Cornwall Gdns
Canterbury CT1 ....88 D7
Margate CT9 ....8 B3
Cornwall Ho Deal CT14 .117 A5
5 Dover CT17 ....166 D7
Cornwall Rd Deal CT14 ..117 C3
Gillingham ME7 ....10 D6
Herne Bay CT6 ....22 B2
Rochester ME1 ....9 C3
Cornwallis Ave
Aylesham CT3 ....112 F6
Chatham ME4 ....9 E1
Folkestone CT19 ....178 B6
Gillingham ME8 ....11 A4
Herne Bay CT6 ....23 C3
Cornwallis Circ CT5 .....20 D1
Cornwallis Cl
Ashford TN24 ....157 B7
Folkestone CT19 ....178 B6
Cornwallis Cotts ME17 ...96 E2
Cornwallis Gdns CT10 ...30 A6
Cornwallis Rd ME16 .....74 D4
Cornwallis Rdbt ME8 ....11 A4
Cornwallis Sch The ME15 96 F2
Coronation Cl CT10 .....29 E7
Coronation Cotts CT19 .177 D6
Coronation Cres
Margate CT9 ....28 B8
Queenborough ME11 ......2 F5
Coronation Dr
Great Chart TN23 ....138 C1
Leysdown-on-S ME12 ......6 D2
Coronation Flats 5 ME4 ..9 F3
Coronation Rd
Chatham ME5 ....10 C2
Ramsgate CT11 ....52 D6
Sheerness ME12 ....1 E1
Coronation Sq TN29 ...203 C6
Corone Cl CT19 ....178 A7
Corporation Rd ME7 .....10 D7
Corporation St ME1 ......9 C6
Corral Cl ME5 ....10 D2
Corrall Almshouses 4
ME15 ....75 A3
Corrance Gn ME15 ......97 A8
Corsican Wlk CT6 ....23 C3
Cortland Cl ME10 ....36 E6
Cortland Mews ME10 ....36 E6
Corunna Cl CT21 ....176 A2
Corunna Pl CT15 ....149 E3
Cory's Rd ME1 ....9 D6
Corylus Dr CT5 ....43 A7
Cossack St ME1 ....9 D3
Cossington Rd
Canterbury CT1 ....88 A7
Chatham ME5 ....32 B1
Cosway Cotts TN25 ....172 C1
Cotswold Cl TN24 ......139 B4
Cotswold Gdns ME15 ....76 A2
Cottage Rd Chatham ME4 ..9 F6
Ramsgate CT11 ....52 E6
Cottage Row CT13 ......72 F1
Cottall Ave ME4 ....9 F2
Cottington Rd CT12 .....51 B5
Cotton Hill Wlk TN26 ...183 A7
Cotton Rd CT1 ....87 E7
Coulman St ME7 ....10 D5
Coulson Gr CT14 ....116 A5
Coulter Rd Ashford TN23 .155 E5
Herne Bay CT6 ....22 B2
Coulters Cl ME14 ....75 D5
Coultrip Cl ME12 ....5 B5
Council Cotts ME15 .....96 A4
Countess Mountbatten Ct
CT8 ....27 E8
Country Ways ME17 ....102 D3
Country's Field TN29 ...195 C8
County Rd ME14 ....75 A5
County Sq 8 TN23 .....139 B2
Court Cotts
St Nicholas at Wade CT7 ..25 E2
Wingham CT3 ....91 A7
Court Dr ME16 ....74 D4
Court Flats CT3 ....91 A7
Court Hall ME11 ....2 F5
Court Hall Mus★ ME10 ..36 E6
Court Hill CT3 ....68 E2
Court Hill Ho CT16 .....148 E4
Court House Farm CT15 113 E5
Court La Detling ME14 ....55 C5
Preston CT3 ....70 B6
Court Lodge CT14 ......117 B6
Court Lodge Cotts ME15 .96 A7
Court Lodge Rd
Appledore TN26 ....190 C7
Gillingham ME7 ....10 F6
Court Mdw ME8 ....11 B2
Court Mdws CT3 ....89 F8
Court Pl CT20 ....178 C4
Court Rd Burham ME1 ....53 A8
Deal CT14 ....117 B1
Sittingbourne ME10 ......36 F7
St Nicholas at Wade CT7 ..25 E2
Court St ME13 ....62 D7
Court Tree Dr ME12 ....5 B5
Court Wurtin TN23 .....156 A7
Courtenay Rd
Boughton Street CT2,ME13 .64 E5
Deal CT14 ....117 C8
Maidstone ME15 ....74 F2
Courteney Rd ME8 ......33 B8
Courtfield Ave ME5 .....32 B3
Courtland Ave CT16 ....149 A6
Courtland Dr CT16 .....148 E4
Courtlands Herne Bay CT6 23 B3
Kingsdown CT14 ....134 D6
Courtlands Cl CT12 ......51 E5
Courtlands Way CT8 ......7 D1
Courts The CT9 ....7 E1
Courtyard The
Ashford TN24 ....156 F6
Gillingham ME8 ....33 A8
Staple CT3 ....92 A6
Coventina Ho CT11 ......52 D7
Coventon La CT14 ....94 A5
Coventry Gdns CT6 .....23 E5
Coverdale Ave ME15 ....97 D6
Coverdale Cl ME5 ....32 B7
Covert TN23 ....138 E1
Covert Rd CT3 ....112 E4
Covert The ME5 ....32 B1
Covet La CT4 ....111 C2
Cow La Canterbury CT1 ...87 D7
Dover CT17 ....166 A7
Cowbeck Cl ME8 ....33 D6
Cowden Rd ME14 ....75 C5
Cowdray Rd CT14 ......117 A3
Cowdray Sq CT14 ......117 A3
Cowdrey Cl
Ashford TN24 ....157 A7
Maidstone ME16 ....74 B2
Rochester ME1 ....9 B2
Cowdrey Pl CT1 ....88 B6
Cowgate Hill CT17 .....166 D7
Cowgate La CT18 ......163 C5
Cowley Rise CT9 ....29 C8
Cowper Cl CT5 ....21 D3
Cowper Rd Deal CT14 ...117 C5
Gillingham ME7 ....10 D3
Margate CT9 ....7 J1
River CT17 ....148 E3
Sittingbourne ME10 ......37 B4
Cowstead Rd ME9 ....34 D2
Cox St ME14 ....55 E6
Coxes Ave CT12 ....29 B3
Coxes La CT12 ....29 B3
Coxett Hill ME13 ....61 D5
Coxheath Prim Sch ME17 96 C3
Coxhill CT15 ....130 C3
Coxhill Cres CT17 ......148 D3
Coxhill Gdns CT17 .....148 D3
Coxland Cotts TN26 ....181 B1
Cozenton Cl ME8 ....11 E1
Crabble Ave CT17 ......149 A2
Crabble Cl CT17 ....148 F2
Crabble Corn Mill★
CT17 ....148 F3
Crabble Hill CT16,CT17 ..149 A2
Crabble La CT17 ....148 E2
Crabble Mdws CT17 ....149 A2
Crabble Rd CT17 ......149 A3
Crabtree La ME17 ......119 B8
Crabtree Rd ME8 ....33 D8
Crabtree Rndbt ME14 ....53 E2
Crackstake CT3 ....71 D2
Craddock Dr 8 CT1 .....67 B1
Craddock Rd CT1 ....67 B1
Craddock Way ME8 .....33 D5
Cradle Bridge Dr TN24 .139 F2
Cradles Rd ME9 ....34 C2
Crafford St CT16 ....149 D1
Craft Ctr TN25 ....159 F2
Cragie Wlk ME8 ....33 E4
Craig Ho ME1 ....9 E1
Craighton Flats 2 CT13 .72 F1
Crampton Ct CT10 ......30 A4
Cranborne Ave ME15 ....75 C1
Cranborne Wlk CT2 .....66 E3
Cranbourne Ave ME15 ...97 B8
Cranbourne Cl CT11 .....52 F8
Cranbrook Cl
Gillingham ME8 ....11 C3
Maidstone ME15 ....97 F7
Margate CT9 ....8 E1
Cranbrook Dr ME10 .....36 D1
Cranbrooks TN25 ......157 D4
Cranford Cl ME8 ....11 D1
Cranleigh Dr CT16 .....149 B7
Cranleigh Gdns
Chatham ME4 ....9 D3
Maidstone ME16 ....74 C7
Whitstable CT5 ....43 E8
Cranmer Ct ME15 ....97 B8
Cranmere Ct ME2 ....9 C8
Cranswick Cotts CT14 ..133 C8
Craufurd Gn CT20 .....177 D5
Craven Cl CT9 ....28 C8
Crawford Gdns CT9 ......8 B2
Crawford Rd CT10 ......29 F5
Crayford Cl ME14 ....75 C6
Craythorne TN30 ......179 B8
Craythorne Cl
Hythe CT21 ....177 B4
New Romney TN28 .....200 B8
Craythorne Ho TN30 ...179 B8
Craythorne La TN28 ...200 B7
Cremer Cl CT4 ....86 C1
Cremer Pl ME13 ....62 A8
Cremers Rd ME10 ....37 B5
Crescent Ho Margate CT9 ..8 A2
Rochester ME2 ....9 C7
Crescent Rd
Birchington CT7 ....27 A7
Broadstairs CT10 ....30 C8
Faversham ME13 ....62 D7
Margate CT9 ....7 H2
Ramsgate CT11 ....52 D7
Crescent St 1 ME10 .....36 F4
Crescent The
Aylesham CT15 ....113 A3
Boughton Street ME13 ....64 A3
Canterbury CT2 ....66 F4
Chartham CT4 ....86 D1
Eythorne CT15 ....131 C7
Folkestone CT20 ....177 E3
Halfway Houses ME12 ......3 E6
Lower Halstow ME9 ......13 C3
Maidstone ME14 ....74 F8
Sandwich CT13 ....93 E6
Sheerness ME12 ....1 D2
Sittingbourne ME10 ......15 A1
St Margaret's at Cliffe
CT15 ....151 A5
Teynham ME9 ....38 D3
Crescent Way ME5 ......31 D5
Cress Way ME13 ....62 A7
Cressey Ct 7 ME4 ....9 E4
Cressfield TN23 ....138 F1
Crest Rd ME1 ....9 C1
Cresta Cl CT6 ....21 F4
Crestway ME5 ....32 B8
Crete Rd E CT18,CT19 ..163 D1
Crete Rd W CT18 ......163 B1
Creteway Cl CT19 ......178 E8
Creve Coeur Cl ME14 ....76 A5
Crevequer Chambers 1
ME8 ....11 F1
Cricketers Cl
Harrietsham ME17 ......100 D6
Hawkinge CT18 ....163 B6
Sittingbourne ME10 ......36 F8
Crimond Ave TN29 .....187 A4
Criol La TN26 ....155 A2
Cripple Hill TN26 ......152 D1
Cripple St ME15 ....97 A7
Cripps Cl CT3 ....112 E5
Cripps' La CT15 ....150 F6
Crisfield Ct TN30 ......167 B2
Crismill La ME14,ME17 ...76 F3
Crispe Cl ME8 ....33 D4
Crispe Park Cl CT8 ......27 B7
Crispe Rd CT7 ....27 A3
Crispin Cl ME13 ....62 D8
Crispin Ct ME17 ....96 C3
Crittenden Bglws ME15 ..96 A4
Crittenden Cotts ME15 ..96 A4
Crocken Hill Rd TN27 ..118 C2
Crockham La ME13 ......64 B6
Crockham Rd ME13 .....64 C6
Crockshard Hill CT3 .....91 B4
Crockshard La CT3 .....91 B4
Croft Cl ME5 ....32 C1
Croft Gdns ME17 ......101 D4
Croft La CT20 ....177 F5
Croft Rd TN24 ....139 D2
Croft's Pl 8 CT10 ....30 B4
Crofters Cl CT21 ....187 E8
Crofters The ME8 ....33 F7
Crofton Cl TN24 ....139 C6
Crofton Rd CT8 ....27 E7
Croftwood TN23 ....155 D6
Croidene Ct ME12 ....4 A6
Cromer Rd Rochester ME2 ..9 B8
Sittingbourne ME9,ME10 ...58 F8
Crompton Gdns ME15 ....75 B3
Crompton Tower
Rly Mus★ CT10 ....30 A4
Cromwell Park Pl CT20 .177 D4
Cromwell Rd
Canterbury CT1 ....88 A6
Maidstone ME14 ....75 B5
West Minst ME11 ....2 F7
Whitstable CT5 ....20 E1
Cromwell Terr ME4 ......10 A3
Crook's Court La CT15 .164 F4
Crooked S Rd CT14 ....133 E7
Crookenden Pl CT4 ....128 F8
Crosier Ct ME9 ....12 E3
Crosley Rd ME7 ....10 D3
Cross Dr ME17 ....99 B1
Cross Keys ME14 ....76 C4
Cross La Faversham ME13 .62 C7
7 Faversham ME13 ......62 D7
Sittingbourne ME10 ....36 E6
Throwley Forstal ME13 ..104 C7
Cross Rd Birchington CT7 ..27 B8
Deal CT14 ....117 A2
St Margaret's at Cliffe
CT15 ....151 A4
Cross St
2 Canterbury CT2 ....66 E1
Chatham ME4 ....10 A4
Gillingham ME7 ....10 C6

218 Dow – Eve

Downside *continued*
St Margaret's at Cliffe CT15 ....151 A6
Downside Rd CT16 ....149 B7
Downsview ME5 ....32 C8
Dragonfly Cl TN23 ....155 D8
Dragonfly Way CT18 ....163 B4
Dragoon Ho [10] CT1 ....67 A1
Drainless Rd CT13 ....93 A5
Drake Ave ME12 ....4 D5
Drake Ct [3] CT11 ....52 F8
Drake Rd TN24 ....157 B7
Drakes Cl ME9 ....12 E2
Drakes Lee TN28 ....200 E5
Drapers Almshouses CT9 29 A8
Drapers Ave CT9 ....28 F8
Drapers Cl CT9 ....29 A8
Drapers Mill (dis)★ CT9 ..8 A1
Drapers Mills Prim Sch CT9 ....29 A8
Drawbridge Cl ME15 ....97 E8
Dray's Field ME9 ....79 A7
Dreadnought Ave ME12 ...4 B6
Dreamland Fun Pk★ CT9 ..7 I2
Dresden Ct CT8 ....27 D8
Drew La CT14 ....117 C4
Drewery Dr ME8 ....33 C5
Drill La CT3 ....69 B1
Drive The Canterbury CT1 ..88 B6
Deal CT14 ....117 C5
Whitstable CT5 ....44 D8
Drop Redoubt Fort★ CT17 ....166 D7
Drop Redoubt Rd CT17 .166 D7
Drove Rd ME12 ....3 E7
Drove The Fordwich CT2 ..68 A4
Monkton CT12 ....49 B6
Northbourne CT14 ....116 A5
Whitfield CT16 ....149 A8
Whitstable CT5 ....44 D8
Drovers Rdbt TN24 ....139 A4
Droveway Gdns CT15 ...151 A6
Droveway The CT15 ...151 B6
Drum La TN23 ....139 B2
Drury Rd TN30 ....167 B1
Drybeck Ave CT11 ....51 F7
Dryden Cl CT1 ....88 C7
Dryden Rd CT16 ....149 B3
Drywall Ind Est ME10 ...37 B6
Dublin Ho [16] ME15 ....97 E7
Duchess Of Kent Dr ME5 32 B3
Duck La Canterbury CT1 ..67 A1
Shadoxhurst TN26 ....169 F7
Duck St CT4 ....144 F4
Duckpit Rd CT4 ....126 A6
Duckworth Cl TN24 ....157 B7
Dudley Ave CT8 ....27 C8
Dudley Rd Ashford TN24 .139 E5
Folkestone CT19 ....178 E5
Duke of Clarence Trad Est The ME12 ....1 B3
Duke of York's Royal Military Sch CT15 ....149 F4
Duke St Deal CT14 ....117 D7
Margate CT9 ....7 I3
Dukes Mdw TN26 ....183 A7
Dukes Meadow Dr ME7 ..32 F6
Dukes Wlk [7] ME15 ....75 A4
Dukeswood CT5 ....44 D6
Dully Rd ME9 ....59 E6
Dumergue Ave ME11 ....3 B5
Dumpton Gap Rd CT10 ..30 A2
Dumpton La CT11 ....29 E1
Dumpton Park Dr CT10, CT11 ....30 A2
Dumpton Park Rd CT11 ..52 E8
Dumpton Park Sta CT11 .29 F1
Duncan Dr CT7 ....26 E8
Duncan Rd
Gillingham ME7 ....10 D5
Ramsgate CT11 ....52 D7
Whitstable CT5 ....43 D7
Dundein Dr CT16 ....149 B3
Dundonald Rd
[11] Broadstairs CT10 ....30 B4
Ramsgate CT11 ....52 C7
Dunedin Cl ME10 ....36 C3
Dunedin House [9] ME15 .97 E5
Dunedin Rd CT12 ....29 A1
Dunera Dr ME14 ....75 A7
Dunes Rd TN28 ....200 D3
Dungeness Nature Reserve★ TN29 205 D8
Dungeness Power Sta Visitor Ctr★ TN29 ....205 E6
Dungeness Rd TN29 ....204 C3
Dungeness Sta★ TN29 .205 F6
Dunkeld Ho [6] ME15 ....97 E7
Dunkery Rise TN24 ....139 B4
Dunkirk Cl TN29 ....195 B7
Dunkirk Dr ME5 ....31 F6
Dunkirk Rd N ME13 ....64 B2
Dunkirk Rd S ME13 ....64 B1
Dunkirk Sq CT15 ....149 F3
Dunkirk Village Sch ME13 ....64 D2
Dunlin Ct TN29 ....195 A3
Dunn Street Rd ME7 ...55 A8
Dunnett Rd CT19 ....177 E6
Dunning's La ME1 ....9 C4
Dunnings The ME16 ....74 A2
Dunnock Rd TN25 ....139 B7
Dunoon Ct CT11 ....29 F1
Dunstall Cl TN29 ....195 A5
Dunstall Gdns TN29 ...195 A5
Dunstall La TN29 ....195 A5
Dunstan Ave CT8 ....27 D7
Dunster Terr [3] ME15 ...97 E8
Dunston Ho CT14 ....117 D8
Durban Cl CT12 ....29 A2
Durban Cres CT16 ....149 C4
Durban House [7] ME15 ..97 E5
Durban Rd CT9 ....8 A1
Durham Cl Canterbury CT1 87 F6
[9] Dover CT17 ....166 D7
Maidstone ME15 ....75 E1
Durham Hill CT17 ....166 D7
Durham Rd ME8 ....33 C7
Durling Ct ME8 ....12 A1
Durlock CT12 ....50 C5
Durlock Ave CT11 ....52 B5
Durlock Rd CT3 ....92 B7
Durlocks The CT19 ....178 E5
Durnford Cl CT2 ....66 E2
Durovernum Ct CT1 ....88 A7
Durrell Gdns ME5 ....10 C1
Duval Dr ME1 ....31 E8
Duvard's Pl ME9 ....35 F1
Dyke Rd CT19 ....178 E5
Dymchurch Ho CT1 ....88 B8
Dymchurch Prim Sch TN29 ....195 C8
Dymchurch Rd
Hythe CT21 ....176 A2
Hythe,Palmarsh CT21, TN29 ....187 C6
St Mary's Bay TN29,TN28 .195 A5
Dymchurch Sta★ TN29 .195 B7
Dyngley Cl ME10 ....36 E6

E

Eagle Hill CT11 ....52 D7
Eagles Cl ME10 ....37 C4
Ealham Cl Ashford TN24 .157 A8
Canterbury CT4 ....88 B5
Ealing Cl ME5 ....32 C4
Earl Cl ME5 ....32 B4
Earl St ME14 ....74 F4
Earl's Ave CT20 ....178 B4
Earls Ave TN24 ....139 F1
Earlsfield TN25 ....173 A6
Earlsfield Rd CT21 ....176 D2
Earlsmead Cres CT12 ....51 C5
Earlsworth Ct TN24 ....156 E6
Earlsworth Rd TN24 ....156 D6
Easole Hts CT15 ....113 D5
Easole St CT15 ....113 D5
East Blean Wood (Nature Reserve)★ CT3,CT6 ....46 B6
East Borough Prim Sch ME14 ....75 B5
East Cliff Dover CT16 ....166 F8
Folkestone CT19 ....178 F6
East Cliff & Warren Ctry Pk★ CT18 ....164 D1
East Cliff Gdns [19] CT19 .178 E5
East Cliff Par CT6 ....23 A5
East Cliff Pas [20] CT19 ..178 E5
East Court (Sch for Dyslexics) CT11 ....52 G7
East Cross TN30 ....179 B7
East Ct ME15 ....75 A1
East End Rd ME4,ME7 ....10 D8
East Farleigh Prim Sch ME15 ....96 B6
East Farleigh Sta ME16 ..96 B8
East Gn ME10 ....15 A1
East Hall La ME10 ....37 C5
East Hill Ashford TN24 ...139 C2
Tenterden TN30 ....179 B8
East Kent Light Rly★ CT15 ....131 A7
East Kent Ret Pk CT10 ...29 B4
East La ME12 ....1 B2
East Langdon Rd
Guston CT15 ....149 F7
Martin Mill CT15 ....133 B2
East Lodge Rd TN23 ....138 F3
East Mountain La TN24 .139 F7
East Norman Rd CT16 ..149 E1
East Northdown Cl CT9 ...8 E1
East Park Rd ME20 ....74 A8
East Ramp CT16 ....166 G8
East Rd Chatham ME4 ....10 A7
Folkestone CT20 ....177 D4
Gillingham ME4 ....10 A8
Sandwich CT13 ....73 A8
East Rise CT12 ....29 B1
East Roman Ditch CT16 .166 F8
East Row ME1 ....9 C5
East St Ashford TN23 ....139 B2
Canterbury CT1 ....67 C3
Chatham ME4 ....10 A3
Dover CT17 ....166 C8
Faversham ME13 ....62 D7
Folkestone CT19 ....178 E5
Gillingham ME7 ....10 D6
Harrietsham ME17 ....100 E5
Herne Bay CT6 ....23 A5
Hythe CT21 ....176 D2
Sittingbourne ME10 ....37 A4
East Stour Ct TN24 ....139 D1
East Stour Prim Sch TN24 ....156 D6
East View
Brookland TN29 ....197 D8
Hersden CT3 ....46 F1
East Weald Dr TN30 ....167 B1
East Wootton Cotts CT4 109 A4
Eastbridge Rd TN29 ....195 B8
Eastbrook Pl CT16 ....166 E8
Eastchurch CE Prim Sch ME12 ....5 D3
Eastchurch Rd Margate CT9 8 E3
Minster (Sheppey) ME12 ....5 B5
Eastcourt Gn ME8 ....11 B4
Eastcourt La
Gillingham ME8 ....11 B3
Gillingham,Lower Twydall ME7,ME8 ....11 B4
Eastern Arm N CT16 ...166 H8
Eastern Arm S CT16 ...166 H8
Eastern Ave
Ashford TN23 ....139 A2
Halfway Houses ME12 ....3 D6
Queenborough ME11 ....3 B4
Eastern Espl
Broadstairs CT10 ....30 B5
Margate CT9 ....8 B3
Eastern Gdns TN24 ....156 E8
Eastern Rd Gillingham ME7 10 F6
Leysdown-on-S ME12 ....6 G2
Lydd TN29 ....203 D7
Eastern Service Rd CT16 ....166 H8
Eastfield House ME16 ...74 B2
Eastfield Rd [1] CT7 ....27 A7
Eastfields CT19 ....178 D6
Eastgate ME1 ....9 C5
Eastgate Cl CT6 ....23 B3
Eastgate Ct ME1 ....9 C5
Eastgate Rd TN30 ....179 C8
Eastgate Terr ME1 ....9 C5
Eastling Cl ME8 ....11 D3
Eastling Prim Sch ME13 .81 F5
Eastling Rd Bayfield ME13 61 D2
Eastling ME13 ....81 F7
Eastmead Ave TN23 ....156 C8
Easton's Cnr TN25 ....172 F4
Eastry CE Prim Sch CT13 93 B2
Eastry Cl Ashford TN23 ...156 A6
Maidstone ME16 ....74 C7
Eastry Ct CT3 ....112 F5
Eastry Park CT13 ....93 C1
Eastwell [5] TN30 ....179 A7
Eastwell Barn Mews TN30 ....179 A8
Eastwell Cl
Maidstone ME14 ....75 C5
Shadoxhurst TN26 ....155 B1
Eastwell Meadows TN30 ....179 A8
Eastwell Terr TN25 ....122 E3
Eastwood Cotts ME9 ....38 E6
Eastwood Rd ME10 ....36 D5
Eaton Hill CT9 ....7 I2
Eaton Rd Dover CT17 ....166 B7
Margate CT9 ....7 I1
Eaves Ct ME10 ....37 B5
Eaves Rd CT17 ....166 A7
Ebbsfleet La CT12 ....51 A3
Ebony Cotts TN30 ....189 A6
Ebony Wlk ME16 ....74 B3
Eccleston Rd ME15 ....74 F2
Echo Cl ME15 ....97 F6
Echo Ho ME10 ....37 B3
Echo Wlk ME12 ....4 D6
Eclipse Dr ME10 ....36 E8
Eddie Willet Rd CT6 ....22 B3
Eddington Cl ME15 ....97 B6
Eddington La CT6 ....22 F3
Eddington Way CT6 ....22 E3
Eden Ave ME5 ....32 A7
Eden Ho TN23 ....156 C8
Eden Rd CT5 ....43 A7
Edenbridge Dr ME12 ....3 B8
Edenbridge Ho CT1 ....88 B8
Edenfield CT7 ....27 B7
Edgar Cl CT5 ....21 D3
Edgar Ho CT14 ....117 B3
Edgar Rd Canterbury CT1 ..67 B1
Dover CT17 ....149 B1
Margate CT9 ....8 A3
Minster (Thanet) CT12 ....50 B6
Edge End Rd CT10 ....29 F4
Edgehill Cl CT20 ....177 D4
Edger Pl [5] ME15 ....75 A4
Edinburgh Ho Deal CT14 117 A5
[7] Dover CT17 ....166 D7
Edinburgh Pl CT20 ....178 B3
Edinburgh Rd
Ashford TN24 ....139 B2
Chatham ME4 ....10 C2
Gillingham ME7 ....10 D5
Margate CT9 ....28 B8
Edinburgh Sq ME15 ....97 D7
Edinburgh Wlk [5] CT9 ...28 B8
Edisbury Wlk ME8 ....33 D5
Edith Rd Faversham ME13 .62 C6
Ramsgate CT11 ....52 C6
Westgate-on-S CT8 ....7 D1
Edmanson Ave CT9 ....7 E1
Edmund Cl ME16 ....74 A3
Edmund St CT3 ....91 A8
Edna Rd ME14 ....74 F8
Edred Rd CT17 ....166 B8
Edward Ct ME5 ....10 C1
Edward Dr CT7 ....27 B7
Edward Rd Canterbury CT1 88 A8
Folkestone CT19 ....178 D6
Kingsdown CT14 ....134 C6
Queenborough ME11 ....3 B5
Edward St Chatham ME4 ..10 A3
Rochester ME2 ....9 B7
Sheerness ME12 ....1 B3
Edward Terr [9] CT20 ...178 E6
Edwards Cl ME8 ....33 C5
Edwards Rd CT16 ....166 D8
Edwin Rd ME8 ....33 C8
Edwina Ave ME12 ....4 A7
Edwina Pl ME9 ....35 C7
Edyngham Cl ME10 ....37 A8
Effingham Cres CT17 ...166 D8
Effingham St
Dover CT17 ....166 D8
Ramsgate CT11 ....52 E6
Egbert Rd Birchington CT7 26 D8
Faversham ME13 ....62 C6
Minster (Thanet) CT12 ....50 B6
Westgate-on-S CT8 ....7 C1
Egerton CE Prim Sch TN27 ....118 F3
Egerton Dr CT9 ....8 E2
Egerton House Rd TN27 118 E4
Egerton Rd
Charing Heath TN27 ....119 C7
Maidstone ME14 ....74 E7
Pluckley TN27 ....119 B1
Temple Ewell CT16 ....148 E5
Eggarton La CT4 ....107 C2
Eggringe TN23 ....138 E1
Egremont Rd ME15 ....75 F2
Eighteen Acre La TN29 .198 D8
Elder Cl ME17 ....99 D2
Elder Ct ME8 ....33 B6
Elders The CT3 ....68 F1
Eldon Pl [4] CT10 ....30 B4
Eldon St ME4 ....10 A4
Eleanor Dr ME10 ....36 F8
Elfrida Cl CT9 ....29 C8
Elgar Pl CT11 ....52 D7
Elham CE Prim Sch CT4 144 F4
Elham Cl Gillingham ME8 ..11 B3
Margate CT9 ....8 C1
Elham Rd CT1 ....87 E6
Elham Valley Railway Mus★ CT18 ..177 A8
Elham Valley Vineyards★ CT4 ....128 D4
Elham Way CT10 ....30 A2
Eling Ct ME15 ....97 A8
Eliot Coll CT2 ....66 E4
Elisons Wlk CT1 ....88 C8
Elizabeth Carter Ave CT14 ....116 F4
Elizabeth Ct
Broadstairs CT10 ....30 B6
Chatham ME5 ....32 A7
Gillingham ME8 ....11 C1
Herne Bay CT6 ....22 F5
Elizabeth Dr CT18 ....164 B2
Elizabeth Gdns CT21 ...176 B1
Elizabeth House ME14 ...75 A6
Elizabeth Kemp Ct CT12 .29 C1
Elizabeth Rd CT11 ....52 F6
Elizabeth St CT17 ....166 D6
Elizabeth Way CT6 ....23 B3
Elizabethen Ct TN27 ....120 C7
Ellen Ave CT11 ....29 E2
Ellen's Hill CT14 ....116 E3
Ellen's Pl ME9 ....35 C6
Ellenden Ct CT2 ....66 C4
Ellens Rd CT14 ....116 F2
Ellenswood Cl ME15 ....76 A1
Ellesmere Mews TN28 ..200 C8
Ellingham Leas ME15 ....97 C7
Ellingham Way TN23 ....156 A5
Ellington Ave CT9 ....28 B8
Ellington High Sch CT11 .52 C7
Ellington Inf Sch CT11 ...52 C7
Ellington Pl CT11 ....52 C7
Ellington Rd CT11 ....52 D7
Elliot Cl CT1 ....67 C3
Elliots Pl ME13 ....62 D7
Elliott Park Sch ME12 ....4 A7
Ellis Dr TN28 ....200 C8
Ellis Ho [7] ME14 ....75 B4
Ellis Rd CT5 ....21 A3
Ellis Way CT6 ....23 C2
Ellison Cl CT5 ....21 C1
Ellison Ct ME13 ....62 E6
Ellison Way ME8 ....12 A2
Elm Ave ME4 ....9 E1
Elm Cl TN27 ....118 F3
Elm Cotts TN25 ....122 E3
Elm Court Ind Est ME7 ...32 E3
Elm Ct CT8 ....27 E8
Elm Fields TN29 ....199 A6
Elm Gdns CT21 ....176 E2
Elm Gr Maidstone ME15 ...75 B3
Manston CT12 ....28 D1
Sittingbourne ME10 ....37 B4
Westgate-on-S CT8 ....27 E8
Elm Ho [11] CT21 ....176 B2
Elm La ME12 ....4 E5
Elm Park Gdns CT17 ...165 F7
Elm Pl TN23 ....155 F7
Elm Rd Aylesham CT3 ...112 E5
[7] Folkestone CT19 ....178 E6
Gillingham ME7 ....10 E6
St Mary's Bay TN29 ....194 F3
Elm Tree Dr ME1 ....9 A2
Elm Wood Cl CT5 ....21 C2
Elm Wood W CT5 ....21 C2
Elmfield Gillingham ME8 ..11 A3
Tenterden TN30 ....179 B8
Elmfield Ct
Coxheath ME17 ....96 C3
Tenterden TN30 ....179 B8
Elmhurst Gdns ME4 ....9 E3
Elmleigh Rd CT3 ....90 A8
Elmley Ind Est ME11 ....3 A2
Elmley Marshes Nature Reserve★ ME12 .16 F4
Elmley Rd ME12 ....4 D3
Elmley Way CT9 ....28 F6
Elms Ave CT11 ....52 D6
Elms Hill CT15 ....165 D6
Elms The Hersden CT3 ...46 E1
Teynham ME9 ....39 A2
Elms Vale Rd CT15,CT17 .165 E7
Elmstead Pl [10] CT20 ...178 E5
Elmstone Cl ME16 ....74 B2
Elmstone Gdns CT9 ....8 E2
Elmstone Hole Rd ME17 ....100 D1
Elmstone La ME16 ....74 B2
Elmstone Rd
Gillingham ME8 ....33 D7
Ramsgate CT11 ....52 D7
Elmton La CT15 ....114 C1
Elmtree TN26 ....181 C1
Elmway ME12 ....5 F6
Elmwood Ave CT10 ....30 A8
Elmwood Cl CT10 ....30 A7
Elventon Cl CT19 ....177 E7
Elverland La ME13,ME9 ...61 B2
Elvington Cl ME16 ....74 D5
Elvington La CT18 ....162 E2
Elwick La [13] TN23 ....139 B2
Elwick Rd TN23 ....139 B2
Ely Cl ME8 ....11 E2
Embassy Cl ME7 ....10 F1
Emerald Cl ME1 ....31 D7
Emerald View ME12 ....6 E4
Emily Rd ME5 ....32 B6
Emmerson Gdns CT5 ...21 D3
Empire Terr CT9 ....28 E8
Empress Gdns ME12 ....6 D4
Emsworth Gr ME14 ....75 D6
Enbrook Rd CT20 ....177 E4
Enbrook Valley CT20 ...177 E5
Encombe CT20 ....177 D3
Enfield Rd CT14 ....117 D7
Engineers Ct [1] TN23 ..139 B2
English Martyrs' RC Prim Sch ME2 ....9 B8
Ennerdale ME13 ....62 E6
Ennerdale Gdns CT3 ...112 F6
Enterprise Bsns Est ME2 ..9 E7
Enterprise Cl ME2 ....9 D8
Enterprise Ctr The ME5 ..54 C8
Enterprise Rd
Maidstone ME15 ....75 A1
Margate CT9 ....29 A6
Enticott Cl CT5 ....21 A1
Epaul La ME1 ....9 C6
Eppe Cl [2] ME2 ....9 B8
Epping Cl CT6 ....23 B2
Epple Bay Ave CT7 ....27 B8
Epple Bay Rd CT7 ....27 A8
Epple Rd CT7 ....27 B8
Epps Rd ME10 ....36 E3
Epsom Cl ME15 ....97 F6
Eric Rd CT17 ....149 B2
Erith Cl ME14 ....75 A8
Erith St CT17 ....149 B1
Ernest Dr ME16 ....74 B5
Ernest Rd ME4 ....10 A3
Ernwell Rd CT19 ....178 D6
Ersham Rd CT1 ....88 A7
Eskdale Ave CT11 ....52 A7
Esmonde Dr CT12 ....27 F2
Esplanade Dover CT17 ..166 D6
Rochester ME1 ....9 B5
Westgate-on-S CT8,CT9 ....7 C1
Essella Pk TN24 ....139 E1
Essella Rd TN24 ....139 E1
Essetford Rd TN23 ....156 A7
Essex Ave CT6 ....22 B4
Essex Gdns CT7 ....26 F6
Essex Rd Canterbury CT1 ..88 D7
Maidstone ME15 ....97 E6
Westgate-on-S CT8 ....27 F8
Essex St CT5 ....43 D8
Estelle Cl ME1 ....31 D7
Esther Ct ME10 ....36 E8
Estuary Cl CT5 ....21 E3
Estuary Rd ME12 ....1 C1
Etchden Rd TN26 ....154 A8
Ethel Rd CT10 ....29 F5
Ethel-Maud Ct ME7 ....10 D7
Ethelbert Cres CT9 ....8 A3
Ethelbert Gdns CT9 ....7 J3
Ethelbert Rd
Birchington CT7 ....26 D8
Canterbury CT1 ....88 B6
Deal CT14 ....95 C1
Dover CT17 ....166 C8
Faversham ME13 ....62 C6
Folkestone CT19 ....178 D7
Margate CT9 ....7 J3
Ramsgate CT11 ....52 D6
Rochester ME1 ....9 C4
Ethelbert Road Inf Sch ME13 ....62 C6
Ethelbert Sq CT8 ....7 C1
Ethelbert Terr Margate CT9 8 A3
Westgate-on-S CT8 ....7 C1
Ethelburga Dr CT18 ...161 B7
Ethelred Ct ME13 ....62 C6
Ethelred Rd CT8 ....7 C1
Eton Cl ME5 ....31 F4
Ettrick Terr CT21 ....176 A2
Eurogate Bsns Pk TN24 139 B5
Eurolink Way ME10 ....36 F4
Eva Rd ME7 ....10 D3
Evans Rd TN24 ....157 A7
Evelings Alley [12] CT5 ....20 D2
Evelyn Cl ME2 ....9 C8
Evelyn Ct CT21 ....177 A2
Evelyn Ho
[9] Folkestone CT20 ....178 D5
[5] Rochester ME2 ....9 C8
Evelyn Rd ME16 ....74 E3

Freshfield La CT21 .....176 B4
Freshland Rd ME16 .....74 B4
Freshlands CT6 ....23 E5
Freshwater Cl CT6 ......22 B3
Freshwater Rd ME5 .....32 B7
Friars Ave ME5 ....31 F2
Friars Cl CT5 ....21 A1
Friars Sch TN23 ....155 B8
Friars The CT1 ....66 F1
Friars Way CT16 ....149 A3
Friary Pl 3 ME2 ....9 B7
Friary Prec ME2 ....9 B7
Friary Way CT2 ....66 D2
Frid Cnr TN26 ....153 E7
Friendly Cl CT9 ....8 D1
Friends Ave CT9 ....29 D8
Friesian Way TN24 .....139 C8
Frindsbury Rd ME2 ....9 B8
Frinstead Wlk ME16 .....74 B7
Frinsted Cl ME8 ....11 C3
Frinsted Rd ME9 ....58 E2
Friston Way ME1 ....31 D8
Frith Rd Aldington TN25 ..172 C6
Dover CT16 ....149 C1
Frithwood Cl ME15 ......75 F1
Frittenden Cl TN23 .....155 E6
Frobisher Cl ME10 ......36 E7
Frobisher Ct 2 CT11 .....52 F8
Frobisher Gdns ME1 ......9 C2
Frog Farm Cotts ME9 ....13 A4
Frog La CT4 ....111 C6
Frogmore Wlk ME17 ....101 C5
Frognal Cl ME9 ....38 B2
Frognal Gdns ME9 ....38 C2
Frognal La ME9 ....38 B2
Front Brents ME13 ......62 D8
Front Rd TN26 ....169 A1
Front St CT14 ....133 F5
Front The CT15 ....151 A4
Frost Cres ME5 ....32 A7
Froyle Cl ME16 ....74 C6
Fruiterer's Cl ME9 ......59 B7
Fulbert Dr ME14 ....75 F5
Fulbert Rd CT16 ....149 B5
Fulham Ave CT9 ....28 C7
Fullers Cl ME14 ....76 A4
Fullers Yd CT9 ....7 J2
Fulmar Ct TN29 ....194 F3
Fulsam Pl CT9 ....7 H1
Fulston Manor Sch ME10 36 F2
Fulston Pl ME10 ....37 A3
Furfield Cl ME17 ....97 E5
Furley Park Prim Sch
TN23 ....156 C2
Furrell's Rd ME1 ....9 D5
Furze Hill Cres ME12 .....3 E6
Fusilier Ave CT20 ......177 B5
Fyndon Ho CT1 ....88 C7

G

Gabriel's Hill ME15 .....75 A4
Gadby Rd ME10 ....36 C5
Gads Hill ME7 ....10 F6
Gadsby La TN26 ....153 A3
Gagetown Terr 1 ME14 ..74 F7
Gainsboro Rd 4 CT7 .....26 F8
Gainsborough Ave CT9 ..29 C8
Gainsborough Cl
Folkestone CT19 ....178 A7
Gillingham ME8 ....33 D6
Sittingbourne ME10 .....36 B5
Gainsborough Dr
Herne Bay CT6 ....23 E5
Maidstone ME16 ....74 B4
Gainsborough Ho ME1 ....9 D5
Galena Cl Chatham ME5 ..32 A1
Sittingbourne ME10 .....36 C6
Gallants La ME15 ....96 A4
Galleon Cl ME1 ....31 C8
Galliard St CT13 ....94 A8
Gallow's Cnr CT21 .....176 A2
Galloway Dr TN25 .....139 C8
Galloways Rd TN29 ....203 C5
Gallwey Ave CT7 ....26 E7
Galway Rd ME12 ....1 D1
Gammon's Farm La
TN29 ....185 B3
Gandy's La ME17 ....97 C2
Gange Mews 5 ME13 ....62 D7
Gann Rd CT5 ....20 F2
Gaol La 13 CT16 ....166 D7
Gap House Sch CT10 ....30 B2
Gap The Blean CT2 ......66 A7
Canterbury CT1 ....88 B5
Garden Cl Maidstone ME15 97 E7
Rough Common CT2 ......66 A2
Garden Cotts CT3 ....91 A7
Garden Hall The TN25 ..124 A1
Garden of England Pk
(Mobile Home Pk)
ME17 ....100 B7
Garden Pl TN24 ....139 E6
Garden Rd CT19 ....178 D6
Garden St ME7 ....10 A6
Gardeners Pl CT4 ....86 F1
Gardens The
Coxheath ME17 ....96 C3
Ivychurch TN29 ....192 F4
Gardiner St ME7 ....10 C6
Garfield Pl 4 ME13 .....62 D7
Garfield Rd
Gillingham ME7 ....10 D6
Margate CT9 ....7 H2
Garlinge Green Rd CT4 .108 E6
Garlinge Inf Sch CT9 ....28 C8
Garlinge Jun Sch CT9 ...28 B8
Garrard Ave CT9 ....28 B8
Garrington Cl ME14 .....75 C6
Garrison Rd ME12 ....1 B3
Gas House Rd ME1 ....9 C6
Gas La ME13 ....63 F3
Gas Rd Sittingbourne ME10 .36 F5
Sittingbourne,Murston
ME10 ....37 B6
Gas St CT1 ....87 F7
Gascoyne Cl ME15 ......76 B2
Gasworks La TN23 .....139 B2
Gatcombe Cl
Chatham ME5 ....32 A5
Maidstone ME16 ....74 B5
Gate Quays CT9 ....7 I2
Gateacre Rd CT5 ....43 A6
Gatefield La 9 ME13 ....62 D7
Gatekeeper Chase ME8 ..33 F8
Gateway Ct 15 CT11 .....52 F7
Gateway The CT16 .....166 E7
Gatland La ME16 ....74 B2
Gault Cl ME15 ....76 A2
Gaunt's Cl CT14 ....117 A4
Gayhurst Cl ME8 ....33 D6
Gayhurst Dr ME10 ......36 C5
Gaze Hill Ave ME10 .....37 A3
Gazedown TN29 ....194 F3
Gean Cl ME5 ....54 A8
Genesta Ave CT5 ....43 B7
Genesta Cl ME10 ....36 E7
Geneva Ave ME8 ....11 A2
Gentian Cl
4 Chatham ME5 ....31 E4
Maidstone ME14 ....75 E5
Geoffrey Ct CT7 ....27 A7
George Alley CT14 .....117 D6
George Cooper Ho 7
CT20 ....178 C4
George Gurr Cres CT19 178 D8
George Hill Rd
Broadstairs CT10 ....29 F8
Margate CT10,CT9 ....8 E1
George La
Boughton Street ME13 ...63 F3
Folkestone CT20 ....178 D4
Leeds ME17 ....99 B7
New Romney TN28 ......200 B7
Rochester ME1 ....9 C6
George Marsham House
ME15 ....96 F3
George Parris Ct ME12 ...4 C6
George Pk CT9 ....7 F1
George Roche Rd CT1 ...88 A6
George Spurgen
Com Prim Sch CT19 ...178 E7
George St Ashford TN23 .139 B1
Deal CT14 ....117 D7
Dover CT17 ....149 C1
Maidstone ME15 ....75 A3
Ramsgate CT11 ....52 E7
Sittingbourne ME10 .....37 B4
George Stone Ho 22
CT20 ....178 E5
George Summers Cl ME2 .9 E8
George V Ave CT9 ....28 C8
George Warren Ct 1 CT9 .7 J1
George Williams Way
TN24 ....139 E5
George Wood Cl TN29 ..203 C6
George's Ave CT5 ....43 A7
Georgian Cl ME11 ....3 A3
Georgian Dr ME17 ......96 D3
Georgian Way ME8 ......33 C4
Gerald Ave ME4 ....9 F2
Gerald Palmby Ct CT14 .117 C7
Geraldine Rd CT19 .....177 F6
Gerrard Ave ME1 ....31 E8
Gerrards Dr ME10 ......36 F2
Gibbons Rd ME10 ......36 B5
Gibraltar Ave ME7 ......10 B7
Gibraltar Hill ME4 ....9 F4
Gibraltar La
Hawkinge CT18 ....163 A2
Maidstone ME14 ....74 F8
Gibraltar Sq CT15 .....149 E3
Gibson St ME10 ....36 E4
Gidd's Pond Cotts ME14 .75 E6
Giddyhorn La ME16 .....74 C5
Gifford Cl ME8 ....11 C3
Gigger's Green Rd TN25 185 C7
Gilbert Cl ME7 ....33 A5
Gilbert Rd
4 Ashford TN24 ....139 B2
Ramsgate CT11 ....52 D8
Gilbert Terr 2 ME14 .....74 F7
Gilchrist Ave CT6 ....22 C2
Giles Gdns CT9 ....28 F8
Giles La CT2 ....66 D4
Giles-Young Ct 8 ME10 ..36 E5
Gilford Rd CT14 ....117 D5
Gilham Gr CT14 ....117 B4
Gill La Mersham TN25 ...172 A8
Ruckinge TN26 ....171 C2
Gillett Rd TN29 ....203 D7
Gillingham Coll The ME7 .10 F4
Gillingham Gate ME7 ....10 C8
Gillingham Gate Rd ME7 10 C8
Gillingham Gn ME7 .....10 E6
Gillingham Rd ME7 .....10 D5
Gillingham Sta ME7 .....10 D5
Gillman Cl CT18 ....162 F4
Gillon Mews 9 CT1 .....67 B2
Gills Terr ME8 ....12 C3
Ginsbury Cl ME2 ....9 E6
Giraud Dr ME13 ....62 B8
Glack Rd CT14 ....116 F4
Glade The Chatham ME5 ..32 A2
Deal CT14 ....116 F6
Gladstone Ct CT10 ......29 F4
Gladstone Dr ME10 .....37 C4
Gladstone Rd
Ashford TN24 ....156 E7
Broadstairs CT10 ....29 F4
Chatham ME4 ....9 E2
Deal CT14 ....117 C4
Folkestone CT19 ....178 E6
Maidstone ME14 ....75 A6
Margate CT9 ....7 I1
Whitstable CT5 ....20 D2
Gladwyn Cl ME8 ....33 D4
Glamis Cl ME5 ....32 A5
Glanville Rd
Gillingham ME7 ....10 D5
Rochester ME2 ....9 A8
Glasgow House 8 ME15 .97 E7
Gleaming Wood Dr ME5 .54 D8
Gleaners Cl ME14 ....75 E4
Gleanings Mews ME1 .....9 C5
Glebe Cl
Biddenden Green TN27 ..135 B2
St Margaret's at Cliffe
CT15 ....150 F6
Glebe Cotts ME13 ....81 E7
Glebe Ct CT12 ....50 B5
Glebe Gdns
Lenham ME17 ....101 E5
6 Margate CT9 ....28 B8
Glebe La Maidstone ME16 .74 A1
Sittingbourne ME10 .....37 B2
Glebe Rd Gillingham ME7 ..10 E3
Margate CT9 ....28 B8
Glebe The TN27 ....120 D7
Glebe Way Ashford TN24 139 D6
Whitstable CT5 ....43 D8
Glebeland TN27 ....118 F4
Glebelands Alkham CT15 147 D1
Ash CT3 ....71 C2
Mersham TN25 ....157 E4
Glemsford Cotts CT2 ....65 E1
Glen Ave CT6 ....23 C5
Glen Gr CT17 ....166 B7
Glen Iris Ave CT2 ....66 C2
Glen Iris Cl CT2 ....66 C2
Glen Rd CT14 ....134 C6
Glen The
Minster (Sheppey) ME12 ...4 B7
Minster (Sheppey) ME12 ...4 C7
Shepherdswell CT15 ....130 D5
Upstreet CT3 ....47 D3
Glen Wlk CT5 ....43 A3
Glenavon Ho CT10 ......30 B7
Glenbervie Dr CT6 ......23 E5
Glenbrook Cl CT6 ....23 D5
Glenbrook Gr ME10 .....36 E7
Glencoe Inf Sch ME4 ....10 A2
Glencoe Jun Sch ME4 ...10 A2
Glencoe Rd Chatham ME4 .10 A2
Margate CT9 ....8 A1
Glendale Rd ME12 ....4 B7
Gleneagles Ct ME5 .....31 F2
Gleneagles Dr ME15 ....75 A1
Glenfield Rd CT16 .....149 B3
Glenside CT5 ....44 A8
Glenside Ave CT1 ....67 B2
Glenwood TN30 ....167 B3
Glenwood Cl
Chatham ME5 ....10 C1
Gillingham ME7 ....33 A7
Maidstone ME16 ....74 C5
St Michaels TN30 ......167 B3
Glenwood Dr ME12 ....4 C6
Glistening Glade ME8 ...33 E6
Globe La ME4 ....9 F5
Gloster Cl CT18 ....163 B3
Gloster Ropewalk CT17 166 C5
Gloster Way CT17 .....166 C5
Gloucester Ave
Broadstairs CT10 ....29 F3
Margate CT9 ....8 D2
Gloucester Cl ME8 .....34 A8
Gloucester Mews TN28 .200 C8
Gloucester Pl 17 CT20 ..178 D5
Gloucester Rd
Maidstone ME15 ....97 D8
Whitstable CT5 ....20 F2
Glover Cl ME10 ....14 F1
Glover Rd TN24 ....139 E1
Glovers Cres ME10 .....36 F3
Glovers Mill ME4 ....9 D3
Glynne Cl ME8 ....33 D6
Goad Ave ME5 ....32 B3
Goat Lees La TN25 .....139 D8
Gobery Hill CT3 ....70 B1
Godden Rd CT2 ....67 A4
Goddings Dr ME1 ....9 A3
Goddington La ME17 ...100 B6
Goddington Rd ME2 ......9 B8
Godfrey Ho CT5 ....43 E8
Godfrey Wlk TN23 .....156 B8
Godfrey's Grave ME13 ...64 B7
Godfreys Cotts ME13 ...105 C8
Godinton* TN23 ....138 C4
Godinton Cty Prim Sch
TN23 ....138 D3
Godinton La TN23,TN26 .138 D5
Godinton Rd TN23 .....139 A2
Godinton Way TN23 ....139 A2
Godwin Bglws CT9 ....8 B3
Godwin Cl ME10 ....14 F1
Godwin Cotts CT9 ....8 A3
Godwin Rd Canterbury CT1 87 C6
Dover CT16 ....166 F8
Margate CT9 ....8 A3
Godwyn Gdns CT20 ....178 A4
Godwyn Rd Deal CT14 ..117 C8
Folkestone CT20 ....178 A4
Godwyne Cl CT16 ......166 D8
Godwyne Ct CT16 ......149 D1
Godwyne Rd CT16 .....149 D1
Gogway CT4 ....126 B4
Gold Hill TN25 ....121 D4
Goldcrest Wlk CT5 ......43 B6
Golden Acre La CT8 .....27 D7
Golden Cl CT8 ....27 D7
Golden Hill CT5 ....43 F6
Golden Sq
New Romney TN28 .....200 A6
Tenterden TN30 ....179 B8
Golden St CT14 ....117 D7
Golden Wood Cl ME5 ...54 D8
Goldfinch Cl
Faversham ME13 ....40 C1
Herne Bay CT6 ....23 C2
Goldings The
Gillingham ME8 ....33 C8
Monkton CT12 ....49 C7
Goldsmith Ct TN30 .....167 B1
Goldsmith Rd ME8 ......33 E5
Goldstone Dro CT3 ......71 E7
Goldstone Wlk ME5 .....32 A1
Goldthorne Cl ME14 .....75 C5
Goldups La CT4 ....84 C1
Goldups Lane Cotts CT4 .84 C1
Goldwell Cl TN25 ......173 A6
Goldwell Hos TN25 .....173 A6
Goldwell La
Aldington TN25 ....173 B7
Great Chart TN23,TN26 ..154 F8
Golf Ct CT14 ....95 C1
Golf Rd CT14 ....117 C8
Golf Road Pl CT14 .....117 C8
Gooch Cl ME16 ....74 D8
Good Hope CT14 ....116 F4
Good Intent Cotts TN27 119 A5
Goodall Cl ME8 ....33 E5
Goodban Sq CT3 ....71 D1
Goodcheap La TN25 ...140 D2
Goodfellow Way 3
CT16 ....166 D8
Goodnestone
CE Prim Sch CT3 ....91 C2
Goodnestone Gdns*
CT3 ....91 C1
Goodnestone Hill CT3 ...91 D2
Goodnestone Rd
Sittingbourne ME10 .....37 B4
Wingham CT3 ....91 B5
Goodwin Ave CT5 ....21 E2
Goodwin Dr ME14 ....75 B8
Goodwin Pk CT9 ....29 A5
Goodwin Rd
Ramsgate CT11 ....52 B5
St Margaret's at Cliffe
CT15 ....151 A4
Goodwood Cl ME15 .....97 F6
Goose Cl ME5 ....32 A7
Gordon Ave ME11 ....3 A4
Gordon Cl Ashford TN24 .139 D2
Sittingbourne ME10 .....37 C4
Gordon Cotts ME9 ......58 B6
Gordon Ct ME17 ....96 E3
Gordon Cty Inf Sch ME2 ..9 A8
Gordon Gr CT8 ....7 C1
Gordon Rd Canterbury CT1 87 F7
Chatham ME4 ....10 B2
Faversham ME13 ....62 E8
Folkestone CT20 ....177 D6
Gillingham ME7 ....10 E5
Gillingham,Brompton ME4 ..10 A7
Herne Bay CT6 ....22 F4
Margate CT9 ....8 A3
Margate, Westwood CT9 ..29 A5
Ramsgate CT11 ....52 D8
Rochester ME2 ....9 A8
Whitfield CT16 ....149 A5
Whitstable CT5 ....43 D8
Gordon Sq Birchington CT7 26 F7
Faversham ME13 ....62 E7
Gordon Terr ME1 ....9 C4
Gore Cl CT13 ....93 B3
Gore Cotts ME9 ....12 E1
Gore Court Rd
Maidstone ME15 ....97 F5
Sittingbourne ME10 .....36 E2
Gore End Cl CT7 ....26 F7
Gore Farm Trails* ME9 .12 D1
Gore La CT13 ....93 B2
Gore Mews 3 CT1 ....67 B2
Gore Rd Eastry CT13 ....93 B3
Silver Street ME9 ....57 F5
Gore St CT12 ....49 A7
Gore Terr CT13 ....93 B3
Gorely Ho 14 CT17 .....166 D7
Goretop La CT14 ....94 C6
Gorham Dr ME15 ....76 A1
Gorrell Rd CT5 ....20 E1
Gorse Ave ME5 ....31 F5
Gorse La CT6 ....23 C2
Gorse Mead TN23 ......155 F8
Gorse Rd ME10 ....37 C5
Goschen Rd CT17 ......166 B8
Gosfield Rd CT6 ....23 A4
Goshawk Ho 1 ME10 ....37 A4
Goss Hall La CT3 ....72 A2
Gosselin St CT5 ....43 E8
Goteley Mere TN24 ....139 C7
Gothic Cl CT14 ....117 B1
Gothic Cotts TN26 .....121 A1
Goudhurst Cl
Canterbury CT2 ....67 A4
Maidstone ME16 ....74 E4
Goudhurst Rd ME8 ......11 B3
Gough Rd CT20 ....177 E3
Gould Rd ME5 ....32 B3
Grace Ave ME16 ....74 D6
Grace Ct 16 CT20 ......178 D5
Grace Hill CT20 ....178 D5
Grace Mdw CT16 ......149 A7
Grace Rd ME12 ....1 B1
Grace Wlk CT14 ....117 A5
Grafton Ave ME1 ....31 E8
Grafton Rd
Broadstairs CT10 ....29 F8
Sittingbourne ME10 .....36 F4
Grafton Rise CT6 ....22 C4
Grain Rd ME8 ....33 C3
Grainey Field ME9 ......34 E4
Gram's Rd CT14 ....134 C8
Grampian Way ME15 ....76 A1
Grampion Cl TN24 .....139 C4
Granada House 8 ME15 .75 A4
Granada St 9 ME15 .....75 A4
Granary Cl Gillingham ME8 11 F1
Maidstone ME14 ....75 E5
Granary Court Rd TN25 .159 A4
Granary Pl CT5 ....43 D8
Grand Ct Folkestone CT20 178 B3
7 Gillingham ME7 ....10 C6
Littlestone-on-S TN28 ...200 E5
Grand Dr CT6 ....22 C4
Grand Mans CT10 ....30 B3
Grand Par TN28 ....200 E5
Grange Cres TN30 .....167 A3
Grange Ct 1 CT20 .....178 C4
Grange Hill ME5 ....10 B3
Grange Ho ME16 ....74 A2
Grange La ME14 ....54 A1
Grange Rd
Broadstairs CT10 ....29 F6
Deal CT14 ....117 B5
Folkestone CT19 ....177 E6
Gillingham,Grange ME7 ...11 A6
Gillingham,Lower Twydale
ME7 ....11 B5
Herne Bay CT6 ....23 C4
Hythe CT21 ....176 B4
Ramsgate CT11 ....52 C6
Rochester ME2 ....9 B7
Tenterden TN30 ....167 A3
Grange Rdbt ME7 ....11 A6
Grange The
Shepherdswell CT15 ....130 D5
Whitstable CT5 ....43 A6
Grange Way
Broadstairs CT10 ....29 F2
Rochester ME1 ....9 C3
Grant Cl Broadstairs CT10 .29 E6
Gillingham ME7 ....11 B1
Grant Dr ME15 ....97 D6
Grant's Cotts ME17 ....101 B5
Grantham Ave CT14 ....117 A5
Grantley Cl TN23 ......156 A8
Granville Ave
Broadstairs CT10 ....30 B3
Ramsgate CT12 ....29 B1
Granville Cl ME13 ......62 C7
Granville Dr CT6 ....22 B2
Granville Farm Mews 19
CT11 ....52 F7
Granville Marina 17 CT11 52 F7
Granville Par CT20 ....177 E3
Granville Pl ME12 ....1 D2
Granville Rd
Broadstairs CT10 ....30 B3
Deal CT14 ....117 C2
Gillingham ME7 ....10 E5
Kingsdown CT14 ....134 D3
Maidstone ME14 ....75 A6
Sheerness ME12 ....1 D2
St Margaret's at Cliffe
CT15 ....151 B6
Granville Rd E CT20 ...177 F3
Granville St Deal CT14 .117 D5
Dover CT16 ....149 C1
Granville The CT15 ....151 B6
Grapple Rd ME14 ....75 A7
Grasmere Ave CT11 .....52 A7
Grasmere Gdns CT19 ..178 B7
Grasmere Rd
Ashford TN24 ....139 C6
Whitstable CT5 ....44 B8
Grasmere Way CT3 ....112 F6
Grasslands Ashford TN23 155 D7
Langley Heath ME17 .....98 E4
Grassmere TN29 ....194 E3
Grassy Glade ME7 ......33 B6
Gravel Castle Rd CT4 ..109 A8
Gravel Hill ME13 ......103 C8
Gravel La CT15 ....165 A4
Gravel Wlk
3 Ashford TN23 ....139 B3
12 Canterbury CT1 ......87 F8
Rochester ME1 ....9 D5
Gravelly Bottom Rd
ME17 ....99 B2
Graveney Prim Sch
ME13 ....41 E1
Graveney Rd
Faversham ME13 ....62 F7
Maidstone ME15 ....97 F7
Gray Cl CT18 ....163 B5
Graylen Cl CT14 ....117 C7
Graylings Ct ME10 .....36 C2
Graylings The ME1 ....9 B3
Grays Way CT1 ....87 B6
Grayshott Cl ME10 .....36 F3
Graystone Rd CT5 ......21 A2
Great Basin Rd ME12 .....1 A2
Great Burton Ho TN24 ..139 E5

Great Chart Prim Sch TN23 155 D8
Great Conduit St CT21 176 C2
Great Ivy Mill Cotts ME15 96 F7
Great Lines ME7 10 B5
Great South Ave ME4 10 A1
Greatstone Prim Sch TN28 200 D2
Grebe Apartments 15 ME15 97 E5
Grebe Cl CT18 163 A4
Grebe Cres CT21 187 C8
Grecian St ME14 75 A6
Green Acres CT15 131 D7
Green Acres Cl CT6 23 B3
Green Bank Cl ME7 33 A5
Green Cl Hawkinge CT18 163 B4
Rochester ME1 9 D2
Green Cloth Mews 2 CT1 67 B2
Green Ct Bridge CT4 89 A1
Folkestone CT19 178 E7
Green Dell CT2 66 F4
Green Gates CT16 149 A8
Green Hedges TN30 179 B8
Green Hill ME15 76 B1
Green Hill La ME17 100 D1
Green Hills CT4 128 D8
Green La Alkham CT15 147 D3
Ashford TN23 155 E5
Bethersden TN26 153 A2
Boughton Monchelsea ME17 97 C3
Broadstairs CT10 29 E5
Capel-le-F CT18 164 B3
Challock TN25 105 A2
Chilham CT4 85 C2
Deal CT14 117 B1
Dover CT16 149 B3
Eythorne CT15 131 D7
Folkestone CT19 178 E7
Goodnestone CT3 92 B3
Hythe CT21 176 A2
Langley Heath ME17 98 E3
Margate CT9 29 E8
Platt's Heath ME17 100 F2
Rhodes Minnis CT4,CT18 143 E2
Rodmersham ME9 59 B7
Smarden TN27 135 A1
St Margaret's at Cliffe CT15 133 F1
Stockbury ME9 34 F1
Temple Ewell CT16 148 E6
Whitfield CT16 148 E7
Whitstable CT5 43 D8
Green Lane Ave CT21 176 A2
Green Lane Cotts ME17 98 E3
Green Leas CT5 21 D1
Green Lees ME13 61 E2
Green Meadows TN29 186 D2
Green Porch Cl ME10 36 F7
Green Rd Birchington CT7 26 F8
Stalisfield Green ME13 103 C6
Green Sands ME5 54 C8
Green St ME7 10 C5
Green The Blean CT2 66 A6
Burmarsh TN29 186 C4
Chartham CT4 86 D3
East Farleigh ME15 96 B7
Harbledown CT2 65 E1
Hythe CT21 176 B4
Littlebourne CT3 89 F7
Lower Halstow ME9 13 B3
Lydd TN29 203 B5
Manston CT12 28 D1
Sheerness ME12 1 I1
Woodchurch TN26 169 A2
Wye TN25 123 E2
Green Way Lydd TN29 203 C5
Maidstone ME16 74 B3
Green's Cotts ME15 96 A4
Greenacre CT4 111 D3
Greenacre Cl ME5 32 A5
Greenacre Dr CT14 117 C1
Greenacre Sch ME5 31 F5
Greenbank Ashford TN24 139 D6
Chatham ME5 32 B8
Greenbanks CT18 161 C6
Greenborough Cl ME15 97 E6
Greencroft TN23 155 E6
Greenfield Cl ME20 53 A6
Greenfield Cotts
9 Canterbury CT1 87 F7
Maidstone ME14 54 A1
Greenfield Rd
Folkestone CT19 178 E7
Gillingham ME7 10 D6
Ramsgate CT12 29 C2
Greenfields
Maidstone ME15 97 E8
Sellindge TN25 159 E2
Greenfinches ME7 32 F6
Greenhill Bridge Rd CT6 22 D3
Greenhill Cl CT12 50 B7
Greenhill Gdns
Herne Bay CT6 22 D3
Minster (Thanet) CT12 50 B7
Greenhill La TN27 135 F7
Greenhill Rd CT6 22 C2
Greenhithe 3 ME15 75 A3
Greenhouse La CT2 66 E2
Greenly Way TN28 200 C6
Greensand Rd ME15 76 A2
Greenside
High Halden TN26 167 E7
Maidstone ME15 75 B3
Greenvale Gdns ME8 11 B2
Greenview Wlk ME8 11 A4
Greenway Chatham ME5 31 D6
Faversham ME13 62 B8
Greenway Court Farm Cotts ME17 78 A1
Greenway Court Rd ME17 78 A1
Greenway La ME17 100 A7
Greenways
Lower Halstow ME9 13 B3
Maidstone ME14 75 F5
Sittingbourne ME10 37 B3
Greenwich Cl
Chatham ME5 32 B4
Maidstone ME16 74 D4
Gregory Cl Gillingham ME8 33 E4
Sittingbourne ME10 37 A8
Gregory Ct TN25 123 E2
Grenadier Cl
Gillingham ME8 12 B2
Maidstone ME15 75 F2
Grenham Bay Ave CT7 26 E8
Grenham Rd CT7 26 F8
Grenville Gdns CT7 26 E8
Grenville Way CT10 29 E4
Gresham Ave CT9 7 E1
Gresham Cl 3 ME8 11 F1
Gresham Rd ME17 96 D3
Greville Homes CT13 93 B2
Grey Friars Cotts 8 CT1 87 F8
Grey Wethers ME14 53 E4
Grey Willow Gdns TN23 155 D8
Greyfriars Cl ME16 74 D5
Greyfriars Ct CT10 8 F1
Greystones Rd
Cliffs End CT12 51 D5
Maidstone ME15 76 A2
Greystones Sch TN24 139 F1
Grieveson Ho ME4 10 A4
Griffin Cotts TN26 181 C2
Griffin St CT14 117 D7
Griffin's Cnr TN25 140 E7
Grimshill Ct CT2 66 C4
Grimshill Rd CT5 43 E8
Grimston Ave CT20 178 B4
Grimston Gdns CT20 178 B4
Grimthorpe Ave CT5 43 C7
Grinsell Hill CT12 50 E6
Grisbrook Farm Cl TN29 203 D6
Grisbrook Rd TN29 203 D6
Grizedale Cl ME1 31 D8
Groombridge Sq 13 ME15 97 F6
Grosvenor Ave ME4 9 E3
Grosvenor Cotts CT7 27 B3
Grosvenor Gdns CT9 7 I1
Grosvenor Hill CT9 7 I2
Grosvenor House 5 ME15 97 F5
Grosvenor Pl CT9 7 I2
Grosvenor Rd
Ashford TN24 139 D7
Broadstairs CT10 30 A4
Gillingham ME7 11 A1
Ramsgate CT11 52 C7
Whitstable CT5 43 D7
Grotto Gdns CT9 7 J2
Grotto Hill CT9 7 J2
Grotto Rd 5 CT9 7 J2
Grove Ave ME12 6 G2
Grove Cl ME13 62 A6
Grove Cotts TN30 179 B6
Grove Court Farm ME13 64 A3
Grove Ct 4 ME2 9 B7
Grove Dairy Farm ME9 36 A6
Grove Ferry Hill CT3 47 E3
Grove Ferry Rd CT3 48 A2
Grove Gdns 6 CT9 7 G1
Grove Green La ME14 75 E5
Grove Green Rd ME14 75 F5
Grove Ho TN27 136 C3
Grove La TN29 191 D3
Grove Park Ave ME10 36 B5
Grove Park Com Prim Sch ME10 36 B6
Grove Pl ME13 62 A6
Grove Rd Chatham ME4 10 B2
Deal CT14 117 D3
Folkestone CT20 178 E6
Gillingham ME7 11 A6
Maidstone ME15 97 C7
Preston CT3 70 B8
Ramsgate CT11 52 D6
Rochester ME2 9 B8
Selling ME13 84 B4
Staple CT3 91 F6
Wickhambreaux CT3 69 D6
Grove Road Cotts
Wickhambreaux CT3 69 C2
Wickhambreaux CT3 69 C3
Grove Terr CT1 87 E7
Grove The Ashford TN24 139 E6
Barham CT4 128 F8
Deal CT14 117 C6
Dover CT16 149 C1
Herne Bay CT6 22 C2
Maidstone ME14 76 A3
Westgate-on-S CT8 27 F8
Grove Way CT3 70 C7
Grovehurst Ave ME10 14 F1
Grovehurst Rd ME10,ME9 14 E2
Grovelands ME17 101 E5
Groveway ME12 6 F2
Grovewood Ct ME14 75 E4
Grovewood Dr ME14 75 E4
Grummock Ave CT11 52 B7
Grundy's Hill 10 CT11 52 E6
Guardian Ct ME8 11 C1
Guestling Mill Ct 1 CT13 72 F1
Guildcount La 5 CT13 72 F1
Guildford Ave CT8 27 E8
Guildford Lawn 1 CT11 52 E6
Guildford Rd CT1 87 F6
Guildhall Ct 10 CT20 178 D5
Guildhall Mus★ ME1 9 C6
Guildhall St
4 Canterbury CT1 87 F8
18 Folkestone CT20 178 D5
Guildhall St N CT19, CT20 178 D5
Guilford Ave CT16 149 A8
Guilford Ct CT14 117 D2
Guilford Rd CT13 94 E8
Guilton CT3 71 B1
Guldeford La TN29,TN31 196 F3
Guldeford Lane Cnr TN31 196 D2
Gulland Ho 4 ME14 75 B4
Gullands ME17 98 E4
Gun La ME2 9 B7
Gundulph Rd ME1 9 E4
Gundulph Sq ME1 9 C6
Gunnis Cl ME8 33 D4
Gurling Rd CT15 133 F1
Guston CE Prim Sch CT15 149 E3
Guston Rd ME14 75 C6
Guy Cl CT10 30 A7
Gwyn Rd CT12 29 C2
Gypsy Cnr CT5 44 D3

H

Hackfield TN23 138 F1
Hackington Cl CT2 66 E4
Hackington Pl CT2 66 F2
Hackington Rd CT2 66 E7
Hackington Terr CT2 66 F2
Hacklinge Hill CT14 94 B2
Hackney Rd ME16 74 C2
Haddon Dene Sch CT10 29 F4
Hadleigh Ct ME7 33 A3
Hadleigh Gdns CT6 23 B5
Hadley Gdns ME17 77 E2
Hadlow Coll of Agriculture & Hort (Horticultural Unit) CT1 88 B8
Hadlow Dr CT9 8 E2
Hadlow Rd ME14 75 C5
Hadrian Gdns TN23 155 F5
Haffenden Meadow TN27 120 C8
Haffenden Rd TN30 167 B1
Haig Ave Chatham ME1 9 D1
Chatham,Luton ME4 10 A2
Gillingham ME7 10 E4
Haine Ind Est CT12 28 F1
Haine Rd CT12,CT10 28 F2
Halden Cl ME15 97 F6
Hales Cl TN30 179 B8
Hales Ct TN30 179 B8
Hales Dr CT2 66 F3
Hales Rd ME10 36 D1
Haleys Pl ME1 53 A8
Halfmile Ride CT9 28 E6
Halford Cl CT6 23 B2
Halfpenny Cl ME16 74 A2
Halfway Houses Prim Sch ME12 3 D6
Halfway Rd ME12 3 D8
Halifax Cl ME5 32 B6
Hall Ave TN24 156 F6
Hall Cl ME10 36 E6
Hall Cres CT14 116 F5
Hall Rd ME5 32 C3
Hallcroft Ct CT11 52 C7
Hallett Wlk 10 CT1 67 B2
Halliday Ct CT21 176 A2
Hallsfield Rd ME5 31 D2
Hallwood Cl ME8 33 D5
Hallwood House ME5 32 C2
Halstatt Rd CT14 117 A3
Halstead Cl CT2 67 B4
Halstead Gdns CT9 8 F3
Halstead Wlk ME16 74 C7
Halstow Cl ME15 97 B6
Halstow Way TN23 155 F8
Halt The Elham CT4 144 F4
Whitstable CT5 44 A7
Ham Farm Cotts CT14 93 F2
Ham La Gillingham ME7 32 E3
Lenham ME17 101 C5
Ham Mill La TN26,TN29 183 A2
Ham Rd ME13 40 C1
Ham Shades La CT5 21 A1
Ham Street Sta TN26 183 A8
Hambledon Ct ME16 74 B3
Hambrook Cl CT4 107 B8
Hambrook La CT4 107 C8
Hambrook Wlk ME10 36 F8
Hamelin Rd ME7 32 F8
Hamels The CT2 67 F5
Hamilton Cl
Littlestone-on-S TN28 200 E5
Ramsgate CT12 29 B1
Hamilton Cres ME10 36 C3
Hamilton Ho ME17 96 C3
Hamilton Rd
Ashford TN24 156 D6
Deal CT14 117 C4
Dover CT17 166 B8
Gillingham ME7 10 D7
Lydd TN29 203 C6
Whitstable CT5 20 D1
Hammond Cl CT15 113 E5
Hammond's Cnr TN29 199 E6
Hammond's Rd CT20 177 E5
Hamond Hill 6 ME4 9 E4
Hampden La TN23 156 A7
Hampden Mews TN23 156 A7
Hampden Rd TN23 156 A6
Hampshire Cl ME5 32 C7
Hampshire Dr ME15 97 C8
Hampshire Rd CT1 88 D7
Hampson Way ME14 76 A4
Hampton Cl Chatham ME5 32 A5
Herne Bay CT6 22 A3
Hampton Gdns CT6 22 A3
Hampton La TN25 141 C3
Hampton Pier Ave CT6 22 B4
Hampton Prim Sch CT6 22 C4
Hampton Rd ME14 75 C6
Hampton Vale CT21 177 B4
Hamstreet Prim Sch TN26 182 F8
Hamstreet Rd
Bromley Green TN26 170 E5
Hamstreet TN26 183 C7
Hamwick Gn ME5 32 C1
Hancocks Field CT14 117 A5
Hangman's La
Ringwould CT14 133 F5
Ripple CT14 133 D5
Hanover Cl Ashford TN23 138 F2
Deal CT14 117 D2
Margate CT9 8 E2
Sittingbourne ME10 36 E2
Hanover Ct
Broadstairs CT10 29 F4
Faversham ME13 62 B8
Hythe CT21 176 C1
Maidstone ME14 75 B5
Hanover Dr ME8 33 C4
Hanover Pl CT2 66 F2
Hanover Rd ME17 96 C3
Hanover Sq CT6 22 F5
Hanover St CT6 22 F5
Hanscomb Ho CT2 66 E2
Hanslett's La ME13 61 D3
Hanway ME8 11 A2
Harbledown Gdns CT9 8 E3
Harbledown Manor ME8 11 B3
Harbledown Pk CT2 66 C1
Harbour Approach Rd CT20 178 E4
Harbour Par CT11 52 E6
Harbour Point CT19 178 F5
Harbour Sch The CT15 165 E7
Harbour St
Broadstairs CT10 30 B4
Folkestone CT20 178 E5
Ramsgate CT11 52 E6
Whitstable CT5 20 D2
Harbour Twrs 13 CT11 52 E6
Harbour Way CT20 178 E5
Harbourland Cl ME14 75 B8
Harbourne La TN26, TN30 167 E5
Harcourt Dr
Canterbury CT2 66 D2
Herne Bay CT6 22 B5
Harcourt Gdns ME8 33 E4
Harcourt Prim Sch CT19 177 E7
Harcourt Rd CT19 177 F7
Harden Rd TN29 203 D7
Hardinge Cl ME8 33 D4
Hardinge Rd TN24 139 C3
Hardres Court Rd
Lower Hardres CT4 110 A3
Stelling Minnis CT4 126 F6
Hardres Rd CT11 52 E8
Hardres St CT11 52 E7
Hards Town ME4 10 A4
Hardwick Rd CT20 178 A4
Hardwicke Rd CT17 166 B6
Hardy Cl Ashford TN24 157 A7
Canterbury CT2 66 C1
Chatham ME5 32 B6
Hardy Rd
Littlestone-on-S TN28 200 D3
St Margaret's at Cliffe CT15 150 E8
Hardy St ME14 75 A6
Hare St 2 ME4 10 B3
Harebell Cl
3 Chatham ME5 31 F4
Maidstone ME14 75 E5
Minster (Sheppey) ME12 4 A4
Haredale Cl ME1 31 D7
Harkness Ct 6 ME10 37 B4
Harkness Dr CT2 66 E2
Harman Ave CT21 174 F3
Harman Ct ME5 32 B3
Harmers Way TN27 118 F3
Harmsworth Gdns CT10 30 A5
Harnet St 6 CT13 72 F1
Harold Ave Gillingham ME7 10 E4
Westgate-on-S CT8 27 E8
Harold Ct ME13 62 C6
Harold Rd Birchington CT7 26 E8
Deal CT14 117 D8
Margate CT9 8 B3
Sittingbourne ME10 37 B4
Harold St Dover CT16 166 D8
Queenborough ME11 3 A4
Harold's Rd CT16 166 E8
Harp Farm Rd ME14 54 C6
Harper Rd TN23 155 F8
Harple La ME14 54 F1
Harps Ave ME12 4 C6
Harpswood ME17 77 F1
Harpswood La CT21 176 A4
Harptree Dr ME5 31 F5
Harrier Dr ME10 37 A2
Harrietsham Sta ME17 100 D6
Harriet Dr ME1 9 B3
Harriets Cnr CT5 43 B5
Harringe La CT21,TN25 174 A6
Harriot Cl CT19 178 B7
Harris Gdns ME10 37 C5
Harris Rd ME12 1 D2
Harris's Alley CT3 91 A7
Harrison Ct 4 ME8 11 F1
Harrison Dr ME17 100 E6
Harrison Rd 4 CT11 52 D6
Harrison Terr ME13 40 A2
Harrow Ct Chatham ME5 32 C4
Stockbury ME9 56 D8
Harrow Dene CT10 29 E6
Harrow Rd ME7 32 F6
Harrow Way
Ashford TN23 155 E5
Maidstone ME14 75 E5
Harry Wells Rd CT6 22 B3
Harrys Rd ME9 38 D3
Hart Cl CT18 163 A4
Hart Hill TN27 103 A2
Hart St ME16 74 F3
Hart Street Bsns Ctr ME16 74 F3
Hartington St ME4 10 A3
Hartley Cl ME15 97 F6
Hartlip Cl ME12 3 B7
Hartlip Endowed CE Prim Sch ME9 34 D5
Hartlip Hill ME9 34 F7
Hartnup St ME16 74 C2
Hartpiece Cl ME8 11 F2
Harts Cotts TN26 183 A8
Harts La 6 CT5 20 D2
Hartsdown Rd CT9 28 D8
Hartsdown Tech Coll CT9 28 D8
Harty Ave ME8 33 B3
Harty Ferry Cotts ME13 40 C5
Harty Ferry Rd ME12 18 E4
Harty Ferry View CT5 43 C6
Harty Terr ME12 5 A5
Harvest La CT4 126 E5
Harvest Way
Ashford TN23 155 D7
Hawkinge CT18 163 B4
Harvesters Cl ME8 33 E7
Harvesters Way ME14 75 D4
Harvey Ct CT19 178 A6
Harvey Dr
Sittingbourne ME10 37 A2
Whitstable CT5 21 B1
Harvey Gram Sch The CT19 178 B6
Harvey Pl
22 Folkestone CT20 178 D5
7 Folkestone CT20 178 E5
Harvey Rd Ashford TN24 139 F1
Gillingham ME8 33 E8
Harvey St CT20 178 E5
Harville Rd TN25 123 C2
Harwich St CT5 43 D8
Harwick Dr TN28 200 C8
Harwood Ho TN25 123 E1
Harwood Rd ME8 12 B1
Hasborough Rd CT19 178 F6
Haskard Cl CT18 162 F4
Haslemere Est ME15 97 F5
Haslewood Cl TN27 135 B2
Hassall Reach CT1 87 B6
Hassell St TN25 124 F2
Haste Hill Cl ME17 97 B3
Haste Hill Rd ME17 97 B3
Hasted Rd ME9 35 B7
Hasteds ME17 77 D2
Hastings Ave CT9 8 A1
Hastings Pl CT13 93 F8
Hastings Rd ME15 75 B3
Hatch La CT4 86 C5
Hatch Rd ME17 101 C5
Hatch St 3 ME13 62 C7
Hatfield Rd Margate CT9 7 G2
Ramsgate CT11 52 D7
Rochester ME2 9 A8
Hathaway Ct
Gillingham ME8 33 D8
Rochester ME1 9 B5
Hatherall Rd ME14 75 B6
Hatherley Ct CT9 8 A3
Hatton Rd ME5 32 C3
Havant Wlk 8 ME15 97 F6
Havelock Pl CT3 71 E1
Havelock Rd CT14 117 C3
Havelock St CT1 67 A1
Haven Cl ME1 9 C2
Haven Dr Hawkinge CT18 163 A4
Herne Bay CT6 23 F6
Haven The Ashford TN23 155 F5
Brenzett TN29 192 A3
Hythe CT21 187 C8
Haventhorpe TN24 139 C3
Havisham Cl ME1 9 D2
Havock La 1 ME14 74 F4
Hawbeck Rd ME8 33 C3
Hawe Cl CT2 67 A4
Hawe Farm Way CT6 23 B2
Hawe La CT2 68 A7
Hawes Ave CT11 52 B7
Hawk Cl CT5 43 C7
Hawk's La CT1 87 F8
Hawkesbury St CT17 166 D5
Hawkhurst Cl CT7 27 B8

Hawkhurst Rd ME8 ... 11 B3
Hawkhurst Way CT10 ... 30 A2
Hawkinge Prim Sch
CT18 ... 163 B4
Hawkins Cl Chatham ME7 . 10 A6
Sittingbourne ME10 ... 36 E7
Hawkins Rd CT19 ... 177 D6
Hawks Rd CT6 ... 22 B2
Hawks Way TN23 ... 155 E7
Hawksdown CT14 ... 134 B8
Hawksdown Rd CT14 ... 134 C8
Hawkshill Rd CT14 ... 134 D8
Hawkwood ME16 ... 74 B5
Hawkwood Cl ME1 ... 9 D5
Hawley Ct ME16 ... 74 E4
Hawley Sq CT9 ... 7 J2
Hawley St CT9 ... 7 I2
Hawser Rd ME1 ... 9 C1
Hawthorn TN26 ... 190 D8
Hawthorn Ave
Canterbury CT2 ... 67 A2
West Minst ME12 ... 3 A8
Hawthorn Cl Hythe CT21 187 E8
Ramsgate CT11 ... 29 E1
River CT17 ... 148 E2
St Mary's Bay TN29 ... 194 F3
Womenswold CT3 ... 112 E4
Hawthorn Cnr
Herne Bay CT6 ... 24 A3
Old Romney TN29 ... 198 E3
Hawthorn House 5 ME5 . 31 F5
Hawthorn Rd
Kingsnorth TN23 ... 156 B4
Sittingbourne ME10 ... 36 E4
Hawthorne Ave ME8 ... 11 C2
Hawthorne Cl CT15 ... 131 D7
Hawthorns ME5 ... 31 F1
Hawthorns The CT10 ... 29 C4
Hay Hill CT13,CT14 ... 93 D2
Hay La CT14 ... 93 F2
Hayes Alley 11 CT5 ... 20 D2
Hayes La ME9 ... 56 F6
Hayfields ME5 ... 32 D2
Haygate Ho ME1 ... 9 C4
Hayle Mill Cotts ME15 ... 96 F8
Hayle Mill Rd ME15 ... 96 F8
Hayle Rd ME15 ... 75 A3
Haymakers La TN23 ... 155 D8
Haymen St ME4 ... 9 E3
Haynes Ho 3 ME14 ... 75 B4
Hayrick Cl ME14 ... 75 E5
Haysel ME10 ... 37 A2
Hayton Rd TN25 ... 160 A2
Haywain Cl Ashford TN23 155 E5
Maidstone ME14 ... 75 F4
Hayward Ave ME2 ... 9 B8
Hayward Cl
Ashford TN24 ... 157 A8
Deal CT14 ... 117 A4
Hayward's Cl TN28 ... 200 B6
Hayward's Hill ME13 ... 82 C4
Hayward's Ho ME1 ... 9 C6
Hazebrouck Rd ME13 ... 62 A7
Hazel Ave ME16 ... 74 C5
Hazel Cl CT15 ... 131 C7
Hazel Ct CT7 ... 26 D8
Hazel Gr Chatham ME5 ... 32 B8
Sheerness ME12 ... 1 H1
Hazel Street Rd ME9 ... 57 A4
Hazel Wlk CT10 ... 29 C4
Hazeldene ME12 ... 5 F6
Hazeldown Cl CT17 ... 148 E2
Hazelmere Dr CT6 ... 23 D5
Hazels The ME8 ... 33 B5
Hazelwood Dr ME16 ... 74 B4
Hazelwood Mdw CT13 ... 93 F7
Hazlemere Dr ME7 ... 11 A5
Hazlemere Rd CT5 ... 43 A7
Hazling Dane CT15 ... 130 F5
Hazlitt Dr ME16 ... 74 D5
Head Hill ME13 ... 63 D7
Head Hill Rd ME13 ... 63 D8
Head Race The ME15 ... 74 D2
Headcorn Dr CT2 ... 67 B4
Headcorn Gdns CT9 ... 8 E2
Headcorn Rd
Gillingham ME8 ... 11 B4
Platt's Heath ME17 ... 100 F1
Headingley Rd ME16 ... 74 B6
Heard Way ME10 ... 37 B5
Heart In Hand Cnr CT3 ... 23 F2
Heart In Hand Rd CT6 ... 23 F2
Heart's Delight La CT3 ... 70 B3
Hearts Delight Rd ME9 ... 36 B1
Heath Cl CT2 ... 67 F7
Heath Ct CT15 ... 150 F6
Heath Gr ME16 ... 74 A2
Heath Ho CT3 ... 46 E5
Heath Rd Coxheath ME17 . 96 C3
Langley Heath ME17 ... 98 E4
Maidstone ME16 ... 74 A2
Heath The
Appledore TN26 ... 181 C1
Whitstable CT5 ... 21 B1
Heath Villas TN26 ... 181 C2
Heather Cl Chatham ME5 ... 31 F4
Margate CT9 ... 28 C8
Sittingbourne ME10 ... 37 A3
Heather Dr
Maidstone ME15 ... 75 B2
St Michaels TN30 ... 167 B3
Heatherwood Cl ME17 ... 99 E2
Heathfield ME17 ... 98 E4
Heathfield Ave
Dover CT16 ... 149 B2
Heathfield Ave *continued*
Maidstone ME14 ... 75 C7
Heathfield Bglws ME17 . 102 B1
Heathfield Cl
Chatham ME5 ... 32 B7
Maidstone ME14 ... 75 B7
Heathfield Rd
Ashford TN24 ... 139 C3
Maidstone ME14 ... 75 C7
Heathfield Way CT4 ... 128 F8
Heathorn St ME14 ... 75 B5
Heathside TN26 ... 181 C1
Heathside Ave ME17 ... 96 C4
Heathwood Dr CT11 ... 29 E1
Heaton Rd CT1 ... 87 F6
Hedgend Ind Est CT7 ... 25 F3
Hedgerow The ME14 ... 75 E5
Hedgerows TN23 ... 155 D7
Hedges The ME14 ... 75 A7
Hedley St ME14 ... 75 A5
Heel La CT2 ... 67 C8
Heel Rd ME13 ... 104 B7
Heights Terr CT17 ... 166 C6
Heights The CT5 ... 43 C6
Helding Cl CT6 ... 23 B2
Helen Thompson Cl ME9 . 14 E4
Helena Ave CT9 ... 28 E8
Helena Corniche CT20 . 177 C3
Helena Rd CT18 ... 164 C2
Hellyar Ct ME1 ... 9 C4
Helmdon Cl CT12 ... 29 C2
Helvellyn Ave CT11 ... 52 B7
Hempstead Inf Sch ME7 . 33 A5
Hempstead Jun Sch ME7 33 A5
Hempstead La ME9 ... 37 E3
Hempstead Rd
Gillingham ME7,ME8 ... 33 B6
Gillingham,Hempstead ME7 . 33 A5
Hempstead Valley Dr
ME7 ... 33 A4
Hempstead Valley Sh Ctr
ME7 ... 33 A3
Hempsted St 11 TN23 ... 139 B2
Henbane Cl ME14 ... 75 E5
Hendon Bsns Ctr TN24 . 139 D2
Hengist Ave CT9 ... 8 B1
Hengist Rd
Birchington CT7 ... 26 C7
Deal CT14 ... 117 D7
Westgate-on-S CT8 ... 27 E8
Henley Bsns Pk ME2 ... 9 D7
Henley Cl Chatham ME5 ... 32 A6
Gillingham ME8 ... 33 D8
Henley Fields
Maidstone ME14 ... 75 E6
St Michaels TN30 ... 167 B2
Henley Meadows TN30 . 167 A2
Henley View TN30 ... 167 B2
Henniker Cl CT16 ... 149 A5
Henry Ct CT1 ... 87 F7
Henry St Chatham ME4 ... 10 B3
Gillingham ME8 ... 12 A1
Henwood TN24 ... 139 D3
Herbert Dane Ct 10
ME13 ... 62 D7
Herbert Rd Ashford TN24 156 D6
Chatham ME4 ... 10 A3
Gillingham ME8 ... 33 E8
Ramsgate CT11 ... 52 C6
Herbert St CT17 ... 149 B1
Herdson Rd CT20 ... 178 A5
Hereford Cl ME8 ... 11 D2
Hereford Gdns CT7 ... 26 F6
Hereford Rd ME15 ... 97 D7
Hereson Rd CT11 ... 52 F8
Hereson Sch The CT11 ... 52 F8
Hereson Sec Boys Sch
CT10 ... 30 A3
Hereward Ave CT7 ... 26 E8
Heritage Cl CT5 ... 43 A6
Heritage Dr ME7 ... 10 F1
Heritage Gdns CT16 ... 166 E8
Heritage Rd Chatham ME5 32 A6
Folkestone CT20 ... 177 D6
Herman Terr ME4 ... 10 A3
Hermitage Cl CT21 ... 176 B2
Hermitage La
Detling ME14 ... 55 B4
Maidstone ME16 ... 74 A4
Herne Ave CT6 ... 23 A4
Herne Bay High Sch CT6 22 D3
Herne Bay Inf Sch CT6 . 22 F4
Herne Bay Jun Sch CT6 . 22 F4
Herne Bay Mus* CT6 ... 22 F5
Herne Bay Rd Sturry CT3 . 45 E2
Whitstable CT5 ... 21 C3
Herne Bay Sta CT6 ... 22 E3
Herne CE Inf Sch CT6 ... 46 B8
Herne CE Jun Sch CT6 ... 46 A8
Herne Ct CT19 ... 177 C6
Herne Dr CT6 ... 22 C2
Herne Rd ME8 ... 11 C2
Herne St CT6 ... 46 A8
Herne Windmill* CT6 ... 23 B2
Herneville Gdns CT6 ... 23 B4
Hernhill CE Prim Sch
ME13 ... 64 B6
Hero Ho ME12 ... 1 C2
Hero Wlk ME1 ... 31 C7
Heron Apartments 3
ME15 ... 97 F5
Heron Cl ME9 ... 13 B3
Heron Dr ME12 ... 4 B5
Heron Forestall Ave
CT18 ... 163 B4
Heron Lodge 6 CT16 ... 149 B2
Heron Way ME5 ... 32 B7
Heron Wlk TN23 ... 155 E8
Heron's Brook TN25 ... 140 E6
Heron's Way CT21 ... 187 D8
Heronden Rd Eastry CT13 . 92 F1
Park Wood ME15 ... 97 F4
Herons Cl CT4 ... 107 C8
Herschell Rd CT7 ... 26 F8
Herschell Rd E CT14 ... 117 C3
Herschell Rd W CT14 ... 117 C3
Herschell Sq CT14 ... 117 C3
Hersden Com Prim Sch
CT3 ... 46 E1
Hertford Ct CT1 ... 88 C8
Hertford Ho
Herne Bay CT6 ... 23 A5
14 Ramsgate CT11 ... 52 E6
Hertford Pl CT11 ... 52 E6
Hertford Rd CT9 ... 29 C8
Hertford St CT11 ... 52 E6
Herts Cres ME15 ... 96 F3
Hever Cl ME15 ... 97 F6
Hever Gdns ME16 ... 74 E3
Hever Pl Canterbury CT2 ... 67 A3
Sittingbourne ME10 ... 36 D3
Hewitt Cl Gillingham ME7 ... 10 F6
Maidstone ME16 ... 74 D7
Hewitt Rd 1 CT16 ... 166 D8
Hewitts Pl TN24 ... 139 F1
Hextable Cl
Ashford TN23 ... 155 F6
Maidstone ME16 ... 74 D7
Heyford Cl CT18 ... 163 B4
Hibernia St 5 CT11 ... 52 E6
Hickory Dell ME7 ... 33 A5
Hicks Forstal Rd CT3 ... 46 B5
Hidden Mdw ME13 ... 62 B7
Higgins' La ME4 ... 9 F5
High Banks Loose ME15 ... 96 F5
Rochester ME1 ... 9 D2
High Dewar Rd ME8 ... 34 A8
High Elms ME8 ... 11 E1
High Halden
CE Prim Sch TN26 ... 167 E7
High Knocke TN29 ... 195 B6
High Mdw CT17 ... 149 C1
High Minnis CT4 ... 143 F8
High Oak Hill ME9 ... 13 E1
High Snoad Wood TN25 105 A1
High St Ashford TN23 ... 139 C2
Aylesford ME20 ... 53 A2
Bridge CT4 ... 89 A1
Broadstairs CT10 ... 29 E5
Broadstairs, St Peter's
CT10 ... 30 A4
Brookland TN29 ... 197 E8
Canterbury CT1 ... 87 F8
8 Canterbury,Northgate
CT1 ... 67 A1
Chatham ME4 ... 10 A4
Deal CT14 ... 117 D6
Dover CT16 ... 166 C8
Dymchurch TN29 ... 195 C8
Eastchurch ME12 ... 5 D3
Eastry CT13 ... 93 B2
Elham CT4 ... 144 F5
Fordwich CT2 ... 68 A4
Gillingham ME7 ... 10 C5
Gillingham,Brompton ME7 ... 10 A6
Gillingham,Rainham ME8 ... 33 F8
Herne Bay CT6 ... 22 F5
Hythe CT21 ... 176 C2
Lenham ME17 ... 101 D5
Littlebourne CT3 ... 89 F7
Lydd TN29 ... 203 B6
Lyminge CT18 ... 161 C6
Maidstone ME14 ... 74 F4
Manston CT12 ... 51 D8
Margate CT9 ... 7 I2
Margate, Garlinge CT9 ... 28 B7
Minster (Sheppey) ME12 ... 4 D6
Minster (Thanet) CT12 ... 50 C6
New Romney TN28 ... 200 B6
Newington ME9 ... 35 C6
Queenborough ME11 ... 2 F5
Ramsgate CT11 ... 52 D7
Rochester ME4 ... 9 E4
Rochester,Strood ME2 ... 9 B7
Rochester,Troy Town ME1 ... 9 C6
Sandwich CT13 ... 73 A1
Sheerness ME12 ... 1 D2
Sheerness,Blue Town ME12 ... 1 B3
Sittingbourne ME10 ... 36 F4
Sittingbourne,Milton Regis
ME10 ... 36 E6
Smarden TN27 ... 135 A1
St Margaret's at Cliffe
CT15 ... 150 F6
Sturry CT2 ... 67 F5
Temple Ewell CT16 ... 148 D5
Tenterden TN30 ... 179 A7
Whitstable CT5 ... 20 D2
Wingham CT3 ... 91 A8
Wye TN25 ... 123 E2
High St The TN27 ... 120 C7
High Street St Lawrence
CT11 ... 52 B7
High Trees Cl TN24 ... 157 A8
High View Ave CT6 ... 22 B5
Higham Cl ME15 ... 74 E2
Higham La CT4 ... 111 B8
Higham Pk* CT4 ... 111 C8
Higham View ME14 ... 53 E4
Highbury Gdns CT12 ... 29 B3
Highbury La TN30 ... 179 A7
Highbury Wlk CT12 ... 29 B2
Highcroft Gn ME15 ... 97 F4
Highfield Cl
Gillingham ME8 ... 33 D7
Hythe CT21 ... 176 A4
Highfield Cl *continued*
Ramsgate CT12 ... 29 B3
Rough Common CT2 ... 66 B3
Highfield Ct
5 Margate CT9 ... 8 B2
Ramsgate CT12 ... 29 B2
Highfield Gdns CT9 ... 7 H1
Highfield Ind Est CT19 ... 178 F6
Highfield La TN24,TN25 . 157 C6
Highfield Rd
Ashford TN24 ... 157 A8
Gillingham ME8 ... 33 D7
Halfway Houses ME12 ... 3 E6
Ramsgate CT12 ... 29 B3
Highfields Ave CT6 ... 23 D4
Highfields View CT6 ... 23 C4
Highgate Rd CT5 ... 21 B1
Highgrove Rd ME5 ... 32 A5
Highland Cl CT20 ... 177 F4
Highland Rd
Chartham CT4 ... 86 D1
Maidstone ME15 ... 97 E6
Highlands Cres TN29 ... 195 A4
Highlands Farm Rare
Breeds Ctr* TN26 ... 169 D1
Highpoint TN24 ... 139 D3
Highridge Gillingham ME7 . 10 F1
Hythe CT21 ... 177 A3
Highridge Cl ME14 ... 75 F5
Highsted Gram Sch ME10 36 E2
Highsted Rd ME9 &10 ... 36 F1
Highsted Valley ME9 ... 58 F7
Highstreet Rd
Waterham ME13 ... 42 D2
Yorklets CT5,ME13 ... 42 E2
Highview Cl
Boughton Street ME13 ... 64 B3
Maidstone ME15 ... 97 A8
Highview Dr ME5 ... 31 D5
Highview Rd ME12 ... 4 C7
Highview Sch CT19 ... 178 D6
Highworth Gram Sch
for Girls TN24 ... 139 A3
Hilary Cl CT6 ... 23 C4
Hilda Rd Chatham ME4 ... 10 A3
Halfway Houses ME12 ... 3 D6
Hildenborough Cres
ME16 ... 74 C7
Hildersham Cl CT10 ... 29 E5
Hill Ave CT15 ... 130 E5
Hill Brow Maidstone ME14 . 76 A5
Sittingbourne ME10 ... 36 D2
Hill Chase ME5 ... 31 E3
Hill Cres Aylesham CT3 . 112 E5
Lenham ME17 ... 101 D5
Hill Ct TN27 ... 103 E1
Hill Dr CT13 ... 93 B3
Hill Green Rd ME9 ... 56 D8
Hill House Dr CT12 ... 50 C7
Hill La CT18 ... 162 B1
Hill Rd Burham ME5 ... 31 A3
Folkestone CT19 ... 178 E8
Folkestone,Ford CT19 ... 178 E7
Rochester ME1 ... 9 A2
Hill The Charing TN27 ... 120 D8
Littlebourne CT3 ... 89 F8
Hill Top Cotts ME17 ... 96 E2
Hill Top Rd CT6 ... 23 B5
Hill View Ashford TN24 . 139 C3
Margate CT9 ... 28 D7
Hill View Terr CT18 ... 161 D3
Hill View Way ME5 ... 31 E5
Hill's Terr ME4 ... 9 F3
Hillary Rd ME14 ... 75 A7
Hillborough Dr CT6 ... 23 F5
Hillborough Gr ME5 ... 32 A3
Hillborough Rd CT6 ... 23 B5
Hillbrow Ave
Herne Bay CT6 ... 23 B2
Sturry CT2 ... 67 F7
Hillbrow La TN23 ... 138 F1
Hillbrow Rd
Ashford TN23 ... 139 A1
Ramsgate CT11 ... 52 D8
Hillcrest TN23 ... 155 B8
Hillcrest Cl TN24 ... 139 E6
Hillcrest Gdns
Deal CT14 ... 117 A2
Ramsgate CT11 ... 52 B6
Hillcrest Rd
Chatham ME4 ... 9 F2
Hythe CT21 ... 176 B3
Kingsdown CT14 ... 134 D4
Littlebourne CT3 ... 89 E8
Hillcroft Rd CT6 ... 23 B3
Hillden Shaw ME15 ... 97 A8
Hiller Cl CT10 ... 30 A6
Hillfield Villas TN26 ... 167 F8
Hillman Ave CT6 ... 22 A4
Hillside
1 Folkestone CT20 ... 177 E3
Rochester ME1 ... 9 A2
Hillside Ave
Canterbury CT2 ... 66 C2
Rochester ME2 ... 9 B8
Rushenden ME11 ... 2 F3
Hillside Ct Hythe CT21 . 176 C2
2 Rochester ME2 ... 9 A7
Hillside Ind Est CT20 ... 177 E4
Hillside Rd
Chatham ME4 ... 10 A4
Dover CT17 ... 149 A2
Minster (Sheppey) ME12 ... 4 B7
Stalisfield Green ME13 ... 103 E6
Whitstable CT5 ... 21 A1
Hillside St CT21 ... 176 C2
Hillstone Ct CT16 ... 166 E8
Hilltop Rd ME12 ... 4 A5
Hilltop Spinning
& Weaving Ctr* TN25 . 160 A2
Hillview Rd
Canterbury CT2 ... 66 C2
Whitstable CT5 ... 43 D8
Hillyfield Rd TN23 ... 156 A8
Hillyfields Jun Sch ME7 . 10 E6
Hillyfields Rise TN23 ... 139 A1
Hilton Bsns Ctr TN23 ... 156 B6
Hilton Dr ME10 ... 36 B6
Hilton Rd TN23 ... 138 F2
Hinchliffe Way CT9 ... 29 D8
Hind Cl TN29 ... 195 C8
Hinde Cl ME10 ... 36 F7
Hinde Ho ME10 ... 36 E6
Hines Terr ME5 ... 10 C1
Hinton Cres ME7 ... 33 A6
Hinxhill Rd TN24,TN25 ... 140 D1
Hirst Cl CT16 ... 149 B4
Historic Dockyard The*
ME4 ... 10 A7
Hither Field TN27 ... 120 C7
Hoades Wood Rd CT2 ... 68 A7
Hoath Cl ME8 ... 33 B7
Hoath La ME8 ... 33 B7
Hoath Prim Sch CT3 ... 46 E5
Hoath Rd CT3 ... 46 C3
Hoath Way ME7,ME8 ... 33 B5
Hobart Cres CT16 ... 149 C3
Hobart Gdns ME10 ... 36 C4
Hobart Rd CT12 ... 29 A1
Hockeredge Gdns CT8 ... 27 F8
Hockers Cl ME14 ... 76 A8
Hockers La ME14 ... 76 A7
Hodge's Gap CT9 ... 8 C3
Hodgson Rd CT5 ... 42 F7
Hog Gn CT4 ... 144 F4
Hog Hill ME14 ... 76 B5
Hogarth Cl CT6 ... 23 E5
Hogbarn La ME17 ... 79 A3
Hogben Cl CT18 ... 161 B7
Hogg La CT4 ... 109 E2
Holbeam Rd ME13 ... 82 A1
Holborn La ME4 ... 9 F5
Holbourn Cl CT6 ... 46 B8
Holbrook Dr CT12 ... 29 B1
Holcombe Rd Chatham ME4 9 F2
Rochester ME1 ... 9 C3
Holdenhurst TN23 ... 155 E6
Holder Cl ME5 ... 32 C6
Holding St ME8 ... 11 F1
Holland Cl Broadstairs CT10 8 G2
Sheerness ME12 ... 1 C1
Holland Ho ME1 ... 9 D5
Holland Rd Chatham ME5 . 31 E4
Maidstone ME14 ... 75 B5
Hollands Ave CT19 ... 178 F7
Hollicondane Rd CT11 ... 52 E8
Hollingbourne Hill ME17 . 77 F4
Hollingbourne Prim Sch
ME17 ... 77 E2
Hollingbourne Rd ME8 ... 11 C2
Hollingbourne Sta ME17 . 77 C3
Hollington Pl TN24 ... 139 B3
Hollingworth Rd ME15 ... 97 F5
Hollow La Canterbury CT1 . 87 E5
Hartlip ME9 ... 34 E5
Hollow Rd CT3 ... 47 B6
Hollow St CT3 ... 47 C5
Hollow Wood Rd CT17 ... 165 E8
Hollowmede CT1 ... 87 E6
Holly Cl Broadstairs CT10 . 29 C4
Chatham ME5 ... 32 C8
Eastry CT13 ... 93 B2
Folkestone CT19 ... 178 E7
Gillingham ME7 ... 10 E6
Hythe CT21 ... 176 D3
Holly Farm Rd ME15 ... 98 C6
Holly Gdns CT9 ... 8 C2
Holly Hill Rd ME13 ... 64 D5
Holly La CT9 ... 8 C2
Holly Rd Ramsgate CT11 ... 52 E8
St Mary's Bay TN29 ... 194 F4
Holly Tree Cl ME17 ... 99 E2
Hollybrook Hill ME10 ... 36 D4
Hollybush Cnr CT4 ... 90 A3
Hollybush La CT3 ... 69 A4
Holm Mill La ME17 ... 100 B6
Holm Oak Gdns CT10 ... 29 F4
Holman Mews CT1 ... 88 A7
Holme Oak Cl CT1 ... 87 F6
Holmesdale Cl ME15 ... 96 F3
Holmesdale Terr 14
CT20 ... 178 D4
Holmestone Rd CT17 ... 148 E1
Holmlea Cl TN24 ... 139 E1
Holmoaks Gillingham ME8 . 11 E2
Maidstone ME14 ... 75 C5
Holmscroft Rd CT6 ... 23 D5
Holmside ME7 ... 10 E3
Holmside Ave ME12 ... 3 D6
Holmwood Rd TN23 ... 155 E7
Holness Rd CT3 ... 71 D2
Holt St CT15 ... 113 C4
Holters Mill CT2 ... 66 F2
Holton Cl CT7 ... 27 A6
Holtwood Cl ME8 ... 33 D6
Holtye Cres ME15 ... 75 B2
Holy Family RC Prim Sch
ME15 ... 97 F4
Holy Trinity & St John's
CE Prim Sch CT9 ... 7 J2
Holy Trinity CE Prim Sch
CT10 ... 30 A1
Holyrood Dr ME12 ... 4 A5
Holywell Ave CT19 ... 178 D8
Holywell Ho CT19 ... 178 D8
Holywell La ME9 ... 12 F2

Middleton Cotts TN25 . .122 E3
Middleton Ct 9 ME10 . . .36 E4
Middletune Ave ME10 . . .36 E2
Midhurst Ct ME15 . . . . . .75 A3
Midley Cl ME16 . . . . .74 C7
Midsummer Hill TN24 . .139 D6
Miers Court Prim Sch
ME8 . . . . .33 F7
Mierscourt Cl ME8 . . . . .34 A8
Mierscourt Rd ME8 . . . .33 E6
Mikyle Ct CT1 . . . . .88 A6
Milbourne Gr ME10 . . . .36 E7
Milburn Rd ME7 . . . . .10 C7
Mildred Cotts CT19 . . . .177 F7
Mile Rd CT12,CT3 . . . . . . .48 F6
Miles Ct CT3 . . . . .91 A8
Miles Pl ME1 . . . . .9 D3
Miles Way CT7 . . . . .26 F7
Milestone Cl CT19 . . . .178 A7
Milestone Rd CT14 . . . .117 B5
Milford Cl ME16 . . . . . . .74 D5
Military Rd
Canterbury CT1 . . . . .67 A1
Chatham ME4 . . . . .9 F5
2 Dover CT17 . . . . .166 D7
Folkestone CT20 . . . . .177 E4
Hythe CT21 . . . . .176 B2
Ramsgate CT11 . . . . .52 E6
Stone in Oxney TN26,TN30 190 B4
Mill Bank TN29 . . . . . . .203 B6
Mill Bank Cotts CT13 . . .93 A2
Mill Bay CT20 . . . . .178 E5
Mill Cl Lenham ME17 . . . .101 C4
River CT17 . . . . .148 F2
Sandwich CT13 . . . . .72 E2
Wickhambreaux CT3 . . . . . .69 C2
Mill Cotts
Queenborough ME11 . . . . . . .3 A5
Ramsgate CT11 . . . . .52 D6
Worth CT14 . . . . .94 A4
Mill Ct Ashford TN24 . . . .139 D2
Sittingbourne ME10 . . . . . . .37 A3
Mill Field Ash CT3 . . . . . . .71 E1
Broadstairs CT10 . . . . .29 F5
Mill Fields Rd CT21 . . . .175 F2
Mill Gn CT13 . . . . .93 A2
Mill Hamlet CT3 . . . . . . .69 C2
Mill Hill CT14 . . . . .117 A3
Mill La Aldington TN25 . . .172 E5
Ashford TN24 . . . . .140 A1
Biddenden Green TN27 . . .135 A2
Birchington CT7 . . . . .26 F6
Bridge CT4 . . . . .88 F1
Canterbury CT1 . . . . .66 F1
Canterbury, Harbledown
CT2 . . . . .87 C8
Chatham,Bluebell Hill ME5 .31 D1
Chatham,Luton ME5 . . . . . .10 C1
Chilham CT4 . . . . .107 D7
Coxheath ME17 . . . . .96 D4
8 Dover CT16 . . . . .166 E7
Eastry CT13 . . . . .93 B2
Hartlip ME9 . . . . .34 E6
Hawkinge CT18 . . . . .163 B5
Herne Bay CT6 . . . . .23 B2
Lydd TN29 . . . . .203 D7
Lynsted ME9 . . . . .60 C5
Maidstone ME14 . . . . .74 F6
Margate CT9 . . . . .7 I2
Nonington CT15 . . . . .113 F4
Northbourne CT14 . . . . . . .115 F4
Preston CT3 . . . . .70 D6
Shepherdswell CT15 . . . . .130 F5
Stelling Minnis CT4 . . . . . .126 F2
Tenterden TN30 . . . . .167 B1
Whitfield CT16 . . . . .149 A8
Worth CT14 . . . . .94 A4
Mill Lane Cotts CT14 . . .116 A4
Mill Mews CT14 . . . . .117 B4
Mill Pl ME13 . . . . .62 D8
Mill Rd Bethersden TN26 .153 E5
Bramling CT3 . . . . .90 E6
Deal CT14 . . . . .117 C4
Dymchurch TN29 . . . . .195 B7
Gillingham ME7 . . . . .10 C6
Hoath CT3 . . . . .46 F5
Hythe CT21 . . . . .176 D2
Lydd TN29 . . . . .203 D7
Rochester ME2 . . . . .9 B8
Staple CT3 . . . . .92 B5
Sturry CT2 . . . . .67 F5
Mill Row CT7 . . . . .26 F6
Mill St Loose ME15 . . . . . .96 F5
Maidstone ME15 . . . . .74 F4
Sittingbourne ME10 . . . . . . .36 E5
Temple Ewell CT16 . . . . . .148 D5
Mill Terr Bridge CT4 . . . . . .88 F1
Chartham CT4 . . . . .86 D3
Mill View Ashford TN24 . .156 F8
Woodchurch TN26 . . . . . . .169 A3
Mill View Rd CT6 . . . . . . .23 A1
Mill Wall Pl CT13 . . . . . . .94 A8
Mill Way ME10 . . . . .36 F6
Mill Wlk ME16 . . . . .74 A3
Millais Rd CT16 . . . . . . .149 C1
Millbank La TN29 . . . . . .198 E7
Millbank Rd TN23 . . . . . .155 F5
Millbrook CT21 . . . . .176 D2
Millbrook Cl ME15 . . . . . .74 F1
Millbrook Meadow
TN23 . . . . .138 E1
Milldale Cl CT14 . . . . . . .117 B4
Millen Rd ME10 . . . . .36 E5
Millen's Row ME13 . . . . . .83 B3
Millenium Terr CT1 . . . . . .87 C6
Millennium Way
Broadstairs CT10 . . . . .29 C4
Sheerness ME12 . . . . .1 C2
Miller Ave CT2 . . . . .87 D8
Miller Cl Ashford TN24 . .139 D2
Sittingbourne ME10 . . . . . .37 A8
Miller Cotts TN24 . . . . . .139 D2
Miller Ct ME12 . . . . .4 A5
Millers Ct Ramsgate CT12 .29 B1
Whitstable CT5 . . . . .43 D7
Millers La CT12 . . . . .49 C7
Millers Wharf ME15 . . . . .74 F2
Millers Yd CT1 . . . . .87 E7
Millfield Ashford TN23 . . .155 D8
Folkestone CT20 . . . . .178 D5
Hawkinge CT18 . . . . .163 C6
High Halden TN26 . . . . . . .167 D7
Sittingbourne ME10 . . . . . . .37 A3
St Margaret's at Cliffe
CT15 . . . . .150 F7
Millfield Cl CT18 . . . . . .163 B5
Millfield Manor CT5 . . . . .20 E1
Millfield Rd
Faversham ME13 . . . . .62 E7
Ramsgate CT12 . . . . .29 B3
Millfields Chatham ME5 . . .32 D2
Shepherdswell CT15 . . . . .130 E4
Millmead Ave CT9 . . . . .8 D1
Millmead Gdns CT9 . . . . . .8 D1
Millmead Rd CT9 . . . . .8 C1
Millpond Cl ME2 . . . . .9 B8
Mills Cl ME12 . . . . .3 F6
Mills Terr ME4 . . . . .10 A3
Millstock Terr ME15 . . . . .74 E2
Millstream Cl
Faversham ME13 . . . . .62 C7
Whitstable CT5 . . . . .20 E1
Millstrood Rd CT5 . . . . . .43 E8
Millwood Ct 4 ME4 . . . . . .9 F4
Milne Rd TN24 . . . . .156 F8
Milner Cl CT15 . . . . .114 B1
Milner Cres CT3 . . . . . . .112 E5
Milner La CT2 . . . . .67 F5
Milner Rd Elvington CT15 114 B1
Gillingham ME7 . . . . .10 D7
Whitstable CT5 . . . . .43 A6
Milstead & Frinstead
CE Prim Sch ME9 . . . . . .58 E1
Milstead Cl
Maidstone ME14 . . . . .75 C5
West Minst ME12 . . . . .3 B7
Milsted Rd ME8 . . . . .11 C3
Milton Ave CT9 . . . . .7 J1
Milton Cl Canterbury CT1 .88 C6
Dover CT16 . . . . .149 B4
Milton Court Prim Sch
ME10 . . . . .36 E6
Milton Rd Ashford TN23 .139 B2
Canterbury CT1 . . . . .88 A6
Dover CT16 . . . . .149 B4
Gillingham ME7 . . . . .10 C3
Sittingbourne ME10 . . . . . . .36 E4
Milton Sq 4 CT9 . . . . .7 J1
Milton St ME16 . . . . .74 C2
Mincers Cl ME5 . . . . .32 C2
Minerva Ave CT16 . . . . .149 C2
Minerva Ho CT11 . . . . . . .52 D7
Minerva Rd ME2 . . . . .9 A8
Minnis Field CT4 . . . . . .126 E2
Minnis Gn CT4 . . . . .126 E2
Minnis La CT15,CT17 . . . .148 C2
Minnis Rd CT7 . . . . .26 E7
Minnis Terr CT17 . . . . . . .149 A2
Minnis Way CT14 . . . . . . .94 B5
Minster Abbey
Minster (Sheppey) ME12 . . . .4 D6
Minster (Thanet) CT12 . . . . .50 C5
Minster CE Prim Sch
CT12 . . . . .50 B5
Minster Cl CT10 . . . . .30 A2
Minster Coll ME12 . . . . . . .3 F6
Minster Dr Herne Bay CT6 22 D4
Minster (Sheppey) ME12 . . . .4 B8
Minster Gatehouse Mus★
ME12 . . . . .4 D6
Minster Lodge CT11 . . . . .52 C6
Minster Rd Acol CT12,CT7 .27 C2
Faversham ME13 . . . . .62 E7
Gillingham ME8 . . . . .11 C3
Minster (Sheppey) ME12 . . . .4 B6
Ramsgate CT11 . . . . .52 B5
Westgate-on-S CT8 . . . . . . .27 F7
Minster Sta CT12 . . . . . . .50 C5
Minster-in-Sheppey
Prim Sch ME12 . . . . .4 C7
Mint The CT2 . . . . .66 C1
Mintching Wood La ME9 .58 F2
Minter Ave CT18 . . . . . . .162 F7
Minter Cl CT18 . . . . .162 F7
Minterne Ave ME10 . . . . .36 D2
Minterne Com Jun Sch
ME10 . . . . .36 D2
Miranda Ct ME12 . . . . .1 C1
Misling La CT4 . . . . .143 C7
Missenden Ct 6 CT20 . .178 D5
Mitcham Rd TN29 . . . . . .195 C8
Mitchell Ave Chatham ME4 .9 F2
Hawkinge CT18 . . . . .163 B5
Mitchell Cl ME17 . . . . . . .101 C5
Mitchell St CT19 . . . . . . .177 D6
Mitre Rd ME1 . . . . .9 B4
Mittell Ct TN29 . . . . .203 B6
Moat Farm Cl CT19 . . . . .178 C7
Moat Farm Rd CT19 . . . .178 C7
Moat Ho Canterbury CT1 . .87 F7
Charing TN27 . . . . .120 C7
Moat La Ash CT3 . . . . .71 E1
Fordwich CT2 . . . . .68 A3
Rough Common CT2 . . . . . .66 B4
Moat Pk TN27 . . . . .120 C6
Moat Sole CT13 . . . . .72 F1
Moat The TN27 . . . . .120 C7
Moat Way ME11 . . . . .3 A5
Moatfield Mdw TN23 . . .156 B4
Mock La TN23 . . . . .155 B6
Mockett Ct 4 ME10 . . . . .36 E4
Mockett Dr CT10 . . . . .29 C7
Molehill Cnr CT5 . . . . . . .44 D8
Molehill Copse Prim Sch
ME15 . . . . .97 D7
Molehill Rd Herne Bay CT6 22 A1
Whitstable CT5,CT6 . . . . . . .44 E8
Molineux Rd CT12 . . . . . . .50 B6
Molland Cl CT3 . . . . .71 C2
Molland La Ash CT3 . . . . . .71 C2
Westmarsh CT3 . . . . .71 D6
Molland Lea CT3 . . . . .71 C2
Molloy Rd TN26 . . . . .155 B1
Monarch Cl ME5 . . . . .32 A6
Monastery Ave CT16 . . . .149 E1
Monastery St CT1 . . . . . . .88 A8
Monckton's Ave ME14 . . .74 F7
Monckton's Dr ME14 . . . .74 E7
Moncktons La ME14 . . . . .74 F7
Moncrif Cl ME14 . . . . .76 B4
Mongeham Church Cl
CT14 . . . . .116 D3
Mongeham Prim Sch
CT14 . . . . .116 F4
Mongeham Rd CT14 . . . .116 E3
Mongeham View CT14 . .116 E4
Monica Cl ME13 . . . . .84 E6
Monins Rd CT17 . . . . . . .166 B7
Monkdown ME15 . . . . . . .76 A1
Monkery La TN25,TN27 .104 D2
Monks Cl Canterbury CT2 .67 A2
Faversham ME13 . . . . .62 B8
Monks Way CT16 . . . . . . .149 A3
Monks Wlk TN27 . . . . . . .120 C7
Monkshill Rd ME13 . . . . . .42 B2
Monkton CE Prim Sch
CT12 . . . . .49 D7
Monkton Court La CT15 131 D7
Monkton Gdns CT9 . . . . . . .8 E3
Monkton Manor CT12 . . .49 B7
Monkton Pl CT11 . . . . . . .52 D7
Monkton Rd CT12 . . . . . . .50 A6
Monkton Rdbt CT12 . . . . .49 D8
Monkton St CT12 . . . . . . .49 B7
Monkwood Cl ME1 . . . . . .31 B8
Monmouth Cl ME8 . . . . . .11 D2
Mons Ct ME10 . . . . .14 F1
Montacue Ct CT20 . . . . .178 B4
Montague Ct ME12 . . . . . . .1 C1
Montague Rd CT11 . . . . . .52 E8
Montague St CT6 . . . . . . .22 D5
Montefiore Ave
Broadstairs CT10 . . . . .30 A1
Ramsgate CT11 . . . . .29 F1
Montefiore Cotts CT11 . .52 F8
Montfort Cl
Ashford TN23 . . . . .155 F7
Canterbury CT2 . . . . .67 A4
Montfort Rd Chatham ME5 31 F2
Rochester ME2 . . . . .9 A8
Montgomery Ave ME5 . . .32 A7
Montgomery Rd ME7 . . . .10 C3
Montgomery Sch CT2 . . . .68 C8
Montgomery Way CT19 .178 E8
Montpelier Ave CT5 . . . . .43 D6
Montpelier Bsns Pk
TN23 . . . . .138 F1
Montpelier Gate ME16 . . .74 B5
Montreal Cl 8 CT16 . . . .149 B3
Montrose Ave ME5 . . . . . .10 E2
Monument Way TN24 . . .156 F5
Moon Hill CT15 . . . . .130 E4
Moonstone Dr ME5 . . . . . .32 B2
Moor La Ivychurch TN29 .192 D4
Woodchurch TN26 . . . . . . .180 E6
Moor Lane Cotts TN26 . .181 C2
Moor Park Cl ME8 . . . . . .34 A8
Moor St ME8 . . . . .34 B8
Moore Cl TN29 . . . . .192 A3
Moore St ME2 . . . . .9 A8
Moorfield CT2 . . . . .66 F4
Mooring Rd ME1 . . . . .9 D1
Moorings The ME9 . . . . . .38 E6
Moorland Rd CT15 . . . . .130 E4
Moorstock La TN25 . . . .159 C2
Moorwell Dr CT15 . . . . . .130 D5
Moray Ave CT7 . . . . .26 F8
Mordaunt Ave CT8 . . . . . .27 E8
Morden St ME1 . . . . .9 C4
Morehall Ave CT19 . . . . .177 F6
Morehall Prim Sch
CT19 . . . . .177 F6
Morella Wlk ME17 . . . . . .101 C5
Morello Cl ME9 . . . . .38 C2
Moreton Ct CT14 . . . . . . .117 C2
Moreton Terr TN26 . . . . .155 A1
Morgan Kirby's Gdn
ME13 . . . . .83 D5
Morgan Rd ME2 . . . . .9 A8
Morris Ave CT6 . . . . .21 F4
Morris Court Cl ME9 . . . .37 D2
Morrison Rd CT20 . . . . . .178 E6
Morry La ME17 . . . . .99 D1
Mortimer Cl TN23 . . . . . .156 B7
Mortimer Rd CT16 . . . . . .166 F8
Mortimer St CT6 . . . . . . .22 F5
Morton Cl ME15 . . . . .97 D6
Mossbank ME5 . . . . .32 A3
Mossend Mews CT11 . . . .29 E2
Mossy Glade ME8 . . . . . . .33 E6
Mostyn Rd ME14 . . . . . . .75 C4
Mote Ave ME15 . . . . .75 B3
Mote Hall Villas ME14 . . .76 C4
Mote Pk ME15 . . . . .75 D2
Mote Rd ME15 . . . . .75 A3
Motney Hill Rd ME8 . . . . .12 A4
Mouat Ct ME5 . . . . .32 A3
Mount Charles Wlk CT4 . .88 F1
Mount Dr ME14 . . . . .76 B4
Mount Ephraim★ ME13 . .64 A4
Mount Field
Faversham ME13 . . . . .62 B6
Queenborough ME11 . . . . . . .3 A5
Mount Green Ave CT12 . .51 D5
Mount La Hartlip ME9 . . . .34 D4
Maidstone ME14 . . . . .76 B4
Mount Lodge ME1 . . . . . . .9 B2
Mount Pleasant
Aldington TN25 . . . . .173 A6
Aylesford ME20 . . . . .53 A3
Blean CT2 . . . . .66 A6
Gillingham ME5 . . . . .10 B3
Kingsdown CT14 . . . . .134 D5
Oare ME13 . . . . .40 B2
Tenterden TN30 . . . . .179 C8
Mount Pleasant Dr ME14 76 A5
Mount Pleasant Rd 4
CT20 . . . . .178 D5
Mount Pleasant Terr
ME17 . . . . .100 E2
Mount Rd Canterbury CT1 .88 C6
Chatham ME4 . . . . .9 F3
Dover CT17 . . . . .166 A6
Rochester ME1 . . . . .9 B2
Mount St CT21 . . . . .176 C2
Mount View ME13 . . . . . . .62 A5
Mount View Ct 3 ME4 . . . .9 F3
Mount View Rd CT6 . . . . .23 A2
Mountain St CT4 . . . . . . .107 B6
Mountbatten Ave ME5 . . .32 A7
Mountbatten Way TN25 158 E6
Mountfield Rd TN28 . . . .200 C6
Mountfield Row TN28 . .200 C6
Mountfield Way CT8 . . . .27 D6
Mountpleasant Cl CT18 .161 C7
Mounts Cl CT14 . . . . . . .117 A5
Mountsfield Cl ME16 . . . .74 D5
Mountview ME9 . . . . .36 B2
Moyes Cl CT12 . . . . .51 D5
Moyle Cl ME8 . . . . .33 D4
Mozart Ct ME4 . . . . .9 E3
Muddy Bush Cnr CT3 . . . .90 F2
Muir Rd Maidstone ME15 . .75 A2
Ramsgate CT11 . . . . .52 F8
Mulberry Cl
Gillingham ME7 . . . . .33 A4
Ramsgate CT11 . . . . .52 F8
Mulberry Ct
Canterbury CT1 . . . . .87 F8
Hythe CT21 . . . . .176 D3
Littlestone-on-S TN28 . . . .200 E5
Maidstone ME14 . . . . .75 B5
Mulberry Field CT13 . . . .72 F1
Mulberry Hill CT4 . . . . . .85 D1
Munday Bois Cotts
TN27 . . . . .135 F8
Munday Bois Rd TN27 . .118 E1
Mundella Prim Sch
CT19 . . . . .178 D6
Mungeam Ho ME1 . . . . . . .9 C4
Munn's La ME9 . . . . .34 E6
Murrain Dr ME15 . . . . . . .76 A1
Murray Rd ME2 . . . . .9 C8
Murston Inf Sch ME10 . . .37 B4
Murston Jun Sch ME10 . . .37 B5
Murston Rd ME10 . . . . . . .37 B4
Murthwaite Ct ME12 . . . . . .4 A5
Murton Pl ME13 . . . . .41 E1
Muscovy Rd TN25 . . . . . .139 C7
Muscovy Way CT6 . . . . . . .22 E3
Museum of
Kent Rural Life★ ME14 .53 D1
Museum St ME14 . . . . . . .74 F4
Musgrave Cl CT12 . . . . . .27 F2
Musgrave Rd ME10 . . . . . .36 F6
Musgrove TN23 . . . . .156 A8
Musket La
Eyhorne Street ME17 . . . . . .77 B2
Silver Hill ME17 . . . . .77 A2
Mustards Rd ME12 . . . . . . .6 D2
Mutrix Gdns CT9 . . . . .7 E1
Mutrix Rd CT9 . . . . .28 B8
Mutton La ME13 . . . . .62 A6
Mymms Cl CT5 . . . . .44 C8
Mynn Cres ME14 . . . . . . .76 A4
Myrtle Cres ME5 . . . . . . .31 F5
Myrtle Rd 5 CT19 . . . . . .178 E6
Mystole La CT4 . . . . .108 C8
Mystole Rd CT4 . . . . .108 A8

N

Nacholt Cl CT5 . . . . .21 A2
Nackington Ct CT1 . . . . . .88 B6
Nackington Pk CT4 . . . . . .88 A4
Nackington Rd CT1,CT4 . .88 A3
Nag's Head La ME1 . . . . . . .9 D4
Nagpur House 4 ME15 . . .97 E5
Nailbourne Cl CT4 . . . . .111 D3
Nailbourne Ct CT18 . . . .161 C7
Naildown Cl CT21 . . . . . .177 A3
Naildown Rd CT21 . . . . . .177 A3
Nairne Cl TN26 . . . . .170 A8
Namur Pl CT15 . . . . .149 F3
Napchester Rd CT16 . . .149 A8
Napier Cl ME10 . . . . .36 C4
Napier Com Sch ME7 . . . .10 D4
Napier Ct ME14 . . . . .74 F7
Napier Gdns CT21 . . . . . .176 C1
Napier Rd
Broadstairs CT10 . . . . .29 E6
Napier Rd *continued*
Dover CT16 . . . . .149 B2
Gillingham ME7 . . . . .10 D4
Napleton Ct CT11 . . . . . . .52 C6
Napleton Rd
Faversham ME13 . . . . .62 C7
Ramsgate CT11 . . . . .52 C6
Napoleon Wlk ME17 . . . .101 C5
Napwood Cl ME8 . . . . . . .33 D6
Nares Rd ME8 . . . . .33 D4
Nargate Cl CT3 . . . . .90 A8
Nargate St CT3 . . . . .90 A8
Narrabeen Rd CT19 . . . . .177 E6
Narrowbush La TN29 . . .198 B7
Naseby Ave CT20 . . . . . . .177 D5
Nash Cl ME5 . . . . .32 C2
Nash Court
Farming World★ ME13 .63 D4
Nash Court Gdns CT9 . . . .28 F8
Nash Court Rd CT9 . . . . . .28 F8
Nash Gdns CT10 . . . . .30 B4
Nash Hill CT18 . . . . .161 D6
Nash La CT9 . . . . .28 F7
Nash Rd Margate CT9,CT10 28 F7
Preston CT3 . . . . .70 D2
Nashenden Farm La ME1 31 A8
Nashenden La ME1 . . . . . . .9 A2
Nasmyth Rd CT7 . . . . .27 A8
Nat's La TN25 . . . . .141 A5
Natal Rd Chatham ME4 . . .10 A3
Dover CT16 . . . . .149 C4
Nativity Cl ME10 . . . . .36 E4
Nautilus Cl ME12 . . . . .4 A6
Nautilus Dr ME12 . . . . .4 A6
Naval Terr ME12 . . . . .1 B3
Naylands CT9 . . . . .7 H1
Naylor's Cotts ME7 . . . . .33 B1
Neal's Place Rd CT2 . . . .66 C3
Neale St ME4 . . . . .9 F2
Neame Rd CT7 . . . . .27 A7
Neames Forstal ME13 . . .84 E7
Neason Ct CT19 . . . . . . .178 F6
Neason Way CT19 . . . . . .178 F6
Neath Rd TN29 . . . . .202 A2
Neatscourt Cotts ME12 . . .3 C4
Nelson Ave ME12 . . . . .4 D5
Nelson Cl Ashford TN24 . .157 B8
West Minst ME12 . . . . .3 A8
Nelson Cres CT11 . . . . . .52 E6
Nelson Ct CT7 . . . . .26 E8
Nelson Ho 8 ME15 . . . . .97 F5
Nelson Park Rd CT15 . . .150 E8
Nelson Pl CT10 . . . . .30 B5
Nelson Rd Gillingham ME7 10 D4
Whitstable CT5 . . . . .20 D1
Nelson St Deal CT14 . . . .117 D7
Faversham ME13 . . . . .62 C6
Nelson Terr ME5 . . . . .10 C1
Nelson Wlk ME10 . . . . . . .36 B5
Neptune Bsns Pk ME2 . . . .9 E7
Neptune Cl ME2 . . . . .9 E7
Neptune Terr ME12 . . . . . .1 E2
Neptune Way ME2 . . . . . . .9 E6
Nesbit Rd TN29 . . . . .194 F4
Ness Rd TN29 . . . . .203 C6
Ness The CT1 . . . . .88 B5
Nether Ave TN28 . . . . . .200 D6
Nethercourt Cir CT12 . . .52 A6
Nethercourt Farm Rd
CT11 . . . . .52 B7
Nethercourt Gdns CT11 . .52 B6
Nethercourt Hill CT11 . . .52 B6
Nethergong Hill CT3 . . . .47 D3
Netherhale Farm Rd CT7 26 B3
Nethersole Cl CT2 . . . . . .67 A4
Nethersole Rd CT4 . . . . .112 F1
Netley Cl ME14 . . . . .75 D6
Nettlefield TN24 . . . . . . .139 E5
Nettlepole La TN27 . . . .119 D1
Nevill Gdns CT14 . . . . . .117 B1
Neville Cl ME14 . . . . .75 B8
Neville Rd ME4 . . . . .9 E2
New Barns Rd ME14 . . . .75 A8
New Beverley Ho CT2 . . .66 F2
New Bridge 10 CT16 . . . .166 E7
New Cotts Guston CT15 . .149 E6
Harbledown CT2 . . . . .65 E1
Teynham ME9 . . . . .38 A4
New Covenant Pl ME1 . . . .9 D4
New Cross St CT9 . . . . . . .7 I2
New Cut Chatham ME4 . . . . .9 F4
Dean Street ME15 . . . . .96 D7
New Cut Rd
Chilham CT4,ME13 . . . . . . .85 A3
Maidstone ME14 . . . . .75 D5
New Delhi House 5
ME15 . . . . .97 E5
New Dover Rd
Canterbury CT1,CT4 . . . . . .88 C6
Capel-le-F CT18 . . . . .164 C2
New Forest La CT4 . . . . .85 B3
New Gardens Rd ME9 . . . .38 C2
New Haine Rd CT12 . . . . .29 A3
New Hall Cl TN29 . . . . . .195 C8
New Hall Mus★ TN29 . .195 C8
New House Cl CT1 . . . . . .87 E4
New House La CT4 . . . . . .87 C2
New Inn Cotts ME15 . . . . .96 C7
New La TN29 . . . . .203 C6
New Rd Chatham ME4 . . . . .9 F4
Egerton TN27 . . . . .119 A2
Elham CT4 . . . . .144 F4
Eythorne CT15 . . . . .131 C7
Harbledown CT2 . . . . .65 D3
Herne CT2,CT6 . . . . .45 C4

Q

Rosebery Rd Chatham ME4 ... 9 E2
Gillingham ME7 ... 10 D7
Rosedale Rd CT9 ... 8 A1
Roseholme ME16 ... 74 D2
Roselands CT14 ... 117 C1
Roselands Gdns CT2 ... 66 D2
Roselawn Gdns 3 CT9 ... 28 B8
Roselea Ave CT6 ... 22 F3
Roseleigh Ave ME16 ... 74 C5
Roseleigh Rd ME10 ... 36 D2
Rosemary Ave
Broadstairs CT10 ... 30 A3
Halfway Houses ME12 ... 3 D6
Rosemary Cl 4 ME5 ... 31 F4
Rosemary Cnr TN29 ... 197 D8
Rosemary Ct ME1 ... 9 D4
Rosemary Gdns
Broadstairs CT10 ... 29 F2
Whitstable CT5 ... 44 A8
Rosemary La 16 CT1 ... 87 F8
Rosemary Rd ME15 ... 76 A3
Rosemount Cl ME15 ... 96 F4
Rosetower Ct CT10 ... 29 F8
Rosiers Ct 1 CT2 ... 66 E1
Ross Gdns CT2 ... 66 B3
Ross St ME1 ... 9 D4
Ross Way CT20 ... 177 E5
Rossendale Ct 10 CT20 ... 178 E6
Rossendale Gdns 8
CT20 ... 178 E6
Rossendale Rd CT20 ... 178 E6
Rossetti Ct CT7 ... 26 F7
Rossetti Rd CT7 ... 26 F8
Rossland Rd CT12 ... 52 A8
Rosslyn Gn ME16 ... 74 B5
Rothbrook Dr TN24 ... 139 C7
Rother Vale ME5 ... 32 C3
Rothley Cl TN30 ... 179 B8
Rothsay Ct CT11 ... 29 F1
Rough Common Rd CT2 ... 66 B3
Round Wood Cl ME5 ... 32 A1
Roundel Cl ME9 ... 38 D2
Roundel The ME10 ... 36 F2
Roundwell ME14 ... 76 D3
Rover Rd ME5 ... 32 B2
Row The Ash CT3 ... 71 E5
Elham CT4 ... 144 F5
Ruckinge TN26 ... 183 F8
Rowan Cl Ashford TN23 ... 138 E2
Staple CT3 ... 92 A6
Sturry CT2 ... 67 F6
Rowan Ct CT10 ... 30 A5
Rowan Ho 4 ME5 ... 31 F5
Rowan Lea ME5 ... 10 B1
Rowan Wlk ME4 ... 9 E3
Rowans The ME12 ... 4 B7
Rowbrocke Cl ME8 ... 33 D3
Rowe Cl CT9 ... 28 F7
Rowena Rd CT8 ... 7 C1
Rowetts Way ME12 ... 5 D3
Rowland Ave ME7 ... 10 E2
Rowland Cl ME7 ... 10 E1
Rowland Cres CT6 ... 23 E5
Rowland Dr CT6 ... 22 C2
Roxburgh Rd CT8 ... 7 D1
Royal Ave CT5 ... 43 C5
Royal Cinque Ports
Golf Links CT13,CT14 ... 95 B4
Royal Cl CT10 ... 29 F4
Royal Cres Margate CT9 ... 7 H2
Ramsgate CT11 ... 52 D5
Royal Eagle Cl ME2 ... 9 E7
Royal Engineers Mus★
ME7 ... 10 B6
Royal Engineers' Rd
ME14 ... 74 F7
Royal Espl Margate CT9 ... 7 F1
Ramsgate CT11 ... 52 C5
Royal Military Ave
CT20 ... 177 D5
Royal Military Rd
Aldington TN25 ... 173 D1
Hythe CT21 ... 175 D1
Royal Mus★ CT1 ... 87 F8
Royal Par CT11 ... 52 E6
Royal Rd Ramsgate CT11 ... 52 D6
Sheerness ME12 ... 1 D2
Royal Sch
for Deaf Children CT9 ... 7 J2
Royal Sovereign Ave
ME4 ... 10 B7
Royal Star Arc 5 ME14 ... 74 F4
Royal Victoria Hospl
CT19 ... 178 C6
Royal Victoria Pl 5
CT16 ... 166 D8
Royds Rd TN24 ... 156 D6
Royston Gdns CT15 ... 150 F6
Royston Rd ME15 ... 76 A3
Roystons Cl ME8 ... 11 F2
Royton Ave ME17 ... 101 D5
Rubery Dro CT3 ... 72 C7
Ruckinge Cnr TN26 ... 183 F8
Ruckinge Rd TN26 ... 183 A7
Ruckinge Way ME8 ... 11 C3
Rudge Cl ME5 ... 32 D2
Rugby Cl Broadstairs CT10 ... 29 F5
Chatham ME5 ... 31 F4
Rugby Gdns TN23 ... 156 C8
Rugby Rd CT17 ... 166 A6
Ruins Barn Rd ME10,ME9 ... 58 D6
Rule Ct ME12 ... 3 B8
Rumfields Rd CT10 ... 29 D4
Rumstead La ME17,ME9 ... 56 D4
Rumstead Rd ME9 ... 56 E4
Rumwood Ct ME17 ... 98 B5
Runcie Ho 6 CT1 ... 87 F7
Runcie Pl CT2 ... 66 D1
Runham La ME17 ... 100 E3
Running Horse Rndbt
The ME14 ... 53 E1
Runnymede Gdns ME15 ... 97 A8
Runnymede Mews ME13 ... 62 C7
Rush Cl Chatham ME5 ... 32 A3
Dymchurch TN29 ... 195 B6
Rusham Rd CT3 ... 70 C1
Rushenden Ct ME11 ... 2 F3
Rushenden Rd ME11 ... 3 A4
Rushmead Cl CT2 ... 66 D2
Rushmead Dr ME15 ... 97 A7
Russel Dr CT5 ... 21 D3
Russell Cl ME10 ... 36 C3
Russell Ct ME4 ... 10 B3
Russell Pl ME13 ... 40 B3
Russell Rd
1 Folkestone CT19 ... 178 D6
Kit's Coty ME20 ... 53 D7
Russell St Dover CT16 ... 166 E7
Sheerness ME12 ... 1 C2
Russells Ave ME8 ... 34 A8
Russet Ave ME13 ... 62 E5
Russet Ct ME17 ... 96 C3
Russet Rd CT1 ... 88 C8
Russets The
Maidstone ME16 ... 74 B5
Whitstable CT5 ... 21 D1
Ruth House ME16 ... 74 E5
Rutherford Coll CT2 ... 66 E4
Rutherford Rd TN24 ... 139 B5
Rutland Ave CT9 ... 8 C2
Rutland Cl CT1 ... 88 D7
Rutland Gdns
Birchington CT7 ... 26 F7
Margate CT9 ... 8 C2
Rutland Ho 3 CT9 ... 8 B2
Rutland Pl ME8 ... 33 C3
Rutland Rd CT16 ... 149 B3
Rutland Way ME15 ... 97 E8
Ryan Dr ME15 ... 76 A2
Rycaut Cl ME8 ... 33 D3
Rydal Ave CT11 ... 52 B7
Ryde Cl ME5 ... 32 B8
Ryde St CT2 ... 66 E1
Ryder's Ave CT8 ... 27 D8
Rye Ct TN23 ... 155 D7
Rye Rd Brookland TN29 ... 197 D8
Wittersham TN30 ... 189 A2
Rye Wlk CT6 ... 23 C2
Ryecault Cl 4 ME16 ... 74 E3
Ryegrass Cl ME5 ... 32 C6
Ryland Ct 4 CT20 ... 178 E5
Ryland Pl 5 CT20 ... 178 E5
Rylands Rd TN24 ... 139 D5
Rype Cl TN29 ... 203 C5
Ryswick Mews TN28 ... 200 C8

S

Sabre Ct ME7 ... 11 A1
Sackett's Gap CT9 ... 8 C3
Sacketts Hill CT10 ... 29 C6
Sackville Cl TN26 ... 138 A7
Sackville Cres TN23 ... 139 A2
Saddler's Wall La TN29 ... 191 B1
Saddlers Cl ME14 ... 75 E5
Saddlers Hill CT3 ... 91 D2
Saddlers Mews CT5 ... 21 D1
Saddlers Way TN23 ... 156 B5
Saddleton Gr CT5 ... 43 D8
Saddleton Rd CT5 ... 43 D8
Sadlers Cl ME5 ... 31 D2
Saffron Way
1 Chatham ME5 ... 31 F5
Sittingbourne ME10 ... 36 F7
Saffron's Pl 12 CT20 ... 178 E5
Sage Rd ME1 ... 9 B3
Sailfield Ct ME4 ... 9 F7
Sailmakers Ct 5 ME4 ... 10 B2
St Agnes Gdns ME12 ... 1 D1
St Alban's Rd CT3 ... 46 E1
St Albans Cl ME7 ... 10 E7
St Alphege CE Inf Sch
CT5 ... 20 D1
St Alphege Cl CT5 ... 43 B7
St Alphege La 8 CT1 ... 66 F1
St Alphege Rd 4 CT16 ... 149 C1
St Ambrose Gn TN25 ... 123 E2
St Andrew Rd ME7 ... 10 D7
St Andrew Terr CT17 ... 149 A2
St Andrew's Cl
Maidstone ME16 ... 74 A2
Whitstable CT5 ... 43 E7
St Andrew's Gdns CT15 ... 130 E5
St Andrew's Lees CT13 ... 94 A8
St Andrew's Rd
Deal CT14 ... 117 C6
Littlestone-on-S TN28 ... 200 E6
Maidstone ME16 ... 74 A3
Ramsgate CT11 ... 52 F8
St Andrews CT19 ... 178 E5
St Andrews Cl
Canterbury CT1 ... 87 E7
Folkestone CT19 ... 178 B7
Herne Bay CT6 ... 23 A4
Margate CT9 ... 28 F7
St Andrews Gdns CT17 ... 149 B2
St Andrews Way CT14 ... 115 A3
St Angela's Sch CT8 ... 27 D7
St Ann's Rd
Dymchurch TN29 ... 195 B7
Faversham ME13 ... 62 B7
St Anne Ct ME16 ... 74 E4
St Anne's Ct
1 Dover CT16 ... 149 B2
Herne Bay CT6 ... 22 E5
St Anne's Dr CT6 ... 22 D4
St Anne's Gdns CT9 ... 28 F8
St Anne's Rd
Ashford TN23 ... 155 F7
Whitstable CT5 ... 20 F2
St Anselm's Catholic Sch
CT1 ... 88 C5
St Anthony's Sch CT9 ... 8 C1
St Anthony's Way CT9 ... 8 C1
St Augustine of Canterbury
RC Prim Sch ME8 ... 33 D3
St Augustine's Abbey
CT11 ... 52 D5
St Augustine's Abbey
(rems of) CT1 ... 88 A8
St Augustine's Ave CT9 ... 28 F8
St Augustine's Cres CT5 ... 21 D3
St Augustine's Ct CT1 ... 88 B8
St Augustine's Pk CT11 ... 52 C6
St Augustine's
RC Prim Sch CT21 ... 176 E2
St Augustine's Rd
Canterbury CT1 ... 88 B7
Deal CT14 ... 116 F4
Ramsgate CT11 ... 52 D5
St Augustines Bsns Pk
CT5 ... 21 E3
St Barnabas Cl
Ashford TN23 ... 155 F7
Gillingham ME7 ... 10 D3
Maidstone ME16 ... 74 C8
St Bart's Rd CT13 ... 93 F8
St Bartholemews Cl 4
CT17 ... 166 C8
St Bartholomew's Hospl
ME1 ... 9 E4
St Bartholomew's Hospl
CT13 ... 94 A7
St Bartholomew's La 4
ME1 ... 9 E4
St Bartholomew's Sch
ME10 ... 36 F7
St Bartholomew's Terr 2
ME1 ... 9 E4
St Benedict's Lawn CT11 ... 52 D5
St Benedicts
RC Prim Sch ME5 ... 32 C2
St Benet's Rd CT8 ... 27 E7
St Benets Ct TN30 ... 179 B8
St Benets Way TN30 ... 179 B8
St Catherine's Dr ME13 ... 62 D6
St Catherine's Gr CT12 ... 28 D1
St Catherine's Hospl
ME1 ... 9 D4
St Catherines TN29 ... 199 A7
St Catherines Ct CT11 ... 29 F1
St Christopher Cl CT9 ... 29 D8
St Christopher's Sch CT1 ... 88 B6
St Christophers Gn CT10 ... 29 F5
St Clare Rd CT14 ... 117 C1
St Clement's Ct CT6 ... 23 A3
St Clement's Ho ME1 ... 9 D5
St Clement's Rd CT8 ... 7 C1
St Clements 8 CT13 ... 73 A1
St Clements Cl ME12 ... 6 D2
St Clements Ct CT10 ... 29 E6
St Clements Rd ME12 ... 6 E3
St Cosmus Cl TN25 ... 105 B1
St Crispin's Com Prim
Inf Sch CT8 ... 27 E7
St Crispin's Rd CT8 ... 27 E7
St David's Cl
Birchington CT7 ... 27 B8
Whitstable CT5 ... 43 E8
St David's Rd Deal CT14 ... 117 C6
Ramsgate CT11 ... 29 F1
St Davids Ave CT17 ... 166 A5
St Denys Rd CT18 ... 163 B5
St Dunstan's Cl CT2 ... 66 E1
St Dunstan's Rd CT9 ... 8 A2
St Dunstan's St CT2 ... 66 E1
St Dunstan's Terr CT2 ... 66 E1
St Dunstans Ct 4 CT2 ... 66 E1
St Eanswythe Way 19
CT20 ... 178 D5
St Eanswythe's
CE Prim Sch CT20 ... 178 D4
St Edmund's RC Sch
CT16 ... 149 D2
St Edmund's Rd CT14 ... 116 E4
St Edmund's Sch CT2 ... 66 C3
St Edmunds Rd CT1 ... 87 F8
St Edmunds Way ME8 ... 12 B1
St Edward's RC Prim Sch
ME12 ... 1 C2
St Ethelbert's RC Prim Sch
CT11 ... 52 F8
St Faith's La ME14 ... 76 B4
St Faith's St ME14 ... 74 F4
St Faiths Sch CT3 ... 71 C1
St Francis Cl Deal CT14 ... 116 F4
Maidstone ME14 ... 75 B7
Margate CT9 ... 29 D8
St Francis RC Prim Sch
ME14 ... 75 B7
St Francis Rd CT19 ... 177 F6
St Francis Sch ME14 ... 75 B7
St Francis' RC Sch
ME14 ... 75 A5
St Gabriel's Ct 12 CT20 ... 178 E6
St George's Ave
Herne Bay CT6 ... 22 D4
Sheerness ME12 ... 1 C1
St George's Bsns Ctr
TN23 ... 138 F2
St George's CE
Foundation Sch CT10 ... 29 C5
St George's CE Mid Sch
ME12 ... 4 E6
St George's Cl CT5 ... 43 E7
St George's Ct ME12 ... 3 B8
St George's Lees CT13 ... 94 A8
St George's Pass CT14 ... 117 D6
St George's Pl
Canterbury CT1 ... 88 A8
Hythe CT21 ... 187 D8
St George's Rd
Broadstairs CT10 ... 30 A4
Deal CT14 ... 117 D6
Folkestone CT19 ... 177 F6
Gillingham ME7 ... 10 C6
Ramsgate CT11 ... 52 F8
Sandwich CT13 ... 94 A8
St George's Sq
3 Ashford TN24 ... 139 B2
Maidstone ME16 ... 74 E3
St George's St CT1 ... 88 A8
St George's Terr CT6 ... 22 E5
St Georges Ave ME12 ... 5 D2
St Georges Bsns Pk
ME10 ... 37 B4
St Georges Cres CT17 ... 166 B5
St Georges Ct CT17 ... 149 A2
St Georges La CT1 ... 88 A8
St Georges Pl
Sandwich CT13 ... 94 B8
St Margaret's at Cliffe
CT15 ... 150 F6
St Georges St CT1 ... 88 A8
St Giles Cl CT17 ... 166 B5
St Giles Rd CT17 ... 166 B5
St Giles Wlk CT17 ... 166 B5
St Gregory's 9 CT1 ... 67 A1
St Gregory's Cl CT14 ... 116 F4
St Gregory's
RC Prim Sch CT9 ... 28 E8
St Gregory's Rd CT1 ... 67 B1
St Helen's Rd ME12 ... 1 E1
St Helier's Cl ME16 ... 74 B2
St Hilda Rd CT19 ... 177 E6
St Hilda's Rd CT21 ... 176 B1
St Jacob's Pl CT1 ... 87 D6
St James Cl ME12 ... 6 E4
St James La 5 CT16 ... 166 E7
St James Rd CT14 ... 134 D5
St James St CT16 ... 166 E7
St James' Ave
Broadstairs CT10 ... 29 E5
Ramsgate CT12 ... 29 B1
St James' Gdns CT5 ... 43 D8
St James' Park Rd CT9 ... 28 A8
St James's Terr CT7 ... 27 B8
St Jean's Rd CT8 ... 27 E7
St John Bsns Ctr The 10
CT9 ... 7 J1
St John Fisher
Catholic Sch ME4 ... 9 E3
St John Fisher
RC Lower Sch ME4 ... 9 F2
St John's Ave
Ramsgate CT12 ... 29 A1
Sittingbourne ME10 ... 37 B3
St John's CE Inf Sch ME4 ... 9 E3
St John's CE Prim Sch
ME14 ... 75 E4
St John's Church Rd
CT19 ... 178 C6
St John's Cl CT18 ... 163 A7
St John's Commandery
(rems of)★ CT15 ... 146 E4
St John's Cotts 11 CT13 ... 72 F1
St John's Ct TN24 ... 157 A6
St John's Hospl 6 CT1 ... 67 A1
St John's La
Ashford TN23,TN24 ... 139 C2
Canterbury CT1 ... 87 F8
St John's Pl CT1 ... 67 A1
St John's Rd Dover CT17 ... 166 C7
Faversham ME13 ... 62 D7
Gillingham ME7 ... 10 C3
Margate CT9 ... 7 J2
New Romney TN28 ... 200 A6
Whitstable CT5 ... 21 D3
St John's St
Folkestone CT20 ... 178 D5
7 Margate CT9 ... 7 J2
St John's Way CT18 ... 163 A7
St Johns Cres CT2 ... 66 D6
St Johns Rd
Elvington CT15 ... 114 B2
Hythe CT21 ... 176 A3
St Johns Way ME1 ... 9 A2
St Joseph's RC Prim Sch
Aylesham CT3 ... 113 A5
Broadstairs CT10 ... 29 F5
St Julien Ave CT1 ... 67 D1
St Katherine Rd ME12 ... 3 E7
St Laurence Ave ME16 ... 74 C8
St Laurence Cl ME9 ... 37 D2
St Laurence Ct CT11 ... 52 C7
St Laurence In Thanet
CE Jun Sch CT12 ... 52 B8
St Lawrence Ave CT11 ... 52 B5
St Lawrence Cl CT1 ... 88 B6
St Lawrence Coll CT11 ... 52 D8
St Lawrence Coll
(Jun Sch) CT11 ... 52 E8
St Lawrence Ct TN28 ... 200 A6
St Lawrence Forstal CT1 ... 88 B6
St Lawrence Gd (Kent
Cty Cricket Club) CT1 ... 88 B6
St Lawrence Ind Est
CT11 ... 52 B7
St Lawrence Rd CT1 ... 88 B6
St Leonard's Rd CT14 ... 117 B4
St Leonards Ave ME4 ... 9 F2
St Leonards Ct CT21 ... 176 B1
St Leonards Rd
Hythe CT21 ... 176 B1
Maidstone ME16 ... 74 C8
St Louis Gr CT6 ... 22 C4
St Luke's Ave
Maidstone ME14 ... 75 B5
Ramsgate CT11 ... 52 E8
St Luke's Cl CT8 ... 27 E8
St Luke's Rd
Maidstone ME14 ... 75 B5
Ramsgate CT11 ... 52 E8
St Luke's Wlk CT18 ... 162 F4
St Lukes Cl CT5 ... 43 E7
St Lukes Ct TN23 ... 155 F7
St Magnus Cl CT7 ... 27 A8
St Magnus Ct CT8 ... 27 A8
St Margaret's at Troy Town
CE Prim Sch ME1 ... 9 C4
St Margaret's Banks ME1 ... 9 D5
St Margaret's CE Jun Sch
ME8 ... 33 E8
St Margaret's Cl CT5 ... 43 A6
St Margaret's Inf Sch
ME8 ... 33 E8
St Margaret's Mews ME1 ... 9 C5
St Margaret's Rd
St Margaret's at Cliffe
CT15 ... 151 A5
Westgate-on-S CT8 ... 27 E7
St Margaret's St
Canterbury CT1 ... 87 F8
Rochester ME1 ... 9 C5
St Margaret's-at-Cliffe
Prim Sch CT15 ... 151 A6
St Margarets Cl ME16 ... 74 B2
St Margarets Ct 1
CT20 ... 178 B5
St Margarets Dr
Deal CT14 ... 134 B8
Gillingham ME8 ... 33 C5
St Margarets Rd CT7 ... 27 F3
St Mark's Cl CT20 ... 177 D5
St Marks Cl CT5 ... 43 E8
St Marks Ho ME7 ... 10 C5
St Martin's CE Prim Sch
CT18 ... 177 B5
St Martin's Cl
Detling ME14 ... 55 A1
Dover CT17 ... 166 B5
St Martin's Hill CT1 ... 88 C8
St Martin's Hospl CT1 ... 88 D8
St Martin's Pl CT1 ... 88 B8
St Martin's Rd
Canterbury CT1 ... 67 B1
Deal CT14 ... 116 F4
Guston CT15 ... 149 E4
St Martin's Sch CT17 ... 166 A7
St Martin's Terr CT1 ... 88 B8
St Martin's View CT6 ... 46 A8
St Martins Ave CT1 ... 88 B8
St Martins Cl
Canterbury CT1 ... 88 B8
Newington ME9 ... 35 C7
St Martins Ct CT1 ... 88 B8
St Martins Rd
Folkestone CT20 ... 177 D6
New Romney TN28 ... 200 B6
St Mary Ct 13 ME13 ... 62 D7
St Mary of Charity
CE Inf Sch ME13 ... 62 D7
St Mary of Charity
CE Jun Sch ME13 ... 62 D7
St Mary's Ave Margate CT9 ... 8 D1
Margate CT9 ... 29 D8
St Mary's CE Prim Sch
Ashford TN23 ... 139 A3
Chilham CT4 ... 107 B8
Dover CT16 ... 166 E8
Folkestone CT19 ... 178 F6
St Mary's Church★ CT6 ... 24 C7
St Mary's Cl Eastry CT13 ... 93 C2
Hamstreet TN26 ... 183 A8
Nonington CT15 ... 113 C5
Woodnesborough CT13 ... 93 B6
St Mary's Ct 17 CT1 ... 87 F8
St Mary's Cty Prim Sch
ME2 ... 9 B7
St Mary's Gdns
Gillingham ME4 ... 10 B7
St Mary's Bay TN29 ... 195 A5
Upstreet CT3 ... 47 E3
St Mary's Gr
Tilmanstone CT14 ... 115 A4
Whitstable CT5 ... 42 F7
St Mary's Mdw CT3 ... 91 A8
St Mary's Pl ME9 ... 35 C7
St Mary's RC Prim Sch
Deal CT14 ... 116 F3
Gillingham ME7 ... 10 D6
Whitstable CT5 ... 20 F2
St Mary's Rd
5 Broadstairs CT10 ... 30 B4
Deal CT14 ... 117 C1
Elham CT4 ... 144 F4
Faversham ME13 ... 62 D7
Gillingham ME7 ... 10 C6
Minster (Thanet) CT12 ... 50 B6
Patrixbourne CT4 ... 89 B3
Rochester ME2 ... 9 B7
St Mary in the Marsh
TN28,TN29 ... 194 C5
West Hythe CT21 ... 175 B1
St Mary's Row ME12 ... 4 A6
St Mary's St CT1 ... 87 F8

Upbury Manor High Sch
ME7 . . . . .10 B4
Upbury Way ME4 . . . . . . .10 A4
Upchurch Wlk CT9 . . . . . . .8 E2
Updown Way CT4 . . . . . . .86 F1
Uphill CT18 . . . . .163 B4
Uplands CT2 . . . . .66 F4
Uplands Way ME12 . . . . . . .3 C5
Uplees Cotts ME13 . . . . . .39 F5
Upleas Rd ME13 . . . . .40 A3
Upnor Ho ME15 . . . . .97 E8
Upnor Rd ME2 . . . . .9 D8
Upper Approach Rd
CT10 . . . . .30 A3
Upper Brents ME13 . . . . .62 D8
Upper Bridge St
Canterbury CT1 . . . . .88 A8
Wye TN25 . . . . .123 F2
Upper Britton Pl ME7 . . .10 B5
Upper Chantry La CT1 . . .88 A7
Upper Corniche CT20 . .177 C3
Upper Dane Ct CT9 . . . . . . .8 B1
Upper Dane Rd CT9 . . . . . .8 B1
Upper Denmark Rd
TN23 . . . . .156 B8
Upper Dumpton Park Rd
CT11 . . . . .52 E8
Upper East Rd ME4 . . . . .10 B8
Upper Fant Rd ME16 . . . .74 D2
Upper Field Rd ME10 . . . .37 B5
Upper Free Down CT6 . . .23 B2
Upper Gore La CT13 . . . .93 A2
Upper Gr CT9 . . . . .7 J2
Upper Hunton Hill ME15 .96 A3
Upper Luton Rd ME5 . . . .10 C2
Upper Malthouse Hill
CT21 . . . . .176 B2
Upper Maltings Pl CT7 . .26 F7
Upper Rd
Dover CT15,CT16 . . . . . . .150 C2
Dover,Eastern Docks
CT16 . . . . .166 H8
Maidstone ME15 . . . . .75 B2
Upper St
Hollingbourne ME17 . . . . .77 E3
Kingsdown CT14 . . . . . . .134 D5
Leeds ME17 . . . . .98 F5
Tilmanstone CT14 . . . . . .115 A3
Upper St Ann's Rd ME13 .62 B6
Upper Stone St ME15 . . .75 A3
Upper Strand St CT13 . . .73 A1
Upper Tickham Cotts
ME9 . . . . .60 D6
Upper Vicarage Rd
TN24 . . . . .139 D7
Upstreet CT18 . . . . .161 D3
Upton Cl CT19 . . . . .178 A7
Upton Jun Sch CT10 . . . .29 F4
Upton Rd CT10 . . . . .29 F5
Urquhart Cl ME5 . . . . . . .32 A5
Ursuline Dr CT8 . . . . .27 D7

V

Vale Cotts ME9 . . . . .57 A8
Vale Dr ME5 . . . . .31 E6
Vale Pl CT11 . . . . .52 D6
Vale Rd Broadstairs CT10 . .29 F4
Loose ME15 . . . . .96 E4
Ramsgate CT11 . . . . .52 D6
Ripple CT14,CT15 . . . . . .133 B8
Whitstable CT5 . . . . .43 D8
Vale Sq CT11 . . . . .52 D6
Vale The CT10 . . . . .30 A4
Vale View Com Sch
CT17 . . . . .166 B7
Vale View Rd
Aylesham CT3 . . . . .112 E5
Dover CT17 . . . . .166 B7
Valebrook Cl CT20 . . . . .177 C5
Valence Ho ME15 . . . . . . .97 C7
Valenciennes Rd ME10 . . .36 E3
Valentine Cl ME7 . . . . . . .11 A1
Valentine Rd ME15 . . . . . .97 E7
Valerian Cl ME5 . . . . .31 E4
Valestone Cl CT21 . . . . .177 B4
Valetta Way ME1 . . . . .9 B4
Valiant Rd ME5 . . . . .32 C2
Valkyrie Ave CT5 . . . . . . .43 C7
Vallance The ME9 . . . . . . .60 A6
Valley Cotts
Alkham CT15 . . . . .147 C1
Stalisfield Green ME13 . . .103 D8
Valley Dr ME15 . . . . .96 F6
Valley Park Com Sch
ME14 . . . . .75 C4
Valley Rd Barham CT4 . . .111 E2
Canterbury CT1 . . . . .87 E6
Folkestone CT20 . . . . . . .177 E4
Gillingham ME7 . . . . .10 E4
Lydden CT9 . . . . .28 E4
River CT17 . . . . .148 E3
Valley Rise ME5 . . . . .31 F1
Valley The ME17 . . . . .96 D3
Valley View CT15 . . . . . . .131 C8
Valley View Rd ME1 . . . . . .9 B1
Valley Wlk CT21 . . . . . . .177 B3
Vancouver Dr ME8 . . . . . .11 C1
Vancouver Rd CT16 . . . . .149 C3
Vange Cottage Mews ME1 9 B4
Vanity La ME17 . . . . .96 D1
Vanity Rd ME12 . . . . .6 F2
Varne Ct 6 CT20 . . . . . . .177 F3
Varne Lodge 5 CT20 . . .177 F3
Varne Mews TN28 . . . . . .200 E4
Varne Pl CT19 . . . . .178 F5
Varne Rd CT19 . . . . .178 F5
Vaughan Dr ME10 . . . . . . .36 F8
Vauxhall Ave
Canterbury CT1 . . . . .67 C3
Herne Bay CT6 . . . . .22 A3
Vauxhall Cres CT1 . . . . . .67 C3
Vauxhall Industrial Rd
CT1 . . . . .67 D4
Vauxhall Rd CT1,CT2 . . . . .67 C4
Vectis Dr ME10 . . . . .36 F8
Ventnor Cl ME5 . . . . .32 C8
Ventnor La 12 CT9 . . . . .7 J2
Venture Cl TN29 . . . . . . .186 D1
Vere Rd CT10 . . . . .30 A4
Vereth Rd 2 CT11 . . . . . .52 D6
Vernon Holme (Kent Coll
Inf & Jun Sch) CT2 . . . .66 A1
Vernon Pl Canterbury CT1 .88 A7
Deal CT14 . . . . .117 D8
Verwood Cl CT2 . . . . .66 E2
Vesper Ct TN27 . . . . . . .135 A1
Vestey Ct CT8 . . . . .7 C1
Viaduct Cl CT12 . . . . .52 C8
Viaduct Terr TN26 . . . . . .182 F7
Viaduct The CT17 . . . . . .166 D5
Viburnum Cl TN23 . . . . . .138 E2
Vicarage Cl ME20 . . . . . . .53 A3
Vicarage Cres 8 CT9 . . . . .7 J2
Vicarage Ct ME9 . . . . .35 B7
Vicarage Gdn CT12 . . . . . .49 C7
Vicarage Gdns CT3 . . . . .91 A7
Vicarage Hill CT4 . . . . . .109 B4
Vicarage La
Ashford TN23 . . . . .139 C2
Blean CT2 . . . . .66 A6
Deal CT14 . . . . .116 F5
East Farleigh ME15 . . . . . .96 B6
Elham CT4 . . . . .144 F4
Faversham ME13 . . . . .62 A4
Lower Halstow ME9 . . . . . .13 C3
Nonington CT15 . . . . .113 C5
4 Sandwich CT13 . . . . .72 F1
Selling ME13 . . . . .84 C6
St Margaret's at Cliffe
CT15 . . . . .150 F6
Tilmanstone CT14 . . . . . .115 A3
Vicarage Pl CT9 . . . . .7 J1
Vicarage Rd
Folkestone CT20 . . . . . . .177 F3
Gillingham ME7 . . . . .10 C5
Minster (Sheppey) ME12 . . . .4 D7
Rochester ME2 . . . . .9 B8
Sittingbourne ME10 . . . . . .36 E6
Vicarage St
Broadstairs CT10 . . . . . . .29 E5
Faversham ME13 . . . . .62 D8
Vicary Way ME16 . . . . . . .74 D5
Vickers Cl CT18 . . . . . . .163 A4
Victor Ave CT9 . . . . .8 D2
Victoria Ave
Broadstairs CT10 . . . . . . .29 E8
Hythe CT21 . . . . .176 B2
Margate CT9 . . . . .8 B1
St Margaret's at Cliffe
CT15 . . . . .151 B6
Westgate-on-S CT8 . . . . . .27 F8
Victoria Cl ME5 . . . . .31 D2
Victoria Cres
Ashford TN23 . . . . .139 B1
Dover CT16 . . . . .166 D8
Victoria Ct Hythe CT21 . .176 C1
6 Maidstone ME16 . . . . . .74 E3
Victoria Dr CT6 . . . . .22 C5
Victoria Gr
12 Folkestone CT20 . . . . .178 D5
Hythe CT21 . . . . .177 B2
Victoria Ho 7 CT5 . . . . . .20 D2
Victoria Hospl CT14 . . . .117 B5
Victoria Par
Broadstairs CT10 . . . . . . .30 B4
Ramsgate CT11 . . . . .52 F7
Victoria Pk Dover CT16 . .166 E8
Herne Bay CT6 . . . . .23 A5
Victoria Pl
Faversham ME13 . . . . .62 C7
Hythe CT21 . . . . .176 B4
Victoria Rd Ashford TN23 139 B1
Broadstairs CT10 . . . . . . .29 E6
Canterbury CT1 . . . . .87 E7
Capel-le-F CT18 . . . . . . .164 B2
Chatham,Luton ME4 . . . . . .10 B2
Chatham,Walderslade ME5 .31 E3
Deal CT14 . . . . .117 D5
Folkestone CT19 . . . . . . .178 C5
Hythe CT21 . . . . .176 C1
Kingsdown CT14 . . . . . . .134 C4
Littlestone-on-S TN28 . . . .200 E5
Lydden CT9 . . . . .28 D4
Margate CT9 . . . . .7 J2
Ramsgate CT11 . . . . .52 F7
Sittingbourne ME10 . . . . . .36 D4
Victoria Rd W TN28 . . . .200 E5
Victoria Road Prim Sch
TN23 . . . . .139 B1
Victoria Row CT1 . . . . . . .67 A1
Victoria St Dover CT17 . .149 B1
Gillingham ME7 . . . . .10 D6
Maidstone ME16 . . . . .74 E3
New Romney TN28 . . . . . .200 A6
Rochester ME2 . . . . .9 B7
Rochester,Troy Town ME1 . . .9 D5
Sheerness ME12 . . . . .1 D1
Whitstable CT5 . . . . .20 D2
Victoria Terr Hythe CT21 .177 B2
Minster (Sheppey) ME12 . . .5 A5
Rochester ME1 . . . . .9 A2
Sittingbourne ME10 . . . . . .36 D4
Victory Manor 1 ME7 . . .10 A6
Victory Pk ME2 . . . . .9 E7
Victory Rd CT15 . . . . . . .133 F1
Victory St ME12 . . . . .1 C2
Vidal Manor ME7 . . . . . . .10 C5
Viewlands ME5 . . . . .10 C3
Vigo Terr ME9 . . . . .38 B1
Viking Cl CT7 . . . . .26 D8
Viking Ct Broadstairs CT10 30 B3
Canterbury CT2 . . . . .66 F2
Margate CT9 . . . . .8 A2
Viking Ship★ CT12 . . . . . . .51 E5
Village View ME5 . . . . . . .10 C2
Village Way TN26 . . . . . .183 A7
Villas The CT3 . . . . .47 A1
Villiers Ct CT17 . . . . . . .166 C7
Villiers Ho CT10 . . . . .30 B7
Villiers Rd CT1 . . . . .67 D1
Vincent Cl
Broadstairs CT10 . . . . . . .29 C3
Folkestone CT20 . . . . . . .177 E5
Vincent Ct ME12 . . . . .1 D1
Vincent Gdns ME12 . . . . . .1 D1
Vincent Pl TN24 . . . . . . .139 F4
Vincent Rd
Kit's Coty ME20 . . . . .53 C7
Lydden CT9 . . . . .28 C4
Sittingbourne ME10 . . . . . .37 C3
Vine Cl CT11 . . . . .29 E2
Vine End CT11 . . . . .29 E2
Vine Lands TN29 . . . . . . .203 B6
Vine Lo CT11 . . . . .29 E2
Vineries The ME7 . . . . . . .10 E5
Viners Cl ME10 . . . . .36 F1
Vines La ME1 . . . . .9 C5
Viney's Gdns TN30 . . . . .167 C1
Vineyard Cres ME8 . . . . . .12 B1
Vinson Cl ME13 . . . . .41 D1
Vinten Cl CT6 . . . . .46 B8
Vinters Rd ME14 . . . . .75 B4
Vintners Way ME14 . . . . . .75 E4
Violet Ave CT12 . . . . .29 C2
Violet Cl ME5 . . . . .54 A8
Virginia Rd
Gillingham ME7 . . . . .10 C7
Whitstable CT5 . . . . .44 A8
Vixen Cl ME5 . . . . .32 C6
Vlissingen Dr CT14 . . . . .117 C8
Volante Dr ME10 . . . . .36 E7
Vulcan Cl Chatham ME5 . .32 B7
Whitstable CT5 . . . . .43 C7

W

Wacher Cl CT2 . . . . .66 F2
Waddenhall Farm CT4 . .126 B6
Waddington Dr CT18 . . .163 A4
Waddle Cnr TN30 . . . . . .189 D3
Wades Cl TN29 . . . . .194 B4
Wadham Pl ME10 . . . . . . .37 B2
Waghorn St ME4 . . . . .10 B2
Wagoners Cl ME14 . . . . . .75 E4
Wain Ct ME12 . . . . .4 A5
Wainwright Ct CT10 . . . . .30 B6
Wainwright Pl TN24 . . . .156 D8
Wake Rd ME1 . . . . .31 C8
Wakefield Way CT21 . . . .176 B1
Wakefield Wlk CT21 . . . .176 D1
Wakehurst Cl ME17 . . . . .96 B3
Wakeley Jun Sch ME8 . . .12 A1
Wakeley Rd ME8 . . . . .12 A1
Wakeleys Cotts ME8 . . . . .34 B8
Walcheren Cl CT14 . . . . .117 C8
Waldens The ME17 . . . . . .99 E2
Waldershare Ave CT13 . . .95 A7
Waldershare Rd CT15 . . .132 A5
Walderslade Ctr ME5 . . . .32 A3
Walderslade Girls Sch
ME5 . . . . .31 F5
Walderslade Prim Sch
ME5 . . . . .32 A3
Walderslade Rd ME5 . . . .31 F6
Walderslade Woods ME5 53 F8
Waldron Dr ME15 . . . . . . .96 F6
Waldron Rd CT10 . . . . . . .30 B2
Walk The ME17 . . . . .99 E2
Walker La CT7 . . . . .26 D8
Walkers Outland (RSPB
Reserve)★ TN29 . . . . . .204 B1
Wall Rd TN24 . . . . .139 B3
Wall The ME10 . . . . .36 E5
Wallace Mews CT19 . . . .178 D7
Wallace Rd ME1 . . . . .31 E8
Wallace Way CT10 . . . . . .29 E4
Wallbridge La ME8,ME9 . .12 D3
Waller Rd TN28 . . . . .204 E7
Wallers Rd ME13 . . . . .62 A7
Wallis Ave ME15 . . . . .97 E5
Wallis Rd TN24 . . . . .139 D2
Wallwood Rd CT11 . . . . . .52 F8
Walmer Castle★ CT14 . .117 D1
Walmer Castle Rd CT14 117 C1
Walmer Ct 3 ME14 . . . . .75 A5
Walmer Gdns
Cliffs End CT12 . . . . .51 D5
Deal CT14 . . . . .117 A2
Sittingbourne ME10 . . . . . .36 D5
Walmer Rd CT5 . . . . .43 E8
Walmer Sch CT14 . . . . . .117 B2
Walmer Sta CT14 . . . . . .117 A1
Walmer Way Deal CT14 . .117 A2
1 Folkestone CT20 . . . . .177 F5
Walmsley Ho 4 CT19 . . .178 E6
Walmsley Rd CT10 . . . . . .29 F5
Walner Gdns TN28 . . . . .200 B7
Walner La TN28 . . . . .200 B7
Walnut Cl Ashford TN24 .139 D6
Chatham ME5 . . . . .32 B8
Walnut Ridge TN25 . . . .173 A6
Walnut Tree Ave ME15 . . .97 A5
Walnut Tree Cl 6 CT7 . . .27 A7
Walnut Tree Cotts ME13 .84 E8
Walnut Tree Dr ME10 . . . .36 D4
Walnut Tree La
Maidstone ME15 . . . . .97 A5
Westbere CT2 . . . . .68 D7
Walpole Rd CT9 . . . . .7 J3
Walsby Dr ME10 . . . . .37 A8
Walseley Terr TN29 . . . .203 C5
Walsham Rd ME5 . . . . . . .31 F1
Walshaw House 2 ME14 .75 A6
Walsingham Cl ME8 . . . . .33 D3
Walsingham House 3
ME14 . . . . .75 A6
Waltham Cl
Ashford TN24 . . . . .140 A2
Margate CT9 . . . . .8 E2
Waltham Rd
Gillingham ME8 . . . . .11 C3
Waltham CT4 . . . . .108 F1
Walton Gdns CT19 . . . . .178 D7
Walton Manor Cl CT19 .178 D7
Walton Rd CT19 . . . . . . .178 D6
Waltons The CT19 . . . . .178 C8
Wanden La TN27 . . . . . .135 C8
Wanstall Ct CT7 . . . . .27 A7
Wansted House Sch CT9 . .8 A3
Wantsum Cl CT6 . . . . .23 F5
Wantsum Mews 7 CT13 . .72 F1
Wantsum Way CT7 . . . . . .25 E3
Wantsume Lees CT13 . . . .72 E2
Warblers Cl 3 ME2 . . . . . .9 A7
Warden Bay Rd ME12 . . . . .6 E3
Warden Cl ME16 . . . . .74 C4
Warden Ct 10 CT17 . . . . .149 C1
Warden House Mews
CT14 . . . . .117 A4
Warden House Prim Sch
CT14 . . . . .117 A5
Warden Point Way CT5 . .43 C6
Warden Rd Rochester ME1 . .9 C2
Warden ME12 . . . . .6 B5
Warden Terr ME12 . . . . . . .5 A6
Warden View Gdns ME12 . .6 D1
Warden Way ME12 . . . . . . .6 B5
Wardour Cl CT10 . . . . .30 B4
Wards Hill Rd ME12 . . . . .4 C8
Wardwell La ME9 . . . . . . .13 C1
Ware St ME14 . . . . .76 A5
Warehorne Rd TN26 . . . .183 A7
Warlingham Cl ME8 . . . . .12 A1
Warmlake ME17 . . . . .98 F1
Warmlake Est ME17 . . . . .98 E1
Warmlake Rd ME17 . . . . .98 C1
Warner St ME4 . . . . .9 F3
Warnford Gdns ME15 . . . .97 A8
Warre Ave CT11 . . . . .52 C5
Warren Cl
Folkestone CT19 . . . . . . .178 F6
Sittingbourne ME10 . . . . . .37 B2
Warren Dr CT10 . . . . .29 E5
Warren Dr The CT8 . . . . .27 D7
Warren Hos TN27 . . . . . .119 E8
Warren Hts TN25 . . . . . .158 E5
Warren La Ashford TN24 .139 A4
Hartlip ME9 . . . . .34 C3
River,Lydden CT15 . . . . . .147 D6
Warren Lo CT1 . . . . .87 B6
Warren Rd
Folkestone CT19 . . . . . . .178 F6
Kit's Coty ME5 . . . . .53 D7
Littlestone-on-S TN28 . . .200 D6
Warren Ret Pk TN24 . . . .139 B4
Warren St
Stalisfield Green TN27 . . .103 A3
Warren Street ME17 . . . . .102 D7
Warren The
Brabourne Lees TN25 . . . .158 E5
Selling ME13 . . . . .84 E7
Whitstable CT5 . . . . .43 C6
Warren View TN23 . . . . .138 F4
Warren Way CT19 . . . . . .178 F6
Warren Wood Cty Prim Sch
& Language Unit ME1 . . .31 C8
Warren Wood Rd ME1 . . .31 C7
Warten Rd CT11 . . . . .29 F1
Warwick Cres ME10 . . . . .36 C5
Warwick Dr CT11 . . . . . . .52 B5
Warwick Pl ME16 . . . . . . .74 E3
Warwick Rd
Ashford TN24 . . . . .139 E5
Canterbury CT1 . . . . .88 C8
Deal CT14 . . . . .117 D2
Margate CT9 . . . . .8 B2
Whitstable CT5 . . . . .20 D2
Washford Farm Rd
TN23 . . . . .155 E5
Washington Cl 4 CT16 .149 B3
Washington La TN29 . . .198 C6
Wass Dro CT3 . . . . .71 B7
Wat Tyler Way ME15 . . . .75 A4
Watchester Ave CT11 . . . .52 C5
Watchester La CT12 . . . . .50 B5
Watchmans Terr 6
ME5 . . . . .10 C2
Water Farm CT4 . . . . . . .144 F4
Water La Bayfield ME13 . . .61 F4
Canterbury CT1 . . . . .87 F8
6 Faversham ME13 . . . . . .62 C7
Harrietsham ME17 . . . . . .100 B5
Kingswood ME17 . . . . .99 F3
6 Maidstone ME15 . . . . . .75 A4
Maidstone,Bearsted ME14 . .76 E6
Sturry CT2 . . . . .67 F5
Water Mdws CT2 . . . . . . .67 F4
Water St CT14 . . . . .117 D7
Waterbrook Ave TN24 . .157 A4
Watercress La
Ashford TN23 . . . . .155 F8
Wingham CT3 . . . . .90 F6
Waterditch La ME17,
TN27 . . . . .102 E5
Waterfall Rd TN26 . . . . .138 B6
Waterham Rd ME13 . . . . .42 C1
Waterlock Cotts CT3 . . . .91 A7
Waterloo Cres CT16,
CT17 . . . . .166 E7
Waterloo Hill ME12 . . . . . .4 D6
Waterloo Mansions 12
CT16,CT17 . . . . .166 E7
Waterloo Mus★ CT10 . . . .30 B5
Waterloo Pl 8 CT11 . . . . .52 F7
Waterloo Rd
Folkestone CT20 . . . . . . .177 D5
Gillingham ME7 . . . . .10 C4
Sittingbourne ME10 . . . . . .36 D5
Whitstable CT5 . . . . .20 D2
Waterloo St ME15 . . . . . .75 A3
Waterloo Terr ME12 . . . . . .5 A5
Waterlow Rd ME14 . . . . .75 A6
Waterman Ho TN23 . . . .156 B8
Watermead Cl TN23 . . . .155 F7
Watermeadow Cl ME7 . . .32 F6
Watermill Cl
Maidstone ME16 . . . . .74 B5
Rochester ME2 . . . . .9 C8
Waters Edge ME15 . . . . . .74 F2
Waters Pl ME7 . . . . .33 A6
Watersend CT16 . . . . . . .148 D5
Waterside TN24 . . . . . . .139 F1
Waterside Ct
5 Hythe CT21 . . . . .176 B2
Rochester ME2 . . . . .9 E6
Waterside Dr CT8 . . . . .7 D1
Waterside La ME7 . . . . . . .10 F7
Waterside View ME12 . . . . .6 E4
Watersmead CT16 . . . . . .148 C5
Waterstone Pl ME13 . . . . .62 A6
Waterworks Hill CT15 . . .133 B3
Waterworks La CT15 . . . .133 B3
Watery La CT4 . . . . .109 C5
Watkin Rd CT19 . . . . . . .178 C6
Watling Ave ME5 . . . . . . .10 D2
Watling Pl ME10 . . . . .37 A3
Watling St Canterbury CT1 .87 F8
Chatham ME5 . . . . .10 D2
Watson Ave ME5 . . . . .31 D5
Watsons Cl TN25 . . . . . .139 C8
Watsons Hill ME10 . . . . . .36 E5
Wattle Cnr TN30 . . . . . . .189 D3
Watts Cotts TN24 . . . . . .139 D7
Watts Yd 12 CT13 . . . . . .72 F1
Watts' Ave ME1 . . . . .9 C4
Watts' St ME4 . . . . .9 E3
Wauchope Rd CT5 . . . . . .42 F6
Wave Crest CT5 . . . . .20 C1
Waverley Ave ME12 . . . . . .4 B7
Waverley Cl Chatham ME5 32 D2
Coxheath ME17 . . . . .96 C3
Waverley Rd CT9 . . . . .28 C8
Way Farm Cotts CT12 . . . .50 E7
Way Hill CT12 . . . . .50 E7
Wayborough Hill CT12 . . .50 D7
Wayfield Cty Prim Sch
ME5 . . . . .32 A7
Wayfield Rd ME5 . . . . .32 A7
Wayne Cl CT10 . . . . .29 E5
Wayside TN30 . . . . .167 B2
Wayside Ave TN30 . . . . .167 B3
Wayside Flats TN30 . . . .167 B2
Weald Cl ME15 . . . . .97 C6
Weald Ct ME10 . . . . .36 D2
Weald The TN24 . . . . . . .139 C3
Wealden Ave TN30 . . . . .167 B1
Wealden Ct 5 ME5 . . . . . .10 B3
Wealden Forest Pk★
CT2,CT6 . . . . .45 D4
Wealdhurst Pk CT10 . . . .29 D5
Wear Bay Cres CT19 . . .178 F6
Wear Bay Rd CT19 . . . . .178 F5
Weatherall Cl ME13 . . . . .64 B2
Weatherly Cl ME1 . . . . . . .9 C4
Weatherly Dr CT10 . . . . . .29 F2
Weavering Cotts ME14 . . .75 E3
Weavering St ME14 . . . . .75 F4
Weavers The ME16 . . . . . .74 B5
Weavers Way
Ashford TN23 . . . . .155 E7
Dover CT16 . . . . .149 A3
Webb Cl CT19 . . . . .178 A7
Webster Rd ME8 . . . . .11 F1
Webster Way CT18 . . . . .163 B4
Weddington La CT3 . . . . .71 E2
Wedgewood Cl ME16 . . . .74 B5
Wedgewood Dr ME5 . . . . .32 A7
Weeds Wood Rd ME5 . . . .31 F4
Week St ME14 . . . . .75 A4
Weekes Ct ME11 . . . . .3 A5
Weigall Pl CT11 . . . . .52 C7
Weighbridge Way CT16 166 H8
Welcombe Ct ME8 . . . . . .33 D8
Well Cl CT2 . . . . .68 A6
Well La Bayfield ME13 . . . .61 B3
Fordwich CT2,CT3 . . . . . . .68 A3
St Margaret's at Cliffe
CT15 . . . . .150 F6
Well Rd Lyminge CT18 . . .161 C6
Maidstone ME14 . . . . .75 A5
Queenborough ME11 . . . . . .3 A5
Rushenden ME11 . . . . .2 F3
Well St ME15,ME17 . . . . . .96 E4
Well Winch Rd ME10 . . . .36 D5

Weller Ave ME1 9 D2
Wellesley Ave CT14 117 C3
Wellesley Cl
Broadstairs CT10 29 E3
Westgate-on-S CT8 27 E7
Wellesley Rd
Ashford TN23 139 C2
Dover CT16 166 E7
Margate CT9 8 B1
Sheerness ME12 1 E2
Westgate-on-S CT8 27 E7
Wellesley Terr CT13 94 A8
Wellesley Villas TN24 139 C3
Wellfield Rd CT20 178 A5
Wellington Cl CT8 7 C1
Wellington Cres CT11 52 F6
Wellington Ct CT14 117 D3
Wellington Gdns
2 Dover CT16 149 B3
Margate CT9 7 J3
Wellington House 6 ME15 97 E5
Wellington Par
Kingsdown CT14 134 E6
Kingsdown,Hawkshill CT14 134 D7
Wellington Pl
Folkestone CT20 177 D3
Maidstone ME14 74 F6
Wellington Rd
Deal CT14 117 D5
Folkestone CT20 177 D5
Gillingham ME7 10 C4
Lydden CT9 28 D4
Sittingbourne ME10 36 B5
Temple Ewell CT16 148 D5
Westgate-on-S CT8 27 E7
Wellington St CT5 43 D5
Wellington Terr CT20 177 D3
Wellis Gdns CT9 7 G1
Wells Ave CT1 88 B7
Wells Cl
New Romney TN28 200 C6
Tenterden TN30 179 B8
Wells Ho ME10 37 B4
Wells Rd CT19 177 F6
Wells Way ME13 40 B1
Welsdene Rd CT9 28 B8
Welson Rd CT20 178 A5
Wemmick Cl ME1 31 D7
Wemyss Ct 13 CT1 67 B2
Wemyss Ho 14 CT1 67 B2
Wemyss Way CT1 67 C1
Wenderton La CT3 70 A2
Wenham's La TN29 192 E2
Wents Wood ME14 75 F5
Wentworth Ave CT9 7 E1
Wentworth Cl CT18 161 C6
Wentworth Dr
Gillingham ME8 33 E7
Ramsgate CT12 29 A1
Sittingbourne ME10 36 C5
Wentworth Gdns CT6 22 D2
Wentworth Ho ME10 36 C5
Wesley Terr CT18 161 C7
West Beach CT5 20 C1
West Borough Prim Sch ME16 74 B3
West Cliff CT5 20 D1
West Cliff Arc 8 CT11 52 E6
West Cliff Ave CT10 30 B3
West Cliff Ct CT10 30 B3
West Cliff Dr CT6 22 B4
West Cliff Gdns
Folkestone CT20 178 D4
Herne Bay CT6 22 B4
West Cliff Prom CT11 52 D5
West Cliff Rd
Broadstairs CT10 30 B3
Ramsgate CT11 52 D6
West Cliff Terr CT11 52 B5
West Ct ME15 75 A1
West Dr ME5 31 D5
West Dumpton La CT11 29 E1
West End TN26 168 F3
West End Cotts ME9 80 D7
West Gn ME10 14 F1
West Hill Rd CT6 22 C5
West Hythe Rd CT21 187 A8
West La Sheerness ME12 1 B2
Sittingbourne ME10 37 A4
West Lane Trad Est ME10 37 A4
West Lawn Gdns CT20 177 D3
West Lea CT14 117 C7
West Minster Prim Sch ME12 3 B8
West Norman Rd CT16 166 E8
West Par CT21 176 B1
West Park Ave CT9 8 D1
West Park Farm North Ret Pk CT19 178 B8
West Park Rd ME15 75 B2
West Pas ME12 1 B2
West Pl TN29 197 D8
West Ramp CT16 166 G8
West Rd Folkestone CT20 177 C4
Gillingham ME4 10 A7
Sandwich CT13 51 A1
West Ridge ME10 36 D3
West Rise CT12 29 B1
West Side CT15 133 A1
West St Ashford TN23 139 B2
Deal CT14 117 D6
Dover CT17 166 C8
West St *continued*
Faversham ME13 62 C7
Gillingham ME7 10 D6
Harrietsham ME17 100 C6
Hothfield TN26 137 F7
Lenham ME17 79 E1
New Romney TN28 200 A6
Queenborough ME11 2 F5
Sheerness ME12 1 B2
Sittingbourne ME10 36 E4
Woodside Green ME17 101 E8
West Street Cotts CT14 94 A1
West Terr CT20 178 D4
West View CT19 178 D8
West View Cl CT6 22 C2
West Wlk ME16 74 B3
West Wood Rd ME9 56 B8
Westbere La CT2 68 B7
Westbourne TN23 155 D6
Westbourne Gdns CT20 178 B4
Westbourne St ME10 36 E4
Westbrook Ave CT9 7 F1
Westbrook Cotts CT9 7 G1
Westbrook Gdns CT9 7 G1
Westbrook La CT6 22 B3
Westbrook Prom CT9 7 G2
Westbrook Rd CT9 7 G2
Westbrook Wlk 8 ME13 62 C7
Westbrooke Cl ME4 10 A2
Westbury Cres CT17 166 B6
Westbury Hts CT17 166 B6
Westbury Rd Dover CT17 166 B6
Westgate-on-S CT8 27 E8
Westcliff Dr ME12 4 D8
Westcliff Gdns CT9 7 F1
Westcliff Ho 4 CT20 178 D4
Westcliff Rd CT9 7 G1
Westcourt La CT15 130 C5
Westcourt Rd ME7 10 A6
Westdean Cl CT17 148 E2
Westenhanger Sta TN25 175 B7
Westerham Cl
Broadstairs CT9 8 F1
Canterbury CT2 67 A4
Gillingham ME8 11 B3
Westerham Rd ME10 36 C3
Westerhill Rd ME17 96 C1
Westerhout Cl CT14 117 C8
Western Ave
Ashford TN23 139 A3
Bridge CT4 89 A1
Gillingham ME4 10 A8
Halfway Houses ME12 3 D6
Herne Bay CT6 22 E4
Western Cl CT17 166 C6
Western Espl
Broadstairs CT10 30 B2
Herne Bay CT6 22 C5
Western Gdns TN24 156 E8
Western Heights Rdbt CT17 166 C5
Western Ho CT14 117 C7
Western Link ME13 62 A8
Western Rd Deal CT14 117 C7
Maidstone ME16 74 C2
Margate CT9 29 C8
Western Service Rd CT16 166 G8
Western Undercliff CT11 52 C5
Westfield CT2 66 A6
Westfield Bsns Ctr ME2 9 C7
Westfield Cotts ME9 13 A2
Westfield La CT18 161 C3
Westfield Rd
Birchington CT7 27 A7
Margate CT9 28 C8
Westfield Sole Rd ME5, ME15 54 D8
Westfields TN27 136 D8
Westgate Ave CT7 28 A4
Westgate Bay Ave CT8,CT9 7 C1
Westgate Cl CT2 66 C1
Westgate Court Ave CT2 66 D1
Westgate Garden Flats CT2 87 E8
Westgate Gr CT2 66 F1
Westgate Hall Rd 5 CT1 66 F1
Westgate Rd ME13 62 E7
Westgate Terr CT5 20 E2
Westgate-on-Sea Sta CT8 27 E8
Westland Way CT18 163 B3
Westlands Ave ME10 36 B4
Westlands Rd CT6 22 A3
Westlands Sch The ME10 36 B4
Westlea Ct CT20 178 A3
Westleigh Rd CT8 27 D8
Westmarsh Cl ME15 97 F7
Westmarsh Dr CT9 8 E2
Westmeads Com Inf Sch CT5 20 E2
Westmeads Rd CT5 20 E2
Westminster Rd CT1 67 C4
Westminster Wlk CT12 29 C1
Westmoors TN23 155 E6
Westmoreland Dr ME9 13 C3
Westmorland Cl ME15 97 E7
Westmorland Gn ME15 97 E7
Westmorland Rd ME15 97 E7
Westmount Ave ME4 9 F3
Westmount Ho 4 CT9 8 B2
Weston Rd ME2 9 A8
Westonville Ave CT9 7 F1
Westover Gdns CT10 29 E7
Westover Rd CT10 29 E6
Westree Ct 7 ME16 74 E3
Westree Rd ME16 74 E3
Westway ME17 96 C3
Westwell La
Charing TN25,TN27 120 F5
Potters Corner TN24,TN25 138 E7
Westwell TN25,TN26 121 B4
Westwood Ind Est CT9 29 A6
Westwood Pl ME13 62 D5
Westwood Rd
Broadstairs CT10 29 C4
Maidstone ME15 97 A7
Westwood Ret Pk CT10 29 A5
Wetheral Dr ME5 32 B4
Wey Cl ME5 32 C5
Wey St TN26 183 D3
Weybridge Cl ME5 32 C4
Weyburn Dr CT12 29 A1
Weyhill Cl ME14 75 C6
Weymouth Cl CT19 177 D7
Weymouth Rd CT19 177 D6
Weymouth Terr CT19 177 D7
Wharf Rd Gillingham ME7 10 C7
Maidstone ME15 74 E2
Wharfedale Rd CT9 8 A1
Wharton Gdns TN24 156 E8
Whatman Cl ME14 75 C6
Whatmer Cl CT2 68 A6
Wheatcroft Cl ME10 37 B4
Wheatcroft Gr ME8 33 F7
Wheatear Way ME5 32 B7
Wheatfields Chatham ME5 32 D2
Maidstone ME14 75 D4
Wheatley Rd
Ramsgate CT12 29 C1
Whitstable CT5 20 E2
Wheatsheaf Cl
Boughton Street ME13 64 A3
Maidstone ME15 97 B8
Wheatsheaf Gdns ME12 1 C1
Wheatsheafe La CT15 133 B2
Wheeler St ME14 75 A5
Wheelers The ME8 33 B6
Wheelwrights The ME17 100 D6
Wheelwrights Way CT13 93 B2
Wheler Rd TN27 120 C8
Whewell Terr 1 CT20 178 E5
Whiffen's Ave ME4 9 F5
Whiffen's Ave W ME4 9 F5
Whigham Cl TN23 155 D7
Whimbrel Cl ME10 36 F8
Whimbrel Wlk ME5 32 C1
Whinfell Ave CT11 51 F7
Whinless Rd CT17 166 A8
Whiston Ave TN26 153 C4
Whitby Rd CT20 177 D6
Whitchurch Cl ME16 74 E4
Whitcombe Cl ME5 32 C3
White Acre Dr CT14 134 B8
White Cliffs 11 CT20 178 D4
White Cliffs Bsns Ctr CT16 149 A6
White Cliffs Bsns Pk CT16 149 B6
White Ct 8 CT20 177 E3
White Hart Mansions CT9 7 I3
White Hill
Boughton Aluph TN25 123 B6
Challock TN25 105 E1
White Hill Cl CT4 110 A8
White Hill Rd ME9,ME14 33 D1
White Horse Hill CT18 163 C3
White Horse La
6 Canterbury CT1 87 F8
Otham ME15 98 A6
Rhodes Minnis CT4 144 A3
White House Farm Ct CT15 113 E5
White Marsh Ct CT5 20 E2
White Mill Mus★ CT13 72 E2
White Post ME17 78 B5
White Post Gdns CT3 71 E1
White Rd ME4 10 A2
White Rock Ct ME16 74 E3
White Rock Pl 5 ME16 74 E3
White Wood Rd CT13 93 B1
Whiteacre La CT4 125 E4
Whitebeam Dr ME17 96 B3
Whitecliff Way CT19 178 F6
Whitefriars Mdw CT13 94 A8
Whitefriars Way 13 CT13 72 F1
Whitegate Ct ME8 33 D5
Whitehall TN29 197 E8
Whitehall Bridge Rd CT2 87 E8
Whitehall Cl CT2 87 E8
Whitehall Dr ME17 99 D3
Whitehall Gdns CT2 66 E1
Whitehall Rd
Broad Street ME14 77 A6
Canterbury CT2 87 E8
Canterbury,Harbledown CT2 87 D7
Ramsgate CT12 29 C1
Sittingbourne ME10 36 E2
Whitehall Way TN25 159 D1
Whiteheads La ME14 76 B4
Whitehorse Hill ME5 10 B3
Whitehouse Cres ME1 53 A8
Whitehouse Dro CT13, CT3 72 D7
Whitelocks Cl CT4 111 D3
Whitenbrook CT21 177 A3
Whiteness Gn CT10 8 F1
Whiteness Rd CT10 8 G1
Whites Hill CT14 115 B2
Whitewall Ctr ME2 9 D8
Whitewall Rd ME2 9 D7
Whitewall Way ME2 9 D7
Whiteway Rd ME11,ME12 2 F6
Whitfeld Rd TN23 156 B8
Whitfield Ave
Broadstairs CT10 29 E7
Dover CT16 149 B2
Whitfield Cotts TN23 156 B8
Whitfield Ct CT16 149 A6
Whitfield Hill River CT16 148 E4
Temple Ewell CT16 148 F4
Whitfield CT16 148 F5
Whitfield Rdbt CT16 149 A6
Whitfield Sch & Aspen Specl Unit CT16 149 A7
Whitgift Ct CT2 66 D1
Whiting Cres ME13 62 A8
Whiting Ho TN29 203 C5
Whitmore St ME16 74 D2
Whitstable & Seasalter Endowed CE Jun Sch CT5 20 D1
Whitstable & Tankerton Hospl CT5 21 A2
Whitstable & Tankerton Sta CT5 20 E1
Whitstable Jun Sch CT5 20 D1
Whitstable Mus & Art Gallery★ CT5 20 D1
Whitstable Rd
Canterbury CT2 66 D2
Faversham ME13 62 E7
Faversham, Goodnestone ME13 63 B6
Herne Bay CT5,CT6 21 F3
Herne Bay, Studd Hill CT6 22 B3
Rough Common CT2 66 B4
Whittaker St ME4 10 A4
Whittington Terr CT15 130 D4
Whybornes Chase ME12 4 C7
Whyman Ave ME4 10 A1
Whytecliffs CT10 30 A2
Wichling Cl CT2 67 A3
Wick La CT4 129 E7
Wicken House ME16 74 E4
Wicken La TN25,TN27 120 E6
Wickenden Cres TN24 157 A8
Wickets The TN24 156 F7
Wickham Ave CT11 52 G8
Wickham Cl ME9 35 B6
Wickham Court La CT3 69 B3
Wickham La CT3 69 B1
Wickham Mill CT3 69 C2
Wickham Pl ME17 101 D5
Wickham Rd CT3 69 B2
Wickham St ME1 9 D3
Wickham Terr ME11 2 F5
Wickhambreaux CE Prim Sch CT3 69 C2
Widgeon Wlk CT18 163 B3
Widred Rd CT17 166 C8
Wierton La ME17 97 E1
Wife Of Bath Hill CT2 87 C8
Wigmore Cotts CT15 131 C8
Wigmore La CT15 131 C8
Wigmore Rd
Gillingham,Park Wood ME8 33 B4
Gillingham,Wigmore ME8 33 B5
Wigmore Wood CT15 131 C8
Wigwam Paddocks CT7 27 A8
Wihtred Rd ME9 37 D2
Wilberforce Rd
Coxheath ME17 96 D3
Folkestone CT20 177 E3
Wilbrough Rd CT7 27 A7
Wilcox Cl CT3 112 D5
Wild Air CT7 26 F8
Wilderness Hill CT9 8 A2
Wildfell Cl ME5 54 C8
Wildish Rd ME13 62 A8
Wildman Cl ME8 33 D3
Wildwood Cl ME17 99 E2
Wildwood Glade ME7 33 B4
Wildwood Rd CT2 67 F6
Wildwood Wildlife Pk★ CT2,CT6 45 D4
Wiles Ave TN28 200 B6
Wiles Ho TN28 200 B6
Wilfred Rd CT11 52 C8
Wilgate Green Rd ME13 82 F6
Wilkes Rd CT10 29 E4
Wilkie Rd CT7 27 A8
Wilks Cl ME8 12 B2
Will Adams Ct 9 ME7 10 C6
Will Adams Rdbt ME8 10 F2
Will Adams Way ME8 10 F1
Willement Rd ME13 62 B7
Willesborough Ct TN24 140 A2
Willesborough Ind Pk TN24 140 A1
Willesborough Inf & Jun Sch TN24 157 A8
Willesborough Rd TN24 139 F4
Willesborough Windmill★ TN24 140 A1
Willetts Hill CT12 49 D7
William Ave
Folkestone CT19 178 B7
Margate CT9 29 C8
William Gibbs Ct 14 ME13 62 D7
William Harvey Hospl The TN24 140 C1
William Judge Cl TN30 179 D7
William Pitt Ave CT14 117 B6
William Pitt Cl CT21 176 D2
William Rd TN23 156 B8
William Rigby Dr ME12 3 E7
William St
Faversham ME13 62 D7
Gillingham ME8 12 A1
William St *continued*
Herne Bay CT6 22 F5
Sittingbourne ME10 36 E4
Whitstable CT5 20 D2
Williamson Rd TN29 204 E5
Willingdon TN23 155 E5
Willingdon Pl CT14 117 C1
Willingdon Rd CT16 149 A5
Willington Gn ME15 97 E7
Willington St ME15 75 F2
Willis Ct ME12 3 F5
Willis Ho ME1 9 C4
Willop Cl TN29 186 F3
Willop Way TN29 186 F3
Willoughby Ct 14 CT1 87 F8
Willow Ave
Broadstairs CT10 29 D4
Faversham ME13 62 A7
Willow Cl Canterbury CT2 67 A2
Hythe CT21 175 E1
Margate CT9 8 C2
Willow Ct
Broadstairs CT10 30 A5
Folkestone CT20 177 E4
Maidstone ME15 97 A6
Willow Dr
Hamstreet TN26 183 A7
St Mary's Bay TN29 194 F3
Willow Ho Sheerness ME12 1 C2
Sittingbourne ME10 37 B3
Willow House 2 ME5 31 F5
Willow Rd
Great Mongeham CT14 116 C3
Whitstable CT5 43 C5
Willow Rise ME15 75 F1
Willow Tree Cl
Ashford TN24 139 F1
Herne Bay CT6 23 D5
Willow Tree Farm Cvn Pk CT21 187 D8
Willow Way
Maidstone ME15 75 B3
Margate CT9 28 C8
Whitstable CT5 44 C8
Willow Waye CT15 131 D7
Willowbank Cl TN29 195 A4
Willowbank Ct 12 ME15 75 B4
Willowby Gdns ME8 33 E4
Willows Ct CT2 66 C4
Willows The
Ashford TN24 139 D6
Gillingham ME8 11 E2
Newington ME9 35 B6
Sheerness ME12 1 I1
Sittingbourne ME10 14 F1
Willson's Rd CT11 52 D6
Wilmecote Ct ME8 33 D8
Wilmington Way ME8 11 B2
Wilmott Pl CT13 93 B2
Wilson Ave Chatham ME1 31 E7
Deal CT14 116 F4
Wilson Cl Ashford TN24 140 A1
Maidstone ME15 97 E7
Wilsons La ME15 96 A5
Wiltie Ct CT19 178 C5
Wiltie Gdns CT19 178 C5
Wilton Cl CT14 117 C5
Wilton Rd
Folkestone CT19 178 B6
Margate CT12 28 F1
Wilton Terr ME10 36 B5
Wiltshire Cl ME5 32 C8
Wiltshire Way 4 ME15 97 E8
Wimborne Pl CT12 52 B8
Wimbourne Dr ME8 33 D6
Win Pine Ho CT21 176 A1
Winant Way CT16 149 B3
Wincheap CT1 87 E7
Wincheap Foundation Prim Sch CT1 87 E6
Wincheap Gn 4 CT1 87 F7
Wincheap Ind Est CT1 87 D7
Winchelsea Ct CT17 166 C7
Winchelsea Rd
Chatham ME5 32 B5
Dover CT17 166 B7
Winchelsea St CT17 166 B7
Winchelsea Terr CT17 166 B7
Winchester Ave ME5 31 F4
Winchester Gdns CT1 88 A6
Winchester Ho 4 ME15 97 D7
Winchester Pl 9 ME14 75 A5
Winchester Way ME8 34 A8
Wind Hill TN27 119 E7
Wind Hill La TN27 119 E7
Windermere ME13 62 E6
Windermere Ave CT11 52 A7
Windermere Ct TN24 139 C4
Windermere Dr ME8 33 D7
Windermere Gdns CT3 112 F6
Windermere Gr ME10 36 D3
Windermere Ho 4 ME15 97 E7
Winding Hill ME13 83 F6
Windmill Ave CT12 29 B3
Windmill Cl
Ashford TN24 140 A1
Bridge CT4 89 A1
Canterbury CT1 88 C8
Herne Bay CT6 23 A2
Windmill Ct
Boughton Monchelsea ME17 97 B3
Whitstable CT5 43 C7
Windmill Hill ME17 100 B1
Windmill Hts ME14 76 B4
Windmill Manor ME7 10 C4
Windmill Par CT11 52 C6
Windmill Quay Rd ME12 4 E2

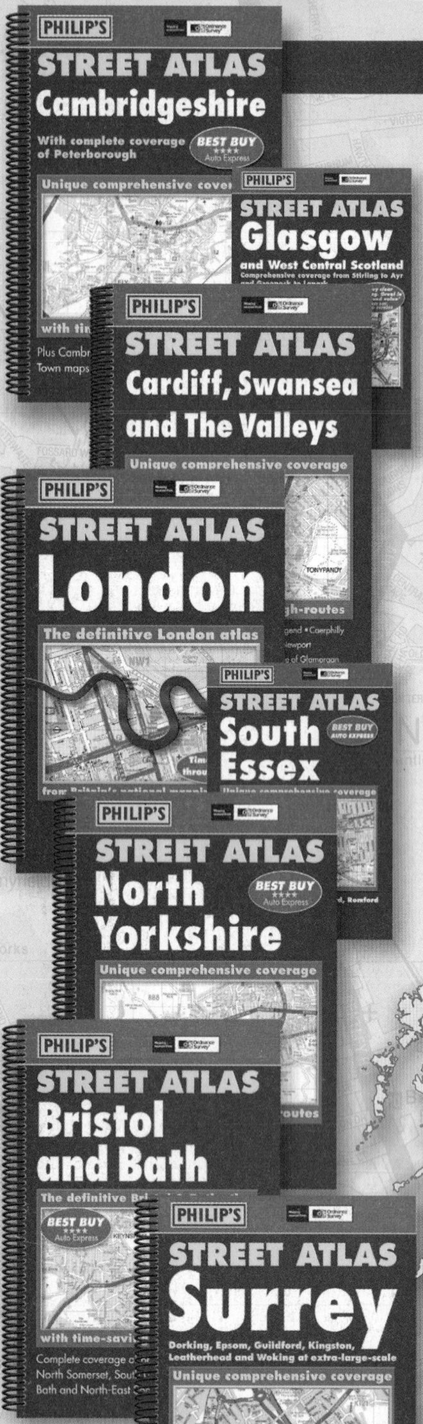

Street Atlases from Philip's

Philip's publish an extensive range of regional and local street atlases which are ideal for motoring, business and leisure use. They are widely used by the emergency services and local authorities throughout Britain.

Key features include:

- **Superb county-wide mapping at an extra-large scale of 3½ inches to 1 mile, or 2½ inches to 1 mile in pocket editions**
- **Complete urban and rural coverage, detailing every named street in town and country**
- **Each atlas available in two handy sizes – standard spiral and pocket paperback**

'The mapping is very clear... great in scope and value'

★★★★ BEST BUY AUTO EXPRESS

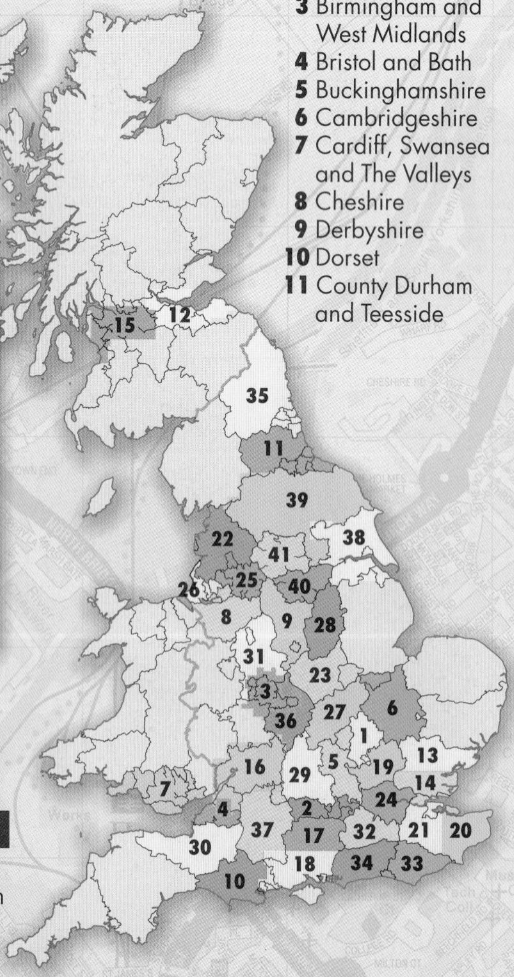

1 Bedfordshire
2 Berkshire
3 Birmingham and West Midlands
4 Bristol and Bath
5 Buckinghamshire
6 Cambridgeshire
7 Cardiff, Swansea and The Valleys
8 Cheshire
9 Derbyshire
10 Dorset
11 County Durham and Teesside
12 Edinburgh and East Central Scotland
13 North Essex
14 South Essex
15 Glasgow and West Central Scotland
16 Gloucestershire
17 North Hampshire
18 South Hampshire
19 Hertfordshire
20 East Kent
21 West Kent
22 Lancashire
23 Leicestershire and Rutland
24 London
25 Greater Manchester
26 Merseyside
27 Northamptonshire
28 Nottinghamshire
29 Oxfordshire
30 Somerset
31 Staffordshire
32 Surrey
33 East Sussex
34 West Sussex
35 Tyne and Wear and Northumberland
36 Warwickshire
37 Wiltshire and Swindon
38 East Yorkshire and Northern Lincolnshire
39 North Yorkshire
40 South Yorkshire
41 West Yorkshire

How to order

The Philip's range of street atlases is available from good retailers or directly from the publisher by phoning 01903 828503

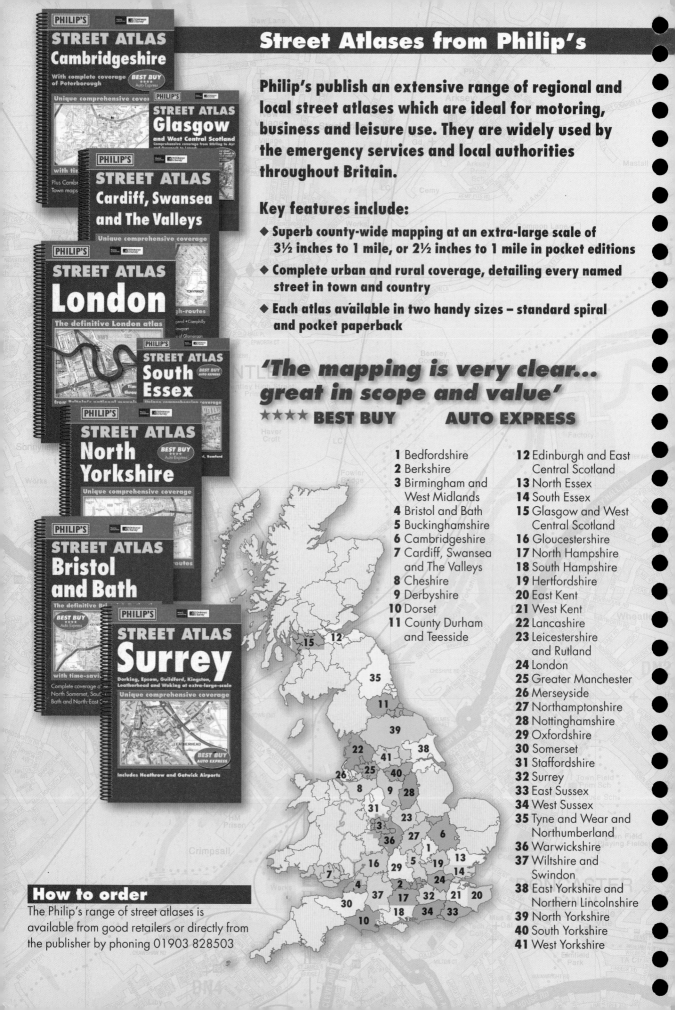